edition **4**

Small Business Management

Entrepreneurship and Beyond

Timothy S. Hatten

Mesa State College

Houghton Mifflin Company   Boston   New York

Executive Publisher: George Hoffman
Executive Editor: Lisé Johnson
Senior Marketing Manager: Nicole Hamm
Senior Development Editor: Julia Perez
Associate Project Editor: Deborah Thomashow
Cover Design Director: Tony Saizon
Senior Photo Editor: Jennifer Meyer Dare
Senior Composition Buyer: Chuck Dutton
Senior New Title Project Manager: Pat O'Neill
Editorial Associate: Katilyn Crowley
Marketing Assistant: Lauren Foye

Cover image: Harold Burch, New York City

Printed in the U.S.A.

Library of Congress Control Number: 2007938106

ISBN-10: 0-618-99936-1
ISBN-13: 978-0-618-99936-1

23456789-CRK-12 11 10 09 08

Brief Contents

Part 1

The Challenge 1

    Chapter 1 Small Business: An Overview **2**

    Chapter 2 Small Business Management, Entrepreneurship, and Ownership **27**

Part 2

Planning in Small Business 59

    Chapter 3 Social Responsibility, Ethics, and Strategic Planning **60**

    Chapter 4 The Business Plan **93**

Part 3

Early Decisions 123

    Chapter 5 Franchising **124**

    Chapter 6 Taking Over an Existing Business **151**

    Chapter 7 Starting a New Business **178**

Part 4

Financial and Legal Management 201

    Chapter 8 Accounting Records and Financial Statements **202**

    Chapter 9 Small Business Finance **235**

    Chapter 10 The Legal Environment **262**

Part 5

Marketing the Product or Service 289

    Chapter 11 Small Business Marketing: Strategy and Research **290**

    Chapter 12 Small Business Marketing: Product **313**

    Chapter 13 Small Business Marketing: Place **341**

    Chapter 14 Small Business Marketing: Price and Promotion **373**

Part 6

Managing Small Business 405

       Chapter 15 International Small Business **406**

       Chapter 16 Professional Small Business Management **435**

       Chapter 17 Human Resource Management **464**

       Chapter 18 Operations Management **496**

Appendix Complete Sample Business Plan **519**

Notes 541

Answers to Test Preppers 550

Index 553

Contents

Preface   xv

PART 1 The Challenge

1 Small Business: An Overview   2

What Is Small Business?   4
Size Definitions   5
Types of Industries   6

Small Businesses in the U.S. Economy   7
Recent Growth Trends   9

Workforce Diversity and Small Business Ownership   10
The Value of Diversity to Business   12

Secrets of Small Business Success   13
Competitive Advantage   13
Getting Started on the Right Foot   16

Understanding the Risks of Small Business Ownership   17
What Is Business Failure?   17
Causes of Business Failure   18
Business Termination versus Failure   19

Mistakes Leading to Business Failure   20
Failure Rate Controversy   21

Manager's Notebook
Straight from the Source   14

Profile in Entrepreneurship
Lifelong Trek   16

Summary   22
Questions for Review and Discussion   23
Questions for Critical Thinking   23
Experience This . . .   23
What Would You Do?   24

Chapter Closing Case
Small Business Lessons from the Movies   24

Test Prepper   26

2 Small Business Management, Entrepreneurship, and Ownership   27

The Entrepreneur-Manager Relationship   28
What Is an Entrepreneur?   29
Entrepreneurship and the Small Business Manager   29

A Model of the Startup Process   31

Your Decision for Self-Employment   35
Pros and Cons of Self-Employment   35
Traits of Successful Entrepreneurs   38
Preparing Yourself for Business Ownership   40

Forms of Business Organization   42
Sole Proprietorship   43
Partnership   45
Corporation   49
Specialized Forms of Corporations   52

Manager's Notebook
Small Business Readiness Assessment   30

Reality Check
Not All Happy Endings   37
College Students as Entrepreneurs   40

Profile in Entrepreneurship
Good Person, Good Business, Good Food   38

Summary   54
Questions for Review and Discussion   54
Questions for Critical Thinking   55
Experience This . . .   55
What Would You Do?   55

Chapter Closing Case
Mixing Business and Friendship   56

Test Prepper   58

PART 2   Planning in Small Business

3   Social Responsibility, Ethics, and Strategic Planning   60

Relationship Between Social Responsibility, Ethics, and Strategic Planning   61

Social Responsibilities of Small Business   62
Economic Responsibility   63
Legal Obligations   63
Ethical Responsibility   65
Philanthropic Goodwill   66

Ethics and Business Strategy   67
Codes of Ethics   68
Ethics Under Pressure   69

Strategic Planning   72
Mission Statement   73
Environmental Analysis   74
Competitive Analysis   76
Strategic Alternatives   84
Goal Setting and Strategies   84
Control Systems   87
Strategic Planning in Action   87

Profile in Entrepreneurship
Doing Well and Doing Good   67

Creating Competitive Advantage
Urban Entrepreneurship   70

Reality Check
It's Not Easy Being Green   72

Manager's Notebook
Playing to Win   85

Summary   88
Questions for Review and Discussion   89
Questions for Critical Thinking   90
Experience This . . .   90
What Would You Do?   90

Chapter Closing Case
Time to Change Strategy?   90

Test Prepper   92

4   The Business Plan   93

Every Business Needs a Plan   94
The Purpose   95
The Practice: Guidelines for Writing a Business Plan   97

Business Plan Contents   101
Cover Page   101
Table of Contents   102
Executive Summary   102
Company Information   102
Environmental and Industry Analysis   102
Products or Services   103
Marketing Research and Evaluation   104
Manufacturing and Operations Plan   106
Management Team   107
Timeline   108
Critical Risks and Assumptions   108
Benefits to the Community   108
Exit Strategy   109
Financial Plan   109
Appendix   114

Review Process   114
Business Plan Mistakes   116

@ e-biz
Cool B-Plan Tools   96

Manager's Notebook
Good, Bad, and Ugly Business Plans   98
How Does Your Plan Rate?   117

Profile in Entrepreneurship
Creating the Buzz   109

Creating Competitive Advantage
Competition, Please   114

Summary   118
Questions for Review and Discussion   118
Questions for Critical Thinking   118
Experience This . . .   119
What Would You Do?   119

Chapter Closing Case
Diamond in the Rough   119

Test Prepper   122

PART

3 Early Decisions

5 Franchising   124

About Franchising   125
Background   125
Franchising Today   126

Franchising Systems   127
Product-Distribution Franchising   127
Business-Format Franchising   128

Why Open a Franchise?   128
Advantages to Franchisee   128
Disadvantages to Franchisee   130
Advantages to Franchisor   132
Disadvantages to Franchisor   133

Selecting a Franchise   134
Evaluate Your Needs   134
Do Your Research   134
Analyze the Market   139
Disclosure Statements   139
The Franchise Agreement   142
Get Professional Advice   145

International Franchising   145

Manager's Notebook
Fast Facts   126
From the Horse's Mouth   136
Franchise Red Flags   143

Profile in Entrepreneurship
Subway To Go   135

Summary   146
Questions for Review and Discussion   147
Questions for Critical Thinking   147
Experience This . . .   148
What Would You Do?   148

Chapter Closing Case
A Franchisor's Dilemma   148

Test Prepper   150

6 Taking Over an Existing Business   151

Business-Buyout Alternative   152
Advantages of Buying a Business   152
Disadvantages of Buying a Business   154

How Do You Find a Business for Sale?   155

What Do You Look for in a Business?   156
Due Diligence   157
General Considerations   158
Why Is the Business Being Sold?   158
Financial Condition   158

What Are You Buying?   161
Tangible Assets   162
Intangible Assets   163
Personnel   164
The Seller's Personal Plans   165

How Much Should You Pay?   165
What Are the Tangible Assets Worth?   166
What Are the Intangible Assets Worth?   167

Buying the Business   168
Terms of Sale   168
Closing the Deal   169

Taking Over a Family Business   169
What Is Different About Family Businesses?   170
Complex Interrelationships   171
Planning Succession   171
General Family Business Policies   172

Creating Competitive Advantage
Do . . . Due Diligence   153

Manager's Notebook
Letter of Confidentiality   159
Declining Value of Aging Accounts
    Receivable   163

Profile in Entrepreneurship
More than Rice and Beans   170

Summary   173
Questions for Review and Discussion   173
Questions for Critical Thinking   174
Experience This . . .   174
What Would You Do?   174

Chapter Closing Case
Tough Sale   175

Test Prepper   177

7   Starting a New Business   178

About Startups   179
Advantages of Starting from Scratch   180
Disadvantages of Starting from Scratch   180

Types of New Businesses   180
E-Businesses   180
Home-Based Businesses   182
Starting a Business on the Side   183
Fast-Growth Startups   183

Evaluating Potential Startups   185
Business Ideas   185
Where Business Ideas Come From   188

Getting Started   190
What Do You Do First?   190
Importance of Planning to a Startup   191
How Will You Compete?   193
Customer Service   194
Licenses, Permits, and Regulations   195
Taxes   195

Reality Check
Startup Myths and Realities   186
Life is Good   191

Creating Competitive Advantage
Creativity is the Key   190

Profile in Entrepreneurship
Über Inventor—Old School   194

Summary   196
Questions for Review and Discussion   197
Questions for Critical Thinking   197
Experience This . . .   198
What Would You Do?   198

Chapter Closing Case
Turning James Prosek into "James Prosek"
   the Brand   198

Test Prepper   200

PART 4   Financial and Legal Management

8   Accounting Records and Financial Statements   202

Small Business Accounting   203

How Important Are Financial Records?   205
Accurate Information for Management   206
Banking and Tax Requirements   206

Small Business Accounting Basics   207
Double- and Single-Entry Systems   207
Accounting Equations   209
Cash and Accrual Methods of Accounting   209
What Accounting Records Do You Need?   210
Using Financial Statements to Run Your Small
   Business   214

Analyzing Financial Statements   215
Ratio Analysis   216
Liquidity Ratios   216
Activity Ratios   217
Leverage Ratios   218
Profitability Ratios   219
Using Financial Ratios   220

Managing Cash Flow   222
Cash Flow Defined   222
Cash-Flow Fundamentals   223
Cash-Flow Management Tools   224
Strategies for Cash-Flow Management   227

Manager's Notebook
Smart to Ask. . . 206
Computerized Accounting Packages   208

Reality check
Do You Have a Business or a Hobby?   215
Open-Book Management   225

Summary   230
Questions for Review and Discussion   231

Questions for Critical Thinking   231
Experience This . . .   231
What Would You Do?   231

Chapter Closing Case
Keep Dancin' with the One Who Brought You   233

Test Prepper   234

9   Small Business Finance   **235**

Small Business Finance   236

Initial Capital Requirements   237
Defining Required Assets   237
The Five Cs of Credit   238
Additional Considerations   239

Basic Financial Vocabulary   240
Forms of Capital: Debt and Equity   240
Other Loan Terminology   243

How Can You Find Capital?   244
Loan Application Process   244
Sources of Debt Financing   244
What If a Lender Says "No"?   250
Sources of Equity Financing   251
Choosing a Lender or Investor   256

@ e-biz
Finding Financing Online   245

Manager's Notebook
What to Do Before You Talk to Your Banker   247

Reality Check
Start a Business with Plastic? Yikes!   251

Profile in Entrepreneurship
Bootstrapping with a Necktie   255

Summary   257
Questions for Review and Discussion   257
Questions for Critical Thinking   258
Experience this . . .   258
What Would you Do?   258

Chapter Closing Case
Stick It Out or Bail?   259

Test Prepper   261

10   The Legal Environment   **262**

Small Business and the Law   263
Laws to Promote Fair Business Competition   264
Laws to Protect Consumers   264
Laws to Protect People in the Workplace   265
Licenses, Restrictions, and Permits   272

Bankruptcy Laws   273
Chapter 7 Bankruptcy   273
Chapter 11 Bankruptcy   274
Chapter 13 Bankruptcy   274

Contract Law for Small Businesses   274
Elements of a Contract   275
Contractual Obligations   275

Laws to Protect Intellectual Property   277
Patents   277
Copyrights   280
Trademarks   282
Global Protection of Intellectual Property   283

Reality Check
Whadda Ya Do?   266
Protect Your IP or No?   278

@ e-biz
Legal Answers Without a Retainer Fee   276

Manager's Notebook
Exercise Your Trademark   282

Summary   283
Questions for Review and Discussion   284
Questions for Critical Thinking   284
Experience This . . .   285
What Would You Do?   285

Chapter Closing Case
Intellectual Property Stolen—Now What?   285

Test Prepper   287

PART

5   Marketing the Product or Service

11   Small Business Marketing: Strategy and Research   290

Small Business Marketing   291
Marketing Concept   291
Of Purple Cows   292

Marketing Strategies for Small Businesses   293
Setting Marketing Objectives   294
Developing a Sales Forecast   294
Identifying Target Markets   297
Understanding Consumer Behavior   300

Market Research   302
Market Research Process   303
Limitations of Market Research   308

Reality Check
And Now a Word from Our Sponsor . . .   293

Profile in Entrepreneurship
A Petunia by Any Other Name   295

Creating Competitive Advantage
Sometimes the Best Marketing Strategy Is a Good
    Defense   296

@ e-biz
Get Found Online   299

Summary   309
Questions for Review and Discussion   309
Questions for Critical Thinking   310
Experience This . . .   310
What Would You Do?   310

Chapter Closing Case
A Fork in the Road   310

Test Prepper   312

12   Small Business Marketing: Product   313

Using Your Marketing Mix   314

Product: The Heart of the Marketing Mix   314
Developing New Products   316
Inventor's Paradox   318
Importance of Product Competitive Advantage
    320
Packaging   321

Purchasing for Small Business   321
Purchasing Guidelines   322
Purchasing Basics   322

Selecting Suppliers   324
Make-or-Buy Decision   324
Investigating Potential Suppliers   324

Managing Inventory   327
How Much Inventory Do You Need?   327
Costs of Carrying Inventory   328

Controlling Inventory   329
Reorder Point and Quantity   330
Visual Control   330
Economic Order Quantity   330

ABC Classification   332
Electronic Data Interchange   332
Just-in-Time   333
Materials Requirements Planning   334

Profile in Enterpreneurship
The Customer is King with
    "Shoppertainment"   317

Reality Check
Slotting Fees: Unfair for Small Businesses?   319
Money on the Shelf   328

Summary   335
Questions for Review and Discussion   336
Questions For Critical Thinking   336
Experience This . . .   336
What Would You Do?   337

Chapter Closing Case
Keeping the Business Social   337

Test Prepper   340

13 Small Business Marketing: Place   341

Small Business Distribution   342

Location for the Long Run   345

State Selection   347

City Selection   349

Site Selection   352
Site Questions   354
Traffic Flow   354
Going Global   355

Location Types   356
Central Business Districts   356
Shopping Centers   356
Stand-Alone Locations   358
Service Locations   358
Incubators   358

Layout and Design   360
Legal Requirements   360
Retail Layouts   360
Service Layouts   362
Manufacturing Layouts   362

Home Office   364

Lease, Buy, or Build?   365
Leasing   365
Purchasing   367
Building   368

Profile in Entrepreneurship
Advantage by Location   345

Manager's Notebook
GIS: "Where" and "Who"   353

Creating Competitive Advantage
Economic Action Downtown   357

Reality check
Incubation Variations   359

Summary   368
Questions for Review and Discussion   369
Questions for Critical Thinking   369
Experience This . . .   370
What Would You Do?   370

Chapter Closing Case
Going Big-Box or Not?   370

Test Prepper   372

14 Small Business Marketing: Price and Promotion   373

The Economics of Pricing   374
Competition   375
Demand   376
Costs   378

Breakeven Analysis   379

Pricing-Setting Techniques   381
Customer-Oriented Pricing Strategies   382
Internal-Oriented Pricing Strategies   383
Creativity in Pricing   384

Credit Policies   384
Extending Credit to Your Customers   385
Collecting Overdue Accounts   388

Promotion   389
Advertising   389
Personal Selling   395
Public Relations   396
Sales Promotions   397
Promotional Mix   399

Reality Check
What Price is Too Low . . . or Too High?   377

Profile in Entrepreneurship
Hitting the Streets   390

Creating Competitive Advantage
Guppy in a Shark Tank: Small Business, Big Trade Shows   391

@ e-biz
Wadda Ya Lookin' At?   398

Summary   400
Questions for Review and Discussion   400
Questions for Critical Thinking   401
Experience this . . .   401
What Would you Do?   402

Chapter Closing Case
Go Big or Go Home   402

Test Prepper   404

PART 6
Managing Small Business

15 International Small Business   406

Preparing to Go International 408
Growth of Small Business 408
International Business Plan 408
Take the Global Test 409

Establishing Business in Another Country 411
Exporting 411
Importing 411
International Licensing 411
International Joint Ventures and Strategic
    Alliances 412
Direct Investment 412

Exporting 413
Indirect Exporting 415
Direct Exporting 416
Identifying Potential Export Markets 417

Importing 420

**Financial Mechanisms for Going International
    421**
International Finance 421
Managing International Accounts 422
Countertrade and Barter 423

Information Assistance 424

The International Challenge 424
Understanding Other Cultures 425
International Trading Regions 427
ISO 9000 429

Profile in Entrepreneurship
Hot Tchotchkes 413

Reality Check
Deepset Darkest Continent 414

@ e-biz
6.6 Billion Potential Customers 423

Summary 430
Questions for Review and Discussion 431
Questions for Critical Thinking 431
Experience This . . . 432
What Would You Do? 432

Chapter Closing Case
Hypergrowth Needed 432

Test Prepper 434

16 Professional Small Business Management   435

Managing Small Business 437
Four Functions of Management 437
What Managers Do 437

Small Business Growth 440
Your Growing Firm 440
Transition to Professional Management 442
The Next Step: An Exit Strategy 444

Leadership in Action 445
Leadership Attributes 446
Negotiation 448
Delegation 449
Motivating Employees 449
Can You Motivate? 453

Employee Theft 455

**Special Management Concerns: Time and Stress
    Management 455**
Time Management 455
Stress Management 457

@ e-biz
Help Me, Help Me, Help Me 438

Manager's Notebook
Entrepreneurial Evolution 447

Creating Competitive Advantage
Motivating Without Breaking the Bank 450

Profile in Entrepreneurship
Smooth Operator 454

Summary 459
Questions for Review and Discussion 459
Questions for Critical Thinking 460
Experience This . . . 460
What Would You Do? 460

Chapter Closing Case
Family Matters 461

Test Prepper 463

17 Human Resource Management   464

Hiring the Right Employees   465

Job Analysis   466
Job Description   466
Job Specifications   467

Employee Recruitment   467
Advertising for Employees   467
Employment Agencies   469
Internet Job Sites   469
Executive Recruiters (Headhunters)   469
Employee Referrals   469
Relatives and Friends   469
Other Sources   470

Selecting Employees   471
Application Forms and Résumés   471
Interviewing   471
Testing   474
Temporary Employees and Professional Employer
    Organization (PEO)   476

Placing and Training Employees   477
Employee Training and Development   477
Ways to Train   479

Compensating Employees   480
Determining Wage Rates   480

Incentive-Pay Programs   481
Benefits   482

**When Problems Arise: Employee Discipline and
    Termination   487**
Disciplinary Measures   487
Dismissing Employees   490

Manager's Notebook
Don't Even Ask!   472
Sixty-Second Guide to Training Your First (or Fiftieth)
    Employee   478
Firing an Employee   489

Profile in Entrepreneurship
Cooking up a Cause   482

Summary   491
Questions for Review and Discussion   492
Questions for Critical Thinking   493
Experience This . . .   493
What Would You Do?   493

Chapter closing case
Switch to an HSA or Not?   494

Test Prepper   495

18 Operations Management   496

Elements of an Operating System   498
Inputs   498
Transformation Processes   498
Outputs   498
Control Systems   499
Feedback   500

Types of Operations Management   500
Operations Management for Manufacturing
    Businesses   500
Operations Management for Service
    Businesses   501

What Is Productivity?   502
Ways to Measure Manufacturing Productivity   502
Ways to Measure Service Productivity   503

What About Scheduling Operations?   505
Scheduling Methods   506
Routing   507
Sequencing   507
Dispatching   507

Quality-Centered Management   508
Six Sigma in Small Business   508

Quality Circles   510

How Do You Control Operations?   510
Feedforward Quality Control   510
Concurrent Quality Control   511
Feedback Quality Control   513

Reality Check
Stretching the Supply Chain   499
How Good Is Good Enough?   507

Profile in Entreprenuership
It's Not Easy   504

@ e-biz
Six-Sigma Online   510

Summary   513
Questions for Review and Discussion   514
Questions for Critical Thinking   514
Experience This . . .   514
What Would You Do?   515

Chapter Closing Case
Made in the U. S. of A.   515

Test Prepper   517

Appendix: Complete Sample Business Plans   **519**

Notes   **541**

Answers to Test Preps   **550**

Index   **553**

Preface

Are you thinking about starting your own business some day? For many students, preparation for small business ownership begins with a course in Small Business Management. My goal as a teacher (and the purpose of this text) is to help students fulfill their dreams of becoming entrepreneurs and achieving the independence that comes with small business success.

The theme of this book revolves around creating and maintaining a *sustainable competitive advantage* in a small business. Running a small business is difficult in today's rapidly evolving environment. At no other time has it been so important for businesses to hold a competitive advantage. Every chapter in this book can be used to create your competitive advantage—whether it be your idea, your product, your location, or your marketing plan. Running a small business is like being in a race with no finish line. You must continually strive to satisfy the changing wants and needs of your customers. This book can help you run your best race.

The writing style is personal and conversational. I have tried to avoid excessive use of jargon by explaining topics in simple, understandable language. The book is written in the first person, present tense, because I, the author, am speaking directly to you, the student. I believe that a good example can help make even the most complex concept more understandable and interesting to read. To strengthen the flow of the material and reinforce important points, examples have been carefully selected from the business press and small business owners I have known.

New to This Edition

In preparing this fourth edition, I incorporated suggestions from teachers and students who used the previous edition. In addition, an advisory board of educators from around the country was consulted to help me determine the best ways to meet the needs of students in this course. Here are some of the changes that have been made in this edition:

- Sixteen of the end-of-chapter cases have been replaced with live *Inc.* magazine case studies. The actual small business owner's decision and expert commentary are included in instructor material.

- Because student learning and comprehension are so important, questions have been revised for content and length at the end of each chapter in a section called *Test Prepper.*

- We listened to adopters and reviewers who told us that highlight boxes are great for focusing attention, but that there should not be too many, and they should not be too long. The best examples of small business practices have been presented in chapter-opening vignettes and feature boxes, then discussed further in the body of the text. Of the 70 highlight boxes, which are limited to 4 per chapter, 47 percent are new, and the others have been updated. Of the 18 chapter openers, 7 are new, and the others have been updated.

- Every effort has been made to prevent "new edition bloat." Attention has been paid to items to delete and not just to add in order to stay current and streamlined.

Highlight Feature Boxes

To highlight important issues in small business management, five types of boxed features are used: *Profile in Entrepreneurship, Manager's Notebook, Reality Check, @e-biz,* and *Creating Competitive Advantage.* In this edition, the number of boxes was reduced to avoid reader confusion, and the length of boxes was shortened to hold the reader's attention. (Believe it or not, a rumor exists that some students actually skip reading these highlight boxes. Of course, you would never do this, as you would miss some of the juiciest stories.) Here are some examples of each type of highlight box:

Profile in Entrepreneurship   New to this fourth edition, these boxes reveal fascinating behind-the-scenes stories of people who have created some very interesting businesses.

- Lifelong Trek
- Good Person, Good Business, Good Food
- Doing Well and Doing Good
- Creating the Buzz
- A Great Ride on the Subway
- More Than Rice and Beans
- Über Inventor—Old School
- A Petunia by Any Other Name
- The Customer Is King with "Shoppertainment"
- Advantage by Location
- Hitting the Streets
- Hot Tchotchkes

Creating Competitive Advantage   One of the most important (if not *the* most important) things you create in your small business is your competitive advantage—the factor that you manage better than everyone else. There are many ways to create a competitive advantage, and these boxes point out some of the most interesting:

- Urban Entrepreneurship
- Competition, Please
- Do . . . Due Diligence
- Creativity Is the Key
- Sometimes the Best Marketing Strategy Is a Good Defense
- Economic Action Downturn
- Guppy in a Shark Tank: Small Business, Big Trade Shows

Manager's Notebook   These features include specific tips, tactics, and actions used by successful small business owners.

- Straight from the Source
- Small Business Readiness Assessment

- Playing to Win
- Good, Bad, and Ugly Business Plans
- How Does Your Plan Rate?
- Fast Facts
- From the Horse's Mouth
- Franchise Red Flags
- Letter of Confidentiality
- Declining Value of Aging Accounts Receivable
- Smart to Ask . . .
- Computerized Accounting Packages
- What to Do Before You Talk to Your Banker
- Exercise Your Trademark
- GIS: "Where" and "Who"
- Entrepreneurial Evolution
- Don't Even Ask!
- Sixty-Second Guide to Training Your First (or Fiftieth) Employee
- Firing an Employee

Reality Check These real-world stories come from streetwise business practitioners who know how it's done and are willing to share the secrets of their success.

- Not All Happy Endings
- College Students as Entrepreneurs
- It's Not Easy Being Green
- Startup Myths and Realities
- Life *Is* Good
- Do You Have a Business or Hobby?
- Open-Book Management
- Start a Business with Plastic? Yikes!
- Whadda Ya Do?
- Protect Your IP or Not?
- And Now a Word From Our Sponsor
- Slotting Fees: Unfair for Small Businesses?
- Money on the Shelf
- Incubation Variations
- What Price Is Too Low . . . or Too High?
- Deepest Darkest Continent
- Stretching the Supply Chain
- How Good Is Good Enough?

@ e-biz Small business owners need to be online-savvy, and these boxes can help.

- Cool B-Plan Tools
- Finding Financing Online
- Legal Answers Without a Retainer Fee
- Get Found Online
- Wadda Ya Lookin' At?
- 6.6 Billion Potential Customers
- Help Me, Help Me, Help Me
- Six Sigma Online

Effective Pedagogical Aids

The pedagogical features of this book are designed to complement, supplement, and reinforce material from the body of the text. The following features enhance critical thinking and show practical small business applications:

- *Chapter opening vignettes, Reality Checks,* and extensive use of examples throughout the book show you what *real* small businesses are doing.
- Each chapter begins with *Learning Objectives,* which directly correlate to the chapter topic headings and coverage. These same objectives are then revisited and identified in each *Chapter Summary.*
- A *running glossary* in the margin brings attention to important terms as they appear in the text.
- *Questions for Review & Discussion* allow you to assess your retention and comprehension of the chapter concepts.
- *Questions for Critical Thinking* prompt you to apply what you have learned to realistic situations.
- End-of-chapter *What Would You Do?* exercises are included to stimulate effective problem solving and classroom discussion.
- End-of-chapter *Experience This . . .* exercises are for student experiential practice.
- *Chapter Closing Cases* present actual business scenarios, allowing you to think critically about the management challenges presented and to further apply chapter concepts.
- *Test Preppers* assure that chapter material is firmly implanted in your gray matter via matching, multiple-choice, true/false, and fill-in-the-blank questions.
- The *complete business plan* for a retail business in the appendix provides you with excellent examples to follow in creating your own business plan.

Complete Package of Support Materials

This edition of *Small Business Management* provides a support package that will encourage student success and increase instructor effectiveness.

Student Support Materials

GoVenture CD This fun and exciting business simulation program allows you to virtually experience the challenges and satisfactions of small business management. As you take on the role of entrepreneur/manager, you are faced with the myriad decisions that must be made—from what type of business you will launch, to what your measures of success will be, to how to keep control of inventory. So much real-life detail is built into this program that you feel you are indeed going through a dry run of the day-to-day realities of small business management.

HM ManagementSPACE™ Student website This valuable resource offers non-passkey protected content such as ACE practice tests, visual glossary terms, career snapshots, outlines, summaries, glossaries (chapter-based and complete), and much more. Content behind the passkey includes ACE+ practice tests, Flashcards, Crossword Puzzles and other Interactive Games, and Audio Chapter Reviews (mp3 chapter summaries and quizzes).

Instructor Support Materials

Online Instructor's Resource Manual (available on Instructor website) The comprehensive *Instructor's Resource Manual* has been written by the author and presents learning objectives for each chapter, a brief chapter outline, comprehensive lecture outlines, answers to review and discussion questions, as well as teaching notes.

HM Testing CD The Computerized Test Bank allows instructors to administer tests via a network system, modem or personal computer, and includes a grading function that lets them set up a new class, record grades from tests or assignments, and analyze grades and produce class and individual statistics.

HM ManagementSPACE™ Instructor website This password-protected site includes valuable tools to help instructors design and prepare for the course such as basic and premium PowerPoint slides, downloadable Instructor's Resource Manual files, the DVD Guide, Classroom Response System content, a sample syllabus, and much more.

HM ManagmentSPACE™ with Blackboard/WebCT These Blackboard and WebCT course cartridges are for instructors who want to create and customize online course materials for use in distance learning or as a supplement to traditional classes. This service helps instructors create and manage their own websites to bring learning materials, class discussions, and tests online. Houghton Mifflin provides all the necessary content for the course in Small Business Management.

DVD This diverse collection of professionally produced videos can help instructors bring lectures to life by providing thought-provoking insights in to real-world companies, products, and issues. A DVD Guide accompanies the program and is designed to help instructors integrate text content with the video series.

Acknowledgments

There are so many people to thank—some who made this book possible, some who made it better. Projects of this magnitude do not happen in a vacuum. Even though my name is on the cover, a lot of talented people contributed their knowledge and skills.

Joanne Dauksewicz, Lynn Guza, and Ellin Derrick played key roles in the book's history. George Hoffman, executive publisher, saw potential in my work. I am lucky that he is my editor and even more fortunate that he is my friend. Julia Perez, my wonderfully patient developmental editor has been tremendous to work with. Deborah Thomashow, senior project editor, was wonderful in coordinating the production process. There are many other people whose names I unfortunately do not know who worked their magic in helping to make the beautiful book you hold in your hands, and I sincerely thank them all. Of course, the entire group of Houghton Mifflin sales reps will have a major impact on the success of this book. I appreciate all of their efforts. Thanks to Morgan Bridge and other faculty contributors.

I am especially grateful to Professor Amit Shah, Frostburg State University, and Professor Margaret Trenholm-Edmunds, Mount Allison University, for their help with the electronic ancillary program. I would also like to thank the many colleagues who have reviewed this text and provided feedback concerning their needs and their students' needs:

Allen C. Amason, *University of Georgia*

Godwin Ariguzo, *University of Massachusett–Dartmouth*

Walter H. Beck, Sr., *Reinhardt College*

Joseph Bell, *University of Arkansas at Little Rock*

Rudy Butler, *Trenton State College*

J. Stephen Childers, Jr., *Radford University*

Michael Cicero, *Highline Community College*

Richard Cuba, *University of Baltimore*

Gary M. Donnelly, *Casper College*

Peter Eimer, *D'Youville College*

Arlen Gastinau, *Valencia Community College West*

Caroline Glackin, *Delaware State University*

Doug Hamilton, *Berkeley College of Business*

Gerald Hollier, *University of Texas at Brownsville*

David Hudson, *Spalding University*

Philip G. Kearney, *Niagara County Community College*

Paul Keaton, *University of Wisconsin–La Crosse*

Mary Beth Klinger, *College of Southern Maryland*

Paul Lamberson, *University of Southern Mississippi–Hattiesburg*

MaryLou Lockerby, *College of Dupage–Glen Ellyn*

Anthony S. Marshall, *Columbia College*

Norman D. McElvany, *Johnson State College*

Milton Miller, *Carteret Community College–Morehead City*

Bill Motz, *Lansing Community College*

Grantley E. Nurse, *Raritan Valley Community College*

Cliff Olson, *Southern Adventist University*

Roger A. Pae, *Cuyahoga Community College*

Nancy Payne, *College of Dupage–Glen Ellyn*

Michael Pitts, *Virginia Commonwealth University*

Julia Truitt Poynter, *Transylvania University*

George B. Roorbach, *Lyndon State College*

Marty St. John, *Westmoreland County College*

Joe Salamone, *SUNY Buffalo*

Gary Shields, *Wayne State University*

Bernard Skown, *Stevens Institute of Technology*

William Soukoup, *University of San Diego*

Jim Steele, *Chattanooga State Technical Community College*

Ray Sumners, *Westwood College of Technology*

Charles Tofloy, *George Washington University*

Barrry Van Hook, *Arizona State University*

Mike Wakefield, *Colorado State University–Pueblo*

Warren Weber, *California Polytechnic State University*

John Withey, *Indiana University*

Alan Zieber, *Portland State University*

Finally, my family: Saying thanks and giving acknowledgment to my family members is not enough, given the patience, sacrifice, and inspiration they have provided. My wife, Jill; daughters, Paige and Brittany; and son, Taylor, are the best. The perseverance and work ethic needed for a job of this magnitude were instilled in me by my father, Drexel, and mother, Marjorie—now gone but never forgotten.

Timothy S. Hatten

About the Author

Timothy S. Hatten is a professor at Mesa State College in Grand Junction, Colorado, where he has served as the chair of business administration and director of the MBA program. He is currently co-director of the Entrepreneurial Business Institute. He received his Ph.D. from the University of Missouri–Columbia, his M.S. from Central Missouri State University, and his B.A. from Western State College in Gunnison, Colorado. He is a Fulbright Scholar. He taught small business management and entrepreneurship at Reykjavik University in Iceland and business planning at the Russian-American Business Center in Magadan, Russia.

Dr. Hatten has been passionate about small and family businesses his whole life. He grew up with the family-owned International Harvester farm equipment dealership in Bethany, Missouri, which his father started. Later, he owned and

Timothy Hatten

managed a Chevrolet/Buick/Cadillac dealership with his father, Drexel, and brother, Gary.

Since entering academia, Dr. Hatten has actively brought students and small businesses together through the Small Business Institute program. He counsels and leads small business seminars through the Western Colorado Business Development Corporation. He approached writing this textbook as if it were a small business. His intent was to make a product (in this case, a book) that would benefit his customers (students and faculty).

Dr. Hatten is fortunate to live on the Western Slope of Colorado where he has the opportunity to share his love of the mountains with his family.

Please send questions, comments, and suggestions to thatten@mesastate.edu.

## part 1

The Challenge

Chapter 1   Small Business: An Overview

Chapter 2   Small Business Management, Entrepreneurship, and Ownership

When most people think of American business, corporate giants like General Motors, IBM, and Wal-Mart generally come to mind first. There is no question that the companies that make up the *Fortune 500* control vast resources, products, and services that set world standards and employ many people. But as you will discover in these first two chapters, small businesses and the entrepreneurs who start them play a vital role in the American economy. **Chapter 1** illustrates the economic and social impact of small businesses. **Chapter 2** discusses the process and factors related to entrepreneurship.

Small Business: An Overview

After reading this chapter, you should be able to:

- Describe the characteristics of small business.

- Recognize the role of small business in the U.S. economy.

- Understand the importance of diversity in the marketplace and the workplace.

- Identify some of the opportunities available to small businesses.

- Suggest ways to court success in a small business venture.

- Name the most common causes of small business failure.

On Patriot's Day 1985, Jim Koch (pronounced "cook") started Boston Beer Company. Koch brewed his beer, called Samuel Adams, according to a family recipe dating from the 1870s. Although he had never been in the beer business before, he became at age 37 a sixth-generation brewer. Intending to compete directly with the best imports, Koch advertised his beer with patriotic slogans like "Declare your independence from foreign beer." The namesake of the beer was a revolutionary war hero who had helped organize the Boston Tea Party.

Like many entrepreneurs, Koch started his business on a shoestring: $100,000 from personal savings and $250,000 borrowed from family and friends—a small amount for a brewery. To reduce overhead expenses, he arranged to use the excess capacity of a brewery in Pittsburgh. For the first several years, Koch was the company's only salesperson, traveling from bar to bar enticing bartenders to taste samples of Samuel Adams that he carried in his briefcase. Sometimes as many as 15 calls were needed before he eventually won the sale.

Jim Koch.

Samuel Adams was not made for the mass market. At first it was brewed in batches of only 6,500 cases each. Koch marketed the beer as being geared toward people who were tired of drinking "ordinary" beer and were willing to pay for premium quality. Koch enjoyed saying that major breweries spill more beer in a minute than he made in a year. Quality was his focus, not quantity.

The company that started with one person and one recipe has grown to have more than 250 employees and 17 different styles of beer that have won more than 650 brewing awards—more than any other beer in history has won. Koch has never been satisfied to make the same beer as others. He has even created a new category he calls extreme beer. These new niche beers, like Triple Bock, Millennium Ale, and Utopia, are very strong and compete with the finest cognac, port, or sherry in blind taste tests. For example, Utopia is about 25% alcohol and sells for about $100 per 25-ounce bottle. Such beverages are a product of Koch's passion for quality. Appropriately, Boston Beer Company's ads stress product and process—not image—by not featuring muscle-bound men or bikini-clad women. Because Samuel Adams was the first beer to have a freshness date stamped on its label, Koch wrote a radio ad touting that fact: "Maybe other beer commercials want you to think that if you drink their beer, you'll get lucky. But I can guarantee with Samuel Adams, you'll always get a date." Anheuser-Busch later mimicked the practice.

. . . Koch takes risks, some of which do not work out well. In August 2002, for example, Koch decided (for some unknown reason) to cooperate with a pair of radio "shock jocks" through a promotion called "Sex for Sam," in which the couple who engaged in carnal knowledge in the riskiest place would win a trip to Boston. When a pair of contenders were arrested in St. Patrick's Cathedral in New York, Koch had to publicly apologize and cancel the promotion. It was not exactly the type of attention he wanted.

In a short time, from austere beginnings, Boston Beer Company has become a $50 million business. Although Samuel Adams is no longer brewed in small batches, its quality remains high. The company was the first to enter the chasm between *micro* brewery and *major* brewery. Boston Beer has about a 0.6 percent share of the U.S. market (that translates to about 1 of every 200 beers consumed). Its incredible growth and success have come from its fanatical attention to quality, its use of marketing tools that no other microbrewery had used—advertising, merchandising, and hard selling—and the perseverance of its founder, Jim Koch, an entrepreneur with a vision.

SOURCES: Adapted from www.samueladams.com, "The World of Beer"; Julie Sloane, "How We Got Started," *Fortune Small Business*, September 2004; Gerry Khermouch, "Keeping the Froth on Sam Adams," *Business Week*, 1 September 2003, 54; Desiree J. Hanford, "Boston Beer Targets Samuel Adams Sales Growth of 6% a Year," *The Wall Street Journal Online*, 19 February 2004; Jenny McCune, "Brewing Up Profits," *Management Review*, April 1994, 16–20; James Koch, "Portrait of the CEO as Salesman," *Inc.*, March 1988, 44–46; Peter Corbett, "Microbrew Boom Starting to Lose Fizz," *The Arizona Republic*, 30 April 1999; Mike Beirne "Brewer Goes to Extremes to Elevate Beer Segment," *Brandweek*, 8 August 2005; Adrienne Carter "Beer Takes Its Place at the Table," *Business Week*, 19 June 2006.

What Is Small Business?

As the driver of the free enterprise system, small business generates a great deal of energy, innovation, and profit for millions of Americans. While the names of huge, *Fortune* 500 corporations may be household words pumped into our lives via a multitude of media, small businesses have always been a central part of American life. In his 1835 book, *Democracy in America*, Alexis de Tocqueville commented, "What astonishes me in the United States is not so much the marvelous grandeur of some undertakings as the innumerable multitude of small ones." If Tocqueville were alive today, aside from being more than 200 years old, he would probably still be amazed at the contributions made by small businesses.

The U.S. Small Business Administration (SBA) Office of Advocacy estimates that there were 25.8 million businesses in the United States in 2005. Census data show that 24 percent of those 25.8 million businesses have employees, and 76 percent do not.[1] The IRS estimate may be overstated because one business can own other businesses, but all of the businesses are nevertheless counted separately. What a great time to be in (and be studying) small business! Check out the following facts. Did you realize that small businesses

- Represent more than 99.7 percent of *all* employers?
- Employ more than half of all private sector employees?
- Employ 41 percent of high-tech employees (such as scientists, engineers, and computer workers)?
- Create 60 to 80 percent of net new jobs annually?
- Represent 97 percent of all exporters of goods?
- Produce 13 to 14 times more patents per employee than large firms?
- Create more than 50 percent of private gross domestic product (GDP)?
- Pay 45 percent of total U.S. private payroll?
- Are 53 percent home-based and 3 percent franchises?[2]

Small businesses include everything from the stay-at-home parent who provides day care for other children, to the factory worker who makes after-hours deliveries, to the owner of a chain of fast-food restaurants. The 25.8 million businesses identified by the SBA included more than 9 million Americans who operate "sideline" businesses, part-time enterprises that supplement the owner's income.[3] Another 12 million people make owning and operating a small business their primary occupation. Seven million of these business owners employ only themselves—as carpenters, independent sales representatives, freelance writers, and other types of single-person businesses. The U.S. Census Bureau tracks firms by number of employees. These data show that approximately 5.9 million firms hire employees, and 19.5 million firms exist with no employees.[4] The firms included in the census figures are those that have a tangible location and claim income on a tax return. Figure 1.1 shows that 61 percent of employer firms (established firms with employees) have fewer than 5 employees. Slightly more than 100,000 businesses have 100 employees or more. Most people are surprised to learn that of the millions of businesses in the United States, only approximately 17,000 businesses have 500 or more workers on their payroll.

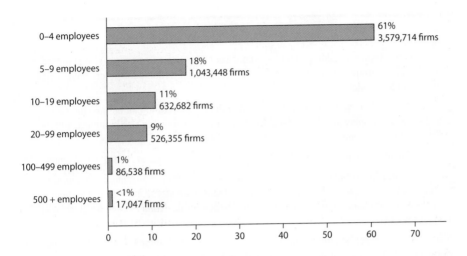

Figure 1.1

ALMOST ALL ESTABLISHED
FIRMS ARE SMALL
BUSINESSES

SOURCE: Small Business Administration, Office
of Advocacy, "Firm Size Data," http://
www.sba.gov/advo/research/data.html

Size Definitions

The definition of **small business** depends on the criteria for determining what is "small" and what qualifies as a "business." The most common criterion used to distinguish between large and small businesses is the number of employees. Other criteria include sales revenue, the total value of assets, and the value of owners' equity. The SBA, a federally funded agency that provides loans and assistance to small businesses, has established definitions of business size that vary by industry. These definitions are based on annual sales revenues or number of employees, and they vary by industry codes now assigned by the North American Industrial Classification System (NAICS), which replaced the Standardized Industrial Code (SIC). The NAICS was adopted by the United States to unify a variety of classifications employed by the United States, Mexico, and Canada. The SBA adopted the size changes effective October 2002.[5]

The SBA's Size Policy Board makes recommendations of business size eligibility based on economic studies. In establishing and reviewing business size standards, it considers the following factors:

- Industry structure analysis
- Degree of competition
- Average firm size
- Startup cost
- Entry barriers, distribution of sales, and employment by firm size
- Effects of different size standard levels on the objectives of SBA programs
- Comments from the public on notices of proposed rulemaking

Small business size standards vary by the industry within which the business operates: construction, manufacturing, mining, transportation, wholesale trade, retail trade, and service. In general, manufacturers with fewer than 500 employees are classified as small, as are wholesalers with fewer than 100 employees, and retailers or services with less than $6 million in annual revenue. Table 1.1 details more specific size standards.

---

small business
A business is generally considered small if it is independently owned, operated, and financed; has fewer than 100 employees; and has relatively little impact on its industry.

Table 1.1

SMALL BUSINESS SIZE STANDARDS

Range of Size Standards by Industry

Construction: General building and heavy construction contractors have a size standard of $31 million in average annual receipts. Special trade construction contractors have a size standard of $13 million.

Manufacturing: For approximately 75 percent of the manufacturing industries, the size standard is 500 employees. A small number have a 1,500-employee size standard, and the balance have a size standard of either 750 or 1,000 employees.

Mining: All mining industries, except mining services, have a size standard of 500 employees.

Retail Trade: Most retail trade industries have a size standard of $6.5 million in average annual receipts. A few, such as grocery stores, department stores, motor vehicle dealers, and electrical appliance dealers, have higher size standards. None exceed $26.5 million in annual receipts.

Services: For the service industries, the most common size standard is $6.5 million in average annual receipts. Computer programming, data processing, and systems design have a size standard of $23 million. Engineering and architectural services have different size standards, as do a few other service industries. The highest annual receipts size standard in any service industry is $32.5 million. Research and development and environmental remediation services are the only service industries with size standards stated in number of employees.

Wholesale Trade: For all wholesale trade industries, a size standard of 100 employees is applicable for loans and other financial programs. When acting as a dealer on federal contracts set aside for small business or issued under the *8(a) program,* the size standard is 500 employees, and the firm must deliver the product of a small domestic manufacturer.

Other Industries: Other industry divisions include agriculture; transportation, communications, electric, gas, and sanitary services; finance; insurance; and real estate. Because of wide variations in the structures of the industries in these divisions, there is no common pattern of size standards. For specific size standards, refer to the size regulations in 13 CFR § 121.201 or the table of small business size standards.

SOURCE: Small Business Administration, "Guide to SBA's Definitions of Small Business—Summary of Size Standards by Industry Division," www.sba.gov/size/indexguide.html

Why is it important to classify businesses as big or small? Aside from facilitating academic discussion of the contributions made by these businesses, the classifications are important in that they determine whether a business may qualify for SBA assistance and for government set-aside programs, which require a percentage of each government agency's purchases to be made from small businesses.

Types of Industries

Some industries lend themselves to small business operation more than others do. In construction, for instance, 90 percent of companies in the industry are classified as small by the SBA. Manufacturing and mining industries have long been associated with mass employment, as well as mass production, yet SBA data show that 30 percent of manufacturers and mining companies are classified as small. More than 64 percent of all retail businesses are small, employing about 15 million people in selling goods to their ultimate consumers. More than three out of every four arts, entertainment, and recreational service businesses are small.[6]

The industry that employs the largest number of people in small business, however, is services. Seventy-one percent of all service businesses are small. More than 28 million people are employed by small businesses that provide a broad range of services from restaurants to lawn care to telecommunications. As indicated by industry percentages and by sheer numbers of employees, small businesses are important to every industry sector (see Figure 1.2).

For purposes of discussion in this book, we will consider a business to be small if it meets the following criteria:

- *It is independently owned, operated, and financed.* One or very few people run the business.
- *It has fewer than 100 employees.* Although SBA standards allow 500 or more employees for some types of businesses to qualify as "small," the most common limit is 100.
- *It has relatively little impact on its industry.* Boston Beer Company, described in the chapter opener, has annual sales of $238 million. Although this is an impressive figure, the firm is still classified as a small business because it has little influence on the Anheuser-Busch or SABMiller breweries, which had 2006 sales of $15 billion and $12.9 billion, respectively.[7]

Small Businesses in the U.S. Economy

Until the early 1800s, all businesses were small in the way just described. Most goods were produced one at a time by workers in their cottages or in small artisan studios. Much of the U.S. economy was based on agriculture. With the Industrial Revolution, however, mass production became possible. Innovations such as Samuel Slater's textile machinery, Eli Whitney's cotton gin, and Samuel Colt's use of interchangeable parts in producing firearms changed the way business was conducted. Factories brought people, raw materials, and machinery together to produce large quantities of goods.

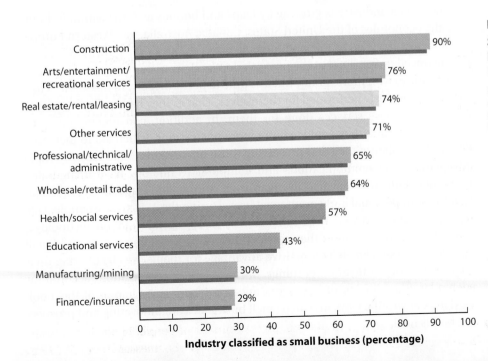

Figure 1.2

SMALL BUSINESS
EMPLOYMENT SHARE
OF NAICS INDUSTRIES

SOURCE: Small Business Administration, Office of Economic Research, "Research Publications—Small Business Share of NAICS Industries," Research Summary #218.

Construction — 90%
Arts/entertainment/recreational services — 76%
Real estate/rental/leasing — 74%
Other services — 71%
Professional/technical/administrative — 65%
Wholesale/retail trade — 64%
Health/social services — 57%
Educational services — 43%
Manufacturing/mining — 30%
Finance/insurance — 29%

Industry classified as small business (percentage)

Although the early manufacturers were small, by the late 1800s businesses were able to grow rapidly in industries that relied on economies of scale for their profitability. *Economy of scale* is the lowering of costs through production of larger quantities: The more units you make, the less each costs. During this time, for example, Andrew Carnegie founded U.S. Steel, Henry Ford introduced the assembly line for manufacturing automobiles, and Cornelius Vanderbilt speculated in steamships and railroads. Although these individuals had begun as entrepreneurs, their companies eventually came to dominate their respective industries. The costs of competing with them became prohibitively high as the masses of capital they had accumulated formed a barrier to entry for newcomers to the industry. The subsequent industrialization of America decreased the impact of new entrepreneurs over the first half of the twentieth century.[8] Small businesses still existed during this period, of course, but the economic momentum that large businesses had gathered kept small businesses in minor roles.

The decades following World War II also favored big business over small business. Industrial giants like General Motors and IBM, and retailers like Sears, Roebuck, flourished during this period by tapping into the expanding consumer economy.

In the late 1950s and early 1960s, another economic change began. Businesses began paying more attention to consumer wants and needs, rather than focusing solely on production. This paradigm shift was called the **marketing concept**—finding out what people want and then producing that good or service, rather than making products and then trying to convince people to buy them. With this shift came an increased importance ascribed to the service economy. The emphasis on customer service by businesses adopting the marketing concept started to provide more opportunities for small business. Today, the **service sector** of our economy is made up of jobs that produce services for customers rather than tangible products. The growth of this sector is important to small businesses, because they can compete effectively in it.

The service industry is growing by leaps and bounds as firms within it dominate the economies of the United States, Canada, Australia, and Western Europe. What factors have led to this phenomenal growth? Part of the growth in services can be traced to the fact that the post–World War II economic boom years provided consumers with more money but less time to perform many of the services that they had previously performed for themselves. That is, they had enough money to pay to have these services done for them. In addition, consumers' increased income meant that they could acquire more possessions, which led to increased demands for maintaining and preserving those possessions. More recently, rapid advances in telecommunications and computer technology have inaugurated entire new industries devoted to organizing, storing, and transmitting information for both personal and commercial uses. During the 1990s, for example, U.S. manufacturers increased their efficiency by adopting information technology; now retailers, banks, and other service businesses are doing the same.[9] Small service businesses create competitive advantage for themselves by offering their customers more time for other things. Because service organizations account for such a large proportion of U.S. economic activity, in each chapter of this book we'll look at specific ways in which small businesses are innovating and prospering in this field.

marketing concept
The business philosophy of discovering what consumers want and then providing the good or service that will satisfy their needs.

service sector
Businesses that provide services, rather than tangible goods.

Recent Growth Trends

By the early 1970s, corporate profits had begun to decline, while these large firms' costs increased. Entrepreneurs such as Steve Jobs of Apple Computer and Bill Gates of Microsoft started small businesses and created entirely new industries that had never before existed. Managers began to realize that bigger is not necessarily better and that economy of scale does not guarantee lower costs. Other startups, such as Wal-Mart and The Limited, both of which were founded in the 1960s, dealt serious blows to retail giants like Sears in the 1970s. Because their organizational structures were flatter, the newer companies could respond more quickly to customers' changing desires, and they were more flexible in changing their products and services.

In the 1980s, and then again in the 1990s, U.S. business saw a period of "merger mania," when businesses acquired other businesses purely for the sake of growth, rather than to exploit a natural fit between the two partners. This period was short-lived because most of the mergers and acquisitions were financed heavily, often with *junk bonds*—funds borrowed at very high interest rates. This debt left the newly expanded businesses at a disadvantage and was often followed by a string of bankruptcies and layoffs.

A new term entered the business vocabulary during the 1990s that continues to affect the business world today—**downsizing.** Downsizing can involve the reduction of a business's workforce to shore up dwindling profits. It can also stem from a business's decision to concentrate on what it does best. Any segment of a business in which its owner does not have special skills can be put up for sale, eliminated, or sent out for someone else to do (*outsourced*). The effects of downsizing and outsourcing on small business are twofold. First, many people who lose their jobs with large businesses start small businesses of their own. Second, these new businesses often do the work that large businesses no longer perform themselves—temporary employment, cleaning services, and independent contracting, for example. While downsizing and outsourcing are often painful to the displaced individuals, they ultimately enhance the productivity and competitiveness of companies.[10]

downsizing
The practice of reducing the size of a business.

The trend of more people working in their homes either via telecommuting or as the owner of a home-based business points out the importance of understanding the history of business. Are we going to come full circle back to where we were in the early 1800s, with all business conducted in private cottages? Probably not, but certainly we can see that history, at least to a certain degree, repeats itself.

Large businesses will always be needed, but in an environment in which competition, technology, and the desires of the marketplace change quickly, as it does in the economy of the twenty-first century, entry barriers fall. Small businesses are better able to take advantage of changing conditions. As Ted Stolberg, a venture capitalist who invests in small businesses, says, "The capital advantage big businesses sometimes have is being eliminated. The technology is helping smaller companies beat up the big guys."[11]

Increased Business Startups   Indeed, the rate of small business growth has more than doubled in the last 30 years. In 1970, 264,000 new businesses were started.[12] In 1980, that figure had grown to 532,000; reaching 585,000 by 1990;

574,000 in 2000 and 671,800 in 2005.[13] Although a lot of attention tends to be paid to the failure rate of small businesses, many people continue going into business for themselves. New businesses compared with closures are consistently close in number. For example, in 2005 there were 671,800 new starts and 544,800 closures—each representing about 10 percent of the total.[14]

Increasing Interest at Colleges and Universities   The growing economic importance of small business has not escaped notice on college and university campuses. In 1971 only 16 schools in the United States offered courses in entrepreneurship. By 2005 that number had grown to 1,600.[15] Other evidence of increased interest in entrepreneurship education at U.S. colleges and universities and those in other countries is the proliferation of centers for entrepreneurship, student-run business incubators, and endowed faculty entrepreneurship positions—406 in the United States and 563 worldwide.[16]

What can explain this phenomenal growth of interest in small business at educational institutions? For one thing, it parallels the explosion in small business formation. For another thing, since mistakes made in running a small business are expensive in terms of both time and money, many prospective business owners attend school in order to make those mistakes on paper and not in reality.

Some students don't wait for graduation to take advantage of hot college trends. Jason Beck and Craig Rabin, both 22 and co-founders of Collegiate Poker Tour Events Inc. in Buffalo Grove, Illinois, got their business idea while at their respective colleges, Beck at the University of Miami and Rabin at Illinois State University. Upon graduation in 2004 the pair wanted to harness the popularity of poker playing for the college set. "I'm a poker player myself, and [we saw it] was a huge trend," says Beck. The company organizes high-profile poker tournaments for college intramural departments. There's strictly no gambling; students play for free and win prizes including gift certificates and scholarship dollars. The company makes money through sponsorships from local and national businesses, who pay for the exposure to the highly coveted college consumers. Beck and Rabin hope to gross about $100,000 in their first full year of business.[17]

Workforce Diversity and Small Business Ownership

Data from the Census Bureau Survey of Business Owners (SBO) and Bureau of Labor Statistics show that self-employment rose 12.2 percent from 1995 to 2004. Women's self-employment increased 20 percent over the same period. Men represented two-thirds of the self-employed in 2004. The trend toward self-employment is reflected in all nonwhite categories by large percentage gains, although in 2004 white Americans still constituted most of the self-employed—88.3 percent.[18] Trends of an aging population, increasing birthrate of minority groups, more attention to the needs and abilities of people with handicaps, and more women entering the workforce are changing the way our nation and our businesses operate. The intent of most civil rights laws (covered in Chapter 10) is to ensure that all groups are represented and that discrimination is not tolerated. Wheels of change tend to move slowly, and inequities persist for all groups of people, but progress is being made, especially among the self-employed.

Within the SBA's Office of Advocacy, the Office of Economic Research produces reports on the economic activity of small minority- and women-owned firms and assesses the effects of regulation on them. Its report "Dynamics of Minority-Owned Employer Establishments, 1997–2001" (see this report and "Women in Business, 2006" at www.sba.gov/advo/stats) reviewed the most recent available statistical information on minority-owned firms, their composition, industrial distribution, legal forms of ownership, growth, and turnover. It also looked at socioeconomic characteristics of minority business owners. The report suggested that although minority-owned businesses are vital to the growth of the U.S. economy, significant issues continue to hamper their growth. Some statistics from the report follow:

People from All Backgrounds Can Find Satisfaction in Their Own Business.

- The number of minority-owned firms and their annual revenues were as follows:[19]
  - Asian-owned firms totaled 1,103,587 and generated $326.7 billion annual revenue.
  - Black-owned firms totaled 1,197,567 and generated $88.6 billion annual revenue.
  - Hispanic-owned businesses totaled 1,573,464 and generated $222 billion annual revenue.
  - American Indian/Alaska Native-owned firms totaled 201,387 and generated $26.9 billion annual revenue.
  - Native Hawaiian- and other Pacific Islander-owned firms totaled 28,948 and generated $4.3 billion annual revenue.
- Of all U.S. businesses, 5.8 percent were owned by Hispanic Americans, 4.4 percent by Asian Americans, 4.0 percent by African Americans, and 0.9 percent by American Indians.
- Of minority-owned businesses, 39.5 percent were Hispanic-owned, 30.0 percent Asian-owned, 27.1 percent African American-owned, and 6.5 percent American Indian-owned.
- *Business density*—the number of individuals in the population divided by the number of businesses in the population, with the lower the number indicating the higher the density—was 10.1 for nonminorities, 11.7 for Asians and Pacific Islanders, 12.6 for American Indians and Alaska Natives, 29.4 for Hispanics, and 42.1 for African Americans. Among Asians, Koreans had the highest business

density, and "other Pacific Islanders" had the lowest. Among Hispanics, Spaniards had the highest, Puerto Ricans the lowest.

- During 1997–2001, 27.4 percent of nonwhite businesses expanded their operations, compared with 34 percent of Hispanic-owned employer establishments, 32.1 percent of Asian/Pacific Islander-owned businesses, 27.8 percent of American Indian/Alaska Native-owned establishments, and 25.7 percent of African American-owned businesses.

- SBA data show that the four-year survival rate for non-minority-owned businesses was 72.6 percent between 1997 and 2001. Those for minority-owned businesses were 72.1 percent for Asian/Pacific Islander-owned business, 68.6 percent for Hispanic-owned businesses, 67 percent for American Indian/Native Alaskan-owned businesses, and 61 percent for African American-owned businesses.[20]

Now consider some of the findings of businesses owned by women, summarized in several SBA Office of Advocacy reports:

- Various measures of the number of women-owned businesses exist, including measures of self-employment and business tax returns. Women owned more than 50 percent of 5.4 million businesses in 2001.

- The 6.5 million women-owned businesses generated $940.8 billion in revenues in 2002, employed more than 7.1 million workers, and had nearly $173.7 billion in payroll in 2002.

- In addition, another 2.7 million firms are owned equally by both women and men; these firms add another $731.4 billion in revenues and employ another 5.7 million workers.

- Women-owned businesses represented 28.2 percent of all nonfarm businesses in the United States.

- In 1998 of all U.S. sole proprietorships, 37 percent were operated by women. Women-operated businesses generated 18 percent of total business receipts and 22 percent of net income.

- Women-owned businesses were concentrated in the wholesale and retail trade and manufacturing industries.

- Women's share of total self-employment increased from 22 percent in 1976 to 33.6 percent in 2004.

- Compared with non-Hispanic white business owners, of whom 28 percent were women, minority groups in the United States had larger shares of women business owners, ranging from 31 percent of Asian American to 46 percent of African American business owners.[21]

These data show that when faced with the choice of working for someone else or working for themselves, people from widely varied backgrounds choose the latter.

The Value of Diversity to Business

Considering the number of problems that most small business owners face, perhaps more of them will make the same discovery that Ernest Drew did in the following story: Diversity in the workplace can provide creative problem-solving ideas.

Ernest Drew, CEO of chemical producer Hoechst Celanese, learned the value of diversity during a company conference. A group of 125 top company officials, primarily white men, were separated into groups with 50 women and minority employees. Some of the groups comprised a variety of races and genders; others were composed of white men only. The groups were asked to analyze a problem concerning corporate culture and suggest ways to change it. According to Drew, the more diverse teams produced the broadest solutions. "They had ideas I hadn't even thought of," he recalled. "For the first time, we realized that diversity is a strength as it relates to problem solving."[22] Drew's conclusion that a varied workforce is needed at every level of an organization can be applied to businesses of any size.

Secrets of Small Business Success

When large and small businesses compete directly against one another, it might seem that large businesses would always have a better chance of winning. In reality, small businesses have certain inherent factors that work in their favor. You will improve your chances of achieving success in running a small business if you identify your competitive advantage, remain flexible and innovative, cultivate a close relationship with your customers, and strive for quality.

It may come as a surprise, but big businesses need small businesses—a symbiotic relationship exists between them. For instance, John Deere Company relies on hundreds of vendors, many of which are small, to produce component parts for its farm equipment. Deere's extensive network of 3,400 independent dealers comprising small businesses provides sales and service for its equipment. These relationships enable Deere, the world's largest manufacturer of farm equipment, to focus on what it does best, while at the same time creating economic opportunity for hundreds of individual entrepreneurs.

Small businesses perform more efficiently than larger ones in several areas. For example, although large manufacturers tend to enjoy a higher profit margin due to their economies of scale, small businesses are often better at distribution. Most wholesale and retail businesses are small, which serves to link large manufacturers more efficiently with the millions of consumers spread all over the world.

Competitive Advantage

To be successful in business, you have to offer your customers more value than your competitors do. That value gives the business its **competitive advantage.** For example, suppose you are a printer whose competitors offer only black-and-white printing. An investment in color printing equipment would give your business a competitive advantage, at least until your competitors purchased similar equipment. The stronger and more sustainable your competitive advantage, the better your chances are of winning and keeping customers. You must have a product or service that your business provides better than the competition, or the pressures of the marketplace may make your business obsolete (see Chapter 3).

Flexibility   To take advantage of economies of scale, large businesses usually seek to devote resources to produce large quantities of products over long periods

competitive advantage
The facet of a business that is better than the competition. A competitive advantage can be built from many different factors.

Straight from the Source

Rieva Lesonsky, editorial director of *Entrepreneur* magazine, shares a few of her favorite inspirational quotes for entrepreneurs and small business owners:

- Only those who dare to fail miserably can achieve greatly—Robert Kennedy.

- Even is you're on the right track, you'll get run over if you just sit there—Will Rogers.

- If everything seems under control, you're just not going fast enough—Mario Andretti.

- Creativity is allowing yourself to make mistakes. Art is knowing which ones to keep—Scott Adams.

- People are always blaming their circumstances for what they are. I don't believe in circumstances. The people who succeed are the people who look for circumstances they want. And if they can't find them, they make them—George Bernard Shaw.

What famous quotations can you find that relate to self-employment?

SOURCE: Rieva Lesonsky, "Words to Live By," *Entrepreneur,* March 2007, 10.

of time. This commitment of resources limits their ability to react to new and quickly changing markets as small businesses do. Imagine the difference between making a sharp turn in a loaded 18-wheel tractor trailer and a small pickup. Now apply the analogy to large and small businesses turning in new directions. The big truck has a lot more capacity, but the pickup has more maneuverability in reaching customers.

Innovation   Real innovation has come most often from independent inventors and small businesses. The reason? The research and development departments of most large businesses tend to concentrate on the improvement of the products their companies already make. This practice makes sense for companies trying to profit from their large investments in plant and equipment. At the same time, it tends to discourage the development of totally new ideas and products. For example, telecommunications giant AT&T has an incentive to improve its existing line of telephones and services to better serve its customers. In contrast, the idea of inventing a product that would make telephones obsolete would threaten its investment.

Small businesses have contributed many inventions that we use daily. The long list would include zippers, air conditioners, helicopters, computers, instant cameras, audiotape recorders, double-knit fabric, fiber-optic examining equipment, heart valves, optical scanners, soft contact lenses, airplanes, and automobiles, most of which were later produced by large manufacturers. In fact, many say that the greatest value of entrepreneurial companies is the way they force larger competitors to respond to innovation. Small businesses innovate by introducing new technology, markets, creating new markets, developing new products, and nurturing new ideas—actions that larger businesses have to compete with, thereby requiring the larger businesses to change.

Economist Joseph Schumpeter called the replacement of existing products, processes, ideas, and businesses with new and better ones **creative destruction.** It is not an easy process. Yet, although change can be threatening, it is vitally necessary in a capitalist system.[23] Small businesses are the driving force of change that leads to creative destruction, especially in the development of new technology.[24]

Recently the SBA researched types of innovation and the role played by small businesses. It identified four types of innovation:

> **creative destruction**
> The replacement of existing products, processes, ideas, and businesses with new and better ones.

- *Product innovation:* Developing a new or improved product.
- *Service innovation:* Offering a new or altered service for sale.
- *Process innovation:* Inventing a new way to organize physical inputs to produce a product or service.
- *Management innovation:* Creating a new way to organize business's resources.

The most common types of innovation relate to services and products. Thirty-eight percent of all innovations are service related, and 32 percent are product related. Interestingly, the SBA found that the majority of innovations originate from the smallest businesses, those with 1 to 19 employees. More than three-fourths of service innovations are generated by very small businesses, which also generate 65 percent of both product and process innovations.[25] Recent research reported to the SBA's Office of Advocacy showed that small patenting firms produce 13 to 14 times more patents per employee as large patenting firms.[26]

The process of creative destruction is not limited to high-technology businesses or to the largest companies. A small business owner who does not keep up with market innovations risks being left behind. Creative destruction occurs in mundane as well as exotic industries, such as chains of beauty salons replacing barber shops. Knowledge is the key to innovation and advancement. For this reason, it is important for you to keep current with business literature by reading periodicals such as *Inc., Fast Company,* or *Fortune Small Business* that cover small business topics and any specialized trade journals that exist for your type of business. Many business schools also have executive education programs, which range from two days to a year or longer, specifically designed for small business owners.

Close Relationship to Customers Small business owners get to know their customers and neighborhood on a personal level. This closeness allows them to provide individualized service and gives them firsthand knowledge of customer wants and needs. By contrast, large businesses get to "know" their customers only through limited samples of marketing research (which may be misleading). Knowing customers personally can allow small businesses to build a competitive advantage based on specialty products, personalized service, and quality, which enable them to compete with the bigger businesses' lower prices gained through mass production. For this reason, you should always remember that the rapport you build with your customers is of vital importance—it is what makes them come back again and again.

Getting Started on the Right Foot

Before starting your own business, you will want to make sure that you have the right tools to succeed. Look for a market large enough to generate a profit, sufficient capital, skilled employees, and accurate information.

Market Size and Definition Who will buy your product or service? Marketing techniques help you find out what consumers want and in what quantity. Armed with this information, you can make an informed decision about the profitability of offering a particular good or service. Once you conclude that a market is large enough to support your business, you will want to learn what your customers have in common and how their likes and dislikes will affect your market, so as to serve them better and remain competitive.

Gathering Sufficient Capital All too often, entrepreneurs try to start a business without obtaining sufficient startup capital. The lifeblood of any young business is cash; starting on a financial shoestring hurts your chances of success. Profit is the ultimate goal, but inadequate cash flow cuts off the blood supply (see Chapter 8).

You may need to be creative in finding startup capital. A second mortgage, loans from friends or relatives, a line of credit from a bank or credit union, or a combination of sources may be sufficient. Thorough planning will give you the

Profile in Entrepreneurship
Lifelong Trek

Ever wonder who made the bicycles that Lance Armstrong rode to the glory of seven Tour de France victories? Maybe the same company that made the bike you rode to class. Even if you are familiar with Trek bikes, you probably don't know the entrepreneur behind the company. Richard Burke started the Trek—and he didn't have training wheels to keep them rolling.

A few years after graduating from Marquette University (calling himself a marginal student with a 2.0 GPA), Burke took a job with Roth Distributing in Milwaukee, WI, distributing appliances. In 1973 he noticed two things happening: gasoline prices rising and the first U.S. boom in physical fitness. He thought of adding bicycles to Roth's lineup, but decided that neither would last, so he passed on that idea. Three years later, after realizing that both were here to stay, Burke started a division of Roth making bike frames in an old red barn. Trek remained a division of Roth until 1997.

In 1998 the average American had never heard of the Tour de France, and there was no news coverage of the event. That year Trek signed a deal to sponsor a team that included Lance Armstrong. No one could have predicted the notoriety and string of victories that Armstrong would bring to Trek. When Burke realized that Armstrong might win the Tour de France, he flew there, arriving just three days before the finish.

Burke admits that if the decision had been up to him, Trek would never have made an endorsement deal with Lance, because, as he puts it, he's "too cheap." He gives all the credit for the marketing coup to his younger marketing managers who told him, "This is something that we want to be part of." Good entrepreneurs trust their instincts, but they listen to others also.

SOURCE: From Leigh Buchanan, "Pulling Away from the Pack," *Inc.*, July 2006, pp. 110–112. Copyright © 2006 Mansueto Ventures LLC, publisher of Inc. Magazine, New York, NY 10017. Reprinted with permission.

best estimate of how much money you will need. Once you have made your best estimate, double it—or at least get access to more capital. You'll probably need it.

Finding and Keeping Effective Employees   Maintaining a capable workforce is a never-ending task for small businesses. Frequently, small business owners get caught up in the urgency to "fill positions with warm bodies" without spending enough time on the selection process. You should hire, train, and motivate your employees before opening for business (see Chapter 17).

Once established, you must understand that your most valuable assets walk out the door at closing time. In other words, your employees are your most valuable assets. It is their skill, knowledge, and information that make your business successful. These intangible assets are called **intellectual capital.**

Getting Accurate Information   Managers at any organization will tell you how difficult it is to make a decision before acquiring all the relevant information. This difficulty is compounded for the aspiring small business owner, who does not yet possess the expertise or experience needed to oversee every functional area of the business, from accounting to sales. Consult a variety of sources of information, from self-help books in your local library to experts in your nearest Small Business Development Center. A more accurate picture can be drawn if you consider several vantage points.

> *intellectual capital*
> The valuable skills and knowledge that employees of a business possess.

Understanding the Risks of Small Business Ownership

The decision to start your own business should be made with a full understanding of the risks involved. If you go in with both eyes open, you will be able to anticipate problems, reduce the possibility of loss, and increase your chances of success. The prospect of failure should serve as a warning to you. Many new businesses do not get past their second or third years. Running a small business involves much more than simply getting an idea, hanging out a sign, and opening for business the next day. You need a vision, resources, and a plan to take advantage of the opportunity that exists.

What Is Business Failure?

Even though business owners launch their ventures with the best of intentions and work long, hard hours, some businesses inevitably fail. Dun & Bradstreet, a financial research firm, defines a *business failure* as a business that closes as a result of either (1) actions such as bankruptcy, foreclosure, or voluntary withdrawal from the business *with a financial loss to a creditor* or (2) a court action such as receivership (taken over involuntarily) or reorganization (receiving protection from creditors).[27]

How long do startup businesses typically last? A recent study on business longevity by the National Federation of Independent Business (NFIB), titled "Business Starts and Stops," found that slightly more than 10 percent of businesses ceased operations in less than one year. Twenty-five percent stopped business between one and two years, while another 20 percent closed their doors between their third and fifth anniversaries. Only 13 percent lasted longer than 21 years.

As measured by Dun & Bradstreet's definition, 76 out of 10,000 businesses failed in 1998 (the latest figures available), as shown in Figure 1.3. Businesses within the agriculture, forestry, and fishing industries enjoy the lowest industry failure rate, whereas businesses within the transportation industry suffer the highest rate of failure.

Causes of Business Failure

The rates of business failure vary greatly by industry and are affected by factors such as type of ownership, size of the business, and expertise of the owner. The causes of business failure are many and complex; however, the most common causes are inadequate management and financing (see Figure 1.4).

Figure 1.3

BUSINESS FAILURE RATE PER 10,000 FIRMS

SOURCE: Dun & Bradstreet Corporation, *Business Failure Record*, as reported in "Business Failures by Industry: 1990 to 1998," *Statistical Abstract of the United States* (Washington, DC: U.S. Government Printing Office, 2001), 561.

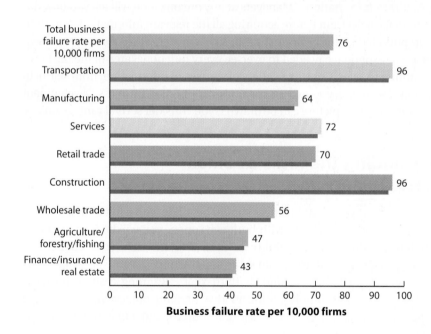

Figure 1.4

CAUSES OF BUSINESS FAILURE

SOURCE: Dun & Bradstreet Corporation, *Business Failure Record, NFIB Foundation/VISA Business Card Primer*, as shown in William J. Dennis, Jr., *A Small Business Primer* (Washington, DC: National Foundation of Independent Business, 1993), 23. Reprinted by permission of the National Federation of Independent Business.

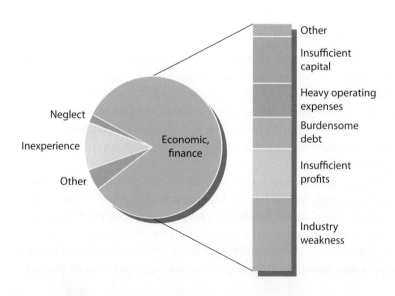

Although financial problems are listed as the most common cause of business failure, consider management's role in controlling them. Could business failure due to industry weakness be linked to poor management? Yes, if the owner tried to enter an industry or market with no room for another competitor or responded only slowly to industry changes. High operating expenses and insufficient profit margins also reflect ineffective management. Finally, business failure due to insufficient capital suggests inexperienced management.

Inadequate Management   *Business management* is the efficient and effective use of resources. For small business owners, management skills are especially desirable—and often especially difficult to obtain. Lack of experience is one of their most pressing problems. Small business owners must be generalists; they do not have the luxury of specialized management. On the one hand, they may not be able to afford to hire the full-time experts who could help avert costly mistakes. On the other hand, their limited resources will not permit them to make many mistakes and stay in business. As a small business manager, you will probably have to make decisions in areas in which you have little expertise.

Entrepreneurs are generally correct in pointing to internal factors as the reason for the failure of their businesses; these factors are the cause of 89 percent of such failures.[28] Internal problems are those more directly under the control of the manager, such as adequate capital, cash flow, facilities/equipment inventory control, human resources, leadership, organizational structure, and accounting systems.

The manager of a small business must be a leader, a planner, and a worker. You may be a "top gun" in sales, but that skill could work against you. You might be tempted to concentrate on sales while ignoring other equally important areas of the business, such as record keeping, inventory, and customer service.

Inadequate Financing   Business failure due to inadequate financing can be caused by improper managerial control as well as shortage of capital. On the one hand, if you don't have adequate funds to begin with, you will not be able to afford the facilities or personnel you need to start up the business correctly. On the other hand, if you do possess adequate capital but do not manage your resources wisely, you may be unable to maintain adequate inventory or keep the balance needed to run the business.

There are a lot of ways to fail in business. You can extend too much credit. You can fail to plan for the future or not have strategic direction. You can overinvest in fixed assets or hire the wrong people. Identifying mistakes that can be made is merely one component of the problem. Figuring out how to avoid them is the hard part.[29]

Business Termination versus Failure

There is a difference between a **business termination** and a **business failure** A *termination* occurs when a business no longer exists for any reason. A *failure* occurs when a business closes with a financial loss to a creditor. Reasons for a termination abound. The owner may have an opportunity to sell her business to someone else for a healthy profit, or be ready to move on to a new business or to retire, or she may have simply lost interest in the business. The market for the business's product may have changed or become saturated. Perhaps the owner

business termination
When a business ceases operation for any reason.

business failure
When a business closes with a financial loss to a creditor.

has decided it would be more appealing to work for someone else. In other cases, businesses may change form. A partnership may be restructured as a corporation, or a business may move to a new location. Businesses that undergo such changes are considered terminated even though they continue in another form.

Mistakes Leading to Business Failure

No one likes to think about failing, yet many small business owners invite failure by ignoring basic rules for success. One of the most common mistakes is to neglect to plan for the future because planning seems too hard or time-consuming. Planning what you want to do with your business, where you want it to go, and how you're going to get there are prerequisites for a sound business. Of course, that doesn't mean you can't change your plans as circumstances dictate. Your plan should provide a road map for your business, showing you both the expressways and the scenic route—and the detours.

Another common mistake is failing to understand the commitment and hard work that are required for turning a business into a success. Having to work long hours and do things you don't enjoy because no one else is available to do them are part and parcel of owning a small business. Yet, when you have the freedom of being your own boss, the hard work and long hours often don't seem so demanding!

Still another mistake that small business owners make, particularly with rapidly growing businesses, is not hiring additional employees soon enough or not using existing employees effectively. There comes a point in the growth of a business when it is no longer possible for the manager to do it all, but she resists delegation in the belief that it means she is giving up control. It is important to recognize that delegating tasks to others isn't giving up control—it's giving up the execution of details.

The last type of mistake discussed here involves finances. Inaccurate estimates of cash flow and capital requirements can swamp a business quickly. Figuring the correct amount of money needed for starting a business is a tough balancing act: Asking for too little may hinder growth and actually jeopardize survival, whereas asking for too much might cause lenders or investors to hesitate. An important rule to remember in terms of arranging financing or calculating cash-flow projections is to figure the unexpected into your financial plans. In this way, you can have more of a cushion to fall back on if things don't go exactly according to plan. After all, without the right amount of capital, it's impossible to succeed.[30]

Business failure, then, is a serious reality. How can a small business owner avoid it? Difficult changes may be needed, and change requires leaders to overcome all sorts of human dynamics, like inertia, tradition, and head-in-the-sand hoping that things will get better. Strategic moments require courage, or at least a lack of sentimentality, which is rare. It is in these moments that the best leaders find a mirror and ask themselves the defining question that the late, great Peter Drucker posed nearly 40 years ago: "If you weren't already in your business, would you enter it today?" If the answer is no, Drucker said, you need to face a second tough question: "What are you going to do about it?" Every leader should heed this good advice and, if need be, follow it through to its conclusion, whether that will be to fix, sell, or close the business.[31]

	New	Closures	Bankruptcies
2005	671,800	544,800	39,201
2003	612,296	540,658	35,037
2000	574,300	542,831	35,472
1995	594,369	497,246	50,516
1990	584,892	531,892	63,912

SOURCE: Small Business Administration, Office of Advocacy, "Frequently Asked Questions," June 2006, www.sba.gov/advo

Table 1.2
U.S. BUSINESS STARTUPS, CLOSURES, AND BANKRUPTCIES

Failure Rate Controversy

Almost everyone has heard the story about the supposedly high rate of failure for small businesses. "Did you know that 90 percent of all new businesses fail within one year?" the story usually begins, as if to confirm one's worst fears about business ownership. For educators and business people, this piece of modern folklore is known as "the myth that would not die." Actually, only about 18 percent of all new businesses are forced to close their doors with a loss to creditors.[32] The rest either close voluntarily or are still in business. Over the past several decades, the number of new businesses that have opened has approached or exceeded the number that have closed. Table 1.2 shows a net increase in business formations (more businesses were started than stopped operations).

Sometimes researchers include business terminations in their failure-rate calculations, resulting in an artificially high number of failures. Economic consultant David Birch describes the misinterpretation of economic data as "like being at the end of a whisper chain. It's a myth everyone agrees to."[33] Fortunately for small business owners, this high number of failures is indeed a myth, not a fact.

Analysis of business closure data as part of the recent U.S. Census Bureau's Characteristics of Business Owners (CBO) reveals some interesting findings—including the finding that about one-third of closed businesses were successful at the time of their closure. The study represented a universe of about 17 million businesses with a sample of 78,147 businesses. It was one of the first major studies to include "closing while successful" as a possible outcome (see Figure 1.5). That option could well challenge the failure myth, or the view that business closure is always negative. Entrepreneurs certainly devise exit strategies to close or sell a business before losses accumulate or to move on to other opportunities.[34]

Starting a business does involve risk, but the assumption of risk is part of life. The divorce rate in 2001 was 40 per 10,000.[35]

Of every 10,000 students who start college, about 52 percent fail to graduate.[36] Would you decide not to get married because the divorce rate is too high? Were you afraid to go to college because of the dropout rate? The point to remember is that if you have a clear vision, know your product and your market, and devote the time and effort needed, your small business, like many others, can succeed.

Figure 1.5
ANALYSIS OF BUSINESS CLOSURE

Business Success as Percentage of New Employer Firms After Four Years of Existence.

SOURCE: Brian Headd, "Redefining Business Success: Distinguishing Between Closure and Failure," *Small Business Economics,* August 2003, 59.

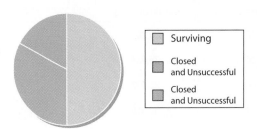

- [ ] Surviving
- [ ] Closed and Unsuccessful
- [ ] Closed and Unsuccessful

Summary

• Characteristics of small business

Small businesses include a wide variety of business types that are independently owned, operated, and financed. Although specific size definitions exist for each type of business, manufacturers with fewer than 500 employees, wholesalers with fewer than 100 employees, and retailers or services with annual revenues less than $3.5 million are typically considered small. By itself, each individual small business has relatively little impact in its industry.

• Role of small business in the U.S. economy

Small businesses provided the economic foundation on which the U.S. economy was built. Today these businesses are creating new jobs even as large businesses continue eliminating jobs. Small businesses are more flexible than large ones in the products and services they offer. Most real product innovations come from small businesses.

• Importance of diversity in small business

As the population becomes more diverse, the owners and employees of small businesses are likewise becoming more diverse. Businesses owned by women and minorities are growing at a faster rate than the overall rate of business growth. Diversity is important in small business because a wide range of viewpoints and personal backgrounds can improve problem solving.

• Opportunities available to small businesses

Small and large businesses need each other to survive—they have a symbiotic relationship. This relationship provides opportunities to small businesses in that they can supply needed parts to large manufacturers and can distribute manufactured goods. Moreover, small businesses often pick up functions that large businesses outsource. Other opportunies exist for small businesses where they enjoy the advantage of being able to profitably serve smaller niches than can their larger counterparts. For all these reasons, small businesses are rapidly becoming important players in international trade.

• Ways to court success in small businesses

To prevent your small business from becoming another casualty noted in business-failure statistics, you must begin with a clearly defined competitive advantage. You must offer a product or service that people want and are willing to buy. You must do something substantially better than your competition does it. You must remain flexible and innovative, stay close to your customers, and strive for quality.

• Causes of small business failure

Ineffective and inefficient management, which shows up in many ways, is the number one cause of business failure. Inadequate financing, industry weakness, inexperience, and neglect are other major causes.

Questions for Review and Discussion

1. How would you define small business?

2. Name a company that seems large but might be classified as small because it has relatively little impact on its industry.

3. Large businesses depend on small businesses. Why?

4. Define *outsourcing*, and describe its impact on small business.

5. Why are small businesses more likely than large businesses to be innovative?

6. Explain the term *creative destruction*.

7. How can being close to your customers give you a competitive advantage?

8. How would you show that small business is becoming a more important part of the economy?

9. The text compares the failure rate for small businesses with the divorce rate in marriage and the student failure rate in college. Are these fair comparisons?

10. Describe four causes of small business failure. How does the quality of management relate to each of these causes?

11. Describe the techniques that a business with which you are familiar has used to prevent its failure.

12. How would the computer industry be different today if there were no businesses with fewer than 500 employees? Would personal computers exist?

13. Predict the future of small business. In what industries will it be most involved? What trends do you foresee? Will the failure rate go up or down? Will the importance of small business increase or decrease by the year 2020?

Questions for Critical Thinking

1. The chapter discussed the evolution of small business in the U.S. economy. On the heels of the rapid growth in the popularity of Internet businesses in the late 1990s and the ensuing bust in 2000, what will be the next stage in small business's evolution? Is the Internet just another business tool, or will it re-create the way business is done?

2. Is *creative destruction* just another economic theory for the foundation of capitalism? Build a case supporting your answer.

Experience This . . .

This chapter discussed the failure rate for small businesses. Call your local Small Business Development Center and ask if the local business failure rate matches the "90 percent failure rate in one year" quote that was questioned in the chapter.

What Would You Do?

Everyone likes to eat. . .you love food. . .why not open a restaurant? It may not be *quite* that easy. Kenny Lao, 30, knew better when he started his New York City Rickshaw Dumpling Bar in 2006. But Lao says, "If you have a strong concept and have your execution and operation strategies down pat, any time is a good time to open a restaurant—even now." Lao built his dumpling empire on six varieties of dumplings (including a chocolate dessert dumpling) and simple add-ons like Asian salad, noodle soup and green-tea milkshakes. It takes approximately 25 minutes from order to delivery. Rickshaw sells about 1.4 million dumplings per year for $1.3 million in revenue.

Questions

1. Evaluate the business idea of Kenny Lao's business. Dumplings are his signature menu item. If you were to venture into the restaurant business, what would be your signature item? What would be your competitive advantage?

2. Look at Figure 1.4, "Causes of Business Failure." If a restaurant business goes under (as Kenny Lao's eventually did), what do you think are the most likely reasons?

SOURCE: Eileen Figure Sandlin, "The Main Ingredients," *Entrepreneur*, March 2007, 100–108.

CHAPTER CLOSING CASE

SMALL BUSINESS LESSONS FROM THE MOVIES

Want to inspire your organization? Earn the undying loyalty of employees?
Turn crises into triumphs? Start by renting these ten videos.

Every year around Christmas, Susan Schreter takes a refresher course in leadership. Her teacher is always the same: George Bailey, the sweetly earnest hero of *It's A Wonderful Life*, who risks his livelihood to prove that compassionate banking need not be an oxymoron. "Every time I see that movie, I want to be more—like George," says Schreter, CEO of Coupons4Everything.com, a Seattle-based startup that offers coupons and rebates for consumer goods over the web. "He reminds me that the important thing is to be respected, not as a rich entrepreneur but as a socially minded, successful member of a community."

Schreter's paean to the saint of Bedford Falls came in response to a recent *Inc.* survey that asked small-company CEOs and senior executives to name the movies that inspired business leaders best. The question isn't a frivolous one: Movies—like *Shakespeare*—are becoming a staple of business school curricula, as professors screen *Wall Street* to teach ethics and leaven Tom Peters with Tom (*Jerry Maguire*) Cruise. "Films are a catalyst. They present dramatic problems, crises, and turnarounds," explains John K. Clemens, who incorporates works like *Hoosiers* and *Citizen Kane* into his graduate management and executive education courses at Hartwick College, in Oneonta, New York, and is the coauthor of *Movies to Manage by: Lessons in Leadership from Great Films* (NTC/Contemporary Publishing Group, 1999). "Films beg to be interpreted and discussed, and from those discussions businesspeople come up with principles for their own jobs."

Academic validation notwithstanding, *Inc.* magazine writers expected the cold shoulder when they recently asked approximately 100 readers to don Roger Ebert hats. Company builders, after all, are generally too busy to haunt the local cineplex, let alone mull over the business implications of what they might see there. Or so they thought. To their surprise, almost two-thirds of those surveyed responded, many almost immediately. Some wrote or called several times to tweak their lists, while others left impassioned voice mail messages extolling their favorites. "If you haven't seen it, rent it today," these messages almost invariably concluded.

A few respondents described movies that had influenced their professional lives. One CEO said that *Baby Boom*, in which Diane Keaton trades the corporate piranha pool for motherhood and a gourmet baby food startup, inspired her to go into business for herself. Another used insights gleaned from the Bill Murray comedy *What About Bob?*—about a psychiatric patient tormenting his shrink—to help him cope with a problem employee.

More often, however, readers praised films that grapple with ethical and personal quandaries played out by realistically nuanced characters. "The best leadership films deal with the fundamentals, such as the presence or absence of integrity and trust," says Clemens. "In *Citizen Kane*, for example, you see the classic trajectory of early integrity followed by its loss as the character climbs the power grid. In *Dead Poets Society*, Keating, an English teacher at a prep school, is fired, and there's a suicide. But he has enormous integrity. And at the end you have to ask yourself, 'Did he succeed or fail?'—which is a wonderful question for anyone interested in leadership."

Readers, no doubt, will disagree with the inclusion of some of the films listed here and become apoplectic over the exclusion of others. But that's to be expected. As the Academy Awards remind us each year, filmmaking is both an art and a science, but film ranking is neither.

Following is a list of movies that ranked highly in the *Inc.* survey. Yes, some of them were made before most students were born, but they are available as rentals. To see a description and analysis of these titles, go to this book's Web page at http://business.college.hmco.com/students, and select "cases."

Apollo 13 (1995)

The Bridge on the River Kwai (1957)

Dead Poets Society (1989)

Elizabeth (1998)

Glengarry Glen Ross (1992)

It's A Wonderful Life (1946)

Norma Rae (1979)

One Flew over the Cuckoo's Nest (1975)

Twelve Angry Men (1957)

Twelve O' Clock High (1949)

SOURCES: Based on "Everything I Know About Leadership, I Learned from the Movies," by Buchanan and Hofman, from *Inc.*, March 2000, pp. 58–70. Adapted with permission of Gruner & Jahr USA; Leigh Buchanan, "Cinema for the Enterprising," *Inc.*, February 2007, 75–77.

Questions

1. What are your personal screen inspirations? What lessons do these or other movies provide in running a small business?

2. In addition to the movies cited in this case, think of other titles for business lessons such as *Risky Business, Pirates of Silicon Valley,* and *Tucker.* What lessons do they provide?

3. What movies portray leaders who think creatively, who keep their heads, who manage communication, and, as for failure, well, that's just not an option (a line from *Apollo 13*)?

4. Bearing in mind that the intent of movies is artistic, rather than educational, what movie lessons do you think illustrate the opposite of what a manager should do or say?

Test Prepper

ACE self-test

college.hmco.com/pic/hatten4e

You've read the chapter, studied the key terms, and the exam is any day now. Think you're ready to ace it? Take this sample test to gauge your comprehension of chapter material. You can check your answers at the back of the book. Want more test questions? Visit the student website at college.hmco.com/pic/hatten4e and take the ACE and ACE+ quizzes for more practice.

Multiple Choice

1. Small businesses represent what share of total U.S. businesses?
   a. 99.7 percent
   b. 88.2 percent
   c. 79.1 percent
   d. 24.3 percent

2. The coding of businesses that was developed to bring consistency among U.S., Canadian, and Mexican business is called
   a. SIC
   b. NAICS
   c. NERD
   d. SAE

3. The replacement of existing products and businesses with new and better ones is called
   a. outsourcing
   b. entrepreneurship
   c. upscaling
   d. creative destruction

4. What share of net new jobs is created by small businesses?
   a. 75 percent
   b. 99.7 percent
   c. 49.9 percent
   d. none

5. The reason for business failure is most commonly
   a. external
   b. inexperience
   c. internal
   d. governmental

Fill in the Blank

1. Small businesses create more than _____ percent of private gross domestic product (GDP).

2. The size standard for most retail businesses to be classified as small is _____ in average annual receipts.

3. Between 1982 and 2000, the minority-owned business share of U.S. firms has _____.

4. Ernest Drew said of his experience, "For the first time, we realized that _____ is a strength as it relates to problem solving."

5. When a business closes with a financial loss to a creditor, it is called a _____.

## chapter 2

Small Business Management, Entrepreneurship, and Ownership

There is an old saying that success is 99 percent perspiration and 1 percent inspiration. Kevin Plank's business inspiration certainly came from his perspiration. In the early 1990s, when Plank played football for the University of Massachusetts, he had to change the soaked cotton T-shirt under his jersey several times during each game. After his graduation from college, Plank developed a skintight, microfiber T-shirt made from various blends of Spandex, nylon, and polyester that share one common ability: They wick moisture away and keep it from the wearer's skin.

The Georgia Tech and Arizona State football teams were first to game-test the new garments. What followed from those humble beginnings was incredible growth for Under Armour, Plank's small business. In 1996, Plank was developing his sportswear in his grandmother's Washington, D.C., townhouse. By 2006 his

After reading this chapter, you should be able to:

- Articulate the differences between the small business manager and the entrepreneur.

- Discuss the steps in preparing for small business ownership.

- Enumerate the advantages and disadvantages of self-employment.

- Describe the three main forms of ownership—sole proprietorship, partnership, and corporation—and their unique features.

Kevin Plank.

company had become the official supplier of performance apparel for Major League Baseball, the U.S. Ski Team, the National Hockey League, National Football League teams, NCAA football teams, and Under Armour was available in over 6,500 stores worldwide. Under Armour owns 70 percent of the compression-performance market it helped create over the last decade—the $500 million worth of form-fitting shirts, shorts, and the like sold each year—leaving giants like Nike, Reebok, and Russell in its dust and making this company a truly amazing success story.

Such phenomenal growth and widespread success did not come without quite a bit of risk and lots of hard work, of course. Plank began with $20,000 of his own money, ran up $40,000 in debt on five personal credit cards, and took out a $250,000 SBA loan. He took a gamble by buying a $25,000 ad in *ESPN: The Magazine.* That bet paid off handsomely, however, when it led to Under Armour's big break—the placement of its product in the movie *On Any Given Sunday.* Word of mouth has also been crucial to the company's success. As Plank explains, "You send a sample to one guy. The next thing you know, the guy in the locker next to him is making fun of him. By day two, he's scratching his ear. By day three, he's asking if he can wear it also. I don't ever see losing that."

Kevin Plank got his entrepreneurial start while still in college. He had both a vision and the guts to make his vision become a reality. That reality ultimately landed Under Armour in the number 2 spot on the *Inc.* 500 list of fastest-growing companies, thanks to revenues of $500 million. This rocket growth rate has not slowed, averaging annual 78.3 percent growth from 2003 to 2006 (hitting $1 billion per year). His success has not gone unnoticed: Under Armour was ranked number 6 on *Business Week's* 2006 Hot Growth companies. Keep watching—Plank will continue to "protect this house." After a November 2006 initial public offering, Plank's personal net worth jumped to $789 million. His story is certainly an inspiration for any would-be collegiate entrepreneur.

SOURCES: Chuck Salter, "Protect This House," *Fast Company,* August 2005, 70–75; John Carey, "Perspiration Inspiration," *Business Week,* June 5, 2006; Karen E. Spaeder, "Beyond Their Years," *Entrepreneur,* November 2003, 76; Mark Hyman, "How I Did It," *Inc.,* December 2003, 102–104; Cara Griffin, "Battling with the Big Boys," *Sporting Goods Business,* December 2002, 32; Kurt Badenhausen,"Over the Top," *Forbes,* 5 June 2006.

The Entrepreneur-Manager Relationship

What is the difference between a small business manager and an entrepreneur? Aren't all small business owners also entrepreneurs? Don't all entrepreneurs start as small business owners? The terms are often used interchangeably, and although some overlap exists between them, there are enough differences to warrant studying them separately.

In fact, entrepreneurship and small business management are both *processes,* not isolated incidents. **Entrepreneurship** is the process of identifying opportunities for which marketable needs exist and assuming the risk of creating an organization to satisfy them. An entrepreneur needs the vision to spot opportunities and the ability to capitalize on them. **Small business management,** by

entrepreneurship
The process of identifying opportunities for which marketable needs exist and assuming the risk of creating an organization to satisfy them.

small business management
The ongoing process of owning and operating an established business.

contrast, is the ongoing process of owning and operating an established business. A small business manager must be able to deal with all the challenges of moving the business forward—hiring and retaining good employees, reacting to changing customer wants and needs, making sales, and keeping cash flow positive, for example.

> " An entrepreneur is a person who takes advantage of a business opportunity by assuming the financial, material, and psychological risks of starting or running a company. "

The processes of entrepreneurship and small business management both present challenges and rewards as the business progresses through different stages.

What Is an Entrepreneur?

An entrepreneur is a person who sees an opportunity or has an idea and assumes the risk of starting a business to take advantage of that opportunity or idea. The risks that go with creating an organization can be financial, material, and psychological. The term *entrepreneur,* a French word that dates from the seventeenth century, translates literally as "between-taker" or "go-between."[1] It originally referred to men who organized and managed exploration expeditions and military maneuvers. The term has evolved over the years to have a multitude of definitions, but most include the following behaviors:

- *Creation.* A new business is started.
- *Innovation.* The business involves a new product, process, market, material, or organization.
- *Risk assumption.* The owner of the business bears the risk of potential loss or failure of the business.
- *General management.* The owner of the business guides the business and allocates the business's resources.
- *Performance intention.* High levels of growth and/or profit are expected.[2]

All new businesses require a certain amount of entrepreneurial skill. The degree of entrepreneurship involved depends on the amount of each of these behaviors that is needed. Current academic research in the field of entrepreneurship emphasizes opportunity recognition, social capital, and trust. For an interesting article reviewing the scholarly development of entrepreneurship topics, see "Is there Conceptual Convergence in Entrepreneurship Research?"[3]

Entrepreneurship and the Small Business Manager

Entrepreneurship involves the startup process. Small business management focuses on running a business over a long period of time and may or may not involve the startup process. Although you cannot study one without considering the other, they are different. In managing a small business, most of the "entrepreneuring" was done a long time ago. Of course, a good manager is always looking for new ways to please customers, but the original innovation and the triggering event that launched the business make way for more stability in the maturity stage of the business.

The manager of a small business needs perseverance, patience, and critical-thinking skills to deal with the day-to-day challenges that arise in running a business over a long period of time.

Small Business Readiness Assessment

Becoming an entrepreneur is not for everyone. In business, there are no guarantees. There is simply no way to eliminate all of the risks. It takes a special person with a strong commitment and specific skills to be successful as an entrepreneur.

Are you ready to start your own business? Use the Readiness Assessment Guide to better understand how prepared you are. This guide is designed to help you better understand your readiness for starting a small business. It is not a scientific assessment tool. Rather, it is a tool that will prompt you with questions and assist you in evaluating your skills, characteristics, and experience as they relate to your readiness for starting a business.

General

1. Do you think you are ready to start a business?
2. Do you have support for your business from family and friends?
3. Have you ever worked in a business similar to what you are starting?
4. Would people who know you say you are entrepreneurial?
5. Have you ever taken a small business course or seminar?

Personal Characteristics

6. Are you a leader?
7. Do you like to make your own decisions?
8. Do others turn to you for help in making decisions?
9. Do you enjoy competition?
10. Do you have willpower and self-discipline?
11. Do you plan ahead?
12. Do you like people?
13. Do you get along well with others?
14. Would people who know you say you are outgoing?

Personal Conditions

15. Are you aware that running your own business may require working more than 12 hours a day, 6 days a week, and maybe Sundays and holidays?
16. Do you have the physical stamina to handle a "self-employed" workload and schedule?
17. Do you have the emotional strength to deal effectively with pressure?
18. Are you prepared, if needed, to temporarily lower your standard of living until your business is firmly established?
19. Are you prepared to lose a portion of your savings?

Skills and Experience

20. Do you know what basic skills you will need in order to have a successful business?

21. Do you possess those skills?

22. Do you feel comfortable using a computer?

23. Have you ever worked in a managerial or supervisory capacity?

24. Do you think you can be comfortable hiring, disciplining, and delegating tasks to employees?

25. If you discover you do not have the basic skills needed for your business, will you be willing to delay your plans until you have acquired the necessary skills?

SOURCE: Online Training—Small Business Primer,
www.sba.gov/services/training/onlinecourses/index.html

A Model of the Startup Process

The processes of entrepreneurship and small business management can be thought of as making up a spectrum that includes six distinct stages (see Figure 2.1).[4] The stages of the entrepreneurship process are innovation, a triggering event, and implementation. The stages of the small business management process are growth, maturity, and harvest.

The **entrepreneurship process** begins with an *innovative idea* for a new product, process, or service, which is refined as you think it through. You may tell your idea to family members or close friends to get their feedback as you develop and cultivate it. You may visit a consultant at a local Small Business Development Center for more outside suggestions for your innovative business idea. Perhaps you even wake up late at night thinking of a new facet of your idea. That is your brain working through the creative process subconsciously. The time span for the innovation stage may be months or even years before the potential entrepreneur moves on to the next stage. Usually a specific event or occurrence sparks the entrepreneur to proceed from thinking to doing—a **triggering event.**

When a triggering event occurs in the entrepreneur's life, he or she begins bringing the organization to life. This event could be the loss of a job, the successful gathering of resources to support the organization, or some other factor that sets the wheels in motion.

Implementation is the stage of the entrepreneurial process in which the organization is formed. It can also be called the *entrepreneurial event.*[5] Risk increases at this stage of the entrepreneurial process, because a business is now formed. The innovation goes from being just an idea in your head to committing resources to bring it to reality. The commitment needed to bring an idea to life is a key element in entrepreneurial behavior. Implementation involves one of the following: (1) introducing new products, (2) introducing new methods of production, (3) opening new markets, (4) opening new supply sources, or (5) industrial reorganization.[6]

Entrepreneurship is, in essence, the creation of a new organization.[7] By defining entrepreneurship in terms of the organization rather than the person involved, we can say that entrepreneurship ends when the creation stage of the organization

> *entrepreneurship process*
> The stage of a business's life that involves innovation, a triggering event, and implementation of the business.
>
> *triggering event*
> A specific event or occurrence that sparks the entrepreneur to proceed from thinking to doing.

> *implementation*
> The part of the entrepreneurial process that occurs when the organization is formed.

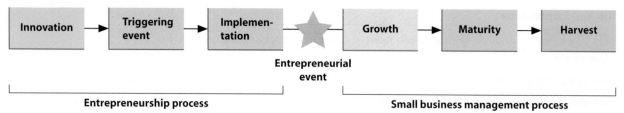

Figure 2.1

THE STARTUP PROCESS

The Stages of Entrepreneurship and Small Business Management Are Unique and Follow This Sequence with Few Exceptions.

SOURCES: Based on, with additions to, Carol Moore, "Understanding Entrepreneurial Behavior: A Definition and Model," *in Academy of Management Best Paper Proceedings,* edited by J. A. Pearce II and R. B. Robinson, Jr., 46th Annual Meeting of the Academy of Management, Chicago, 1989, 66–70. See also William Bygrave, "The Entrepreneurial Paradigm (I): A Philosophical Look at Its Research Methodologies," *Entrepreneurship: Theory and Practice,* Fall 1989, 7–25.

---

small business management process
The stage of a business's life that involves growth, maturity, and harvest.

growth
Achievement of a critical mass in the business, a point at which an adequate living is provided for the owner and family, with enough growth remaining to keep the business going.

maturity
The stage of the organization when the business is considered well established.

harvest
The stage when the owner removes himself from the business. Harvesting a business can be thought of as picking the fruit after years of labor.

---

ends. This is the point where the **small business management process** begins. The rest of this book will concentrate on the process of managing a small business from growth through harvest.

The small business manager guides and nurtures the business through the desired level of **growth.** The growth stage does not mean that every small business manager is attempting to get her business to *Fortune* 500 size. A common goal for growth of small businesses is to reach a critical mass, a point at which an adequate living is provided for the owner and family, with enough growth remaining to keep the business going.

The **maturity** stage of the organization is reached when the business is considered well established. The survival of the business seems fairly well assured, although the small business manager will still face many other problems and challenges. Many pure entrepreneurs do not stay with the business until this stage. They have usually moved on to other new opportunities before this point is reached. Small business managers, by contrast, are more committed to the long haul.

This stage could be as short as a few months (in the case of a fad product) or as long as decades. Maturity in organizations can be similar to maturity in people and in nature. It is characterized by more stability than that of the growth and implementation stages. Of course, organizations should not become too complacent or stop looking for new ways to evolve and grow, just as people should continue learning and growing throughout their lives.

In the **harvest** stage, the owner removes himself from the business. Harvesting a business can be thought of as picking the fruit after years of labor. In his book *The Seven Habits of Highly Effective People,* Steven Covey says that one of the keys of being effective in life is "beginning with the end in mind."[8] This advice applies to effectively harvesting a business also. Therefore, it is a time that should be planned for carefully.

The harvest can take many forms. For example, the business might be sold to another individual who will step into the position of manager. Ownership of the business could be transferred to its employees via an *employee stock ownership plan (ESOP).* It could be sold to the public through an *initial public offering (IPO).* The business could merge with another existing business to form an entirely new business. Finally, the harvest could be prompted by failure, in which case the doors are closed, the creditors paid, and the assets liquidated. Although made in a different context, George Bernard Shaw's statement, "Any darned fool can start a love affair, but it takes a real genius to end one successfully," can also apply to harvesting a business.

Not every business reaches all of these stages. Maturity cannot occur unless the idea is implemented. A business cannot be harvested unless it has grown.

Figure 2.2 adds **environmental factors** to our model to show what is going on outside the business at each stage of development. Management guru Peter Drucker points out that innovation occurs as a response to opportunities within several environments.[9] For example, other entrepreneurs might serve as role models when we are in the innovation and triggering-event stages. Businesses in the implementation and growth stages must respond to competitive forces, consumer desires, capabilities of suppliers, legal regulations, and other forces. The environmental factors that affect the way in which a business must operate change from one stage to the next.

The personal characteristics of the entrepreneur or the small business manager that are most significant in running a business will vary from one stage to the next. As you will see in the next section, personal characteristics or traits are not useful in predicting who will be a successful entrepreneur or small business manager, but they do affect the motivations, actions, and effectiveness of those running a small business (see Figure 2.3). For example, in the innovation and triggering-event stages, a high tolerance for ambiguity, a strong need to achieve, and a willingness to accept risk are important for entrepreneurs. In the growth and maturity stages, the personal characteristics needed to be a successful small business manager are different from those needed to be a successful entrepreneur. In these stages the small business manager needs to be persevering, committed to the long run of the business, a motivator of others, and a leader.

> *environmental factors*
> Forces that occur outside the business that affect the business and its owner.

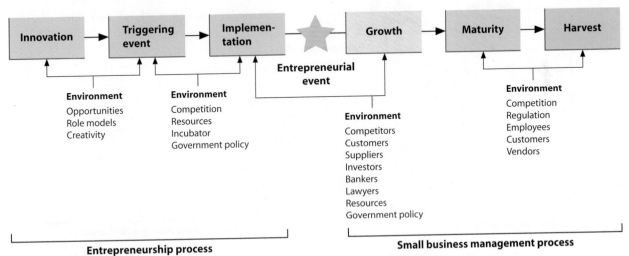

Figure 2.2
ENVIRONMENTAL FACTORS AFFECTING THE STARTUP PROCESS

At Each Stage in the Startup Process, the Small Business Owner Must Confront a New Set of Concerns. Here the Arrows Show What Those Concerns Are and How They Overlap.

SOURCES: Based on, with additions to, Carol Moore, "Understanding Entrepreneurial Behavior: A Definition and Model," *in Academy of Management Best Paper Proceedings,* edited by J. A. Pearce II and R. B. Robinson, Jr., 46th Annual Meeting of the Academy of Management, Chicago, 1989, 66–70. See also William Bygrave, "The Entrepreneurial Paradigm (I): A Philosophical Look at Its Research Methodologies," *Entrepreneurship: Theory and Practice,* Fall 1989, 7–25.

The business also changes as it matures. In the growth stage, attention is placed on team building, setting strategies, and creating the structure and culture of the business. In the maturity stage, more attention can be directed to specific functions of the business. The people within the business gravitate toward, specialize in, and concentrate on what they do best, be it marketing, finance, or managing human resources.

The purpose of the entrepreneurship and small business management model is to illustrate the stages of both processes and factors that are significant in each. The purpose of this book is to assist you as you proceed from the innovation stage through the management of your successful business to a satisfying harvest.

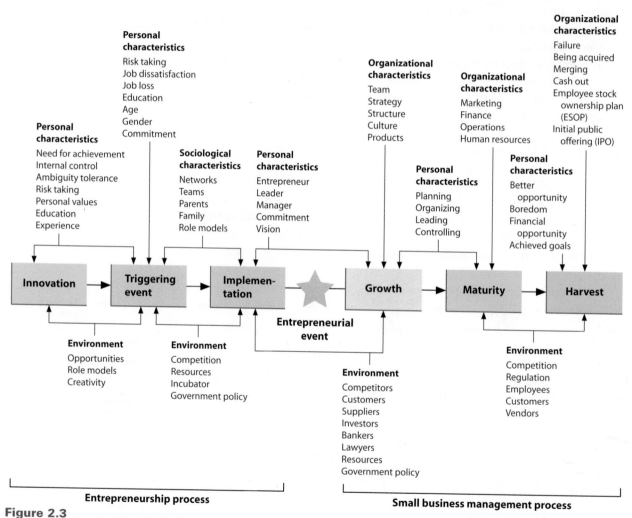

Figure 2.3

A MODEL OF THE ENTREPRENEURSHIP/SMALL BUSINESS MANAGEMENT PROCESS

In Each Stage of the Startup Process, Different Personal Characteristics Will Be More Important to the Owner as the Business Takes on New Attributes. This Model Shows How Entrepreneurial Skills Are Required Early in the Process, Then Give Way to Management Skills Once the Business Is Established.

SOURCES: Based on, with additions to, Carol Moore, "Understanding Entrepreneurial Behavior: A Definition and Model," *in Academy of Management Best Paper Proceedings,* edited by J. A. Pearce II and R. B. Robinson, Jr., 46th Annual Meeting of the Academy of Management, Chicago, 1989, 66–70. See also William Bygrave, "The Entrepreneurial Paradigm (I): A Philosophical Look at Its Research Methodologies," *Entrepreneurship: Theory and Practice,* Fall 1989, 7–25.

Your Decision for Self-Employment

Readers of this text are probably considering the prospect of starting their own business now or at some time in the future. To help you decide whether owning a small business is right for you, we will consider some of the positive and negative aspects of self-employment. Then we will look at the reasons why other people have chosen this career path, what they have in common, and what resources they had available. Finally, we will address the issue of how you can prepare yourself for owning a small business.

Pros and Cons of Self-Employment

Owning your own business can be an excellent way to satisfy personal as well as professional objectives. Before starting your own business, however, you should be aware of the drawbacks involved as well as the payoffs. We will discuss the advantages first, such as the opportunity for independence, an outlet for creativity, a chance to build something important, and rewards in the form of money and recognition (see Figure 2.4).

Opportunity for Independence   To many people, having their own business means having more control over their lives. They feel that they cannot reach their full potential working for someone else. Business ownership seems to offer a way to realize their talents, ambitions, or vision. This search for independence has led many people to leave jobs with large corporations and strike out on their own.

Opportunity for a Better Lifestyle   The desire to use one's skills fully is the most common motivation for self-employment. The idea is to provide a good or service that other people need while enjoying what you do. The lifestyle provided by owning your own business can make going to work fun. Working becomes a creative outlet that gives you the opportunity to use a combination of your previously untapped talents.

Also attractive to most entrepreneurs is the challenge presented by running their own business. Such people are often bored working for someone else. As a business owner, the only limitations you face arise from a challenge to your own perseverance and creativity, not from barriers placed before you by other people or the constraints of an organization.

About half of small business owners are motivated by familial concerns (refer again to Figure 2.4). They may feel that not only is self-employment the best way to provide for their children now, but also that their business is a legacy for their children. Children, in turn, may enter the family business out of self-interest or to help ease their parents' burden.

Opportunity for Profit   Less than 20 percent of small business owners express a desire to earn lots of money. Most people do not start businesses to get rich, but rather to earn an honest living. Nonetheless, the direct correlation between effort and compensation is a powerful motivation to work hard. The fact that you can keep all the money you earn is a strong incentive for many entrepreneurs.

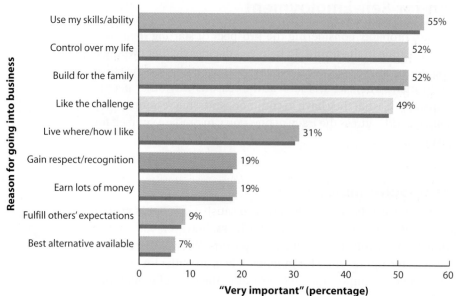

Figure 2.4

REASONS PEOPLE GO INTO BUSINESS FOR THEMSELVES

Small Business Owners Are Driven by a Variety of Motives, but a Desire for Independence Is the Primary One.

SOURCE: Arnold C. Cooper et al., "New Business in America," *NFIB Foundation/ VISA Business Card Primer,* as shown in William J. Dennis, Jr., *A Small Business Primer* (Washington, DC: National Federation of Independent Business, 1993), 31.

Risks of Self-Employment   Small business ownership offers ample opportunities to satisfy your material and psychological needs, but it also poses certain risks of which you should be aware. Personal liability, uncertain income, long working hours, and frequently limited compensation while the business grows are some of the disadvantages of self-employment. Moreover, not having anyone looking over your shoulder may leave you with fewer places to turn for advice when the going gets tough. And even though you are your own boss, you are still answerable to many masters: You must respond to customer demands and complaints, keep your employees happy, obey government regulations, and grapple with competitive pressures.

The uncertainty of your income is one of the most challenging aspects of starting a business. There is no guaranteed paycheck at the end of the pay period, as exists when you are working for someone else. Your young business will require you to pump any revenue generated back into it. As the owner, you will be the last person to be paid, and you will probably have to live on your savings for a while. Going through the first year of business without collecting a salary is common for entrepreneurs.

The reliable, if dull, nine-to-five work schedule is another luxury that small business owners must do without. To get your business off the ground during the critical startup phase, you may find yourself being the company president during the day and its janitor at night. Owning and running a business require a tremendous commitment of time and effort. You must be willing to make sure that everything that must be done actually gets done. In a recent study conducted by the Families and Work Institute, among the 3,500 small business respondents, 43 percent worked more than 50 hours per week, while 38 percent worked between 35 and 50 hours per week. (The same study also showed those same small business owners earned an average of $112,800 per year—so there *is* a payoff!)[10]

When you own a business, it becomes an extension of your personality. Unfortunately, it can also take over your life, especially at the beginning. Families, friends, and other commitments must sometimes take a back seat to the business. This problem is complicated by the fact that people often start businesses in their child-rearing years. Married couples going into business together face a volatile mix of business and marital pressures that do not always lead to happy endings.

> "A small business manager needs perseverance, patience, and intelligence to meet the ongoing challenges of keeping a company vibrant."

Reality Check
Not All Happy Endings

Mary and Phil Baechler started their company, Racing Strollers, with a rented garage and a phone listing in *Runner's World* magazine. A devoted runner, Phil had designed a stroller, the Baby Jogger, with three bicycle wheels, which enabled him to take their six-month-old child with him when he went running. The product was very successful, and the business grew quickly. Within ten years, Racing Strollers had become a $5 million company. Unfortunately, the Baechlers differed in their levels of interest in the business. This compounded the strain of living and working together. Mary became hooked on the challenges of running a growing business, whereas Phil wanted to cultivate a life away from work. Phil couldn't understand why Mary always chose work over family. Mary couldn't understand why Phil wouldn't always put in the extra effort for the business. Can two people with different obsessions live in peace?

Mary thinks the secret might be in accepting the other person the way he or she is, but they couldn't do that for each other. Mary wanted to change Phil into a manager embroiled in every detail of the business. Phil longed for the sweet girl he had met 15 years earlier. At some point, Mary chose the business over her marriage. The pressure she felt to build the business is common to entrepreneurs. She used typical rationalizations like, "As soon as this current problem is over, I'll spend more time with the family," and, "I just gotta get through this month," to justify her actions to herself.

Small problems in the marriage accumulated, building a wall one brick at a time—critical comments made in passing, patterns of neglect here and there. Soon the success of the business brought in offers from prospective buyers and very different reactions from the Baechlers. Phil saw the business as a winning lottery ticket to be cashed in. Mary couldn't let go of it.

The Baechlers' marriage ended because they had different answers to the fundamental question, Why are we here? Phil is an artist and designer who wanted financial security from the business, which would allow him to play golf and paint in Hawaii. Mary loved being needed by the business. She needed the thrills and magic that the problems and victories of running a business provided. They still loved each other, but they couldn't love each other and run a business together.

Can you separate family and business? How can you maintain a balance between them? When is enough sacrifice enough? What are the economic and emotional impacts on the post-divorce family unit? Does the cumulative effect of work and family roles overload or strengthen "co-preneurs"?

SOURCES: Mary Baechler, "Death of a Marriage," *Inc.*, April 1994, 74–78; Matthew Goldstein, "Breaking Up Is Hard to Do," *Crain's New York Business*, 28 September 1998, 27; Craig Galbraith, "Divorce and the Financial Performance of Small Family Businesses: An Exploratory Study," *Journal of Small Business Management*, vol. 41(3) 2003, 296–309.

Traits of Successful Entrepreneurs

Since the early 1960s, researchers have tried to identify the personal characteristics that will predict those people who will be successful entrepreneurs. The conclusion of more than 30 years of research is that successful entrepreneurs cannot be predicted. They come in every shape, size, and color, and from all backgrounds. Still, in this section we will briefly examine some characteristics seen among individuals who tend to rise to the top of any profession. The point to remember when you are considering starting a business is that no particular combination of characteristics guarantees success. People possessing all the positive traits discussed here have experienced business failure. However, certain qualities seem to be prerequisites of success.

First, You need to have a *passion* for what you are doing. Caring very deeply about what you are trying to accomplish through your business is imperative. If you go into business with a take-it-or-leave-it, it-will-go-or-it-won't attitude, you are probably wasting your time and money. *Determination* is also critical. You must realize that you have choices and are not a victim of fate. You need to believe that you can succeed if you work long enough and hard enough. *Trustworthiness* is important to entrepreneurs because of their many interpersonal, institutional, or organizational relationships (often untested) under conditions of uncertainty.[11] Finally, you need a deep *knowledge* of the area in which you are working. Your customers should see you as a reliable source in solving their wants and needs. Virtually every successful entrepreneur possesses these four characteristics of passion, determination, trustworthiness, and knowledge.[12] In other words, perseverance, the

Profile in Entrepreneurship

Good Person, Good Business, Good Food

In 1985 George Schenk did not intend to create a new category of food. He was interested in what he could cook in wood-fired, earthen ovens, and over an open flame. At the time that he founded American Flatbread Company in Wakefield, Vermont, Schenk was tinkering.

But tinkering is an integral part of entrepreneurship—creating a synthesis of previously unconnected parts. Schenk was very familiar with the health-food push that began in the 1960s and 1970s. He was also interesting in the gourmet eating trend of the 1980s—eating foods that tasted better and were more exotic. American Flatbread became an organic, all-natural pizza empire, with Schenk emphasizing the hand-crafted quality of his foods.

The flatbread, pizza, and company are all means of his self-expression.

Entrepreneurs like Schenk often lead by example. A real turning point in the company's evolution came when he realized that he couldn't do it all himself. He wisely avoided the Founder's Syndrome, in which company founders believe they have all the answers, by encouraging and rewarding new ideas from all his employees and management team.

All small businesses face adversity. American Flatbread has weathered two crises so far: a flood and the death of an employee. The company survived because of the way George Schenk showed his concern for his employees, customers, and community. This man exemplifies successful entrepreneurship by virtue of his personality traits, ability to take advantage of a business opportunity, and people skills that benefit employees and customers alike.

technical skills to run a business, belief in yourself, and the ability to inspire others to trust you are all important for success.

A pioneer in entrepreneurial research, David McClelland identified entrepreneurs as people with a higher **need to achieve** than nonentrepreneurs.[13] People with a high need to achieve are attracted to jobs that challenge their skills and problem-solving abilities, yet offer a good chance of success. They equally avoid goals that seem almost impossible to achieve and those that pose no challenge. They prefer tasks in which the outcome depends on their individual effort.

Locus of control is a term used to explain how people view their ability to determine their own fate. Entrepreneurs tend to have a stronger internal locus of control than people in the general population.[14] People with a high internal locus of control believe that the outcome of an event is determined by their own actions. Luck, chance, fate, or the control of other people (external factors) are less important than one's own efforts.[15] When faced with a problem or a difficult situation, internals look within themselves for solutions. Internal locus of control is the force that compels many people to start their own businesses in an effort to gain independence, autonomy, and freedom.

Successful entrepreneurs and small business owners are innovative and creative. *Innovation* results from the ability to conceive of and create new and unique products, processes, or services. Entrepreneurs see opportunities in the marketplace and visualize creative new ways to take advantage of them.

How do entrepreneurs tend to view *risk taking*? A myth about entrepreneurs is that they are wild-eyed, risk-seeking, financial daredevils. While acceptance of financial risk is necessary to start a business, the prototypical entrepreneur tends to accept moderate risk only after careful examination of what she is about to get into.

Consider the case of Scott Schmidt, the entrepreneurial athlete who started what has become known as "extreme skiing." Basically, he jumps from 60-foot cliffs on skis for a living. Ski equipment companies sponsor him for endorsements and video production. If you saw him from the ski lift, you would say, "That guy is a maniac for taking that risk." The same is often said of other entrepreneurs by people looking in from outside the situation. Actually, Schmidt very carefully charts his takeoff and landing points, and he does not see himself as reckless. An analogy can be drawn between Schmidt's adventurous style of skiing and the risks of starting a new business.

Entrepreneurs carefully plan their next moves in their business plans. Once they are in the air, entrepreneurs must trust their remarkable talent to help them react to what comes their way as they fall. Entrepreneurs don't risk life and limb, because they look for ways to minimize their risks by careful observation and planning, just as Schmidt precisely plans his moves. They commonly do not see unknown situations as risky, because they know their strengths and talents, are confident of success, and have analyzed the playing field. In similar fashion, Scott Schmidt doesn't consider himself reckless. He considers himself very good at what he does.[16] That is a typical entrepreneurial attitude.

Other traits that are useful in owning your own business are a high level of energy, confidence, orientation toward the future, optimism, desire for feedback, high tolerance for ambiguity, flexibility/adaptability, and commitment. If one characteristic of successful entrepreneurs stands out above all others across all types of businesses, however, it would have to be their *incredible tenacity*.

need to achieve
The personal quality, linked to entrepreneurship, of being motivated to excel and choose situations in which success is likely.

locus of control
A person's belief concerning the degree to which internal or external forces control his or her future.

Reality Check

College Students as Entrepreneurs

As many of you reading this textbook already realize, now is a great time to be studying entrepreneurship and small business management. But not all of you are waiting until graduation to launch your ventures.

Megan Wettach opened a store in her hometown of Mt. Pleasant, Iowa, selling prom dresses while she was still in high school. After the 22-year-old junior at the University of Iowa took a class in entrepreneurship, she moved the company to the proverbial next level. Without the knowledge, bigger-picture thinking, and skills gained in that class, Wettach may well have remained content with a little dress store in a small Iowa town. But after the class, she is now aiming to become a global force in fashion. Megan designs original gowns, contractually outsources production in China, and successfully negotiated a deal with no less than Nordstrom to carry her line.

Alex Farkas's double major of art history and entrepreneurship at the University of Arizona gave him a unique perspective on a need in the marketplace and an opportunity to acquire the skills necessary to create

a mechanism to capitalize upon it. Farkas, with partners Stephen Tanenbaum and Greg Rosborough, knew that unknown art students salivate for an outlet to show their creations. They also knew that many consumers would much rather have a piece of truly original art than a mass-produced poster. Their class-produced business plan for Ugallery.com won the trio of 23-year-olds over $22,000 in startup capital via business-plan competitions.

Hard work by student entrepreneurs not only helps them score an A but serves as a wise investment. Professor Bill Guerrero of Purchase College, State University of New York, says, "I wouldn't worry about the grade. I would worry about understanding the entrepreneurial lifestyle and risks to help avoid some pitfalls that most entrepreneurs go through. It doesn't guarantee them success as entrepreneurs, but it will certainly help alleviate some of the common mistakes."

SOURCES: Nichole L. Torres, "Get Schooled" Entrepreneur, October 2006, 96–101; Patricia Gray, "Can Entrepreneurship Be Taught?" *Fortune Small Business*, 1 March 2006, http://money.cnn.com/magazines/fsb/fsb_archive; Nichole L. Torres, "Real Smart," *Entrepreneur*, December 2006, 134–135.

Preparing Yourself for Business Ownership

How do you prepare for an undertaking like owning your own business? Do you need experience? Do you need education? The answer to both questions is always "yes." But what kind? And how much? These questions are tougher to answer because their answers depend on the type of business you plan to enter. The experience you would need to open a franchised bookstore differs from that needed for an upscale restaurant.

Entrepreneurs and small business owners typically have higher education levels than the general public. About 60 percent of new business owners have had at least some college education (see Figure 2.5).[17] Exceptions do exist, however—people have dropped out of school and gone on to start successful businesses—so it is difficult to generalize. Even so, in a majority of cases we can conclude that more education increases the chances of success. Note should be taken that, for the most successful small businesses, the CEOs of *Inc.* 500 companies have significantly higher education levels (refer again to Figure 2.5).

Entrepreneurship and small business management are the fastest-growing classes in business schools across the country.[18] In 1971 Karl Vesper of the University of Washington found that 16 U.S. schools offered a course in entrepreneurship. In his 1993 update of that study, that number had grown to 370. By 2006,

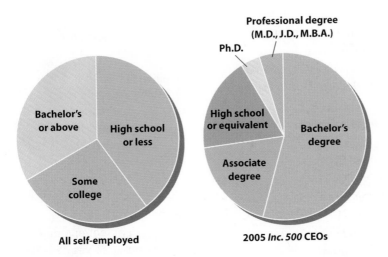

Figure 2.5
EDUCATION LEVEL OF NEW
BUSINESS OWNERS

*Although Individual Exceptions
Exist, Small Business Owners as
a Group Have More Formal
Education Than the General
Population, and Inc. 500 CEOs
Have Even Higher Education
Levels.*

SOURCES: U.S. Small Business Administration,
Office of Advocacy, "Characteristics of Small
Business Employees and Owners,"
www.sba.gov/stats; "Meet the Founders—CEO
Survey," *Inc. (The Inc. 500 Special Issue),*
November 2005, 126.

1,600 institutions offered courses in entrepreneurship.[19] Some of the nation's top business schools, such as University of Arizona, Syracuse, De Paul, Temple, and University of Dayton (ranked as the top five Best Undergrad Programs for Entrepreneurs by *Entrepreneur* magazine in 2006), as well as many other four-year colleges and community colleges, are offering degrees in entrepreneurship and small business management.[20] Until very recently, the leaders of most business schools argued that entrepreneurship could not be taught. Now, however, the increased academic attention is constructing a body of knowledge on the processes of starting and running small businesses, which proves that entrepreneurial processes can and are being learned.

The SBA and other nonacademic agencies offer start-your-own-business seminars to prospective entrepreneurs. Executive education programs offered through college extension departments are providing curricula specifically designed for entrepreneurs and small business owners. These one-day to one-year programs provide valuable skills without a degree.

Obtaining practical experience in your type of business is an important part of your education. You can learn valuable skills from various jobs that will prepare you for owning your own business. For example, working in a restaurant, in retail sales, or in a customer service department can hone your customer relations skills, which are crucial in running your own business but difficult to learn in a classroom.

The analytical and relational skills that you learn in formal educational settings are important, but remember that your future development depends on lifelong learning. (*Commencement,* after all, means "beginning"—the beginning of your business career!) Finally, don't overlook hobbies and other interests in preparing for self-employment. Participating in team sports and student organizations, for instance, can cultivate your team spirit and facility in working with others. Your marketing skills can be improved through a knowledge of languages or fine art. Sometimes an avocation can turn into a vocation. For example, more than one weekend gardener has become a successful greenhouse owner.

Of course, no amount of experience or education can completely prepare you for owning your own business. Because every person, situation, and business is

Figure 2.6

OWNERSHIP FORMS OF U.S. BUSINESSES

The Sole Proprietorship Is the Most Common Business Form in the United States.

SOURCE: *The 2007 Statistical Abstract,* U.S. Census Bureau, Table 724, "Number of Returns, Receipts, and Net Income by Type of Business," www.census.gov/compendia/statab.

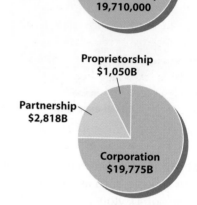

Partnership
3,375,000

Corporation
5,401,000

Proprietorship
19,710,000

Figure 2.7

SALES REVENUE BY OWNERSHIP TYPE

Corporations Produce the Majority of Revenues Earned.

SOURCE: *The 2007 Statistical Abstract,* U.S. Census Bureau, Table 724, "Number of Returns, Receipts, and Net Income by Type of Business," www.census.gov/compendia/statab.

Proprietorship
$1,050B

Partnership
$2,818B

Corporation
$19,775B

Figure 2.8

NET INCOME BY OWNERSHIP TYPE

Corporations Also Earned the Bulk of Net Income.

SOURCE: *The 2007 Statistical Abstract,* U.S. Census Bureau, Table 724, "Number of Returns, Receipts, and Net Income by Type of Business," www.census.gov/compendia/statab.

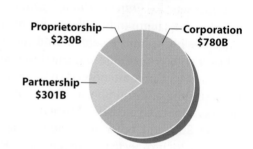

Proprietorship
$230B

Corporation
$780B

Partnership
$301B

different, you are certainly going to encounter situations for which you could not have possibly prepared. Get as much experience and education as you can, but at some point you must "take off and hang on." You have to find a way to make your business go.

Forms of Business Organization

One of the first decisions you will need to make in starting a business is choosing a form of ownership. This section will lead you through your options and present the advantages and disadvantages of each.

Several issues should be considered when making this decision. To what extent do you want to be personally liable for financial and legal risk? Who will have controlling interest of the business? How will the business be financed? The three basic legal structures you can choose for your firm are sole proprietorship, partnership, or corporation, with specialized options of partnerships and corporations available.

About 72 percent of all businesses that exist in the United States are sole proprietorships, making this the most common form of ownership (see Figures 2.6, 2.7, and 2.8). Yet, sole proprietorships account for only 4 percent of the total revenue generated by businesses and only 18 percent of the net profits earned. By comparison, corporations bring in 84 percent of business-generated revenue and 59 percent of the net income earned, even though they account for only 20 percent of the total number of businesses. Partnerships are also in the minority, with 9 percent of the total number of businesses, 12 percent of the revenue, and 23 percent of the net income earned.

Figure 2.9 shows that proprietorships increased in number and as a percentage of the total of the 27 million small businesses that existed in the United States from 1980 to 2003. This trend illustrates the rise of very small businesses. The number of corporations grew gradually, whereas the number of partnerships remained relatively constant. Changes in tax laws have an effect on the number of businesses of each type that are formed.

There is no single best form of organization. The choice depends on your short- and long-term needs, your tax situation, and your personal preferences, abilities, and resources. Don't confuse legal form of ownership with the size of the business. When you walk into a small neighborhood business, can you assume that it is a sole proprietorship? Not necessarily. A one-person flower shop may be a corporation, or a multimillion-dollar factory could be a sole proprietorship.

Sole Proprietorship

A **sole proprietorship** is a business that is owned and operated by one person. There are no legal requirements to establish a sole proprietorship. In most states, if you are operating under a name other than your full first and last legal names, you must register the business as a trade name with the state department of revenue (see Table 2.1).

sole proprietorship
A business owned and operated by one person.

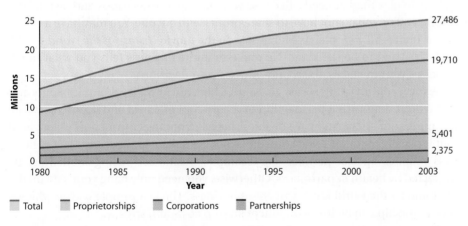

Figure 2.9
GROWTH IN THE BUSINESS POPULATION

While the Number of All Forms of Ownership Has Risen, Business Tax Returns Show That the Number of Proprietorships Has Increased the Most.

SOURCE: *The 2007 Statistical Abstract,* U.S. Census Bureau, Table 724, "Number of Returns, Receipts, and Net Income by Type of Business," www.census.gov/compendia/statab.

Advantages	Disadvantages
Independence	Unlimited liability
Easy to set up	Limited resources
Easy to close	Limited skills
Tax benefits	Lack of continuity

Table 2.1
BALANCING THE ADVANTAGES AND DISADVANTAGES OF SOLE PROPRIETORSHIPS

Sole Proprietorships Create Pride of Ownership.

Advantages   As the owner of a sole proprietorship, you have complete control of the business. The sole proprietorship is well suited to the aspiring entrepreneur's desire for independence. You don't have to consult with any partners, stockholders, or boards of directors. As a result of this independence, you are free to respond quickly to new market needs. Because you make all the decisions and bear all the responsibility, you do not have to share profits with anyone. You may have a smaller pie, but it's all *your* pie. As Mel Brooks in the movie *History of the World, Part I,* said, "It's good to be the king." No one else in the business tells you what to do, criticizes your mistakes, or second-guesses your decisions.

A sole proprietorship is easy to set up. There are fewer legal requirements and restrictions than with a partnership or a corporation. Legal and license costs are at a minimum. An inexpensive business license from the city or county clerk is all that is usually required—and sometimes not even that—unless your type of business requires special permits. For example, businesses selling food must be inspected by health departments. Otherwise, you need only hang your sign on the door and let the world know you are in business. The fast, simple way in which a proprietorship can be formed reduces startup costs and stress.

The Internal Revenue Service (IRS) regards the business and the owner in a sole proprietorship as being a single entity. If your business shows a loss the first year or two (which is common), those losses can be deducted from any other income you have for the year. This tax advantage is short-lived, however. The tax code states that your business must make money three out of five years. According to the IRS, only moneymaking ventures are considered businesses. Anything else is a hobby. Even so, this deduction can give you a boost if you are starting your business on a part-time basis and have other income.

Just as proprietorships are easy to open, they are easy to close. If you choose, you can liquidate your assets, pay your bills, turn off the lights, and take your sign

off the door, and you are then out of business. This is not the case with partnerships and corporations.

Disadvantages   The biggest disadvantage of a sole proprietorship is its **unlimited liability.** As a sole proprietor, you are personally liable for all debts incurred by the business. If the business should fail, you could lose more than you invested in it. Personal assets, such as your home and car, might have to be liquidated to cover the business debt. Thus, although there are few caps on the potential for return with a sole proprietorship, there are similarly few caps on the amount you could lose.

unlimited liability
The potential for an owner to lose more than has been invested in a business.

The sole proprietorship is the most difficult form of business for which to raise capital from outside sources. As one individual, you have access to fewer financial resources than a group of people could gather. Lenders believe that their chances of seeing a return on their investment are reduced in a sole proprietorship and therefore are not as likely to loan money to this type of business.

The total responsibility of running a sole proprietorship may mean independence, but it can also be a disadvantage. Just as you are limited to the amount of capital you can raise, so you are limited to and by your own skills and capabilities. You may be an expert in some areas of running a business but be deficient in others.

Total responsibility can also mean a lack of continuity in the business. If you should become unable to work through illness, disability, or death, the business will cease to exist. Long vacations can become virtually impossible to take.

Partnership

If two or more people are going into business together, they have two choices: form a partnership or form a corporation. A **partnership** is defined as an association of two or more persons to carry on as co-owners of a business for profit. Legally you can have a partnership without a written agreement (although it is not recommended), so the paperwork requirements for starting a partnership are about the same as those for a proprietorship.

partnership
An association of two or more persons to carry on as co-owners of a business for profit.

When you form a partnership with friends, family, or associates, you may not think it is necessary to have a written agreement because you are so familiar with each other. You do. Problems are inevitable for every partnership, and the human memory is far too frail to depend upon in times of business difficulty. An agreement that is well thought out when the partnership is formed can save the business—and a friendship—later. Without a written agreement, a partnership operates according to the rules of the state under the Uniform Partnership Act (UPA). The intent of the UPA is to settle problems between partners. For example, without a written agreement that states otherwise, each partner shares equally in the profit and management of the business. The UPA is discussed in more detail later in this chapter.

Partners should bring complementary skills and resources to the alliance to give it a better chance of success. For instance, if one partner has creative abilities, the other partner should have a good business (financial) sense. Partners may also complement each other by providing different business contacts or amounts of capital. Think of the relationship this way: if both partners possess the same qualities, one of them probably isn't needed.

general partnership
A business structure in which the business owners share the management and risk of the business.

There are two types of partnerships: general and limited. Most of this discussion will focus on the **general partnership,** which is more common. In a general partnership, each partner faces the same personal liability as a sole proprietor. In a limited partnership, at least one of the partners has limited liability. This section will concentrate on general partnerships, with limited partnerships being discussed at the end of the section.

Advantages   The biggest advantage of partnerships should be the pooling of managerial talent and capital to create a product or service that is better than any of the partners could have created individually (see Table 2.2).

Access to additional capital is an advantage of partnerships. Partners can pool their money. Moreover, credit is easier to obtain than for a proprietor. The reason is that the creditor can collect the debt from any one or all of the partners. Partnerships can also benefit from more management expertise in decision making. With more partners involved, there is a higher chance of someone knowing what to do or having prior experience in any given situation.

Partnerships, like proprietorships, have a tax advantage in that the owners pay taxes as individuals. Therefore, profits are taxed only once on each partner's share of the income. The partnership must file an informational return that reports how much money it earned or lost during the tax year and what share of the income or loss belongs to each partner.

Partnerships are easy to create. All you need are the appropriate business licenses and a tax number, and you're in business—for better or for worse.

Disadvantages   As with sole proprietorships, a disadvantage of partnerships is that the general partners carry the burden of unlimited liability. Each general partner's liability is not limited to the amount of his investment but rather extends to his personal property as well. Even if the partnership agreement specifies a defined split in profits, each partner is 100 percent responsible for all liabilities.

In a partnership, you can be held liable for the negligence of your partners. A great deal of trust, a comprehensive agreement, and a good lawyer are, therefore, needed before opening such a business. Similarly, each partner can act as an agent of the partnership. In other words, any partner can enter into a contract for the partnership, incurring debt or other responsibilities, or selling assets, unless limited by the *articles of partnership*, discussed in detail later in this chapter. The choice of a business partner is much like choosing a partner for marriage. You need to know and be able to live with the other person's character, work habits, and values to make sure you are compatible.

Table 2.2
BALANCING THE ADVANTAGES AND DISADVANTAGES OF PARTNERSHIPS

Advantages	Disadvantages
Pooled talent	Unlimited liability
Pooled resources	Potential for management conflict
Easy to form	Less independence than proprietorships
Tax benefits	Continuity or transfer of ownership

The potential for managerial conflict within the partnership is one of the most serious problems that can threaten its viability. If partners disagree on matters that involve core issues, such as a future direction for the business, the partnership could literally split at the seams.

If a common reason to go into small business is independence, entering into a partnership limits that independence. For example, what happens if you want to reinvest profits in the business, but your partner wants to start holding your business meetings in Hawaii and have the company buy each of you new cars? Some resolution must be found, or the entire business could be in jeopardy. Being a partner requires compromise and cooperation.

Although the ability to raise capital is better with a partnership than with a proprietorship, a partnership still cannot usually gather as many resources as a corporation.

Another financial problem could occur when the partnership decides to retain some of its income and reinvest it in the business. All partners must pay income tax on their share of the partnership's income, even if they do not receive those funds. This requirement could prove financially difficult for some partners.

Continuity can also be a problem for partnerships. Difficulties may arise if a partner wants to withdraw from the partnership, dies, or becomes unable to continue in the business. Even if the partnership agreement identifies the value of each owner's share, the remaining partners may not have the financial resources to buy out the one who wants to leave. If a partner leaves, the partnership is dissolved. The remaining partners must find a new partner to bring in, contribute additional capital themselves, or terminate the business. This problem can be avoided in advance by including a *buy-sell agreement* in the *articles of partnership*, which will be discussed in detail later in this chapter. The buy-sell agreement spells out what will happen if one of the partners wants to leave voluntarily, becomes disabled, or dies. A sensible solution is a "right of first refusal" clause, which requires the selling partner to give the remaining partners the first chance to buy the exiting partner's share. This proactive solution is highly recommended for all partnerships and corporations.

Limited Partnership   The **limited partnership** was created to avoid some of the problems of a general partnership while retaining its basic benefits. A limited partnership must have at least one general partner who retains unlimited liability and all of the other responsibilities discussed in the general partnership section. In addition, any number of limited partners with limited liability is allowed. Limited partners are usually passive investors. All they can lose is the amount they invest in the business. With very few exceptions, limited partners cannot participate in the management of the business without losing their liability protection. Limited partnerships are a good way for the general partners to acquire capital— from the limited partners—without giving up control, taking on debt, or going through the process of forming a corporation.

The cost and complication of organizing a limited partnership can be as high as those for forming a corporation. A document called a *limited partnership agreement* is required in most states. This agreement identifies each partner's potential liability and the amount of capital each partner supplies. Most limited partnerships are formed for real estate investment because of the tax advantages to the

limited partnership
A business structure in which one or more of the owners may be granted limited liability as long as one partner is designated as a general partner with unlimited liability.

limited partners, who can write off depreciation and other deductions from their personal taxes.[21]

Uniform Partnership Act   Signed in 1917 and revised in 1994, the Uniform Partnership Act (UPA) covers most legal issues concerning partnerships and has been adopted by every state in the union except Louisiana. The intent of the UPA is to settle problems that arise between partners. The best way for partners to protect their individual interests and the interests of the business is to draft their own articles of partnership (discussed later). Because partnerships can be formed by two people simply verbally agreeing start a business, however, not all of them write such articles. Even if the partners do not draw up a written agreement, the UPA provides some measure of protection and regulation for them, including the following provisions:

- All partners must agree to any assignment of partnership property.
- Each partner has one vote, no matter what percentage of the partnership she owns, unless a written agreement states otherwise.
- Accurate bookkeeping records are required, and all partners have the right to examine them.
- Each partner owes loyalty to the partnership by not doing anything that would intentionally harm the partnership or the other partners.
- Partners may draw on their share of the profits. This ability provides partners with access to their own capital.
- Salaries must be part of a written agreement. If a loss is incurred, partners must pay their share.

State-specific revisions to this act primarily involve the way in which a general partnership can become a *limited-liability partnership (LLP)*,[22] which is very similar to a *limited-liability company (LLC)*, which is discussed in detail later in this chapter.

articles of partnership
The contract between partners of a business that defines obligations and responsibilities of the business owners.

Articles of Partnership   The formal contract between the principals, or people forming a partnership, is called the **articles of partnership**. The purpose of this contract is to outline the partners' obligations and responsibilities. As a legal document, it helps to prevent problems from arising between partners and provides a mechanism for solving any problems that do arise. A partnership agreement can save your business and your friendship. Articles of partnership usually specify the following items:

- *The name, location, and purpose of the partnership.* States the name of the partnership, where it is located, and why it exists.
- *The contribution of each partner in cash, services, or property.* Describes what each partner brings to the company.
- *The authority of each partner and the need for consensual decision making.* Specifies, for example, that large purchases (say, over $5,000) or contracts require the approval of a majority (or both) of the partners.
- *The management responsibilities of each partner.* Specifies, for example, that all partners must be actively involved and participate equally in the management and the operation of the business.

- *The duration of the partnership.* States whether the partnership is created to last indefinitely or for a specific period of time or for a specific project, such as building a new shopping center. The latter type of partnership is called a **joint venture.**

- *The division of profits and losses.* Specifies the distribution of profits or losses, which does not have to be exactly equal. The distribution could be allocated according to the same percentages that the partners contributed to the partnership. If not exactly equal, the division must be clearly stated.

- *The salaries and draws of partners.* States how the partners will be compensated, a decision which is made after the decision about how to divide profits and losses at the end of the accounting period. A *draw* is the removal of expected profits by a partner.

- *The procedure for dispute settlement or arbitration.* Describes a procedure for mediation or arbitration to solve serious disagreements, thus saving a costly trip to court.

- *The procedure for sale of partnership interest.* Provides veto power to partners in case one partner tries to sell his interest in the business.

- *The procedure for addition of a new partner.* States whether the vote for adding a new partner can be a simple majority or must be unanimous.

- *The procedure for absence or disability of a partner.* Describes the procedure for dealing with an accident, illness, or death of a partner.

- *The procedure and conditions for dissolving the partnership.* Describes what will happen if and when the partnership ends.

> **joint venture**
> A partnership that is created to complete a specified purpose and is limited in duration.

Corporation

The **corporation** is the most complicated business structure to form. In the eyes of the law, a corporation is an autonomous entity that has the legal rights of a person, including the ability to sue and be sued, to own property, and to engage in business transactions. A corporation must act in accordance with its charter and the laws of the state in which it exists. These laws vary by state.

This section is concerned with the type of corporation most common among small businesses—a **closely held corporation.** With this type of business, relatively few people (usually fewer than ten) own stock. Most owners participate in the firm's management, and those who don't are usually family or friends. By contrast, corporations that sell shares of stock to the public and are listed on a stock exchange are called **public corporations.** Public corporations must comply with more detailed and rigorous federal, state, and Securities and Exchange Commission (SEC) regulations, such as disclosing financial information in the company's annual report. These are different animals from the closely held corporations of small businesses.

This discussion will begin with the regular, or *C,* corporation. Later we will look at variations called the *S corporation* and the *limited-liability company (LLC).* The **C corporation** is a separate legal entity that reports its income and expenses on a corporate income tax return and is taxed on its profits at corporate income tax rates.

> **corporation**
> A business structure that creates an entity separate from its owners and managers.

> **closely held corporation**
> A corporation owned by a limited group of people. Its stock is not traded publicly.

> **public corporation**
> A corporation that sells shares of stock to the public and is listed on a stock exchange.

> **C corporation**
> A separate legal entity that reports its income and expenses on a corporate income tax return and is taxed on its profits at corporate income tax rates.

Advantages   By far the biggest advantage of forming a corporation is the limited liability it offers its owners. In a corporation, the most you stand to lose is the amount you have invested in it. If the business fails or if it is sued, your personal property remains protected from creditors (see Table 2.3).

As an example of how limited liability can be an advantage to a small business, consider the case of Kathy, owner of a local pub. Kathy is worried that one of her employees might inadvertently or intentionally serve alcohol to a minor or to an intoxicated person. If the intoxicated person were to get into an automobile accident, Kathy could be sued. In addition to buying liability insurance, Kathy has also incorporated her business so that her personal assets will be protected in the event of a lawsuit.

Corporations generally have easier access to financing, because bankers, venture capitalists, and other lending institutions tend to regard them as being more stable than proprietorships or partnerships. Corporations have proven to be the best way to accumulate large pools of capital.

Corporations can also take advantage of the skills of several people and draw on their increased human and managerial resources. Boards of directors can bring valuable expertise and advice to small corporations. Also, because a corporation has a life of its own, it continues to operate even if its stockholders change. Transfer of ownership can be completed through the sale of the stock.

Disadvantages   Complying with requirements of the state corporate code poses challenges that are not faced by proprietorships or partnerships. Even the smallest corporation must file *articles of incorporation* (described later in this chapter) with the secretary of state, adopt bylaws, and keep records from annual stockholder and director meetings. Directors must meet to show that they are setting policy and are actively involved in running the corporation. Fulfilling these requirements is necessary to prevent the IRS, creditors, or lawsuits from removing the limited-liability protection of a corporation. If a business does not meet these requirements, it is not considered to be operating as a corporation, and therefore forfeits the limited-liability protection of its directors and stockholders, leaving them personally responsible for liabilities. The process of denying limited-liability protection is referred to as "piercing the corporate veil."[23]

The legal and administrative costs incurred in starting a corporation can be a sizable disadvantage. *Self-incorporation kits* exist, but be careful about going through the incorporation process without the aid of an attorney. The cost of incorporating can easily reach $1,000 before the business is even open.

Corporate profits face double taxation in that the profits are taxed at the corporate level first and can be taxed again once the profits are distributed to

Table 2.3

BALANCING THE ADVANTAGES AND DISADVANTAGES OF CORPORATIONS

Advantages	Disadvantages
Limited liability	Expensive to start
Increased access to resources	Complex to maintain
Transfer of ownership	Double taxation*

* C corporation only

stockholders. If a stockholder also works in the corporation, she is considered to be an employee and must be paid a "reasonable wage," which is subject to state and federal payroll taxes.

Even the limited liability that incorporation affords may not completely protect your personal property. If you use debt financing or borrow money, lenders will probably expect you to secure the loan with your personal property. Therefore, if the business must be liquidated, your personal property can be attached.

If you sell stock in your corporation, you inevitably give up some control of your business. The more capital you need to raise, the more control you must relinquish. If large blocks of stock are sold, you may end up as a minority stockholder of what used to be your own business. Raising capital in this way may be necessary for growth, but you lose some measure of control in the process.

Forming a Corporation   The process of incorporating your business includes the following steps: First, you must prepare **articles of incorporation** and file them with the secretary of state where you are incorporating. You must choose a board of directors, adopt bylaws, elect officers, and issue stock. At the time you incorporate, you must also decide whether to form a C corporation, an S corporation, or a limited-liability company (LLC), all of which will be described in this chapter.

You are not required to use an attorney to file articles of incorporation, but attempting the process and making a mistake could end up costing you more than an attorney would have charged for the job. Although states vary in their requirements, articles of incorporation usually include the following items:

> *articles of incorporation*
> A document describing the business that is filed with the state in which a business is formed.

- *The name of your company.* The name you choose must be registered with the state in which it will operate. This registration prevents companies from operating under the same name, which could create confusion for the consumer. Your corporation's name must not be deceptive about its type of business.

- *The purpose of your corporation.* You must state the intended nature of your business. Being specific about your purpose will give financial institutions a better idea of what you do. Incorporating in a state that permits very general information in this section allows you to change the nature of your business without reincorporating.

- *The names and addresses of the incorporators.* Some states require at least one incorporator to reside in that state.

- *The names and addresses of the corporation's initial officers and directors.*

- *The address of the corporation's home office.* You must establish headquarters in the state from which you receive your charter or register as an out-of-state corporation in your own state.

- *The amount of capital required at time of incorporation.* The proposed capital structure includes the amount and type of capital stock you issue at the time of incorporation.

- *Capital stock to be authorized.* In this section, you specify the types of stock and the number of shares that the corporation will issue.

- *Bylaws of the corporation.* A corporation's bylaws are the rules and regulations by which it agrees to operate. Bylaws must stipulate the rights and powers of shareholders, directors, and officers; the time and place for the annual share-holder meeting and the number needed for a quorum (the number needed to transact business); how the board of directors is to be elected and compensated; the dates of the corporation's fiscal year; and who within the corporation is authorized to sign contracts.

- *Length of time the corporation will operate.* Most corporations are established with the intention that they will operate in perpetuity. However, you may specify a duration for the corporation's existence.

Some small business owners minimize the legal costs of forming a corporation by doing much of the background work themselves. Several software companies have jumped on this do-it-yourself bandwagon. For instance, the PC Law Library, published by Cosmi Corporation of Rancho Dominguez, California, contains more than 200 legal documents for both business and personal situations. Nolo Press of Berkeley, California, a publisher of legal reference books, has developed Nolo's Partnership Maker and Incorporator Pro. These software packages provide standard and alternative clauses that can be included in partnership agreements and articles of incorporation.

If you decide to use such software, it is highly advisable that you have an attorney who is familiar with your state's incorporation or partnership laws review your papers to make sure that all the required information has been covered.

Specialized Forms of Corporations

You have two other options to consider in addition to the C corporation. S corporations and limited-liability companies are corporations that are granted special tax status by the Internal Revenue Service. A competent tax advisor can assist you to determine whether one of these options could provide a tax advantage for your business.

> *S corporation*
> A special type of corporation in which the owners are taxed as partners.

S Corporation   An **S corporation** provides you with the limited-liability protection of a corporation while allowing the tax advantages of a partnership. It avoids the double-taxation disadvantage of regular corporations and lets you offset losses of the business against your personal income tax. The S corporation files an informational tax return to report its income and expenses but it is not taxed separately. Income and expenses of the S corporation "flow through" to the shareholders in proportion to the number of shares they own. Profits are taxed to shareholders at their individual income tax rate.

To qualify as an S corporation, a business must meet the following requirements:

- Shareholders must be individuals, estates, or trusts—not other corporations.
- Nonresident aliens cannot be shareholders.
- Only one class of outstanding common stock can be issued.
- All shareholders must consent to the election of the S corporation.
- State regulations specify the portion of revenue that must be derived from business activity, not from passive investments.
- There can be no more than 100 shareholders.[24]

Limited-Liability Company   A relatively new form of ownership, the **limited-liability company (LLC),** is quickly becoming the "hot" business form on its way to becoming the entity of choice for the future. First recognized by the IRS in 1988, LLCs offer the limited-liability protection of a corporation and the tax advantages of a partnership without the restrictions of an S corporation. The LLC is still evolving, so it is wise to keep a watchful eye on its development. For example, although the LLC is provided pass-through treatment of revenue for federal taxation purposes, individual states may tax it differently. Most states tax it as a partnership, but some, such as Florida, tax it as a corporation.[25] Check with your tax accountant to see how LLCs are taxed in your state. Furthermore, some states allow the formation of an LLC by a single individual, in which case the IRS will treat it as a sole proprietorship.

> **limited-liability company (LLC)** A relatively new type of corporation that taxes the owners as partners yet provides a more flexible structure than an S corporation.

The owners of an LLC are called *members.* Unlike the situation for C and S corporations, shares of stock do not represent ownership by the members. Rather, the rights and responsibilities of members are specified by the operating agreement of the LLC, which is like a combination of the bylaws and a shareholder agreement in other corporations. LLCs offer small business owners greater flexibility than either C or S corporations in that they can write the operating agreement to contain any provision desired regarding the LLC's internal structure and operations. In particular, LLCs are not constrained by the regulations imposed on C and S corporations dictating who can and cannot participate in them, what they can or cannot own, or how profits and losses will be allocated to members. For example, the owners of an LLC can allocate 50 percent of the business's profits to a person who owns 30 percent of the company. This distribution is not allowable in C or S corporations.

Although the requirements and rules that govern LLCs vary from state to state, there is some consistency. For example, almost every state requires an LLC designator (such as LLC, L.C., Limited Company, or Ltd.) in the business name. Still, it is a good idea to check your local regulations when starting an LLC.

You should seriously consider forming an LLC if you need flexibility in the legal structure of your business, desire limited liability, and prefer to be taxed as a partnership rather than as a corporation.

Nonprofit Corporation   The **nonprofit corporation** is a tax-exempt organization formed for religious, charitable, literary, artistic, scientific, or educational purposes. Nonprofit corporations depend largely on grants from private foundations and public donations to meet their expenses. People or organizations that contribute to a nonprofit can deduct their contributions from their own taxes.

> **nonprofit corporation** A tax-exempt corporation that exists for a purpose other than making a profit.

Assets dedicated to nonprofit purposes cannot be reclassified. If its directors decide to terminate the corporation, its assets must go to another nonprofit organization.[26] The details of forming and running a nonprofit corporation are beyond the interest of most readers of this book. To learn more about this business form, consult the sources listed in the endnotes.

Summary

- ## The differences between the small business manager and the entrepreneur

An entrepreneur is a person who takes advantage of an opportunity and assumes the risk involved in creating a business for the purpose of making a profit. A small business manager is involved in the day-to-day operation of an established business. Each faces significant challenges, but they are at different stages of development in the entrepreneurship/small business management model.

- ## The steps in preparing for small business ownership

The entrepreneurship process involves an *innovative* idea for a new product, process, or service. A *triggering event* is something that happens to the entrepreneur that causes him to begin bringing the idea to reality. *Implementation* is the stage at which the entrepreneur forms a business based on her idea. The first stage of the small business management process is *growth*, which usually means the business is becoming large enough to generate enough profit to support itself and its owner. The *maturity* stage is reached when the business is stable and well established. The *harvest* stage occurs when the small business manager leaves the business because of its sale, merger, or failure.

- ## The advantages and disadvantages of self-employment

The advantages of self-employment include the opportunity for independence, the chance for a better lifestyle, and the potential for significant profit. The disadvantages include the personal liability you would face should the business fail, the uncertainty of an income, and the long working hours.

- ## The characteristics of the forms of small business ownership

There are several choices for the form of ownership of your small business. The most common is the sole proprietorship. If you choose a partnership, you have the choice of a general partnership, in which all partners are fully liable for the business, or a limited partnership, in which at least one partner retains unlimited liability. A corporation offers its owners limited liability. In forming a corporation, you are creating a legal entity that has the same rights as a person. Variations of corporations include S corporations, limited-liability companies, and nonprofit corporations.

Questions for Review and Discussion

1. What do entrepreneurs do that distinguishes them from other persons involved in business?

2. Why might personality characteristics be good predictors of who will be a successful entrepreneur?

3. If a friend told you that entrepreneurs are high-risk takers, how would you set the story straight?

4. Describe the significance of triggering events in entrepreneurship. Give examples.

5. How is small business management different from entrepreneurship?

6. Why would an entrepreneur be concerned about harvesting a business that has not yet been started?

7. Explain why people who own a small business may not enjoy pure independence.

8. If personal characteristics or personality traits do not predict who will be a successful entrepreneur, why are they significant to the study of entrepreneurship or small business management? Which characteristics do you think are most important?

9. Sole proprietorships account for 76 percent of all U.S. businesses and generate 6 percent of all business revenue. Only 18 percent of all sole proprietorships are incorporated, but they generate 90 percent of all revenue. What do these statistics tell you about the two forms of ownership?

10. Under what conditions would you consider joining a partnership? Why would you avoid becoming a partner?

11. When would forming a limited-liability company be more advantageous than creating a C corporation or a partnership?

Questions for Critical Thinking

1. Think of an activity that you love to do; it could be a personal interest or a hobby. How could you turn your passion for this activity into a business? What questions would you have to answer for yourself before you took this step? What triggering events in your personal life would it take for you to start this business?

2. Imagine that the principal from the high school you attended (and graduated from) called to invite you to make a presentation to a newly founded entrepreneurship club at the school. What would you tell this group of high school students about owning their own business as a career option?

Experience This . . .

Do you really know what it's like to start a business? Interview a person you consider an entrepreneur to get some insight. Because time is valuable, have a set of questions prepared before the interview. The following set may be a place for you to start:

1. How did you develop a vision for your business?

2. How long did you envision this business before you took action to start it?

3. What triggering event prompted you to take action to start this business?

4. What are the most important entrepreneurial characteristics that have helped you succeed?

5. What were your biggest challenges?

6. What would you do differently the next time you start a business?

What Would You Do?

"Gardeners love this crap." That's the slogan for Pierce Ledbetter's Memphis, Tennessee–based company, Zoo Doo. In 1990, while still a student at Cornell University, Ledbetter returned home to Memphis and talked the managers at the local zoo into selling him composted animal manure from the enormous amounts produced by the zoo's animals daily. Why would any sane individual want animal manure? Well, it's extremely rich in soil nutrients. Wanting to cash in on the gardening craze just beginning to sweep across the United States, Ledbetter saw a marketing opportunity. He began selling his "Zoo Doo" in attractively designed pails. He even had the unique idea of having the manure compressed into various animal-shaped sculptures that gardeners could place in their gardens to decompose naturally and organically. His designs caught the eye of garden centers and mass merchandisers across the United States. Ledbetter's Zoo Doo now claims sales of about $1.5 million.

But having a great product and a great slogan isn't enough to make any small business a success. It's important to choose a form of business ownership that best meets your individual needs, goals, and constraints. Factors such as availability of adequate funding, amount of management expertise, product liability possibilities, and willingness to share decision making can influence which form of ownership is most appropriate.

SOURCE: Cyndee Miller, "Entrepreneur Steps Firmly into the Field of Manure," *Marketing News*, 22 June 1992, 15, 18.

Questions

1. Put yourself in Pierce Ledbetter's shoes (and watch where you step!). Discuss the advantages and disadvantages of organizing Zoo Doo as a sole proprietorship, a partnership, or a corporation. Think of all the possible factors that might influence your choice.

2. Now that you've looked at the various ways to organize Zoo Doo, it's time to convince your management professor at Cornell University of your decision. Write a letter describing the approach you've decided to take in organizing your Zoo Doo business and why.

CHAPTER CLOSING CASE

MIXING BUSINESS AND FRIENDSHIP

His rock club was in ruins. His partnership was crumbling. Could Allan Fingerhut save his business and his friendship?

The bill arrived early last year. According to the notice, Allan Fingerhut's Minneapolis nightclub, First Avenue, owed $170,000 in overdue real estate taxes. It wasn't the first indication of trouble at the club—which Fingerhut had entrusted to his childhood friend Byron Frank after moving to California and starting a new business. And it wouldn't be the last. Staring at the notice, Fingerhut wondered whether mixing friendship and business had been such a great idea after all.

First Avenue had been a Minneapolis institution since the 1970s, helping launch the careers of artists such as Prince and the Replacements. But revenue at the club had been sliding since 2002. Fingerhut's relationship with Frank was suffering as well. Since moving west in 1988, Fingerhut had had little direct involvement with the nightclub. Though he reviewed quarterly financial results and wrote the occasional check, he no longer knew who was headlining on a Saturday night; he visited just once a year. For years, the arrangement had worked out fine. But Fingerhut had come to regret his hands-off approach. Was it too late to step in and save his business?

Doing so would not be easy. Fingerhut and Frank had been pals since they were 8 years old. In 1969, at the age of 25, Fingerhut signed a lease on a former Greyhound bus station in downtown Minneapolis and transformed it into a live music venue, the Depot, which he later renamed First Avenue. Frank soon joined him. Though Fingerhut was the club's sole owner, the two ran the place like partners. Fingerhut focused on marketing and strategy, while

Frank, a CPA, maintained the books. Nightclub veterans Steve McClellan and Jack Meyers handled day-to-day operations, from overseeing the bar staff to booking acts. Throughout the 1970s, the club was a critical and financial success.

In 1983, First Avenue was the setting for Prince's cult movie *Purple Rain*, which sent the club's fortunes soaring even higher. But the years of late nights and loud music were taking a toll, and Fingerhut was getting burnt out. In 1988, he and his wife, Rose, decided to focus on a more subdued business in a warmer climate. They moved to Marin County, California, where they established a fine-art publishing company in San Rafael and an art gallery in Sausalito. Fingerhut says he never had a doubt about leaving First Avenue in the hands of his buddies back home. "I knew these guys shared my objective to keep the arts alive in Minneapolis," he says. "I thought they would never do anything to risk losing it."

And First Avenue continued to prosper. In fact, Fingerhut was so pleased with the business that in 2000, along with Frank, McClellan, Meyers, and Fingerhut's brother, Ron, he formed a partnership that purchased the building that housed the club. Frank, for the first time, now had a financial stake in the business; indeed, he was the building's largest single shareholder, though Fingerhut remained sole owner of the club itself.

But two years later, things took a turn for the worse. "After 9/11, people didn't want to come out in big groups to see music," says Meyers. What's more, R&B and hip-hop had grown increasingly popular in the Twin Cities, making First Avenue's all-rock format seem outdated. Meanwhile, a slew of new bars and clubs were cutting into the club's customer base. In 2003, revenue plunged nearly 25 percent, to $3.1 million, Fingerhut says. He urged his associates to shift the club's strategy by scheduling more DJs and dance nights. But Frank disagreed, insisting that the club remain true to its rock 'n' roll roots. Now that his own money was on the line, he was in no mood to compromise—and McClellan and Meyers agreed. "In this industry, you have to roll with it and hang on through the trends," McClellan says.

As First Avenue's financial problems mounted, the arguments increased in both frequency and ferocity. Fingerhut was horrified when Frank spent some $200,000 on renovations, which included a plush new VIP lounge. His trust in his old friend eroding, Fingerhut decided he had to make a drastic move. If he allowed his buddies to continue running

First Avenue their way, he was convinced, the business was bound to go bankrupt. But if he returned to the club, things could get ugly. For Fingerhut, it was beginning to look like a no-win situation.

Questions

1. As an outside consultant to Allan Fingerhut, what would you recommend that he do? Should he try to make the business work with his partners? Should he take control of the business himself?

2. From what you have read in this chapter about entrepreneurs and partners, is it possible for true entrepreneurs to work well with partners? Why or why not?

SOURCE: From Lora Kolodny, *Inc.*, May 2005, 51–52. Copyright © 2005 Mansueto Ventures LLC, publisher of Inc. Magazine, New York, NY 10017. Reprinted with permission.

Test Prepper

You've read the chapter, studied the key terms, and the exam is any day now. Think you're ready to ace it? Take this sample test to gauge your comprehension of chapter material. You can check your answers at the back of the book. Want more test questions? Visit the student website at college.hmco.com/pic/hatten4e and take the ACE and ACE+ quizzes for more practice.

 ACE self-test   college.hmco.com/pic/hatten4e

Matching

_____ 1. the potential to lose more than an owner has invested in a business

_____ 2. a specific event that sparks an entrepreneur to proceed from thinking to doing

_____ 3. the personal quality in which people are motivated to excel and choose situations in which success is likely

_____ 4. the ability to see, conceive, and create new products.

_____ 5. the process of identifying opportunities for which marketable needs exist and assuming the risk of creating an organization to satisfy them

_____ 6. the stage in the life of a business in which the owner reaps the fruits of her labor

_____ 7. the primary reason people seek self-employment

_____ 8. the process of owning and operating an established business

_____ 9. a business owned and operated by one person

_____10. a business structure that creates an entity separate from its owners and managers

     a. innovation

     b. harvest

     c. locus of control

     d. need to achieve

     e. sole proprietorship

     f. partnership

     g. corporation

     h. LLC

     i. limited liability

     j. joint venture

     k. entrepreneurship

     l. triggering event

     m. independence

     n. money

     o. risk taking

     p. unlimited liability

     q. small business management

True/False

1. T   F   The word "entrepreneur" has origins that date back to early eleventh-century Arabic traders.

2. T   F   In the maturity stage of the SBM process, survival is pretty much assured.

3. T   F   Because there are so many unknown variables of a business, the harvest stage cannot be planned in the beginning.

4. T   F   Environmental factors remain constant during each business stage.

5. T   F   Running a business always strengthens marriages.

6. T   F   Entrepreneurs typically have a high internal locus of control.

7. T   F   Entrepreneurs are born, not made.

8. T   F   Sole proprietorships generate the highest sales revenue.

9. T   F   Buy-sell agreements are strongly recommended for all nonproprietorships.

10. T   F   Income and expenses "flow through" S corporations and LLCs.

## part 2

Planning in Small Business

Chapter 3   Social Responsibility, Ethics, and Strategic Planning

Chapter 4   The Business Plan

Getting a small business started and keeping it successful will not happen by accident. Planning is required to gather the resources needed and to allocate them wisely. Although some successful businesses have been established without a formal plan, none was created without planning. The most important thing about business planning is not the written plan that is produced, but rather the strategic thinking that goes into the writing. The next two chapters will take you through several facets of business planning. **Chapter 3** discusses social responsibility and strategic planning. **Chapter 4** concentrates on the operational side of business planning.

Social Responsibility, Ethics, and Strategic Planning

After reading this chapter, you should be able to:

- Explain the relationship between social responsibility, ethics, and strategic planning.

- Name the levels of social responsibility.

- Discuss how to establish a code of ethics for your business.

- Describe each step in the strategic planning process, and explain the importance of competitive advantage.

In 2002, 19-year-old Princeton sophomore Tom Szaky (pronounced *zack*-y) was feeding red worms with dining hall refuse and diving into Dumpsters for recyclable packaging. What he and classmate Jon Beyer were actually creating was a company that would sell garbage. Starting with six unpaid employees, the two invested $20,000 and 10 months to perfect a conveyor that passes garbage through a sieve of worms. Within a week soil comes out the other side. They sell what those in the industry politely refer to as worm castings: excrement that is a nutrient-rich alternative to potting soil. The process of unleashing worms on organic waste such as food scraps and grass clippings is known as *vermicomposting.* Amateur horticulturists and hippies have been doing it on a small scale for decades. Szaky says his system is fast, relatively small, and odorless—unlike traditional composting, which so far has been commercially impractical. The company that Szaky created is named TerraCycle.

Tom Szaky.

TerraCycle has grown to 12 employees and had a revenue of $2 million in 2006. It has waste-management contracts from restaurants, schools, and penitentiaries on the input side and sells completely organic fertilizer to such giants as Wal-Mart and Home Depot. Think about this business model: Worms do most of the work, never take a day off, produce their body weight in waste every 24 hours, double their population every three months, and eat stuff that would otherwise go to a landfill. Szaky says that theoretically TerraCycle could get paid to haul away garbage—creating a negative cost of raw materials.

Two national environmental groups, Zerofootprint and the Clean Air Foundation, have both identified TerraCycle's products as "The Most Eco-Friendly Product available today." Notes a press release announcing the awards, "Unlike the production of any other consumer product, which produces waste, TerraCycle actually consumes waste in manufacturing their product. TerraCycle's plant foods are the world's first product that is made from (worm poop) and packaged (used soda bottles) entirely in waste!"

TerraCycle's social responsibility goes beyond recycling trash and making organic fertilizer. For example, elementary schoolchildren can collect used soda bottles for TerraCycle, which then contributes five cents per bottle to the school—twice as much as the school would pay the recycling center— so solid waste is circulated, needy schools receive money, environmental conscious-ness is raised, and the company sends out a marketing message that your plants and your planet will benefit. Szaky also bought a 10-bedroom, four-story house as its headquarters in Trenton, NJ, where its college interns live during the summer.

In April 2003, Szaky and company got some great news: They had won $1 million in the Carrot Capital Business Plan Challenge. Pretty exciting...until Szaky was eventually told that the venture capitalists were interested only in him, not his partner buddies. Szaky walked away from the deal and the seven-figure check. He is obviously a young man who understands the connection between social responsibility, ethics, and strategic planning.

SOURCES: Bo Burlingham, "The Coolest Little Start-Up in America," *Inc.*, July 2006, 78–85; Alison Stein Wellner, "The Green 50—The Recyclers," *Inc.*, November 2006, 101–103; Tahl Raz, "Talking Trash," *Inc.*, November 2002, 36–37; Kim Shiffman, "Tom Szaky," *Profit*, September 2005.

Relationship Between Social Responsibility, Ethics, and Strategic Planning

What do concepts like social responsibility and ethics have to do with strategic planning in business? They are rarely covered together in textbooks, but the con-nection between them is especially strong in small businesses because of the inseparability of the owner and the business. The direction in which the business is heading is the same direction in which the owner is going. What is important to the business is what is important to the owner. In many cases, a small business is an extension of the owner's life and personality.

Strategic planning is the guiding process used to identify the direction for your business. It spells out a long-term game plan for operating your business. *Social responsibilities* are the obligations of a business to maximize the positive effects it has on society and minimize the negative effects. *Ethics* are the rules of moral values that guide decision making—your understanding of the difference between right and wrong.

Let's look at the relationship between social responsibility, ethics, and strategic planning in the following way: When you assess your company's external environment for opportunities and threats, you identify what you might do. When you look at your internal strengths and weaknesses, you see what you can do and cannot do. Your personal values are ingrained in the business; they are what you want to do. Your ethical standards will determine what is right for you to do. Finally, in responding to everyone who could be affected by your business, social responsibility guides what you should do.

The connection between social responsibility, ethics, and strategic planning is especially strong in small business. In fact, at a very fundamental level, they are more difficult to separate than to connect.

Social Responsibilities of Small Business

Social responsibility means different things to different people. In this chapter, we will define it as the managerial obligation to take action to protect and improve society as a whole, while achieving the goals of the business.[1] The manager of a socially responsible business should attempt to make a profit, obey the law, act ethically, and be a good corporate citizen.

social responsibility
The obligation of a business to have a positive effect on society on four levels—economic, legal, ethical, and philanthropic.

Your level of commitment to these responsibilities and the strategic planning process you conduct form the heart of your business—the foundation and philosophy on which the business rests. Knowing what is important to yourself, your business, and everyone affected by its actions (social responsibility) is significant in deciding where you want to go and how to get there (strategic planning). The business you start or operate takes on a *culture,* or a set of shared beliefs, of its own. When you create a business, *your* values have a strong influence on the culture of the business you create. The values and culture of your business are demonstrated by your socially responsible (or irresponsible) actions.

As noted earlier, social responsibilities are the obligations of a business to maximize the positive effects it has on society and minimize the negative effects. There are four levels of social responsibility: economic, legal, ethical, and philanthropic (see Figure 3.1).[2] Although the primary responsibility of a business is economic, our legal system also enforces what we, as a collective group or society, consider proper behavior for a business. In addition, the firm itself decides what is ethical behavior, or what is right beyond legal requirements. Finally, a business is be expected to act like a good citizen and help improve the quality of life for everyone—a philanthropic obligation. Although all four of these obligations have always existed, ethical and philanthropic issues have received considerable attention recently.

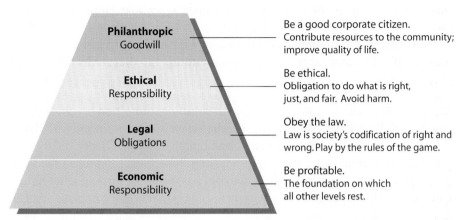

Figure 3.1
PYRAMID OF SOCIAL
RESPONSIBILITY

*Businesses Are Expected to Act in
a Responsible Manner in Four
Interconnected Areas.*

SOURCE: Reprinted with permission from
Business Horizons, July/August 1991, by Archie
B. Caroll, Copyright © 1991 by Elsevier. "The
Pyramid of Corporate Social Responsibility:
Toward the Moral Management of Organizational
Stakeholders–Balancing Legal, Economic, and
Social Responsibilities." Copyright © 1991, with
permission from Elsevier.

Economic Responsibility

As a businessperson in a free enterprise system, you have not only the fundamental right but also the responsibility to make a profit. You are in business because you are providing a good or a service that is needed. If you do not make a profit, how can you stay in business? If you don't stay in business, how can you provide that good or service to people who need it?

Historically, the primary role for business has been economic. When entrepreneurs assume the risk of going into business, profit is their incentive. If you don't attend to the economics of your business, you can't take care of anything else. Therefore, the economic responsibilities of your business include a commitment to being as profitable as possible; to making sure employees, creditors, and suppliers are paid; to maintaining a strong competitive position; and to maintaining efficient operation of your business.

Economist Milton Friedman emphasizes the economic side of social responsibility. Friedman contends that business owners should not be expected to know what social problems should receive priority or how many resources should be dedicated to solving them. He states, "There is one and only one social responsibility of business: to use its resources and energy in activities designed to increase its profits so long as it stays within the rules of the game . . . [and] engages in open and free competition, without deception and fraud."[3] His point of view is that business revenues that are diverted to outside causes raise prices to consumers, decrease employee pay, and may support issues with which some of the business's stakeholders do not agree. Friedman quotes another believer in free enterprise, Adam Smith, who in 1776 said, "I have never known much good done by those who profess to trade for the public good."[4] Basically, Friedman's argument is that businesses should produce goods and services and let concerned individuals and government agencies solve social problems.

Legal Obligations

Above making a profit, each of us is expected to comply with the federal, state, and local laws that lay out the ground rules for operation. Laws can be seen as society's codes of right and wrong; in other words, laws exist to ensure that individuals and businesses do what is considered right by society as a whole. These codes change continually, as laws are added, repealed, or amended in an attempt to match changes in public sentiment. Laws regulating business activity generally involve four areas: (1) consumers, (2) the competition, (3) the environment, and (4) employees

Consumer Protection   Laws geared toward consumer protection became popular when Ralph Nader started the *consumer protection movement* in the early 1960s. Beginning with his safety campaign in the automotive industry, Nader and the consumer activist group he formed, Nader's Raiders, have fought to protect the safety and rights of consumers. Consumer activism has taken the form of letter-writing campaigns, lobbying of government agencies, and boycotting of companies that are perceived to be irresponsible.

Of course, consumer protection did not start in the 1960s. Laws protecting consumers from unsafe business practices date back to 1906, when the Pure Food and Drug Act was passed, largely in response to Upton Sinclair's 1905 book about the meat-packing industry, *The Jungle*. Today, government agencies such as the Consumer Product Safety Commission and the Food and Drug Administration (FDA) set safety standards and regulations for consumer products, food, and drugs.

Trade Protection   Laws that protect competition date back to the Sherman Antitrust Act of 1890, which prohibits monopolies. These laws see competition and unrestrained trade as creating a series of checks and balances on businesses, prompting them to provide quality products and services at reasonable prices. The Federal Trade Commission (FTC) enforces many of these laws.

Environmental Protection   Laws protecting the environment were passed beginning in the 1960s to set minimum standards for business practices concerning air, water, and noise. The Environmental Protection Agency (EPA) was created to enforce many of these laws.

Employee Protection   The 1960s saw the passage of legislation regarding equality in the workplace. The Civil Rights Act of 1964 prohibits discrimination in employment on the basis of race, color, sex, religion, or national origin. The Equal Employment Opportunity Commission (EEOC) enforces these laws in addition to the Age Discrimination in Employment Act (ADEA) and the Equal Pay Act (EPA).[5] Although the Americans with Disabilities Act (ADA) of 1990, equal employment opportunity (EEO), and affirmative action regulate diversity in the workplace (see Chapter 10 for more details on these issues), a small business owner must keep the big picture in mind. The key to managing diversity is to see people as individuals with strengths and weaknesses and to create a climate where all can contribute.[6]

Consequences for Small Business   Some laws have unexpected consequences that place a heavier burden on small business than on large ones. For example, the intent of the Sarbanes-Oxley Act was to make publicly traded firms more trustworthy, but instead it has prevented many successful small businesses from making initial public offerings of their stock. Initial compliance for firms covered by the legislation may cost as much as several hundred thousand dollars, and maintaining that compliance may add another $50,000 per year in accounting and legal fees.[7] Because of this legal burden, and the auditing requirements of Section 404 that can be crushing for small businesses, many entrepreneurs who would like to go public have decided against taking that step—at least for now.[8]

Sexual harassment is an ongoing problem in small businesses, although it generally doesn't receive as much public attention as multimillion-dollar corporate settlements of sexual harassment lawsuits. Sexual harassment can damage a person's dignity, productivity, and eagerness to come to work, which is costly both to that person and to the business.[9] EEOC guidelines define sexual harassment as unwelcome sexual advances, requests for sexual favors, and other verbal or physical conduct of a sexual nature when (1) sexual activity is required to get or keep a job or (2) a hostile environment is created in which work is unreasonably difficult.[10] To help keep your small business free of harassment, the American Management Association recommends that you take the following steps:

- Have a clear written policy prohibiting sexual harassment.
- Hold mandatory supervisory training programs on policies and prevention of harassment.
- Ensure that the workplace is free of offensive materials.
- Implement a program for steps to take when a complaint of harassment is received.
- Keep informed of all complaints and steps taken.
- Make sure the commitment against harassment exists at every level.[11]

Public attitudes ebb and flow on many subjects. Society's attitude toward office romances (not including extramarital affairs and boss-employee relations) is swinging toward greater tolerance and away from the dictum to "keep it professional." In a recent survey by the American Management Association, two-thirds of the managers questioned said that it is acceptable to date a colleague.[12] The Society of Human Resource Management, however, reports that most businesses ban fraternization between people in the same chain of command.

How do you, as a small business owner, allow love to bloom in the workplace and still guard against sexual harassment lawsuits? Some employers ask coworkers who are dating to sign a "love contract," or *consensual-relationship agreement,* in which both parties acknowledge that they are willing participants.[13]

Ethical Responsibility

Although economic and legal responsibilities are shown in Figure 3.1 as separate levels of obligation, they actually coexist, because together they represent the minimum threshold of socially acceptable business behavior. *Ethics* are the rules of moral values that guide decision making by groups and individuals. They represent a person's fundamental orientation toward life—what she sees as right and wrong. Ethical responsibilities of a business encompass how the organization's decisions and actions show concern for what its stakeholders (employees, customers, stockholders, and the community) consider fair and just.

The literature of business ethics identifies four dominant ethical perspectives:

- *Idealism* includes religious and other beliefs and principles.
- *Utilitarianism* deals with the consequences of one's own actions.
- *Deontology* is a rule-based, or duty-based, principle.
- *Virtue ethics* is concerned with the character of an individual.[14]

As individuals, we resolve ethical issues by being guided by one of these perspectives. Research has shown no single ethical perspective dominates among small business owners. Rather, they consider ethical considerations in general to be very important in the way they conduct their businesses, no matter which principle actually influences their individual behavior at a given time.

Changes in ethical standards and values usually precede changes in laws. As described in the previous section on legal obligations, society's expectations changed dramatically in the 1960s, which led to the passage of new laws. Changing values cause constant interaction between the legal and ethical levels of social responsibility. Even businesses that set high ethical standards and try to operate well above legal standards, however, may have difficulty keeping up with expectations that perpetually rise.

Philanthropic Goodwill

Philanthropy is the highest level illustrated on the social responsibility pyramid of Figure 3.1. It includes businesses participating in programs that improve the quality of life, raise the standard of living, and promote goodwill. The difference between ethical responsibility and **philanthropic goodwill** is that the latter is seen not so much as an obligation but rather as a contribution to society to make it a better place. Businesses that do not participate in these activities are not seen as unethical, but those that do tend to be seen in a more positive light.

> *philanthropic goodwill*
> The level of social responsibility in which a business does good without the expectation of anything in return.

Philanthropic activity is not limited to the wealthy or to large corporations writing seven-figure donation checks. Average citizens and small businesses can be and are philanthropic. A small business can sponsor a local Special Olympics meet, contribute to a Habitat for Humanity project, lead a community United Way campaign, or sponsor a Little League baseball team. Albert Vasquez allows a church group to convert his Tucson, Arizona, El Saguarito Mexican food restaurant into a center of worship on Sunday mornings. Kerry Stratford, co-owner of Boelts Bros. Associates, and his partners have donated more than 500 hours in their studios creating designs and advertising for nonprofit groups.[15]

One small business owner can make a difference. Over the past few years, the term *social entrepreneur* has emerged as a way to describe the use of business skills to marshal resources, create organizations that operate efficiently and effectively, and aspire to change society. In 2004, *Fast Company* created the Social Capitalist Awards to recognize new companies created to accomplish missions such as reinventing public education, employing homeless people, and building libraries in Nepal. The award for the top change-making organization is based on five major criteria:

- *Entrepreneurship:* the ability to do a lot with a little, gather needed resources, and build an organization
- *Innovation:* a "big idea" that represents a dramatic leap from any solution that has existed previously

Profile in Entrepreneurship
Doing Well and Doing Good

Gary and Meg Hirshberg are co-founders of Stonyfield Farms, makers of premium organic yogurt. From the beginning, Stonyfield has prided itself on its social responsibility, going far beyond its motto, "For a healthy planet." Under the Hirshbergs' management, Stonyfield has tied its fortunes to improving the environment (10 percent of profits go to environmental causes), providing a healthy and enjoyable workplace, educating consumers, being profitable, and, yes, giving investors a return.

Stonyfield Farm manufactures and distributes organic milk products. The Vermont-based firm helps family farms by paying them premium prices for their milk. Stonyfield has built up a group of New England dairy farmers who don't use hormones to boost production, making their milk more expensive. Customers seem impressed: Stonyfield's yogurt sales have grown at an annual rate of 22 percent over the past 12 years. The Hirshbergs are always looking for ways to be even more socially responsible. For example, to cut down waste, they use rejects from the plastic container production as feedstock to make handles for toothbrushes and razors. About two cups go into each handle. Cups are shipped to processors that grind the plastic into pellets that are then converted into handles and other products. Marketed under the Preserve brand, the products are sold in more than 2,000 natural food stores nationwide and increasingly in supermarkets in the Northeast.

In 2001 the Hirshbergs sold a controlling interest in the company to Groupe Danone. Stonyfield Europe was created in June 2006 as an independent entity within Groupe Danone's Fresh Dairy Products division. Paris-based Groupe Danone, the largest fresh dairy company in the world, also owns 85 percent of Stonyfield Farm. The new, locally developed French product line will promote Stonyfield's highly successful "healthy people, healthy planet" mission.

Gary and Meg Hirshberg are two very special entrepreneurs. See more of their story in the video clip that accompanies this chapter.

SOURCES: Diane Brady, "The Organic Myth," *BusinessWeek*, 16 October 2006, 51–56; David Phillips, "An American in Paris," *Dairy Foods*, October 2006,18; Julie Rose, "Selling [His Soul] to Dannon?," *Fortune Small Business*, December 2001/January 2002; Matthew Phan, "Beyond the Bottom Line," *Fortune Small Business*, December 2004/January 2005; "Recycling Company Partners with Yogurt Maker to Produce Toothbrushes," *In Business*, January/February 2005, 7.

- *Social impact:* pure and simple results
- *Aspiration:* lofty goals that are in line with resources available
- *Sustainability:* the ability to last and produce results into the future[16]

Ethics and Business Strategy

Business ethics means more than simply passing moral judgment on what should and should not be done in a particular situation. It is part of the conscious decisions you make about the direction you want your business to take. It is a link between morality, responsibility, and decision making within the organization.[17]

In 2003 the Ethics Resource Center (ERC) conducted its National Business Ethics Survey and found some interesting results regarding small businesses. Ninety percent of U.S. small business respondents considered their top managers ethical; only 18 percent had ever observed misconduct at work. Only 58 percent had written codes of ethics, 41 percent offered ethical training, and slightly fewer than half had a way for employees to report bad behavior anonymously.[18]

> *business ethics*
> The rules of moral values that guide decision making—your understanding of the difference between right and wrong.

A poll by RISE business published in *BusinessWeek* magazine asked people who run small and large businesses whether they found certain business practices to be acceptable or unacceptable. A greater percentage of those who ran small businesses, called "entrepreneurs" in this study, disapproved of questionable business practices than did managers of large businesses. Compare their responses to your own (see Figure 3.2).

Codes of Ethics

code of ethics
The tool with which the owner of a business communicates ethical expectations to everyone associated with the business.

A **code of ethics** is a formal statement of what your business expects in the way of ethical behavior. It can serve as a guide for employee conduct to help employees determine what behaviors are acceptable. Because the purpose of a code of ethics is to let everyone know what is expected and what is considered right, it should be included in an employee handbook (see Chapter 17 on human resource management).

Your code of ethics should reflect *your* ethical ideals, be concise so that it can be easily remembered, be written clearly, and apply equally to all employees, regardless of level of authority.[19] Your expectations and the consequences of breaking the code should be communicated to all employees. Small businesses, especially in fast-paced, high-tech industries, often ignore formal codes of conduct because of their push for rapid growth. This mistake can cause expensive legal problems later.

An explicit code of ethics and the expectation that employees must adhere to it can reap many benefits for your small business, including the following:

- Obtaining high standards of performance at all levels of your workforce
- Reducing anxiety and confusion over what is considered acceptable employee conduct
- Allowing employees to operate as freely as possible within a defined range of behavior
- Avoiding double standards that undermine employee morale and productivity
- Developing a public presence and image that are consistent with your organization's ideals[20]

If you want to maintain and encourage ethical behavior in your business, it must be part of your company's goals. By establishing ethical policies, rules, and standards in your code of ethics, you can treat them like any other company goal, such as increasing profit or market share. Establishing ethical goals allows you to take corrective action by punishing employees who do not comply with company standards and by rewarding those who do. If your code of ethics is supported and strictly enforced by you and your management team, it will become part of your company's culture and will improve ethical behavior. Conversely, if your managers and employees see your code of ethics as a window-dressing facade, it will accomplish nothing. Don't just take a three "Ps" approach—print it, post it, and pray they read it. Instead, talk about your code when it is implemented, review it annually, and use employee suggestions to improve it.[21]

> " Ethical dilemmas can be magnified by differences in language, culture, and business practices. "

Another recommendation is to include a *frequently asked questions (FAQs)* section in the code of ethics section of your employee handbook. Have these FAQs

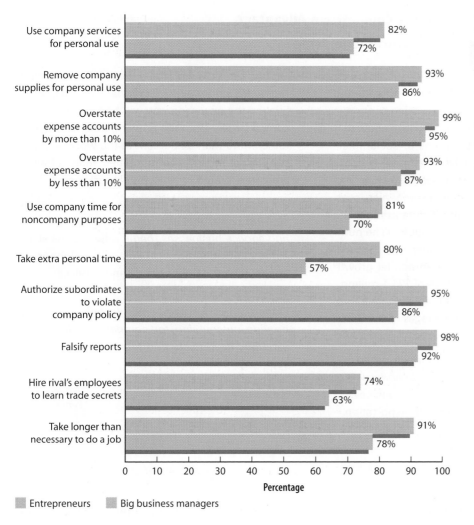

Figure 3.2
WHAT IS UNACCEPTABLE CONDUCT?

A Greater Percentage of Entrepreneurs Tend to Regard Questionable Business Practices as Unacceptable Than Do Managers of Large Businesses.

SOURCE: "The Entrepreneurial Ethic,"
BusinessWeek, 5 October 1998.

relate specifically to your industry, because many of your new employees will have the same questions.[22]

Ethics Under Pressure

Businesses face ethical dilemmas every day. How can they maintain high ethical standards when the effects of doing so will hit their bottom line?

> *You run a construction company and receive a bid from a subcontractor. You know a mistake was made; the bid is accidentally 20 percent too low. If you accept the bid, it could put the subcontractor out of business. But accepting it will improve your chance of winning a contract for a big housing project. What do you do?*[23]

Robert George, CEO of Medallion Construction Company of Merrimack, New Hampshire, was the manager who faced this dilemma. Medallion was bidding to become the general contractor for a $2.5 million public housing contract. An electrical contractor from the area submitted a bid that was $30,000, or 20 percent, lower than the quotes from four other subcontractors. Subcontractor bids come in

Creating Competitive Advantage

Urban Entrepreneurship

Harvard professor Michael Porter started researching economic opportunities in blighted neighborhoods to show that no amount of government programs or social intervention helps communities unless the local economy works. What evolved from his research was an *Inc.* magazine list of the fastest-growing companies located in inner cities, and a nonprofit organization, the Initiative for a Competitive Inner City (ICIC). The number one company on the 2006 Inner City 100 list, Commodity Sourcing Group, had an annual growth rate of 10,028 percent and revenues of $21.1 million.

Inner cities are a hotbed of entrepreneurship. Four principal competitive advantages draw businesses to these areas:

- A *strategic location at the core of major urban areas, highways, and communication nodes with potent logistical advantages.* Inner-city businesses' proximity to customers and to transportation infrastructure is a key advantage.

- *An underutilized workforce with a high retention rate amid a tight overall national labor market.* Fueling the new economy will be labor that comes largely from the growing inner-city workforce. More than 54 percent of the workforce will come from minority communities, many of which are concentrated in cities and inner cities.

- *An underserved local market with substantial purchasing power that can support many more retail and service businesses than it now has.* As standards of living improve in inner-city neighborhoods, the quantity of goods and services demanded in those areas will increase.

- *Opportunities for companies to link up with and provide outsourcing for competitive clusters (for example, health care and tourism) in the regional economy.*

SOURCES: Leigh Buchanan "The 2006 Inner City 100" *Inc.*, June 2006, 109–120; Mike Hofman, "Q&A with Michael Porter," *Inc.*, May 2004, 98–110.

only a few hours before the general contractors must deliver their bids so that subcontractors cannot be played off against one another. George was tempted to take the bid that he knew was a mistake because it would have almost guaranteed that Medallion would win the contract. Then he reconsidered for several reasons. Accepting the bid could have caused problems if the subcontractor went belly-up once the project was underway. Then Medallion would have been forced to find a replacement, which might have caused time delays and cost overruns.

Aside from the pragmatic problems, the ethical ramifications troubled George. He asked himself, "Is it fair to allow someone to screw up when they don't know it and you do?" He decided that the money wasn't worth the damage to his reputation of ruining a fellow small business person. George called the subcontractor and said, "Look, I'm not going to tell you what your competitors bid, but your number is very low—in my opinion, too low." The subcontractor withdrew his bid. Medallion still won the contract.

A year later, the same subcontractor submitted another low bid on a different project. This time the low bid was intentional. The subcontractor offered a 2 percent discount because he remembered how honestly George had treated him earlier. Sometimes high ethics can have material rewards. Having a reputation for high ethical standards can give you an "ethical edge," a competitive advantage for your business. Being known for doing what is right can help you attract talented people, win loyal customers, forge relationships with suppliers, and earn the public's trust.

> *You spend months trying to negotiate a deal to sell your equipment in Japan. You deliver your product as agreed, but the Japanese distributor tells you it is not what the customer expected. The distributor wants you to reengineer the equipment even though it clearly meets the written specifications.* What do you do?

David Lincoln is president of Lincoln Laser Company, a manufacturer located in Phoenix, Arizona. Lincoln thought he had a done deal with a distributor from Japan that had spent months scrutinizing Lincoln's $300,000 machine that scans printed circuit-board wiring for very small cracks or breaks. The distributor finally ordered eight machines. Unfortunately, the Japanese client wasn't happy after delivery. Lincoln said, "They thought it should inspect *every type* of printed circuit board, even though we explained repeatedly that it was suitable only for a certain class of boards." To change the machine so that it could inspect every type of circuit board would require Lincoln to have the software rewritten, pull engineers from another project, and borrow funds to pay for the additional work.

Lincoln's first instinct was to say, "This is what you agreed to; we supplied what we said we would. You bought it, so now pay up." He could have said "no" and been acting ethically according to common business practices in the United States. Instead, he decided to go beyond his basic obligation and do what he felt was the right thing under the circumstances. As Lincoln reflected on the differences between American and Japanese customers, he realized that he had expected Japanese customers to act like American clients without taking into account the differences in adaptation levels between the two groups. In other words, he hadn't taken the time to become sensitive to cultural differences. Fortunately, Lincoln was able to secure financing to accommodate its customers—keeping the ethical principles, credibility, and Japanese market for his company intact.

Here are some more ethical situations to consider:

- Your company, a maker of data storage products, has just released a new external hard drive with special padding to reduce damage if dropped. You discover that the new hard drive includes an unintentional little bonus: a software worm that will turn every customer's PC into a spam distributor. What do you do?[24]

- You own a high-tech business in a very competitive industry. You find out that a competitor has developed a scientific discovery that will give it a significant competitive advantage. Your profits will be severely cut, but not eliminated, for at least a year. If you had some hope of hiring one of your competitor's employees who knows the details of its secret, would you hire him or her?

- A high-ranking government official from a country where payments regularly lubricate decision-making processes asks you for a $200,000 consulting fee. For this fee, he promises to help you obtain a $100 million contract that will produce at least $5 million of profit for your company. What do you do?

- You recently hired a manager who is having a problem with sexual harassment from another manager. She informs you, as the business owner, what is happening and tells you she is considering legal action. Unfortunately, you have been so busy dealing with incredible growth that you haven't had a chance to write formal policies. What do you do?

Reality Check

It's Not Easy Being Green

Efforts of businesses to act in a socially responsible manner toward the environment are usually called *green marketing.* Small businesses can show concern for the environment (and cut costs at the same time) by recycling paper products and office supplies, purchasing environmentally benign products, and using environmentally safe product packaging. Each business must decide how it can have the greatest positive environmental impact. Not every business can affect issues such as vehicle-related air pollution or ozone depletion, of course, but every business should recognize the power of the green movement and the rise in environmental consciousness. Here are some guidelines for incorporating a green marketing program into your business:

- Environmentalism is not a passing fad—it is strongly supported—so pay attention to what your target market supports and buys.

- The number of people concerned about environmental issues is growing. They buy environmentally friendly products. Sales of organic foods are increasing by 20 percent per year.

- Get an energy audit. Most local utilities offer businesses free consultations on how they can reduce usage and save money.

- Green marketing can be a sustainable competitive advantage leading to long-term profit.

- Tell suppliers that you're interested in sustainable products, and set specific goals for buying recycled, refurbished, or used products. Make the environment, and not just price, a factor in your purchasing decisions.

- Green marketing involves the actual production of your product, raw material procurement, and disposal.

- A successful green marketing strategy depends on effective communication with customers and suppliers about your efforts.

- Green marketing needs to be integrated into the strategic planning process.

- Don't limit your vision with thoughts like "SUV owners are not green consumers." Just look at the SUVs parked at any suburban Whole Foods Market.

SOURCES: "How to Make *Your* Business Greener," *Inc.*, November 2006, 103; Cait Murphy, "The Next Big Thing," *Fortune Small Business,* June 2003, 64; Jacquelyn Ottman, "Green Marketing: The Systems That Surround You," *Business,* July/August 2000, 29.

- An advertising agency has created and released a marketing and advertising campaign for your consumer product. The campaign has proven to be offensive to some minority groups (who do not buy your product), and those parties have expressed their objections. Sales for your product have increased by 45 percent since the campaign started. What do you do?[25]

Strategic Planning

strategic plan
A long-term planning tool used for viewing a business and the environments in which it operates in broadest terms.

Recall from Chapter 1 that poor management is the major cause of business failure. Since the first function of good management is good planning, a good **strategic plan** is a priority for the small business owner. Strategic planning is a long-range management tool that helps small businesses be proactive in the way they respond to environmental changes. The process of strategic planning provides an overview of your business and all the factors that may affect it in the next

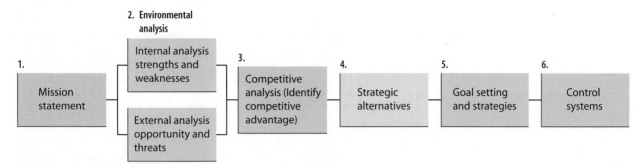

Figure 3.3

STRATEGIC PLANNING PROCESS

A Strategic Plan Can Be Drafted in Six Sequential Steps.

three to five years. It will help you formulate goals for your business so as to take advantage of opportunities and avoid threats. From your goals, you can determine the most appropriate steps you need to take to accomplish them—an *action plan.*

At the beginning of this chapter, the question was posed about the connection between social responsibility, ethics, and strategic planning. If the intent of the strategic planning process is to produce a working document for your business to follow, the relationship can be seen in this way: When you assess your company's external environment for opportunities and threats, you identify what you *might do.* When you look at the internal strengths and weaknesses, you see what you *can do* and *cannot do.* Your personal values are ingrained into the business; they are what you *want to do.* Your ethical standards will determine what is *right for you to do.* Finally, in responding to everyone who could be affected by your business, social responsibility guides what you *should do.* When viewed in this manner, not only are social responsibility, ethics, and strategic planning connected, but impossible to separate.

Writing a strategic plan generally involves a six-step process, as shown in Figure 3.3: (1) formulating your mission statement, (2) completing an environmental analysis, (3) performing a competitive analysis, (4) analyzing your strategic alternatives, (5) setting your goals and strategies, and (6) setting up a control system.

Yogi Berra once said, "You've got to be very careful if you don't know where you're going, because you might not get there."[26] Strategic planning is how entrepreneurs determine how to "get there."

Mission Statement

A **mission statement** provides direction for the company by answering a simple question: What business are we really in? The mission statement should be specific enough to tell the reader something about what the business is and how it operates, but it should *not* be a long, elaborate document detailing all of your business philosophies.

By accurately describing the purpose, scope, and direction of your business, your mission statement communicates what you want your business to do and to be.

mission statement
A description of the reason why an organization exists.

It is the foundation on which all other goals and strategies are based. Without a concrete statement of organizational mission, the values and beliefs of a small business must be interpreted from the actions and decisions of individual managers.[27] The result may not be what you, as the owner, desire. Another value of a mission statement derives from the commitment you make by printing and publicizing your strategy and philosophy. You have more incentive to stick to your ideas and expect others to follow them if they are written down and shared than if you keep them to yourself.

Management consultant and author Tom Peters writes that a company's mission statement should be 25 words or less in length.[28] This brevity will allow everyone in the organization to understand and articulate it. Great Harvest Bakery's mission statement is a good example of a brief, but heartfelt statement of values:

- Be loose and have fun.
- Bake phenomenal bread.
- Run fast to help customers.
- Create strong, exciting bakeries.
- Give generously to others.

Good mission statements, like Great Harvest's, maintain a balance between ideas and reality. From Great Harvest's statement, you can tell what the company wants to achieve and how. It says what the business is and, by implication, what it is not. Does Great Harvest intend to diversify into wedding cakes and frozen pies to become a major force in the baking industry? No, the company intends to focus on making and selling the best bread possible.

Because the mission statement lies at the heart of the strategic planning process, you can see in Great Harvest's statement and principles the connection between strategic planning and social responsibility. You can even see evidence of the pyramid of social responsibility in its stated principles. The importance of making a profit corresponds with the economic-responsibility level of the pyramid. The principle of treating one another with respect and dignity incorporates ethics into its strategic plan. The company's principle of contributing positively to the community and the environment shows ethics and philanthropy.

Environmental Analysis

Large and small businesses alike must operate in constantly changing environments. The ability to adapt to change is a major determinant of success or failure for any business in a free enterprise system. Essentially, *environmental analysis* is the process in which a manager examines what is going on within any sector that could affect the business, either within the business or outside of it.

Environmental analysis is also called **SWOT analysis** because you examine **S**trengths, **W**eaknesses, **O**pportunities, and **T**hreats. An analysis of the *internal* environment identifies strengths and weaknesses that exist within your own business. An analysis of the *external* environment identifies opportunities and threats—factors outside your control—that may affect your business.

Because of their speed, flexibility, and sensitivity to customer preferences, small businesses are in a position to quickly take advantage of changes in the environment. Environmental analysis is important to small businesses because

SWOT analysis
The step of strategic planning in which the managers identify the internal strengths and weaknesses of a business and the opportunities and threats that exist outside the business.

they have fewer resources to risk. No business can afford many mistakes, but the larger the operation, the more breadth it generally has to absorb the cost of errors. A small business may be significantly affected by detrimental environmental changes that a larger business could more easily weather.

External Analysis   *Opportunities* are positive alternatives that you may choose to help attain your company's mission. Although you should always be scanning for opportunities, you cannot pursue every one. Your strategic plan will help you identify those that are right for your business.

Threats are obstacles to achieving your mission or goals. They are generally events or factors over which you have no control: a change in interest rates, new government regulations, or a competitor's new product. Although you cannot control these threats, you can prepare for them or take positive action to cope with them. Threats and opportunities can be found by scanning developments in the following environments:

- *Economic.* Much of the economic data readily available on the international and national levels are very valuable to small businesses operating in smaller, more isolated markets. As a small business owner, you need to be aware of economic conditions that affect your target markets, such as unemployment rates, interest rates, total sales, and tax rates within your community.

- *Legal/regulatory.* Some factors can affect small businesses in more than one environment. For example, the passage of the North American Free Trade Agreement (NAFTA) changed both regulations and the competitive environment. With regulations altered to encourage trade between the United States, Canada, and Mexico, many small businesses have found a wealth of new opportunity in new markets. Other businesses have seen the changes as a threat because they brought new competition.

- *Sociocultural.* What members of society value and desire as they pass from one life stage to another has an effect on what they purchase. For example, the increased popularity of tattoos among teens and twenty-somethings means opportunity for skin artists who are able to provide this service in a small business. Will the next opportunity for an entrepreneur be an innovative new process for removing those tattoos?

- *Technological.* Technology is the application of scientific knowledge for practical purposes. Few environmental forces have caused as much excitement in the business community as the emergence of the Internet. Entrepreneurs are scrambling to find ways to take advantage of the opportunities of e-business.

- *Competitive.* Actions of your competitors are considered forces within your competitive environment. You face a difficult task in not only tracking what your competitors are currently doing, but also predicting their reactions to your moves. If you drop the price of your product to gain more market share, will competing business managers react by holding their prices constant or by cutting their prices below yours? This situation could escalate into an expensive price war.

Are opportunities and threats easy to identify? No, and they never have been. Writer Mark Twain once said, "I was seldom able to see an opportunity until it had ceased to be one."

Internal Analysis   An *internal analysis* assesses the strengths and weaknesses of your company. It identifies what it is that your company does well and what it could do better. Internal analysis is important for two reasons. First, since your personal opinion of your own business is sure to be biased (we tend to look at ourselves through the proverbial rose-colored glasses), you need an objective analysis of the capacity and potential of your business. Second, an internal analysis can help you match the strengths of your business with the opportunities that exist. The idea is to put together a realistic profile of your business to determine whether you can take advantage of opportunities and react to the threats identified in the environmental analysis. This isn't as easy as it sounds, because you have to view your environments not as if they are snapshots, but rather as several videos playing simultaneously. The key is to match opportunities that are still unfolding with resources that are still being acquired.

Although most of us have no problem identifying our strengths, some of us may need help realizing our weaknesses. The following diagnostic tests can help you evaluate your business realistically:

- Visit your newest, lowest-level employee. Can she tell you why the business exists? Name major competitors? Say what you do well? List major customers? If not, your vision isn't coming across.

- Can that same employee describe what he is doing to contribute to your competitive advantage?

- Ask a long-term employee how things went yesterday. If you get answers like "Okay" or "Fine . . . just fine," you may have a potential problem. If you hear specifics, consider it a good sign.

- Observe what the business looks like after hours. Is the place neat and orderly, or does it look like a tornado struck? Although neatness doesn't guarantee success, you should be able to find the checkbook, phone book, and most of the furniture.

- Observe your business during work hours. Invent a reason to be where you can watch and hear what goes on. What impression do you get of the business?

- Select a few customers at random to call or visit. Ask them how they were treated the last time they were in your business, and emphasize that you would like an *honest* answer.

- Call your business during the busiest part of the day. How quickly is the phone answered? Is the response efficient, friendly, surly, or overly chatty?

- Ask a friend to visit your business as a mystery shopper. Would he come back again?[29]

Competitive Analysis

If you were forced to condense the description of your business down to the one factor that makes you successful and sets your business apart from all other similar businesses, you would recognize your **competitive advantage,** which is found by means of a *competitive analysis*. The heart of your company's strategy and reason for being in business is your competitive advantage. You must do *something* better than everyone else; otherwise, your business isn't needed. Furthermore, your

---

competitive advantage
The facet of a business that it does better than all of its competitors.

Remember, champ – he may be bigger, stronger, an' faster, but he ain't got yer reach!!

www.CartoonStock.com

competitive advantage must be sustainable over time to remain a benefit to you. If it can be easily copied by competitors, you have to find a new way to stay ahead.

Without analysis, competition will likely be viewed with bias. Competitors are rarely as slow, backward, and inferior in all areas as we would like to believe they are. Competition should be viewed as formidable and serious. In competitive analysis, you are trying to identify *competitive weaknesses*. In what areas is the competition truly weak and therefore vulnerable? Some bias may be removed if you are as specific as possible in writing your competitive analysis. For example, instead of saying that your competitors offer poor service, qualify your remarks with references to return policies, delivery, schedules, or fees.

" Competitive advantage must be defined from the customer's perspective. A brand of tight-fitting jeans may prove popular among the young and slim, while losing market share among the not-so-young and not-so-slim. "

How can you analyze the competition? The process of gathering competitive intelligence doesn't have to be prohibitively expensive. A little effort and creativity combined with keeping your eyes open can yield a lot of information. Here are common ways that can help small business owners gather information for compiling their competitive analyses:

- Read articles in trade publications. A proliferation of specialized publications in every industry makes your gathering easier—for example, read *Progressive Grocer* if you are selling food products, or *Lodging Hospitality* if you are interested in travel accommodations.

- Listen to what your customers and salespeople say about competitors. These groups make the most frequent comparisons of you and the competition.

- Keep a file on key competitors. Information is useless unless you can access it easily. Include published information, notes of conversations, or competitors' sales, product, or service brochures. These readily available sources of information can help you determine how your competitors position themselves.

- Establish a regular time, perhaps a monthly meeting, to meet with key employees to evaluate the information in these competitive information files.

- Attend industry trade shows, exhibits, and conferences. A lot can be learned from competitors' booths and through the networking (or socializing) that goes on at such events.

- Buy competitors' products and take them apart to determine their quality and other advantages. Consider incorporating the best elements of competing products into your own products. This process is called *reverse engineering* and is part of a process of establishing comparison standards called *benchmarking*.

- Consult published credit reports on your competitors. Companies like Dun & Bradstreet (D&B) make standard credit reports available. See what D&B says about the competition.[30]

For a practical application of competitive analysis that small business owners can use, try this: Rank your business and four competitors you have identified in each of the following areas. Using Figure 3.4 as a guide, rank each business from 1 to 5, with 5 being the lowest and 1 the highest. Assign only one 1 per area, one 2, and so on. No ties are allowed, so you will end up with a ranked list of the five companies. This exercise will help you improve your competitive position and possibly point out new areas in which your business might enjoy a competitive advantage.

Areas of Comparison (For example only; add or delete areas that most apply to your business.)

1. *Image.* How do consumers perceive the reputation and the physical appearance of the business?

Figure 3.4
COMPETITIVE ANALYSIS

Areas of Comparison	Your Business	Competitor A	Competitor B	Competitor C	Competitor D
1. Image	_____	_____	_____	_____	_____
2. Location	_____	_____	_____	_____	_____
3. Layout	_____	_____	_____	_____	_____
4. Atmosphere	_____	_____	_____	_____	_____
5. Products	_____	_____	_____	_____	_____
6. Services	_____	_____	_____	_____	_____
7. Pricing	_____	_____	_____	_____	_____
8. Advertising	_____	_____	_____	_____	_____
9. Sales methods	_____	_____	_____	_____	_____
TOTALS	_____	_____	_____	_____	_____

2. *Location.* Is the business convenient to customers in terms of distance, parking, traffic, and visibility?

3. *Layout.* Are customers well served with the physical layout of the business?

4. *Atmosphere.* When customers enter the business, do they get a feeling that it is appropriate for your type of business?

5. *Products.* Can customers find the products they expect from your type of business?

6. *Services.* Do customers receive the quantity and quality of services they expect?

7. *Pricing.* Do customers perceive the prices charged to be appropriate given the quality of the products sold? Do they receive the value they expect?

8. *Advertising.* Does the advertising of the business reach its target market?

9. *Sales methods.* Are customers comfortable with the methods the business uses to sell products?

Defining Your Competitive Advantage   Your strategic plan helps you define a competitive advantage by analyzing different environments, studying your competition, and choosing appropriate strategies. Advantages you have over your competitors could include price, product features and functions, time of delivery (if speed is important to customers), place of business (if being located near customers is needed), and public perception (the positive image your business projects). Remember, a competitive advantage must be sustainable. If competitors can easily copy it, then it is not a true competitive advantage.

Three core ideas are valuable in defining your competitive advantage. First, keep in mind that any advantage is relative, not absolute. What matters in customers' minds is not the absolute performance of your product or service, but its performance compared with that of other products. For example, no toothpaste can make teeth turn pure white, but you could build an advantage if you developed a toothpaste that gets teeth noticeably whiter than competing toothpastes do.

Second, you should strive for multiple types of competitive advantage. Doing more than one thing better than other businesses will increase the chances that you can maintain an advantage over a longer period of time.

Third, remember that areas of competition change over time. Customers' tastes and priorities change as products and the processes for making them evolve, as the availability of substitute products changes, and for a variety of other reasons that can affect your competitive advantage. For example, in the past consumers compared watches based on their ability to keep time accurately. The introduction of the quartz watch, however, changed customer priorities. The cheapest quartz watch in the display case kept time more accurately than the most expensive mechanical watch, so the differentiating factors for watches became styles (types of watch faces) and features (built-in calculators, stopwatches, and television remote controls).[31]

Five Basic Forces of Competition   One of the leading researchers and writers on the topic of competitive advantage is Michael Porter, a professor at Harvard

Figure 3.5
FIVE FORCES OF COMPETITION

The Interplay of Competitive Forces Helps to Determine Which Products and Companies Succeed in the Marketplace— and Which Don't.

SOURCE: Michael Porter, "Know Your Place," *Inc.,* September 1991, 91. Reprinted from "The Five Forces for Competition" from "Know Your Place" by Porter, Inc., September 1991.

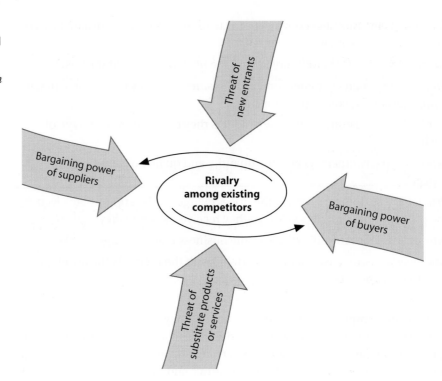

Business School. Porter has identified five basic forces of competition that exist within every industry. Analyzing these forces for your chosen industry can help you determine the attractiveness of the industry and the prospects for earning a return on your investment (see Figure 3.5).

The degree of "rivalry among existing competitors" in Figure 3.5 refers to how passively or aggressively the businesses within an industry compete. If they consistently attack one another, the attractiveness of the industry is reduced because the potential to make a profit is decreased. For example, compare the airline industry, where strong rivalries produce low profits, with the packaged consumer goods industry, where companies try to attract different groups of customers.

The "threat of new entrants" in the figure is a function of how easily other businesses can enter your market, which keeps prices and profits down. If a certain type of food, such as Cajun bagels, becomes popular, very little prevents new bakeries from opening or converting to produce this popular item. Low barriers to entry reduce profitability for incumbents.

The "bargaining power of suppliers" affects the price you will have to pay to produce your goods. If the supplies in question are commodities carried by several companies, suppliers will have little power to raise the prices they charge. By contrast, if you have only one or two choices of vendors, or if you require very specialized goods, you may have to pay what the suppliers ask.

The "bargaining power of buyers" affects how much latitude you have in changing your prices. The more potential substitutes your buyers have, the more power they have to influence your prices or the extent of services you must provide to keep their business.

The "threat of substitute products or services" is determined by the options your customers have when buying your product or service. The greater the number of substitutes available, the more your profit margin can be squeezed. Overnight delivery services must consider the threat of fax machines and e-mail, for example, even though they are entirely different ways to transmit messages.

The following five fatal flaws are associated with misapplying strategic thinking to specific competitive situations.

- *Misreading industry attractiveness.* The highest-tech, most glamorous, fastest-growing field may not be the best for making a profit because of its attractiveness to competition.

- *Failure to identify a true competitive advantage.* Imitation can put you in the middle of the pack. Yet, being different from competitors is both risky and difficult.

- *Pursuing a competitive advantage that is not sustainable.* Porter recommends that if small businesses cannot sustain an advantage, the owner should view the business as a short-term investment rather than an ongoing enterprise. This business philosophy might be stated as "Get in, grow, and get out."

- *Compromising a strategy in an attempt to grow faster.* If you are fortunate enough to identify a significant competitive advantage, don't give it up in a quest to become more like your larger competitors. Remember what made you successful in the first place.

- *Not making your strategy explicit or not communicating it to your employees.* Writing your strategy down and discussing it with your key people sets up an atmosphere in which everyone in your organization feels compelled to move toward a common goal. Each of your employees makes decisions every day. If your overall strategy is to offer products at the lowest possible cost, decisions by everyone in your business need to reinforce that goal.[32]

Importance of Competitive Advantage   Having a competitive advantage is critical. Your business must do *something* better than other organizations or it is not needed. To cope with a quickly changing competitive environment, small businesses need to be market driven.[33] Part of becoming market driven includes closely monitoring changing customer wants and needs, determining how those changes will affect customer satisfaction, and developing strategies to gain an edge. Small businesses cannot rely on the inertia of the marketplace for their survival.[34] When running a small business, you cannot solve problems simply by throwing money at them. Instead, you need to see your competitive environment with crystal clarity, then identify and secure a position you can defend.

In developing your competitive advantage, you will inevitably make decisions under conditions of uncertainty. This is the art, rather than the science, of marketing-related decision making. In his book *Marketing Mistakes,* Robert Hartley notes that we can seldom predict with any exactitude the reactions of consumers or the countermoves and retaliations of competitors.[35] Although it may be easy to play Monday-morning quarterback, viewing mistakes with twenty-twenty hindsight, we will do better to decide to learn from others' mistakes, especially when looking for a competitive advantage. Of course, no one ever deliberately set out to design a bad product or start a business that would fail. Nevertheless, what seems to be a good idea for achieving a competitive advantage often may not be, for one reason or another.

The lack, or loss, of competitive advantage exists in every size of business. Apple Computer, which began small, has fought to maintain the competitive advantage of ease of use. In 1983 Apple tried to break into the business market for personal computers with the Lisa. Although that computer was easy to use and had nice graphics, its advantages were not noticed by the business community because of its limited software and expensive price tag ($10,000).[36] Similar problems (performance below customer expectations and high price) plagued Apple's Newton MessagePad when it came out in 1993. Occasionally, competitive advantages are gained well after a product is introduced. For instance, the unsuccessful Lisa evolved into the Macintosh, one of the world's most popular models.

The list of products and businesses that have failed to gain a competitive advantage is long and distinguished. Entrants include Ford's Edsel (a car with lots of innovations—and lots more problems), To-Fitness Tofu Pasta, Gerber Singles (adult-modified baby foods that looked like dog food), Cucumber Antiperspirant Spray, and R. J. Reynolds' Premier (cigarettes that didn't burn or smoke). Premier appealed to nonsmokers . . . but nonsmokers don't buy cigarettes, and even Reynolds' president admitted that they "tasted like crap."[37] As you see, there are many lessons to learn from others' mistakes.

Benefits of Competitive Advantage   Gaining a sustainable competitive advantage can help you establish a self-sustaining position in the marketplace. Whether your edge comes from external factors, such as luck or the failure of a competitor, or internal factors, such as exceptional skills or superior resources, it can set up a cycle of success (see Figure 3.6).[38]

Because of your competitive advantage, your customers will be more satisfied with your business than with your competitors'. You will, in turn, gain market

Steve Jobs Demonstrates an Early Apple Model, Lisa, Which Had Competitive Advantages but Not Enough of Them.

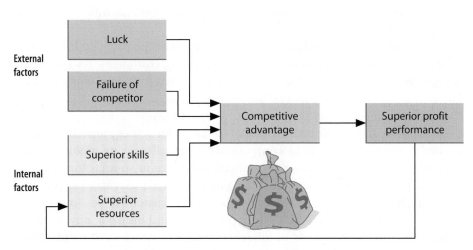

Figure 3.6
COMPETITIVE ADVANTAGE
CYCLE

However It Is Created, a Competitive Advantage Will Increase Your Profit Margins, Providing More Resources for Your Small Business to Use to Strengthen Itself.

SOURCE: "Competitive Advantage Cycle," from *Competitive Marketing Strategy,* Czepiel. Copyright © 1992. Reprinted by permission of Pearson Education, Inc.

share. Increased market share translates into larger sales and profits, which in turn give you more resources for improving your products, facilities, and human resources—all of which allow you to improve your competitive advantage. As additional resources come into the business from outside the company, they can be used to build and fortify operational sources of advantage.[39] Businesses that don't gain competitive advantage, therefore, lose out in this cycle. Their customers receive less value and are less satisfied. Their market share, sales volume, and profit fall. Without profits, they have fewer resources to reinvest in the business, so positioning is difficult to maintain. The gap between follower and leader grows wider.

How to Create Competitive Advantage   Three generic competitive strategies exist through which a business can gain a competitive advantage: lower cost, differentiation, and focus strategies.[40] Using *focus strategies* means aiming at a narrow segment of a market. By definition, all small businesses target niches or narrow market segments, so let's concentrate on the first two strategies.

You must find a way to lower your costs if you intend to compete primarily on price. If you try to compete on price without obtaining a cost advantage, your business is headed for trouble. Such an advantage can come from reduced labor costs, less expensive raw materials or supplies, more efficient distribution, or any number of other factors.

A competitive advantage based on *differentiation* means that your product or service is different from those offered by your competitors. Its value comes from the fact that you can show customers why your difference is better, not just cheaper. In this way, differentiation can effectively remove direct competition. For example, when a mass merchandiser such as Wal-Mart or Target enters a town, small retailers are not necessarily run out of business. Studies that measured the impact of Wal-Mart's entrance on local retailers in Iowa have shown that as long as the small retail stores stock different merchandise than Wal-Mart, they actually benefit due to the increased number of shoppers coming into town. Small stores should differentiate rather than try to compete head-to-head with the giants.[41] Wal-Mart pushes its manufacturing clients (70 percent of its inventory comes from China) to make more, faster, in order to keep shelves full of homogenous items. Small manufacturers and retailers can compete via different product design, service, and quality.[42]

An advantage does not have to involve features of the product. It can come from anything your business does—including quality, customer service, or distribution. Research shows that competitive advantage has four key components: the competitor identification process, the sources of the advantage, the positions of the advantage, and the performance outcomes achieved.[43]

To create a sustainable competitive advantage, your strategy must incorporate a combination of methods to continuously differentiate your product and to improve it in areas that make a meaningful difference to your customers.[44] But how can you keep up with the ever changing tastes and preferences of your customers? There are so many questions about your customers you must try to answer. The products and services that people like and dislike at any particular time are shaped by hundreds of influences, many of which can't be identified. Nevertheless, you need to gather as many facts as possible about your markets in an objective and orderly manner. *Market research* offers a way to answer at least some questions about your customers' changing wants and needs, so as to help you create and hold on to your competitive advantage.

Strategic Alternatives

The process of defining *strategic alternatives* begins by identifying problems based on information gained in earlier steps. Next is the drafting of a list of alternatives. Thus, in this two-step process, you identify what is wrong, then determine what you can do about it.

Problem identification is the most difficult part of strategic planning. It takes thorough SWOT and competitive analyses and a lot of analytical thinking to pinpoint problems like a current strategy that no longer suits your environment or a mismatch between your strengths and an opportunity that you have discerned. Bracing up one of your weaknesses and preparing for an upcoming threat are tasks that demand your attention. If completion of your SWOT and competitive analyses identifies no major problems or new strategies needed, don't fix anything. Always look to be proactive, but don't ignore the possibility that keeping to the status quo might be the best choice.

Few problems can be solved with a single solution or with the first idea that comes to mind. Therefore, you should try to generate as many potential solutions as possible. Don't evaluate ideas as you generate them, as criticism stifles creativity. Only after you've exhausted the possibilities should you evaluate whether each alternative would solve your particular problem or work in your company. Once your list of alternative strategies is compiled, you need to consider its potential effects on your company's resources, environment, and people.

Although there is a strong temptation to list strategic alternatives informally in one's mind, research has shown that putting ideas down on paper leads to a wider range of alternatives and stimulates the creativity and insightful thinking that are the bases for good strategic change.[45]

Goal Setting and Strategies

Your mission statement sets the broadest direction for your business. SWOT and competitive analyses help you refine or change that direction, but the goals that

Playing to Win

Winners in business often play rough and do not apologize for it. Toyota, Dell, and Wal-Mart don't pull any punches when going head-to-head with their competitors. They play hardball. They exemplify single-minded pursuit of a competitive advantage and all the benefits that accompany it.

Playing hardball means working with intensity. It makes your company strong and vibrant, which results in more affordable products for satisfied customers. To use a baseball analogy, if an aggressive batter (competitor) is crowding the plate, a hardball player (a successful entrepreneur) will throw a hard, inside, brush-back pitch to establish strength. Hardball players play tough, but stay within the rules—they don't cheat.

Stalk and Lachenauer described their Hardball Manifesto in a recent *Harvard Business Review* article. The manifesto includes five key points:

- *Focus relentlessly on competitive advantage. Always try to widen the gap* with competitors. Don't be satisfied with today's competitive advantage— go for tomorrow's also.

- *Strive for "extreme" competitive advantage.* Try to develop a facet that puts your advantage out of the reach of competitors.

- *Avoid attacking directly.* Hardball players tend to prefer the economies of force gained by an indirect attack over direct confrontation.

- *Exploit people's will to win.* Hardball entrepreneurs understand that people have a natural desire to win, and they build upon that desire in their employees.

- *Know the caution zone.* Hardball players know where the boundaries of legal and social conventions are; they may play close to those lines, but don't cross them.

SOURCES: George Stalk, Jr., and Rob Lachenauer, "Hard Ball," *Harvard Business Review,* April 2004, 62; Joshua Kurlantzick, "Ready to Rumble?" *Entrepreneur,* May 2004, 61–63.

you set must stem from your mission statement. Obviously, goals are needed before you can build a set of strategies. As the cliché goes, "If you don't put up a target, you won't hit anything." Goals need to be

- *Written in terms of outcomes rather than actions.* A good goal states where you want to be, not how you want to get there. For example, a goal should focus on increasing sales rather than on your intention to send one of your brochures to every address in town.

- *Measurable.* In order to tell whether you have accomplished a goal, you must be able to measure the outcome.

- *Challenging, yet attainable.* Goals that are too easy to accomplish are not motivating. Goals that are not likely to be accomplished are self-defeating and decrease motivation.
- *Communicated to everyone in the company.* A team effort is difficult to produce if some of your players don't know the goals.
- *Written with a time frame for achievement.* Performance and motivation increase when people have goals accompanied by a time frame as compared with open-ended goals.

Writing usable goals isn't easy at first. If you state that your goal is to be "successful," is that a good goal? It sounds positive; it sounds nice. But is it measurable? No. How can you tell whether you have achieved a goal such as this? You can't, because there is no defined outcome. There is also no time frame. Do you intend to be successful this year? By the time you are 90? Goals need the characteristics listed previously to be useful.

Although you will have only one mission statement, you will have several business-level goals that apply to your entire organization. Each functional area of your business (for example, marketing, finance, human resources, and production) will have its own set of specific goals that relate directly to achieving your business-level goals (see Figure 3.7). Even if you are the only person performing marketing, finance, human resource management, and production duties, these areas of your small business must still be addressed individually.

- Your *mission statement* describes who you are, what your business is, and why it exists.
- A *business-level goal* describes what you want your overall business to accomplish to achieve your company mission.
- A *function-level goal* describes the performance desired of specific departments (or functional areas, such as marketing, production, and so on) to achieve your business-level goals.
- A *strategy* is a plan of action that details how you will attain your function-level goals.

In the final stage of goal setting, specific strategies are developed to accomplish your goals. For example, a *marketing strategy* might be to hire Jerry Seinfeld to be spokesperson for your new standup comedy computer program. This strategy should help you attain your *function-level marketing goal* of capturing 20 percent market share of the total comedy software market. Your marketing goal should help you attain your *business-level goal* of increasing third-quarter profits by 8 percent, which in turn ensures that you accomplish your company *mission* of satisfying the entertainment needs of lonely computer operators and thereby earn a profit.

Function-level goals and strategies must coordinate with one another and with business-level goals for the business to run smoothly. For example, the marketing department may develop a strategy of advertising on the Internet that will bring in orders from all over the globe. This result is great as long as the production department can increase capacity, the human resource department can hire and train enough new employees, and all other areas of the business are prepared. Each functional area must see itself as an integral part of the entire business and act accordingly.

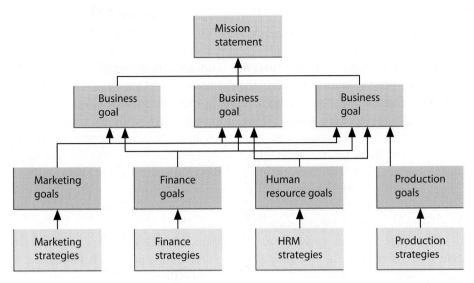

Figure 3.7
LEVELS OF GOALS

The Goals You Set for Each Functional Area of Your Small Business Should Help You Achieve the Overall Goals of Your Business, Which in Turn Issue from Your Mission Statement.

Control Systems

Planning for the future is an inexact science. Very rarely do the actual outcomes of your plans exactly match what you anticipated. When things don't turn out as you planned, you must ask, "Why was there a deviation?" Having a control process built into the strategic planning process will help answer this question.

Your strategic plan, including all of its separate parts, sets a standard of comparison for your business's actual performance. The purpose of control systems is to provide you with information to start the planning process all over again. After checking your controls, you either readjust the standards of your plan or create new goals for your plan, and off you go for another planning period. This is why goals must be (1) written in terms of outcomes rather than actions; (2) measurable; (3) challenging, yet attainable; (4) communicated; and (5) written with a time frame for achievement. You need to collect accurate data about what you have done so you can compare this information with your planned standards. Control systems don't need to be expensive and elaborate. They should be simple enough to become a natural part of your management process.

> " Strategic planning requires you to broaden your thinking and forces you to look at the general issues over the next three to five years—countering the realities of the competitive world with concrete plans instead of wishful thinking. "

Strategic Planning in Action

Strategic plans are different from *business plans* (see Chapter 4). Business plans and strategic plans support each other and overlap to some degree, but they seek to accomplish different purposes. Business plans are written primarily to test the feasibility of a business idea, acquire financing, and coordinate the startup phase. Strategic plans are needed both before the business is started and continuously while it is in operation, to match the direction of the business with changes that occur within its environments.

Strategic planning addresses strategic growth: where you are going. Business planning addresses operational growth: how you will get there. Strategic planning looks outward from the business at the long-term prospects for your products, your markets, your competition, and so on. Business planning, or organizational growth, focuses on the internal concerns of your business, such as capital, personnel, and marketing. Eventually, the two plans will converge, as your long-term strategic goals will be strongly influenced by operational decisions made when the business was started.[46] Strategic planning requires you to broaden your thinking and forces you to look at general issues over the next three to five years—countering the realities of the competitive world with concrete plans instead of wishful thinking. Most sections of a strategic plan will not be extremely detailed but will provide outlines for direction. A business plan, by comparison, needs to be as detailed as possible.

Planning is difficult; consequently, many small business owners would like to ignore it. The reason the planning process is difficult is because it forces you to identify realities that exist in a competitive world rather than relying on emotions, guesses, and assumptions.

What is the best kind of strategic or business plan to write? The one that you will *use!* A balance must be struck between floundering around with no direction or being stuck in an unrealistic, rigid planning process that strangles flexibility and is based on hard data that are not really hard. You need to remember that the *planning process* is actually more important and valuable than the plan that is created because of the *strategic thinking* required to write it.

When you begin writing the first draft of your plan, don't worry about the fine points of its structure—simply get your ideas down on paper. Once the plan is written, you should revise it to reorder your ideas into a logical and clear format. An informal plan written in a format that you are comfortable with and will use is 100 percent better than a formal plan that fits someone else's definition of "correct" form but sits on a shelf.

Get advice and suggestions from as many sources as practical when you are formulating your plans. Ask colleagues, bankers, accountants, other executives, and lawyers for their input. If your business is already in operation, including employees in decisions is a great way to show them that their opinions count. They can all provide valuable insight to enhance your plans.

Summary

• The relationship between social responsibility, ethics, and strategic planning

The social responsibility and ethics of your business are the commitments you make to doing what is right. Strategic planning is the process of deciding where you want your business to go and how it will get there. All three concepts work together to form the foundation on which your entire business rests.

• Levels of social responsibility

You have an economic responsibility to make your business profitable. Without profit, your business cannot contribute anything to society. Your legal obligation to obey the law describes the minimal behavior expected for your firm to be part of society. Your ethical responsibility covers your obligation to do what is right. Philanthropic goodwill is contributing to others without expecting anything in return.

• Importance of a code of ethics

Business ethics encompasses more than deciding what should and should not be done in a particular situation. It supplies the fundamental basis for the course you want your business to take. A code of ethics offers a way for you to communicate your ethical expectations to everyone involved in your business. The code should represent your ethical ideals, be concise enough to be remembered, be written clearly, and apply to everyone in the organization.

• Steps in the strategic planning process and the importance of competitive advantage

The strategic planning process includes defining your mission statement, conducting an environmental analysis (internal and external, or SWOT, analysis), analyzing the competition and defining your competitive advantage, identifying strategic alternatives, setting goals, and establishing systems to measure effectiveness. A competitive advantage is the facet of your business that gives your company an edge over the competition. The strategic plan helps you to identify and establish competitive advantage by analyzing the environment and the competitive landscape.

Questions for Review and Discussion

1. Write a brief summary of the connection between social responsibility, ethics, and strategic planning in a small business setting.

2. Discuss the four groups of laws that generally regulate business activity in this country, and give some historical background on the major laws that affect all entrepreneurs today.

3. Define the purpose of a code of ethics, and write a brief code that would be suitable for a small business.

4. Although a certain practice may be widely accepted in the business community and be perfectly legal, does that necessarily mean it is always moral? Qualify your answer with examples.

5. Write a mission statement for a small business that not only functions as a strategic planning guide but also incorporates the company's philosophy of social responsibility and ethical standards.

6. Explain how cultural differences between countries can have either a positive or a negative effect on an entrepreneur who is pursuing a

contract either outside the United States or with persons of different ethnic backgrounds in the United States.

7. Why is environmental analysis more crucial to the small business owner than to larger corporations?

8. You are an entrepreneur and wish to perform a self-evaluation of your business environment. How would you go about this task? Be specific about what you hope to discover through the evaluation of your employees, product, management, and so on.

9. What is the value of competitive analysis to the small business owner? What sorts of things should you know about your competition, and what analytical methods can you use to find out this information?

10. Goal setting is a major part of the entrepreneur's business plan. Outline specific methods for setting goals that are realistic, fit into the overall mission of the company, and can be related to the strategic planning process that is in place at the organization.

Questions for Critical Thinking

1. How can a small business show that it is socially responsible? Think of evidence of social responsibility (like sponsoring a Little League team) that a small business can demonstrate.

2. What does strategic planning mean to the small business owner? How does the size of the organization affect the strategic planning process, and how much input should be sought from outside sources while outlining the strategic plan?

Experience This . . .

Small businesses in the area where you live make impacts on your local society. Some make a positive impact, others a negative impact. Identify two local companies—one that is a good citizen and one that is not. Find newspaper and magazine articles to support your classifications (so that you are dealing with as many facts and as little opinion as possible). Write a two- to three-page paper explaining the possible strategic business implications of the actions of these two small businesses. Will either of them need to change in the near future as a consequence of past behavior?

What Would You Do?

Some small businesses, by the very nature of what they produce or market, find it difficult to clarify how they plan to fulfill the four levels of social responsibility (economic, legal, ethical, and philanthropic). Through strategic planning, even companies in somewhat controversial and questionable industries can define how they will be socially responsible. Consider Grand Casinos of Minneapolis. As more and more states have legalized gambling in selected locations, Lyle Berman, CEO of Grand Casinos, has been there to develop and manage the casinos. His company has proved so successful that it ranked first on *Fortune*'s list of America's 100 fastest-growing companies. Yet Grand Casinos' business—gambling—tends to arouse considerable controversy. Obviously, Berman could use strategic planning to help identify areas in which his company could fulfill its social responsibilities.

Question

1. You're in charge of strategic planning for Grand Casinos. The company wants to open and manage a casino in rural Iowa. Community residents have asked you and your strategic planning team to attend a town meeting to discuss the casino. You'll need to prepare a description of how your company is fulfilling its social responsibility. (Use Figure 3.1 as a guide.) Other members of the class will act as community residents. As a resident, prepare your questions and concerns for confronting the Grand Casinos team.

CHAPTER CLOSING CASE

TIME TO CHANGE STRATEGY?

The four men huffed and puffed their way up a steep hiking trail in the Rocky Mountains. Russell Straub urged them on. "Let's go," he called out. "Got to get that blood flowing!" The men were all top managers at Loan Bright, Straub's online mortgage company, and they had gathered for a weeklong retreat at his home in Evergreen, Colorado, to make some important decisions. A little exercise would help, Straub thought. He wanted everyone's head clear for what would be one of the toughest calls in the company's history: whether to abandon Loan Bright's high-end financial services clients and head down-market. It would be a radical move, but something had to be done. After five years of rapid growth, the former *Inc.* 500 company had stagnated. Straub was eager to kick-start it and thought he had the answer.

Straub had founded Loan Bright with two of his University of Vermont fraternity brothers in 1999. The idea was to connect mortgage lenders with potential home buyers. People seeking mortgages would visit the company's website, CompareInterestRates.com. After entering some basic information, they would get a list of lenders and available terms. Loan Bright, based in Evergreen, made money by selling that home-buyer data—including contact information, home value, and credit rating—to mortgage lenders, which handed them out as leads to their sales teams.

Loan Bright's first customers tended to be small mortgage brokers eager for leads. But from the outset, the company aspired to move up the food chain and take on more lucrative clients. To Straub, the logic seemed impeccable: "Would you rather have a million customers paying you a dollar a month, or one paying you a million a month?" he asked himself. By 2004, the company had successfully made the shift, with a dream list of fat clients including Wells Fargo, Bank of America, and Chase Manhattan Mortgages. And the strategy appeared to be paying off. Sales reached $4.5 million and the company came in at number 162 on the 2004 *Inc.* 500 list.

But Straub was noticing some worrisome issues. With about 60 percent of the firm's revenue divided among its 10 largest clients, Loan Bright couldn't afford to displease a single one. "You'd have a hiccup with one client and it felt like it could put you out of business," he says. But demands from some big customers were becoming difficult to fulfill. One key client began requesting lead lists sorted by increasingly narrow criteria; it asked for a list of mortgage seekers with less-than-perfect credit who were purchasing a property above a certain value and financing a particular percentage of the purchase.

The problem was, Loan Bright's Web traffic wasn't great enough to create a meaningful list of those superspecialized leads. Indeed, Straub performed some calculations and estimated that Loan Bright would have to increase traffic tenfold. Doing that, of course, would involve some heavy advertising and marketing expenses.

That customer wound up getting frustrated and leaving. Loan Bright was able to land a new customer to make up for the lost revenue, but other longtime clients also were growing more demanding, and Loan Bright's difficulty in serving them was proving similarly frustrating. Straub realized that the company was treading water: lose a customer, gain a customer. "We just couldn't get any traction," he says. By September 2005, Loan Bright had lost money every month for the previous nine months. The company laid off seven employees and was "cutting into bone and muscle" to save on expenses, says Straub.

The problem began consuming more and more of his time. And soon new issues began to emerge. A group of salespeople, for example, came to see him one day. They begged him to stop advertising Loan Bright's services on Google. The ads were generating plenty of phone calls, they explained, but the calls usually came from individual loan officers who wanted to buy only a few leads. When the salespeople pressed them to buy more, or to connect them to higher-level decision makers who could authorize a substantial contract, the loan officers invariably balked. For Loan Bright salespeople, who were paid by the size of the deals they closed, a Google phone call was a nightmare.

As Straub thought about the Google problem, he had an epiphany. "Wait a minute," he thought. "*Why are these loan officers calling us?*" Obviously they needed help, and coincidentally Loan Bright needed to tweak its business model. Perhaps the emphasis on large clients was misplaced. "Maybe we should shift gears and embrace these folks," Straub thought.

On the first Monday of September 2005, Loan Bright's management team gathered in the great room of Straub's house nestled deep in woods at the base of a small mountain. The top agenda item for the weeklong retreat: how to get Loan Bright back on track.

Questions

1. Was it time for Loan Bright to change markets? When a company sets a strategy, should it be changed? Why? When?

2. If Loan Bright does not change markets, what other aspects of the business should it change?

SOURCE: From Phaedra Hise, "Russell Straub's High-End Clients Were Straining His Business with Tougher and Tougher Demands," *Inc.*, September 2006, 47–51. Copyright © 2006 Mansueto Ventures LLC, publisher of Inc. Magazine, New York, NY 10017. Reprinted with permission.

Test Prepper

ACE self-test

college.hmco.com/pic/hatten4e

You've read the chapter, studied the key terms, and the exam is any day now. Think you're ready to ace it? Take this sample test to gauge your comprehension of chapter material. You can check your answers at the back of the book. Want more test questions? Visit the student website at college.hmco.com/pic/hatten4e and take the ACE and ACE+1 quizzes for more practice.

True/False

1. Every business can be socially responsible.

2. Inner cities are crime-ridden, poor locations for businesses.

3. Making a profit diminishes any social good a business creates.

4. Social responsibility, ethics, and strategic planning are not merely connected, but inseparable.

5. If a goal is not measurable, you cannot tell whether you have attained it.

6. Green marketing is generally a scam to sell products for more money.

7. Economist Milton Friedman contends that businesses should produce goods and social experts should solve social problems.

8. Small businesses generally cannot afford to make strategic mistakes.

9. A small business needs either a business plan or a strategic plan, but not both.

10. The organizational culture of your small business affects employees' ethical decisions.

Fill in the Blank

1. The value of the planning process involved in writing a strategic plan is the _____ required to write it.

2. An important value of internal analysis is matching _____ with _____.

3. If your SWOT and competitive analyses identify no major problems, _____ _____ _____.

4. Ideally, all your strategies and goals ensure that you accomplish your _____ _____.

5. Regulation of business activity generally applies to these groups: consumers, _____, environment, and employees.

The Business Plan

A few years ago the author of this book had the opportunity to teach the process of writing business plans to budding entrepreneurs in the Russian city of Magadan. Magadan (population 130,000) is located on the Sea of Okhotsk, not far below the Arctic Circle. The University of Alaska–Anchorage has set up Russian–American Business Training Centers throughout the Russian Far East as a means of developing entrepreneurship—a much-needed commodity in this economically troubled country.

There is no question that entrepreneurship—with its creation of new businesses offering new products and ideas—is the engine that runs a free market economy like the one Russia is still trying to establish. But a very real question remains: How do you start that engine of new business in times of economic crisis? At a time when many Russians had not been paid for 6, 9, or even 12 months or longer, the fuel (currency) to run the economic engine was scarce. Nevertheless, more than 40 aspiring entrepreneurs enrolled in the author's classes to learn how to write a business plan.

When resources are scarce, the need for creativity and innovation increases. This was evident in Magadan. Although the banks had no money with which to

After reading this chapter, you should be able to:

- Explain the purpose and importance of the business plan.

- Describe the components of a business plan.

- Recognize the importance of reviewing your business plan.

Timothy Hatten.

make loans, students identified "alternative sources" of financing in their business plans, such as extensive use of barter of goods and services, and multiple friends and family from whom to borrow small amounts of money. Their willingness to innovate demonstrated the essence of *bootstrapping*—the perseverance and desire to make business happen despite formidable obstacles. Remember the term *bootstrapping,* or picking yourself up by your own bootstraps, as you contemplate entering into self-employment.

What types of businesses were planned in Magadan? As wide a variety as you might find in the class you are probably attending now. A range of cafés, importing of used cars and trucks, a crematorium, and an ambitious expansion and upgrade of the Magadan airport (estimated cost, 900 million rubles). A preponderance of talent in artistic areas also emerged from among the Russian students. A man named Dmitri, who was trained as a geologist, had built and collected machinery for cutting, shaping, and polishing stone. During the summer, he would scour the hills near Magadan collecting agate, geodes, and other stones and minerals. Dmitri then spent the long Russian winters in his workshop transforming those raw materials into beautiful chess sets, mosaics, and other creations. He and a partner wrote a business plan to export his treasures.

If entrepreneurship involves identifying a need and creating a business to satisfy that need (and it does), then the Magadan entrepreneurial prize went to a man named Anatoli. Anatoli was trained as an electrical engineer, and like many of us, he likes to see what he can find in salvage piles. One day Anatoli found a compact heating element, and he immediately thought of a new use for this relic. Magadan, like most Russian cities, has a central, coal-fired heating plant where water is heated, sent via underground pipes to all business and government buildings and apartments, and finally enters cast-iron radiators to heat the rooms. Because "underground" means "permafrost" in this region of the world, centralized heating is not exactly an efficient system. When the system is operating at peak performance, you can still see your breath indoors. At worst, when the city's coal supply runs short, the entire heating system shuts down for hours. Anatoli adapted the heating element he found so that it would electrically heat the water as it enters an individual apartment's radiator. He wrote a business plan to import similar heating elements, which he planned to retrofit to existing heating units to keep Russian apartments more comfortable. Now that's an entrepreneur with a plan!

Every Business Needs a Plan

Successful small business owners know where they want to go and find a way to get there. To see their dreams of owning a profitable business become a reality, they know they must plan each step along the way. Starting a business is like going on vacation—you don't reach your destination by accident. Whether you want to hike through Denali National Park in Alaska or sell frozen yogurt to tourists in Miami, you need a map and adequate provisions.

A **business plan** is a written document that demonstrates persuasively that enough products or services can be sold at a profit for your firm to become a viable business. Planning is an essential ingredient for any successful business. Although we all create mental plans, those thoughts need to be committed to writing before starting a business.[1] A written plan can help us find omissions and flaws in our ideas by allowing other people to critically review and analyze them.

> **business plan**
> A document describing a business that is used to test the feasibility of a business idea, to raise capital, and to serve as a road map for future operations.

A business plan tells the reader what your business objectives are; *when, where, why,* and *how* your business will accomplish its objectives; and *who* will be involved in running the business. When planning, you must define the goals of your business, determine the actions that need to be taken to accomplish them, gather and commit the necessary resources, and aim for well-defined targets. A business plan can mean the difference between running a business proactively and reactively. When NASA launched *Apollo 7,* the first manned spacecraft to land on the moon, it didn't aim at the moon. Instead, NASA pointed the rocket to the point in space where the moon would be, factoring in the time needed to get there. Similarly, a business plan should aim at the point where you want your business to be in the future.

The Purpose

The three primary reasons for writing business plans are (1) to aid you in determining the feasibility of your business idea, (2) to attract capital for starting up, and (3) to provide direction for your business after it is in operation.

Proving Feasibility   Writing a business plan is one of the best ways to prevent costly oversights. Committing your ideas to paper forces you to look critically at your means, goals, and expectations. Many people thinking of starting a small business get caught up in the excitement and emotions of the process. It is a truly exciting time! Unfortunately, business decisions based purely on emotion are often not the best long-term choices.

Wanting to have a business does not automatically mean that a market exists to support your desire. You may love boats and want to build a business around them, but if you live 100 miles from the nearest body of water and are unwilling to move, it is unlikely that you can create a viable boat business. Norm Brodsky is a successful entrepreneur who writes a column in *Inc.* magazine titled "Street Smarts." Brodsky states, "The initial goal of every business is to survive long enough to see whether or not the business is viable—no matter what type of business, or how much capital you have. You never know for sure if a business is viable until you do it in the real world."[2] Writing your plan can help remove strong personal emotions from the decision-making process. You need to be passionate about the business you are in, but emotion must be balanced and tempered with logic and rationality.

Attracting Capital   Almost all startups must secure capital from bankers or investors. One of the first questions a banker or investor will ask when approached about participating in a business is, "Where is your plan?" You need to appreciate bankers' position. They have to be accountable to depositors for the

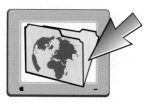

@ e-biz

Cool B-Plan Tools

Need to write a business plan and want some online help? Many Web pages provide a plethora of information, ranging from free to far from free. Check out the following:

CCH Business Owner's Toolkit (www.toolkit.cch.com). You'll find free sample business plans written for service, retail, and manufacturing businesses—in downloadable files.

BizPlanit.com (www.bizplanit.com). The consultants who created BizPlanit.com will review and critique your plan section by section for several hundred dollars or draft your plan from scratch for several thousand bucks. Yikes! That's a good incentive to write your own plan. This site also includes a lot of freebies.

North of the Border Business Plan (http://smallbusinessbc.ca/startup). The British Columbia Business Service Centre created this comprehensive site. It includes tools for small businesses such as an Interactive Business Planner, an Online Small Business Workshop, and Small Business Guides with sample business plans.

The Queen Mother of Business Plan Sites (www.sba.gov/starting_business). In addition to all the other information available at the Small Business Administration website, you will find some outstanding advice on creating a business plan.

"Next Stop . . ." Businesstown (www.businesstown. com/planning/creating.asp). This comprehensive small business site is crammed full of helpful information. The business-planning section has so many detours that anyone writing a business plan will find it bookmark-worthy.

Business Plan Center (www.businessplans.org). This site provides full business plans from Moot Corporation, billed as "the Super Bowl of Business Plan competitions," guideline articles for planning, strategy insight, and Web resources.

money entrusted to their care. Bankers in general are financially conservative, so before they risk their capital, they will want assurances that you are knowledgeable and realistic in your projections. Therefore, a complete business plan is needed before you can raise any significant capital. Your business plan will show that you know what you are doing and have thought through the problems and opportunities. Potential investors will also have questions about your plan. They will want to know when your business will break even, when it will be profitable, and if your numbers are real.[3]

Providing Direction   Business plans should provide a road map for future operation. "Can't see the forest for the trees" and "It's difficult to remember that your initial objective was to drain the swamp when you're up to your hips in alligators" are clichés that well apply to starting a small business in that so much of your time can be consumed by handling immediate problems ("management by spot fire," or paying attention to the latest dilemma to flare up) that you have trouble concentrating on the overall needs of the business. By having a road map to guide you over the long term, you are more likely to stay on course.

Don't misunderstand—providing direction does not mean that directions (and plans) don't change. Craig Knouf understands that point very well. He calculates that he has revised his original business plan more than 120 times since he first wrote it in 1997 for Associated Business Systems, an office-equipment supplier in

Craig Knouf at Associated Business Systems, an Office-Equipment Supplier in Portland, Oregon.

Portland, Oregon. Knouf meets with his seven vice presidents to take a look at the 30-page document every month to review current goals and every quarter for three-month goals, and he holds a two-day meeting to discuss annual long-term objectives. Knouf says, "If you only looked at the plan every quarter, by the time you realize the mistake, you're five months off. You're done. You're not going to get back on track." His original product line did not place much emphasis on scanning software, but a monthly review caught a rise in demand for scanners. Knouf acted quickly, and his flexibility paid off to the tune of software revenue doubling to more than $3 million between 2003 and 2004. Seasons change, and Craig Knouf is ready to change even faster.[4]

> " Free or inexpensive business planning assistance is available to entrepreneurs from such sources as Small Business Development Centers. "

The Practice: Guidelines for Writing a Business Plan

No rigid formula for writing business plans exists that would fit every new business. Plans are unique to each business situation. Even so, some general guidelines should be followed.

Consider Your Audience   You need to show the benefit of your business to your reader. Investors want their money to go into market-driven businesses, which satisfy the wants and needs of customers, rather than technology-driven ones, which focus more on the product or service being offered than on what people want.[5]

Keep It Brief   Your business plan should be long enough to cover all the major issues facing the business, yet not look like a copy of *War and Peace.* Your final plan should be complete, yet concise. Including financial projections and appendices, it

Good, Bad, and Ugly Business Plans

In their jobs, loan officers at a bank and small business consultants are constantly examining business plans. A discussion with them about good and poor business plans reveals that they've seen the gamut from excellent to just plain awful. Let's look at selected pages from two specific examples of business plans—one well written and one that needs a lot of revision. (Needless to say, the poorly written business plan has been altered to protect the identity of the guilty writer.)

Company A The business plan for Cameo's Fine Jewelry & Timepieces was written as a class project by an undergraduate business student. Although the student chose to take a different career direction, the plan summary in Figure 4.1(a) and the full plan in the appendix to this book are solid and fundable.

Company B Jay's Quarterback Club was the idea for a sports bar and restaurant in Norcross, Georgia. When Jay M. went looking for financing of his idea, however, he found that potential investors and lenders were reluctant to loan him the startup capital. A close look at his business plan reveals mistakes that might explain their reluctance. Selected pages from that plan follow in Figure 4.1(b).

should be less than 40 pages long. Your first draft will probably be longer, but you can sharpen your ideas by editing the final document to 40 or fewer pages.

Point of View   Try to write your business plan in the third person (do not use "I" or "we"). This approach helps maintain objectivity by removing your personal emotions from the writing process.

Create a Professional Image   The overall appearance of your business plan should be professional and attractive, but not extravagant. Having your document laser-printed on white paper, with a colored-stock cover, dividers, and spiral binding, is perfectly acceptable. Think of the message your business plan will send to bankers and investors: Having it bound in leather with gold leaf–trimmed pages is not a good sign. Does the plan's appearance suggest that you really need the money or will spend it wisely? Conversely, what might potential investors think of a business plan scratched out on a Big Chief tablet with a crayon? Would it look as if you were really serious about your business?

As you write the first draft of your plan, have several people who are not involved in your business read your work to get their initial reactions. Do they quickly grasp the essence of your proposal? Are they excited about your idea? Do they exclaim, "Wow!"? Getting feedback while you are still writing the plan can help you refine your work and get the reader to say "Wow!"

Where to Get Help   Who should write the business plan for your proposed venture? You should! The person who is best qualified and who receives the most

Cameo's Fine Jewelry & Timepieces Executive Summary

Cameo's Fine Jewelry & Timepieces is designed to be the Western Slope of Colorado's finest, most exquisite jewelry store available. Located in the heart of Grand Junction, Cameo's will offer jewelry and watches from world-renowned artists and designers from countries known for their quality such as Switzerland, Germany, Italy, and the U.S. Galleries will feature the work of Cartier, Rolex, Pippo Italia, Hearts on Fire, Paul Klecka, and many more.

The experience our customers receive through our atmosphere and customer service will be as fine as the jewelry itself. Our retail format will take on the elements of both a gallery and a lounge. Saltwater fish tanks will enhance the environment, and a wine and cocktail bar will be available to our customers. The sales staff and on-duty gemologist will be able to assist in finding that perfect piece of jewelry, and if it's not available, they will be able to order it or create a custom piece. Socials will invite the community to come enjoy the galleries and become more educated on the different qualities of jewelry.

Location and Target Market   Grand Junction serves as an ideal location, being that it is the largest city on the Western Slope of Colorado and acts as a retail hub for the surrounding communities. Since Cameo's will be the only jewelry store on the Western Slope that offers this level of quality, it will draw from a four-county region including Mesa, Garfield, Delta, and Montrose counties, which have a total population of 254,666. After taking into account age, percent of population who purchase jewelry, yearly weddings, and salary, there are 101,096 jewelry consumers within this geographic market. My goal is to obtain a 1 percent market share during the first year of business, which would provide 1,011 customers.

With this market penetration, and an average jewelry purchase of $2,000, Cameo's would sell $2,022,000 worth of products in the first fiscal year. The cash position at the end of the first fiscal year will equal $460,052, making this a very attractive and profitable venture to pursue.

Competitive Advantage   Cameo's defining strengths will be that of location and facility as well as inventory. Cameo's will be housed in a 6,850 square foot renovated building on 4th and Main in Grand Junction. Being downtown means that Cameo's will fall under the guidance of the Downtown Partnership. The purpose of the Downtown Partnership is to oversee the promotion of the downtown area and provide community benefiting events. Some events held downtown include an October fest, a farmer's market, parade of lights, and an art hop.

Cameo's exclusive inventory will also set it apart from other jewelry stores. Many pieces in inventory will be rare or hard to find and certainly the only one available within this geographic market.

There are several things that make the jewelry industry as a whole very attractive, including strong growth, a stable position, and new product creation, innovation, and trends. Currently the jewelry industry is growing annually at a rate of 9 percent, allowing for more retail outlets in one geographic region.

Jewelry is very stable because it is never going away, nor is it a fad item. Jewelry is often considered a necessity in times of marriage and anniversary, and is often used as a gift. There are many new jewelry products entering the market all the time that are technologically, fashion, and trend driven, which creates an increase in demand.

Management   My passion for watches, and the jewelry industry, combined with previous work experience will enable me to make this business a success. Previous employment has provided me with experience in the necessary functions of this business, including management, marketing, event planning, and financials.

My skills in marketing and event planning will prove most beneficial to the startup of this business. The product costs in this industry are very high, and general knowledge is low; therefore, providing information and educating the consumer is crucial.

Figure 4.1(a)

(Continued).

Special events will draw consumers into the store in order to show them what it has to offer.

Finances   Financial projections show that equipment, supplies, fixtures, and leasehold improvements totaling $111,000 are needed, along with a beginning inventory of $513,500 and operating expenses of just over $90,000, which all together will create total initial capitalization costs of $730,000. The owner brings $73,000 of equity and seeks a bank loan of $657,000 at competitive terms.

Cash-flow projections show positive cash flow in year 1, totaling approximately $380,000.

Figure 4.1(b)

EXAMPLE OF POOR BUSINESS PLAN

A Sloppy Appearance Can Hurt the Chances of Your Plan Being Taken Seriously by Lenders and Investors.

JAY'S QUARTERBACK CLUB CLUB

Proposed Business

My idea is to open a bar/restaurant that have a sports theme. Sports are big business right now and the timing is perfect. I think that people are really interested in sports and will be willing to pay good money for this type of dining experience. People eat out a lot and my business will give them another place to spend their money.

Marketing Research and Marketing Plan

I've done some research in the community and haven't seen any restaurant or bar like Jay's Quarterback Club. Since there's nobody else doing this type of business, I won't have no direct competition. So marketing expenses will be minimal. Perhaps I'll run some newspaper advertisements and put out coupons iif I need to when sales aren't enough to help me pay the expenses.

Operations Plan

As soon as I get word on my financing, I'll start looking for an appropriate location for my business. If I can't find something that fits my needs, I'll just build one. I've been checking into suppliers for food and other materials I'll need. I feel confident that I can dedvelop good contacts and have reliable sources.

As far as employees goes, with the level of business that I know we can accomplish in the first few months of operations, I will be hiring 4 additional employees: cook, bartender, and 2 waitpersons. This will leave me free to do the scheduling, ordering, and managing.

Sales Projections

I've worked in restaurants in the past and have a lot of experience there so I believe that my bar/restaurant can make lots of money. I believe that my first year's sales will be $500,000 and expenses will be $410,000. That means I'll make $90,000. I intend to have several cost controls but, still it's really hard to tell exactly what my expenses will be, though. In the second year, because we'll be familiar to the customer, I know we can increase sales by 20% for total revenue of $510,000. I think I can hold my expenses constant at $90,000.

Conclusion

Since I've had a lot of experience working in restaurants, I am positive that I can make this venture work. The theme will be unique and there's not anyone else doing this, so there shouldn't be any problem attracting paying customers. If you'd like more information, I'd be happy to share my idea for Jay's Quaterback Club with you in person. Just call me at my home number. Thanks for your consideration.

benefit from the planning process is the person who is going to implement the plan. It is *your* business, after all, and it needs to be *your* plan. With that stated, can you get aid in writing the plan? Of course you can, and you should seek such help if you need it. Here are some sources:

- The Small Business Administration home page at www.sba.gov
- Your local Small Business Development Center
- A local SCORE (Service Corp of Retired Executives) chapter
- Your local Chamber of Commerce
- A college or university near you
- One of the many paperback guides written on business plans available at any bookstore

Computer software is available to perform many functions of our daily lives. We can balance our checkbook or design our dream house using software, for example. Although software packages can make our lives easier, you need to be careful not to use one to generate a "cookie-cutter" business plan. Filling in a few blanks on a master document does not produce a workable business plan any more than a paint-by-numbers kit produces valuable art. Because your business will be different from others, you need to emphasize your competitive advantage and show your objectives.

This is not to imply that you should not use word processing, spreadsheets, or graphics packages to produce your plan. You should, because they can be extremely helpful. Instead, this caveat applies to "canned" business plans. If you wish to investigate business-planning software, check out Jian's BizPlanBuilder Interactive and Palo Alto Software's Business Plan Pro, but remember that writing a business plan is as much an art as it is a science.[6]

Business Plan Contents

A business plan should be tailored to fit your particular business. Write the plan yourself, even if you seek assistance from lawyers, accountants, or consultants. In 40 or fewer pages, the plan should present your strengths clearly and in a logical order.

Although a plan's contents will vary from business to business, its structure is fairly standardized. Your plan should contain as many of the following sections as appropriate for your type of venture.[7] Not every business will require every one of these sections. For example, if your business is a startup, it won't have a history section, but you can describe your management experience.

Cover Page

The cover page should include the name of the business, its address and phone number, and the date the plan was issued. If this information is overlooked, you have a problem if a potential investor tries to reach you to ask additional questions (or send a check).

Table of Contents

You want the business plan to be as easy to read as possible. An orderly table of contents will allow the reader to turn directly to the sections desired.

Executive Summary

executive summary
A condensed abstract of a business plan used to spark the reader's interest in the business and to highlight crucial information.

The **executive summary** gives a one- to two-page overview of your entire plan. It is the most important section of the plan because readers do not want to wade through 35 to 40 pages to get the essential facts. If you do not capture the reader's attention here, he is not likely to read the rest of the plan.

The executive summary should include the following components:

- *Company information*—what product or service you provide, your competitive advantage, when the company was formed, your company objectives, and the background of you and your management team.
- *Market opportunity*—the expected size and growth rate of your market, your expected market share, and any relevant industry trends.
- *Financial data*—financial forecasts for the first three years of operations, equity investment desired, and long-term loans that will be needed.

The information in the preceding list is a lot to condense into two pages, but all of it is important, and if you truly understand what you are writing about, you will find that you can explain it simply and succinctly. A first-rate executive summary provides you with a two-sentence "elevator pitch," so named in case you would ever find yourself contained in an elevator with a venture capitalist and need to explain your business concept quickly.[8]

Although the executive summary is the first section of the plan, it should be written last. You are condensing what you have already written into the summary, not expanding the summary to fill the plan. Here's a hint for writing the executive summary: As you compose all the other sections of the plan, highlight a few key sentences that are important enough to include in your executive summary. To see examples of executive summaries, refer to the complete plan included in Appendix A and the sample plans on this book's website.

Company Information

In the next section you should describe the background of your company, your choice of legal business form, and the reasons for the company's establishment. How did your company get to the point where it is today? Give the company's history by describing in some detail what your business does and how it satisfies customers' needs. How did you choose and develop your products or services to be sold? Don't be afraid to describe any setbacks or missteps you have taken along the way to forming your business. They represent reality, and leaving them out could make your plan and projections look "too good to be true" to lenders or investors.

Environmental and Industry Analysis

In the section on environmental and industry analysis you have an opportunity to show how your business fits into larger contexts. An *environmental analysis* shows identified trends and changes that are happening at the national and international levels that may influence the future of your small business. Introduce environmental categories such as economic, competitive, legal, political, cultural, and technological arenas that affect and are affected by your business. Discuss the future outlook and trends within these categories. For example, a cultural trend of "Buy American" might create a competitive advantage for your small manufacturing business. Changes in the legal or political arena can provide opportunities as well. Suppose the Environmental Protection Agency (EPA) banned lead fishing sinkers because of possible contamination of water supplies. What if you had just created a line of fishing sinkers produced from some material other than lead?

While you generally cannot control such external environments, you can describe the opportunities that changes in them present in your business plan. As an entrepreneur, you have to understand the world in which you operate and how you can best assess the opportunities that arise there.

After completing the environmental analysis, you should do an *industry* analysis describing the industry within which your business operates. Here you will focus on specific industry trends. Describe industry demand—pertinent data will likely be readily available from industry trade publications or other published sources. How do you determine what other businesses or products should be included as part of your industry? One helpful way to draw the line between what and whom to include in your industry is to consider possible substitutes for your product. If you own a business that sells ice cream, do your customers view frozen yogurt or custard as a potential substitute for your frozen treats? If so, you should consider businesses that sell these products to be part of your industry. What competitive reactions and industrywide trends can you identify? Who are the major players in your industry? Have any businesses recently entered or exited the field? Why did they leave? Is the industry growing or declining? Who are the new competitors in the industry?

Lenders want to see that you have a clear understanding of how your industry operates. Specifically, which of Porter's five forces (threat of new entrants, bargaining power of customers, threat of substitutes, bargaining power of suppliers, and rivalry among existing competitors; see Chapter 3) are rated as high or low for the industry you intend to enter?[9]

The environmental and industry analyses are tricky sections of your business plan to write. As stated earlier, your plan must be concise, but in this section especially you must cover huge, comprehensive issues and factors that could fill volumes. Feel like you are being pulled in several different directions at once? Good—now you are starting to realize the complexity of what you are getting into. Think of the environmental and industry analysis section in the following way: As a small business owner, you have to be knowledgeable about all current and potential factors that could affect your business. Of course, the business plan is not the place to describe every possible development in detail. Instead, treat this section as if you are showing only the tip of the iceberg that represents your accumulated knowledge, and make it clear that you are prepared to answer questions relating to less critical factors that you chose not to include in your business plan.

Products or Services

In the next section you can go into detail describing your product or service. How is your product or service different from those currently on the market? Are there any other uses for it that could increase current sales? Include drawings or photos if appropriate. Describe any patents or trademarks that you hold, as these give you a proprietary position that can be defended. Describe your competitive advantage. What sets your product or service apart as better than the competition's?

What is your product's potential for growth? How do you intend to manage your product or service through the product life cycle? Can you expand the product line or develop related products? In this section of your business plan you can discuss potential product lines as well as current ones.

Marketing Research and Evaluation

You need to present evidence that a market exists for your business. A section on marketing research and evaluation, presenting the facts you have gathered on the size and nature of your markets, will tell investors if a large enough market exists and if you can be competitive in that market. State the market size in dollars and units. Give your sales forecast by estimating from your marketing research how many units and dollars worth of your product you expect to sell in a given time period. That sales forecast becomes the basis for projecting many of your financial statements. Indicate your primary and secondary sources of data, and the methods you used to estimate total market size and your market share.

Target Markets and Market Segmentation   You must identify your target markets and then concentrate your marketing efforts on these key areas. These markets must share some identifiable need that you can satisfy. What do the people who buy your product have in common with one another? To segment your markets, you could use a demographic characteristic (for example, 18- to 25-year-old females), a psychographic variable (similar lifestyles, usage rate of product, or degree of loyalty), a geographic variable (anyone who lives within a five-mile radius of your business), or other variable. Describe actual customers who have expressed a desire to buy your product. What trends do you expect will affect your markets?

Market Trends   Markets and consumer tastes change, so you will need to explain how you will assess your customers' needs over time. A danger of segmentation and target marketing is that it encourages the belief that those segments and markets will stay the same—they won't. Specify how you will continue to evaluate consumer needs so that you can identify market trends and, based on that information, improve your market lines and aid new product development.

Competition   Among three or four primary competitors, identify the price leader, the quality leader, and the service leader. Realistically discuss the strengths and weaknesses of each. Compare your products or services with those of competitors on the basis of price, product performance, and other attributes.

This section offers a good opportunity to include the SWOT analysis you completed in the strategic planning chapter (Chapter 3). Identify the strengths and weaknesses of your business and the opportunities and threats that exist outside your business.

Market Share   Because you have identified the size of your market and your competitors, you can estimate the *market share* you intend to gain—that is, the percentage of total industry sales. Market share can effectively be shown and explained using a pie chart.

Your job in writing the marketing-research section of your business plan is to convince the reader that a large enough market exists for your product for you to achieve your projected sales forecasts.

Marketing Plan   Your *marketing plan* shows how you intend to achieve your sales forecast. You should start by explaining your overall marketing strategy, identifying your potential markets, and explaining what you have decided is the best way to reach them. Include your *marketing objectives* (what you want to achieve) and the strategies you will use to accomplish these objectives.

Pricing as Part of Marketing Plan   Your pricing policy is one of the most important decisions you will have to make. The price must be "right" to penetrate the market, to maintain your market position, and especially to make profits. Compare your pricing policies with those of the competitors you identified earlier. Explain how your gross margin will allow you to make a profit after covering all expenses. Many people go into business with the intent of charging lower prices than the competition. If this is your goal, explain how you can follow this strategy and still make a profit: through greater efficiency in manufacturing or distribution of the product, lower labor costs, lower overhead, or whatever else allows you to undercut the competition's price.

You should discuss the relationship between your price, your market share, and your profits. For example, by charging a higher price than the competition, you may reduce your sales volume but realize a higher gross margin and increase your business's bottom line.

Promotion as Part of Marketing Plan   How will you attract the attention of and communicate with your potential customers? For industrial products, you might use trade shows and advertise in trade magazines, via direct mail, or through promotional brochures. For consumer products, you should describe your plans for advertising and promotional campaigns. You should also give the advertising schedule and costs involved. Examples of advertising or brochures may be included in the appendix of the business plan.

Place as Part of Marketing Plan   Describe how you intend to sell and distribute your products. Will you use your own salesforce or independent sales representatives or distributors? If you will hire your own salesforce, describe how it will be structured, the sales expected per salesperson per year, and the pay structure. Your own salesforce will concentrate more on your products because it will sell them exclusively. If you will use sales representatives, describe how those individuals will be selected, the territories they will cover, and the rates they will charge. Independent sales representatives may also handle products and lines other than yours, but they are much less expensive for you because they are not your employees. Your place strategy should describe the level of coverage (local, regional, or national) you will use initially and as your business grows. It should include the channels of distribution you will use to get and to sell products.

Service Policies as Part of Marketing Plan   If you sell a product that may require service, such as cameras, copy machines, or bicycles, describe your service and warranty policies. These policies can be important in the customer's decision-making process. How will you handle customer-service problems? Describe the terms and types of warranties offered. Explain whether you will provide service via your own service department, subcontract out the service work, or return products to the factory. Also state whether service is intended to be a profit center or a breakeven operation.

Manufacturing and Operations Plan

The *manufacturing and operations plan* will stress elements related to your business's production. It will outline your needs in terms of facilities, location, space requirements, capital equipment, labor force, inventory control, and purchasing. Stress the areas most relevant to your type of business. For instance, if you are starting a manufacturing business, outline the production processes and your control systems for inventory, purchasing, and production. The business plan for a service business should focus on your location, overhead, and labor force productivity.

Geographic Location   Describe your planned geographic location and its advantages and disadvantages in terms of wage rates, unionization, labor pool, proximity to customers and suppliers, types of transportation available, tax rates, utility costs, and zoning. Again, you should stress the features most relevant to your business. Proximity to customers is especially important to a service business, whereas access to transportation will be of greater concern to a manufacturing business.

Facilities   What kind of facilities does your business need? Discuss your requirements for floor space (including offices, sales room, manufacturing plant space, and storage areas), parking, loading areas, and special equipment. Will you rent, lease, or purchase these facilities? How long will they remain adequate: One year? Three years? Is expansion possible?

Make-or-Buy Policy   In a manufacturing business, you must decide what you will produce and what you will purchase as components to be assembled into the finished product. This is called the *make-or-buy decision*. Many factors go into this decision (see Chapter 12). In your business plan, you should justify the advantages of your policy. Describe potential subcontractors and suppliers.

Control Systems   What is your approach to controlling quality, inventory, and production? How will you measure your progress toward the goals you have set for your business?

Labor Force   At the location you have selected, is there a sufficient quantity of adequately skilled people in the local labor force to meet your needs? What kinds of training will you need to provide? Can you afford to offer this training and still remain competitive? Training can be a hidden cost that can turn a profit into a loss.

Management Team

A good management team is the key to transforming your vision into a successful business. Show how your team is balanced in terms of technical skills (possessing the knowledge specific to your type of business), business skills (the ability to successfully run a business), and experience. As when building any other kind of team, the skills and talents of your management team need to complement one another. Include a job description for each management position, and specify

> "A successful management team unites people with complementary business knowledge, technical skills, and life experience."

the key people who will fill these slots. Can you show how their skills complement one another? Have these individuals worked together before? An *organization chart* can be included in the appendix of your plan to graphically show how these positions fit together. Résumés for each key manager should be included in the appendix.

State how your key managers will be compensated. Your chances of obtaining financing are very slim unless the managers are willing to accept substantially less than their market value for salary while the business is getting started. Managers must be committed to putting as many proceeds as possible back into the business.

Discuss the management training your key people have had and may still need. Be as specific as possible on the cost, type, and availability of this management or technical training.

Like your managers, you may need professional assistance at times. Identify other people with whom you will work, including a lawyer, a certified public accountant, an insurance agent, and a banker. Identify contacts you have supporting you in these areas.

Anyone who is considering putting money into your business will scrutinize this section thoroughly. Therefore, your plan must answer the following questions about the management team members, which were first posed by Harvard professor William Sahlman:

- Where are the founders from?
- Where have they been educated?
- Where have they worked, and for whom?
- What have they accomplished—professionally and personally—in the past?
- What is their reputation within the *business* community?
- What experience do they have that is directly relevant to the opportunity they are pursuing?
- What skills, abilities, and knowledge do they have?
- How realistic are they about the venture's chances for success and the tribulations it will face?
- Who else needs to be on the team?
- Are they prepared to recruit high-quality people?
- How will they respond to adversity?
- Do they have the mettle to make the inevitable hard choices?
- How committed are they to this venture?
- What are their motivations?[10]

"CAN YOU COME BACK TOMORROW? HE'S DOING HIS COMMUNITY SERVICE TODAY."

www.CartoonStock.com

Timeline

Create a timeline outlining the interrelationships and timing of the major events planned for your venture. In addition to helping you calculate your business needs and minimize risk, the timeline is an indicator to investors that you have thoroughly researched potential problems and are aware of deadlines. Keep in mind that people tend to underestimate the time needed to complete projects. Your schedule should be realistic and attainable.

Critical Risks and Assumptions

All business plans contain implicit assumptions, such as how your business will operate, what economic conditions will be, and how you will react in different situations. Identification and discussion of any potentially major trends, problems, or risks that you think you may encounter will show the reader that you are in touch with reality. These risks and assumptions could relate to your industry, markets, company, or personnel.

This section gives you a place to establish alternate plans in case the unexpected happens. If potential investors discover unstated negative factors after the fact, they may quickly question the credibility of both you and the business. Too many businesses are started with only a plan A and no thought about what will happen if X, Y, or Z occurs.[11] Possible contingencies that you should anticipate include the following scenarios:

- *Unreliable sales forecasts.* What will you do if your market does not develop as quickly as you predicted or, conversely, if your market develops too quickly? Each of these situations creates its own problems. Sales that are too low may cause serious financial problems. Sales that are too high may cause bottlenecks in production, difficulties in purchasing enough products from vendors or suppliers, trouble hiring and scheduling employees, or dissatisfied customers who must wait longer than they expected for your product or service.

- *Competitors' ability to underprice or to make your product obsolete.*

- *Unfavorable industrywide trends.* Not long ago, businesses that produced asbestos made up a thriving industry supplying products for automotive and building construction firms. Then reports linking asbestos with cancer drastically affected the demand for that product and virtually eliminated the industry.

- *Appropriately trained workers not as available as predicted.*

- *Erratic supply of products or raw materials.*

- *Any one of the 10,000 other things you didn't expect.*

Benefits to the Community

Your new business will affect the lives of many other people besides yourself. Describe the potential benefits to the community that the formation of your business could provide.

This chapter's entrepreneurship profile is about a group from a fictitious bicycle company called Freeriders Inc. Freeriders is a young company about to launch a new product. The point of this story is to show how people from different areas of a business approach business planning. It is interesting to note just how predictable behaviors can be.

In the video clip that accompanies the book, you will be introduced to Sandra, the chief financial officer; Bryce, national sales manager; Lisa, production and design manager; and Noah, marketing manager. Many small businesses are run by teams, so Freeriders' organization is a common one. Some of the decisions the team has to agree upon in planning their new product include the following:

- Do we put our finite money into more expensive bike components or hiring an expensive celebrity endorser?
- How do we select the correct price point—production costs versus what the target market will pay?
- How do we create marketing buzz in a crowded market?

See how the entrepreneurial team interacts with each other, and decide what you might do differently.

- *Economic development*—number of jobs created (total and skilled), purchase of supplies from local businesses, the multiplier effect (which shows the number of hands that new dollars brought into the community pass through before exiting).
- *Community development*—providing needed goods or services, improving physical assets or the appearance of the community, contributing to a community's standard of living.
- *Human development*—providing new technical skills or other training, creating opportunities for career advancement, developing management or leadership skills, offering attractive wages, and providing other types of individual growth.

Exit Strategy

Every business will benefit by devoting some attention to a succession plan. Before you begin your business is a good time to consider how you intend to get yourself (and your money) out of it. Do you intend to sell it in 20 years? Will your children take it over? How will you prepare them for ownership? Do you intend to grow the business to the point of an initial public offering? How will investors get their money back?

Financial Plan

Your *financial plan* is where you demonstrate that all the information from previous sections of your business plan, such as marketing, operations, sales, and strategies, can come together to form a viable, profitable business. Potential investors will closely scrutinize the financial section of your business plan to ensure that it is feasible before they become involved. Projections should be your best estimates of future operations. Your financial plan should include the following statements (existing businesses will need historical statements and pro forma projections, whereas startups will have only projections):

- Sources and uses of capital (initial and projected)
- Cash-flow projections for three years
- Balance sheets for three years
- Profit-and-loss statements for three years
- Breakeven analysis

We will discuss how to prepare these documents in later chapters. (See Chapter 8 for cash-flow projections, balance sheets, and profit-and-loss statements, and Chapter 9 for sources and uses of capital.) With the financial statements, you need to show conclusions and important points, such as how much equity and how much debt are included, the highest amount of cash needed, and how long the payback period for loans is expected to be.

Sources and Uses of Funds   The simple **sources and uses of funds** form shows where your money is coming from and how you are spending it (see Figure 4.2).

Cash-Flow Statement   The most important financial statement for a small business is the **cash-flow statement,** because if you run out of cash, you're out of business. In a cash-flow statement, working from your opening cash balance, you add all the money that comes into your business for a given time period (week, month, quarter), and then you subtract all the money you spend for the same time

sources and uses of funds
A financial document used by startup businesses that shows where capital comes from and what it will be used for.

cash-flow statement
A financial document that shows the amount of money a business has on hand at the beginning of a time period, receipts coming into the business, and money going out of the business during the same period.

Figure 4.2
SOURCES AND USES OF FUNDS WORKSHEET

A Sources and Uses of Funds Worksheet Shows Where Money Comes From and What It Is Used for.

Sources of Funds:

Debt:
Term loans $ _____
Refinancing of old debt   _____
Lines of credit   _____
Line 1   _____
Line 2   _____
Mortgage   _____

Equity:
Investments   _____

Total Sources: $ _____

Uses of Funds:

Property $ _____
Inventory   _____
Equipment (itemize)   _____
                                          _____
                                          _____
                                          _____
Working capital   _____
Cash reserve   _____
Total Uses: $ _____

Opening cash balance		
Add:	Cash receipts	
	Collection of accounts receivable	
	New loans or investment	
	Other sources of cash	
	Total receipts	
Less:	Utilities	
	Salaries	
	Office supplies	
	Accounts payable	
	Leased equipment	
	Sales expenses	
	Loan payments	
	General expenses	
	Total disbursements	
Cash increase (or decrease)		
Closing cash balance		

Figure 4.3

SAMPLE COMPONENTS OF CASH-FLOW STATEMENT

A Cash-flow Statement Shows How Money Enters and Exits Your Business.

period. The result is your closing cash balance, which becomes your opening balance for the next time period (see Figure 4.3).

You should project a cash-flow statement by month for the first year of operation and by quarter for the second and third years. *Cash flow* shows you what the highest amount of working capital will be. It can be especially critical if your sales are seasonal in nature or cyclical.

Balance Sheet   The **balance sheet** shows all the assets *owned* by your business and the liabilities, or what is *owed* against those assets (see Figure 4.4). The difference between the two is what the company has *earned,* or the net worth of the business, which is also called *capital.* From the balance sheet, bankers and investors will calculate some key ratios, such as debt-to-equity and current ratio (see Chapter 8) to help determine the financial health of your business. You need to prepare balance sheets ending at each of the first three years of operation.

> *balance sheet*
> A financial document that shows the assets, liabilities, and owner's equity for a business.

Profit-and-Loss Statement   Don't expect the pro forma **profit-and-loss statement** for your business plan to be a finely honed, 100 percent accurate projection of the future. Your objective is to come up with as close an approximation as possible of what your sales revenues and expenses will be. In making your projections, it is helpful to break sales down by product line (or types of services) and then determine a best-case scenario, a worst-case scenario, and a most likely scenario somewhere between the two extremes for each category. This practice helps create realistic projections. Remember that lenders and investors (especially venture capitalists) are professionals at picking apart business plans.[12]

> *profit-and-loss statement*
> A financial document that shows sales revenues, expenses, and net profit or loss.

Start preparing this statement in the left-hand column to show what your sales and expenses would be under the worst of conditions (see Figure 4.5). Assume that you have difficulty getting products, that the weather is terrible, that your salespeople are out spending all their time playing golf instead of selling, and that the state highway department closes the road that runs in front of your only location for repairs. Imagine that anything bad that can happen will happen. Now, in the right-hand column, make projections assuming that

Figure 4.4
BALANCE SHEET

A Balance Sheet Shows What You Own and Whom You Owe.

For year ended [month] [day], [year]	Year 1	Year 2	Year 3
Current Assets			
Cash	$ _____	$ _____	$ _____
Accounts Receivable	_____	_____	_____
Inventory	_____	_____	_____
Supplies	_____	_____	_____
Prepaid Expenses	_____	_____	_____
Fixed Assets			
Real Estate	_____	_____	_____
Equipment	_____	_____	_____
Fixtures and Leasehold Improvements	_____	_____	_____
Vehicles	_____	_____	_____
Other Assets			
License	_____	_____	_____
Goodwill	_____	_____	_____
TOTAL ASSETS	$ _____	$ _____	$ _____
Current Liabilities			
Accounts Payable	_____	_____	_____
Notes Payable (due within 1 year)	_____	_____	_____
Accrued Expenses	_____	_____	_____
Taxes Owed	_____	_____	_____
Long-Term Liabilities			
Notes Payable (due after 1 year)	_____	_____	_____
Bank Loans	_____	_____	_____
TOTAL LIABILITIES	$ _____	$ _____	$ _____
NET WORTH (assets minus liabilities)	$ _____	$ _____	$ _____

everything goes exactly your way. What would your sales and expenses be if customers with cash in their hands are waiting in line outside your door every morning at opening time, if suppliers rearrange their schedules so that you never run out of stock, and if competitors all close their doors for a month of vacation just as you are beginning operations? This is a lot more fun, of course, but not any more likely to happen than the first scenario, although either could happen. Your most realistic estimate will fall between these two extremes in the center column.

Question and test your projections. Is there enough demand for you to reach your sales goal? Do you have enough space, equipment, and employees to reach your sales goal? Break your sales down into the number of units, then the number of units bought per customer, and then the number of units sold per day. When viewed this way, you may find that every person in town would have to buy eight bagels per day, 365 days per year, for you to achieve your sales projections for your proposed bagel shop. (Yes, real business plans get written with such projections.) Obviously, you would need to revise your goal, expand your menu, do more to control your expenses, or convince people to eat more bagels than is humanly possible for your business to succeed to meet such a projection.

Breakeven Analysis   How many units (or dollars' worth) of your products or service will have to be sold to cover your costs? A *breakeven analysis* will give you

	Low	Most Likely	High
SALES:			
Product/service line 1	$ _____	$ _____	$ _____
Product/service line 2	_____	_____	_____
Product/service line 3	_____	_____	_____
Product/service line 4	_____	_____	_____
TOTAL SALES REVENUE			
Cost of Goods Sold:			
Product/service line 1	_____	_____	_____
Product/service line 2	_____	_____	_____
Product/service line 3	_____	_____	_____
Product/service line 4	_____	_____	_____
TOTAL COST OF GOODS SOLD	$ _____	$ _____	$ _____
GROSS PROFIT	$ _____	$ _____	$ _____
EXPENSES:			
Variable:			
Payroll	$ _____	$ _____	$ _____
Sales commission	_____	_____	_____
Freight and delivery	_____	_____	_____
Travel and entertainment	_____	_____	_____
Semivariable:			
Advertising/promotion	_____	_____	_____
FICA/payroll tax	_____	_____	_____
Supplies	_____	_____	_____
Telephone	_____	_____	_____
Fixed:			
Rent	_____	_____	_____
Utilities	_____	_____	_____
Property taxes	_____	_____	_____
Dues and subscriptions	_____	_____	_____
TOTAL EXPENSES	_____	_____	_____
Profit before depreciation	_____	_____	_____
Depreciation	_____	_____	_____
NET PROFIT	$ _____	$ _____	$ _____

Note: Expense items for your business will vary from these three categories. For illustration purposes only.

Figure 4.5
PROFIT-AND-LOSS STATEMENT

Projecting the Best and the Worst That Could Happen Helps You Calculate What Your Profits or Losses Are Likely to Be.

1. Total sales $ _____
2. Fixed costs $ _____
3. Gross margin $ _____
4. Gross margin as percentage of sales (line 3/line 1)   _____ %
5. Breakeven sales (line 2/line 4) $ _____
6. Profit goal $ _____
7. Sales required to achieve profit goal [(line 2 + line 6)/line 4] $ _____

Figure 4.6
BREAKEVEN ANALYSIS

At What Point Will You Make Money?

a sales projection of how many units or dollars need to be sold to reach your **breakeven point**—that is, the point at which you are neither making nor losing money (see Figure 4.6; see also Chapter 14).

To reinforce your financial projections, you may want to compare them to industry averages for your chosen industry. *Robert Morris Associates Annual Statement* publishes an annual index showing industry averages of key manufacturing,

> *breakeven point*
> The point at which sales and costs are equal and a business is neither making nor losing money.

Creating Competitive Advantage
Competition, Please

You're in this class, and maybe you've even finished writing your assigned business plan. How about entering it into a collegiate business plan competition? There are a lot of them around now—nearly 3,500 students competed in some 70 contests at the regional, national, and international levels. The prizes can include hundreds of thousands of dollars plus access to venture capital. The Carrot Capital VentureBowl offers a top prize of $750,000; however, most B-school competitions generally offer less than $100,000.

Matt Ferris and Bruce Black wrote a business plan for KidSmart Vocal Smoke Detector while in the University of Georgia's MBA program. KidSmart includes a personalized message in a parent's own voice giving instructions to children in case of fire. Ferris and Black's plan won second place in the Carrot Capital VentureBowl, but the pair turned down the $750,000 prize because they felt the offer was too restrictive. They went on to win Moot Corp.'s prize and bagged $100,000, without having to give up as much company ownership as the other competition required. That $100,000 will come in handy as the alarms go on sale on QVC and in catalogs like those produced by Sharper Image, Hammacher Schlemmer, and SkyMall.

And here is another college-student success story: Medical students Jon Mathy, Eshan Alipour, Eric Allison, and Amita Shukla came up with a device that bypasses an artery blockage the way water in a river flows around a big boulder and eliminates the need for surgery. They identified a huge market and wrote a business plan that won Stanford University's business plan annual competition. And so VisiVas was born.

SOURCES: Jennifer Merritt, "Will Your Plan Win a Prize?" *BusinessWeek*, 15 March 2004, 108; Elaine Pofeldt et al., "Here Comes the Competition," *Fortune Small Business*, November 2003, 38; Carolina Braunschweig, "No Business Plans, Please," *Venture Capital Journal*, August 2003, 24–31.

wholesale, and retail business groups. Compare your projected financial ratios with industry averages to give the reader an established benchmark (see Chapter 8).

Appendix

Supplemental information and documents not crucial to the business plan, but of potential interest to the reader, are gathered in the appendix. Résumés of owners and principal managers, advertising samples, brochures, and any related information can be included. Different types of information, such as résumés, advertising samples, organization chart, and floor plan, should each be placed in a separate appendix labeled with successive letters of the alphabet (Appendix A, Appendix B, and so on). Be sure to identify each appendix in your table of contents (for example, "Appendix A: Advertising Samples").

Review Process

Writing a business plan is a project that involves a long series of interrelated steps. Beginning with your idea for a business, you want to determine its feasibility through the creation of your business plan. The technique illustrated in Figure 4.7 will allow you to identify the steps you need to take in writing your plan. Steps connected by lines show that lower-numbered steps need to be completed before moving on to higher-numbered ones. Steps that are shown as being parallel take place simultaneously. For example, steps 6 through 10 can be completed at the

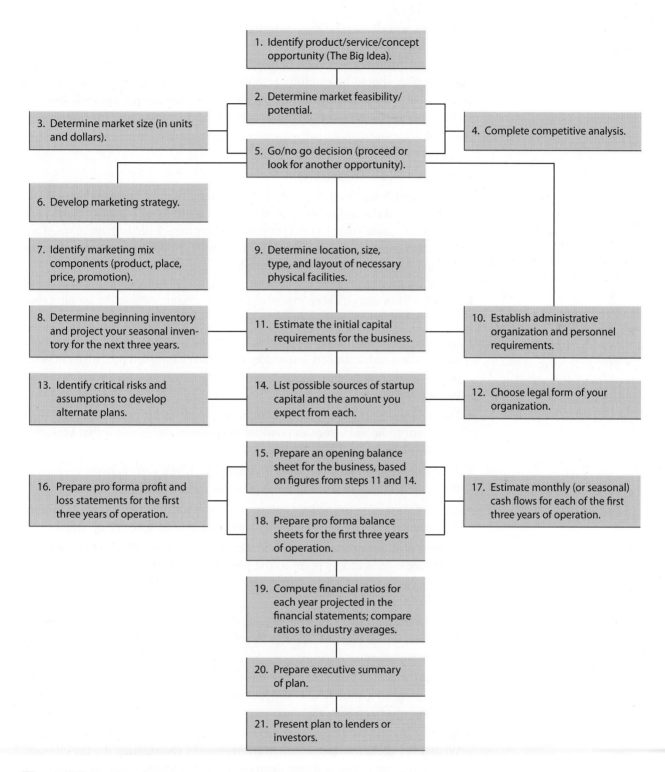

Figure 4.7
BUSINESS PLAN

Writing a Business Plan Is a Long Process of Progressive Steps That Generally Follow the Sequence Shown Here.

same time, and all must be accomplished before you can estimate how much capital you need in step 11.

Like any project involving a number of complex steps and calculations, your business plan should be carefully reviewed and revised before you present it to potential investors. After you have written your plan, rate it yourself the way lenders and investors will evaluate it (see Manager's Notebook, "How Does Your Plan Rate?").

Business Plan Mistakes

Often we can learn from the mistakes of others. Writing business plans is no exception. Bankers and investors who assess hundreds of business plans each year look for reasons to reject the proposals. This practice helps them to weed out potentially unworthy investments and to identify the likely winners—the most organized, focused, and realistic proposals.

Your business plan says a lot about your level of financial and professional knowledge. How can you keep investors focused on your ideas while keeping your plan out of the "reject" pile? It helps to avoid the most common errors.

- *Submitting a "rough copy."* Your plan should be a cleanly typed copy without coffee stains and scratched-out words. If you haven't worked your idea out completely enough to present a plan you're proud of, why should the investor take you seriously?

- *Depending on outdated financial information or industry comparisons.* It is important to be as current as possible to convince the investor that you are a realistic planner.

- *Trying to impress financiers with technojargon.* If you can't express yourself in common language in your business plan, how will you be able to market it?

- *Lacking marketing strategies.* Getting your product/business known by potential buyers is key. "We'll just depend on word-of-mouth advertising" won't cut it.

- *Making unsubstantiated assumptions.* Explain how and why you have reached your conclusions at any point in the plan. Don't assume that the competition will roll over without a fight or that phenomenal growth will begin the moment you get the money.

- *Being overly optimistic.* Too much "blue sky and rainbows" will lead the investor to wonder if your plan is realistic. Describe potential pitfalls and your strategies to cope with them.

- *Misunderstanding financial information.* Even if you get help from an accountant in preparing your financial documents, be sure you understand and can interpret what they say.

- *Ignoring the macroenvironment.* How will competitors react to your business? What other economic factors are likely to change? Considering the business climate and environment will help demonstrate the breadth of your understanding.

- *Avoiding or disguising potential negative aspects.* If you fail to mention possible problems, or misrepresent them, you will give the impression that you are either naive or devious, and lenders find neither trait especially charming.

How Does Your Plan Rate?

On the following checklist, take the perspective of a potential lender or investor who is rating your business plan. Give each section a grade ranging from A to F, with A being the best grade. Would you want to invest your money in a business that doesn't earn an A in as many categories as possible? Use your rating to identify areas that can be improved.

Grade	Model (A) Plan
Business Description	
Company	Simply explained and feasible
Industry	Growing in market niches that are presently unsatisfied
Products	Proprietary position; quality exceeds customer's expectations
Services	Described clearly; service level exceeds customer expectations
Previous success	Business has past record of success
Competitive advantage	Identified and sustainable
Risks turned into opportunities	Risks identified; how to minimize risks is shown
Orientation of business	Market oriented, not product oriented
Marketing	
Target market(s)	Clearly identified
Size of target market(s)	Large enough to support viable business
User benefits identified	Benefit to customers clearly shown
Management Team	
Experience of team	Successful previous experience in similar business
Key managers identified	Managers with complementary skills on team
Financial Plan	
Projections	Realistic and supported
Rate of return	Exceptionally high; loans can be paid back in less than one year
Participation by owner	Owner has significant personal investment
Participation by others	Other investors already involved
Plan Packaging	
Appearance	Professional, laser-printed, bound, no spelling or grammatical errors
Executive summary	Concise description of business that prompts reader to say, "Wow!"
Body of plan	Sections of plan appropriate and complete
Appendices	Appropriate supporting documentation
Plan standardized or custom	Plan custom-written for specific business, not "canned"

- *Having no personal equity in the company.* If you aren't willing to risk your own money in the venture, why should the investor? A vested interest in the business will help to convince potential lenders that you will work as hard as possible to make the business succeed. Or, if you have invested only $1,000, is it reasonable to seek $20 million in capital?[13]

Summary

• The importance of the business plan

Business plans are important to (1) raise capital, (2) provide a road map for future operations, and (3) prevent omissions.

• The components of a business plan

The major sections of a business plan include the cover page, table of contents, executive summary, company, environmental and industry analysis, products or services, marketing research and evaluation,

manufacturing and operations plan, management team, timeline, critical risks and assumptions, benefits to the community, exit strategy, financial plan, and appendix.

• The review process

Like any project involving a number of complex steps and calculations, your business plan should be carefully reviewed and revised before you present it to potential investors. After you have written your plan, evaluate it as you think lenders and investors will.

Questions for Review and Discussion

1. Why wouldn't a 100-page business plan be four times better than a 25-page business plan?

2. Should you write a business plan even if you do not need outside financing? Why or why not?

3. Who should write the business plan?

4. If successful companies like Pizza Hut have been started without a business plan, why does the author claim they are so important?

5. Why do entrepreneurs have trouble remaining objective when writing their business plans?

6. Why do some prospective business owners refuse to plan?

7. Why is the executive summary the most important section of the business plan?

8. Talk to the owner of a small business. Did she write a business plan? A strategic plan? If he received any assistance, where did it come from?

Questions for Critical Thinking

1. When you reach the point in your career where you are ready to start your own business (or your next one), will you write a business plan before beginning? Why or why not? If you would choose to start a business without a business plan, what would be an alternative for testing feasibility?

2. You are an investor in small businesses, and you have three business plans on your desk. Which of the following potential business owners do you think would be the best bet for an investment (if you could pick only one)?

a. A recent college grad, full of energy and ideas, but short on experience

b. A middle-management corporate refugee desiring a business of her own after experiencing frustration with bureaucratic red tape

c. A serial entrepreneur who has previously started seven businesses, three of which were huge successes and four of which failed, losing their entire investment

Experience This . . .

Do a keyword Internet search for "business plans." When you find a sample business plan that interests you, complete a thorough analysis of it. How do the section headings compare with the headings described in this chapter? Have any sections been added or deleted? Does the executive summary make you say, "Wow, this is a great idea!"? Review the business plan you found by using Figure 4.7 and the Manager's Notebook, "How Does Your Plan Rate?" Does the plan appear to present a feasible idea for a business? Do you find any "holes" in it? If this were a plan for your business, would you proceed? Why or why not? If you were an investor approached about financing this plan, would you put your money into this business without being able to run it? Why or why not?

What Would You Do?

Early one morning your telephone rings. It is your small business/entrepreneurship professor, who tells you he just received notification that he has won the first Nobel Prize in Entrepreneurship. His plane leaves soon for Stockholm, where he will pick up the award, so he won't be in class today. Because you are one of the star students in this class, the professor asks you to conduct class today covering Chapter 4, "The Business Plan." Write an outline of how you would teach this class and what you would cover to effectively teach this material. Would you lecture? How would you keep discussion going? Would you show business plan samples? Where would you find them? Would you show Web pages? Which ones? You can do anything (except cancel class!) that your professor would do, but *what would you do*?

CHAPTER CLOSING CASE

DIAMOND IN THE ROUGH

Micky McDonald ran Westbeach for five years. Then it went bankrupt. Was it time to walk away—or buy it?

Micky McDonald figured that the little snowboard-clothing company he had been running for the previous five years was history. His boss, the owner of Vancouver-based Westbeach Sports, had decided not to invest any more dollars in a business that had lost $1.4 million in 2005 and was looking at additional red ink in 2006. The company filed for bankruptcy in May, and McDonald agreed to stay on, helping the trustee look for buyers for the Westbeach brand.

There were a few nibbles, but all of the buyers were dragging out their due diligence and McDonald just assumed he would soon be out of a job; he already was getting calls from headhunters.

If creditors didn't doom the company, McDonald figured, the marketplace would probably do the job. If the company canceled its orders for the following season, its jackets and pants would be out of stores for at least a full year. By then, Westbeach would be of little interest to anyone.

But before the trustee found a bidder, McDonald received an intriguing phone call from Frankie Hon, owner of Westbeach's Hong Kong manufacturer, Charterlink, which was on the hook for the fabric required in filling those orders. What if the production run were made on Charterlink's dime? And what if the company were reorganized, with McDonald, Charterlink, and a third partner as the new owners? "The clock was ticking, and we had to get a deal done in order to get these goods to market," McDonald says.

It would be a big risk. Snowboard apparel, once a cottage industry made up of several hundred tiny companies, is now a $137 million business in the United States alone and includes major players such as Burton, Quiksilver, and Billabong. Their combined marketing and merchandising muscle dwarfs anything coming out of Westbeach, which has 10 employees, $7.3 million in revenue, and little or no presence in the United States (Canada and Europe are its main markets).

And yet, McDonald felt a connection to Westbeach, where he had weathered three ownership changes over nine years. The company had been part of snowboarding culture since the 1980s, around the time he was introduced to the sport in the Austrian Alps. Maybe it was worth a chance.

McDonald had been a sportswear sales and marketing manager in the United Kingdom when he came across Westbeach during a vacation in British Columbia. In those days snowboarding was still the province of young daredevils looking for thrills that went beyond skiing down a sculpted hill. Commercially, no one paid much attention to the activity, and snowboard apparel was typically an extension of the tight-fitting bright-colored jackets and pants found in alpine skiing. But Westbeach and its looser-fitting clothes stood out. "They were almost indestructible, very waterproof, and very rugged," McDonald remembers. In 1990 he became a Westbeach distributor in the United Kingdom, and

several years later he opened a subsidiary in Innsbruck, Austria.

By the mid-1990s, the sport's popularity was sky-rocketing. Yet the industry lacked experienced businesspeople. Inventory levels and marketing costs ballooned under the assumption that the sport would keep growing at stupendous rates. When that didn't happen, Westbeach and others began to struggle. Oregon-based Morrow Snowboards, which was looking to get into apparel, wound up buying Westbeach in 1997, but that company soon stumbled and was forced into bankruptcy. In 1999 the snowboard side of Morrow's business was sold to K-2, with Westbeach eventually taken over by a partnership. Two years later, one of the partners bought out the others, and McDonald was sent back to Canada to be president.

His marching orders: expand the business without losing money. One of his first steps was pulling out of the U.S. market. The company had been spending 80 percent of its marketing budget on advertising in American publications even though just 5 percent of total revenue was coming from U.S. buyers. On the production side, he moved manufacturing from China to Vietnam, where costs were lower and import duties and quotas more favorable. That boosted margins without raising retail prices. The company lost $600,000 in 2002, broke even in 2003, and made a little money in 2004.

But there was no room for missteps, and in 2005 a six-week dock strike in Vancouver proved disastrous. "When you're in a season-sensitive and time-sensitive business and you don't make deliveries on time to your customers, they start to ask for discounts," McDonald says. Westbeach lost $700,000 after retailers and suppliers canceled orders. There were other problems, such as overspending on marketing efforts in an attempt to compete with the bigger sports and apparel companies. Smaller names got squeezed out; at a major trade show last year, there were just 95 snowboard brands, compared with 360 in 1995.

But McDonald knew that the Westbeach brand had proved popular and resilient, despite his employer's refusal to invest in it. Perhaps the company did have a future. To be sure, he was concerned about taking on the responsibility—and financial risk—of co-owning a business. As president,

McDonald often found himself making mistakes and learning on the fly. "I took my eye off the ball on really fundamental things," he admits. A more seasoned chief executive might have kept the company out of bankruptcy. But the more McDonald thought about it, the more Frankie Hon's suggestion to buy the company made sense.

Questions

1. How would creating a business plan help McDonald decide whether to buy the business or run away?

2. What would you emphasize in writing a business plan for Westbeach?

3. Snowboarding is obviously a very dynamic, changeable business. Why write a plan for this type of business?

SOURCE: Mark Lacter, "Case Study—Anatomy of a Business Decision," *Inc.*, February 2007, 53–55. Copyright © 2006 Mansueto Ventures LLC, publisher of Inc. Magazine, New York, NY 10017. Reprinted with permission.

Test Prepper

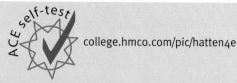

You've read the chapter, studied the key terms, and the exam is any day now. Think you're ready to ace it? Take this sample test to gauge your comprehension of chapter material. You can check your answers at the back of the book. Want more test questions? Visit the student website at college.hmco.com/pic/hatten4e and take the ACE and ACE+ quizzes for more practice.

Multiple Choice

1. When considering starting up a business, a business plan can
   a. prove feasibility
   b. attract money
   c. provide direction
   d. all the above

2. The cover letter should
   a. praise the management team
   b. inform the reader why you are sending the plan
   c. include at least two pages on competitors
   d. include segmentation variables

3. Benefits to the community cited in this chapter include
   a. attracting celebrities
   b. economic development
   c. community development
   d. human development

4. Analysis that illustrates the point at which your business neither makes nor loses money is called
   a. loss leader analysis
   b. make-or-buy analysis
   c. breakeven analysis
   d. profit-and-loss analysis

5. Business-plan appendices could include all of the following *except*
   a. résumés
   b. advertising samples
   c. college transcripts
   d. purchase orders from customers

Fill in the Blank

1. Writing a business plan is a long series of _____ steps.

2. The section of the business plan in which you describe how to eventually separate the owner from the business is called the _____. _____.

3. As described in the @ e-biz feature, Moot Corp. is a famous _____ competition.

4. A common business plan mistake is making unsubstantiated _____.

5. In the Manager's Notebook feature, you saw that "A" plans are those in which the owner has significant personal _____.

## part 3

Early Decisions

Chapter 5   Franchising

Chapter 6   Taking Over an Existing Business

Chapter 7   Starting a New Business

A small business owner has three primary options for getting into business: A franchise can be purchased, an existing business can be bought, or a new venture can be created. Each strategy has its advantages and disadvantages, but which one is right for your business? Circumstances may mean that only one or two of these options are available to you. The correct path depends on several factors that will be explored as you make your early decisions. **Chapter 5** introduces us to franchising, **Chapter 6** covers the purchase of an existing business, and **Chapter 7** focuses on the excitement and risks of starting from scratch.

Franchising

After reading this chapter, you should be able to:

- Explain what a franchise is and how it operates.

- Articulate the difference between product-distribution franchises and business-format franchises.

- Compare the advantages and disadvantages of franchising.

- Explain how to evaluate a potential franchise.

- Explore franchising in the international marketplace.

What's one of the hottest businesses in franchising today? Ice cream—but not just any ice cream. Try super-premium, personalized ice cream. Cold Stone Creamery is at the forefront of the craze that has customers lined up to get freshly made ice cream blended with "mix-ins" ranging from fruit to nuts to candy.

Cold Stone Creamery believes that people want not just treats high in the "Oh my gosh, this is good" factor, but also entertainment. So the company hires energetic performers who can sing and dance while they scoop ice cream. It values the experience it offers its customers—a feeling of taking a ten-minute vacation.

To set the proper in-store mood, Cold Stone Creamery uses imported Italian ice cream cabinets, called *gheas,* that are designed to keep ice cream at just the right temperature and consistency. The wallpaper is covered with a subtle image of the company "icone" logo. The icone's ice cream colors reflect the colors of the fruit, nuts, and candy mix-ins. The photographs lining the walls are designed to win over the strongest plain-vanilla fans. Creations are mixed on a "cold stone," a granite slab kept cooled to 61 degrees at all times.

Cold Stone Creamery.

Cold Stone is unique among franchisors in the preferred financing programs it has established through lenders like Comerica and UPS Capital to make the borrowing process easier for newcomer franchisees. Cold Stone has also developed a guide for franchisees detailing lender expectations to streamline the borrowing process.

According to Doug Ducey, president and CEO of Cold Stone Creamery, in August 1999 company leaders set the big, hairy, audacious goal of having 1,000 profitable stores by the end of 2004 (at the time the firm had only 74 stores in operation). They met that goal and blew by it to have over 1,400 franchises by the start of 2007. Ducey believes that getting the right people on the team—both in the franchises and in corporate headquarters—is the key to hitting their target. The overall company goal is to reinvent the traditional ice cream shop, to keep growing and never look back. Cold Stone Creamery plans to do for ice cream what Starbucks did for coffee. Realizing that lofty goal could turn a lot of individual franchisees into wealthy business owners.

Since opening its first unit outside the United States in 2001, in St. Thomas, Virgin Islands, Cold Stone has been rapidly expanding internationally. Today it operates 8 out of a planned 20 to 30 stores in Japan. Plans also call for 105 stores in China and 60 in Taiwan through a joint-venture deal with Presidents Chain Store Corporation, a large convenience-store operator.

SOURCES: C. J. Prince, "Show Me the Money," *Entrepreneur,* January 2007, 108–116; David Farkas, "Cold Front," *Chain Leader,* February 2007, 49–50; Ryan Underwood, "Fast Talk," *Fast Company,* May 2004, 57; Erin McCarthy, "New York Screams for Ice Cream," *Display & Design Ideas,* August 2003, 18; Devlin Smith, "What's Hot: Ice Cream," *Entrepreneur.com,* 25 August 2003; Kathy Heasley, "Casting Call: Cold Stone Creamery Is Hottest Gig in Town," *Franchising World,* July/August 2000, 16.

About Franchising

Over the past 50 years or so, franchising has become a very attractive means of starting and operating a small business. Some of the most familiar franchises are McDonald's, H&R Block, AAMCO Transmissions, GNC (General Nutrition Centers), and Dairy Queen. A **franchise** is an agreement that binds a **franchisor** (a parent company of the product, service, or method) with a **franchisee** (a small business that pays fees and royalties for exclusive rights to local distribution of the product or service). Through the franchise agreement, the franchisee gains the benefit of the parent company's expertise, experience, management systems, marketing, and financial help. Franchisors benefit because they can expand their operations by building a base of franchisees rather than by using their own capital and resources.

Background

Franchises have experienced considerable growth since the 1950s. However, contrary to popular belief, the concept did not originate with McDonald's. In fact, franchises have existed since the early 1800s.

> *franchise*
> A contractual license to operate an individually owned business as part of a larger chain.
>
> *franchisor*
> The parent company that develops a product or business process and sells the rights to franchisees.
>
> *franchisee*
> The small business person who purchases the franchise so as to sell the product or service of the franchisor.

Fast Facts

The International Franchise Association Educational Foundation conducts and reports research studies to provide a statistical basis for answering key questions posed about franchising. The five-part study titled "The Profile of Franchising: 2006" shows multiple views of franchising today from 2,500 companies representing 18 main industry segments. Some interesting findings emerged:

- The median initial franchise fee for standard franchises was $25,147.
- Franchises classified as Standard Programs—either stand-alone or in-line stores—totaled 93 percent.
- Franchises that were home-based totaled 6 percent.
- Franchises that were vehicle- or mobile-based totaled 7 percent.
- Franchises that were started with an initial investment of $240,000 or less totaled 80 percent.
- Franchisors had been in operation one year or less totaled 15 percent.
- The minimum total initial investment for a lodging franchise was reported as $4.1 million.
- Most franchise systems charged royalties based on a percentage of gross sales—the average was 6.7 percent.
- Companies offering an exclusive territory to franchisees totaled 73 percent.

SOURCES: International Franchise Association Educational Foundation series, "The Profile of Franchising: 2006," 3 August 2006, www.franchise.org/education.aspx

In the 1830s, Cyrus McCormick was making reapers, and Isaac Singer began manufacturing sewing machines. As America's economic system began to shift from being based on agriculture and small business to being based on industry and big business, business methods needed to change as well. Early manufacturers also had to provide distribution of their products. To do so, they faced the choice of setting up a company-owned system or developing contracts with independent firms to represent them. The choice was not an easy one. Direct ownership guaranteed complete control and ensured quality levels of service. On the other hand, direct ownership was expensive and difficult to manage. McCormick and Singer were two of the first to use agents in building sales networks quickly, at little cost to themselves.[1] This use of exclusive agents laid the groundwork for today's franchising. The exclusive contractual agreement between franchisor and franchisee has evolved past agency, but it has become a viable business alternative.

Franchising Today

Today franchising is found in almost every industry (see Figure 5.1). More than 767,000 U.S. businesses are franchised. Interest in international franchising is also growing quickly. Franchised businesses generate annual sales of $1.53 trillion, or nearly 10 percent of the U.S. private-sector economy and 40 percent of all retail sales![2] Franchised businesses directly produce almost 10 million jobs—roughly the same number of people employed by all manufacturers of durable goods.

A study titled "The Economic Impact of Franchised Businesses in the United States" for the International Franchise Association reported economic activity that happened (1) within franchised businesses and (2) because of franchised businesses. In total, franchised businesses supported more than 18 million jobs and had a payroll exceeding $500 billion.

> "Franchising dominates the fast-food, automobile, and lodging segments of the U.S. economy."

Franchising Systems

There are two types of franchises: product-distribution franchises and business-format franchises. These two forms are used by producers, wholesalers, and retailers to distribute goods and services to consumers and other businesses.

Product-Distribution Franchising

Product-distribution franchising allows the franchisee (or dealer) to buy products from the franchisor (or supplier) or to license the use of its trade name. This approach typically connects a single manufacturer with many dealers. The idea is to make products available to consumers in a specific geographic region through exclusive dealers. Soft-drink bottlers and gasoline stations, for example, use this type of franchising. Auto manufacturers also use this system to make their cars, service, and parts available. Your local Chevrolet dealer, for instance, has full use of the Chevrolet trade name, brand names (like Corvette), and logos (like the bow tie symbol) to promote the dealership in your area. Product franchisors regulate their franchisees' locations to avoid excessive competition between them. As a consequence, Chevrolet would not allow a new dealership that sells its products to set up across the street from your established local dealer.

> *product-distribution franchising*
> A type of franchising in which the franchisee agrees to purchase the products of the franchisor or to use the franchisor's name.

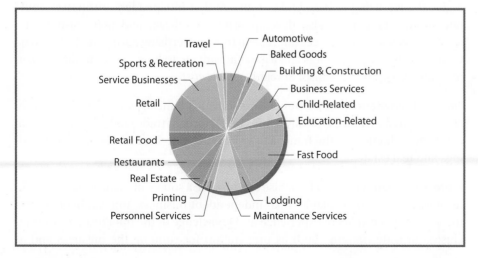

Figure 5.1
NOT ALL FRANCHISES SELL FRENCH FRIES

The Distribution of 2,471 Franchise Systems Across 18 Industry Categories in 2002–2006 Shows a Wide Diversity of Products and Services.

SOURCE: International Franchise Association Educational Foundation series, "The Profile of Franchising: 2006," August 3, 2006, www.franchise.org/education.aspx

Business-Format Franchising

Business-format franchising is more of a *turnkey* approach to franchising. In other words, the franchisee purchases not only the franchisor's product to sell, but also the entire way of doing business, including operation procedures, marketing packages, physical building and equipment, and full business services. Business-format franchising is commonly used in quick-service restaurants (56.3 percent), lodging (18.2 percent), retail food (14.2 percent), and table/full-service restaurants (13.1 percent).

Why Open a Franchise?

If you are considering the purchase of a franchise, you should compare its advantages and disadvantages to those of starting a new business or buying an existing nonfranchised business (see Chapters 6 and 7). You should also determine whether the unique characteristics of franchising fit your personal needs and desires. Some small business owners would rather assume the risk and expense of starting an independent business than have to follow someone else's policies and procedures. Others prefer the advantages that a franchise's proven system can provide. Sometimes it makes sense not to reinvent the wheel (see Table 5.1).

Advantages to Franchisee

For the franchisee, there are eight major advantages of franchising: proven product or service, marketing expertise, financial assistance, technical and managerial assistance, an opportunity to learn the business, quality control standards, efficiency, and opportunity for growth.[3]

Proven Product   The most valuable advantage to a franchisee is that you are selling a proven product or service. Customers are aware of the product; they know the name and what to expect. For example, travelers may not know anything about the Ramada Inn in Colorado Springs, but they know Ramada's reputation and are more likely to stay there than at some independent, unknown motel.

Marketing Expertise   Franchisors spend millions of dollars on national or regional advertising to help build an image that independent businesses could not afford. Franchisors also develop print, broadcast, and point-of-purchase advertising. Local franchisees do share in these advertising costs, usually based on their gross revenues, but it is still a great advantage to have access to the marketing expertise of the franchisor at relatively low cost.

Financial Assistance   Some franchisors provide financial assistance to new franchisees. This assistance typically comes in the form of trade credit on inventory or overhead reduction by the franchisor's choosing, purchasing, and owning buildings and real estate.

Professional Guidance   A franchise can provide a source of managerial and technical assistance not available to an independent business. You can benefit from the accumulated years of experience and knowledge of the franchisor. Most franchisors provide training, both as preparation for running the business and as

Table 5.1

ADVANTAGES AND
DISADVANTAGES
OF FRANCHISING

Franchisee's Perspective	Franchisor's Perspective
Advantages	**Advantages**
1. Proven product or service	1. Expansion with limited capital
2. Marketing expertise	2. Multiple sources of capital
3. Financial assistance	3. Controlled expansion
4. Technical and managerial assistance	4. Motivated franchisees
5. Opportunity to learn business	5. Bulk-purchasing discounts
6. Quality control standards	
7. Efficiency	
8. Opportunity for growth	
Disadvantages	**Disadvantages**
1. Fees and profit sharing	1. Loss of control
2. Restrictions of freedom	2. Sharing profit with franchisees
3. Overdependence or unsatisfied expectations	3. Potential for disputes with franchisees
4. Risk of fraud or misunderstanding	
5. Termination of the agreement	
6. Performance of other franchisees	

instruction after the business gets off the ground. This training can allow a person without prior experience to be successful in owning a franchise. A good franchisor is available to provide day-to-day assistance and professional guidance should a crisis arise. In addition, franchisees can receive a great deal of technical help regarding store layout and design, location, purchasing, and equipment.

Opportunity to Learn   Although it is not usually advisable to go into a business in an unfamiliar field, franchising can provide an opportunity to become successful doing exactly that. Thus, franchising can be helpful for a mid-career change of direction. In fact, some franchisors prefer their franchisees not to have experience in that particular field. They prefer to train their business owners from scratch so there are no bad habits to break.

Recognized Standards   Franchisors impose quality standards for franchisees to follow, a feature that might not seem advantageous at first glance—if independence is your motive for self-employment, why would you want to meet standards set by someone else? The benefit, though, is that the practice ensures consistency to customers. Consumers can walk into a McDonald's anywhere in the world and know what to expect. A franchisor's quality control regulations help franchisees to maintain high standards of cleanliness, service, and productivity. As a franchisee, you will benefit from standardized quality control, because if another franchisee in your organization provides inferior service, it will affect attitudes toward *your* business.

Efficiency   Because of increased efficiency, a franchise can sometimes be started and operated with less capital than it takes to start an independent business. Franchisors have already been through the learning curve and worked most of the bugs out of the process. Inventory needs, such as what to stock and what will sell quickly, are known before you open the doors, so you won't waste money on equipment, inventory, or supplies that you don't need. Many franchisors often provide financial resources for startup and working capital for inventory.

Potential for Business Growth   If you are successful with a franchise, you will often have the opportunity to multiply that success by expanding to other franchises in other locations. Most franchisors have provisions to open other territories.

These eight advantages share a common theme—the opportunity to benefit from someone else's experience. In other words, as a franchisee, you have the chance to learn from someone else's mistakes.

Disadvantages to Franchisee

Of course, franchising has its drawbacks, too. You must give up some control, some decision-making power, and some freedom. Other disadvantages to the franchisee include fees, problems caused by overdependence on the franchisor or by not receiving what was expected from the franchisor, the possibility of fraud or misunderstanding, termination of the agreement, and the potentially negative effect of poor performance of other franchisees.

Cost of Franchise   The services, assistance, and assurance in buying a franchise come at a price. Every franchisor will charge a fee and/or a specified percentage of sales revenue (see Table 5.2). The disadvantage to the franchisees is that they are usually required to raise most of the capital before they begin operations. The total investment can range from $500 for a windshield repair franchise to $45 million for a Hilton Inn.

These fees and percentages may begin to seem excessive after you have been in business for a while and see how they affect your bottom line. It is not uncommon for franchisees to be grateful for the assistance that a franchisor provides in starting the business, only to become frustrated by the royalties that have to be paid a few years later.

Restrictions on Freedom or Creativity   The restrictions placed on their freedom may be a problem for some franchisees. Most people open their own businesses because they have a desire for independence, but franchises have policies and procedures that must be followed to maintain the franchise agreement. Also, the size of your market will be limited by territorial restrictions. And although you may feel that some products, promotions, or policies are not appropriate for your area, you will have little recourse after the franchise agreement has been signed.

Overdependence or Unsatisfied Expectations   Even though a franchisee is bound by contractual agreement, overdependence on the franchisor can still pose

Table 5.2   Getting In

Franchise	Franchise Startup Fee	Costs	Royalty (Percentage)
Maaco Auto Painting & Bodyworks	$40,000	$296,500	8%
Meineke Car Care Centers	$30,000	$190,000–350,000	3%–7%
Jazzercise	$325/$650	$2,900–33,100	Up to 20%
Sign-A-Rama	$39,500	$50,000–144,000	6%
Big Apple Bagels	$25,000	$228,300–367,500	5%
Rocky Mountain Chocolate Factory	$24,500	$129,000–435,000	5%
Bad Ass Coffee	$25,000	$225,000	6%
Cold Stone Creamery	$42,000	$294,300–438,900	6%
Taco Time	$30,000	$139,800–698,500	6%
Subway	$15,000	$74,900–222,800	8%
Hilton Hotels and Resorts	$85,000+	$33M–57M	5%
Merry Maids	$19,000–27,000	$24,400–55,500	5%–7%
It's Just Lunch Dating Service	$25,000–35,000	$96,000–170,000	9%
McDonald's	$45,000	$506,000–1,600,000	12.5% or more
Cartridge World	$30,000	$107,100–175,100	6%
Century 21 Real Estate	$25,000	$118,000–522,800	6%
Kumon Math & Reading Centers	$1,000	$15,200–38,700	$30+/student/mo
Play It Again Sports	$20,000	$190,200–351,000	5%

SOURCE: "28th Annual Franchise 500," *Entrepreneur*, January 2007, 169–259. Reprinted with permission of Entrepreneur Magazine, January 2007, www.entrepreneur.com/franchise500

a problem. Franchisors do not always know what is best for every set of local conditions. The franchisee must be willing and able to apply his own managerial decisions in running the business in the way best suited to the local market and avoid being overly dependent on the franchisor's guidance. The flip side of overdependence is dealing with a franchisor that does not provide all the assistance that the franchisee expected.

Risk of Fraud or Misunderstanding   Less than scrupulous franchisors have been known to mislead potential franchisees by making promises that are not fulfilled. To avoid being taken in by a fraudulent franchise, consult an attorney and talk with as many current franchisees as possible. Do not think that because the agreement looks standard, it is unnecessary for you to understand every section. Look especially at the fine print.

Problems of Termination or Transfer   Difficulty in terminating the franchise agreement or having it terminated against your will can be a disadvantage to the franchisee. Before entering into the franchise, you should understand the section of the agreement that describes how you can get out of the deal. For instance, what if you want to transfer your rights to a family member, or sell the franchise to someone else, or otherwise terminate your agreement? What provisions does the contract make for you to renew the agreement? Most franchise agreements cover a specific period of time—typically, between 5 and 20 years. Some may be renewed in perpetuity if both parties agree. Otherwise, both sides must consider franchise renewal when the term of the agreement expires. Check the agreement to see whether the franchisee has a *right of first refusal,* which means that the franchisee must decline to continue the agreement before the franchisor can offer the franchise to someone else. Check whether the franchisor must provide *just cause* for termination or must give a definite reason why the agreement is not being continued. Remember that a franchise is a contract. Any questions regarding it should be directed to your legal counsel.

Poor Performance of Other Franchisees   Poor performance on the part of other franchisees can lead to problems for you. If the franchisor tolerates substandard performance, a few franchisees can seriously affect the sales of many others. Customers view franchises as an entire unit, because the implicit message from franchises is that "we are all alike"—for good or ill. If customers are treated unsatisfactorily in one location, they are likely to believe the same treatment will occur elsewhere.

Advantages to Franchisor

Now let's look at franchising from the franchisor's perspective. First we will consider the positive aspects: smaller capital investment required than if outlets were formed independently, multiple sources of capital coming into the business, expansion of the business happening much faster than if the franchisor were in business alone, synergy created by a group of motivated franchisees, and volume discounts for bulk purchasing.

Expansion with Smaller Capital Investment   From the perspective of the franchisor, the biggest advantage of offering franchises is the expansion of its distribution sources with limited equity investments. The franchise fees from franchisees provide capital to the franchisor. The franchisor therefore does not have to borrow from lenders or attract outside investors. For a business with limited capital, franchising, in which franchisees share the financial burden, may be the only viable way to expand.

Multiple Sources of Revenue   Franchisors often build several sources of revenue into their franchise agreements. These sources might include the franchise fee, which is paid when the agreement is signed; a percentage of the franchise's monthly gross operating revenues; and revenue from selling the necessary products and supplies to the franchisees. For example, a fast-food restaurant franchisee could have a franchise fee of up to $200,000; pay 3 to 8 percent of monthly gross sales as a royalty fee; and be required to purchase all food items (from hamburger to condiments), office supplies, and restaurant supplies (napkins, coffee filters, paper cups) from the franchisor.

Controlled Expansion   When compared with the expansion of a corporate chain, expanding via franchising can be accomplished with a simpler management structure. Very rapid growth of a corporation can be more of a problem than an opportunity, however, if the growth outpaces central management's capacity to control and monitor it. When this happens, problems with inconsistency, communications, and especially cash flow generally appear. Although franchisors still face these problems to some degree, the franchise network reduces them.

Motivated Franchisees   Because franchisees own their own businesses, they are almost always more highly motivated to make it succeed than an employee working for someone else. Franchisees have a direct personal interest in the entire operation, so they are inspired to perform and thus create positive synergy within the franchise.

Bulk Purchasing   Centralized purchasing of products and supplies allows franchisors to take advantage of volume discounts, because they are buying for all the franchise locations. This economy of scale can increase profit margins and hold down costs for franchisees.

Disadvantages to Franchisor

Problems exist in every method of business operation, and franchising is no exception. Loss of control over the business is the biggest disadvantage faced by franchisors. Other potential problems relate to profit sharing and disputes with franchisees.

Loss of Control   Franchisees who do not maintain their businesses reflect poorly not only on other franchisees, but also on the franchisor. Although the franchisor does control the organization to the limit specified by the franchise agreement, franchisees are still independent businesspeople. After the franchise agreement has been signed, the franchisor must get permission from franchisees before any products or services are changed, added, or eliminated. Permission is often negotiated individually. This system makes it difficult for the franchisor to adapt products to meet changing customer needs, especially if a wide variety of consumer tastes are being served over a large geographic area.

One way franchisors have dealt with this problem is by establishing some company-owned units. Because these sites are not independently owned businesses, the franchisor can test-market new products, services, and procedures in them. In this way, the franchisor can track and respond to changing customer needs, as well as use these units as examples when negotiating with franchisees.

Profit Sharing   If franchisees are able to recover their initial investment within two or three years, they could be enjoying a 30 to 50 percent return on investment. This return can provide motivation for the franchisees, but it represents profit that the franchisor is not making with a company-owned unit.

Franchisee Disputes   Friction between franchisees and franchisors may arise over such issues as payment of fees, expansion, and hours of operation. These potential conflicts point to the importance of good communication between both sides and the need to have a clearly written franchise agreement.

Selecting a Franchise

Choosing the right franchise is a serious decision. Investing in a franchise represents a major commitment of time and money. Before taking the plunge into franchising, determine what you need in a business and evaluate what several different franchises can offer you and your customers.

Evaluate Your Needs

The choice of which franchise to buy is not an easy one. You need to find a franchise opportunity that matches your interests, skills, and needs. Ask yourself the following questions to determine whether franchising is the appropriate route to small business ownership for you:

- How much equity capital will you need to purchase the franchise and operate it until your income equals your expenses? Where are you going to get it?

- Are you prepared to give up some independence of action to secure the advantages offered by the franchise?

- Do you really believe you have the innate ability, training, and experience to work smoothly and profitably with the franchisor, your employees, and your customers?

- Are you ready to make a long-term commitment to working with this franchisor, offering its product or service to your public?[4]

Do Your Research

Inc., Fortune Small Business, The Wall Street Journal, and *Entrepreneur* are general business periodicals that contain advertising and articles related to franchising. Trade journals and magazines that specialize in franchising include *Franchise, Franchising Opportunities World,* and *Quarterly Franchising World.*

Trade associations can be valuable sources of information when you are investigating franchise opportunities. The major trade association of franchising is the International Franchise Association (IFA), which can be found at www.franchise.org. The IFA is a leading source of information for franchisors and franchisees alike, offering publications that contain industry-wide data as well as company-specific information. Also check *The Franchise Handbook,* which gives you an idea of the requirements, expectations, and assistance available for each franchise at www.franchise1.com. Figure 5.2 shows examples of the types of franchise descriptions you can find in this handbook.

Other Information Sources   The American Franchisee Association (AFA), based in Chicago (www.franchisee.org), and the American Association of Franchisees and Dealers (AAFD), headquartered in San Diego (www.aafd.org), are trade associations that provide information and services, represent the interests of members, and were formed to help negotiate better terms and conditions from franchisors. The AAFD has developed a Franchisee Bill of Rights as a code of ethical business conduct for franchised businesses.

On Yahoo!, under the Business and Economy category, Small Business Information, you will find a link to another source of franchise information, called

Profile in Entrepreneurship
Subway To Go

When one peruses *Entrepreneur* magazine's Franchise 500 list, the name Subway pops up regularly, taking the top spot 15 times in the 28 times the list has been compiled. Subway has been in business for four decades and has grown to over 26,000 franchises. That's 26,000 individual businesses! How big can one franchise system grow? The entrepreneur who started and oversaw the growth of this juggernaut, Fred DeLuca, thinks there is still a lot of room to grow.

In 1965 seventeen-year-old DeLuca was looking for a way to fund his college education. Family friend Pete Buck agreed to provide him with $1,000 on the condition that Fred would start a sandwich shop (operating under the principle that it is better to teach someone to fish than to give him a fish). Fred found a location in Bridgeport, Connecticut; built a counter and did other remodeling himself; and got the place open. The requirement for a specialty $550 sink almost kept the whole empire from forming, but Pete came through with another thousand dollars.

Some lessons that Fred learned are ones that don't come from business school. He tells the story of what happened during Subway's first year of operation this way: His car had broken down, and while he was walking, "this kid picked me up, we get to talking, and we passed by my store. He says to me, 'That is a great place to eat. They make terrific sandwiches, and you get all the soda you want for free.' I said, 'How does it work?' he said, 'You order some sandwiches, and when the kid'—he was referring to me—'when the kid turns around to make them, you just take a case of soda out of the cooler and sneak it out to your car.'" DeLuca and Subway have come far since those days.

Watch the video clip accompanying this chapter for more insight into entrepreneur Fred DeLuca's success in building a company that now receives more than 2,000 inquiries from potential franchisees each week. And to answer the question of how big can one franchise system grow, note that DeLuca has set a goal increase of 50 percent for sandwich sales at each of the 20,000-plus North American locations and of doubling the number of international stores to 7,500 by 2010.

SOURCES: "The Billionaire Bootstrapper," *Inc.,* July 2006, 108; Nicole Torres, "Full Speed Ahead," *Entrepreneur,* January 2007, 162–163; Nicole Torres, "Staying Power," *Entrepreneur,* January 2006, 130–135.

FranNet. FranNet (www.frannet.com) can provide you with the information needed to help you select the right franchise. Additional information on franchises can be found by using any of the popular search engines and doing a keyword search for "franchise." Better yet, go to a full-text online database like ABI-INFORM, Business Source Premier or Lexis-Nexis to search for general and company-specific information on franchises.

You might also want to check out the Better Business Bureau's website (www.bbb.org/bbb). There you'll find a publications directory, membership list, and contact information for Better Business Bureaus nationwide. You can also access the bureau's newsletter, check the scam alerts, and even file a complaint online.

Still another source of franchise information is the Institute of Management and Administration's Web page (http://ioma.com/ioma), which provides links to hundreds of other business sites, including many industry-specific resources.

From the Horse's Mouth

A good place to get information about a particular franchise is from the people who are currently running one. Ask the following questions to get the real scoop:

- What does the business cost to operate on a monthly basis?
- How long did it take to break even?
- How profitable is the franchise?
- How much does the company charge for advertising fees? (Be careful if this number is more than 1 percent to 3 percent of gross sales.)
- Does the money go toward ads in the local market or mainly toward building the parent company's national image? (You should expect about 50 percent to benefit the franchisee.)
- How many units have failed?
- How rapid is unit turnover?
- How many stores does the parent company own? (About 25 percent is acceptable. Too many could weaken franchisee bargaining power; too few could indicate a weak system.)
- Would you buy the franchise again? (The bottom line.)

Remember when you are talking with these current franchise owners that many of them are struggling to internally validate the decision they have made regarding this business. They will often tell you that things are going great, sales are up, and they would definitely do it all over again. They may be trying to convince themselves. To get a realistic picture of what you are facing, push them to tell you exactly how much profit they have made in each year of operation. Might you have to go two years without making a profit? Could you do that?

SOURCES: Todd D. Maddocks, "Write the Wrongs," *Entrepreneur,* January 2001, 152–155; Federal Trade Commission, "Consumer Guide to Buying a Franchise," 2003, www.franchise.org/resourcectr/

Questions to Ask   When you have a general idea of the franchise you are interested in, contact the company and ask for a copy of its *disclosure statement* (discussed shortly). Before you sign the required contracts with a chosen franchisor, talk to current and former franchisees. They can provide priceless information that you could not learn anywhere else.

Once you have found a franchise you would consider buying (or possibly a few from which to choose), evaluate the opportunities represented by asking yourself the following questions:

- Did your lawyer approve the franchise contract you are considering after she studied it paragraph by paragraph?

Figure 5.2   FRANCHISE INFORMATION

Marble Slab Creamery
3100 S. Gessner, # 305
Houston, TX 77063
www.marbleslab.com
Contact: marbleslab@marbleslab.com

Company Description: Marble Slab Creamery offers home-made, superpremium ice cream that is prepared to order on a marble slab. Customers can create their own ice cream concoctions by combining any flavor of ice cream with "mix-ins" such as fresh fruit, candy, cookies, or nuts. The ice cream and mix-ins are then folded together on a frozen marble slab and served on a freshly baked waffle cone. Other products include smoothies, shakes, sundaes, banana splits, ice cream pies/cakes, specialty coffees, and bakery items
# of Franchised Units: 380 in 30 states in 2 countries
Company-Owned Units: 1
In Business Since: 1983
Franchising Since: 1984
Franchising Fee: $28,000
Royalties: 6%
Capital Requirements: $250,000 net worth, $60,000 liquid
Financing Options: None
Training and Support: Assistance is available on site selection, lease negotiation, architectural layout, and construction supervision. A ten-day training program in Houston, Texas, is required.

Play It Again Sports
Grow Biz International, Inc.
4200 Dalhberg Dr.
Minneapolis, MN 55422-4837
www.playitagainsports.com
Contact: mpeterson@growbiz.com

Company Description: Play It Again Sports buys and sells new and used sporting goods. Stores carry items such as golf clubs and bags, baseball bats and gloves, in-line skates, and fitness equipment. Play It Again Sports is owned by Grow Biz International, which also franchises Music Go Round, Once Upon a Child, Plato's Closet, and Re-Tool.
# of Franchised Units: 556
Company-Owned Units: 2
In Business Since: 1983
Franchising Since: 1988
Franchise Fee: $20,000
Capital Requirements: $153,000–$265,000 total investment. $50,000–$75,000 startup cash
Financing Options: Assistance in preparation of a comprehensive business plan.
Training and Support: Training includes such topics as site selection, lease negotiations, store build-out, POS inventory management, business operating system, evaluating product, and local store marketing.

Subway
325 Bic Dr.
Milford, CT 06460
www.subway.com
Contact: franchise@subway.com

Company Description: Today, Subway is the world's largest and fastest-growing franchise. In 1965, 17-year-old Fred DeLuca and family friend Peter Buck started a tiny sandwich shop as a way to get through college. In 2004, *Entrepreneur* magazine chose Subway as the overall number one franchise in all categories for the twelfth time. More than 50% of franchises purchased are sold to existing owners who choose to reinvest.
# of Franchised Units: 17,500+ in 74 countries
Company-Owned Units: 1
In Business Since: 1965
Franchising Since: 1974
Franchise Fee: $12,500
Royalty Fee: 8%
Capital Requirements: $63,900–$191,000
Financing Options: Franchise fee financing, startup financing, and equipment leasing are available.
Training and Support: Two weeks training with 50% in classroom and 50% hands-on. Follow-up support is given by field staff and headquarters' staff.

General Nutrition Centers
GNC Franchising
300 Sixth Ave.
Pittsburgh, PA 15222
www.gncfranchising.com

Company Description: In 1935 David Shakarian started a health-food store in Pittsburgh called Lackzoom. It specialized in yogurt (which his father introduced to the United States) but also carried health-food products such as honey and grains. Today, as the leading national specialty retailer of vitamins, minerals, herbs, and sports nutrition supplements, GNC capitalizes on the accelerating trend toward self-care. *Entrepreneur* magazine has ranked GNC as the industry's number one franchise for 14 consecutive years.
# of Franchised Units: 1,878 in 50 states in 28 countries
Company-Owned Units: 2,933
In Business Since: 1935
Franchising Since: 1988
Franchise Fee: $40,000
Royalty Fee: 6%
Capital Requirements: $132,681–$182,031
Financing Options: GNC offers direct company financing for startup fees, equipment, inventory, and accounts receivable to qualified individuals.
Training and Support: New franchisees receive three weeks of initial training, including an intensive one-week training class at corporate headquarters. On-site assistance

is provided prior to opening, with ongoing support. Franchisees benefit from GNC's multimillion-dollar national advertising program.

Merry Maids
P.O. Box 751017
Memphis, TN 38175-1017
www.merrymaids.com

Company Description: The world's largest residential cleaning service. *Entrepreneur* magazine ranked Merry Maids as number one in the industry for 10 consecutive years. Name recognition for the Merry Maids brand is very high. The company is committed to training and support, and it provides a comprehensive software and equipment/supply package. Products and supplies are available online. The company is a member of the ServiceMaster family of industry-leading brands.
# of Franchised Units: 1,399 in 48 states in 7 countries
Company-Owned Units: 143
Franchise Fee: $19,000–$27,000
Capital Requirements: $19,550–$26,950+. A larger investment is required to buy an existing franchise.
Financing Options: Up to 80% available toward franchise fee.
Training and Support: Includes an eight-day training session at headquarters; all startup equipment and supplies for two teams; Buddy Program; educational programs; toll-free number

for assistance; national TV ads; free web site for each franchise; weekly intranet bulletin board; newsletters; regional meetings; national convention; proprietary intranet web site; 17 field regional coordinators.

Dunkin' Donuts
14 Pacella Park Dr.
Randolph, MA 02368
www.dunkindonuts.com

Company Description: In 1946, William Rosenberg founded Industrial Luncheon Services, a company that delivered meals and snacks to workers in the Boston area. That success led him to start the Open Kettle, a doughnut shop in Quincy, Massachusetts. Two years later he changed the name to Dunkin' Donuts. Today, the company sells doughnuts, muffins, bagels, coffee, and fruit drinks.
# of Franchised Units: 6,892 in 43 states in 20 countries
Company-Owned Units: 0
In Business Since: 1950
Franchising Since: 1955
Franchise Fee: $40,000–80,000
Capital Requirements: $600,000 in liquid assets, $1.2 million net worth
Financing Options: Yes
Training and Support: Yes

SOURCES: *Entrepreneur Franchise 500 issue*, January 2007, 164–259, www.entrepreneur.com; www.franchisehandbook.com; individual company web pages.

- Does the franchise call on you to take any steps that are, according to your lawyer, unwise or illegal in your state, county, or city?

- Does the franchise give you an *exclusive territory* (discussed later in this chapter) for the length of the franchise, or can the franchisor sell a second or third franchise in your territory?

- Is the franchisor connected in any way with any other franchise company handling similar merchandise or services? If so, what is your protection against this second franchisor organization?

- Under what circumstances can you terminate the franchise contract and at what cost to you, if you decide for any reason at all that you wish to cancel it?

- If you sell your franchise, will you be compensated for your goodwill, or will the goodwill you have built into the business be lost by you?

  Evaluate what the franchisor will offer you and your customers by asking the following questions about the franchisor:

- How many years has the firm offering you a franchise been in operation?

- Does it have a reputation for honesty and fair dealing among the local firms holding its franchise?

- Has the franchisor shown you any certified figures indicating exact net profits of one or more going firms that you personally checked with the franchisee(s)?

- Will the firm assist you with
    - A management training program?
    - Capital?
    - An employee training program?
    - Credit?
    - A public relations program?
    - Merchandise ideas?
- Will the firm help you find a good location for your new business?
- Is the franchising firm adequately financed so that it can carry out its stated plan of financial assistance and expansion?
- Is the franchisor a one-person company or a corporation with an experienced management trained in depth (so that there will always be an experienced person at its head)?
- Exactly what can the franchisor do for you that you cannot do for yourself?
- Has the franchisor investigated you carefully enough to assure itself that you can successfully operate one of its franchises at a profit to both of you?
- Does your state have a law regulating the sale of franchises, and has the franchisor complied with that law?

Analyze the Market

What do you know about your market, the people buying your product or service? In answering the following questions, you can determine whether a franchise is the best way to match what the franchisor has to offer with your skills and your customers' needs:

1. Have you made any study to determine whether the product or service that you propose to sell under franchise has a market in your territory at the prices you will have to charge?
2. Will the population in your proposed territory increase, remain static, or decrease over the next five years?
3. Will the product or service you are considering be in greater demand, in about the same demand, or in less demand five years from now?
4. What competition already exists in your territory for the product or service you contemplate selling?
    a. Nonfranchise firms?
    b. Franchise firms?

Disclosure Statements

Franchisors are required by the Federal Trade Commission (FTC) to provide **disclosure statements** to prospective or actual franchisees. Comparing disclosure statements from each franchise you are considering will help you identify risks, fees, benefits, and restrictions involved. Figure 5.3 provides a sample table of

disclosure statement
Information that franchisors are required to provide to potential franchisees.

Figure 5.3

FRANCHISE DISCLOSURE STATEMENT

Table of Contents

Section

1. Franchisor and Any Predecessors
2. Identity and Business Experience of Persons Affiliated with the Franchisor
3. Litigation
4. Bankruptcy
5. Developer's/Franchisee's Initial Franchise Fee or Other Initial Payment
6. Other Fees
7. Franchisee's Initial Investment
8. Obligation of Franchisee to Purchase or Lease from Designated Sources
9. Obligations of Franchisee to Purchase or Lease in Accordance with Specifications or from Approved Suppliers
10. Financing Arrangements
11. Obligations of the Franchisor: Other Supervision, Assistance, or Services
12. Exclusive Area or Territory
13. Trademarks, Trade Names, and Service Marks
14. Patent and Copyrights
15. Obligation of Franchisee to Participate in the Actual Operations of the Franchise
16. Restrictions on Goods and Services Offered by Developer/Franchise
17. Renewal, Termination, Repurchase, Modification, and Assignment of the Franchise Agreement and Related Information
18. Arrangements with Public Figures
19. Statement of per-Franchise Average Gross Sales and Ranges of Gross Sales for the Year Ended Month, Day, Year
20. Other Franchises of the Franchisor
21. Financial Statements
22. Contracts

EXHIBIT A	Franchise Agreement
EXHIBIT B	Area Development Agreement
EXHIBIT C	Preliminary Agreement
EXHIBIT D	Royalty Incentive Rider
EXHIBIT E	Disclosure Acknowledgment Statement
EXHIBIT F	List of Franchisees as of Month, Day, Year
EXHIBIT G	List of Franchisees Who Have Ceased Doing Business in the One-Year Period Immediately Preceding Month, Day, Year
EXHIBIT H	Financial Statements of Franchisor

contents for a disclosure statement. The entire document can be several hundred pages long. As a prospective franchisee, you would want to read the document carefully and consult a lawyer to review the franchise agreement. Disclosure statements identify and provide information on the following 20 items:

1. *The franchisor.* Information identifying the franchisor and its affiliates and describing their business experience.

2. *Business experience of the franchisor.* Information identifying and describing the business experience of each of the franchisor's officers, directors, and management personnel responsible for franchise services, training, and other aspects of the franchises in the franchise program.

3. *Litigation.* A description of the lawsuits in which the franchisor and its officers, directors, and management personnel have been involved.

4. *Bankruptcy.* Information about any previous bankruptcies in which the franchisor and its officers, director, and management personnel have been involved in the past 15 years.

5. *Initial fee.* Information about the initial franchise fee and other initial payments that are required to obtain the franchise. The franchisor must also tell how your fee will be used and whether you must pay in one lump sum or can pay in installments. If every franchisee does not pay the same amount, the franchisor must describe the formula for calculating the initial fee.

6. *Other fees.* A description of the continuing payments franchisees are required to make after the franchise opens, and the conditions for receiving refunds.

7. *Estimate of total initial investment.* The franchisor must provide a high-range and a low-range estimate of your startup costs. Included expenses would cover real estate, equipment and other fixed assets, inventory, deposits, and working capital.

8. *Purchase obligations.* Information about any restrictions on the quality of goods and services used in the franchise and where they may be purchased, including restrictions requiring purchases from the franchisor or its affiliates.

9. *Financial assistance available.* Terms and conditions of any assistance available from the franchisor or its affiliates in financing the purchase of the franchise.

10. *Product or service restrictions.* A description of restrictions on the goods or services that franchisees are permitted to sell. This could include whether you are required to carry the franchisor's full line of products or if you can supplement them with other products.

11. *Exclusive territory.* A description of any territorial protection or restrictions on the customers with whom the franchisee may deal. Franchisees of Subway sandwich shops and other franchises have alleged that the franchisor has placed franchises too close together and overlapped territories. This practice cuts into the sales volume and market size of individual stores.

12. *Renewal, termination, or assignment of franchise agreement.* A description of the conditions under which the franchise may be repurchased or refused renewal by the franchisor, transferred to a third party by the franchisee, and terminated or modified by either party.

13. *Training provided.* A description of the training program provided to franchisees, including location, length and content of training, cost of program, who pays for travel and lodging, and any additional or refresher courses available.

14. *Public figure arrangements.* A disclosure of any involvement by celebrities or public figures in promoting the franchise. If celebrities are involved, you need to be told if they are involved in actual management and how they are being compensated.

15. *Site selection.* A description of any assistance in selecting a site for the franchise that will be provided by the franchisor. Some franchises, like McDonald's, complete all site analysis and make all location decisions without input from franchisees. Others give franchisees complete discretion in site selection.

16. *Information about franchisees.* You will receive information about the present number of franchises; the number of new franchises projected; and the number that have been terminated, chose not to renew, or were repurchased.

Franchisors must give you the names, addresses, and phone numbers of all franchisees located in your state; contact several of them.

17. *Franchisor financial statements.* The audited financial statements of the franchisors are included to show you the financial condition of the company.

18. *Personal participation of franchisees.* A description of the extent to which franchisees must personally participate in the operation of the franchise. Some permit franchisees to own the franchise but hire a manager to run the day-to-day business. Others require franchisees to be personally involved.

19. *Earning capacity.* A complete statement of the basis for any earnings claims made to the franchisee, including the percentage of existing franchises that have actually achieved the results that are claimed. Franchisors do not have to make any projections of what a franchisee may earn, but if they do, they must also describe the basis and assumptions used to make claims.

20. *Use of intellectual property.* The franchisor must describe your use of its trademarks, trade names, logos, or other symbols. You should receive full use of them because they account for a great deal of the value of a franchise.[5]

The FTC has revised the *Uniform Franchise Offering Circular (UFOC)* several times in the past 25 years. The changes were intended to replace much of the "legalese" wording of disclosure statements with plain English and to provide more standardized information for comparing franchises. The UFOC still has a way to go before it qualifies as "easy reading," but stay with it. This is a very important document to understand.[6]

> "Don't assume that the disclosure statement tells you everything you need to know about the franchise."

When you receive a disclosure statement, you will be asked to sign and date a statement indicating that you received it. The franchisor may not accept any money from you for ten working days from the time you sign the disclosure. This cooling-off period allows you the time to study, evaluate, and prepare your financing.[7]

The Franchise Agreement

franchise agreement
The legal contract that binds both parties involved in the franchise.

The **franchise agreement** is a document that spells out the rights and obligations of both parties in a franchise. This contract defines the precise, detailed conditions of the legal relationship between the franchisee and the franchisor. Its length, terms, and complexity will vary from one franchise and industry to another, so as to maintain the delicate balance of power between franchisees and franchisors.[8] It may or may not be possible for you to negotiate the contents of the contract, depending on how long the franchisor has been established and what the current market conditions are.

You should remember that the franchisor wrote the contract and that most of the conditions contained in it are weighted in the franchisor's favor. Read this document carefully yourself, but never sign a franchise agreement without getting your lawyer's opinion. Make sure your attorney and accountant have experience with franchising. Some of the most important topics that you should understand in franchise agreements are fees to be paid, ways in which the agreement can be terminated or renewed, and your rights to *exclusive territory* (discussed later in this chapter).

franchise fee
The one-time payment made to become a franchisee.

Franchise, Royalty, and Advertising Fees   The **franchise fee** is the amount of money you have to pay to become a franchisee. Some agreements require you to

Franchise Red Flags

Manager's Notebook

The American Franchisee Association strongly recommends that you do not sign a franchise agreement if it contains one of these provisions:

- *Gag Rules.* Franchise agreements may not allow current franchisees to discuss any aspect of their business experience with anyone outside the system—which defeats the purpose of the FTC disclosure rules.

- *Franchisor Venue Provisions.* These provisions may require any disputes to be litigated or arbitrated in the home state of the franchisor, increasing the franchisee's travel costs and giving franchisors home field advantage.

- *Lack of Reciprocal Cure Periods.* Agreements need to provide equal remedies if the other party defaults, but not all do.

- *Nonreciprocal Noncompete Covenants.* Franchisors have a lot of leeway in placing new franchisees wherever they want, but agreements can include oppressive noncompete covenants.

- *Sole-Sourcing Requirements.* Product-oriented franchises often require franchisees to purchase goods only from the franchisor. Allowing purchase from alternate sources (with quality standards) is better.

- *Mandatory Subleases with Rent Overrides.* Many franchise systems require the franchisee to sublease real estate from the franchisor, allowing the franchisor to gain profit without risk.

- *Lack of Accountability for Advertising Funds.* Franchisors do not always have to spend advertising dollars in markets where franchisees have paid in.

- *Lack of Reciprocal Legal Fee Provisions.* Many agreements require franchisees to pay all of the franchisor's legal expenses if litigation arises between parties.

- *Radically Different Franchise Agreements on Renewal.* Many franchisees are surprised to find that they are not really renewing their existing deal, but entering into a wholly new, sometimes very different franchise agreement.

- *Unilateral Amendments to the Franchise Agreements.* Franchisors have the latitude to change operations and policies from time to time, thereby unilaterally changing the franchisee agreement.

SOURCE: Eric Karp, "The Twelve Worst Franchise Agreement Provisions," The American Franchisee Association, www.franchisee.org. Reprinted with permission of The American Franchisee Association and Eric Karp, www.WitmerKarp.Warner.com.

have a percentage of the total franchise fee from a non-borrowed source, meaning, obviously, that you can't borrow that amount. Agreements may or may not allow you to form a corporation to avoid personal liability.

Royalty fees are usually a percentage of gross sales that you pay to the franchisor. Remember that royalties are calculated from gross sales, not from profits. If your business generates $350,000 of sales and the royalty fee is 8 percent, you

royalty fees
The ongoing payments that franchisees pay to franchisors—usually a percentage of gross sales.

have to pay $28,000 to the franchisor whether you make a profit or not. And you still have all your other operating expenses to cover.

When comparing two franchises, look at the combination of franchise fees and royalties. For example, suppose franchise X charges $25,000 for the franchise fee and a 10 percent royalty (not including advertising fees), and franchise Y charges a $37,500 franchise fee with a 5 percent royalty (no advertising fees, either). Assume that gross sales for each franchise would be $250,000 per year. The total fee you would pay for either would be $50,000 for the first year. But for each year after the first, you would pay $25,000 ($250,000 × 10%) with franchise X and only half that with franchise Y ($250,000 × 5%).

If the franchise agreement requires you to pay advertising fees, you want to be sure that a portion of your fee goes to local advertising in your area. If you operate a franchise on the outer geographic fringe of the franchise's operations, the franchisor could spend all of your advertising dollars where there is a greater concentration of other franchises, but none of *your* customers.

When it comes to total fees in franchising, you generally get what you pay for. If a deal looks too good to be true (unlimited potential earnings with no risk), it probably is.[9]

Termination of the Franchise Agreement   The agreement should state how you, as the franchisee, could lose your franchise rights. Also described should be the franchisee's obligations if you choose to terminate the agreement. Make sure the franchisor must show "good cause" to terminate the agreement—that is, there must be a good reason to discontinue the deal. Some states require a good-cause clause.

Terms and Renewal of Agreement   The franchise contract includes a section that specifies how long the agreement will remain in effect and what renewal process will apply. Most franchise contracts run from 5 to 15 years. Will you have to pay a renewal fee, or, possibly worse, negotiate a whole new franchise agreement? Because fees and royalties are generally higher for well-established franchises, your royalties and fees would probably increase if you have to sign a new agreement 10 years from now.

Exclusive Territory   You need to know the geographic size of the territory and the exclusive rights the franchisee would have. Franchisors may identify how many franchises a territory can support without oversaturation and then issue that many, regardless of the businesses' specific locations. Rights of first refusal, advertising restrictions, and performance quotas for the territory are addressed in this section.[10]

This issue of *exclusive territory* is the subject of much controversy in the franchising world. Patrick Leddy, Jr., had run a Baskin-Robbins franchise for 13 years when he learned that the franchisor was planning to open a new store less than two miles away from his site. He protested, but Baskin-Robbins opened the new store anyway. Leddy's sales plunged. When he tried to sell his store, he could not find a buyer because of his declining sales. Many franchisees cite examples like Leddy's case when they called for a federal law to prevent what they called widespread unfair treatment by franchisors.[11]

In reviewing the franchise opportunity, a potential franchisee should gather and verify the accuracy of the information included in the franchise agreement and all other information provided by the franchisor. This process is called **due diligence.** It means doing your homework and investigating the franchise on your own, rather than accepting everything the franchisor says at face value. This is a big commitment, so you should investigate matters thoroughly. Some information you can find yourself; some you will need professional assistance to gather and interpret.

due diligence
The process of thoroughly investigating the accuracy of information before signing a franchise (or any other) agreement.

Get Professional Advice

Consult a lawyer and a CPA before you sign any franchise agreement. Ask your accountant to read the financial data in the company's disclosure statements to determine whether the franchisor would be able to meet its obligation to you if you buy a franchise. Then ask a lawyer who is familiar with franchise law to inform you of all your rights and obligations contained in the franchise agreement—it *is* negotiable, but you have to push. Query your lawyer about any state or local laws that would affect your franchise. The cost of consulting professionals is small compared to the amount of time and money you will invest in a franchise. Do not assume that the disclosure statement tells you everything you need to know about the franchise. That is not the intent of the document.

International Franchising

Overseas franchising has become a major activity for U.S. companies faced with constantly increasing levels of domestic competition. Some franchises are signing few new franchises domestically, but are still rapidly adding foreign operations. Carlos Poza, of the U.S. Commercial Service of the Department of Commerce, reminds us that "95 percent of the world's consumers live outside the U.S. Because the world's consumers know U.S. products are excellent, our companies enjoy a competitive advantage—which means big opportunities for U.S. franchisors."[12]

Ray Kroc, who built McDonald's into a franchise giant, once said, "Saturation is for sponges." What Kroc was saying is that by expanding less crowded or underserved markets, you can increase sales and profits.

Canada is an increasingly attractive market for U.S. franchises because it is close and its markets are similar. With the passage of the North American Free Trade Agreement (NAFTA), franchise opportunities south of the border have become a dominant force in both the retailing and restaurant sectors. For example, TCBY Enterprises is quickly opening stores in Mexico. Both Eastern and Western European and Pacific Rim countries (especially Taiwan, Thailand, Indonesia, and Singapore) are also attractive targets for franchise expansion. When expanding abroad, however, franchisors must be sensitive to the demographic, economic, cultural, and legal climates of the host country.

The success of U.S. franchises is spreading all over the globe. In response, many governments are enacting legislation to regulate franchise operations. Following are some highlights of franchise legislation from a variety of countries:

- *United States.* This chapter has highlighted the federal laws covering disclosure statements, registration requirements, and restrictions on the sale and offering of franchises.

A Great Ride on the Subway.

- *Canada.* Unlike the United States, Canada has no federal legislation uniquely directed toward franchising. Only the province of Alberta has a specific franchise law, which relates to timely disclosure of information.

- *France.* Although French law does not use the word *franchising*, disclosure documents are required to be received by franchisees 20 days prior to execution of the franchise agreement.

- *Mexico.* The Industrial Property Law calls for disclosure; however, the franchisor may, if desired, exclude any confidential information that would benefit a competing franchise system. This is probably the single best place for franchisors to test their international exposure. For example, Dairy Queen tripled its franchisees in Mexico between 2001 and 2004, from 13 to 50.[13]

- *Brazil.* Federal law does not seek to regulate the relationship between franchisor and franchisee, but the franchisee must receive full information at least ten days before execution of the franchise agreement. Brazil is a strong marketplace that is worth the challenges.[14]

- *Spain.* In January 1996 the Spanish government enacted the Retail Trade Act, which requires franchisors to register their company name with the federal government and disclose full information in writing to potential franchisees.

- *Australia.* The Australian government enacted the Franchising Code of Conduct in 1998 to help franchisees make informed decisions.

- *Indonesia.* The government of Indonesia passed the Government Regulation on Franchising in 1997 to provide order in the business of franchising and protection to consumers.

- *Russia.* The Civil Code of Russia regulates the contractual agreement between franchisors and franchisees.

- *Republic of China.* Under legislation passed in 1997, it was required that prospective franchisees receive specific information at least 10 days before signing an agreement. China is McDonald's seventh-largest market by revenue, with 600 stores in 94 Chinese cities. KFC is the largest U.S. restaurant chain in China, with more than 900 locations.[15]

Summary

• What franchising is and how it operates

Franchising is a legal agreement that allows a franchisee to use a product, service, or method of the franchisor in exchange for fees and royalties. A franchisee is an independent businessperson who agrees to operate under the policies and procedures set up by the franchisor.

• The difference between product-distribution franchises and business-format franchises

Product-distribution franchises allow the franchisee to purchase the right to use the trade name of the manufacturer and to buy or sell the manufacturer's products. Business-format franchises allow the franchisee to duplicate the franchisor's way of doing business.

- **The advantages and disadvantages of franchising**

There are eight major advantages of franchising from the franchisee's perspective: proven product or service, marketing expertise, financial assistance, technical and managerial assistance, opportunity to learn, quality control standards, efficiency, and opportunity for growth. The primary disadvantages to the franchisee include fees, restrictions on his freedom to operate the business, overdependence on the franchisor, unsatisfied expectations of the franchisor, termination of the agreement, and poor performance of other franchisees.

- **Evaluating the franchise opportunity**

To evaluate a franchise opportunity, you should send for a copy of the company's disclosure statement (the company is required to send it to you), research the company through business periodicals, talk to current and former franchisees, and check out the franchisor's reputation with the International Franchise Association.

- **Franchising in the international marketplace**

Franchises are rapidly exploring opportunities for international expansion when faced with saturated domestic markets. Foreign markets are often less crowded and more underserved.

Questions for Review and Discussion

1. What is the difference between a franchise, a franchisee, and a franchisor?

2. How would you explain the difference between franchises and other forms of business ownership?

3. Why would you prefer to buy a franchise than to start a new business or buy an existing business?

4. Why is franchising important in today's economy?

5. What is the difference between product-distribution franchises and business-format franchises? Give an example of each that has not been cited in the text.

6. What are the biggest advantage and the biggest disadvantage of franchising? Justify your answer.

7. What do you expect to get in return for paying a franchise fee?

8. What is a royalty fee?

9. Is the disclosure statement the *only* source of information you need to check out a potential franchise? Why or why not?

10. After reading about the topics included in a franchise agreement, who do you think controls most of the power in a franchise: the franchisee or the franchisor? Explain.

11. What are potential sources of conflict between franchisees and franchisors?

12. You are worried that someone else will buy a specific franchise in your area before you do. Would it be appropriate to sign the franchise agreement before talking to your lawyer or accountant if you intend to meet with them later? Explain.

13. If you are the franchisee of a bookstore and are offered twice the business's book value to sell it to a third party, should you or the franchisor collect the additional money? Take a position and justify it.

14. What do you think will be the growth areas (in products, services, and geographic areas) for franchises in the near future?

Questions for Critical Thinking

1. Explain how a franchise could be considered a partnership. What makes a franchise agreement simpler than a partnership that you would start with another individual?

2. After having read about entrepreneurship in Chapter 2, would you consider someone who buys a franchise to be an entrepreneur? Does franchising stifle entrepreneurship?

Experience This . . .

Contact a local franchise owner and set up an appointment to visit her business. Ask if you can see a copy of the franchise agreement, or at least discuss the terms and conditions of the agreement with her.

What Would You Do?

You're convinced that purchasing a franchise is your method of choice for becoming a small business owner. Before you jump in, though, you'd better do your homework. For this exercise, we'll first present some basic information about two possible franchise operations; then it's your turn.

Snip 'N Clip (SNC Franchise Corporation)

This franchisor began business in 1958 and started franchising in 1985. Its business is providing all kinds of hair care procedures. There are 84 locations throughout the United States, 43 of which are owned by franchisees. The initial franchise fee is $10,000, and total investment ranges from $50,950 to $58,450. The company doesn't offer financing.

Smoothie King

This smoothie company finished on top of the juice bar category in *Entrepreneur* magazine's 2007 Franchise 500 list (and it finished as number 91 overall). Smoothie King began franchising in 1988, selling healthy snacks in Covington, LA. There were 437 independent franchises in 2006. The franchise fee is $25,000, the royalty fee is 6 percent, and startup costs range from $121,000 to $250,000. The company offers financing for the franchise fee, startup costs, equipment, and inventory.

Questions

1. Choose one of the two franchises presented and draft a business-plan outline.

2. Divide the class into teams to discuss the merits and potential drawbacks of each of these franchises.

CHAPTER CLOSING CASE

A FRANCHISOR'S DILEMMA

Marc Shuman was determined to expand fast. Then a quarter of his franchisees started to struggle. Was shutting them down the best solution?

Marc Shuman couldn't bear to open another e-mail. Hunkered down in his office in Syosset, New York, the president of GarageTek was reviewing the financial statements of his company's 57 franchises. It was fall 2003—three years after he'd launched his garage makeover business—and he was starting to worry.

A quarter of GarageTek's locations were losing money or barely breaking even, and complaints from disgruntled franchisees were pouring in. Meanwhile, Shuman and his corporate team were struggling to create operational systems that would help the unprofitable franchises get back on track. It had begun to feel like a losing battle. As Shuman analyzed one disappointing financial statement after another, he started thinking about shuttering the failing locations altogether.

GarageTek had seemed like a no-brainer when Shuman founded it in 2000. He got the idea when he and his father, with whom he outfitted department store interiors, designed and built a set of slotted wall panels with moveable shelves for a retail client.

When several of his employees began using the panel systems to organize their own garages and basements, Shuman realized he had a potential hit on his hands. And the timing seemed perfect: The housing market was heating up, garages were getting bigger, and closet organizers were all the rage. Shuman decided to sell the display business and open GarageTek.

Rather than simply selling the panels at home-improvement stores, Shuman decided to build a garage-makeover business. GarageTek would perform in-home consultations, then design and install the systems—complete with shelves, cabinets, bike racks, and workbenches. Homeowners, Shuman figured, were likely to pay a premium for the service. The biggest risk was competition. After all, anyone could have the same idea. But if Shuman could establish a foothold in markets around the country, GarageTek had a better chance of survival. Franchising seemed like the best way to pull off such an ambitious expansion.

In early 2001, Shuman placed an ad soliciting franchisees in *The Wall Street Journal*, and phone calls poured in. His attorney advised him to choose carefully. But Shuman, eager to get started, approved anyone with a business background, a $25,000 franchise fee, and $200,000—which, according to Shuman's calculations, was enough to purchase supplies, buy newspaper ads, and turn a profit within 18 months. Each franchise would pay GarageTek 8 percent of annual sales, a portion of which would help fund national advertising campaigns. In exchange, the franchisee received three days of basic training and a manual written by Shuman. "If they had the money and they had a strong sales and marketing background, we felt they were qualified," Shuman says.

At first, everything seemed to go according to plan. In the first half of 2001 GarageTek franchises opened in Connecticut, New Jersey, and New York. By 2003, 57 franchises had sprung up in 33 states, and annual revenue at the corporate office was on track to top $12 million. That summer, however, Shuman began to realize that while many franchises were thriving, 15 were struggling. One franchisee in California begged Shuman to send executives out west to train his staff. Another complained that GarageTek's suggested marketing method—ads in local newspapers—was ineffective, costing as much as $500 per lead. Desperate for help, Shuman enlisted iFranchise Group, a consulting firm in Homewood, Illinois, to help him develop a strategy. Meanwhile, the corporate team tapped franchisees for tips on which sales tactics worked best—a move that frustrated many of the struggling franchisees, who began to wonder why they were paying GarageTek at all.

Determined to get a handle on the situation, Shuman and his managers compiled a spreadsheet with information on every GarageTek franchise, including the size and demographics of each territory, overhead costs, pricing models, management assessments, and the amount of capital being invested by owners. The data revealed a distinct trend: The failing franchises were either underfunded or being run by nonowner managers hired by hands-off investors.

Shuman was torn. On the one hand, it was his fault for green-lighting those franchises in the first place and providing inadequate training and support. But he couldn't help blaming the struggling franchisees. After all, most GarageTek locations were doing well with minimal handholding. Shuman, who prides himself on being tough, was leaning toward folding the failing franchises—a decision supported by his management team and iFranchise.

But his lawyer warned him that things could get messy. GarageTek's contract stipulated that the corporate office could shut down franchises that failed to meet specific sales goals. However, the attorney warned, disgruntled franchisees could still file lawsuits and ensnare GarageTek in costly litigation. Shuman also worried about GarageTek's reputation. If he shuttered a quarter of the company's locations, it was bound to hurt the brand, especially if angry franchisees griped to customers or the press. "I envisioned a bloodbath," Shuman says.

Questions

1. Was shuttering the failed franchises the right move for Shuman? What are his other options?

SOURCE: From Stephanie Clifford, "Case Study: Hooked On Expansion," *Inc.*, March 2006, 44–50. Copyright © 2006 Mansueto Ventures LLC, publisher of Inc. Magazine, New York, NY 10017. Reprinted with permission.

Test Prepper

college.hmco.com/pic/hatten4e

You've read the chapter, studied the key terms, and the exam is any day now. Think you're ready to ace it? Take this sample test to gauge your comprehension of chapter material. You can check your answers at the back of the book. Want more test questions? Visit the student website at college.hmco.com/pic/hatten4e and take the ACE and ACE+ quizzes for more practice.

f. business-format franchise

g. bulk-purchase discounts

h. franchisee

i. disclosure statement

j. franchise

Matching

_____ **1.** the process of thoroughly investigating the accuracy of information before signing an agreement

_____ **2.** the small business owner who purchases the franchise so as to sell the product of the franchisor

_____ **3.** a one-time payment made to become a franchisee

_____ **4.** ongoing payments made to franchisors—usually a percentage of gross sales

_____ **5.** a type of franchise that represents a turnkey approach

_____ **6.** the information document that the FTC requires franchisors to provide to potential franchisees

   a. franchisor

   b. franchise fee

   c. due diligence

   d. product franchise

   e. royalty fee

True/False

1. T F Franchises account for 95 percent of all small business revenue.

2. T F Franchise revenues exceed $1.5 trillion per year.

3. T F Franchising has existed in the United States since the early 1800s.

4. T F An advantage to the franchisee is the ability to sell a proven product.

5. T F A disadvantage to the franchisee is the cost of the franchise.

6. T F An advantage to the franchisor is the huge amount of capital required for expansion.

7. T F A disadvantage to the franchisor is the high individual motivation of its franchisees.

8. T F Disclosure statements require franchisors to provide audited financial statements of the franchisor.

9. T F Royalties are paid as a percentage of franchisee profits.

10. T F It is extremely difficult for U.S. franchisors to expand into Mexico.

## chapter 6

Taking Over an Existing Business

We discussed the failure rate of small businesses in Chapter 1, where it was pointed out that most businesses do not survive to see their twentieth birthday. Family-owned businesses are much hardier, but still not invincible. Fewer than 30 percent survive into the second generation, barely 10 percent make it into the third generation, and only about 4 percent last until the fourth generation. Thus one way to measure business success, beyond revenues generated, profits earned, or societal impact, would be longevity. Ever wonder what the oldest family business in the United States might be? Perhaps not, but it's an interesting question. Making the list of the top 100 are some household names like number 68, Levi Strauss (founded 1853), and number 88, Anheuser-Busch (founded 1860).

But the hands-down endurance award goes to a business that has lasted through *14 generations* and was started in 1623! Zildjian Cymbal Company of Norwell, Massachusetts, was founded in Constantinople by Avedis I, who discovered a metal alloy that created superior-sounding, more durable cymbals. The sultan named him "Zildjian," Armenian for "cymbalsmith."

After reading this chapter, you should be able to:

- Compare the advantages and disadvantages of buying an existing business.

- Propose ways of locating a suitable business for sale.

- Explain how to measure the condition of a business and determine why it might be offered for sale.

- Differentiate between tangible and intangible assets, and assess the value of each.

- Calculate the price to pay for a business.

- Understand factors that are important when finalizing the purchase of a business.

- Describe what makes a family business different from other types of business.

Craigie Zildjian (the company's CEO), Armand, and Debbie Zildjian (vice president of human resources)

The Zildjian family arrived in the United States in 1910, moving here to escape persecution of Christian Armenians in their native land. The company was brought here in 1929. It was good timing, as Avedis Zildjian III was able to supply his cymbals to the jazz drummers of the day. Those instruments have remained synonymous with hot drummers throughout the Jazz Age, the big band era, and today's rock and roll. Avedis's son Armand applied new technology to the company's traditional approach by creating a modern factory.

As you might have guessed, not all has gone smoothly over the past 385-plus years. When company leader Avedis died in 1979, his sons Robert and Armand locked horns in a nasty courtroom battle for control over the company (cymbaling rivalry?). Robert left Zildjian and set up a competing cymbal company, Sabian, in Canada. He was legally barred from referencing the family history or name in his business or even using the letter "Z" in his company name.

Today Armand's daughters Craigie (the company's CEO) and Debbie (vice president of human resources) are the first female chiefs in Zildjian's long history.

Since you are undoubtedly wondering, the oldest family business in the world is Kongo Gumi, founded in 578. For more than 1,400 years and 40 generations, the Kongo family has built and repaired religious temples from its base in Osaka, Japan.

SOURCES: Kathleen Martin, "Global Cymbals," *Marketing*, 22 March 2004, 13; "America's Oldest Family Companies," May 2004, www.familybusinessmagazine.com; Paul I. Karofsky, "A Commitment to Passion: The Succession Story of the Avedis Zildjian Company," www.fambiz.com/articles

Business-Buyout Alternative

Suppose you are a prospective small business owner. You possess the necessary personal qualities, managerial ability, and capital to run a business, but you haven't decided on the approach you should take to get into business. If you aren't inheriting a family business, then you have three choices for getting started:

- You may buy out an existing establishment.
- You may acquire a franchised business.
- You may start a new firm yourself.

This chapter discusses the many factors to be considered in buying an existing business and taking over a family business.

Advantages of Buying a Business

The opportunity to buy a firm already in operation is appealing for a number of reasons. Like franchising, it offers a way to avoid some beginners' hazards.[1] The existing firm is already functioning—maybe it is even a proven success. Many of the serious problems typically encountered by startups should have been either avoided or corrected by now. The ongoing business is analogous to a ship after its "shakedown cruise," a new automobile after the usual small adjustments have been made, or a

Creating Competitive Advantage

Do . . . Due Diligence

Vern Crosby almost cut corners in due diligence and came close to paying quite a price. Crosby was in charge of marketing for a Maryland-based company that provided facilities, janitorial, and grounds maintenance for military bases. The company's annual revenue was $1 million when Crosby started. Thanks to his marketing skills, sales soon shot to $8.5 million, then $15 million within five years. When the business's partner-owners began fighting and announced they wished to part ways, they offered Crosby right of first refusal to purchase the business.

Given his track record with the company, Crosby thought he knew everything he needed to know. He conducted his own appraisal. He received input from an accountant and a mentor, but from no one else, not even a lawyer. Bad move. Crosby's offer of $2 million was accepted for assets valued at $600,000—plus $1.2 million of debt.

If you understand anything about purchasing a business, catch this—if you purchase the stock of a business, you're getting not just the assets but also all of its liabilities, debt, litigation, and history. Vern Crosby just about got caught on this point.

Crosby found out that the company he planned to buy hadn't been paying its vendors, so he began digging deeper. He had a hard time tracking cash flow through the business, because the owners had been commingling money among several businesses they owned. He says, "They were robbing Peter to pay Paul. It was a nightmare." Amazingly, he was still anxious to buy. Finally, the banks that were providing financing found that the tax debt was actually larger than the $250,000 stated. It was more than $1 million. That killed the deal.

Ironically, the feuding owners' sons co-owned two businesses, and they, too, were fighting to the point where they wanted out. Crosby had learned his lessons about due diligence the first time, so now he conducted proper investigation with the help of an accountant and an acquisitions attorney to handle the valuation of the sons' business. He ended up purchasing both businesses and continues to run them separately.

For another view on purchasing an existing business, watch the video that accompanies this chapter about a *very* unusual furniture store bought by America's wealthiest investor.

SOURCE: Joyce Jones, "Shopping for an Enterprise," *Black Enterprise*, September 1998, 75–83.

---

computer program that has been "debugged." But remember one thing: Just as there are no perfect ships, cars, or software for sale out there, neither are there any perfect businesses on the market. You are searching for an opportunity, so *some* flaws in a business can make it more attractive. You just have to be able to correct them while keeping all the parts that work going strong.

> **" Existing businesses must be scrutinized carefully to determine whether they are a worthy investment of your time and money. "**

Buying an existing business is a popular way for would-be owners to acquire a small business. Of the 6 million U.S. businesses with 19 or fewer employees, at least 1 million are for sale at any given time.[2]

There are several advantages to buying an existing business as compared with the other methods of getting into business. Because customers are used to doing business with the company at its present address, they are likely to continue doing so once you take over. If the business has been making money, you will break even sooner than if you start your own business from the ground up. Your planning for an ongoing business can be based on actual historical figures, rather than relying on projections, as with a startup. Your inventory, equipment, and suppliers are

Table 6.1

ADVANTAGES AND DISADVANTAGES OF BUYING A BUSINESS

Advantages
1. Customer base is established.
2. Location is already familiar to customers.
3. Planning can be based on known historical data.
4. Supplier relationships are already in place.
5. Inventory and equipment are already in place.
6. Employees are experienced.
7. Possibility of owner financing exists.
8. Quick entry is available.
9. Control systems are already in place (e.g., accounting, inventory, and personnel controls).
10. Business image is already set in minds of customers
Disadvantages
1. Business image may be difficult to change.
2. Employees may be ones you would not choose.
3. Business may not have operated the way you like and could be difficult to change.
4. Inventory or equipment may be obsolete.
5. Financing costs could drain your cash flow and threaten the business's survival.
6. Business's location may be undesirable, or a good location may be about to become not so good.
7. Potential liability exists for past business contracts.
8. Misrepresentation is possible (yes, the person selling the business may be lying).

already in place, managed by employees who already know how to operate the business. Financing may be available from the owner. If the timing of the deal occurs when you are ready to buy a business and the owner needs to sell for a legitimate reason, you may get a bargain (see Table 6.1).

Disadvantages of Buying a Business

Could this business that you're considering buying be what is called in the used-car business a "lemon"? Most people don't sell their cars until they feel the vehicle needs considerable mechanical attention. Is the same true of selling businesses?

There are disadvantages to buying an existing business as a way to become your own boss (see Table 6.1 again). The image of the business already exists and may prove difficult to change should you desire to improve it. The employees who come with the business may not be the ones whom you would choose to hire. The previous owners may have established precedents that can be difficult to change. The way the business operates may be outmoded. The inventory or equipment may be outdated. The purchase price may create a burden on future cash flow and profitability. You may pay too much for the business due to misrepresentation or inaccurate appraisal. The business's facilities or location may not be the best. You may be held liable for contracts left over from previous owners.

How Do You Find a Business for Sale?

If you have decided that you're interested in purchasing an existing business and have narrowed your choices down to a few types of businesses, how do you locate one to buy? Perhaps you are currently employed by a small business. Is there a chance that it may be available for purchase sometime soon? Because you know the inner workings of the business, it might be a good place to start. Newspaper advertising is a traditional place for someone who is actively trying to sell a business to start marketing it. Don't stop your quest with the newspaper, however, because many good opportunities are never advertised. Word of mouth through friends and family may turn up businesses that don't appear to be available through formal channels.

> "Don't overlook the direct approach to finding a business for sale. If you are attracted to a business where you have been a customer, why not politely ask the owner if he has thought of selling?"

People who counsel small businesses on a regular basis, such as bankers, lawyers, accountants, and Small Business Administration representatives, can be good sources for finding firms for sale. Real estate brokers often have listings for business opportunities, which include real estate and buildings. Trade associations generally have publications that list member businesses for sale.[3]

Don't overlook a direct approach to finding a business. If you have been a regular customer of an establishment and have an attraction to it, why not politely ask the owner if she has ever thought of selling it? The timing may be perfect if the owner is considering a move to another part of the country or is exploring another new business. Perhaps this is an unlikely way to find a business, but what do you have to lose by asking?

Nearly every city has one or more **business brokers.** Most inspect and appraise a business establishment offered for sale before listing and advertising it. Some also assist a buyer in financing the purchase, but not all of them will provide you with the same level of service. A few will work very hard for you in trying to find a business that matches your talents and needs. Most will tell you what is available at the moment, but not much more than that. Some will do you more harm than good. Remember, business brokers normally receive their commission from the seller, so their loyalty is to the seller, not to you.

> **business broker**
> A business intermediary that brings sellers of their businesses together with potential buyers.

Unfortunately for prospective buyers, the market is rife with "business opportunity" scams. As with any scam, the individuals most likely to be targeted are those venturing into unknown territory and trusting the wrong people. The practice of selling unprofitable (and unfixable) businesses to unwary buyers has been around as long as business itself. The ruse is most common in the retail field, where a single business unit can wreck a dozen or more owners through successive sales and resales to a steady stream of newcomers, each confident that he can succeed where others have failed. Naturally, the brokers who promote these sales make more in commissions the more frequently the business changes hands. Check for recommendations from bankers, accountants, and other businesspeople who have used the broker in the past. You need to be on guard to keep from being included among that group immortalized by the late P. T. Barnum, who allegedly said, "There's a sucker born every minute."

Brokers must take classes and pass examinations to become *certified business intermediaries (CBIs)*. To find a reliable business broker, check the International Business Brokers Association at www.ibba.org.

What Do You Look for in a Business?

To successfully analyze the value of any business, you should have enough experience to recognize specific details that are most relevant in that type of business. You need enough knowledge to take the information provided by sales, personnel, or financial records and (1) evaluate the past performance of the business and (2) predict its probable future developments. You need objectivity to avoid excess enthusiasm that might blind you to the facts. *Don't let emotions cloud your business decisions.*

At a minimum, you should ask the following questions to gather information about the business you are considering buying:

- How long has the business existed?

    Who founded it?

    How many owners has it had?

    Why have others sold out?

- What is the profit record?

    Is profit increasing or decreasing?

    What are the true reasons for the increase or the decrease?

- What is the condition of the business?

    Equipment

    Inventory

    Building

- How long does the lease run?

    Is it a satisfactory lease for your needs?

    Can it be renewed?

    - Are there dependable sources of supply?

- Does the company have an established distribution network and sales force?

- What about present and future competition? Are new competitors or substitute materials or methods visible on the horizon?

- What is the condition of the area around the business? Are traffic routes or parking regulations likely to change?

- Does the present owner have family, religious, social, or political connections that have been important to the success of the business?

- Why does the present owner want to sell?

    Where will he go?

    What is she going to do?

What do people (customers, suppliers, local citizens) think of the present owner and of the business?

• Are the existing personnel satisfactory? Are key people willing to remain?

• How does this business, in its present condition, compare with one that you could start and develop yourself in a reasonable amount of time?[4]

Are you bored with the idea of shopping for a business the old-fashioned ways, such as through classified ads and business brokers? Then go online—specifically, go to www.bizbuysell.com, a very comprehensive site for buying or selling a business that offers a database of thousands of established businesses for sale. You begin by choosing where you want your business to be. All 50 states, plus Africa, Asia, Australia/New Zealand, Canada, the Caribbean, Central America, Europe, and South America, are represented. Next, you choose the type of business that interests you. You can choose all business categories or pick from retail, service, manufacturing, wholesale, construction, transportation, finance, and several other miscellaneous categories.

Due Diligence

For the buyout entrepreneur, preparation is the key to a successful business purchase. You need to analyze your own skills, find good advisors, write a business plan, and, most importantly, do **due diligence.** Due diligence means the disclosure and assimilation of public and proprietary information relating to the business for sale. Many prospective buyers mistakenly view due diligence as a financial review, but in fact it goes far beyond the numbers. This step comprises a complete investigation and review of a business that begins the moment you become interested in a business.[5]

> **due diligence**
> The process of fact finding to determine the total condition of a business being considered for purchase.

Due diligence begins by addressing the overall financial health of the company. What trends have occurred with revenues, expenses, and profit margins? Have they grown, stagnated, or declined? Will the products become obsolete in the foreseeable future? If a small business does not have audited financial statements signed by an accountant (and many don't), then insist on seeing the owner's tax returns (because it's more difficult to lie about those documents). Beyond inspecting the owner's financial documents, you should visit the local county courthouse to check for any existing or pending litigation or liens filed against the business or its owners. The Better Business Bureau can tell you about past or current complaints.

Although the financial scandals of the past few years have centered on large corporations, they have created a heightened level of skepticism about mergers and acquisitions of all sizes of businesses—and increased the emphasis placed on due diligence.[6] The Sarbanes-Oxley Act increases the extent to which executives are held responsible for the accuracy of their company's financial statements. Because business buyers may be liable for any financial reporting discrepancies found after the business purchase, they have a strong incentive to be thoroughly knowledgeable about the firm's accounting practices.[7]

Since buying a business is risky no matter how much due diligence is performed, a new type of insurance has recently been developed to shift some risk to a third party. This insurance, consisting of *representations and warranties policies,* covers financial losses suffered if a seller makes false claims in the representations and warranties section of a sale contract.[8]

General Considerations

If you aspire to try entrepreneurship by buying an existing business, don't rush into a deal. Talk with the firm's banker and verify account balances with its major customers and creditors. Be sure you get any verbal understandings in writing from the seller.

Put the earnest money in escrow with a reputable third party. Before an agreement to purchase is signed, have all papers checked by your accountant and attorney.

If the business you are buying involves inventory, you need to be familiar with the *bulk-sales provisions* of the Uniform Commercial Code. Although the law varies from state to state, it generally requires a seller to provide a list of all business creditors and amounts due to each buyer. You, as the buyer, must then notify each creditor that the business is changing hands. This step protects you from claims against the merchandise previously purchased.

Why Is the Business Being Sold?

When the owner of a business decides to sell it, the reasons he gives to prospective buyers may be somewhat different from those known to the business community, and both of these explanations may be somewhat different from the actual facts. There are at least as many factors that could contribute to the sale of a business as there are reasons for business liquidations. Be careful. Business owners who are aware of future problems (such as a lost contract for a strong line of merchandise or a new law that will affect the business unfavorably) may not tell you everything they know. For a prospective buyer, a discussion with the firm's customers and suppliers is recommended. Check with city planners about proposed changes in streets or routing of transportation lines that might have a serious effect on the business in the near future.

Although anyone can be misled or defrauded, a savvy business buyer with good business sense will rely on her ability to analyze the market, judge the competitive situation, and estimate the profits that could be made from the business, rather than relying on the present owner's reasons for selling. These "reasons" are often too difficult to verify.

One point to consider as you search for a business is the list of alternatives in which you could invest your money, such as the stock market, money market funds, or even a savings account. By viewing the purchase of a business as an investment, you can compare alternatives on the same terms.

Financial Condition

A study of the financial statements of the business will reveal how consistently the business has rewarded its previous owner's efforts. As a prospective purchaser, you must decide if the income reported thus far would be satisfactory to you and your family. If it is not, could it be increased? You will want to compare the firm's operating ratios with industry averages to identify where costs could be reduced or more money is needed.

The seller's books alone should not be taken as proof of stated sales or profits. You should also inspect bank deposits for at least five years or for as long as the present owner has operated the business.

When analyzing the financial statements of the business, don't rely strictly on the most recent year of operation. Profits can be artificially pumped up and expenses cut

Letter of Confidentiality

Elaine Niblic, CEO

Cheatum Products, Inc.

Dear Ms. Niblic:

It was a pleasure to talk with you last week concerning the possible purchase of your business. Our conversation has brought my interest in your business to the point where I would like to examine your financial records for the past five years. Along with the company records I also wish to see tax returns filed for that period of time.

I realize that this information is confidential in nature and that you are concerned about improper use of these records. I assure you that I request this information strictly for the purpose of making a purchase decision regarding your business and the terms of the deal. The only persons to whom I will disclose this confidential information are my spouse, my attorney, and my accountant. I will obtain signed confidentiality statements from them before showing them your records.

I will return all of your records, including any copies made, within two weeks of their delivery to me. Thank you for your trust. I will not violate it, and I look forward to continuing our business transaction.

Sincerely,

James Rocky

temporarily for almost every business. Check whether the business employs the same number of people as in previous years; most businesses can operate short-handed for a while to cut labor expenses. Maintenance on equipment, vehicles, or the building can be cut to increase short-term profit figures. Profits that appear on the books may also be overstated by insufficient write-offs of bad debts, inventory shortages and obsolescence, and under-depreciation of the firm's fixed assets.

Ask to see the owner's tax returns. This request shouldn't create a problem if everything is legitimate. Compare bills and receipts with sales-tax receipts. Reconcile past purchases with the sales and markup claimed. Make certain that all back taxes have been paid. Make sure that interest payments and other current obligations are not in arrears.

Realize that the financial information you need in order to analyze the overall condition of the business is sensitive information to the seller, especially if the two of you don't know each other. You can decrease the seller's suspicions about your using this information to aid a competing business or some other improper use by writing a *letter of confidentiality* (see the example of one in the Manager's Notebook feature).

Independent Audit   Before any serious discussion of purchasing a business takes place, an *independent audit* should be conducted. This exercise will identify the condition of the financial statements. You will want to know whether the business's accounting practices are legitimate and whether its valuation of inventory, equipment, and real estate is realistic.

Even audited statements need some subjective interpretation, however. For example, owners may underreport their income for tax reasons. A family member may be on the payroll and paid a salary although unneeded by the business. Business owners who use a company car or a credit card for non-business purposes also misrepresent their business expenses.

Profit Trend   The financial records of the business can tell you whether sales volume is increasing or decreasing. If it is going up, which departments or product lines account for the increased volume? Did the increased volume lead to increased profitability? In other words, what is the *profit trend?* Many businesses have failed by concentrating on selling a high volume of goods at such low margins that making net profits proved impossible.

If the sales volume is decreasing, is it due to the business's failure to keep up with competition or its inability to adjust to changing times? Or is the decline simply due to a lack of effective marketing?

Interpret net profit of the business you are considering in terms of the amount of capital investment you will have to make in the business as well as sales volume. In other words, a $5,000 annual net profit from a business that requires a $10,000 investment and sales of $20,000 is much more attractive than a business that generates the same profit but requires a $100,000 investment and sales of $200,000.[9]

Expense Ratios   Industry averages comparing expenses to sales exist for every size and type of business. Industrywide *expense ratios* are calculated by most trade associations, many commercial banks, accounting firms, university bureaus of business research, and firms like Dun & Bradstreet and Robert Morris Associates (RMA).

For example, RMA publishes industry averages for 392 specific types of businesses in the manufacturing, wholesale, retail, and service sectors in *RMA Annual Statement Studies.*[10] Comparisons are made in terms of percentages of assets, liabilities, and income data. RMA also provides industry averages of 16 common financial ratios, such as current ratio, quick ratio, sales/working capital, and sales/receivables. (These and other financial ratios are explained further in Chapter 8.)

Imagine you are interested in buying a health club. The location is good, the advertising has caught your attention for several months, and the club boasts state-of-the-art equipment. You are very excited about the possibilities and are now looking over the financial statements. You divide the total current assets by the total current liabilities to calculate the club's *current ratio,* which shows the ability of a business to meet its current obligations. Let's suppose you get a current ratio of 0.5 for this business.

Now you want to get an idea of management performance, which is shown by the *operating ratio,* so you divide the profit before taxes by total assets and multiply by 100 (to convert to a percentage). This computation gives you 4.8 percent. You ask yourself, "Are a current ratio of 0.5 and an operating ratio of 4.8 percent good or bad for a health club?" They could be either. You need something to compare them with to tell you whether they are in line. You go to the library at a nearby university to compare your figures with RMA industry averages. You look in the RMA reports under "Service—Physical Fitness Facilities," where you find the median current ratio listed at 0.9 and the median percentage profit before taxes divided by total assets at 7.5 percent. Your figures are well below the industry averages, so you decide to dig deeper to find out why such large deviations exist between the business you are interested in buying and the average for other similar-sized businesses in the health club industry.

Discoveries in Fields like Life-Sciences, Energy, and Physics Create Business Opportunities.

Expense ratios are standards or guides for comparison. Their effective use depends on your ability to identify existing problems and to change conditions that have caused any ratios to be appreciably lower than the standard.

Other Measures of Financial Health   Profit ratios are excellent indicators of a business's worth, but you should also examine other aspects of its financial health. A complete financial health examination consists of the calculation and interpretation of a variety of other financial ratios in addition to those relating to profit. Of particular interest to you and your accountant will be the following factors:

1. The working capital and the cash flow of the business (is there enough of both to adequately keep the business going?)

2. The relationship between the firm's fixed assets and the owner's tangible net worth

3. The firm's debt load, or leverage

Another key factor in business valuation is what other companies in your industry have sold for. Each year *Inc.* magazine, in parnership with Business Valuation Resources of Portland, Oregon, publishes an issue that contains a comprehensive business valuation guide with graphics and tables that illustrate different companies selling for a premium or below their annual revenue. For example, in 2007 companies in the life sciences, energy, financial services, and technology sectors boasted high sale prices and robust sale multiples.[11]

What Are You Buying?

When buying an existing business, you need to realize that the value of that business comes from what the business owns (its assets and what it earns), its cash flow, and the factors that make the business unique, such as the risk involved (see Figure 6.1).

Figure 6.1

WHAT SHOULD YOU PAY?

The Price You Offer for a Business Should Begin with Adding the Value of Tangible and Intangible Assets to the Profit Potential of the Business.

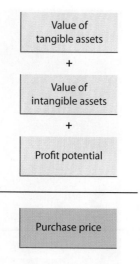

---

tangible assets
Assets owned by a business that can be seen and examined.

Tangible Assets

The **tangible assets** of a business, such as inventory, equipment, and buildings, are generally easier to place a fair market value on than intangible assets, such as trade names, customer lists, and goodwill. If the firm is selling its accounts receivable, you should determine how many of these accounts are collectible and discount them accordingly. Receivables that are 120 days or older are not worth as much as those less than 30 days old, because the odds are greater that you will not collect them. This process is called *aging accounts receivable.* Of the other tangible assets of a business that are up for sale, inventories and equipment should be examined the most closely, because they are most likely to be outdated and therefore worth less than what the seller is asking.

Inventory   Inventory needs to be timely, fresh, and well balanced. One indication that the business has been well managed is an inventory of goods that people want, provided in the proper sizes, designs, and colors, and priced to fit the local buying power and purchasing habits.

Your biggest concern about inventory should be that you aren't buying *dead stock* (merchandise that has no, or very little, value) that the seller has listed as being worth its original value. The loss in value of dead stock should be incurred by the original buyer, and you must ensure that the loss is not passed on to you as part of the sale.

Equipment   It is important that a business be equipped with current, usable machines and equipment. *Book value* (discussed under "What Are the Tangible Assets Worth" later in this chapter) of electronic office equipment, especially computers, becomes outdated quickly. A cash register designed for the bookkeeping requirements of a generation ago, for example, will not record the information now required for tax reporting or scan UPC codes for efficient inventory control.

Often the usefulness of the firm's equipment was outlived long ago and its value depreciated. The owner may have delayed so long in replacing equipment that it has no trade-in value, and without this discount she finds the price of new equipment to be exorbitant. This reason alone could lead to her decision to sell the business. Anything the owner makes on the fixtures and equipment is new, clear profit, an extra bonus on his period of operation.

Manager's Notebook

Declining Value of Aging Accounts Receivable

Not all accounts receivable are created equal. Those that have been owed the longest are worth less because they are the least likely to be collected. In other words, the longer someone takes to pay her account, the more likely it is that she will never pay the debt. Therefore, in valuing a business for sale, you need to reduce the cash value of long overdue accounts so as to reflect the odds that they will not be paid.

Determining how much to reduce the value of old accounts should be based on the debtor company's past payment trends. In the hypothetical example of a company we'll call Fabio's Floral Wholesalers, accounts receivable 30 days and younger have a 100 percent likelihood of being paid. Accounts 31 to 60 days old have historically had a 70 percent probability of being paid, those 61 to 90 days old have had a 50 percent probability of being paid, and those older than 90 days have had a 25 percent probability of being paid. These percentages were determined by looking at the company's accounts receivable history—a fair and logical request to make of the business owner.

Accounts Receivable	Probability Percentage	Book Value	Aged Value
30 days and younger	100	$ 75,000	$ 75,000
31 to 60 days	70	50,000	35,000
61 to 90 days	50	30,000	15,000
Over 90 days	25	30,000	7,500
Total Value		$185,000	$132,500

You can see that there's a significant difference in the aged value and the book value of the accounts receivable: $52,500! When you're buying an existing business, play it smart and be sure to value accounts receivable accurately.

SOURCES: Bridget McCrea and Alan Hughes, "Turning Receivables into Received," *Black Enterprise*, February 2004, 46; Frederick Daily, *Tax Savvy for Small Business*, 7th ed. (Berkeley, CA: Nolo Press, 2003), 16/6. For an alternative method for aging accounts receivable, see Institute of Management and Administration, "New A/R Analysis Technique Improves Cash-Flow Forecasts," *Report on Financial Analysis, Planning & Reporting*, January 2004, 1–10, *www.ioma.com*.

Intangible Assets

Businesses are also made up of **intangible assets** that may have real value to the purchaser. Among these are goodwill; favorable leases and other advantageous contracts; and patents, copyrights, and trademarks.

> *intangible assets*
> Assets that have value to a business but are not visible.

goodwill
The intangible asset that allows businesses to earn a higher return than a comparable business with the same tangible assets might generate.

Goodwill   **Goodwill** is an intangible asset that enables a business to earn a higher return than a comparable business with the same tangible assets might generate. Few businesses that are for sale have much goodwill value.

We all know businesses in existence for years that have not established enough goodwill for the average customer to see the business as being "special." If strong competition existed, such companies would have been driven out of business long ago. From a consumer-preference standpoint, they are at the bottom of the scale. This public attitude cannot be changed quickly. A good name can be ruined in far less time than it takes to improve a bad one.

A successful business has goodwill as an asset. Taking over a popular business brings with it public acceptance that has been built up over a period of many years, which is naturally valuable to the new owner. (Goodwill is discussed further later on in this chapter.)

Leases and Other Contracts   A lease on a favorable location is a valuable business asset. If the selling firm possesses a lease on its building, or if it has any unfulfilled sales contracts, you should determine whether the lease and other contracts are transferable to you or whether they must be renegotiated.

Patents, Copyrights, and Trademarks   *Intellectual property*—which includes patents, copyrights, and trademarks—can also be a valuable intangible asset. *Patent rights* give protection of your machine, process, or a combination of the two against unauthorized use or infringement for only a limited period of time, after which they are open to use by others. Thus it is important for the prospective buyer of an existing business to determine precisely when the firm's patent rights expire and to value these rights based on the time remaining.

Copyrights offer the best protection for books, periodicals, materials prepared for oral presentation, advertising copy, pictorial illustrations, commercial prints or labels, and similar intellectual property. Unlike patent rights, copyrights are renewable.

Registered *trademarks* protect you against unauthorized use or infringement of a symbol, such as the Mercedes-Benz star or McDonald's arches, used in marketing goods. The function of trademarks is to identify specific products and to create and maintain a demand for those products. Because trademark protection lasts as long as the trademark is in continuous use, you should consider its value when purchasing a business that owns a trademark.

Personnel

When purchasing a business, you should regard the people working there as being equally important as profits and production. Retention of certain key people will keep a successful business going. New employees rarely come in as properly trained and steady workers. To help you estimate expenses related to finding, hiring, and training new employees, you will want to know if there are enough qualified people presently employed. Will any of these people depart with the previous owner? Are any key individuals unwilling or unable to continue working for you? The loss of a key person or two in a small business can have a serious impact on future earnings.

The Seller's Personal Plans

As a prospective purchaser of an existing business, you should not feel that all sellers of businesses have questionable ethical and moral principles. Nevertheless, you should remember that "*Caveat emptor*—Let the buyer beware" has been a reliable maxim for years. There are laws against fraud and misrepresentation, but intent to defraud is usually very difficult to prove in court.

You can reduce your risk by writing protective clauses into contracts of sale, such as a **noncompete clause,** in which the seller promises not to enter into the same kind of business as a competitor within a specified geographic area for a reasonable number of years. If the seller resists agreeing to such a clause, it may be a signal that she intends to enter into a similar business in the future.

For a noncompete clause to be legally enforced, it must be reasonable. For example, setting a 25-mile noncompete zone when selling a New York City business would take in a market of about 20 million people—probably an unreasonable restraint that might prevent the seller from earning a living in the future.

An example of a noncompete clause would read as follows:

> Seller shall not establish, engage in, or become interested in, directly or indirectly, as an employee, owner, partner, agent, shareholder, or otherwise, within a radius of ten miles from the city of _____, any business, trade, or occupation similar to the business covered by this sales agreement for a period of three years. At the closing, the seller agrees to sign an agreement on this subject in the form set forth in Exhibit _____.[12]

> *noncompete clause*
> A provision often included in a contract to purchase a business that restricts the seller from entering the same type of business within a specified area for a certain amount of time.

How Much Should You Pay?

Even if you don't plan to buy an existing business, the methods of evaluating one are useful to know so that you can appraise the success of a firm. But if you are planning to buy a business, certain additional factors come into play. When you make a substantial financial investment in a business, you should expect to receive personal satisfaction as well as an adequate living. A business bought at the wrong price, at the wrong time, or in the wrong place can cost you and your family more than the dollars invested and lost. After you have thoroughly investigated the business, weighed the information collected, and decided that the business will satisfy your expectations, a price must be agreed on.

Determining the purchase price for a business involves analyzing several important factors: (1) valuation of the firm's tangible net assets; (2) valuation of the firm's intangible assets, especially any goodwill that has been built up; (3) expected future earnings; (4) market demand for the particular type of business; and (5) general condition of the business (including completeness and accuracy of its records, employee esprit de corps, and physical condition of facilities).[13]

A beginning point (not a finely tuned ending point) for business valuation is the *multiple method.* This approach is based on a formula that applies a weighting factor to the owner-benefit figure of the previous year(s) so as to arrive at a possible purchase price. The *owner benefit* is a combination of several factors:

Pretax Profit + Owner's Salary + Additional Owner Perks + Interest + Depreciation

Most small businesses will sell for a one- to three-times multiple of this figure. Granted, this is a wide range, so how do you determine which multiple to apply? Use a multiple of 1 for those businesses where the seller is "the business"—such as consulting businesses, professional practices, and one-person businesses. Multiples of 3 are more appropriate for businesses that have been in existence for several years, have demonstrated sustainable growth, boast a solid base of clients, own assets that will not have to be replaced in the immediate future, and are involved in growth industries, among other things. A study of hundreds of businesses sold in a recent year in the state of Florida indicated that the average multiple was 2.1 times the owner benefit.[14]

Approaches to valuing a business that focus on the value of the business's assets are called **balance-sheet methods of valuation.** They are most appropriate for businesses that generate earnings primarily from their assets rather than from the contributions of their employees. Approaches that focus more on the profits or cash flow that a business generates are called **income-statement methods of valuation.** As a methodology, *discounted cash flow* (an income-statement method) is often considered the preferred tool with which to value businesses. What sets this approach apart from the other approaches is that it is based on future operating results rather than on historical operating results. As a result, companies can be valued based on their future cash flows, which may be somewhat different than the historical results, especially if the buyer expects to operate some aspects of the business differently.

Discounted cash-flow analysis consists of projecting future cash flows (generally for five years) before debts are subtracted and after taxes are paid. A *discount rate* (expressed as a percentage that represents the risk associated with the investment) is then derived and applied to the future cash flows and *terminal value* (a current value for a company's long-term future cash flows). This detailed analysis depends on accurate financial projections and specific discount-rate assumptions.[15]

balance-sheet methods of valuation
A method of determining the value of a business based on the worth of its assets.

income-statement methods of valuation
A method of determining the value of a business based on its profit potential.

What Are the Tangible Assets Worth?

The worth of tangible assets is what the balance-sheet method of valuation seeks to establish. Their value is determined based on one of three factors:

- *Book value.* What the asset originally cost or what it is worth from an accounting viewpoint; the amount shown on the books as representing the asset's value as a part of the firm's worth
- *Replacement value.* What it would cost to buy the same materials, merchandise, or machinery today; relative availability and desirability of new items must be considered
- *Liquidation value.* How much the seller could get for this business, or any part of it, if it were placed on the open market

There are significant differences in these three approaches to determining value. Book value may not hold up in the marketplace. Buildings and equipment may not be correctly depreciated, whereas land may have appreciated. Replacement value may not be a reliable figure because of opportunities to buy used equipment. It is significant as a measure of value only in comparison to what it would cost to start your own business. Liquidation value is the most realistic approach in determining the value of tangible assets to the buyer of a business. It may represent the lowest figure that the seller would be willing to accept.

You have to determine the value of the following physical assets before serious bargaining can begin:

1. Cost of the inventory adjusted for slow-moving or dead stock

2. Cost of the equipment less depreciation

3. Supplies

4. Accounts receivable less bad debts

5. Market value of the building

Don't make an offer for a business based on the seller's asking price. You may feel as if you got a real bargain if you talk the seller down to half of what she is asking—but half might still be twice as much as the business is worth.[16]

What Are the Intangible Assets Worth?

An established business may be worth more than the sum of its physical assets, and its owner may be unwilling to sell for liquidation value alone. The value of a business's intangible assets is difficult to determine. Intangible assets are the product of a firm's past earnings, and they are the basis on which its earnings are projected.

Goodwill is the term used to describe the difference between the purchase price of a company and the net value of the tangible assets. Goodwill is the most difficult asset to value at a price that the seller will think is fair. It includes intangible but very real assets with real value to the prospective purchaser. Goodwill can be regarded as (1) compensation to the owner for his losses on beginner's mistakes you might have made if you had started from scratch and (2) payment for the privilege of carrying on an established and profitable business.[17] It should be small enough to be made up from profits within a reasonably short period.

What is goodwill worth? To determine a company's goodwill, you can start by using the income-statement method of valuation. To do so, you should capitalize your projected future earnings at an assumed rate of interest that would be in excess of the "normal" return (earnings adjusted to remove any unusual occurrences like a lawsuit settlement or a one-time gain from the sale of real estate) in that type and size of business. The *capitalization rate* is a figure assigned to show the risk and expected growth rate associated with future earnings.

For example, suppose that the liquidation value of the firm's tangible net assets is $224,000 and that the normal before-tax rate of return on the owner's investment in this business is 15 percent, or $33,600 per year. We will assume that the actual profit during the past few years has averaged $83,600, exclusive of the present owner's salary (which may have been overstated or understated).

From the profit, we will deduct a reasonable salary for the owner or manager—what she might earn by managing this type of business for someone else. If we assume a going-rate annual salary of $40,000, then the excess profit to be capitalized (that is, the amount of profit based on goodwill) is $10,000 ($83,600 minus $40,000 salary minus a normal profit of $33,600).

The rate of capitalization is negotiated by the buyer and the seller of the business. It should be appropriate to the risk taken. The more certain you are of the

Table 6.2

CALCULATING PURCHASE
PRICE OF EXISTING BUSINESS

1.	Adjusted value of tangible net worth	$224,000
2.	Earning power at 15 percent	33,600
3.	Reasonable salary for owner or manager	40,000
		73,600
4.	Average annual net earnings before subtracting owner's salary	83,600
5.	Extra earning power of business (line 4: total of lines 2 and 3)	10,000
6.	Value of intangibles using four-year profit figure for moderately well-established firm in (4 years: line 5)	40,000
7.	Offering price (line 1; line 6)	$264,000

estimated profits, the more you will pay for goodwill. The less certain you are (the higher you perceive your risk to be), the less you will pay.

If you assume a 25 percent rate of return on estimated earnings coming from goodwill, then the value of the intangible assets is $10,000/0.25, or $40,000. Usually this relationship is expressed as a ratio or multiplier of 4, "four times (excess) earnings." You would expect to recover the amount invested in goodwill in no more than four years. When you put these two figures together, you come up with an offering price of $264,000 for the business—net tangible assets of $224,000 at liquidation value plus goodwill valued at $40,000. The calculations for this price are shown in Table 6.2.

If the average annual net earnings of the business before subtracting the owner's salary (line 4) was $73,600 or less, then there is no goodwill value. Even though the business may have existed for a long time, the earnings would be less than you could earn through outside investment. In that case, your price would be determined by capitalizing the average annual profit (net earnings minus all expenses and owner's salary) by the normal or expected rate of return on investment in this business. For example,

$$\text{Profit} = \$73,600 - \$40,000 = \$33,600$$

$$\text{Offering Price} = \$33,600/0.15 = \$224,000$$

Valuing goodwill is a highly subjective process. The value of intangible assets comes down to what you think they are worth and what you are willing to pay. You will need to negotiate with the seller to reach a consensus.

Buying the Business

To complete the purchase of your business, you need to negotiate the terms of the deal and prepare for the closing.

Terms of Sale

After a price for the business has been agreed upon, the terms of sale need to be negotiated. Few buyers are able to raise the funds required to pay cash for a business. A lump-sum payment may be in neither the buyer's nor the seller's best interests for tax reasons, unless the seller intends to reinvest in another business. Paying in installments is often the most practical solution.

By building installment payments into your cash-flow projection, you should be assured that the business can be paid for out of earnings. Installments assure the seller that his investment in the business will be returned on a tax-deferred basis, as opposed to paying all taxes at one time with a lump-sum payment. With an installment sale, the seller has some motivation to help with the buyer's success.

A seller may need to take steps to make the business more affordable. One way to do so is by *thinning the assets*. That is, the seller can adjust the assets to be more manageable for the new owner in one or more of the following ways:

- Separate real estate ownership from business ownership. The new owner leases rather than purchases the building. The buyer has less to borrow, and the seller receives a steady rental income.

- Lease equipment and/or fixtures in the same manner as real estate.

- Sell off excess inventory.

- Factor accounts receivable or carry the old accounts.

If you are buying the stock of a business rather than just the assets, you need protection from unknown tax liabilities. The best way to accomplish this is to place part of the purchase price (anywhere from 5 percent to 30 percent) in an escrow account. This *holdback money* is earmarked to pay for any corporate liabilities, including taxes owed, that arise after the deal has closed.

Closing the Deal

When you and the seller have reached an agreement on the sale of the business, several conditions must be met to ensure a smooth, legal transaction. Closing can be handled by using either a settlement attorney or an escrow settlement.

A *settlement attorney* acts as a neutral party by drawing up the necessary documents and representing both the buyer and the seller. Both parties meet with the settlement attorney at the agreed-upon closing date to sign the papers after all the conditions of the sale have been met, such as financing being secured by the buyer and a search completed to determine whether any liens against the business's assets exist.

In an *escrow settlement,* the buyer deposits the money, and the seller provides the bill of sale and other documents to an escrow agent. You can find an escrow agent at most financial institutions, such as banks and trusts that have escrow departments, or through an escrow company. The escrow agent holds the funds and documents until proof is shown that all conditions of the sale have been satisfied. When these conditions are met, the escrow agent releases the funds and documents to the rightful owners.

Taking Over a Family Business

A fourth route into small business (besides starting from scratch, buying an existing business, or franchising) is taking over a family business. This alternative offers special opportunities and risks.

What Is Different About Family Businesses?

Family businesses are those in which two or more members of the same family control, are directly involved in, and own a majority of the business. Family businesses account for 80 percent of all businesses in the United States and are responsible for nearly 50 percent of the U.S. gross domestic product (GDP).[18] They are obviously an important part of our economy, but what makes them different from nonfamily businesses? Two critical factors are (1) the complex interrelationships of family members interacting with one another and interacting with the business, and (2) the intricate succession planning needed.

> "Family businesses account for more than 50 percent of the U.S. GDP"

Profile in Entrepreneurship
More Than Rice and Beans

Goya Foods Vice President and Chief Operations Officer Andy Unanue gets the same e-mail forwarded to him almost daily: "You're Hispanic if . . . ."And inevitably the first item on the list is "You have Goya foods in your kitchen cabinet."

The e-mail makes Unanue and many other Hispanic Americans smile, because we know it's true. From Cubans' beloved black beans and Venezuelans' cornmeal arepas to Mexicans' flautas and Spaniards' gazpacho, Goya's got the globe's kitchens and dining room tables covered with adobos, salsitas, fruit nectars, and a thousand other foodstuffs.

Goya Foods is the largest Hispanic family-owned food company in the United States. Headquartered in Secaucus, New Jersey, it had $750 million in sales in 2002 and looks forward to a projected 7 percent jump in the future.

Talk about a family affair: Don Joe is one of Goya founder Prudencio's four sons. Don Joe's nephew and Andy's cousin Peter is Goya's vice president of distribution. One of Don Joe's brothers, Frank, ran Goya's Puerto Rican operation until his death. Another brother, Ulpiano, left the company in 1969. Andy's introduction into the business began after seventh grade; during that summer and those that followed, he worked in every department. By the time he was 30 and a graduate of the University of Miami and Thunderbird graduate school in Arizona, he had done everything from unloading trucks in the warehouse to running the company's Dominican Republic facility.

But he had little executive experience. The turning point came in 1998, when his older brother Joseph was diagnosed with a bone-marrow cell disorder. Andy was named interim vice president while his brother underwent a bone-marrow transplant. Before leaving, Joseph gave Andy a crash course in running the company; then Andy flew to Seattle, where he became his brother's main bone-marrow donor. During their time together, the siblings talked business—and Joseph taught Andy things like the importance of building a loyal staff.

Talk about stress. "My key incentive was trying to keep my brother alive, but it's stressful when you don't have daily contact with your management team."

Joseph died in late 1998, whereupon Andy was made vice president. He worked hard at carrying out his brother's legacy by building a loyal workforce, understanding his customers, and keeping quality high. His father made him chief operating officer in June 2000.

SOURCE: Gigi Anders, "More Than Rice and Beans," *Hispanic Trends*, www.hispaniconline.com/hh03/mainpages/culture/cruisne-goya.htm

Complex Interrelationships

When you run a family business, you have three overlapping perspectives on its operation (see Figure 6.2).[19] For example, suppose a family member needs a job. From the family perspective, you would see the business as an opportunity to help one of your own. From the ownership perspective, you might be concerned about the effect of a new hire on profits. From a management perspective, you would be concerned about how this hire would affect nonfamily employees.

Everyone involved in a family business will have a different perspective, depending on each person's position within the business. The successful leader of this business must maintain all three perspectives simultaneously.

Planning Succession

Many entrepreneurs dream of the time when they will be able to "pass the torch" of their successful business on to their children. Unfortunately, many factors, such as jealousy, lack of interest, or ineptitude, can cause the flame to go out. Less than one-third of family businesses survive through the second generation, and fewer than one in ten makes it through the third generation.[20] The major cause of family business failure is lack of a business succession plan. There appear to be four reasons for family inability to create such a document:

1. It is difficult for senior family members to address their own mortality.

2. Many senior family members are worried that the way younger family members run the business will not maintain its success. Only 20 percent are confident of the next generation's commitment to the business.[21]

3. Transfer of control is put off until too late because of seniors' concern for their personal long-term financial security.

4. Seniors (like most small business owners) are too personally tied to the business and lacking in outside interests to be attracted to retirement.[22]

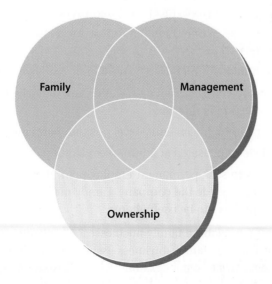

Figure 6.2
FAMILY BUSINESS
PERSPECTIVES

The Family Business Owner Views the Business and What Goes on Within It from Three Different Overlapping Perspectives.

Figure 6.3
SUCCESSION MODEL OF
FAMILY BUSINESS

*Passing on the Ownership of a
Family Business Is a Difficult
Process. The Successor Must Earn
the Trust of Employees Before
Becoming a Successful Leader.*

If the potential successor wants to take over the family business, she must gain acceptance and trust within the organization (see Figure 6.3). When a family member enters the business, he is not usually immediately accepted by nonfamily employees. This skepticism increases when that person moves up to a leadership position within the business. The successor must earn credibility by showing that she is capable of running the business. Only after being accepted and earning credibility will the new manager have legitimate power and become successful as the new leader.[23]

General Family Business Policies

Because family businesses have situations and problems unique to them, they need a set of policies that are not needed in other types of businesses. Such a set of policies can help prevent problems such as animosity from nonfamily employees, which can decrease their motivation and productivity.[24]

- To be hired, family members must meet the same criteria as nonfamily employees.
- In performance reviews, family members must meet the same standards as nonfamily employees.
- Family members should be supervised by nonfamily employees when possible.
- If family members are younger than age 30, they are only eligible for "temporary" employment (less than one year).
- No family member can stay in an entry-level position permanently.
- All positions will be compensated at fair market value.
- For family members to seek permanent employment, they must have at least five years' experience outside the company. Family members must prove their worth to another employer to be useful here.[25]

Want more information about family businesses? Check out www.fambiz.com (more than 300 articles on family business issues and additional links) and www.familybusinessmagazine.com/index.html (*Family Business* magazine online).

Summary

- **The advantages and disadvantages of buying an existing business**

The advantages of buying an existing business include the fact that it is an already functioning operation, customers are used to doing business with it, and you will break even sooner than if you started from the ground up. The disadvantages include the difficulty of changing the business's image or the way it does business, outdated inventory and equipment, too high a purchase price, poor location, and liabilities for previous contracts.

- **How to find a business for sale**

Newspaper advertising is one source for finding a business for sale, and word of mouth through friends and family may be another. Bankers, lawyers, accountants, real estate brokers, business brokers, and Small Business Administration representatives can be other good sources.

- **The means of measuring a business's condition and determining why it is being sold**

Profitability, profit trends, comparison of operating ratios to industry standards, and total asset worth are all measures of the financial health of a business. There are as many reasons for selling a business as there are businesses to sell. As a prospective buyer, you must cut through what is being said to determine the reality of a situation. You must develop an ability to analyze a market and estimate potential profits and worth.

- **The difference between tangible and intangible assets**

Tangible assets are those that can be seen and examined. Real estate, inventory, and equipment are important tangible assets. Intangible assets, though unseen, are no less valuable. Goodwill; leases and contracts; and patents, copyrights, and trademarks are examples.

- **The price to pay for a business**

The offering price to pay for a business is calculated by adding the adjusted value of tangible assets to the value of intangible assets (including goodwill, if appropriate).

- **Factors important when finalizing the purchase of a business**

Once the price of a business is agreed upon, the terms of sale need to be negotiated—including setting up installment provisions and thinning of the assets. Before the closing date the buyer puts an agreed upon amount of money into an escrow account.

- **What makes family businesses different from other types of businesses**

The two primary differences between family businesses and other businesses are the complex interrelationships among family members and their interaction in the business, and the intricate succession planning needed.

Questions for Review and Discussion

1. What are some arguments for buying an established business rather than starting one yourself?

2. When buying an established business, what questions should you ask about it? From whom might you seek information about the business?

3. Which is more important in appraising a business: profitability or return on investment? Discuss.

4. Should one ever consider purchasing a presently unsuccessful business (that is, a business with relatively low or no profits)? Explain.

5. What factors warrant special attention in appraising a firm's (a) inventory, (b) equipment, and (c) accounts receivable?

6. What should a prospective buyer know about the seller's inventory sources and other resource contacts? How is this information obtained?

7. Does competition help or hurt the valuation of a business? Explain.

8. Discuss the ways in which the tangible assets of a business may be valued. What is the most realistic approach to determining a business's true value? Why?

9. What is goodwill, and how may its value be determined?

10. How can a buyer determine the rate of return to use in evaluating the worth of a business?

11. What is meant by "thinning the assets"? Cite examples.

12. Discuss the advantages of working through a business broker. What precautions should one take when dealing with a business broker?

Questions for Critical Thinking

1. You are analyzing the financial records of a business you have been thinking about buying. You discover that although the firm has excellent current and quick-asset ratios by industry standards (meaning its current assets are higher than its current liabilities), its cash is low, and it hasn't paid its bills on time. What might have caused this problem? Would it influence your decision to buy the business?

2. A mother believes that all of her family's children should have equal ownership of the family business regardless of their participation in the business. The father sees the situation completely differently; he believes that the children who are actively involved should receive more ownership. How can this dispute be resolved?

Experience This . . .

Look in your local Yellow Pages for the name of a business broker in your community. Call the broker and ask about the process of buying an existing business.

What terms and conditions are common? What businesses does the broker currently represent?

What Would You Do?

A family in the Pacific Northwest owns a retail clothing store. Two brothers work in the business, and their mother is president of the company. Sibling rivalry was a problem while the boys were growing up, and now that they are in the family business together, it is reappearing. In addition to her role as president, the mother often finds herself playing the role of referee and "chief emotional officer" when the young men fight. The continued rivalry between the brothers and the mother's need to intervene between them has interfered with a normally functional business. The family realizes that its business

system is entangled with its family system, but they are not sure what to do about it.

Questions

1. What should the mother do to help her family (and her business) operate more normally?

2. Would bringing in a nonfamily manager with direct-line control over each brother help or cause more problems? How can they ever decide who will eventually take over control of the business?

CHAPTER CLOSING CASE

TOUGH SALE

Stephen Sullivan just couldn't stomach the idea. He and his partner and friend, Brian Cousins, had spent seven years building Cloudveil, an outdoor sportswear company devoted to hard-core skiers and mountain climbers. And it had been a blast. Cloudveil, based in Jackson, Wyoming, was the kind of place where the partners designed a prototype garment one day and tested it on the slopes the next. Yet, despite 2004 revenue of about $5 million, the company was cash-strapped, in a never-ending struggle to raise enough money to fuel production. The best solution, it seemed, would be to sell the business to a larger company with the capital and infrastructure Cloudveil so desperately needed. And that's what had Sullivan so worried. Selling out, he feared, could mean squandering the brand credibility he and Cousins had created. And that could mean the end of Cloudveil.

The partners, who had both moved to Jackson for its world-class skiing, met in the early 1990s while working in a local ski shop. When they weren't working, they skied the rugged Teton Mountains. Off the slopes, they dreamed of designing their own line of outdoor apparel. That dream became a reality in early 1997, after Sullivan received a pair of ski pants from a friend who had just returned from the French Alps. Every day for a week, Sullivan wore the lightweight pants on the slopes. Flexible and breathable, yet warm, they were unlike any ski pants he had worn. He set up shop in his cabin and started designing ski apparel using the same soft shell fabric. Cloudveil's first line appeared in 13 retail stores nationwide that fall.

From the beginning, Cousins and Sullivan focused on serving Jackson's hard-core backcountry skiing community. They sponsored ski competitions and rock-climbing festivals, and the grass-roots approach worked. By 2002 Cloudveil had 150 products, 15 employees, and about $2 million in sales.

Along with that growth came unexpected headaches. The biggest problem was managing cash flow. It took five or six months for clothes to be manufactured and distributed, which meant Cloudveil had to find a way to finance the next season's production before collecting on the current one. Sullivan began to spend less time on product development and more on financial issues—dealing with complaints from unpaid designers, for example. They brought on two partners—seasoned executives Jon Boris and Michael McGregor—who streamlined operations by automating Cloudveil's order fulfillment process.

Still, even as sales continued to climb, cash remained a persistent problem. By the summer of 2004, the partners knew they had to do something and began exploring financing options with venture capitalists and private equity groups. Cloudveil also began receiving cold calls from would-be strategic buyers who wanted to purchase the company outright. In many ways, that option made the most sense. After all, Cloudveil needed more than just money. The business also needed infrastructure and time to expand the brand without pressure from investors looking for big returns.

But a sale had never been in the game plan, and the idea of it was a tough pill to swallow—especially for Sullivan, who had been the company's creative force and feared that the Cloudveil brand would be neglected, or diluted, by a larger company with several apparel lines. Even so, the partners agreed to meet with suitors and weigh their options.

The process came to a head last October, when Cloudveil's winter catalogs arrived at the company's Jackson warehouse. The catalogs, which were expected to drive about a third of the company's annual sales, were ready to be mailed to 300,000 potential customers. There was only one problem: The company didn't have enough money to pay for the postage. Cousins and Sullivan quickly scheduled a call with Boris and McGregor to find a way to raise the $56,000 needed. The four partners decided to forego their salaries for four months until the catalog sales began to roll in.

But enough was enough, the partners agreed. Just before the catalog debacle, Cousins had received an e-mail from Jim Reilly, senior vice president at Sports Brand International, a New York City apparel company that owns the Italian sportswear lines Fila and Ciesse. SBI was interested in an acquisition, the note said. Cousins called Reilly and liked what he heard. SBI was eager to capture a piece of the growing outdoor apparel market, and Cloudveil had the expertise it needed. Reilly seemed frank and sincere, Cousins recalls.

Questions

1. Can Steven and Brian sell the sportswear business without selling out?

SOURCE: From Dimitra Kessenides, "For Cash-Strapped Cloudveil, It Was a Very Hard Offer to Refuse," *Inc.*, August 2005, 44–45. Copyright © 2006 Mansueto Ventures LLC, publisher of Inc. Magazine, New York, NY 10017. Reprinted with permission.

Test Prepper

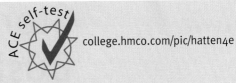

college.hmco.com/pic/hatten4e

You've read the chapter, studied the key terms, and the exam is any day now. Think you're ready to ace it? Take this sample test to gauge your comprehension of chapter material. You can check your answers at the back of the book. Want more test questions? Visit the student website at college.hmco.com/pic/hatten4e and take the ACE and ACE+ quizzes for more practice.

Multiple Choice

1. The value of tangible assets plus the value of intangible assets plus profit potential results in a starting point for
   a. due diligence
   b. purchase price
   c. goodwill
   d. dead stock

2. The critical process of investigation that begins at the moment of interest in a business is called
   a. due diligence
   b. goodwill
   c. forensic investigation
   d. due scrutiny

3. The tactic of making a business more affordable by doing things like separating the real estate from a business is called
   a. churning the butter
   b. dividing the loaves
   c. thinning the assets
   d. cooking the books

4. Which of the following is *not* an overlapping perspective of running a family business?
   a. family
   b. management
   c. ownership
   d. in-laws

5. Family businesses are important to the U.S. economy, generating what percentage of the U.S. GDP?
   a. 10 percent
   b. 25 percent
   c. 50 percent
   d. 90 percent

Fill in the Blank

1. Money that is paid for a business but placed into an account unavailable to the seller for a specific period of time to make sure taxes and liabilities have been paid is called _____.

2. In general, business buyers should be at least very _____, if not to the point of being cynical.

3. Compensation to a business seller for helping a buyer prevent beginner's mistakes is called _____.

4. Business valuation is a subjective process at best. No matter what method is used, it still merely sets points from which _____ can begin.

5. One of the most difficult issues in family business is _____ planning.

## chapter 7

Starting a New Business

After reading this chapter, you should be able to:

- Discuss the advantages and disadvantages of starting a business from scratch.

- Describe types of new businesses and discuss the characteristics commonly shared by fast-growth companies.

- Evaluate potential startups and suggest sources of business ideas.

- Explain the most important points to consider when starting a new business.

A lot of people create new products, new services, and new businesses—not many create whole new worlds. That's exactly what 38-year-old Philip Rosedale did with his startup company, Linden Lab, and its only product, 3-D virtual world Second Life.

In Second Life, people create virtual "second lives" by downloading the program, installing it, creating a new account, and following a series of prompts such as how to interact with the environment and how to customize the character's or avatar's look (which can be anyone or anything your imagination can dream up). Then you can wander (or fly or crawl) from location to location chatting with others or checking stuff out. Or you can really engage by buying land and starting your own virtual business. The currency for Second Life is Linden Dollars—which can be converted back into U.S. dollars. And converted they are! As of March 2007, Second Life businesses are earning $15 million (real dollars) worth of goods and services per month.

Everything in Second Life was created by residents—from houses to clothes to a detailed replica of Rockefeller Center and human-size raccoons. Real-world

Philip Rosedale, Founder of Second Life.

companies like Toyota and American Apparel have a presence. So your avatar can test-drive a new Toyota Scion or buy clothes from American Apparel for your virtual persona.

Rosedale started a database system business for car dealerships when he was 17 to put himself through college. In 1994 he got a job in the Bay Area with an office next to an early Internet service provider. They ran a line over the ceiling for an Internet connection. He remembers thinking, "Man, you could use the Internet to hook together a lot of computers. You could simulate a world, and then we could all go in there."

Of course, at that time computers were not powerful enough for 3-D video. In 1996 Rosedale had met Rob Glaser, CEO of RealNetworks, and decided to get the experience he would need creating complex systems working at RealNetworks. By 1999 Philip was creating what would become Second Life. After six years of ups and downs, by 2003 they thought the whole thing was dead—until they had an idea: Let it go. They had a core group who liked what was happening. Rosedale said to them, "What they have in Second Life is real and all yours." Instead of seeing Second Life as a video game, people saw that by owning intellectual property and virtual real estate, they had incentive to make it grow. That change in mind-set lit the fuse, and Second Life took off.

Go to www.secondlife.com, look around, and imagine what it would take for you to create a new virtual business. Pretty cool.

SOURCES: Sara Wilson, "Unreal World," *Entrepreneur,* March 2007, 42; Philip Rosedale, as told to Michael Fitzgerald, "Only the Money is Real," *Inc.*. February 2007, 80–85; Gary Eastwood, "How to Do Business in a Second Life," *Computer Weekly,* March 6, 2007, 42–44; David Kirkpatrick, "It's Not a Game," *Fortune,* February 2007, 34–38 ; David Carr, "Is Business Ready for Second Life," *Baseline,* March 2007, 30–47; Joe Hutsko, "Living a Second Life," *Macworld,* April 2007, 82–83.

About Startups

Starting a business from the ground up is more difficult than buying an existing business or a franchise, because nothing is in place. There is also more risk involved. However, to many people, the process of taking an idea through all the steps, time, money, and energy needed to become a viable business is the essence of entrepreneurship. The period in which you create a brand new business is an *exciting* time.

Would you prefer to be totally independent? Can you set up an accounting system that is readable to you and acceptable to your bank and the Internal Revenue Service? Can you come up with a promotional campaign that will get you noticed? Are you willing to devote the time and sources needed to succeed? Can you find sources of products, components, or distribution? Can you find employees with the skills your business will need? If so, you may be ready to start your own business.

" Do you want to be totally independent at work? If so, you may be ready to start your own business "

Advantages of Starting from Scratch

When you begin a business from scratch, you have the freedom to mold your new creation into whatever you feel is appropriate. Other advantages of starting from scratch include the ability to create your own distinctive competitive advantage. Many entrepreneurs thrive on the challenge of beginning a new enterprise. You can feel pride when creating something that didn't exist before and in realizing your own goals. The fact that the business is all new can be an advantage in itself—there is no carryover baggage of someone else's mistakes, location, employees, or products. You establish your own image.

Disadvantages of Starting from Scratch

The risk of failure is higher with a startup than with the purchase of an existing business or franchise. You may have trouble identifying market needs in your area that you are able to satisfy. You must make people aware that your business exists—it can be tough to get noticed. Also, you must deal with thousands of details that you didn't foresee, from how to choose the right vendors, to where to put the coffeepot, to where to find motivated employees.

Types of New Businesses

No matter what type of business you are starting, your most important resource is your time. Nothing happens until you make it happen. You have to create and build on the enthusiasm that will attract others to your idea and your business. In the beginning, the only thing you have is your vision, and only you will be responsible for its success.

As the service industry plays an ever greater role in the U.S. economy, startup businesses are becoming increasingly popular. The reason? Service businesses tend to be more **labor intensive,** or dependent on the services of people, as opposed to manufacturing businesses, which are more **capital intensive,** or dependent on equipment and capital.

labor intensive
A business that is more dependent on the services of people than on money and equipment.

capital intensive
A business that depends greatly upon equipment and capital for its operations.

Start by finding out all you can about your industry and trade area from books, newsletters, trade publications, magazines, organizations, and people already in business. After all your questions are answered and your investigation is complete, if you are ready for the challenge, you will find several possible routes for starting your business.

Let's look at a few of those routes that people take, aside from seeking to achieve the typical goal of a low-growth, stable startup that will provide the small business owner with a comfortable, modest living.

e-business
A business that shares information, maintains customer relationships, and conducts transactions by means of telecommunications networks.

E-Businesses

Nothing has changed the small business landscape quite like the Internet. It is the ultimate in making one-to-one connections—which is where small businesses have always thrived. You can begin an **e-business** with relatively low overhead and potentially reach markets all over the world. But keep in mind that the Internet, though a powerful tool, doesn't make all other business metrics obsolete. You still have to make a profit, keep employees happy and motivated, provide customer service, and offer a product that inspires customers to turn over their hard-earned money to obtain. Contrary to popular opinion at one time, electronic business is not all about "click here to buy." As the Internet has begun to mature, the e-business model has evolved into "click here to get more information," "click here to start the just-in-time inventory flow," or "click here to let a new employee go through the orientation process." In other words, e-business has evolved into part of a multi-channel marketing strategy that benefits from traditional business models and lessons that don't have to be thrown out with the emergence of new media such as the Internet.[1]

Describing electronic business in a few paragraphs is a difficult task, because one simple model does not exist. Your e-biz may be something as simple as taking a current avocation (like tying flies for fishing or making custom pillows) and selling your concoctions on eBay, business to consumer. You may not ever personally touch a product, but provide value by connecting other businesses, business to business. In these few paragraphs we won't get into the technical details of mips, megs, and browsers. You, as a webpreneur, will need an understanding of the leading edge of technology. Unfortunately (or fortunately), that edge moves so quickly that we can't do justice to it here. What we can cover here are basic characteristics that a successful Web business must possess.

- *Have a sound business strategy, beginning with having a good reason to be online.* But how do you commit to long-term strategic planning in an economy that moves at the speed of the Internet? John Noble, vice president of corporate Internet strategy at Putnam Investments, suggests that you need to figure out which strategic moves you want to make first. Only then can you figure out how to use technology to accomplish your strategy. If you make decisions based strictly on what is technically possible today, you will be out of position in 6 to 12 months. Doing business on the Internet has become a two-pronged endeavor: You need both bright ideas and the capacity to execute them. As a consequence, Internet strategy has evolved into more of a team effort among people who provide an overarching vision and the *information technology (IT)* people who turn those visions into reality.[2]

- *Have a clear market analysis and create traffic coverage.* Believe it or not, not everyone is on the Web! Are your customers? If they aren't, why are you? The "if you build it, they will come" model seldom works.[3] As with brick-and-mortar businesses, you need to generate traffic into your site. Jonathan Wall of online IT reseller dabs.com says that IT skills such as Java and .NET programming are not difficult for him to source. The most complex and sophisticated part of his business is actually marketing.[4]

- *Logistics are huge.* When people buy online, something usually has to get shipped. As Wall notes, "It's not hard to build a website that takes orders 24/7. But being able to take an order at 9:30 p.m. and have it delivered by 10 a.m. the next day takes a massive investment and a lot of hard work."

- *Use the Internet to save money.* E-business is as much about reducing costs as it is about generating revenue. Creating value-chain efficiencies and meeting increasing customer expectations is what e-biz is about.

- *Build your competitive advantage.* E-business can be boiled down to four ideas: accelerating the *speed* of business, reducing *costs,* enhancing *customer* service, and improving the business *process.* The field is still wide open. Indeed, 78 percent of chief information officers report that they have not tapped the full competitive advantage of e-business.[5]

Home-Based Businesses

The fastest-growing segment of business startups comprises those operated out of people's homes. According to the American Association of Home-Based Businesses (AAHBB), the number of people running businesses from home tops 24 million.[6] Approximately 30 percent of **home-based businesses** deal with financial or computer-related services. Two points stand out as advantages for this type of business: schedule flexibility and low overhead.

> **home-based businesses**
> A popular type of business that operates from the owner's home, rather than from a separate location.

Technology has done much to make this trend possible. Notebook computers, DSL and cable Internet connections, wireless modems, facsimile machines, PDAs (personal digital assistants, such as a Palm Pilot), cellular phones, and laser printers all contribute to flexibility, with quality results now readily available while working at home. The idea is becoming more widely accepted.

Meg Gottemoller left her position as a vice president of Chase Manhattan Bank in New York to start her own communications and training consultancy. Martha Gay runs her own corporate research business from her home in Fort Washington, Pennsylvania. Both of these businesses are successful because they take advantage of the trend toward *corporate outsourcing.* As larger companies reduce the sizes of their workforce, they must contract out work that was once performed by their own workers. Such outsourcing provides many opportunities for small businesses.

Running a business out of your home can provide flexibility in your personal life, but it takes serious organization and self-discipline. Let's look at some of this approach's advantages and disadvantages.

Running a Home-Based Business Provides Flexibility to Also Care for Other Important Things.

Advantages of Home-Based Business   Advantages of a home-based business include the following:

- Control over work hours
- Convenience
- Ability to care for domestic responsibilities (such as children, parents, or the household)
- Low overhead expenses
- Lack of workplace distractions (coworkers popping in, chatting around the coffee machine)
- Decreased commute time
- Tax advantages

Disadvantages of Home-Based Business Disadvantages of a home-based business include the following:

- Difficulty setting aside long blocks of time
- Informal, cramped, insufficient workspace at home

- Demands on family members to cooperate
- Lack of respect (will people think you are unemployed or doing this as a hobby?)
- Domestic interruptions (houses can get noisy and crowded.)
- Lack of workplace camaraderie (houses can get quiet and lonely.)
- Zoning issues[7]

What kind of businesses can you run from your home? According to *Entrepreneur's Start-Ups* magazine, some possibilities include specialty travel tours, computer consultant, personal chef, concierge service, website consultant, event planner, cart or kiosk business, translation service, feng shui consultant, online auctioneer, and technology writer. Check out this magazine and other articles to brainstorm ideas.[8]

Starting a Business on the Side

Many people start businesses while keeping their regular jobs. Although this approach is generally not recommended as a way to enter business, the Bureau of Labor Statistics estimates that more than 1.2 million people take this step each year.[9] Working a full-time job while getting a business off the ground may require superhuman organizational skills and discipline, yet it can offer some notable advantages. A transitional period can allow you to test the waters without pursuing complete immersion in the marketplace. You can also prepare yourself psychologically, experientially, and financially, so that when—or if—you leave your job, you will have a running start. Before taking this route, however, you should be absolutely clear on your company's moonlighting policy and avoid doing anything that might resemble a conflict of interest. Moonlighting policies could include not starting an identical business or not soliciting current customers.

Fast-Growth Startups

Not every new business can be or desires to be a hypergrowth company like, for example, the top company on the 2007 *Inc.* 500 list, MemberHealth, had a three-year growth rate of 20,129 percent! It is informative to see what characteristics and patterns these fast-growth companies shared in *Inc.*'s database (see Figure 7.1).

1. *They rely on team effort.* In contrast to low-growth firms, most fast-growth companies are started by partnerships. In an increasingly complex and competitive environment, teams can deal with a much wider range of problems than can an individual operating alone. Fifty-six percent of the fast-growth CEOs started with partners or cofounders.

2. *They're headed by people who know their line of work.* A majority of the CEOs of high-growth companies had at least 10 years of experience in the industry. In contrast, owners of low-growth companies typically have just a few years of prior experience.

3. *They're headed by people who have started other businesses.* Research shows that 63 percent of the founders of high-growth companies had previously started other companies, and 23 percent had started three or more businesses. This compares to only 20 percent of all business owners who had been self-employed previously. Some 61 percent started in the founder's home.

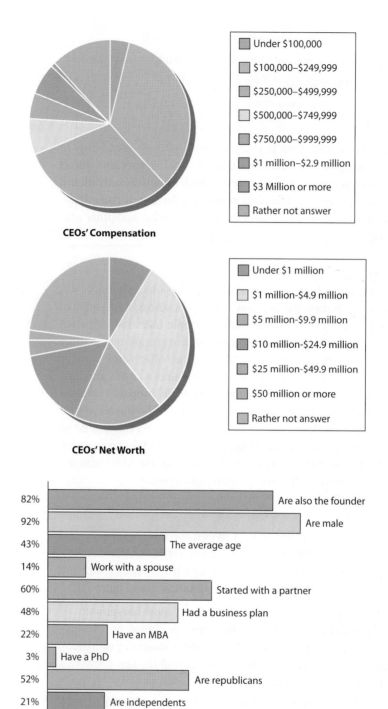

Figure 7.1
INC. 500 BY THE NUMBERS

Information About the CEOs and Companies Included in the Inc. *500 Provides Some Interesting Insights.*

4. *They're making big bucks.* The 445 men and 57 women who run *Inc.* 500 companies take risks and are handsomely rewarded for their derring-do. Forty percent take home more than $500,000 annually, and more than 20 percent have generated a net worth in excess of $7.5 million.

5. *They're high-tech.* Of the fast-growth companies, 41 percent use new technology to achieve a competitive advantage. Another 40 percent say that new technology gives them somewhat of an edge.

6. *They're better financed—but not by much.* This factor is more difficult to measure because of the subjectivity in determining what "well financed" means. Thirteen percent of *Inc.* 500 companies started with an investment of less than $1,000, and 23 percent began with between $1,000 and $10,000. Only 27 percent had initial startup capital exceeding $100,000. Fifty-three percent of CEOs used personal assets as sole startup funds.

7. *Their markets aren't just local.* Successful companies seek to expand their horizons. The majority of *Inc.* 500 companies get more than half of their revenues from outside their home region, and 38 percent are international players. They are looking for **strategic alliances** as well. One-third have entered into agreements with large companies, which in turn have expanded their markets.[10]

> **strategic alliance**
> A partnership between two businesses that join forces to produce a product or serve a market, in a step that neither could take alone. Often used as a means to enter a foreign market.

Evaluating Potential Startups

The first thing you need to start your own business is an idea. Of course, not every idea is automatically a viable business opportunity. You must be able to turn your idea into a profitable business. How do you tell when an idea is also an opportunity? Where do people come up with viable business ideas that are opportunities?

Business Ideas

Although there is no shortage of ideas for new and improved products and services, there is a difference between ideas and opportunities. Are all ideas business opportunities? No. A business opportunity is attractive, durable, timely, and anchored in a product or service that creates or adds value for its buyer or end user. Many ideas for new products and businesses do not add value for customers or users. Maybe the time for the idea has yet to come, or maybe it has already passed.

Consider the idea for a new device for removing the crown caps that were common on bottles of soft drinks for many years. You could concoct an exotic and ingenious tool that would be technically feasible to produce, but is there an opportunity to build a business from it? Not since soft drink and beer companies switched to resealable bottles and screw-off tops to solve the same consumer problem that your invention does. Good idea—but no opportunity.

An idea that is too far ahead of the market can be just as bad as one that is too far behind consumer desires. In 1987 Jerry Kaplan left his job as a software writer for Lotus Development to start Go Computers because he thought the world was ready for portable, pen-based computers. He had some big-time backing from IBM and AT&T, which together pitched in $75 million to help with the startup. Kaplan had a vision of salespeople, lawyers, insurance adjusters, and millions of

Reality Check

Startup Myths and Realities

The human mind has a remarkable ability to rationalize just about anything. If we want to do something, we often tell ourselves it will work—whether or not there is a realistic chance of success. But you can build competitive advantage only by basing actions on reality, not myth. Consider the following myths:

Myth 1: I'm Smart—I Can Just Wing It

Reality: Face it—you need a plan. One of the few things that a group of small business lenders, advisors, and consultants would agree on is the need for a business plan.

Myth 2: I Can Do It on a Shoestring

Reality: While no one ever has enough money, having too little can be doom. Most businesses require a great deal of spending before they can begin to develop cash flow.

Myth 3: No Sweat—I Have a Great Idea

Reality: About 5 percent of the success equation is having a good idea. Great ideas are an important start for businesses, but ideas alone won't get you far. You also need the resources, skills, and products.

Myth 4: I've Got Nothing Better to Do

Reality: You cannot start a successful small business halfheartedly. Starting a business because you have been laid off from your job and just need something to do is not a good idea.

Myth 5: Maybe Starting a Business Will Help Our Marriage

Reality: A risky bet. The stress involved in starting a business can amplify marital weaknesses. Marriage counselors advise people not to start businesses until they are emotionally stable.

Myth 6: A Bad Economy Will Mean Fewer Competitors

Reality: Maybe, but it can also make the survivors fiercer competitors.

Myth 7: I'm Mad as Hell and I'm Not Going to Take It Anymore

Reality: The frustration that you have built up with your current job can be a good rationale for starting your own business if your anger is focused on positive outcomes. Anger in general won't get you ahead.

Myth 8: If I Can't Think of Anything Else, I'll Open a Bar

Reality: Despite common opinion, restaurants and bars are not easy businesses to start or run. The rationale that everyone likes to eat and drink does not hold up. Having dined out regularly or bellied up to a bar does not qualify as experience in this business.

SOURCE: From "Don't Believe It," by David Kansas, *Wall Street Journal: Report on Small Business*, October 15, 1993, p. R8. Copyright © 1993 by Dow Jones & Co., Inc. Reproduced with permission of Dow Jones & Co., Inc. via Copyright Clearance Center.

---

other people writing away on Go computers as if they were paper. Unfortunately, consumers at the time found that computers could not recognize their handwriting or convert it into print. The market was ready, but the technology was not. Nearly two decades later, many consumers regularly use a PDA-like palm-sized computer that can do exactly what Kaplan envisioned. Even with a great idea, a talented leader, and strong financial backing, Go Computers sold only 20,000 units and lasted only three years—it was ahead of its market. When Go closed, Kaplan said that he believed that "a new class of computing devices will come into being . . . it's just a question of when."[11] He was right—just look around today at the success of handheld computers. But a startup, even one with substantial resources, can't wait for technology or markets to catch up with an idea.

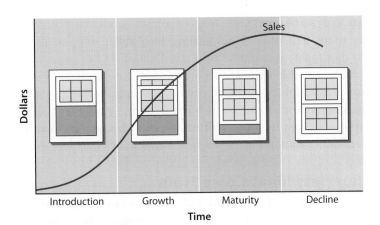

Harvard Business School professor Clayton M. Christiansen, in his book titled *The Innovator's Dilemma: When New Technologies Cause Great Firms to Fail,* discusses how some innovations *sustain* industries—offering better performance, more features, everything that existing customers are seeking. Other innovations *disrupt* an industry—bringing out useful products that people have never seen before.[12]

You've probably heard of the term **window of opportunity.** These windows constantly open and close (sometimes rapidly) as the market for a particular product ("product" meaning either goods or services) or business changes. Products go through stages of introduction, growth, maturity, and decline in the **product life cycle.** During the introduction stage, the window of opportunity is wide open because little or no competition exists. As products progress through this cycle, competition increases, consumer expectations expand, and profit margins decline so that the window of opportunity is not open quite as wide (see Figure 7.2).

Optimally, you want to get through while the window is still opening—if the opportunity is the right one for you. To decide whether you should pursue an opportunity, ask yourself the following questions about your business idea:

- Does your idea solve a consumer want or need? This answer can give you insight into current and future demand.
- If there is a demand, are there enough people who will buy your product to support a business? How much competition for that demand exists?
- Can this idea be turned into a *profitable* business?
- Do you have the skills needed to take advantage of this opportunity?
- Why hasn't anyone else done it? If others have, what happened to them?

In the idea stage of your thinking (before you actually pursue an opportunity), you should discuss your idea with a wide variety of people to get feedback on it. Although praise may make you feel good at this stage, what you really need are people who can objectively look for possible flaws and point out the shortcomings of your idea.

Your final decision as to whether your idea represents an opportunity that you should pursue will come from a combination of research and intuition. Both are valuable management tools, but don't rely exclusively on either. Although

> *window of opportunity*
> A period of time in which an opportunity is available.
>
> *product life cycle*
> Stages that products in a marketplace pass through over time.

research has kept some good ideas from becoming products or businesses, it has kept many more bad ones from turning into losing propositions. Do your homework; thoroughly investigate your possibilities. At the same time, don't get "analysis paralysis," which prevents you from acting because you think you need more testing or questioning—while the window of opportunity closes. Managerial decision making is as much an art as it is a science. Sometimes you will have to make decisions without the benefit of having every last shred of evidence possible. Get all the information that is practical, but also listen to your gut instincts.

Where Business Ideas Come From

The National Federation of Independent Business reports that prior work experience generates the majority of ideas for new businesses for both men and women, although it is a more common source for men. Women look slightly more to hobbies and personal interests for ideas for their businesses (see Figure 7.3).

Prior Work Experience   Experience can be a wonderful teacher. Working for someone else in your area of interest can help you to avoid many errors and begin to build competitive advantages. It gives you the chance to ask yourself, "What would I do differently, if I ran this business?"

One startup may even lead to another. Seeing opportunities for new ventures after starting the first business is known as the **corridor principle**.[13] Entrepreneurs start second, third, and succeeding businesses as they move down new venture corridors that did not open to them until they got into business. As we saw with fast-growth startups, 63 percent of fast-growth CEOs had started other companies in the past, suggesting that one idea really does lead to another.

Research shows that big ideas occur to small business owners almost twice as often after the business is already running as before it begins.[14] This trend illustrates that experience pays off whether you are working for someone else or for yourself.

> *corridor principle*
> The idea that opportunities become available to an entrepreneur only after the entrepreneur has started a business.

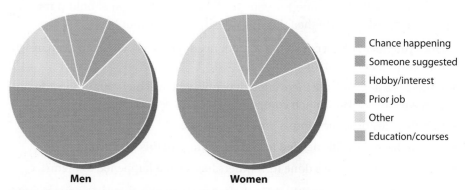

Men   **Women**

Figure 7.3

SOURCES OF NEW BUSINESS IDEAS AMONG MEN AND WOMEN

Prior Work Experience Is the Most Common Source of Ideas for New Businesses for Both Men and Women.

SOURCE: Arnold C. Cooper et al., "New Business in America," 1990, NFIB Foundation/VISA Business Card Primer, in William J. Dennis, Jr., *A Small Business Primer* (Washington, DC: National Federation of Independent Business, 1993), 17. Reprinted by permission of National Federation of Independent Business.

Hobbies and Avocations   Turning what you do for pleasure into a part-time or full-time business is a possibility that you should consider. It helps ensure that your business will be one that you enjoy and understand. If you enjoy fishing, could you potentially use your skills to become a guide? If you love pets, could you channel your affections into a dog-grooming or pet-sitting business?

Julian Bayley has turned an ice-carving hobby into a nice little business. When Elton John hosted his annual White Tie and Tiara charity gala at his mansion near Windsor Castle, ordinary dishes would not do. He called on Bayley's Canadian company, Ice Culture, to use its computer-aided machinery to mill caviar hors d'oeuvre trays for his 450 guests. Bayley has come a long way from his ice-carving hobby to designing and building a $45,000 computer-guided router modified for shaping crystal-clear ice. He also developed an ice lathe that can produce ice vases and oversized bottles. Pretty cool.

Chance Happening (Serendipity)   *Serendipity* means finding something valuable that you were not looking for. Sometimes business opportunities come to you unexpectedly. The ability to recognize them takes an open mind, flexibility, a sense of adventure, and good business sense.

Brother and sister Ethan and Abby Margalith had to borrow a truck in the summer of 1973 to move a few things to a local swap meet. Both were just out of high school and out of work. While driving the truck to the swap meet, the pair realized that moving could be their summer job. Their first truck was a 1944 weapons carrier that they got for free by rescuing it from a mudslide. Starving Student Moving Company became the low-priced alternative to other movers that were characterized by full uniforms and high prices. The Margaliths used their sense of humor in their advertising—one ad stated that they offered "24-hour service for lease breakers." Even without knowing what they were doing, they had more business than they could handle. Ethan has stated that it wasn't until he got to law school that he realized he and his sister were really running a business. He finished law school but decided that the moving business is fun, exciting, and profitable, so he stayed in the field with his sister. By 1999 Starving Student had 35 locations from California to Virginia. The company has proudly moved families, companies, government agencies like the U.S. Secret Service and the FBI, and even celebrities like Cher, Jerry Seinfeld, and Tom Hanks—and it all started with digging a truck out of the mud![15]

Hung Van Thai has struggled to make his entrepreneurial ideas work in a very tough environment—communist Vietnam. Thai started his first two private businesses successfully, only to have the government take them away. The first was a soap manufacturing operation that had sales of $5,000 per day, half of which was net profit. All too soon, however, government authorities shut down his operations because he was undercutting the state-owned soap producers. After that, Thai started his second business, making plastic slippers. Again, because of his success, he attracted government attention. But this time Thai offered to turn his business into a state-owned facility if the government would leave him alone, and his offer was accepted. In the late 1980s, as the Vietnamese government began easing up on economic controls, Thai saw his chance to once again start his own private company. His third startup, Hunsan Company, a manufacturer and retailer of sports shoes, has since thrived. Hunsan's sales have topped $12 million.

Creating Competitive Advantage

Creativity Is the Key

Once you have your business up and going (because of your creativity), how do you keep yourself and others in your business creative? Creativity is a matter of providing the proper business environment—your key to sustaining a competitive advantage. Almost every business has a creative pool with potential that is greater than its performance. How do you provide a spark that keeps your company's employees motivated and competitive?

- *Clearly articulate creativity as a core value of your company.* Put it in your mission statement, make it part of evaluations, and reinforce it.

- *Set aside time to deliberately evoke creativity.* Experiment with different ways to generate ideas.

- *Add a creative exercise to meeting agendas.* Build time into meeting agendas for a creative exercise to encourage people to think innovatively.

- *Study creativity.* There is no shortage of books and articles on the subject.

- *Constantly seek new input.* New experiences will create different mental associations and connections.

- *Learn how to sidestep tension.* Stress limits your ability to be creative.

- *Develop a stance of openness and curiosity.* Delay making judgments. What may sound like a crazy idea at first may evolve into a creative solution.

SOURCE: From "Fuel the Fire: Seven Tips to Keep Your Company's Creativity Sizzling," by Juanita Weaver, December 2003. Reprinted with permission of *Entrepreneur* magazine. www.entrepreneur.com.

Thai hopes to become a viable player in the intensely competitive global shoe industry. He's living proof that the corridor principle—whereby one business naturally leads to another—is alive and well in the global marketplace.[16]

Getting Started

Most of the topics involved in starting your own business are covered in detail in other sections or entire chapters of this book. Let's look at what else is needed to get a business off the ground.

What Do You Do First?

You must first decide that you want to work for yourself rather than for someone else. You need to generate a number of ideas for a new product or service, something that people will buy, until you come up with the right opportunity that matches your skills and interests.

Whether you are starting a business because you have a product or service that is new to the world or because it is not available locally, you must get past some basic questions: Is there a need for this business? Is this business needed here? Is it needed now? These questions address the most critical concern in getting a business off the ground—the feasibility of your idea. Owning a business is a dream of many Americans, but there is usually a gap between that dream and bringing it to reality. Careful planning is needed to bridge that gap.

Reality Check

Life Is Good

Back in 1989, free-wheeling brothers Bert and John Jacobs started selling T-shirts on the streets of Boston. That fall the pair decided to quit their jobs as substitute teachers and sell those T-shirts from dorm room to dorm room on campuses up and down the East Coast. Sleeping on their inventory in the back of a van, they met Jake in about 1994. Technically, John drew the character he called Jake in 1994, and the beatnik with the beret, jack-o'-lantern smile, and pipe-cleaner body has become Life Is Good's mascot.

On the Jacobses' T-shirts Jake appears mountain-biking, skiing, or hanging out on an Adirondack chair, quoting idioms like "Life is good" (what did you expect?). Jake's optimistic messages sell shirts. *Lots* of shirts. Sales have topped $80 million with 5,000 distributors in 14 countries. Life Is Good offers over 900 items in 14 categories targeted to just about every demographic—

babies, surfers, grandmothers, and skaters. Bert says that he is not worried about their shirts falling out of fashion because the foundation of the brand is optimism, and optimism never goes out of style.

The Jacobses did not come from a business background, Bert majored in communications at Villanova, and John studied art and English at the University of Massachusetts–Amherst. But both men understand an important function of marketing—they get positioning. Their spot in the casual garment industry is premium, but not exclusive. They use the best quality cotton available, most of it made in Peru, and use double-reinforced stitching and garment dye for a weathered look. They also reject the homogenization that comes from a cookie-cutter product approach. Rather, they prefer an eclectic product line that adapts to local markets.

Bert and John are interesting, unique guys who have created a company that reflects their own personal spin. Watch the video that accompanies this chapter for more insight into the Life Is Good story.

SOURCES: Leigh Buchanan, "Life Lessons," *Inc.,* October 2006, 86–92; Ryan Thomas, "Lust for Life," *SGB,* January 2006, 30–31; Gwen Moran, "The Good Life," *Entrepreneur,* June 2005, 95; www.lifeisgood.com/about

Importance of Planning to a Startup

Before you launch your business, you should write a comprehensive *business plan* (see Chapter 4). A business plan not only helps you determine the direction of your business and keeps you on track after it opens, but also will be required if you need to borrow money to start your business. It shows your banker that you have seriously evaluated the business opportunity and considered how you will be able to pay back the loan.

In addition to writing your business plan, you need to decide and record other important steps in starting your business.

- *Market analysis.* For your small business to be successful, you must get to know your market by gathering and analyzing facts about your potential customers so as to determine the demand for your product. Market analysis takes time and effort, but it does not have to be statistically complex or expensive. Who will buy your product? What do your customers have in common with each other? Where do they live? How much will they spend?

- *Competitive analysis.* Your business needs a competitive advantage that separates it from your competitors. Before you can develop your own uniqueness, you need to know what other businesses do and how they are perceived. An exercise to help you remove some of the subjectivity of the competitive-analysis process begins with you identifying four of your direct competitors and setting up a grid on which you will rank your business as it compares to those competitors.

- *Startup costs.* How much money will you need to start your business? Before you can seek funding, you must itemize your expected expenses (see Figure 7.4). Although some of these expenses will be ongoing, others will be incurred only when you start business. There will be many expenses that you do not expect; therefore, add 10 percent to your subtotal to help offset them.

- *Capital equipment assets.* Assets such as computers, office equipment, fixtures, and furniture—capital equipment assets—have a life of more than one year. List the equipment you need along with the rest of your startup costs. Beware of the temptation to buy the newest, most expensive, or fastest equipment available before you open your doors. You don't have any revenue yet, and more small businesses have failed due to lack of sales than due to lack of expensive "goodies." Is good used equipment available? Should you lease rather than buy? If sales do materialize, you can replace used equipment with new items by paying for them from actual profits.

- *Legal form of business.* As discussed in Chapter 2, when starting a business you need to consider the appropriate legal form of business: sole proprietorship, partnership, or corporation. Your decision will be based on tax considerations, personal liability, and cost and ease of organizing.

Figure 7.4

HOW MUCH MONEY WILL YOU NEED?

Initial Capital Item	Estimated Cost
Capital equipment	
_____	_____
_____	_____
_____	_____
Beginning inventory	_____
Legal fees	_____
Accounting fees	_____
Licenses and permits	_____
Remodeling and decorating	_____
Deposits (utilities, telephone)	_____
Advertising (preopening)	_____
Insurance	_____
Startup supplies	_____
Cash reserve (petty cash, credit accounts)	_____
Other expenditures:	_____
_____	_____
_____	_____
Subtotal startup expenses:	$ _____
Add 10% safety factor:	_____
TOTAL STARTUP EXPENSES	$ _____

- *Location of business.* Consider how important the location of your business is to your customers (see Chapter 13). If customers come to your business, your location decision is critical. If your business comes to them, or if you don't meet with customers face to face, location is a less critical decision.

- *Marketing plan.* The marketing decisions you need to make before you open your business include who your customers are, how you will reach your potential customers, what you will sell them, where it will be available, and how much it will cost (see Chapter 11).

As you see, some important aspects of starting your business are not included in the business plan. Now let's look at what your business will focus on, how you will approach customer service, what licenses you will need to acquire, and what kinds of taxes you must withhold to begin business.

How Will You Compete?

Before you begin your small business, consider what you want to be known for. Because no business can be all things to all people, you need to determine what your customers value and then strive to exceed their expectations. For instance, if your customers value low price, you must set up your business to cut costs wherever possible, so that you can keep your prices low. If your customers value convenience, you need to set up your business with a focus on providing speed and ease of use for them.

In providing value to your customers, we can identify three grounds on which companies compete: operational excellence, product leadership, and customer intimacy.[17] In choosing to focus on one of these disciplines, you are not abandoning the other two. Instead, you are defining your position in consumers' minds. Visualize your choice by picturing each discipline as a mountain on which you choose to compete by raising the expectation levels of customers in that area (see Figure 7.5). By becoming a leader in that discipline, you will be better able to defend against competing companies below you on that figurative mountain.

Companies that pursue **operational excellence** know that their customers value low price, so they concentrate on the efficiency of their operations in an effort to hold down costs. They don't have the very best products or cutting-edge innovations. Instead, they strive to offer good products at the lowest price possible. Dell Computer is an example of a company that competes on operational excellence.

> *operational excellence*
> Creates a competitive advantage by holding down costs to provide customers with the lowest-priced products.

Figure 7.5
ON WHICH MOUNTAIN WILL YOU COMPETE?

When Setting up Your Small Business, You Must Decide How You Will Satisfy Your Customers. Do You Need to Offer Them the Best Product, the Best Price, or the Best Service?

product leader
A business that creates a competitive advantage based on providing the highest-quality products possible.

customer intimacy
Maintaining a long-term relationship with customers through superior service that results in a competitive advantage.

Companies that are **product leaders** constantly innovate to make the best products available even better. This kind of commitment to quality is not inexpensive, but product leaders know that price is not the most important factor to their customers. New Balance athletic shoes are known for their technical excellence, not for their inexpensive price or their customer service.

Companies that focus on developing **customer intimacy** are not looking for a one-time sale. Rather, they seek to build a long-term, close working relationship with their customers. Their customers want to be treated as if they are the company's only customer. The Lands' End operator you speak with on the telephone sees records of clothing sizes, styles, and colors from your previous orders as soon as you call. Customer-intimate companies offer specific rather than general solutions to their customers' problems.

Customer Service

Your business relationship with your customers does not end with the sale of your product or service. Increasing your level of customer service and adopting

In a chapter on starting a business from scratch based on innovation, it seems appropriate to profile one of the greatest inventors of all time—Thomas Edison. Born in 1847, Edison had very little formal education. In fact, he was home-schooled by his mother.

The list of inventions and companies that Edison created is far too long to fully discuss here, but his 1,093 patents remain a record. Go to http://inventors. about.com/library/inventors for a description of all his patents.

Edison's first patent was for an "electrographic vote-recording machine" to be used in the House of Representatives to end long sessions of filibustering and expedite the political process. Members of Congress were amazed by the technology but ultimately rejected the invention. Edison then vowed to never again invent anything that was neither practical nor marketable. That approach made Edison more of an entrepreneur than an inventor—inventors are typically more interested in seeing what they can make rather than what will sell.

Profile in Entrepreneurship

Über Inventor—Old School

Contrary to popular belief, Edison did not "invent" the light bulb. Instead, he improved upon a 50-year-old idea to develop the first device that was even remotely practical for home use. Imagine the challenge he faced in bringing his works to market. To make money from incandescent lighting, for example, he had to first develop the following:

• The parallel circuit

• A durable light bulb

• An improved dynamo

• The underground conductor network

• Devices for maintaining constant voltage

• Safety fuses and insulating materials, and light sockets with on-off switches

Fortunately, Edison did consider the market value of his inventions. For example, he founded General Electric, he created the first motion pictures, and he made the first sound recording. Remember his many contributions as you listen to MP3s while on your way to see the latest action-adventure movie.

SOURCES: Daniel Wren and Ronald Greenwood, *Management Innovators: The People and Ideas That Have Shaped Modern Business* (New York: Oxford University Press, 1998), 16–24; Mary Bellis, "The Inventions of Thomas Edison," www.inventors.about.com

professional standards in this area are critical endeavors, especially in an industry where all competitors appear to be the same. Satisfying the customer is not a means to achieve a goal; *it is the goal.* Customer service can be your competitive advantage.

The importance of a startup business providing an emphasis on the highest-quality customer service cannot be overstated. Very often the difference between one business and another is the people in it—and the way they treat customers. What is really different between car rental companies? They have basically the same cars. The prices, contracts, and advertisements are all nearly identical. The difference appears when someone answers the telephone. How long does it take to answer? Is the person's voice pleasant and professional, or hostile and bored? Does he have quick access to the information that the customer called for, or does he offer to call back and never does? Does she take the time to understand the customer's needs and make truly helpful suggestions, or does she just try to push any car on the customer? Customer service can be a huge competitive advantage.[18]

Licenses, Permits, and Regulations

If your business has no employees, you have fewer legal requirements to meet. First, let's look at the common requirements for all businesses. You need to file your business name with the secretary of state of the state in which you are forming your business. This step ensures that the name you have chosen for your business is not registered by another company. If it is, you will have to find another name for your business.

You must obtain the appropriate local licenses from the city hall and county clerk's office before you start your business. Find out if you can operate your business in the location you have picked by checking local zoning ordinances. You may need a special permit for certain types of businesses. For example, if your business handles processed food, it must pass a local health department inspection.

Most states collect sales tax on tangible property sold. If your state does, you must apply for a state sales-tax identification number to use when paying the sales taxes you collect. Contact the department of revenue in your state for information regarding your requirements. Many types of businesspeople, such as accountants, electricians, motor vehicle dealers, cosmetologists, and securities dealers, require specific licenses. These licenses are obtained from the state agency that oversees the particular type of business.

Very few small businesses are likely to need any type of federal permit or license to operate. If you will produce alcohol, firearms, tobacco products, or meat products, or give investment advice, contact an attorney regarding regulations.

Taxes

When your business begins operation, you must make advance payments of your estimated federal (and possibly state) income taxes. Individual tax payments are due in four quarterly installments—on the fifteenth day of April, June, September, and January. It is important that you remember to set money aside from your revenues so that it will be available when your quarterly taxes are due. The Internal Revenue Service is not known for its sense of humor if funds are not available.

If your business is a sole proprietorship, you report your self-employment income on IRS Form 1040 Schedule C or C-EZ, or Schedule F if your business is farming. A partnership reports partnership income on IRS Form 1065, and each partner reports her individual share of that income on Schedule SE and Schedule E. Corporations file tax returns on IRS Form 1120. Any payment in excess of $600 made for items like rent, interest, or services from independent contractors must be shown on Form 1096, and copies of Form 1099 must be sent to the people you paid.

When you begin employing other people, you become an agent of the U.S. government and must begin collecting income and Social Security taxes. You must get a federal employer identification number, which identifies your business for all tax purposes. Your local IRS office can supply you with a business tax kit that contains all of the necessary forms. You must withhold 7.51 percent of an employee's wages for Social Security tax, and you must pay a matching 7.51 percent employer's Social Security tax. You pay both halves of the tax on a quarterly basis when you submit your payroll tax return.

> **independent contractor**
> A person who is not employed by a business and, unlike employees, is not eligible for a benefit package.

If a person provides services to your business but is not an employee, he is considered to be an **independent contractor.** Because independent contractors are considered to be self-employed, you do not have to withhold Social Security taxes, federal or state income taxes, or unemployment taxes from their earnings—an obvious advantage to you. Because of the advantage of classifying a person as an independent contractor rather than an employee, the IRS imposes stiff penalties on businesses that improperly treat employees as independent contractors.

You must deposit a percentage of each employee's earnings for federal and state unemployment tax purposes with a federal tax deposit coupon. The federal unemployment tax rate is 6.2 percent of the first $7,000 per employee, but a credit of up to 5.4 percent is allowed for state unemployment tax. In reality, only 0.8 percent goes toward the federal tax. The state rate you pay depends on the amount of claims filed by former employees. The more claims, the higher your unemployment tax will be, within certain limits.

Summary

• **The advantages and disadvantages of starting a business from scratch**

When starting a business from scratch, the small business owner is free to establish a distinct competitive advantage. There are no negative images or prior mistakes to overcome, as may occur when purchasing an existing business. The creation of a new business builds pride of ownership. However, the risk of failure is higher for a startup because there are more uncertainties regarding the size and existence of a market for the business.

• **The common types of new businesses and characteristics of fast-growth companies**

E-businesses have completely changed the small business landscape. Other types of new businesses include home-based businesses and part-time businesses. Some small businesses start with the intention of becoming hypergrowth companies. These companies are generally led by teams of people with prior experience in starting that type of business (usually high-tech manufacturing). They are well financed and constantly looking for opporunities to expand into new markets.

• **Evaluating potential startups and ideas**

When a new product idea is introduced to the market, the window of opportunity is open the widest (assuming it is a product that people want and will buy), because little competition exists. As a product progresses through the product life cycle, the window of opportunity closes, as more competition enters the market and demand declines.

Most people get ideas for new businesses from their prior employment. Turning a hobby or outside interest into a business is also a common tactic. Ideas may come from other people's suggestions or spring from information gained while taking a class. Sometimes business ideas even occur by chance.

• Getting started

The entrepreneur needs to begin by questioning the feasibility of her idea. Then, to bridge the gap between dream and reality, careful planning is needed. Entrepreneurs need to carefully consider the costs of starting a new business, and they must analyze the market and competitive landscape to ensure that their competitive advantage really exists.

Providing customers with outstanding service during and after the sale of a product is of utmost importance in business startups. Customer service is the basis for establishing a long-term relationship with customers.

Startups also have legal requirements. Entrepreneurs must file the business name with the state of origin and obtain local business licenses and any industry-specific permits required. They must also apply for a tax identification number to collect and process sales taxes, if necessary.

Questions for Review and Discussion

1. Compare and contrast the advantages and disadvantages of starting a business from the ground up. Be sure to include the different types of businesses in your analysis.

2. Define *hypergrowth* companies, and evaluate the reasons for their phenomenal rate of growth. What are the most valid explanations for the rate of success found in these companies?

3. Explain the concept of *window of opportunity* as it relates to new startups, from idea conception through the final decision about whether to turn the idea into a reality.

4. Entrepreneurs get their ideas for business startups from various sources. Name these sources, and identify the ones most likely to lead to success.

5. Give some examples of things the new entrepreneur should immediately investigate to ensure to the maximum extent possible that the business will "get off the ground."

6. Is a business plan really necessary for a very small startup business? How much market analysis and competitive analysis should the new entrepreneur conduct prior to startup?

7. What are some of the tangible resources that the new entrepreneur might need in order to go into business? What are some options for obtaining capital for a business that is brand-new and therefore has no financial history?

8. After startup, what is the *single* most important tool the small business owner has at his disposal to ensure the success of the business? Why is it so crucial?

9. What are some examples of consumer preferences and values? What are some examples of things the new business owner can do to ensure capturing some of the market for the good or service being produced?

10. Discuss the legal ramifications of starting your own business. Where should the new entrepreneur seek information and advice regarding laws that govern the type of business that is being promoted?

Questions for Critical Thinking

1. What criteria do you see as most critical in differentiating an idea from an opportunity?

2. Many entrepreneurs test the waters of a market by starting a sideline business. What are the advantages and disadvantages of selling items on Internet auctions like eBay? Is a person who regularly has 20 or 25 items for sale at any given time an entrepreneur? What types of products would be most appropriately sold in this manner?

Experience This . . .

A good idea is nothing more than a tool in the hands of an entrepreneur. Spend a class session in a brainstorming exercise to stimulate creativity. Brainstorming begins by defining a purpose. In this case we want to generate ideas for a business that undergraduate business students can start before they graduate. Choose a student to serve as the facilitator, who will record every idea on the board—with no criticism. Encourage brainstorming to occur spontaneously and abundantly (although you may wish to set a parameter that the idea be legal in nature). Students should strive to fill a known or perceived void. Don't spend time getting committed to one idea.

Once a sizable list has been generated (about 50 ideas, or when the exercise runs out of gas), identify the most promising ideas. Refine and prioritize the ideas. Have the group choose about 10 percent (five or six ideas) and discuss their opportunity potential. Could they stand on their own as viable opportunities—or, better yet, could two, three, or all six be combined into a feasible venture?

What Would You Do?

Carrie Ann thinks she has identified a hot opportunity. She has watched the demand for tattoos and body art increase over the last several years. Carrie Ann believes that this trend is now leveling off and that in the near future many people who have gotten tattoos will want them removed. In anticipation, she has developed a nonsurgical approach to tattoo removal that consists of a cream applied to the tattoo. The area is then covered with gauze, and the cream must be reapplied every day for two weeks. At the end of two weeks, the tattoo is gone. A tube of Carrie Ann's cream will retail for about $50.

Questions

1. Carrie Ann is concerned about the timing of her product's introduction. She is not sure the window of opportunity is open wide enough at this time for her business to succeed, but she worries that if she waits for the opportunity to develop more fully, another product will beat her cream to market. How would you advise her in her opportunity analysis?

2. Carrie Ann's business could become a fast-growth player as described in this chapter. What would she need to do to become a fast-growth company?

CHAPTER CLOSING CASE

TURNING JAMES PROSEK INTO "JAMES PROSEK" THE BRAND

James Prosek, 23, is not going into business for himself; he's going into business *as* himself. At least that's how his big sister Jennifer, 30, sees the plan. Jennifer is part owner of Jacobs & Prosek, a $1.5 million public relations firm based in Stamford, Connecticut. As an MBA candidate at Columbia University's School of Business, Jennifer and her classmates developed a 67-page business plan to turn "James Prosek" into a profit-making concern.

Capitalizing on Fame

When James was a 20-year-old Yale undergraduate, he parlayed his passion for fishing into an encyclopedic coffee-table book, *Trout: An Illustrated History*, which has sold more than 60,000 copies. His watercolors of the angling world fetch as much as $6,000. He has published two more books. His fans include *Rolling Stone* magazine founder Jann Wenner and broadcaster Tom Brokaw, who fished with Prosek in front of NBC news cameras.

Jennifer wants to help James garner the multimillion-dollar opportunities available through his fame in the literary, art, and fishing worlds. She spends much of her free time dreaming up ways her brother can generate ever-greater revenues ($220,000 in one recent year). Yet James says his foremost objective "is to be recognized as a relatively serious author and painter."

Setting Profit Goals

The business plan's goal is to post revenues of close to $3 million with $1.5 million in profits within three years. The plan identifies James as company president, creative director, and product manager for books and fine art. The company's purpose is to help James establish a diversified product line and a brand image—to put James's stamp of approval on everything from smoked-trout gift baskets to fish-themed wrapping paper, calendars, and even throw rugs, already available for $40 apiece. James, however, has reservations: "I don't want the licensing stuff to take over from books. I don't want to become known for throw rugs."

The "James Prosek" business plan is a bid for James to become the personification of a brand like Martha Stewart. While the comparison makes James frown, Jennifer has found it helpful in talking up the plan to potential investors. James may resist the comparison, but "James Prosek's" goal is to transform the individual from a fish aficionado to the standard-bearer for an entire way of life. Despite representing simplicity and naturalness, the "James Prosek" lifestyle will be highly accessorized. The company's overriding mission, says the plan, is "to awaken the minds of all individuals to the beauty of the natural world, trout, and the experience of fishing through the words, paintings, products, and services of James Prosek." As Jennifer says, "I was always frustrated that he had more notoriety than he did dollars. One of my dreams has been, 'Can we leverage all this great exposure James has been getting?'"

Own One Word

Such personal-brand models as the one Jennifer would like to establish already exist, say experts such as Al Ries, coauthor of *Positioning: The Battle for Your Mind.* This branding is what practically every CEO wants these days. "I say to them, 'Think of a word you can own in the mind,'" says Ries. "Regardless of whether you're good at everything, you should emphasize one aspect of your personality and de-emphasize everything else. Become known for one thing."

Right now, James is simply a professional-services provider. He gets paid only if he produces something. The business plan concedes that he can create only so many paintings or write so many books. And none of that is guaranteed. The plan warns that "personal injury could seriously affect Prosek's ability to write and paint." Unlike accountants or consultants, James can't recruit junior partners, taking a percentage of their billings.

James is not slavishly following the business plan. For example, he decided not to host the TV show the plan described. The show would have featured James fishing with top-drawer CEOs and "could have been a huge opportunity," says Jennifer. James says, "I couldn't see the shape of it. I sometimes entertain things just so my sister won't be discouraged."

James expressed reservations about a travel-tour package that Jennifer developed. Jennifer found a partner to finance and market the tour, but the advertising made James uneasy. "They ran a full-page ad in *Yale Alumni Magazine* that said 'created and hosted by James Prosek,'" he says. "I was not going to be there for more than two or three days. I think the tour idea is a great one, but the idea of using me as a poster boy is the unsettling part." As it turned out, only four people signed up for the $10,900 tour and it was canceled.

"The biggest problem is James's personal struggle with wanting to be commercial," Jennifer says. "Nine out of 10 things I offer James, which can be profitable, he'll decline. If I were James Prosek, I'd grow the empire."

SOURCE: Adapted from "Brand in the Making," by Mike Hofman, *Inc.,* October 1999, pp. 52–62. Reprinted with permission of Gruner & Jahr USA.

Questions

1. Describe the niche that 23-year-old James Prosek is filling with his diversified product line. What "business" is he really in as himself?

2. Analyze the opportunities and challenges that James and Jennifer face in creating this business.

3. What would be your advice to the Proseks? Do you agree with Al Ries's suggestion to "become known for one thing"?

4. Is James committed enough to start and run this business, or is he being manipulated?

Test Prepper

You've read the chapter, studied the key terms, and the exam is any day now. Think you're ready to ace it? Take this sample test to gauge your comprehension of chapter material. You can check your answers at the back of the book. Want more test questions? Visit the student website at college.hmco.com/pic/hatten4e and take the ACE and ACE+ quizzes for more practice.

college.hmco.com/pic/hatten4e

Matching

_____ 1. businesses that are more dependent on the services of people than on money or equipment

_____ 2. businesses that connect a company with customers via telecommunication networks

_____ 3. businesses located within the entrepreneur's domicile

_____ 4. the period of time that an opportunity is available

_____ 5. inaction due to additional testing and questioning

_____ 6. the process of finding something valuable that was not looked for

_____ 7. opportunities that become available to an entrepreneur only after preceding decisions have been made

_____ 8. competitive advantage based on holding down business costs in an effort to offer low prices

_____ 9. competitive advantage based on offering the highest-quality products possible

_____10. competitive advantage based on long-term customer relationships

a. labor-intensive business

b. product leadership

c. analysis paralysis

d. home-based business

e. window of opportunity

f. product life cycle

g. serendipity

h. avocation

i. corridor principle

j. customer intimacy

k. operational excellence

l. capital-intensive business

m. e-business

Multiple Choice

1. The risk of business failure for businesses starting from scratch is
   a. higher
   b. lower
   c. no difference
   d. not measurable

2. Which of the following is *not* an advantage of home-based business?
   a. control over working hours
   b. lower overhead expenses
   c. domestic interruptions
   d. tax advantages

3. Fast-growth CEOs have previously started _____ businesses than/as other owners.
   a. more
   b. fewer
   c. about the same number of
   d. less strategic

4. Which of the following was *not* a suggested question to ask about business ideas?
   a. Does this idea solve a customer problem?
   b. Can this venture become a national franchise?
   c. Can this idea be turned into a profitable business?
   d. Do I have the skills to take advantage of this opportunity?

4. Thomas Edison is credited with how many patents?
   a. 133
   b. 555
   c. 755
   d. 1,093

## part 4

Financial and Legal Management

Chapter 8   Accounting Records and Financial Statements

Chapter 9   Small Business Finance

Chapter 10   The Legal Environment

As a small business owner, you will need to depend on the advice of several professionals—most significantly, accountants, lenders, and lawyers. To make the best decisions for your business based on their advice, however, you need a thorough understanding of accounting systems, financial management, and the law. You have to understand your own accounting system and financial-statement analysis, ways to finance your business, and the laws and regulations that apply to your business. **Chapter 8** covers accounting systems and financial statements and their use, **Chapter 9** discusses small businesses' financial needs, and **Chapter 10** examines the legal environment of small business.

Accounting Records and Financial Statements

After reading this chapter, you should be able to:

- Discuss the importance and uses of financial records in a small business.

- Itemize the accounting records needed for a small business.

- Explain the 11 ratios used to analyze financial statements.

- Illustrate the importance of and procedures for managing cash flow.

Linda Nespole of Hi-Shear Technology foresaw some leaner times ahead, so she created a blueprint for saving boatloads of cash. Hi-Shear provides pyrotechnic, mechanical, and electronic products to the aerospace and defense markets. In the late 1990s the company faced some formidable challenges: A recession was about to hit, federal funding for military and space programs was running low, and customers had begun delaying orders. Cash flow became a problem.

Nespole stepped up by devising a cost-control system to pump up Hi-Shear's bottom line. To do so, she went back to basics. First, she examined a year's worth of the firm's utility bills and found that water, gas, and electricity costs were soaring each month. From this information, Nespole deduced that the company had leaky pipes and inefficient lights. Fundamental repairs and adjustments lowered the water and gas bills immediately, and new lighting paid for itself in six months.

Linda Nespole.

Next, Nespole applied the simple process of charting expenses and acting on her findings to other operational costs. The result? Hi-Shear switched telecommunications and insurance providers and saved 30 percent on its 401(k) costs just by threatening to switch its plan provider. "They have no incentive to reduce costs unless you threaten to leave them," Nespole says.

Cash-flow monitoring is now a priority for Hi-Shear. Although it took a bit of a crisis to initiate cost-cutting procedures, all 125 employees are now concerned about saving money on a daily basis. The maintenance staff tracks meters every day. Administrators review utility bills quarterly, and Nespole comparison-shops for all insurance policies annually, even calling human resource directors at other companies to ask about their providers. Hi-Shear doesn't pay outside consultants to help control its costs because Nespole has shown that the time required to find such specialists might be better spent evaluating a business's current service providers. "It's very easy," she says. "You just have to make the time."

Cost-control systems can be so valuable that venture capitalists have even started to require them or help implement them. Venture capitalists contribute to entrepreneurial firms in ways other than writing checks, such as providing services and monitoring the entrepreneurial firm's operations and perform-ance. Recent research shows that cost-control systems contribute positively to the entrepreneurial firm's financial performance.

SOURCES: Frits Wijbenga, Theo Postma, Rebecca Stratling, "The Influence of the Venture Capitalist's Governance Activities on the Entrepreneurial Firm's Control Systems and Performance," *Entrepreneurship: Theory & Practice*, March 2007, 257–277, 21; Ilan Mochari, "A Simple Little System," *Inc.*, October 1999, 87; "Hi-Shear Ships Satellite Assemblies," *Business Wire News*, 29 June 2004, http://money.excite.com

Small Business Accounting

> "The accounting process helps you to translate numbers— the language of business—into plain English."

Are you intimidated by the thought of accounting systems, with row after row and column after column of numbers? If you are, you aren't alone. But you shouldn't be frightened by or dread the numbers of your business, because accounting isn't about making rows and columns of numbers. Rather, it is about organizing and communicating what's going on in your business. Think of numbers as the language of business.

Computers help us take piles of raw *data* and turn them into usable *informa-tion* with which to make managerial decisions. For example, consider a marketing research project you have conducted. You have received thousands of completed questionnaires, each with 20 responses. You would have a very difficult time inter-preting these thousands of pages because they contain raw, unprocessed data. If you were to enter all of these data into a statistical program on a computer, however, you could organize them into means, trends, and a few meaningful numbers—in other words, into *information* that would enable you to make mar-keting decisions.

Accounting systems accomplish a similar purpose. Think of the many piles of checks, receipts, invoices, and other papers your business generates in a month as

> *accounting*
> The system within a business for converting raw data from source documents (like invoices, sales receipts, bills, and checks) into information that will help a manager make business decisions.

Figure 8.1
ACCOUNTING PROCESS

An Accounting System Works via a Cycle to Convert Raw Data into Usable Information for Making Decisions About How to Run Your Small Business.

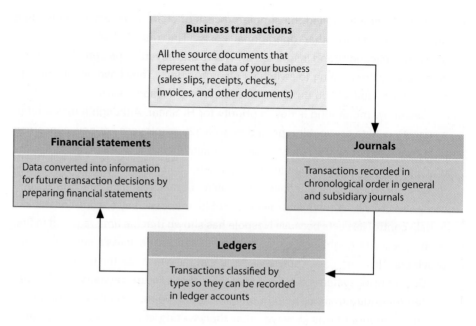

Business transactions

All the source documents that represent the data of your business (sales slips, receipts, checks, invoices, and other documents)

Journals

Transactions recorded in chronological order in general and subsidiary journals

Ledgers

Transactions classified by type so they can be recorded in ledger accounts

Financial statements

Data converted into information for future transaction decisions by preparing financial statements

data. Everything you need to know about the financial health of your business is contained in those piles, but it is not in an easily usable form. Accounting systems transform piles of data into smaller bites of usable information by first recording every transaction that occurs in your business in *journals,* then transferring (or posting) the entries into *ledgers* (both of which are described in this chapter). The process is basically the same whether you use pencil and paper or an accounting program on a PC. From the ledger you make *financial statements* like a balance sheet, income statement, and statement of cash flow. These statements communicate how your business is faring much better than the stacks of papers you started with.

In the last step in the accounting process, you take certain numbers from your financial statements to compute key *ratios* that can be compared to industry averages or historical figures from your own business to help you make financial decisions. The intent of this chapter is not to turn you into an accountant, but rather to help you understand the communication process—or accounting language—better (see Figure 8.1).

So how is a new entrepreneur supposed to get the accounting process started? How can you create an orderly system from nothing without having prior expertise in accounting? Many business owners start by purchasing a simple accounting software package (see Manager's Notebook, "Computerized Accounting Packages"). Another stellar piece of advice is to pay an accounting firm that specializes in small businesses to set up your accounting system. You don't have to use the firm to handle all of your accounting needs like payroll preparation, tax-form preparation, and creation of monthly financial statements, although you could. Money would be wisely spent getting a system that will work for your business from the very beginning—as opposed to throwing all receipts, invoices, and paperwork into a shoebox and panicking when the time comes to file quarterly taxes. Do yourself and your business a favor, and get started correctly by using the services of a professional.

The Sarbanes-Oxley Act set new accounting, auditing, and other financial-oriented standards that require compliance checks in an effort to prevent fraud. The act is yet another reason that small businesses need the services of an accountant.[1] A recent survey of small business owners by Intuit Professional Accounting Solutions revealed that tax advice is the primary service for which these businesspeople rely on their accountants. Financial-statement preparation, bookkeeping, and payroll also rank highly as reasons to consult an accountant.[2]

How Important Are Financial Records?

Financial records are important to businesses for several reasons. Remember when we discussed common reasons for failure of small businesses in Chapter 1? Most of the mismanagement decisions that spell the doom of many small businesses are related to financial and accounting issues.

All too often, the last thing small business owners think of is careful accounting, but it should really be the first issue addressed. While you are plagued with a lot of worries—from making payroll to buying products to selling your services—you can put yourself at a competitive disadvantage by not being accounting oriented from the beginning. Many small business owners don't hire an accountant right away because they are afraid of the cost, but many accounting firms specialize in small business and are available at reasonable prices. It's like the advice you

"It's up to you now, Miller. The only thing that can save us is an accounting breakthrough."

Smart to Ask . . .

Small business owners need a good accountant—especially when the topic is taxes. Here are some questions to ask your number cruncher:

• *What are your qualifications?* If your business and tax return are on the complex side, you'll want a *certified public accountant (CPA)*.

• *How aggressive are you?* There is surprisingly more art than science in tax preparation. Are you financially conservative or aggressive? You'll want an accountant with a comparable approach.

• *Can you look over my QuickBooks?* Many CPAs get irritated with client's QuickBooks when preparing tax returns because a lot of people don't do a good job of tracking income and expenses. Fixing messes takes time, and time is a premium for accountants in tax season.

• *What if I get audited?* You want expertise if the IRS sends you an audit notice. You need to know in advance what your accountant's role will be. CPAs and tax attorneys will handle your case themselves. Bookkeepers and part-time accountants probably won't or can't.

SOURCES: Jennifer Gill, "Smart Questions for Your Accountant," *Inc.*, November 2006, 36; Amy Feldman, "SpecTaxUlar—What to Ask Your Accountant," *Inc.*, March 2006, 100–107.

have probably heard your whole life: Getting things right the first time costs less than fixing mistakes the second or third time.

Accurate Information for Management

You need to have accurate financial information to know the financial health of your business. To make effective management decisions, you must know things like how much your accounts receivable are worth, how old each account is, how quickly your inventory is turning over, which items are not moving, how much your firm owes, when debts are due, and how much your business owes in taxes and FICA (Social Security taxes). Good records are needed to answer these and many other similar questions. Without good records, these questions are impossible to answer. Accurate financial records also allow you to identify problems before they become threats to your business.

Banking and Tax Requirements

The information on your financial statements is needed to prepare your tax returns. If the Internal Revenue Service audits your business, you will be expected to produce the relevant accounting records and statements.

Bankers and investors use your financial statements to evaluate the condition of your business. If you need the services of either, you must not only produce statements, but also be ready to explain and defend their contents.

Small Business Accounting Basics

The accounting system provides you with information for making decisions about your small business. To access this information, you need to understand which entry systems you can use and how accounting equations work. Your accounting system should be easy to use, accurate, timely, consistent, understandable, dependable, and complete.

Double- and Single-Entry Systems

Double-entry accounting systems revolve around three elements: assets, liabilities, and owner's equity. **Assets** are what your business owns. **Liabilities** are what your business owes. **Owner's equity** is what you (the owner) have invested in the business (it can also be called *capital* or *net worth*).

As the name implies, with a double-entry system, all transactions are recorded in two ways—once as a *debit* to one account and again as a *credit* to another account. Every "plus" must be balanced by a "minus" so that each transaction shows how assets are affected on one side and how liabilities and owner's equity are affected on the other.

A double-entry accounting system increases the accuracy of your system and provides a self-checking audit. If you make a mistake in recording a transaction, your accounts will not balance, indicating that you need to go back over the books to find the error. Debits must always equal credits. To increase an asset, you debit the account. To increase a liability or equity, you credit the account.

A **single-entry accounting** system does exist and may be used by small sole proprietorships. With a single-entry system, you record the flow of income and expenses in a running log, basically like a checkbook. It allows you to produce a monthly statement but not to make a balance sheet, an income statement, or other financial records. The single-entry system is simple but not self-balancing, as a double-entry system is.

Popular computer programs like Quicken employ a single-entry accounting system. These programs provide attractive features like the ability to track expense categories, post amounts to those accounts, and print reports, but they are still pretty much electronic check registers. Many small, one-person businesses begin with them because of their simplicity and then graduate to more powerful, full-feature systems like the Peachtree or Great Plains accounting programs. There is no one-size-fits-all computer accounting program that is suitable for all small businesses.[3] You may have to adjust your system as your business grows.

On the subject of beginning simply: *Always* use separate checkbooks for your business and your personal life. Avoid the temptation to combine the two by thinking that "the business money and personal money are all mine—I'll just keep them together." At some point you will need to separate them, which can be very difficult to do later. Also, write checks instead of paying for items with cash. They serve as an accurate form of record keeping. Finally, reconcile your bank accounts monthly, and make sure all errors are corrected.

double-entry accounting
An accounting system in which every business transaction is recorded in an asset account and a liability or owner's equity account so that the system will balance.

assets
Any resource that a business owns and expects to use to its benefit.

liabilities
A debt owed by a business to another organization or individual.

owner's equity
The amount of money the owner of a business would receive if all of the assets were sold and all of the liabilities were paid.

single-entry accounting
An accounting system in which the flow of income and expenses is recorded in a running log, basically like a checkbook.

Manager's Notebook

Computerized Accounting Packages

A computerized accounting information system can help a small business manager get accounting information efficiently and quickly. Computerized accounting can save time in entering accounting data and generating accounting statements, can improve the traceability of income and expenses (which could prove important for audits), and can increase the timeliness and frequency of your accounting statements.

Selecting appropriate hardware and accounting software can pose a major challenge. To facilitate your decision making, let's examine some of the better-known accounting packages.

QuickBooks Pro (www.quickbooks.com). Quick-Books Pro will automate all money matters, including check writing, invoicing, billing, payroll, and receipts. Modules include an integrated merchant credit card service, electronic postal service, and web site creation using 250 templates.

Peachtree Complete Accounting (www.peachtree.com). Peachtree Complete Accounting, a powerful, comprehensive accounting package, is by far the dominant one for small businesses. It comes with payroll, inventory, job-cost, and order-entry functions to create an extensive array of reports, forms, and financial statements.

MYOB Plus (www.myob.com). MYOB (Mind Your Own Business) is another excellent general-purpose accounting program. It has more than 150 predefined reports and more than 100 custom charts of accounts.

Simply Accounting (www.simplyaccounting.com). Simply Accounting is a package aimed at the very small business market. It does not offer all the features of the other software discussed here but is powerful and appropriately named.

Intacct Small Business (us.intacct.com). Intacct Small Business is a package aimed at companies that have outgrown Excel and QuickBooks. It has a suite of applications to run a multitude of financial operations.

Sageworks' ProfitCents (www.profitcents.com). While not a complete accounting package, Sageworks ProfitCents is a financial analysis software that can be pretty handy. When you enter in your financials, you get a detailed assessment (in plain English) of your liquidity, asset management, sales performance and other metrics.

Keep in mind that your choice of an accounting software package depends on the size of your business and its accounting needs. Generally speaking, the more features and customization options provided in the package, the more expensive it will be and the more complex to install and use.

SOURCES: Michael Fitzgerald, "Winning the Numbers Game," *Inc.*, March 2007, 40–41; Rick Telberg, "Make Money with Basic Accounting Software," *Journal of Accountancy*, January 2004, 67; Ted Neeleman, "Mid-range Accounting Software: The Next Step," *Accounting Today*, 15 March 2004, 26; Seth Fineberg, "Online Accounting Gathers Steam in the SMB Market," *Accounting Today*, 5 April 2004, 18.

Accounting Equations

As stated earlier, numbers are the language of business. Three equations are the foundation of that language:

$$\text{Assets} = \text{Liabilities} + \text{Owner's equity}$$

$$\text{Profit} = \text{Revenue} - \text{Expenses}$$

$$\text{Cash flow} = \text{Receipts} - \text{Disbursements}$$

The first equation, Assets = Liabilities + Owner's equity, is the basis of the *balance sheet*. Any entry that you make on one side of the equation must also be entered on the other side to maintain a balance. For example, suppose you have a good month and decide to pay off a $2,000 note you took out at the bank six months ago. You would credit your cash account (an asset) by $2,000 and debit your notes payable account (a liability) by $2,000. Your balance sheet remains in equilibrium. Of course, any equation can be rearranged if you understand it. For example:

$$\text{Owner's equity} = \text{Assets} - \text{Liabilities}$$

You can also think of this equation as follows:

$$\text{What you have} = \text{What you own} - \text{What you owe}$$

The second equation, Profit = Revenue – Expenses, represents the activity described on the *income statement*. In other words, the money you get to keep equals the money your business brings in minus what you have to spend.

The third equation, Cash flow = Receipts – Disbursements, is the basis of the *cash-flow statement*. The money you have on hand at any given time equals the money you bring in minus what you have to pay out.

We will discuss the balance sheet, the income statement, and the cash-flow statement in more detail later in this chapter.

Cash and Accrual Methods of Accounting

One decision you need to make in your accounting system is whether to use cash or accrual accounting. The difference between the two relates to how each shows the timing of your receipts and your disbursements.

Most businesses use the **accrual-basis method** of accounting. With this method, you report your income and expenses at the time they are earned or incurred, rather than when they are collected or paid. Sales you make on credit are recorded as accounts receivable that have not yet been collected. The accrual method also allows you to record payment of expenses over a period of time, even if the actual payment is made in a single installment. For example, you may pay for insurance once or twice a year, but you can record the payments on a monthly basis.

With the **cash-basis method** of accounting, you record transactions when cash is actually received and expenses are actually paid. The cash method is simpler to keep than the accrual method. Although it may be appropriate for very small businesses, for businesses with no inventory, or for businesses that deal strictly in cash, the cash method can distort financial results over time.

Taxpayers can generally adopt any permissible accounting method, as long as it clearly reflects income.[4] You should not use the cash basis if your business extends credit, because credit sales would not be recorded as sales until you receive payment. Also, your accounts payable would not be recorded as an expense until the bill is paid.

accrual-basis method
A method of accounting in which income and expenses are recorded at the time they are incurred rather than when they are paid.

cash-basis method
A method of accounting in which income and expenses are recorded at the time they are paid, rather than when they are incurred.

What Accounting Records Do You Need?

To turn data into management information, you need to follow certain guidelines, or standards, called **generally accepted accounting principles (GAAP)** The group that monitors the appropriateness of these principles is the Financial Accounting Standards Board (FASB).[5] The GAAP guidelines are intended to create financial-statement formats that are uniform across industries. Because business is complex, flexibility in GAAP methods is acceptable as long as consistency is maintained within the business.

Journals and Ledgers   Your accounting actually begins when you record your raw data, from sources such as sales slips, purchase invoices, and check stubs, in journals. A **journal** is simply a place to write down the date of your transactions, the amounts, and the accounts to be debited and credited. You will have several journals, such as sales, purchases, cash receipts, and cash disbursements journals.

At some regular time interval (daily, weekly, or monthly), you will post the transactions recorded in all your journals in a general ledger. A **general ledger** is a summary book for recording all transactions and account balances. One of the advantages of using a computerized accounting system is that it can perform the monotonous task of posting electronically. To speed the posting process and to facilitate access to accounts, each account is assigned a two-digit number. The first digit indicates the class of the account (1 for assets, 2 for liabilities, 3 for capital, 4 for income, and 5 for expenses). The second digit is assigned to each account within the class. For example, your cash account could be assigned account number 11. The first 1 shows that the account is an asset, whereas the second 1 means that it is your first asset listed. Your inventory could be assigned the account number 13, meaning that it is the third asset listed.

At the end of your accounting period or fiscal year, you will close and total each individual account in your general ledger. At this point, or at any time you wish if you are using a computerized accounting package, you can prepare your financial statements to see where your business stands financially. The three most important statements for providing financial information about your business are the income statement, the balance sheet, and the statement of cash flow.

Income Statement   The **income statement**, also called the *profit-and-loss (P&L) statement*, summarizes the income and expenses that your company has totaled over a period of time (see Figure 8.2). The income statement illustrates the accounting equation of Profit = Revenue – Expenses. This statement can generally be broken down into the following sections:

- Net sales
- Cost of goods sold
- Gross margin
- Expenses
- Net income (or loss)

Not only does the income statement show an itemization of your sales, cost of goods sold, and expenses, but it also allows you to calculate the percentage relationship of each item of expense to sales. Including these percentages on your

INCOME		Percentage of Sales
Net Sales	$450,000	100.00
Cost of Goods Sold	270,000	60.00
GROSS PROFIT ON SALES	$180,000	40.00
EXPENSES		
Selling Expense		
Advertising	$ 12,000	2.67
Delivery and Freight	10,000	2.22
Sales Salaries	25,000	5.56
Miscellaneous Selling Expenses	1,000	0.22
Administrative Expense		
Licenses	$ 150	0.03
Insurance	2,400	0.53
Nonsales Salaries	38,000	8.44
Payroll Taxes	6,300	1.40
Rent/Mortgage	12,400	2.76
Utilities	6,000	1.33
Legal Fees	1,500	0.33
Depreciation	42,000	9.33
Miscellaneous Administrative Expenses	500	0.11
TOTAL EXPENSES	$157,250	34.94
INCOME FROM OPERATIONS	$ 22,750	5.06
OTHER INCOME		
Interest Income	$ 300	0.07
OTHER EXPENSES		
Interest Expense	$ 15,000	3.33
NET PROFIT (LOSS) BEFORE TAXES	$ 8,050	1.79
INCOME TAXES	$ 3,220	0.72
NET PROFIT (LOSS) AFTER TAXES	$ 4,830	1.07
NOTE:		
Cash Flow from Operations Equals Net Profit or Loss After Taxes plus Depreciation	$ 46,830	

Figure 8.2
STEREO CITY INCOME STATEMENT

financial statements produces a **common-size financial statement.** Common-size financial statements are valuable tools for checking the efficiency trends of your business by measuring and controlling individual expense items.

Consider the example of Stereo City, a retail company that sells home electronic equipment. Stereo City's net sales for the accounting period covered by Figure 8.2 were $450,000. The business had a 40 percent gross profit (or margin), which means that, out of net sales, Stereo City acquired $180,000 with which to cover its operating expenses. Total expenses were $157,250 (34.94 percent of sales). After adding interest income and deducting interest expenses and taxes, the company's net profit—the bottom line—was $4,830.

Balance Sheet   While the income statement shows the financial condition of your business over time, the **balance sheet** provides an instant "snapshot" of your business at any given moment (usually at the end of the month, quarter, or fiscal year; see Figure 8.3). A balance sheet has two main sections—one showing the assets of the business and one showing the liabilities and owner's equity of the business. As explained previously under "Accounting Equations," these two sides must balance.

On Stereo City's sample balance sheet, you will see a column of percentages of total assets, liabilities, and owner's equity. As with the common-size income

common-size financial statement
A financial statement that includes a percentage breakdown of each item.

balance sheet
A financial statement that shows a firm's assets, liabilities, and owner's equity.

Figure 8.3
STEREO CITY BALANCE
SHEET

ASSETS		Percentage of Total Assets
Current Assets:		
Cash	$ 3,500	1.08
Accounts Receivable	12,000	3.71
Inventory	125,000	38.64
Prepaid Expenses	5,000	1.55
Short-Term Investments	10,000	3.09
Total Current Assets	$155,500	48.07
Fixed Assets:		
Building	$150,000	46.37
Equipment	25,000	7.73
Leasehold Improvements	20,000	6.18
Other Fixed Assets	15,000	4.64
Gross Fixed Assets	$210,000	64.91
Less: Accumulated Depreciation	42,000	12.98
Net Fixed Assets	$168,000	51.93
Total Assets	$323,500	100.00

LIABILITIES AND OWNERS' EQUITY		Percentage of Liability and Equity
Current Liabilities:		
Accounts Payable	$ 75,000	23.18
Accruals	7,500	2.32
Current Portion of Long-Term Debt	17,500	5.41
Other Current Liabilities	5,000	1.55
Total Current Liabilities	$105,000	32.46
Long-Term Liabilities:		
Mortgage Loan	$ 93,000	28.75
Term Loan	39,500	12.21
Total Long-Term Liabilities	$132,500	40.96
Total Liabilities	$237,500	73.42
Owners' Equity		
Paid-in Capital	$ 75,000	23.18
Retained Earnings	11,000	3.40
Total Owners' Equity	$ 86,000	26.58
Total Liabilities and Owners' Equity	$323,500	100.00

statement, these percentages on the common-size balance sheet can indicate accounts and areas that are out of line compared to industry averages, such as those published by Financial Research Associates, Robert Morris Associates, or trade associations.

statement of cash flow
A financial statement that shows the cash inflows and outflows of a business.

Statement of Cash Flow   The **statement of cash flow** highlights the cash coming into and going out of your business. It is summarized by the accounting equation of Cash flow = Receipts – Disbursements (see Figure 8.4). The importance of tracking and forecasting your cash flow is difficult to overstate because it is often more critical to survival of the business than profits. Many businesses show considerable profit but have problems paying their bills—meaning that they have a cash-flow problem.

It is common for new businesses to experience a situation in which more cash goes out than comes in, which is called *negative cash flow*. This condition is not too alarming if it happens when the business is very young or if it happens only

Figure 8.4   STEREO CITY CASH FLOW STATEMENT

	October	November	December	January	February	March	April	May	June	July	August	September	Total
Cash Receipts:													
Retail Receipts (a)	$46,875	$46,875	$46,875	$28,125	$28,125	$28,125	$37,500	$37,500	$37,500	$37,500	$37,500	$37,500	$450,000
Interest Income				100				100				100	300
Total Cash Receipts	$46,875	$46,875	$46,875	$28,225	$28,125	$28,125	$37,500	$37,600	$37,500	$37,500	$37,500	$37,600	$450,300
Cash Disbursements:													
Cost of Goods Sold (b)	$28,125	$28,125	$28,125	$16,875	$16,875	$16,875	$22,500	$22,500	$22,500	$22,500	$22,500	$22,500	$270,000
Sales Expenses	2,603	2,603	2,603	1,562	1,562	1,562	2,083	2,083	2,083	2,083	2,083	2,090	25,000
Advertising	1,000	1,000	1,000	1,000	1,000	1,000	1,000	1,000	1,000	1,000	1,000	1,000	12,000
Insurance	0	600	0	0	600	0	0	600	0	0	600	0	2,400
Legal and Accounting	0	0	375	0	0	375	0	0	375	0	0	375	1,500
Delivery Expenses	1,042	1,042	1,042	625	625	625	833	833	833	833	833	834	10,000
**Fixed Cash Disbursements	4,328	4,328	4,328	4,328	4,328	4,328	4,328	4,328	4,328	4,328	4,328	4,328	51,930
Mortgage (c)	1,033	1,033	1,033	1,033	1,033	1,033	1,033	1,033	1,033	1,033	1,033	1,037	12,400
Term Loan (d)	1,466	1,466	1,466	1,466	1,466	1,466	1,466	1,466	1,466	1,466	1,466	1,466	17,592
Total Cash Disbursements	$39,596	$40,197	$39,972	$26,889	$27,489	$27,264	$33,243	$33,843	$33,618	$33,243	$33,843	$33,630	$402,822
Net Cash Flow	$ 7,279	$ 6,679	$ 6,904	$ 1,337	$ 637	$ 862	$ 4,258	$ 3,758	$ 3,883	$ 4,258	$ 3,658	$ 3,971	$ 47,478
Cumulative Cash Flow	$ 7,279	$13,957	$20,861	$22,197	$22,834	$23,695	$27,953	$31,710	$35,593	$39,850	$43,508	$47,478	

**FCD

Fixed Cash Disbursements:	
Utilities	$ 6,000
Non-sales Salaries	38,000
Payroll Taxes and Benefits	6,300
Licenses	150
Misc. Selling Expenses	1,000
Miscellaneous	480
Total FCD	$51,930
Avg FDC per month	$ 4,328

Cash on Hand:	October	November	December	January	February	March	April	May	June	July	August	September
Opening Balance	$ 3,500	$10,779	$17,457	$24,361	$25,697	$26,334	$27,195	$31,453	$35,210	$39,093	$43,350	$47,008
– Cash Receipts	46,875	46,875	46,875	28,225	28,125	28,125	37,500	37,600	37,500	37,500	37,500	37,600
– Cash Disbursements	(39,596)	(40,197)	(39,972)	(26,889)	(27,489)	(27,264)	(33,243)	(33,843)	(33,618)	(33,243)	(33,843)	(33,630)
Total = New Cash Balance	$10,779	$17,457	$24,361	$25,697	$26,334	$27,195	$31,453	$35,210	$39,093	$43,350	$47,008	$50,978

(a) This assumes that all sales are collected in the month the sale is made.

(b) This is just the Cost of Goods row from the monthly income projection worksheet. Cost of Goods is calculated as 60 percent of the estimated total sales for the month.

(c) The mortgage payments (including both principal and interest) are for a $93,000 15-year loan at 10.6 percent. You can use the spreadsheet function @PMT( ) to calculate this:
Payment = @PMT (loan amount, rate per month, number of months)
        = @PMT (93,000, .106/12, 15*12)

(d) The loan is $39,500 for 2½ years at 8.5 percent. The amount shown includes both principal and interest and is calculated as follows: Payment = @PMT (39500, .85/12, 2.5*12)

(e) A typical strategy for established businesses with fairly predictable revenues and expenses is to open an account such as a "Money Market Deposit Account" with their bank. This account, which is interest earning, is used to store excess cash balances and cover cash shortages.

occasionally. However, if you experience negative cash flow regularly, you may be *undercapitalized,* which is a serious problem.[6] Managing your cash flow will be covered in more detail later in this chapter.

What If You Are Starting a New Business?   If you are starting a new business, you don't have historical data to compile in financial statements. Even so, you must estimate how much money you will need, what your expenses will be at different sales levels, and how much money you can expect to make. Financial planning and budgeting are important parts of the business-planning process. Making financial projections can reveal whether you should even start the business. Are the financial risks you are about to take worth the *realistic* return you can expect? Such projections are made in **pro forma financial statements,** which are either full or partial estimates, because you are making projections rather than recording actual transactions. (*Pro forma* is Latin for "for the sake of form.") Because these statements help you determine your future cash needs and financial condition, a new business should prepare them at least every quarter, if not every month.

In preparing pro forma statements, you need to state the assumptions you are making for your projections. How did you come up with the numbers? Did you grab them out of the air? Did the owner of a similar (but noncompeting) business share his actual numbers for you to use as a base? Are they based on industry averages, such as Robert Morris Associates' *RMA Annual Statement Studies*?

> *pro forma financial statements*
> Financial statements that project what a firm's financial condition will be in the future.

Using Financial Statements to Run Your Small Business

Creating financial statements is one thing, but using them to make informed decisions to run your small business is another. Here's an analogy: When you are driving a vehicle, how do you know when something needs attention? By looking at the instruments on your dashboard. Think of financial statements as your instruments for running your business. Just as in driving, to make correct management decisions you need to know what to look at and when to check. Here's a *Financial Status Checklist* for checking the gauges:

Daily

1. Check your cash balance on hand.
2. Check your bank balance.
3. Calculate daily summaries of sales and cash receipts.
4. Note any problems in your credit collections.
5. Record any money paid out.

Weekly

1. *Cash flow.* Update a spreadsheet of regular receipts and disbursement entries. The discipline required by this endeavor will help you see what is going on in your business.
2. *Accounts receivable. Note* especially slow-paying accounts.
3. *Accounts payable.* Note discounts offered.

4. *Payroll.* Calculate the accumulation of hours worked and total payroll owed.
5. *Taxes. Note* when tax items are due and which reports are required.

Monthly

1. If you use an outside accounting service, provide records of your receipts, disbursements, bank accounts, and journals.
2. Review your income statement.
3. Review your balance sheet.
4. Reconcile your business checking account.
5. Balance your petty cash account.
6. Review federal tax requirements and make deposits.
7. Review and age your accounts receivable.

Analyzing Financial Statements

Your ability to make sound financial decisions will depend on how well you can understand, interpret, and use the information contained in your company's financial statements. This section gives an overview of the most common form of financial analysis: ratio analysis.

Ratio Analysis

Suppose that two entrepreneurs are comparing how well their respective businesses performed last year. The first entrepreneur, Ms. Alpha, determines that her store made 50 percent more profits last year than the store owned by the second entrepreneur, Mr. Beta. Should Ms. Alpha feel proud? To answer this question, we need more information.

The profit figures tell us only part of the story. Although generating 50 percent more profits *seems* good, we need to see how profit relates to other aspects of each business. For example, what if Ms. Alpha's store is four times the size of Mr. Beta's store? Or what if Ms. Alpha's store made three times as many sales as Mr. Beta's store? Now does 50 percent more profits seem as good?

The reality is that fair comparisons can be made only when we demonstrate the relationships between profit and other financial features of the businesses. The relationships that show the relative size of some financial quantity to another financial quantity of a firm are called **financial ratios.** Four important types of financial ratios are the liquidity, activity, leverage, and profitability ratios.[7]

financial ratios
Calculations that compare important financial aspects of a business.

Liquidity Ratios

Liquidity ratios are used to measure a firm's ability to meet its short-term obligations to creditors as they come due. *Liquidity* refers to how quickly an asset can be turned into cash—the more quickly it can become cash, the more liquid it is said to be. The financial data used to determine liquidity are the firm's current assets and current liabilities found on the balance sheet. There are two important liquidity ratios: the current ratio and the quick (or acid-test) ratio.

liquidity ratios
Financial ratios used to measure a firm's ability to meet its short-term obligations to creditors as they come due.

Current Ratio   The **current ratio** measures the number of times the firm can cover its current liabilities with its current assets. The current ratio assumes that both accounts receivable and inventory can be easily converted to cash. Current ratios of 1.0 or less are considered low and indicative of financial difficulties. Current ratios of more than 2.0 often suggest excessive liquidity that may be adverse to the firm's profitability.

current ratio
A financial ratio that measures the number of times the firm can cover its current liabilities with its current assets.

$$\text{Current ratio} = \frac{\text{Current assets}}{\text{Current liabilities}}$$

Using Stereo City's balance sheet, we compute the company's current ratio as follows:

$$\frac{\$155,000}{\$105,000} = 1.48$$

Thus Stereo City can cover its current liabilities 1.48 times with its current assets. Another way of looking at this ratio is to recognize that the company has $1.48 of current assets for each $1.00 of current liabilities.

Quick Ratio   The **quick (acid-test) ratio** measures the firm's ability to meet its current obligations with the most liquid of its current assets. The quick ratio is computed as follows:

quick acid-test ratio
A financial ratio that measures the firm's ability to meet its current obligations with the most liquid of its current assets.

$$\text{Quick ratio} = \frac{\text{Current assets} - \text{Inventory}}{\text{Current liabilities}}$$

Using the data from Stereo City's balance sheet, we compute the quick ratio as

$$\frac{\$155,000 - \$125,000}{\$105,000} = 0.29$$

Stereo City has only $0.29 in liquid assets for each $1.00 of current liabilities. The company obviously counts on making sales to pay its current obligations.

Activity Ratios

Activity ratios measure the speed with which various accounts are converted into sales or cash. These ratios are often used to measure how efficiently a firm uses its assets. Four important activity ratios exist: inventory turnover, average collection period, fixed asset turnover, and total asset turnover.

activity ratios
Financial ratios that measure the speed with which various accounts are converted into sales or cash.

Inventory Turnover   **Inventory turnover** measures the liquidity of the firm's inventory—how quickly goods are sold and replenished. The higher the inventory turnover, the more times the firm is selling, or "turning over," its inventory. A high inventory ratio generally implies efficient inventory management. Inventory turnover is computed as follows:

inventory turnover
An activity ratio that measures the liquidity of the firm's inventory—how quickly goods are sold and replenished.

$$\text{Inventory turnover} = \frac{\text{Cost of goods sold}}{\text{Inventory}}$$

Using data from Stereo City's income statement and balance sheet, we compute the inventory turnover as

$$\frac{\$270,000}{\$125,000} = 2.16$$

Thus Stereo City restocked its inventory 2.16 times last year.

Average Collection Period   The **average collection period** is a measure of how long it takes a firm to convert a credit sale (internal store credit, not credit card sales) into a usable form (cash). All firms that extend credit must compute this ratio to determine the effectiveness of their credit-granting and collection policies. High average collection periods usually indicate many uncollectible receivables, whereas low average collection periods may indicate overly restrictive credit-granting policies. The average collection period is computed as follows:

average collection period
A measure of how long it takes a firm to convert a credit sale (internal store credit, not credit card sales) into a usable form (cash).

$$\text{Average collection period} = \frac{\text{Accounts receivable}}{\text{Average sales per day}}$$

Using the data from Stereo City's balance sheet and income statement, we compute the average collection period as

$$\frac{\$12,000}{\$450,000/365} = 9.93$$

Stereo City collects its receivables in fewer than ten days.

Fixed Asset Turnover   The **fixed asset turnover** ratio measures how efficiently the firm is using its assets to generate sales. The higher the ratio, the more effective is the firm's asset utilization. A low ratio often indicates that marketing efforts are ineffective or that the firm's core business areas are not currently feasible. The fixed asset turnover ratio is calculated as follows:

fixed asset turnover
An activity ratio that measures how efficiently a firm is using its assets to generate sales.

$$\text{Fixed asset turnover} = \frac{\text{Sales}}{\text{Net fixed assets}}$$

Using the data from Stereo City's income statement and balance sheet, we compute the fixed asset turnover ratio as

$$\frac{\$450,000}{\$168,000} = 2.68$$

Stereo City turns over its net fixed assets 2.68 times per year.

Total Asset Turnover   The **total asset turnover** ratio measures how efficiently the firm uses all of its assets to generate sales, so a high ratio generally reflects good overall management. A low ratio may indicate flaws in the firm's overall strategy, poor marketing efforts, or improper capital expenditures. Total asset turnover is calculated as follows:

$$\text{Total asset turnover} = \frac{\text{Sales}}{\text{Total assets}}$$

Using the data from Stereo City's income statement and balance sheet, we compute the total asset turnover as

$$\frac{\$450,000}{\$323,500} = 1.39$$

Stereo City turns its assets over 1.39 times per year.

Leverage Ratios

Leverage ratios measure the extent to which a firm uses debt as a source of financing and its ability to service that debt. The term *leverage* refers to the magnification of risk and potential return that comes with using other people's money to generate profits. Think of the increased power that is gained when a fulcrum is moved under a simple lever. The farther the fulcrum is from the point where you are pushing on the lever, the more weight you can lift. The more debt a firm uses, the more financial leverage it has. Two important leverage ratios are the debt ratio and the times interest earned ratio.

Debt Ratio   The **debt ratio** measures the proportion of a firm's total assets that is acquired with borrowed funds. Total debt includes short-term debt, long-term debt, and long-term obligations such as leases. A high ratio indicates a more aggressive approach to financing and is evidence of a high-risk, high-expected-return strategy. A low ratio indicates a more conservative approach to financing. The debt ratio is calculated as follows:

$$\text{Debt ratio} = \frac{\text{Total debt}}{\text{Total assets}}$$

Using the data from Stereo City's balance sheet, we compute the debt ratio as

$$\frac{\$237,5000}{\$323,500} = 0.73$$

This ratio indicates that the company has financed 73 percent of its assets with borrowed funds. That is, $0.73 of every $1.00 of funding for Stereo City has come from debt.

Times-Interest-Earned Ratio   **Times interest earned** calculates the firm's ability to meet its interest requirements. It shows how far operating income can decline before the firm will likely experience difficulties in servicing its debt obligations.

---

total asset turnover
An activity ratio that measures how efficiently the firm uses all of its assets to generate sales; a high ratio generally reflects good overall management.

leverage ratios
Financial ratios that measure the extent to which a firm uses debt as a source of financing and its ability to service that debt.

debt ratio
A leverage ratio that measures the proportion of a firm's total assets that is acquired with borrowed funds.

times interest earned
A leverage ratio that calculates the firm's ability to meet its interest requirements.

A high ratio indicates a low-risk situation but may also suggest an inefficient use of leverage. A low ratio indicates that immediate action should be taken to ensure that no debt payments will go into default status. Times interest earned is computed as follows:

$$\text{Times interest earned} = \frac{\text{Operating income}}{\text{Interest expense}}$$

Using the data from Stereo City's income statement, we compute times interest earned as

$$\frac{\$22,750}{\$15,000} = 1.52$$

Thus the company has operating income 1.52 times its interest obligations.

Profitability Ratios

Profitability ratios are used to measure the ability of a company to turn sales into profits and to earn profits on assets committed. Additionally, profitability ratios allow some insight into the overall effectiveness of the management team. There are three important profitability ratios: net profit margin, return on assets, and return on equity.

profitability ratios
Financial ratios that are used to measure the ability of a company to turn sales into profits and to earn profits on assets committed.

Net Profit Margin   The **net profit margin** measures the percentage of each sales dollar that remains as profit after all expenses, including taxes, have been paid. This ratio is widely used as a gauge of management efficiency. Although net profit margins vary greatly by industry, a low ratio indicates that expenses are too high relative to sales. Net profit margin can be obtained from a common-size income statement or computed with the following formula:

net profit margin
A profitability ratio that measures the percentage of each sales dollar that remains as profit after all expenses, including taxes, have been paid.

$$\text{Net profit} = \frac{\text{Net income}}{\text{sales}}$$

Using the data from Stereo City's income statement, we compute the net profit margin as

$$\frac{\$4,830}{\$450,000} = 0.0107$$

This company actually generates 1.07 cents of after-tax profit for each $1.00 of sales.

Return on Assets   Also known as *return on investment*, **return on assets** indicates the firm's effectiveness in generating profits from its available assets. The higher this ratio is, the better. A high ratio shows effective management and good chances for future growth. The return on assets is found with the following formula:

return on assets
A profitability ratio that indicates the firm's effectiveness in generating profits from its available assets; also known as *return on investment.*

$$\text{Return on assets} = \frac{\text{Net profit after taxes}}{\text{Total assets}}$$

Using the data from Stereo City's income statement and balance sheet, we compute the return on assets as

$$\frac{\$4,830}{\$323,500} = 0.0149$$

This company generates approximately 1.5 cents of after-tax profit for each $1.00 of assets the company has at its disposal.

Return on Equity   The **return on equity** measures the return the firm earned on its owner's investment in the firm. In general, the higher this ratio, the better off financially the owner will be. However, return on equity is highly affected by the amount of financial leverage (borrowed money) used by the firm and may not provide an accurate measure of management effectiveness. The return on equity is calculated as follows:

$$\text{Return on equity} = \frac{\text{Net profit after taxes}}{\text{Owner's equity}}$$

Using the data from Stereo City's income statement and balance sheet, we compute the return on equity as

$$\frac{\$4,830}{\$86,000} = 0.0562$$

This company generates a little more than 5.5 cents of after-tax profit for each $1.00 of owner's equity. This ratio tells a business owner if he or he is receiving enough return from invested money. In the Stereo City example, 5.5 percent return is not much for the risk involved. That $86,000 could be placed in a relatively safe investment like a corporate bond, where it could earn a much higher return with less risk. This kind of information can tell a business owner whether a business is a good investment compared with other alternative uses for her money.

Using Financial Ratios

Financial ratios by themselves tell us very little. For purposes of analysis, ratios are useful only when compared with other ratios. Two types of ratio comparisons can be employed: **cross-sectional analysis**, which compares different firms' financial ratios at the same point in time, and **time series analysis**, which compares a single firm's present performance with its own past performance.

Cross-Sectional Analysis   Cross-sectional analysis is often done by comparing an individual firm's ratios against the standard ratios for the firm's industry. Such industry ratios may be found in resources available in most college or large public libraries. Look for Robert Morris Associates' *RMA Annual Statement Studies* or Dun & Bradstreet's *Industry Norms and Key Business Ratios.* Another good source is *Financial Studies of the Small Business* from Financial Research Associates.

Table 8.1 shows how some of Stereo City's ratios compare with the median ratios for stereo equipment retail stores with an asset size between $10,000 and $1,000,000. From the data we can conclude that Stereo City potentially has three major problems.

First, Stereo City's quick ratio is only about half the industry average. This could mean that the company has excessive amounts of inventory and faces the possibility of illiquidity if the inventory does not sell in a timely manner.

Second, Stereo City appears to have an excessive amount of debt in relation to its sales. The firm's times-interest-earned ratio is less than one-fourth the industry average, indicating a strong probability that the company will not be able to service its debt in the future.

Third, Stereo City's total asset turnover and return on asset ratios are both considerably below the industry averages. The likely cause is that the firm has insufficient

Table 8.1

COMPARING COMPANY
AND INDUSTRY RATIOS

	Stereo City	Industry
Liquidity		
Current Ratio	1.48	1.60
Quick Ratio	0.29	0.50
Activity		
Average Collection	9.7	8.0
Total Asset Turnover	1.4	4.2
Leverage		
Debt Ratio	73.0	61.5
Times Interest Earned	1.5	6.1
Profitability		
Return on Assets*	2.5	6.2

*Uses pretax Profit

SOURCE: *Financial Studies of the Small Business,* 17th ed. (Winter Haven, FL: Financial Research Associates, 1994).

sales to support the size of the business. The company must either downsize by sell-ing off some assets or work harder to increase sales.

Time Series Analysis   Time series analysis is used to uncover trends in the firm's financial performance. If there is potential trouble in any of the four main areas of analysis (liquidity, activity, leverage, and profitability), managers will have time to correct these problems before the problems become overbearing. The key to potential solutions is found in the ratios themselves. For example, if the time series analysis shows that the firm's liquidity is diminishing, the managers will want to take action to enhance the firm's liquidity position. By looking at the liq-uidity ratios, a number of possible solutions will become apparent.

Because ratio analysis has revealed that Stereo City needs to increase its current assets (especially cash and short-term investments) without any commensurate increase in current liabilities, possible solutions are to borrow cash through a long-term loan, get a cash infusion from the firm's owner, or sell off some fixed assets for cash. An alternative approach would be to reduce current liabilities by restructuring short-term debt into long-term debt or by using the proceeds of the sale of a fixed asset to retire some accounts payable. Any action that boosts the firm's liquidity helps to avoid the risk of Stereo City's becoming insolvent because of diminishing liquidity.

Reviewing financial ratios annually can help you circumvent difficult situa-tions before they have the opportunity to occur. Thus ratio analysis allows small business owners and managers to become proactive directors of the financial aspects of their ventures.

If you find that you enjoy working with accounting information or creating accounting systems, you might even consider starting a small business to provide those services. Finding a unique accounting-services niche can be profitable. Consider, for instance, what Combined Resource Technology (CRT) of Baton Rouge, Louisiana, did. CRT started out as a real estate development company. However, when the oil and gas price crash battered Louisiana's economy, CRT found that it owed some $14 million to banks on loans it had taken out to buy a shopping center and apartment buildings. To avoid failure of their business, CRT partners Darwyn Williams and Chris Moran had to do something quickly. Although their properties' values had plunged, the pair found that the tax assessor's property valuations hadn't changed. Out of desperation was born their new accounting-services business. In its new life, CRT peruses tax rolls to identify overassessed properties and contacts the owners about getting the taxes reduced—for a fee, of course. CRT has since expanded its cost-reduction services beyond taxes, to include utilities, waste disposal, freight, leases, and any other areas where the firm can help business owners reduce costs. CRT provides a unique accounting service that others have been willing to pay for.[8]

Managing Cash Flow

Each business day, approximately a dozen U.S. small businesses declare bankruptcy. The majority of these business failures are caused by poor cash-flow management.[9] Companies from the smallest startups to the largest conglomerates all share the same need for positive cash flow. A company that does not effectively manage its cash flow is poised for collapse.

Cash Flow Defined

cash flow
The sum of net income plus any noncash expenses, such as depreciation and amortization, or the difference between the actual amount of cash a company brings in and the actual amount of cash a company disburses in a given time period.

The accounting definition of **cash flow** is the sum of net income plus any noncash expenses, such as depreciation and amortization. This treatment of cash flow is largely misunderstood by many small business owners. A more "bottom-line" approach is to define cash flow as the difference between the actual amount of cash a company brings in and the actual amount of cash a company disburses in a given time period.

The most important aspects of this refined definition are the inclusion of the terms *actual cash* and *time period.* The goal of good cash-flow management is to have enough cash on hand when you need it. It doesn't matter if your company will have a positive cash balance three months from now if your payroll, taxes, insurance, and suppliers all need to be paid today.

Cash-flow management requires as much attention as developing new customers, perfecting products and services, and engaging in all other day-to-day operating activities. The basic strategy is to maximize your use of cash. This means not only ensuring consistent cash inflows, but also developing a disciplined approach to cash outflows.

Could your cash-flow management system be computerized? As noted earlier in the chapter, single-entry general ledger accounting software packages are certainly easy to use. However, these packages can provide an unrealistic view of your business's cash flow. In a single-entry system, all cash coming into the business is put on the left-hand side of the ledger, and cash flowing out of the business appears on the right-hand side. However, if your business has accounts receivable or accounts payable, a single-entry system can fool you into thinking you have enough cash on hand to meet expenses or to pursue business expansion.

Cash-Flow Fundamentals

The first step in cash-flow management is to understand the purpose and nature of cash flow. Why do you need cash flow? How is cash flow generated? How do firms become insolvent even though they are profitable? To answer these questions, we need to look at the motives for having cash, the cash-to-cash cycle, and the timing of cash inflows and outflows.

> "A company that does not effectively manage its cash flow—by balancing its income and expenses on a day-to-day basis—is poised for collapse."

Motives for Having Cash   A firm needs cash for three reasons: (1) to make transactions, (2) to protect against unanticipated problems, and (3) to invest in opportunities as they arise. Of these, the primary motive is to make transactions—to pay the bills incurred by the business. If a business cannot meet its obligations, it is insolvent. Continued insolvency leads directly to bankruptcy.

Businesses, like individuals, occasionally run into unanticipated problems. Thefts, fires, floods, and other natural and human-made disasters affect businesses in the same way they affect individuals. Those businesses that have "saved for a rainy day" are able to withstand such setbacks. Those that have not planned ahead often suffer—and may even fail—as a result.

Finally, sometimes a business is presented with an opportunity to invest in a profitable venture. If the business has enough cash on hand to do so, it may reap significant rewards. If not, it has lost a chance to add to its cash flow in a way other than through normal operations.

Each of these three motives is important to understand, as they combine to create the proper mentality for the cash-flow manager. If a firm does not proactively manage its cash flow, it will be exposed to many risks, any of which may spell disaster.

Cash-to-Cash Cycle   The **cash-to-cash cycle** of the firm, sometimes known as the *operating cycle*, tracks the way cash flows through the business. It identifies how long it takes from the time a firm makes a cash outlay for raw materials or inventory until the cash is collected from the sale of the finished good. Figure 8.5 shows a typical cash-to-cash cycle.

cash-to-cash cycle
The period of time from when money is spent on raw materials until it is collected on the sale of a finished good.

The firm begins with cash that is used to purchase raw materials or inventory. It will normally take some time to manufacture or otherwise hold finished goods until they sell. As sales are made, cash is replenished immediately by cash sales, but accounts receivable are created by credit sales. The firm must then collect the receivables to secure cash.

The cash-flow process is continuous, with all activities occurring simultaneously. When the process is operating smoothly, cash flow is easy to monitor and control. However, for most firms, it is often erratic and subject to many complications, which makes cash-flow management a challenge.

Timing of Cash Flows   The major complication of cash-flow management is timing. While some cash inflows and outflows will transpire on a regular schedule

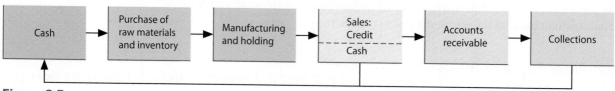

Figure 8.5
CASH-TO-CASH CYCLE

A Chart of the Cash-to-Cash Cycle of Your Small Business Shows the Amount of Time That Passes Between Spending Money for Raw Materials or Inventory and Collecting Money on the Sale of Finished Goods.

(such as monthly interest income or payroll costs), other cash flows occur on no schedule whatsoever. For example, when a firm needs to make periodic purchases of capital equipment, which are not part of the daily cash-to-cash process, it will cause a major disruption in the firm's cash flow.

Even though a firm might send out all of its billings to credit customers at one time, you can be sure that these customers will not all pay at the same time. Uncollected receivables may count as revenue on an accrual-based income statement, but they are worthless from a cash-flow standpoint until they turn into real money.

The small business owner needs to become well versed in the patterns of cash inflows and outflows of the firm. The nuances of timing become critical. A few tools are available that can assist in this process, which we will now discuss.

Cash-Flow Management Tools

Once you have a good idea about the purpose and nature of cash flow, you are ready to take steps to manage it. Using cash budgets, aging schedules, and float to control the inflow and outflow of cash is paramount for effective management.

Cash Budgets   **Cash budgets** (also known as *cash forecasts*) allow the firm to plan its short-term cash needs, paying particular attention to periods of surplus and shortage. Whenever the firm is likely to experience a cash surplus, it can plan to make a short-term investment. When the firm is expected to experience a cash shortage, it can plan to arrange for a short-term loan.

A cash budget typically covers a one-year period that is divided into smaller intervals. The number of intervals is dictated by the nature of the business. The more uncertain the firm's cash flows are, the more intervals required. Using monthly intervals is common, but some firms require daily cash budgets.

The cash budget requires the small business owner to determine all the known cash inflows and outflows that will occur during the year. Both the amount of cash involved and the cycle's length of time must be disclosed. This information is then put into a format like that shown in Table 8.2. The table lists some of the most common types of cash inflows and outflows experienced by a typical small business. Its categories should be modified to fit the particulars of each individual business. The most important point is to include all relevant sources of and demands for cash.

> *cash budget*
> A plan for short-term uses and sources of cash.

Reality Check

Open-Book Management

At bulletin boards in the lobbies, conference rooms, and cafeterias of businesses across the country, many of today's employees are studying a type of information that once was off-limits—the company's financial statements. This practice, called *open-book management (OBM)*, involves showing everyone in the business the numbers that are critical to the business's performance. When employees know and understand the numbers, they can measure their contributions to the company's bottom line and assess how their performance can make a difference in those numbers.

OBM is being used successfully by many small businesses. However, you cannot simply hand out income statements and expect employees to care about the information or understand how their efforts affect it. You must teach them what the numbers mean to them.

One of the first proponents of OBM was Jack Stack, president and CEO of Springfield Remanufacturing Company. In *The Great Game of Business,* he stated that you need to teach employees the rules of the game, give them the information (the financials) they need to play the game, and make sure they share in the risks and rewards. Stack draws an analogy between open-book management and a game of baseball. He asks, "Can you imagine taking a spectator to a baseball game and not explaining the rules, not showing them how they keep score, and not giving them a stake in the outcome? Can you imagine sitting in those stands trying to figure out why those crazy people are running around on that field and hitting this little ball with a stick? The same thing occurs every single day when someone goes to work. They aren't taught the rules; they don't know what business is all about. They're only taught a little circle, a little piece of the process. We tried to convert it into a game—move everybody from a spectator to a player."

OBM is almost certainly the best communication approach organizations can adopt to dramatically improve productivity. Despite being around for about 20 years and being enormously successful in many American private- and public-sector organizations, OBM has not really achieved the level of popularity it deserves, especially outside the United States.

SOURCES: Rodney Gray, "Open-Book Management," *Strategic Communication Management,* February/March 2006, 34–34; Raj Aggarwal, "Open Book Management," *Business Horizons,* September/October 2001, 5–14; Rick Maurer, "The Task of Moving from Why to How," *Journal for Quality & Participation,* Spring 2003, 36; Jack Stack, "Are Your Employees Invested in the Bottom Line?" *Harvard Management Update,* October 2002, 3.

Many businesses find that adding a *reconciliation* component to the bottom of the cash budget is helpful. This reconciliation summarizes the total cash inflows and outflows for the period. When this summary is combined with the beginning cash balance, you have the current cash status of the firm. Because there will be some minimum cash balance required to begin the next period, the ending cash figure is compared to this minimum figure. If there is a positive difference (ending cash minus minimum cash balance), the firm has cash to invest. If there is a negative difference, the firm must arrange for financing before beginning the new cycle.

By forecasting the inflows and outflows of cash, the small business owner will have a picture of when the firm will have cash surpluses and cash shortages. This knowledge allows the cash flow to be managed proactively rather than reactively.

Table 8.2
CASH BUDGET FORMAT

	January	February	March	April	May
Beginning Cash					
Plus Receipts:					
Cash Sales					
Receivable Collections					
Interest					
Owner Contributions					
Other Receipts					
Total Receipts					
Minus Disbursements:					
Cash Purchases					
Payment of Accounts Payable					
Wages and Salaries					
Payroll Taxes					
Advertising					
Office Supplies					
Rent/Mortgage					
Utilities					
Telephone					
Insurance					
Legal/Accounting					
Taxes and Licenses					
Interest Payments					
Loan Principal Payments					
Dues and Subscriptions					
Travel					
Miscellaneous Disbursements					
Total Disbursements					
Ending Cash (Beginning Cash + Receipts − Disbursements)					

- *Pay bills on time, but not before they are due.* Unless you receive enough trade discount incentive to pay early, don't rush to send payments.

- *Be smart in designing your invoice.* Make sure that the amount due, due date, discount for early payment, and penalty for late payment are clearly laid out.[10]

Inventory   Inventory is another area that can drain cash flow. According to James Howard, chairman of the board of Asset Growth Partners, Inc., a New York City financial consulting firm for small businesses, inventory costs are often overlooked or understated by many small businesses. "A typical manufacturing company pays 25 to 30 percent of the value of the inventory for the cost of borrowed money, warehouse space, materials handling, staff, lift-truck expenses, and fixed costs."[11]

Cash flow determines how much inventory can safely be carried by a firm while still allowing sufficient cash for other operations. The inventory-turnover ratio lends insight to this situation. If, for example, a firm has an inventory ratio of 12, it has to keep only one month's worth of projected sales in stock before enough cash returns to pay for the next month's worth of inventory. By comparison, if the firm has a ratio of 4, it must keep three months' worth of projected sales on the shelves. This system ties up cash for as much as 90 days. In this case the firm should try to find suppliers that have terms extending to 90 days. Otherwise, it may have to borrow to meet current cash needs. The cash-flow management goal is to commit just enough cash to inventory to meet demand.

Banks   Ideally, your bank should be your partner in cash-flow management. The small business owner should request the firm's bank to provide an *account analysis*. This analysis shows the banking services the business used during the month, the bank's charge for each service, the balances maintained in all accounts during the month, and the minimum balances required by the bank to pay for the services.

A review of the account analysis will indicate whether any excess account balances are on deposit. These should immediately be removed and invested. Also, your firm may be better off removing all account balances that are earning little or no interest and reinvesting them at higher rates, even if it means having to pay fees for bank services.

Finally, determine how quickly checks that your firm deposits in the bank become available as cash. Banks normally require delays of up to two business days. They should have an *availability schedule,* and the small business owner needs to request one from each bank in the area to determine whether his bank is competitive. Remember—the faster a deposited check becomes available as cash, the sooner your business has use of the money for other purposes.

Other Areas of Cash-Flow Concern   Although receivables, inventory, and bank services are the most

Inventory in a Warehouse is Just like Cash Sitting on a Shelf.

likely places on which to concentrate cash-flow management strategies, several other areas also deserve attention:

1. *Compensation.* Look for duplication of effort and lack of productivity within the firm's workforce. Cut personnel hours in those areas to save on wage and payroll tax costs.

2. *Supplies.* Review all petty cash accounts. Show employees the cost of supplies by marking the cost of each item, such as tablets, on the boxes.

3. *Deliveries.* Keep track of local delivery costs to the business. It may be cheaper to hire a part-time worker to pick up supplies than to pay other companies to deliver items.

4. *Insurance.* Ask insurance carriers about ways to reduce premiums. One independent grocery store reduced premiums for its stock personnel by 15 percent simply by requiring them to wear supports while working.

5. *Borrowing.* Take the cost of borrowing into account when determining operational expenses. Even short-term loans can have a large effect on profit and cash flow.

The process of cash-flow management may seem confusing to you in the beginning, but you may find it relatively easy to monitor once everything is in place. Armed with a cash budget, aging schedules, and a set of feasible strategies, you can avoid cash-flow problems and maximize your use of this precious resource.

Summary

• **The importance of financial records to a small business**

You need financial records so you can make managerial decisions on topics concerning how much money is owed to your business, how much money you owe, and how to identify financial problems before they become serious dilemmas. Financial records are also needed to prepare your tax returns and to inform your banker and investors about your business's financial status. Without accurate financial records, you cannot exercise the kind of clear-sighted management control needed to survive in a competitive marketplace.

• **The accounting records needed for a small business**

The accounting records of your small business need to follow the standards of generally accepted accounting principles (GAAP). From your source documents, such as sales slips, purchase invoices, and check stubs, you should record all the transactions in journals. Information from your journals should then be posted in (transferred into) a general ledger.

Financial statements like your balance sheet, income statement, and statement of cash flow are produced from the transactions in your general ledger.

• **Ratios used to analyze financial statements**

Ratio analysis enables you to compare the financial condition of your business to its performance in previous time periods or to the performance of similarly sized businesses within your industry. Four important types of financial ratios discussed in this chapter are liquidity (current and quick, or acid-test, ratios), activity (inventory turnover, average collection period, fixed asset turnover, total asset turnover), leverage (debt and times interest earned), and profitability ratios (net profit margin, return on assets, return on equity).

• **The importance of managing cash flow**

Cash flow is the difference between the amount of cash actually brought into your business and the amount paid out in a given period of time. Cash flow represents the lifeblood of your business because if you do not have enough money to pay for your operating expenses, you are out of business.

Questions for Review and Discussion

1. How can financial records allow you to identify problems in your business?

2. Assets = Liabilities + Owner's equity. How would you restate this equation if you wanted to know what your liabilities are? Your owner's equity?

3. What purpose do GAAP and FASB serve for a small business owner?

4. Explain the difference between cash and accrual accounting.

5. Define the term *leverage* as it applies to accounting.

6. How can profitability ratios allow insight into the effectiveness of management? Liquidity ratios? Activity ratios? Leverage ratios?

7. If you were setting up open-book management in your business, what would you teach employees to make it work?

8. Explain the difference between macro-aging and micro-aging accounts receivable schedules.

9. Cash flow has been described as the lifeblood of a business. How would you explain this description to someone who does not understand business finance?

10. The sales projection for your retail business is $650,000. The industry average for the asset turnover ratio is 5. How much inventory (total assets) should you plan to stock?

Questions for Critical Thinking

1. You need to write a business plan for a startup business. How do you come up with the numbers for your pro forma financial statements? Do you just guess and make them up? (*Hint:* The process starts with a sales forecast.)

2. Cash flow is more important than profit for a small business. Why? If your income statement shows a profit at the end of the month, how can anything be more important than that?

Experience This . . .

Choose a type of small business that is of interest to you. Go to the library and find industry-standard ratios in Robert Morris Associates' *RMA Annual Statement Studies* or Dun & Bradstreet's *Industry Norms and Key Business Ratios.* What do these standards tell you about the financial needs of this type of business? For example, is inventory turnover high or low in your chosen industry? Are profit margins tight or high?

What Would You Do?

The popularity of soccer as a participation sport attracted Leo Hernandez and Gil Ferguson to open an indoor soccer arena with retail shops selling soccer-related merchandise. Last year's financial statements for their business OnGoal are shown here. Leo and Gil are hoping to expand their business by opening another facility. However, before they approach banks or potential investors, they need to look closely at what the accounting statements show them.

Questions

1. Calculate liquidity, activity, leverage, and profitability ratios for OnGoal.

2. Pair off and compare your ratios. Discuss which of the ratios look weak and which look positive. Develop a one-page explanation of the company's ratios that you can show to potential lenders.

OnGoal
Balance Sheet
December 31, 20—

ASSETS

Current Assets:

Cash	$ 7,120	
Accounts Receivable	2,400	
Merchandise Inventory	18,200	
Prepaid Expenses	3,040	
Total Current Assets		$ 40,760

Fixed Assets:

Fixtures	$16,800	
Less Accumulated Depreciation	3,600	
Building	78,000	
Less Accumulated Depreciation	7,800	
Equipment	12,000	
Less Accumulated Depreciation	4,000	
Total Fixed Assets		$ 91,400
TOTAL ASSETS:		$132,160

LIABILITIES/EQUITY

Current Liabilities:

Accounts Payable	$ 6,000	
Notes Payable	4,000	
Contracts Payable	8,000	
Total Current Liabilities		$ 18,000

Fixed Liabilities:

Long-term Note Payable	$75,000	

Owners' Equity:

Shares Held by Hernandez and Ferguson	$39,160	
TOTAL LIABILITIES/EQUITY:		$132,160

OnGoal
Income Statement
Year Ended December 31, 20—

SALES			$178,000
Cost of Goods Sold:			
Beginning Inventory, January 1	$18,000		
Purchases During Year	22,000		
Less Ending Inventory, December 31	18,200		
Cost of Goods Sold		$ 21,800	
GROSS MARGIN			$156,200
Operating Expenses:			
Payment on Building Note	$34,000		
Salaries	68,000		
Supplies	7,460		
Advertising/Promotion	3,000		
Insurance Expense	18,000		
Utilities Expense	10,000		
Miscellaneous Expenses	4,000		
Total Operating Expenses		$144,460	
NET PROFIT FROM OPERATIONS:			$ 11,740

CHAPTER CLOSING CASE

KEEP DANCIN' WITH THE ONE WHO BROUGHT YOU

For 10 years, Karl De Abrew and Sam Chandler had a happy, productive relationship with Adobe, developing plug-ins to enhance Acrobat PDF software and consulting with the software giant, based in San Jose, California, on developer support. And Adobe seemed just as happy with ARTS PDF, De Abrew and Chandler's Melbourne, Australia–based company; it even sponsored ARTS PDF's online community of PDF users, Planet PDF. By 2003 ARTS PDF had 30 full-time employees and half of its $3 million in annual revenue came from Adobe-related projects.

But the two partners were plotting a move that once would have seemed insane—severing the relationship and instead competing with Adobe with a PDF product of their own. The problem was the way Adobe had begun treating third-party developers like ARTS PDF. Since the release of Adobe Acrobat in 1993, such developers had been key to Adobe's strategy. The company created the application with an open standard, giving any developer access to the software's specifications and a free license to create applications to extend its capabilities. Hundreds of third-party developers had based their businesses on Acrobat. ARTS PDF, for example, scored a big hit with a plug-in that, among other things, allows users to activate Web links in PDF documents, and sells the software on its own website, PDF Store.

But Adobe's CEO, Bruce Chizen, who took over from co-founder John Warnock in 2000, had grown wary of working with outsiders. Warnock used to refer to the hundreds of third-party developers as Adobe's "ecosystem." Under Chizen's leadership, however, the company began reengineering the third-party plug-ins itself, incorporating them into new and increasingly complicated versions of Acrobat. That sparked concern among developers. If consumers could buy Acrobat software loaded with the latest extras, they would no longer need plug-ins.

De Abrew and Chandler were as tuned into the PDF community as anyone, and they knew what was coming: Their plug-in business was disappearing before their eyes. At the same time, they sensed that there was a market for an Acrobat alternative. People were changing the way they used PDF applications. Instead of using the software simply to create and read files, more businesses were embracing the PDF format

as a collaboration tool to let workers share digital documents, inserting revisions and comments along the way. Acrobat can do all those things, but the cost can sting when a company needs to push out the software to large groups of employees. What's more, many companies don't need Acrobat's whiz-bang graphics capabilities, which tend to slow down performance.

De Abrew began asking customers what they thought about Adobe. Their responses backed up his hunch. He says he heard complaints from many executives who were tired of paying between $350 and $450 per user to license the software. Acrobat, they said, was sometimes overwhelming and confusing. They wanted a cheaper version that was faster and easier to use. And if ARTS PDF built it, they'd buy it.

De Abrew and his colleagues had been kicking around the idea of creating an alternative to Adobe for years but had never seriously pursued it. Now it seemed like a good idea. Adobe was huge, with revenue of $700 million. But a 2003 research report found that the PDF market had the potential to reach $1 billion. De Abrew and Chandler were confident that ARTS PDF had the industry knowledge and engineering chops to pull off a cheaper, scaled-down version of Acrobat. What's more, the open PDF standard meant anyone could develop applications to compete with Acrobat, so there was little possibility of a lawsuit.

The way De Abrew and Chandler saw it, they had two options. They could stick it out and hope that Adobe reconsidered its approach toward third-party developers, the chances of which seemed pretty slim. Or they could try to get a slice of the PDF market for themselves. That would mean alienating their biggest partner. It would also mean refocusing most of their limited resources on developing the new product and all but abandoning the plug-in business that had been so profitable. The stakes couldn't be higher: If the competing product failed, Adobe wasn't likely to let them return to the fold. There would be no turning back.

What do you think? Should ARTS PDF have gone head-to-head with Adobe?

SOURCE: From David Miller, "Adobe Had Always Been ARTS PDF's Best Partner, Then Everything Changed," *Inc.,* May 2006, 60–62. Copyright © 2006 Mansueto Ventures LLC, publisher of Inc. Magazine, New York, NY 10017. Reprinted with permission.

Test Prepper

You've read the chapter, studied the key terms, and the exam is any day now. Think you're ready to ace it? Take this sample test to gauge your comprehension of chapter material. You can check your answers at the back of the book. Want more test questions? Visit the student website at college.hmco.com/pic/hatten4e and take the ACE and ACE+ quizzes for more practice.

ACE self-test
college.hmco.com/pic/hatten4e

Matching

_____ 1. a business system that converts raw data into usable information

_____ 2. a record tracking income and expenses only, like a checkbook

_____ 3. a resource that a business owns

_____ 4. an accounting method that records income and expenses at the time they are incurred

_____ 5. a financial statement that shows revenues and expenses

_____ 6. a financial statement that shows conditions in the future

_____ 7. an activity ratio that measures inventory liquidity

_____ 8. a profitability ratio that indicates the firm's effectiveness in generating profit from available assets

_____ 9. the period of time from when money is spent on raw materials until it is collected on the sale of a finished good.

_____10. a list of accounts receivable based on the length of time they are outstanding

    a. accounting system

    b. fuel system

    c. double-entry accounting

    d. asset

    e. cash-to-cash cycle

    f. aging schedule

    g. inventory

    h. cash flow

    i. cash basis

    j. balance sheet

    k. statement of cash flow

    l. inventory turnover

    m. pro forma

    n. quick ratio

    o. debt ratio

    p. return on investment

    q. single-entry accounting

    r. liability

    s. accrual basis

    t. income statement

True/False

1. T F Accounting systems are more important to large corporations than to small businesses.

2. T F It is acceptable to use the same checking account for your small business and your personal life.

3. T F Accounting software commonly used by small business includes packages from QuickBooks, Peachtree, and MYOB.

4. T F A journal is a chronological record of all business transactions.

5. T F Liquidity ratios measure a business's ability to meet its short-time obligations.

6. T F Time series analysis compares a company's performance with the performance of different firms.

7. T F Cash flow is more important than profit to a small business.

8. T F Timing is the critical factor in cash flow.

9. T F Employees always understand and appreciate open-book management.

10. T F Armed with a cash budget, aging schedules, and a set of feasible strategies, you can avoid cash-flow problems and maximize your use of this precious resource.

## chapter 9

Small Business Finance

One of the hottest buzz phrases in small business finance is the *elevator pitch.* "If the person standing next you in the elevator wanted to know about your business, what would you say?" asks Bill Joos, vice president of business development at Garage.com. An elevator pitch is a 30-second spiel designed to pique an investor's interest in your business. By concentrating your thoughts into 30 seconds, you are forced to focus on what really matters, or "the distilled essence of your dreams." Passion is important to the success of an elevator pitch. According to Joos, "If you can't talk about your business in a passionate way, you can't be an entrepreneur."

For an example of an elevator pitch, consider the following for Sistahs of Harlem, a clothing company with lots of "creativity, buzz, and attitude" that needs $250,000:

The Pitch: "We run a women's clothing line that has a point of reference. Our clothes are about conscientiousness, caring, and awareness—all with a sense of fun—and each collection is inspired by a powerful female figure, such as Bessie

After reading this chapter, you should be able to:

- Determine the financing needs of your business.
- Define basic financing terminology.
- Explain where to look for sources of funding.

Carmen Webber and Carmia Marshall, Owners of Sistahs of Harlem.

Coleman, the first black female pilot. We have something for everyone, but our typical clients are metropolitan women who range from age 15 to 50 and are eclectic and socially conscious. The tags on our clothes inform our customers that we make all of our garments in the United States. Each tag also includes biographical information on the inspirational female figure behind a given collection."

Company: Sistahs of Harlem

Owners: Carmen Webber, Carmia Marshall

Location: New York City

Employees: 2

Founded: 2001

2005 Revenue: $28,000

2006 Revenue: $32,000

Investment Needed: First, $250,000 to fund five trade shows in 2007. Then, $5 million to hire a production manager and a salesperson, pursue deals with chains such as Target (NYSE: TGT), and open a retail store

Clientele: Shoppers at five New York City boutiques and 100 regular custom clients, including singer Erykah Badu

Recent Buzz: Mentions in *Nylon* and *Vibe* magazines, guest spots on the Style Channel's *The Look for Less*, and their book, *T-Shirt Makeovers*

If you were an investor, would you loan them the $250k they are asking for? How about the $5 million later? Okay, read this chapter first, then decide.

SOURCES: Stephanie Clifford, "Apparel Company Sistahs of Harlem has Creativity, Buzz, and Attitude to Spare," *Inc.*, January 2007; Carole Matthews "Capital Training," *Inc.*, February 2000, www.inc.com

Small Business Finance

Although some entrepreneurs are well versed in determining their need for capital and knowing where to find it, the failure of many businesses can be traced to undercapitalization. A common approach is "not to worry about it" until the situation gets out of hand. However, every small business owner should understand how to define the amount of funding required to efficiently operate his business. Furthermore, the ability to be a proactive manager of the financial aspects of a business is of paramount importance in a dynamic economy. As you've seen in earlier chapters, when circumstances change quickly, you must be prepared to adapt to the new milieu. This chapter covers issues of financing that every entrepreneur should understand before starting a business.

Because service businesses often require the purchase of fewer fixed assets at startup than do retailers or manufacturers, they can offer a good route to self-employment. A survey by the national accounting and professional services firm Coopers & Lybrand (now called PriceWaterhouseCooper) found that many fast-growing companies now outsource certain service functions to outside providers. For small financial service firms, for instance, this trend means new opportunities. How? The same survey found that the services most commonly outsourced were payroll services, tax compliance, employee benefits, and claims administration. It's a win-win situation for all parties involved. For the outsourcing firm, this approach offers a way to reduce operating costs, because providers of a single type of service have a lower cost structure resulting from economies of scale. For the small service business, it's a prime market to exploit.[1]

Initial Capital Requirements

The fundamental financial building blocks for an entrepreneur are recognizing what assets are required to open the business and knowing how those assets will be financed. This knowledge relates to the business's *initial capital requirements*. Recall from Chapter 8 the importance of the balance sheet. The balance sheet lists the investment decisions of the business owner in the asset column and the financing decisions in the liabilities and owner's equity column. The financing necessary to acquire each asset required for the business must come from either owner-provided funds (equity) or borrowed funds (liabilities).

The process of determining initial capital requirements begins with identifying the short-term and long-term assets necessary to get the business started. Once you have this list of required assets, you must then determine how to pay for them.

> "Each business must have its assets in place—cash, inventory, patents, equipment, buildings, whatever it needs to operate—before it ever opens its doors."

Defining Required Assets

Every business needs a set of short-term and long-term assets in place before the business ever opens its doors. Typical **short-term assets** include cash and inventory but may also include *prepaid expenses* (such as rent or insurance paid in advance) and a *working capital* (cash) reserve. Because many businesses are not profitable in the first year or so of operation, having a cash reserve with which to pay bills can help you avoid becoming insolvent.

The most common **long-term assets** are buildings and equipment, but these assets may also include land, leasehold improvements, patents, and a host of other items. Each of these assets must be in the business *before* the enterprise earns its first dollar of sales. This means you must carefully evaluate your situation to determine exactly what has to be in place for the business to operate effectively. A useful exercise to help accomplish this task is to prepare a list of the assets the business would have if money were no object. Next, review this "wish list" to determine the essential assets that are needed to operate the business on a "bare-bones" basis. Finally, try to calculate the cost of these assets under each scenario.

As an example, suppose you are an entrepreneur starting a restaurant and want seating for 100 people. If money were no object, you could choose brand-new oak dining sets at a cost of $1,200 per six-piece place setting. As a less expensive alternative, at an auction of restaurant supplies and equipment, you could purchase used pine dining sets at a cost of $200 per six-place setting. Either choice will allow the seating requirement to be met.

After carefully completing this exercise for all assets, you will end up with a list of assets with a minimum-dollar investment and another list of assets needed for the dream business. Often your actual business will wind up somewhere in the middle of those two lists as you make final decisions.

> **short-term assets**
> Assets that will be converted into cash within one year.

> **long-term assets**
> Assets that will not be converted into cash within one year.

With the final list of required assets and corresponding dollar costs in hand, you can then determine your financing requirements. Remember that each dollar of assets must be supported by a dollar of equity or liability funds. How much equity can you contribute personally to the enterprise? Note that this contribution does not necessarily have to be all in the form of cash.

The total market value of the owner's assets used in the business plus all cash contributions from the owner to purchase assets or set up cash reserves constitute the *owner's equity*. For example, if your business requires a delivery vehicle and you already own a van with a market value of $12,000 that would be suitable for deliveries, the asset will be listed as "Delivery Vehicle—$12,000," and the balancing entry would be $12,000 of owner's equity.

The final step in the process is to subtract the total dollar value of the owner's equity from the total dollar value of the required assets. Generally, this step yields the dollar amount that must come from other sources. Sometimes there will be more owner's equity than needed to finance the required assets. In this situation, the entrepreneur can afford to invest in more assets or in more expensive assets—such as the new oak dining sets rather than the used pine dining sets for the restaurant mentioned earlier. More commonly, however, businesses will need additional capital to finance the required assets. This additional capital will come from one or more sources, which are most likely external to the business.

It may not take as much startup money as you might think to launch a new business. Of the 2004 *Inc.* 500 (the latest year that startup money needed for the fastest-growing companies was provided), 36 percent needed less than $20,000 in capitalization (see Figure 9.1).

The Five Cs of Credit

When an entrepreneur decides to seek external financing, she must be able to prove creditworthiness to potential providers of funds. A traditional guideline used by many lenders is the *five Cs of credit*, where each C represents a critical qualifying element:

1. *Capacity.* Capacity refers to the applicant's ability to repay the loan. It is usually estimated by examining the amount of cash and marketable securities available, and both historical and projected cash flows of the business.

Figure 9.1
KICK-OFF DOLLARS

Percentages of Inc. 500 Companies That Had Differing Amounts of Startup Capital.

SOURCE: "Crunching the Numbers," *Inc.* 500, 2004, 111.

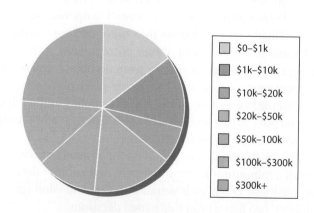

- $0–$1k
- $1k–$10k
- $10k–$20k
- $20k–$50k
- $50k–100k
- $100k–$300k
- $300k+

Collateral Type	Bank	SBA
House	(Market value × 0.75) – mortgage balance	(Market value × 0.80) – mortgage balance
Car	Nothing	Nothing
Truck and heavy equipment	Depreciated value × 0.50	Same
Office equipment	Nothing	Nothing
Furniture and fixtures	Depreciated value × 0.50	Same
Inventory: perishables	Nothing	Nothing
Jewelry	Nothing	Nothing
Other	10% – 50%	10% – 50%
Receivables	Under 90 days × 0.75	Under 90 days × 0.50
Stocks and bonds	50% – 90%	50% – 90%
Mutual funds	Nothing	Nothing
IRA	Nothing	Nothing
CD	100%	100%

SOURCE: U.S. Small Business Administration, "Borrowing Money,"www.sba.gov/financing

Table 9.1

GENERAL APPROXIMATION OF DIFFERENT FORMS OF COLLATERAL VALUATIONS

2. *Capital.* Capital is a function of the applicant's personal financial strength. The net worth of a business—the value of its assets minus the value of its liabilities—determines its capital. The bank wants to know what you own outside of the business that might be an alternate repayment source.[2]

3. *Collateral.* Assets owned by the applicant that can be pledged as security for the repayment of the loan constitute collateral. If the loan is not repaid, the lender can confiscate the pledged assets. The value of collateral is not based on the assets' market value, but rather is discounted to take into account the value that would be lost if the assets had to be liquidated (see Table 9.1).

4. *Character.* The applicant's character is considered important in that it indicates his apparent willingness to repay the loan. Character is judged primarily on the basis of the applicant's past repayment patterns, but lenders may consider other factors, such as marital status, home ownership, and military service, when attributing character to an applicant. The lender's prior experience with applicant repayment patterns affects its choice of factors in evaluating the character of a new applicant.

5. *Conditions.* The general economic climate at the time of the loan application may affect the applicant's ability to repay the loan. Lenders are usually more reluctant to extend credit in times of economic recession or business downturns.

Additional Considerations

Potential investors will want to know more about you and your business than just the "five Cs." For startups, simply having a good idea will not be enough to convince many investors to risk their capital in your business. You will need to show that you are a competent manager with a track record of prior business success. If possible, you should have an informal board of directors made up of people whom you may contact for assistance. Potential members of such a board might include bankers, attorneys, CPAs, and successful business owners.

If yours is a growing or emerging business, you will need to stand ready to provide well-audited financial statements and show a solid record of earnings. It is difficult to attract investors without proven performance and a high likelihood of continued growth and success. The old adage, "You have to have money to make money," is largely true in the area of financing. However, it might be amended to say, "You have to show an ability to make money to attract money."

A common myth suggests that the sheer strength of a business idea can win funding for a venture. In reality, a banker's first question is often, "How much money can you put in?" Bankers are not venture capital partners; they will expect you to put in at least 25 percent of total project costs, and perhaps much more if the loan is viewed as a risky one.[3]

Basic Financial Vocabulary

Before an entrepreneur can begin looking for sources of funds, she needs to understand the terminology associated with the two basic types of funds, debt and equity.

Forms of Capital: Debt and Equity

Two kinds of funds are potentially available to the entrepreneur: debt and equity. *Debt funds* (also known as *liabilities*) are borrowed from a creditor and, of course, must be repaid. Using debt to finance a business creates **leverage**, which is money you can borrow against the money you already have (see Chapter 8). Leverage can enable you to magnify the potential returns expected due to investing your equity in the business.

> *leverage*
> The ability to finance an investment through borrowed funds.

Of course, debt funding can also constrain the future cash flows generated by the business and potentially magnify losses. Debt creates the risk of your becoming technically insolvent if you cannot make each debt payment on time. Continued nonrepayment of debt will ultimately lead to the bankruptcy of the business. Debt is burdensome, which is why some business owners shed it as quickly as possible. Bill Howell of Safe Handling, a transportation and warehouse business in Auburn, Maine, has paid off loans early to prevent collateralization requirements from stifling growth.[4]

Equity funds, by contrast, are supplied by investors in exchange for an ownership position in the business. They need not be repaid. Providers of equity funds forgo the opportunity to receive periodic repayments in hopes of later sharing in the profits of the business. As a result, equity financing does not create a constraint on the cash flows of the business. However, equity providers usually demand a voice in the management of the business, thereby reducing the business owner's autonomy to run the business as he would like.

It is easy to see that the decision to seek outside funds is both critical and complex. Therefore, a more detailed view of each kind of financing is presented in this

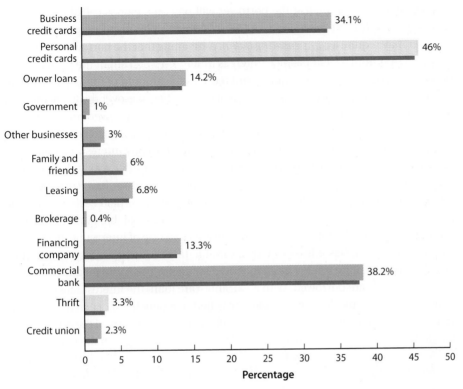

Figure 9.2

WHERE CAPITAL COMES FROM

*Percentages of All Small Firms
Using Credit Are Shown Here
According to Supplier.*

SOURCE: U.S. Small Business Administration,
Office of Advocacy, "Financing Patterns of Small
Firms," September 2003, www.sba.gov/ADVO

chapter. Figure 9.2 contains the results of a survey conducted by the SBA's Office of Advocacy, called the "Survey of Small Business Finance in the United States." In particular, the bar graph shows the sources of capital used by small businesses.

Debt Financing   Three important parameters associated with **debt financing** are the amount of principal to be borrowed, the loan's interest rate, and the loan's length of maturity. Together they determine the size and extent of your obligation to the creditor. Until the debt is repaid, the creditor has a legal claim on a portion of the business's cash flows. Creditors can demand payment and, in the most extreme case, force a business into bankruptcy because of overdue payments.

The **principal** of the loan is the original amount of money to be borrowed. You should try to minimize the size of the loan to reduce your financial risk. The pro forma balance sheet estimates the amount of funds needed (see Chapter 8). The amount you need to borrow is the difference between the total of pro forma assets and total owner's equity.

The **interest rate** of the loan determines the "price" of the borrowed funds. In most cases it will be based on the current prime rate of interest. In the past, the *prime rate* was defined as the rate of interest banks charge their "best" customers—those with the lowest risk. More recently, it has developed into a benchmark for determining many other rates of interest. Interest rates for small business loans are normally the prime rate plus some additional percentage points. For example, if the prime rate is 8.5 percent, a bank might offer small business loans at "prime plus four," or 12.5 percent. Additional factors, such as default risk and maturity, will also affect the cost of a loan.

debt financing
The use of borrowed funds to finance a business.

principal
An amount of money borrowed from a lender.

interest rate
The amount of money paid for the use of borrowed funds.

The actual rate of interest the borrower will pay on a loan is called the *effective rate of interest.* It is often higher than the stated rate of interest for several reasons. A lender may require a *compensating balance,* meaning that the borrower is required to keep a minimum dollar balance (often as much as 10 percent of the principal) on deposit with the lender. This requirement reduces the amount of funds accessible to the borrower and increases the actual rate of interest because over the life of the loan the borrower pays the same amount of interest dollars but has fewer funds available.

The frequency with which interest is compounded can also increase the cost of a loan. *Compounding* refers to the intervals at which you pay interest. Lenders may compound interest annually, semiannually, quarterly, monthly, weekly, daily, or even continuously. For example, quarterly compounding involves four compounding periods within a year—one-fourth of the stated interest rate is paid each quarter. The more compounding periods, the higher the effective rate will be. Financial institutions are required to inform borrowers of the effective rate of interest on all loans.

Whether a loan has a fixed rate or a variable rate of interest affects its ultimate cost. A **fixed-rate loan** retains the same interest rate for the entire length of time for which the funds are borrowed. With a **variable-rate loan**, the interest rate may fluctuate over time. Typically, the variable rate is tied to a benchmark such as the prime rate or federal funds rate. Every year (normally on the anniversary of the original loan date), the variable interest rate is adjusted according to changes in the benchmark.

A fixed-rate loan typically has a higher interest rate than the initial rate on a variable-rate loan. Therefore, the cost of a fixed-rate loan is higher in the first year (or longer). But because the variable interest rate could increase each year, it eventually might exceed the rate on the fixed loan by far. Thus a variable-rate loan represents much more of a gamble than a fixed-rate loan when borrowing for a long period of time.

Your goal is to find the lowest possible effective interest rate, given your current circumstances, by investigating different funding sources. For example, a particular bank may have excess funds available to lend and be willing to offer lower rates than its competitors. A startup business may want to consider a variable-rate loan to help offset its lower cash flows in the first year of operation.

The **maturity** of a loan refers to the length of time for which a borrower obtains the use of the funds. A short-term loan must be repaid within one year, an intermediate-term loan must be repaid within one to ten years, and a long-term loan must be repaid within ten or more years. Typically, the purpose of the loan will determine the length of maturity chosen. For example, you would use a short-term loan to purchase inventory that you expect to sell within one year, yielding the funds to repay the loan. For the purchase of a building, which presumably will serve the business for decades, a long-term loan is preferable. The maturity of the loan should essentially match the borrower's use of the loan proceeds.

The maturity of the loan also affects its interest rate. Ordinarily, the longer the maturity is, the higher the rate of interest. The reason for this rule is that a lender must be compensated for the opportunity cost of not being able to use those loaned funds in other ways. As a consequence, lenders will add a "premium" to the price that the borrower pays for a longer-maturity loan.

Your goal regarding loan maturity is to obtain as much flexibility as possible. On the one hand, a loan with a shorter maturity will usually have a lower rate of interest but must be repaid quickly, thus affecting cash flow more dramatically. On the

fixed-rate loan
A loan whose interest rate remains constant.

variable-rate loan
A loan whose interest rate changes over the life of the loan.

maturity
The length of time in which a loan must be repaid.

other hand, a loan with a longer maturity has a higher rate but gives you more time to repay the loan, resulting in smaller payments and reduced constraints on your current cash flow. Flexibility is created by maximizing the maturity of a loan while retaining the option of repaying the loan sooner than the maturity date, if cash flows allow. Make sure that the lender does not charge a penalty for early repayment.

Consider the principal, effective rate of interest, and maturity very carefully when attempting to obtain debt financing. By ascertaining the proper amount of principal needed, comparing the effective rates of interest at your disposal, and matching the maturity of the loan with the projected availability of cash flows with which to make repayments, you will be able to make the greatest possible use of debt financing.

Equity Financing   As stated earlier, **equity financing** does not have to be repaid. There are no payments to constrain the cash flow of the business. There is no interest to be paid on the funds. Providers of equity capital wind up owning a portion of the business and are generally interested in (1) getting dividends, (2) benefiting from the increased value of the business (and thus their investment in it), and (3) having a voice in the management of the business.

> *equity financing*
> The sale of common stock or the use of retained earnings to provide long-term financing.

Dividends are payments based on the net profits of the business and made to the providers of equity capital. These payments often are made on either a quarterly, a semiannual, or an annual basis. Many small businesses keep net profits in the form of retained earnings to help finance future growth, and dividends are paid only when the business shows profits above the amount necessary to fund projected new development.

> *dividends*
> Payments based on the net profits of the business and made to the providers of equity capital.

Increased value of the business is a natural result of a successful business enterprise. As a successful business grows and prospers, the owners prosper as well. Because the providers of equity capital own a "piece of the action," the value of their investment increases in direct proportion to the increase in the value of the business. The investors are frequently not as concerned about dividends as they are about the business's long-term success. If the business is successful, the equity providers will have the opportunity to sell all or part of their investment for a considerable profit.

A voice in management is an additional consideration for providers of equity capital. The rationale underlying this concept is that because the owners of a business have the most to lose if the business fails, they are entitled to have a say about how their money is used. Not all equity providers are interested in running a business, of course, but many can contribute important expertise along with their capital. They can enhance your business's chances of success.

Other Loan Terminology

Two additional sets of terms that you will often encounter while searching for financing relate to *loan security* and *loan restrictions*. These terms can be of great importance and should be thoroughly understood.

Loan Security   **Loan security** refers to the borrower's assurance to lenders that loans will be repaid. If the entrepreneur's signature on a loan is not considered sufficient security by a lender, the lender will require another signature to guarantee the loan. Other individuals whose signatures appear on the loan are known as *endorsers*. Endorsers are contingently liable for the notes they sign. Two types of endorsers are comakers and guarantors.

> *loan security*
> Assurance to a lender that a loan will be repaid.

Comakers create a joint liability with the borrower. The lender can collect from either the maker (original borrower) or the comaker. *Guarantors* ensure the repayment of a note by signing a guarantee commitment. Both private and government lenders often require guarantees from officers of corporations to ensure continuity of effective management.

Loan Restrictions   Sometimes called *covenants,* loan restrictions spell out what the borrower cannot do (*negative covenants*) or what she must do (*positive covenants*). These restrictions are built into each loan agreement and are generally negotiable—as long as you are aware of them.

Typical negative covenants preclude the borrower from acquiring any additional debt without prior approval from the original lender or will prevent the borrower from issuing dividends in excess of the terms of the loan agreement. Common positive covenants require that the borrower maintain some minimum level of working capital until the loan is repaid, carry some type of insurance while the loan is in effect, or provide periodic financial statements to the lender.

By understanding that lenders will sometimes require the additional assurance of an endorser and will likely create covenants on loan agreements, you can be better prepared to negotiate during the search for financing. Doing your homework on loan terminology and processes improves your chances for successfully obtaining funds.[5]

How Can You Find Capital?

Once you determine how much capital is needed for the startup or expansion, you are ready to begin looking for capital sources. To prepare for this search, you need to be aware of what these sources will want to know about you and your business before they are willing to entrust their funds to you. You also need to understand the characteristics of each capital source and the process for obtaining funds from it.

Loan Application Process

Typically, to determine creditworthiness, a lending institution will collect relevant information from financial statements supplied by the applicant and by external sources, such as local or regional credit associations, credit interchange bureaus, and the applicant's bank. This procedure is known as *credit scoring.* If the applicant meets or exceeds some minimal score (set by the lender) on key financial and credit characteristics, the institution will be willing to arrange a loan. Most lenders hesitate to make loans to startup businesses, however, unless either a wealthy friend or a relative will cosign the loan, or unless loan proceeds will be used to purchase assets that could be repossessed and easily resold in case of default.

> "Government loan programs for small businesses are intended to help create jobs and tax revenues—there are no government grants for starting a business."

Sources of Debt Financing

The wide array of credit options available confuses many entrepreneurs. A thorough understanding of the nature and characteristics of these debt sources will help ensure that you are successful in obtaining financing from the most favorable source for you.

@ e-biz
Finding Financing Online

Less than one-tenth of 1 percent of small businesses are funded with venture capital, so why give space to this topic in a small business text? Because sometimes you need to aim high. To take a look at the playbook from the other team, visit the Web page for the National Venture Capital Association (NVCA), at www.nvca.org. This trade association represents the U.S. venture capital industry. A member-based organization, it consists of venture capital firms that manage pools of risk equity capital designated to be invested in high-growth companies.

A major aid you find here are model documents, such as a model term sheet, stock purchase agreement, certificate of incorporation, and right of first refusal. These model documents indicate what is normal in the venture capital industry, and they include explanatory commentary. While you are visiting NVCA's website, check out the Resource section. It will lead you to a plethora of other sites related to venture capital.

SOURCE: www.nvca.org

Commercial Banks Most people's first response to the question, "Where would you borrow money?" is the obvious one: "A bank." Commercial banks are the backbone of the credit market, offering the widest assortment of loans to creditworthy small businesses. Bank loans generally fall into two major categories: short-term loans (for purchasing inventory, overcoming cash-flow problems, and meeting monthly expenditures) and long-term loans (for purchasing land, machinery, and buildings or renovating facilities).

Most short-term loans are **unsecured loans**, meaning that the bank does not require any

The Primary Source of Small-Business Funding Is the Local Commercial Bank.

collateral as long as the entrepreneur has a good credit standing. These loans are often *self-liquidating,* which means that the loan will be repaid directly with the revenues generated from the original purpose of the loan. For example, if an entrepreneur uses a short-term loan to purchase inventory, the loan is repaid as the inventory is sold. Types of short-term loans include lines of credit, demand notes, and floor planning.

A **line of credit** is an agreement between a bank and a business that specifies the amount of unsecured short-term funds the bank will make available to the business over a specific period of time—normally one year. The agreement allows the business to borrow and repay funds up to the maximum amount specified in the agreement throughout the year. The business pays interest only on the amount of funds actually borrowed but may be required to pay a setup or handling fee.

unsecured loans
A short-term loan for which collateral is not required.

line of credit
An agreement that makes a specific amount of short-term funding available to a business as it is needed.

demand note
A short-term loan that must be repaid (both principal and interest) in a lump sum at maturity.

installment loans
A loan made to a business for the purchase of fixed assets such as equipment and real estate.

balloon notes
A loan that requires the borrower to make small monthly payments (usually enough to cover the interest), with the balance of the loan due at maturity.

unsecured term loans
A loan made to an established business that has demonstrated a strong overall credit profile.

floor planning
A type of business loan generally made for "big-ticket" items. The business holds the item in inventory and pays interest, but it is actually owned by the lender until the item is sold.

A **demand note** is a loan made to a small business for a specific period of time, to be repaid in a lump sum at maturity. With this type of loan, the bank reserves the right to demand repayment of the loan at any time. For example, a bank might loan a business $50,000 for one year at 12 percent interest. The business would repay the loan by making one payment of $56,000 ($50,000 principal plus 0.12 x $50,000 interest) at the end of one year. The only reason a bank is likely to demand repayment sooner is if the business appears to be struggling and is potentially unable to repay the loan in full at the end of the specified time period.

Types of long-term bank loans include installment loans, balloon notes, and unsecured term loans. **Installment loans** are made to businesses for the purchase of fixed assets such as equipment and real estate. These loans are to be repaid in periodic payments that include accrued interest and part of the outstanding principal balance. In the case of many fixed assets, the maturity of the loan will equal the usable life of the asset, and the principal amount loaned will range from 65 to 80 percent of the asset's market value. For the purchase of real estate, banks will often allow a repayment schedule of 15 to 30 years and typically lend between 75 and 85 percent of the property's value. In every case, the bank will maintain a security interest in, or lien on, the asset until the loan is fully repaid.

Balloon notes are loans made to businesses in which only small periodic payments are required over the life of the loan, with a large lump-sum payment due at maturity. A typical balloon note requires monthly payments to cover accrued interest, with the entire principal coming due at the end of the loan's term. This scheme allows you more flexibility with your cash flow over the life of the loan. If you are unable to make the final balloon payment, it is common for the bank to refinance the loan for a longer period of time, allowing you to continue making monthly payments.

Unsecured term loans are made to established businesses that have demonstrated a strong overall credit profile. Eligible businesses must show excellent creditworthiness and have an extremely high probability of repayment. These loans are usually made for very specific terms and may come with restrictions on the use of the loan proceeds. For example, a bank might agree to lend a business a sum of money for a three-year period at a given rate of interest. As the business owner, you must then ensure that the funds are used to finance some asset or activity that will generate enough revenue to repay the loan within the three-year time horizon.

Commercial banks remain a primary source of debt financing for small businesses. The type, maturity, and other terms of each loan, however, are uniquely a function of the financial strength or creditworthiness of the borrower.

Commercial Finance Companies   Commercial finance companies extend short- and intermediate-term credit to firms that cannot easily obtain credit elsewhere. Because these companies are willing to take a bigger risk than commercial banks, their interest rates are often considerably higher. Commercial finance companies perform a valuable service to small businesses that have yet to establish their creditworthiness.[6]

Among the most common types of loans provided by commercial finance companies are floor planning, leasing, and factoring accounts receivable.

Floor planning is a special type of loan used particularly for financing high-priced inventory items, such as new automobiles, trucks, recreational vehicles,

What to Do Before You Talk to Your Banker

Manager's Notebook

The idea of meeting with a banker can be intimidating to some people. To get your relationship off to a good start, take these steps:

- Don't ask anyone to do something you aren't willing to do yourself. You have to put your own assets on the line to get a business loan.
- Start talking with your banker before you are in dire need. Bankers are naturally conservative because they have to protect their depositors' money.
- Don't surprise your banker. Don't go in on Thursday to say that you can't make your payroll on Friday.
- Have routine meetings with your banker to keep her up to date on how your business is progressing.
- Tell your banker in person when your business is having trouble and explain how you intend to overcome the problem.
- Take time to educate your banker about your business and industry. The better your banker understands your business, the better he can help you.
- Be timely with your payments and any financial information the bank may request from you.
- Give your banker all your business—both your personal accounts and your firm's deposits.
- Refer potential customers to your banker.
- Keep a positive attitude. A banker asking for more documentation isn't necessarily looking for a reason to turn your loan down. Rather, she needs more information. Bankers look for reasons to say "yes."

SOURCES: Julie Cripe, "Small Business Financing: What to Do Before You Talk to the Bank," *San Antonio Business Journal*, October 2000, 2; Jeffrey Moses, "The Most Important Part of a Loan Application," National Federation of Independent Business, June 2004, www.nfib.com; Jeffrey Moses, "Focus on the Plan," National Federation of Independent Business, June 2004, www.nfib.com

and boats. A business borrowing money for this purpose is allowed to display the inventory on its premises, but the inventory is actually owned by the bank. When the business sells one of the items, it will use the proceeds of the sale to repay the principal of the loan. The business is generally required to pay interest monthly on each item of inventory purchased with the loan proceeds. Therefore, the longer it takes the business to sell each item, the more the business pays in interest expenses. This is one instance in which the short-term loan is a **secured loan**. That is, the assets purchased with the loan proceeds serve as collateral.

Leasing is a contract arrangement whereby a finance company purchases the durable goods needed by a small business and rents them to the small business for a specific period of time. The rent payment includes some amount of interest. Due to current tax laws, this activity is very lucrative for finance companies and often allows entrepreneurs to have the use of state-of-the-art equipment at a fraction of the cost.

> *secured loan*
> A loan that requires collateral as security for the lender.

factoring
The practice of raising funds for a business through the sale of accounts receivable.

Another important type of loan available from commercial finance companies is accounts receivable **factoring**. Under this arrangement, a small business either sells its accounts receivable to a finance company outright or uses the receivables as collateral for a loan. The purchase price of the receivables (or the amount of the loan) is discounted from the face value of what the business is owed to allow for potential losses (in the form of unpaid accounts) and for the fact that the finance company will not receive full repayment of the loan until sometime in the future.

Typically, the finance company will either purchase the receivables for or will lend the small business somewhere between 55 and 80 percent of the face value of the business's accounts receivable, based on their likelihood of being paid in a timely manner. If a finance company purchases the receivables outright, it will collect payments on them as they come due. If the small business uses its receivables as collateral for a loan, in a process known as *pledging*, as the business collects these accounts due, the proceeds are forwarded to the finance company to repay the loan.

Factoring has historically been viewed as one of the least desirable approaches to financing, but competition from new small- and mid-sized factors is changing that perception. Bryan Bradley, co-founder and designer of Tuleh's, a high-end New York fashion design house, says that he would not even be in business, let alone hosting a runway show for the 2006 Fashion Week, without his factor. When Tuleh makes a sale to an upscale retailer, like Neiman Marcus, the invoice is e-mailed to his factor, Hilldun. The invoice amount is deposited into Tuleh's account minus about 9 percent, providing immediate cash for Bradley to pay for new runway shows or pay his vendors. Factor Hilldun also holds back 20 percent of the receivables in case companies dispute or for some other reason don't pay bills. When payment comes due, Hilldun collects directly from the retailer and sends Bradley the remaining 20 percent minus any adjustments.[7]

policy loans
A loan made to a business by an insurance company, using the business's insurance policy as collateral.

Insurance Companies   For some entrepreneurs, life insurance companies have become a principal source of debt financing. The most common type of loan, **policy loans,** are made to entrepreneurs based on the amount of money paid in premiums on an insurance policy that has a cash surrender value. Although each insurance company varies its methods for making these loans, a typical arrangement is for the insurance company to lend up to 95 percent of a policy's cash surrender value.

The collateral for the loan is the cash that the entrepreneur has already paid into the policy. In essence, the insurance company is lending the entrepreneur his own money. Because the default risk is virtually zero (defaulting on the loan merely reduces the cash surrender value of the policy), the rate of interest is often very favorable.

If an entrepreneur has been paying premiums into a whole-life, variable-life, or universal-life policy, it is likely that the option to borrow funds against it will be available. Term insurance policies, however, have no borrowing capacity. One caution about this type of borrowing is that the amount of insurance coverage is usually reduced by the amount of the loan.

Federal Loan Programs   Government lending programs exist to stimulate economic activity. The underlying rationale for making these loans is that the borrowers will become profitable and create jobs, which in turn means more tax dollars in the coffers of government agencies providing the funds for the loans.

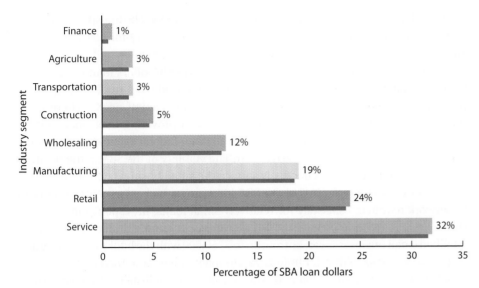

SOURCE: U.S. Small Business Administration, www.sba.gov

Figure 9.3
WHO GETS SBA LOANS?

The SBA Guarantees $10.5 Billion in 7(a) Business Loans. The Average Loan Is $250,656 with a Maturity of 11.5 years; 21 Percent of the Loans Went to Businesses Less Than Two Years Old.

The most active government lender is the Small Business Administration (SBA), a federal agency. **SBA loan** programs include guaranteed loans, direct loans, and the 504 loan program. For full descriptions of all SBA loan programs, see www.sba.gov/services/financialassistance. The majority of these loan funds go to service, retail, and manufacturing businesses (see Figure 9.3).

Guaranteed loans are generally known as the *7(a) program.* Under this program, private lenders—usually commercial banks—make loans to entrepreneurs that are guaranteed up to 85 percent of loans up to $150,000 and up to 75 percent of loans above $150,000 by the SBA. This means that the lender's risk exposure is reduced by the amount of the SBA guarantee. The SBA's 7(a) maximum loan amount is $2 million with SBA maximum exposure of $1.5 million.

To be eligible for the 7(a) program, a business must be operated for profit and must fall within the size standards set by the SBA (see Chapter 1). Loans cannot be made to businesses engaged in speculation or real estate rental. Existing businesses must provide, among other things, financial statements for the past three years and financial projections for the next three years. Startup businesses must provide three years of projected financial statements, a feasible business plan, and proof of adequate investment by the owners (generally about 20 to 30 percent equity).

Successful applicants pay interest rates up to 2.25 percent above the prime rate for loans with maturities of less than seven years and interest rates up to 2.75 percent above the prime rate for loans with maturities of seven years or longer. The borrower must repay the loan in monthly installments, which include both principal and interest. The first payment may be delayed up to six months, and the loans carry no balloon payments, prepayment penalties, or application fees.

The *504 loan* program provides small businesses with funding for fixed assets when conventional loans are not possible. These funds are distributed through a **certified development company**, which is a nonprofit organization sponsored either by private interests or by state or local governments. In a typical arrangement, a private lender will provide 50 percent of the total value of the loan, the borrower 10 percent, and the certified development company the remaining 40 percent of the necessary funds. Because the 504 portion of the funds—that contributed by the

SBA loan
A loan made to a small business through a commercial bank, of which a portion is guaranteed by the Small Business Administration.

certified development company
A nonprofit organization sponsored either by private interests or by state or local governments.

certified development company—is 100 percent guaranteed by the SBA, the private lender's risk exposure is significantly reduced. The maturity for 504 financing is 10 years for equipment purchases and 20 years for real estate.[8]

In addition to the preceding loan programs, the SBA offers loan programs to support small businesses engaged in international trade and rural development, those with women owners, and those with working-capital needs. There is no doubt that the SBA plays a very significant role in providing debt financing for small businesses. However, the agency, like all other federal agencies, is subject to policy changes and budget cuts each year. The viability of the SBA in the future is dependent on its ability to effectively service the small business community.

One of the main criticisms of the SBA loan programs has been the amount of paperwork required, especially for relatively small loans. In response to this concern, the SBA recently created the **SBA Express program**.[9] Under this program, qualified small businesses can borrow up to $350,000 with the bank's own forms and receive a response within 36 hours.. Additionally, there is a *Microloan* program, which provides very small loans to startup, newly established, or growing small business concerns. Under this program, the SBA makes funds available to nonprofit community-based lenders (intermediaries), which in turn make loans to eligible borrowers in amounts up to a maximum of $35,000. The average loan size is about $13,000. Applications are submitted to the local intermediary, and all credit decisions are made on the local level. Each of these programs has been very successful.

State and Local Government Lenders   Many state and local governments lend money to entrepreneurs through various programs. As noted earlier, they can sponsor a certified development company to assist small businesses with the acquisition of fixed assets. Other loan programs are usually tied to economic development goals—for instance, some loans are made contingent on the number of jobs that will be created by the small business. Most state and local government programs have lower interest rates than conventional loans, often with longer maturities. It is clearly to your advantage to find out if these programs would be available to you.

Trade Credit   The last major source of debt financing covered here is the use of **trade credit,** or *accounts payable*. Recall from Chapter 8 that accounts payable are the amounts owed by a business to the creditors that have supplied goods or services to the business. Although startups may find it difficult to obtain everything on credit right away, many manufacturers and wholesalers will ship goods at least 30 days before payment is required. This 30-day grace period is essentially a loan to the small business. Because no interest is charged for the first 30 days, the loan is "free." For this reason, you should take advantage of as much trade credit as possible.

What If a Lender Says "No"?

Not every deal gets approved. Not every loan package is accepted. When rejection happens to you, get past the blow to your ego and try to learn what you did wrong. When a lender says "no," do the following:

- Thank the lender for the time spent reviewing your package. Do not show resentment. Lenders almost always consider applications in a highly professional, objective manner. If you remain professional yourself, you will improve the odds of favorably impressing the lender when you return for future loans.

SBA Express program
A relatively new loan program available through the SBA that simplifies the paperwork that has historically been required.

---

trade credit
The purchase of goods from suppliers that do not demand payment immediately.

Reality Check

Start a Business with Plastic? Yikes!

Credit cards for financing small business? Your loan officer will say, "Don't use them." Your SCORE (Service Corp of Retired Executives) counselor will say, "Don't even think about it." Today many small business owners are using credit cards as a partial source of funding, but this approach isn't for the faint of heart.

Diana Frerick loved to belt out Whitney Houston songs on karaoke nights. When she tried to turn her passion into a business, however, no one wanted to listen. Frerick used two credit cards to spend $5,000 on a karaoke system and music and started hosting private parties and corporate functions. Three years later she and a partner opened Karaoke Star Store & Stage, again using her cards to pay for inventory and supplies. Now they employ 14 people and generate revenues of $2 million.

Credit cards are enticing because most offer extremely low introductory rates—3.9 percent, 2.9 percent, even 0 percent—for a limited time. When those introductory rates end, the annual percentage rate charged can jump as high as 22 percent within a matter of months. Think of it this way: If you aren't earning 22 percent on your equity, how can you afford to pay 22 percent for credit? Answer: You can't. Are you anxious to see how bankruptcy court works?

If you choose to finance via credit cards, how do you tell if you are overextended?

- *You are unaware of your bills.* You should know how much you owe and whom you owe it to. Evaluate your credit report and your monthly credit card statement.

- *You are paying the minimum.* Pay off the credit-card balances on a regular basis. If you are paying only the minimum payment allowed, it is a sign that you are in over your head.

- *You max out.* If your credit cards are close to or at their limit, you are in debt overload.

SOURCES: Robert Janis, "Small-Business Credit Card Use on the Rise," *Black Enterprise*, April 2007, 48–48; Bobbie Gossage, "Financing with Plastic: A Recipe for Disaster?" *WSJ Startup Journal*, June 2004, www.startupjournal.com; Jeffrey Moses, "Managing and Taking Maximum Advantage of Your Credit Cards, Personal and Business," National Federation of Independent Business, 6 June 2004, www.nfib.com/toolsandtips.

- Ask what specific information, or lack thereof, counted against you. Federal regulations require a lender to prepare a detailed explanation for its loan rejection. Talk about the points cited, but don't argue—you are trying to learn as much as you possibly can.

- Ask the lender for specific, personal recommendations. Straight out ask for any personal advice the lender may have.

- Understand that business loans are generally turned down for one (or more) of four main reasons: a poor credit score, lack of collateral, uncertainty of cash flow, and/or a poorly written business plan.

- Ask whether the bank can rework your application so that it meets the lending criteria. This effort may require substantial changes in your business structure or adding personal collateral.[10]

Sources of Equity Financing

From our discussion of debt financing, you know that lenders will expect entrepreneurs to provide equity funds in the amount of at least 20 percent, and possibly 50 percent or more, of the business before approving a loan. The higher the risk assumed by the lender, the more of your own money you must put into the business. The most common sources of equity financing are personal funds, family and friends, partners, venture capital firms, small business investment companies (SBICs), angels, and various forms of stock offerings.

Personal Funds   Most new businesses are originally financed with their creators' funds. The Department of Commerce estimates that nearly two-thirds of all start-ups are begun without borrowed funds. The first place most entrepreneurs find equity capital is in their personal assets. Cash, savings accounts, and checking accounts are the most obvious sources of equity funds. Additional sources are the sale of stocks, bonds, mutual funds, real estate, or other personal investments.

Family and Friends   The National Federation of Independent Business reported that more than one-fourth of new businesses are at least partially funded by the family and friends of the entrepreneurs. Family and friends are more willing to risk capital in a venture owned by someone they know than in ventures about which they know little or nothing. This financing is viewed as equity as long as there is no set repayment schedule.

Financing a business with capital from family and friends, however, creates a type of risk not found with other funding sources. If the business is not successful and the funds cannot be repaid, relationships with family and friends can become strained. You should explain the potential risk of failure inherent in the venture before accepting any money from family and friends. The key is to be sure you have a written contract with an investment letter that clearly outlines who approached whom about the funds in question and explains the specific terms of the funding.[11]

Partners   Acquiring one or more partners is another way to secure equity capital (see Chapter 2). Approximately 10 percent of U.S. businesses are partnerships. Many partnerships are formed to take advantage of diverse skills or attributes that can be contributed to the new business. For example, one person may have the technical skills required to run the business whereas another person may have the capital to finance it. Together they form a partnership to accomplish a common goal.

Partners may play an active role in the venture's operation or may choose to be "silent," providing funds only in exchange for an equity position. The addition of one or more partners expands not only the amount of equity capital available for the business, but also the ability of the business to borrow funds. This is due to the cumulative creditworthiness of the partners versus that of the entrepreneur alone.

Venture Capital Firms   *Venture capital firms* are groups of individuals or companies that invest in new or expanding firms. Of the more than 600 venture capital firms operating in the United States, approximately 500 are private independent firms, about 65 are major corporations, and the rest are affiliated with banks. Obtaining capital from them is not easy.

Most venture capital firms have investment policies that outline their preferences relative to industry, geographic location, investment size, and investment maturity. These firms look for businesses with the potential for rapid growth and high profitability. They provide funds in exchange for an equity position, which they hope to sell off within five to ten years or less.

A recent study showed that the average sum invested by venture capital firms is between $1.5 million and $2 million per business, with an overall range between $23,000 to more than $50 million. An excellent business plan is essential when approaching a venture capital firm, and a referral from a credible source—such as a banker or attorney familiar to the venture capital firm—may also be necessary. It takes an average of six to eight months to receive a potential investment decision. It has been estimated that less than 10 percent of the plans submitted to venture capital firms are ultimately funded.

Venture capital firms rarely invest in retail operations. Instead, they tend to focus on high-technology industries, growth industries, and essential services. Ventures within these fields with strong, experienced management teams have the best chance of being funded. *Pratt's Guide to Venture Capital Success* is a good source of information on this source of financing.

Small Business Investment Companies   *Small business investment companies (SBICs)* are venture capital firms licensed by the SBA to invest in small businesses. SBICs were authorized by Congress in 1958 to provide equity financing to qualified enterprises. In 1969 the SBA, in cooperation with the Department of Commerce, created *minority enterprise small business investment companies (MESBICs)* to provide equity financing to minority entrepreneurs. Any business that is more than 50 percent owned by African Americans, Hispanic Americans, Native Americans, Alaska Natives, or socially and economically disadvantaged Americans is eligible for funding.

SBICs and MESBICs are formed by financial institutions, corporations, or individuals, although a few are publicly owned. These investment companies must be capitalized with at least $500,000 of private funds. Once capitalized, they can receive as much as $4 from the SBA for each $1 in private money invested.

SBICs and MESBICs are excellent sources of both startup and expansion capital. Like venture capital firms, however, they tend to have investment policies regarding geographic area and industry. There are approximately 300 SBICs and MESBICs currently in operation in the United States. They are listed in the *Directory of Operating Small Business Investment Companies* available from any SBA office.

Angels   An **angel** is a wealthy, experienced individual who has a desire to assist startup or emerging businesses. Most angels are self-made entrepreneurs who want to help sustain the system that allowed them to become successful. Usually they are knowledgeable about the market and technology areas in which they invest.

> **angel**
> A lender, usually a successful entrepreneur, who loans money to help new businesses.

According to a study on business angels, there are more than 250,000 such investors in the United States. A typical angel investment ranges from $20,000 to $50,000, although nearly one-fourth are for more than $50,000. An angel can add much more than money to a business, however. His business know-how and contacts can prove far more valuable to the success of the business than the capital invested.

Several types of angel investors exist. *Corporate angels* are typically former senior managers of *Fortune* 1000 companies. In addition to getting their cash, you may persuade them to fill a management position in your company (they generally do the biggest deals, ranging from $200,000 to $1 million). *Entrepreneurial angels* own and operate their own businesses and are looking for ways to diversify their portfolios. They almost always want a seat on the board, but rarely want a management spot (deals run from $200,000 to $500,000). *Enthusiast angels* generally do smaller deals ($10,000 to $200,000), are older and wealthy, and invest for a hobby. *Professional angels* include doctors, lawyers, accountants, and other professionals. They like to invest in companies that offer products with which they are familiar. They can offer value through their expertise. *Micromanagement angels* are very serious investors. They are typically self-made, wealthy individuals who definitely want to be involved in your company strategy.[12]

Finding an angel is not easy. The best ways for an entrepreneur to locate one are to maintain business contacts with tax attorneys, bankers, and accountants in the closest metropolitan area and to find out whether a regional venture capital network exists.

Mergers and Acquisitions (M&A)   Merging with a company flush with cash can provide a viable source of capital. Such transactions may trigger many legal, structural, and tax issues, however, that you must then work out with your accountant and lawyer. Deals for small to midsize companies have become increasingly popular as consolidation in technology-based industries occurs.[13]

Stock Offerings   Selling company stock is another route for obtaining equity financing. The entrepreneur must consider this decision very carefully, however. The sale of stock results in the entrepreneur's losing a portion of the ownership of the business. Furthermore, certain state and federal laws govern the way in which stock offerings are made. Private placements and public offerings are the two types of stock sales.

Private Placements   A *private placement* involves the sale of stock to a selected group of individuals. This stock cannot be purchased by the general public. Sales may be in any amount, but placements less than $500,000 are subject to fewer government-imposed restrictions and trigger less onerous disclosure requirements than those in excess of $500,000. If the company selling the stock is located and doing business in only one state, and stock is sold only to individuals within that same state, the sale is considered an *intrastate stock sale* subject only to that state's regulations. If the sale involves more than one state, then it is an *interstate stock sale*, and the federal Securities and Exchange Commission's regulations will apply.

What if one partner wants out of a business and the remaining partner or partners don't have the cash for a buyout? *Recapitalization* means rearranging the financial structure of a business—generally by using a combination of debt and third-party investors like private equity firms. Once again, competition in the fast-growing private equity market (the number of private equity firms has increased by 16 percent from 2000 to 2006) has made terms for recapitalization more attractive.[14]

Public Offerings   A *public offering* involves the sale of stock to the general public. These sales always are governed by Securities and Exchange Commission regulations. Complying with these regulations is both costly and time-consuming. For public offerings valued between $400,000 and $1 million, the legal fees, underwriting fees, audits, printing expenses, and other costs can easily exceed 15 percent.

Profile in Entrepreneurship
Bootstrapping with a Necktie

When lenders—everybody from bankers to private investors—say "no," tough small business owners turn to themselves. They raise money by *bootstrapping*. Bootstrapping involves saving, rather than borrowing money. It requires being as frugal as possible. You must have discipline, determination, and a serious desire to succeed, so not everyone has the guts to bootstrap.

Brothers Shep and Ian Murray knew they had a high tolerance for risk when they decided to launch Vineyard Vines, a necktie company located in Greenwich, Connecticut. Shep says, "We didn't have a penny to our names, but we had a vision and just went for it," to the tune of $40,000 charged on the Murrays' credit cards.

They took several months working out details. Shep's employer had a fashion division that introduced them to suppliers and allowed them to use a design studio. The pair had their designs and production for their first line of neckties before they even quit their jobs. Most employers will not be equally gracious about their employees moonlighting and launching their own businesses, but keeping a steady income during the planning stage is a great way to bootstrap.

Shep and Ian lived with their parents and sold their first batch of neckties out of their car. Every penny went into the best materials needed for the $65 ties. Neither took a salary for the first year. That kind of dedication is part of bootstrapping.

Bootstrapping can free the new company from excessive debt loads that constrain growth in early years and open doors for outside investment later. Bootstrapping has paid off for Vineyard Vines, which has been getting exposure on the necks of President George Bush, Senator John Kerry, and former presidents George Herbert Walker Bush and Bill Clinton. But, as Murray points out, the company is "tie-partisan."

SOURCE: Steve Forbes, "Tie One On," *Forbes*, June 21, 2004, 32; Ryan Underwood, "Things I Can't Live Without," *Inc.*, November 2004, 82–82; David Worrell, "Bootstrapping Your Startup," *Entrepreneur's Start-Ups*, October 2002; Nancy Carter, Candida Brush, Patricia Greene, Elizabeth Gatewood, and Myra Hart, "Women Entrepreneurs Who Break Through to Equity Financing," *Venture Capital*, January 2003, 1–28.

The first time a company offers its stock to the general public is called an **initial public offering (IPO)**. To be a viable candidate for an IPO, a company must be in good financial health and be able to attract an underwriter (typically a stock brokerage firm or investment banker) to help sell the stock offering. In addition, the market conditions must be favorable for selling equity securities.

There are three main reasons companies choose public offerings:

1. When market conditions are favorable, more funds can be raised through public offerings than through other venture capital methods, without imposing the repayment burdens of debt.

2. Having an established public price for the company's stock enhances its image.

3. The owner's wealth can be magnified greatly when owner-held shares are subsequently sold in the market.

One critical caution about public stock offerings is that they require companies to make financial disclosures to the public. If a company fails to live up to its self-reported expectations, shareholders can sue the company, charging that the company withheld or misrepresented important information.

> **initial public offering (IPO)**
> The first sale of stock of a business made available to public investors.

Choosing a Lender or Investor

A key decision facing entrepreneurs is determining which sources of financing to pursue. Your choice will often be limited by the degree to which you meet the requirements of each lending or investing source. If you decide to pursue *debt financing,* you must have the minimum down payment or other capital requirements necessary to secure the loan. Assuming that these requirements can be met, you will have to determine which lending source to approach. Usually the foremost criterion will be finding the lowest cost or interest rate available. However, according to small business expert G. B. Baty, other important lender-selection considerations are

1. *Size.* The lender should be small enough to consider the entrepreneur an important customer, but large enough to service the entrepreneur's future needs.

2. *Desire.* The lender should exhibit a desire to work with startup and emerging businesses, rather than considering them too risky.

3. *Approach to problems.* The lender should be supportive of small businesses facing problems, offering constructive advice and financing alternatives.

4. *Industry experience.* The lender should have experience in the entrepreneur's industry, especially with startup or emerging ventures.[15]

The best guideline may be to seek the lenders with which you feel the most comfortable. A loan relationship can last for a decade or more. Finding a lending source that is pleasant to work with is often as important as finding the lowest cost of debt.

If you decide to pursue *equity financing,* you should consider the fact that close personal relationships can become strained when money is involved. Although the use of funds obtained from family members, friends, or partners is perhaps conceivable, none of these sources may be acceptable or feasible for personal reasons.

Autonomy is another important consideration. Equity financing always requires that you give up a portion of ownership in the venture. If independence is critical to you, then think carefully about the source of equity you pursue.

The most important criterion in choosing investors should be matching what the business needs with what the investors can offer. If the business requires only money, then you should attempt to find a "silent" partner—one who is willing to provide capital without playing an active role in the management of the business. Conversely, if your business needs a particular type of expertise, in addition to money, then you should seek an investor who can provide management advice or other assistance along with needed capital. For example, a new business in a high-tech industry might pursue angel financing from a successful individual who has prospered in that industry.

Entrepreneurial guru Jeffry A. Timmons offers a few more cautions when choosing an investor. Each of the following "sand traps," he says, imposes a responsibility on the entrepreneur:

1. *Strategic circumference.* A fund-raising decision can affect future financing choices. Raising equity capital may reduce your freedom to choose additional financing sources in the future, due to the partial loss of ownership control that accompanies equity financing.

2. *Legal circumference.* Financing deals can place unwanted limitations and constraints on the unwary entrepreneur. It is imperative to read and understand the details of each financing document. Competent legal representation is recommended.

3. *Opportunity cost.* Entrepreneurs often overlook the time, effort, and creative energy required to locate and secure financing. A long search can exhaust the entrepreneur's personal funds before the business ever gets off the ground.

4. *Attraction to status and size.* Many entrepreneurs seek financing from the most prestigious and high-profile firms. Often a better fit is found with lesser-known firms that have firsthand experience with the type of business the entrepreneur is starting.

5. *Being too anxious.* If the entrepreneur has a sound business plan, more than one venture capital firm may be interested in investing in it. By accepting the first offer, the entrepreneur could overlook a better deal from another source.[16]

Clearly, choosing a lender or investor takes time and patience. The process is similar to finding a spouse. The relationship that is forged between the entrepreneur and the source of financing can be long-lasting and should be mutually beneficial.

Summary

• **The financing needs of your business**

A straightforward process for determining financing need is to (1) list the assets required for your business to operate effectively; (2) determine the market value or cost of each asset; (3) identify how much capital you are able to provide; and (4) subtract the total of the owner-provided funds from the total of the assets required. This figure represents the minimum amount of financing required.

• **Basic financing terminology**

To procure financing, you must understand the basic financial vocabulary. Each major form of capital (debt and equity) has unique terminology that defines the details underlying financing agreements. Each form of capital has pros and cons that make it more or less desirable to the entrepreneur under given circumstances.

• **Where to look for sources of funding**

The search for capital and the application process can be unsettling as you sort through the various sources of funds. Major sources of debt financing include commercial banks, finance companies, government lenders, and insurance companies. Sources of equity include partners, venture capital firms, angels, and stock offerings. Finding capital is one of the most important tasks you face in starting and managing a business. A thorough understanding of the issues involved will enhance your chances of finding the best source for your business.

Questions for Review and Discussion

1. Define "initial capital requirements." How can you determine these?

2. What are the five Cs of credit, and how do lenders use them?

3. What are the differences between debt funds and equity funds?

4. What kinds of businesses would depend on floor planning?

5. What does "pledging accounts receivable" mean?

6. What are the advantages of borrowing through the SBA?

7. Why do suppliers extend trade credit to other businesses? What are the advantages and disadvantages of using trade credit?

8. How do private placements and public offerings differ?

9. Discuss the types of interest rates that may apply to a loan.

10. What is the difference between a secured loan and an unsecured loan?

Questions for Critical Thinking

1. According to *Inc.* magazine, of the approximately 600,000 companies that started in the year 2000, only about 5,000 received funding from venture capitalists. If just this small percentage actually received venture capital, why do small business magazines print such a disproportionately large number of articles about venture capital?

2. How does a small business's capital structure change over time?

Experience this . . .

Make arrangements with your instructor to invite a commercial banker to speak to your class. Discuss what factors bankers find most important in making small business loans. Do they really want to see a business plan? What should be included in it? Which section do they look at first? Second? In what order of importance would they rank the five Cs of credit? Does the visitor's bank make SBA loans? What is different about them? What other alternatives to direct loans does the bank offer? Lines of credit? Access to factoring? Does the bank make recommendations (and arrange meetings) to send a small business owner to meet with angel investors or venture capitalists?

What Would you Do?

Finding money to finance your small business can be a real challenge. You might look to the traditional avenues, such as using personal funds, tapping the resources of family and friends, or even relying on partners for financial backing. In the mid-1990s, however, a new approach to finding financing has emerged—one that utilizes the networking capability of the Internet. That's what Pam Marrone of AgraQuest, Inc., tapped into when she needed additional financing.

Marrone's Davis, California, company develops and manufactures all-natural pesticides. She needed $2.5 million to pay the research, development, and production costs of two pest-control products. Marrone knew how to find money the old-fashioned way. After all, she had raised $300,000 in startup financing to launch her company. But when she began looking to expand her business's product line, she decided to experiment with a more direct link to potential investors via the Internet.

Marrone chose to list her business idea (at a minimal charge) with Venture Connect, a website designed to match investors and entrepreneurs. She also developed her own company home page, which included an extensive business summary and job postings, and promoted it through Yahoo!'s business directory. "This is a potential way to get directly to investors," Marrone said. "The responses have been fast." Marrone was confident that her unique search for financing would pay off, yet she was being just as cautious in her search for financing in this high-tech approach as if she had taken a more traditional approach. After all, we're still talking about money.

Questions

1. What are the advantages and disadvantages of financing via the Internet, as Marrone did?

2. Should Marrone use her Internet financing source exclusively, or should she maintain a relationship with her local bank commercial loan officer? Why or why not?

CHAPTER CLOSING CASE

STICK IT OUT OR BAIL?

The trip to India was supposed to distract Heather Antonelli from her company's financial woes. But as she sat before a bonfire in Rajasthan in November 2004, business was the only thing on her mind. Antonelli, the CEO of Austin-based furniture wholesaler Eminence Style, had just defaulted on a $700,000 line of credit from Bank of America. Before departing for India, she had laid off five of her 11 employees. Faced with declining sales and a huge pile of debt, she was wrestling with a tough decision: Should she shut down her company and declare bankruptcy?

A few years earlier, such a situation would have been unthinkable. Antonelli founded Eminence Style with her mother, JoAnn, in Atlanta in 1996. They had always self-funded the business, using profits from completed orders to finance the manufacturing of the next. Sales grew slowly and steadily, reaching $3 million in 2000. Then, in 2001 a buyer from Sears ordered $2 million worth of tables and armoires for the retailer's Great Indoors division. It was a thrilling opportunity, but there was a hitch: Antonelli didn't have enough cash to pay a factory to make the furniture. For the first time, she began to shop for loans.

Landing financing was surprisingly easy—and exhilarating. In February 2002 she received a $200,000 loan from the SBA. That same week, Bank of America came through with a $700,000 line of credit. Meanwhile, she rounded up $55,000 from friends and family. "It was like Monopoly money," she recalls.

Eminence Style was on track to book 2002 sales of $5.5 million, with a healthy 10 percent profit. But then the value of the dollar began to slip against the euro. A few months earlier, Antonelli had paid her factory in Hungary a one-third deposit of $210,000 to complete the Sears job, and budgeted $420,000 to pay off the balance. As the dollar tanked, the total bill increased by one-third, to $840,000. She paid in full, but eked out a profit of only $10,000.

At first, Antonelli saw it as a minor setback. But in early 2003 her contact at Sears left the company, and his replacement wasn't interested in reordering.

The news couldn't have come at a worse time. Bank of America expected Antonelli to pay her entire $700,000 line of credit, which she had maxed out, in February. She pulled together $350,000 and persuaded her loan officer to give her more time. "I was convinced I could turn things around," she says.

Instead, the situation grew worse, as Antonelli began losing customers to lower-priced rivals that outsourced manufacturing to China, where costs were 50 percent of those in Hungary. While she searched for a Chinese factory that met her standards, she raised prices by 30 percent to stay afloat. Further complicating matters, she moved the company's headquarters to Austin, Texas, where her boyfriend lived, leaving her mother behind to run Eminence Style's show room in Atlanta. As Antonelli struggled to get the company on track, her relationship with her mother became increasingly strained.

Her relationship with her creditors also suffered. In May 2004 Bank of America called in the line of credit, giving Antonelli two months to pay off the remaining $350,000 she owed. A collection specialist began to call her regularly. "I spent the summer doing the bank dance," she says. "It was horrible."

When she returned from India, Antonelli reviewed her options with a business coach, Richard Russakoff, president of Richmond, Virginia-based Bottom Line Consultants. When the two compiled projected profit and loss statements, budget forecasts, and sales predictions, it became clear that it would take at least four years to break even, mainly because the business could no longer afford the employees and marketing necessary to generate substantial sales. "I'd be 37 years old and back where I started," Antonelli says.

The other option wasn't much better. Antonelli and her mother had personally guaranteed their loans. By shutting down the business and declaring Chapter 7 bankruptcy, they could free themselves from the debt, but they both cringed at the thought of not making good on their loans. "It was against my better sense of morals," Antonelli says. She also worried about her reputation: "I didn't want to feel like a failure." JoAnn, meanwhile, begged her daughter to keep the company open. "I had fifty thousand questions," JoAnn recalls. "What would happen to our customers? Would I lose my home?"

The burden of the decision lay on Heather, who handled the company's finances. She was torn, but she knew she had to make up her mind soon. Orders were backed up and worried customers were calling. What's more, Congress was about to pass a stricter bankruptcy law that would require Antonelli to sign up for credit counseling and possibly set up a repayment schedule instead of wiping the debt clean.

What do you think? Was bankruptcy the right decision for Heather Antonelli?

SOURCE: From Nadine Heintz, "Was Bankruptcy the Answer?" *Inc.*, December 2005, 59–60. Copyright © 2006 Mansueto Ventures LLC, publisher of Inc. Magazine, New York, NY 10017. Reprinted with permission.

Test Prepper

You've read the chapter, studied the key terms, and the exam is any day now. Think you're ready to ace it? Take this sample test to gauge your comprehension of chapter material. You can check your answers at the back of the book. Want more test questions? Visit the student website at college.hmco.com/pic/hatten4e and take the ACE and ACE+ quizzes for more practice.

ACE self-test

college.hmco.com/pic/hatten4e

Multiple Choice

1. What percentage of the value of your vehicle will banks or the SBA use as collateral for a loan?
   a. 10 percent
   b. 40 percent
   c. 80 percent
   d. nothing

2. In the chapter-opening vignette, Sistahs of Harlem was preparing their elevator pitch. How much time did they expect to have to make it?
   a. about an hour
   b. 30 seconds
   c. 10 minutes
   d. as long as the "sistahs" need

3. Restrictions to loan agreements are called
   a. covenants
   b. collateral
   c. intrusions
   d. illegal

4. A special type of loan used to fund high-priced items like vehicles is called
   a. installment loan
   b. line of credit
   c. floor planning
   d. ceiling finance

5. Investors who look for businesses that offer extremely high growth and profit potential, plus have a willingness to exchange equity and show potential to cash out in five years, are called
   a. commercial bankers
   b. venture capitalists
   c. private placement specialists
   d. IPO agents

Fill in the Blank

1. Fixed-interest rate loans typically have _____ rates than variable-rate loans.

2. An applicant's ability to repay a loan is called _____.

3. The SBA loan program that slashed paperwork and approval time is the _____ program.

4. Businesses in the _____ sector receive the highest percentage of SBA 7(a) loans.

5. The first time a company offers sale of its stock to the general public is called an _____ _____ _____.

## chapter 10

The Legal Environment

After reading this chapter, you should be able to:

- Name the laws and regulations that affect small business.

- List and explain the types of bankruptcy.

- Describe the elements of a contract.

- Discuss how to protect intellectual property.

David S. Pearl II was stunned when he found that counterfeit products that appeared to be made by his company, Uniweld, had started showing up in Saudi Arabia. But Pearl does not make items that we usually think of when we consider pirated goods—designer handbags, watches, software, or movies—he makes gauges to test refrigeration units and air conditioning compressors. Still, his manifolds had been knocked off right down to the American flag on the packaging. Soon customers in Saudi Arabia who thought they had purchased authentic manifolds for testing and repairing air conditioning systems in the sweltering Mideast were experiencing Freon leaks and inaccuracy.

The U.S. Department of Commerce reports U.S. businesses lose an estimated $200 billion annually to the counterfeiting of trademarked and copyrighted products. The International Chamber of Commerce also estimates that counterfeit goods of all kinds account for 6 percent of all world trade.

A recent study by consulting firm KPMG, notes several ways to mitigate counterfeiting. Among them: use *radio frequency identification (RFID)* and other product-tracking technologies; coordinate with trade groups and business partners to respond to counterfeiting; partner with and assist police agencies in detecting and busting counterfeiters. Pearl started by changing his packaging to be harder to duplicate, but it only took about six months for the counterfeiters to copy that also.

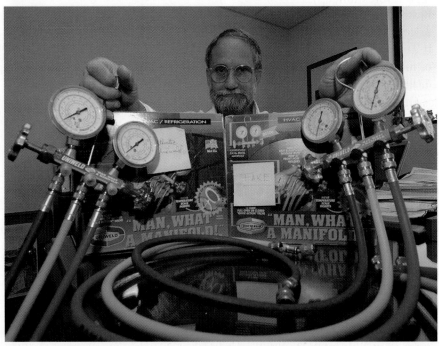

David S. Pearl II.

Uniweld hired a law firm in Saudi Arabia to register trademarks, but fakes continued to cost the company $1 million per year in revenue. None of Pearl's industry or law enforcement contacts could help find who was copying his products until Uniweld's new regional salesman attended a trade show in Duibai. Four people (none of them authorized dealers) offered to sell him phony Uniweld manifolds. More investigative work traced the origin to a Palestinian distributor. The case continues to move slowly through the Saudi Arabia legal system and Uniweld has lost several millions of dollars and suffered a damaged reputation because of the inferior quality of the counterfeited products.

This story shows that businesses both large and small from about any industry may be forced to fight against counterfeiters. Pearl says, "We've been working hard to regain the market, but it's not easy. The only way to survive is by being constantly vigilant."

SOURCES: Thomas Haire, "Ending the Scourge of Counterfeit Products," *Response,* January 2007, 54–57; Erik Sherman, "Fighting Fakes," *Inc.,* February 2006, 45–46; Bill Roberts, "Knocking Off the Counterfeiters," *Electronic Business,* June 2006, 10–12; "Fighting the Phonies," *Aftermarket Business,* January 2007, 1–1; Roger Parloff, Clay Chandler, Alice Fung, "Not Exactly Counterfeit," *Fortune,* May 1 2006, 108–116; Stuart Whitnell "Faking It Can Be Good," *Brand Strategy,* May 2006, 30–31.

Small Business and the Law

Would you like to live in a place with no laws? You could drive as fast as you wanted. You could drink alcohol at any age. You could do whatever you wanted, and, just think, there would be no taxes to pay because there would be no government making up rules and regulations! Although such absolute freedom might sound exciting at first thought, you don't have to picture this scenario for long to realize that it also includes no protection for anyone or any groups—it would be chaos. Orderly, civilized societies are built on laws.

"We need laws to ensure competition, enforce contracts, and protect our rights as consumers, workers, and property owners."

We need laws to ensure fair competition between businesses, to protect the rights of consumers and employees, to protect property, to enforce contracts and agreements, and to permit bankruptcy when things go bad. And we need tax laws to collect the money needed for government to provide these protections. The balance of how much or how little protection we need or we want changes over time. Through elections and open debate, our laws evolve to reflect the needs of and changes in society. But, as an old saying goes, "It's a good thing that we don't get half the government we pay for."

Small business owners face a never ending job of keeping up with the laws and regulations by which they must abide. One problem is that the wording of many laws and regulations is often baffling and easy to misunderstand. A second problem for small businesses is the enormous amount of paperwork required to generate the many reports and records mandated by regulations. This paperwork imposes time and resource burdens on business owners who are often strapped for both. A third problem is the cost (for administrative and actual expenses) and difficulty in complying with regulations.

Running a small business does not require a law degree, but you do need two things to avoid trouble: a working knowledge of legal basics and a good lawyer. The best time to find a lawyer for your small business is when you are writing your business plan—not when you are already in trouble.

A study by the National Federation of Independent Business (NFIB) titled "Small-Business Problems and Priorities" showed that the top 10 small business problems are split between costs, such as health care, and dealing with government regulations. NFIB Senior Research Fellow Bruce Phillips noted, "Small business owners' most serious problems are politically generated, rather than spawned from free-market competition." Small business owners consider managing the daily burdens of health care costs, taxation, and regulation mandates to be far more difficult than what they do best—running a business. Figure 10.1 shows the top 10 responses from more than 4,600 small business owners to a 2004 survey dealing with cost- and regulation-related issues.

Regulations and the legal environment of small business cover a lot of ground. This chapter will discuss several major areas of business affected by the law: regulations, licenses, bankruptcy, contracts, and protection of intellectual property.

Laws to Promote Fair Business Competition

Competition among businesses lies at the heart of a free enterprise system (see Chapter 1). Healthy competition provides the balance needed to ensure that buyers and sellers are both satisfied. It decreases the need for government intervention in the market.

> **antitrust laws**
> Legislation that prohibits firms from combining in a way that would stifle competition within that industry.

Antitrust laws like the Sherman Antitrust Act of 1890 and the Clayton Act of 1914 were written to prevent large businesses from forming *trusts*—large combinations of firms that can dominate an industry and stifle competition, thereby preventing new or small businesses from participating. Under such laws, any agreements or contracts that restrain trade are illegal and unenforceable. The Sherman Antitrust Act and the Clayton Act are two of the best-known antitrust laws and are still widely used in preventing business mergers and acquisitions judged to decrease competition. These laws are worthy of mention here because small businesses benefit from open competitive environments.

The Federal Trade Commission Act of 1914 created the Federal Trade Commission (FTC), the agency that regulates competition, advertising, and pricing in the U.S. economy. The five-member commission has the power to conduct hearings, direct investigations, and issue *cease-and-desist orders*, which prohibit offending companies from unfair or deceptive practices such as *collusion* (acting together to keep prices artificially high). These cease-and-desist orders are enforceable in federal court.

Laws to Protect Consumers

Up until the past few decades, U.S. consumer laws were based on the rule of *caveat emptor:* "Let the buyer beware." Now laws have largely abandoned this precept to offer ever increasing protection for consumers, administered by a wide

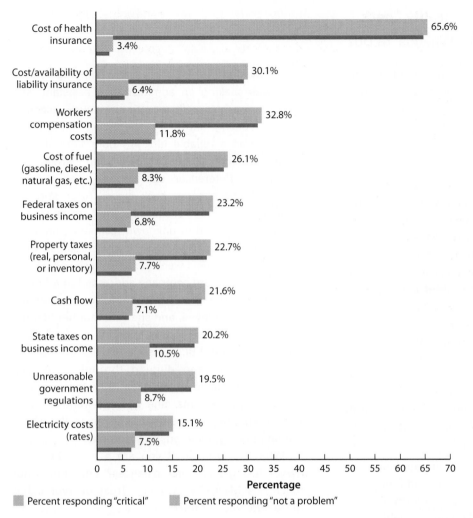

Figure 10.1

GET OFF OUR BACKS

Most Small Business Owners Struggle with Costs and Regulations.

SOURCE: National Federation of Independent Business/Wells Fargo & Co., "Health Insurance Costs: A 'Critical' Problem for Small Business," press release, 25 May 2004.

Cost of health insurance — 65.6% / 3.4%

Cost/availability of liability insurance — 30.1% / 6.4%

Workers' compensation costs — 32.8% / 11.8%

Cost of fuel (gasoline, diesel, natural gas, etc.) — 26.1% / 8.3%

Federal taxes on business income — 23.2% / 6.8%

Property taxes (real, personal, or inventory) — 22.7% / 7.7%

Cash flow — 21.6% / 7.1%

State taxes on business income — 20.2% / 10.5%

Unreasonable government regulations — 19.5% / 8.7%

Electricity costs (rates) — 15.1% / 7.5%

Percentage

■ Percent responding "critical"   ■ Percent responding "not a problem"

variety of state and federal agencies. The most common practices that government protects consumers against involve extension of credit, deceptive trade practices, unsafe products, and unfair pricing.

The FTC, for instance, is involved in product-labeling standards; banning hazardous products; ensuring consumer product safety; regulating the content and message of advertising; ensuring truth-in-lending practices, equal credit access to consumers and fair credit practices; and many other areas. Many laws that are intended to protect consumers fall under the jurisdiction of the FTC, including the Nutrition Labeling and Education Act, the Fair Debt Collection Practices Act, the Truth-in-Lending Act, and the Consumer Product Safety Act, to name but a few. The FTC is an agency of the federal government with broad and deep power when it comes to protecting consumers.

Laws to Protect People in the Workplace

A major thrust of federal employment legislation today is ensuring equal employment opportunity. This goal is based on the belief that an individual should be considered for employment on the basis of her individual merit, without regard to

Reality Check

Whadda Ya Do?

Unfortunately, some employees turn out to be unscrupulous individuals. Small business owners have trouble defending themselves against these offenders. For example:

- When a sweet elderly lady asked the founder of a small woman's clothing manufacturer for a job "at any wage, just to fill up my time," he hired her to clean desks. After exactly 10 days of work, she asked for a leave of absence. Still sentimental, the business owner said, "Give a call when you are ready to come back." The sweet lady didn't call back, but her lawyer did. She had filed a suit against the company claiming that she developed double carpal tunnel syndrome that prevented her from doing work of any kind—to the tune of $20,000 per wrist! Many months and many legal fees later, the owner ended up settling on the courthouse steps, even though he found out that the ex-employee had lined up her lawyer before she applied at the business.

- A regional law firm hired an applicant who claimed on her résumé that she had a bachelor's degree in MIS (management information systems) and an MBA. Based on those qualifications, she was hired as information systems director at a $105,000 annual salary. Two years later, the firm discovered that the employee had embezzled more than $2 million by creating two fictitious suppliers.

- The owner of a small Midwestern shipping company was seeking an administrative assistant who could also help with receptionist duties, accounting, invoicing, and filing. The owner thought she had found a reliable hire in Abbie Normal, who was "very capable, smart, quick, and learned really well." References checked out, and a background check came back clean. After about a month, mysterious packages started arriving at the office, addressed to unknown recipients, often on days that Normal was out, so the packages were sent back. The next week the office received a letter from a credit card company addressed to a former employee. That didn't seem right, so they contacted the ex-employee, and she said that her identity had been stolen a few months earlier." That brought in the FBI. Investigators discovered that Normal had been digging through employee records to steal identities, then using them to open credit card accounts. She was apparently buying the items that were being delivered to the office, then relaying the goods to accomplices.

What can you do if you are a small business owner facing such circumstances? Sometimes not much. As Mark Twain said, "Trust everyone, but make sure you cut the cards."

SOURCES: Phaedra Hise, "Employees from Hell," *Fortune Small Business*, March 2007, 18–28; Joseph Wells, "Protect Small Business," *Journal of Accountancy*, March 2003, 26; "Do You Know the Best Way to Detect Employee Fraud?" *IOMA Security Director's Report*, July 2002, 1–12; Robert Marnis, "Employees from Hell," *Inc.*, January 1995, pp. 50–56.

---

race, color, religion, sex, age, national origin, or disability. This goal dates back to the U.S. Constitution, and it was fortified by passage of the Fourteenth and Fifteenth Amendments in the 1860s. Beginning in the early 1960s, in response to great social change and widespread unrest, Congress acted to strengthen the legal underpinnings of this belief, passing several comprehensive pieces of legislation, outlined here.

Fair Labor Standards Act   The Fair Labor Standards Act is the primary law, passed in 1938, regulating worker's pay. It sets the minimum wage for all covered employees, overtime pay for nonexempt workers, equal pay for men and women, and rules for child labor.

Five categories of workers are exempt from the minimum wage and overtime pay requirements: executive, administrative, and professional employees; outside salespeople; and people in certain computer-related occupations. Each state also has its own (generally complicated) minimum wage guidelines.

Compliance is regulated by the Equal Employment Opportunity Commission (EEOC). Employers covered by the law must provide, on request, detailed records of compensation, including rates of pay, hours worked, overtime payments, deductions, and other related pay data. In addition, supporting documents, such as wage surveys, job descriptions, job evaluation studies, and collective bargaining agreements, may be requested.

Stampp Corbin Started His Business Recycling Computers Because He Wanted to Do Something Environmentally Friendly.

Civil Rights Act of 1964   The Civil Rights Act (CRA) of 1964 prevents discrimination on the basis of sex, race, color, religion, or national origin in any terms, conditions, or privileges of employment. Discrimination on the basis of pregnancy, childbirth, and related medical conditions is also prohibited as a result of a 1978 amendment. Title VII of this legislation applies to all organizations with 15 or more employees working 20 or more weeks per year in commerce or in any industry or activity affecting commerce. As amended, state and local governments, labor unions, employment agencies, and educational institutions are also covered.

Provisions of the act are enforced by the Equal Employment Opportunity Commission (EEOC). Private employers with 100 or more employees are required to file annually Form EEO-1, detailing the makeup of the company's workforce. In addition, all employers are required to keep employment-related documents for at least six months from the time of their creation or, in the case of a personnel action such as a discharge, from the date of the action.

Immigration Reform and Control Act   The Immigration Reform and Control Act (IRCA) was passed in 1986 with two intended goals. First, it seeks to discourage illegal immigration into the United States by denying employment to aliens who do not comply with the Immigration and Naturalization Service regulations. It achieves this goal by requiring employers to document worker eligibility. All U.S. employers must complete Form I-9 for new hires, for which the employee must provide documentation proving his identity and work authorization. Permissible documents include a birth certificate, U.S. passport, certificate of U.S. citizenship, certificate of naturalization, unexpired foreign passport, resident alien card, or a combination of documents attesting to identity and employment authorization as outlined on Form I-9.[1]

A second goal of the act was to strengthen the national-origin provisions of Title VII of the 1964 CRA by extending coverage to "foreign-sounding" and "foreign-looking" individuals, and to all employers with four or more employees (rather than the "15 or more employees" limit established by the CRA). If found guilty of discrimination under the IRCA, you may be assessed back pay for up to two years and civil fines of up to $2,000 per violation and $10,000 for multiple violations.[2] Enforcement responsibilities were assigned to the Office of the Special Counsel for Immigration-Related Unfair Employment Practices, a division of the Department of Justice.

The ongoing debate and recent demonstrations surrounding immigration reform are being watched closely by politicians, citizens, and business people alike—especially small business owners. According to a recent survey from the National Federation of Independent Business (NFIB), more than 90 percent of NFIB small business owners surveyed believe that illegal immigration is a problem, with 70 percent ranking it as a "very serious" or "serious" problem, and 86 percent saying it should have a "very high" or "high" priority for Congress and the Bush administration. So, keep watch for more regulation regarding immigration.[3]

Americans with Disabilities Act   The 1990 Americans with Disabilities Act (ADA) was passed to guarantee individuals with disabilities the right to obtain and hold a job, to travel on public transportation, to enter and use public facilities, and to use telecommunication services. One or more of the act's provisions affects almost all businesses, regardless of size.

If you are a private employer with 15 or more employees (including part-time employees) working 20 or more calendar weeks per year, you are covered by Title 1, the employment discrimination provision. As such, you cannot discriminate against qualified disabled individuals with regard to any employment practice or terms, conditions, and privileges of employment. Under the act, a *disabled person* is one who (1) has a physical or mental impairment that substantially limits one or more major life activities, (2) has a physical or mental impairment, or (3) is regarded as having such an impairment. Specifically included within this definition are recovering drug addicts, alcoholics, and individuals who are infected with HIV or who have AIDS.

In turn, a *qualified applicant* is one who (1) meets the necessary prerequisites for the job, such as education, work experience, or training, and (2) can perform the essential functions of the job with or without *reasonable accommodation*, meaning any modification of the work environment that makes it possible for an individual to enjoy equal employment opportunities without imposing *undue hardship* (defined shortly) on the employer. Once a set of effective accommodations has been identified—which might include restructuring a job, modifying work schedules, providing readers and interpreters, or obtaining and modifying equipment—you are free to select the option that is the least expensive or easiest to provide. Even then, you need make the accommodation only if it does not present an *undue hardship* on the operation of your business, meaning an action that is "excessively costly, extensive, substantial, or disruptive, or that would fundamentally alter the nature or operation of the business."[4] In determining undue hardship, you should consider the nature and cost of the accommodation in relation to your business's size, its financial resources (including available tax credits, as discussed later), the nature and structure of its operation, and the impact of the accommodation on its operation.

In addition to the necessity of making reasonable accommodation for disabled people, you should keep the following points in mind:

- Prior to making a conditional offer of employment, inquiries of others about the applicant's disability, illness, and workers' compensation history are prohibited.

- Required medical or physical examinations are prohibited prior to making a conditional offer of employment. Drug tests may be given at any point in the employment process, however, because they are not considered medical examinations under the law.

- Any selection or performance standards should be job related, be based on a thorough job analysis, and be prepared prior to advertising the position.

- Asking the applicant about the nature, origin, or severity of a known disability is prohibited. You may, however, question the applicant about his ability to perform the essential functions of the job and describe or demonstrate how to perform such functions.

- An employer may not refuse to hire an individual simply because she might or will require accommodation under the act.

- All application materials and processes from the application form to the interview and beyond must be free of references to or inquiries about disabilities.

Under Title III of the ADA, virtually all businesses serving the public must make their facilities and services accessible to the disabled. This may require you to modify your operational policies, practices, and procedures; remove structural barriers; and provide auxiliary aids and services to the disabled. Technical standards for building and site elements, such as parking, ramps, doors, and elevators, have been set forth in the *ADA Accessibility Guidelines for New Construction and Alterations* handbook. The handbook is available from the Office of the Americans with Disabilities Act, U.S. Department of Justice.

Tax incentives are available to aid businesses in complying with the ADA. The Disabled Access Credit allows small businesses to take a tax credit amounting to one-half the cost of eligible access expenditures that are more than $250 but less than $10,500.[5] You may also qualify for tax deductions under the Architectural and Transportation Barrier Removal and Targeted Job Tax Credit provisions. Contact your local IRS or vocational rehabilitation office for additional information.

While the ADA has literally broken down barriers for Americans with disabilities, and most small business owners say they want to comply with the act, many also believe that its requirements are growing vaguer and more onerous. They support the law's aims but find it vaguely written and hard to comply with. A young man with cerebral palsy went out for breakfast at the Blue Plate Café in Memphis. He arrived in a wheelchair, accompanied by a service dog to help him with tasks such as opening doors. The restaurant was crowded, so owner Mike Richmond says he made a decision: Because eight people came with the man and were available to help him, the dog would not be allowed into the dining area. The party then left. Not long afterward, in June 2004, Richmond was served with a lawsuit under the federal Americans with Disabilities Act. To head off a legal battle, he quickly settled. He agreed to pay $3,500 in damages to the man, as well as legal fees and a $1,000 fine. "I was shocked," says Richmond. "But with some of these ADA lawsuits, you don't even know the rules until you get hit."[6]

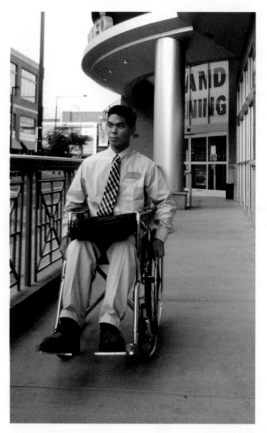

The ADA Assures Business Access to Employees and Customers.

Civil Rights Act of 1991   Title VII of the Civil Rights Act applies to businesses with more than 15 employees. Some of its provisions are outlined here:

- The act prohibits *race norming,* an illegal activity in which different test standards are set for different groups.

- It provides that, in cases where an otherwise neutral employment practice results in an underrepresentation of minorities (called *disparate impact cases*), employers must show that (1) the practice is job related; (2) the practice is consistent with a *business necessity,* meaning that it exists in the best interests of the firm's employees and the general public; and (3) a less discriminatory practice does not exist.

- In cases of intentional discrimination, the act provides for both compensatory and punitive damages and allows for jury trials.

- It places a cap on the amount of punitive and compensatory damages that can be awarded, depending on company size.

Title VII applies to all employment practices, including help-wanted ads, employee reviews, and daily working conditions.

The Civil Rights Act also added teeth to the EEOC guidelines on *sexual harassment* (see Chapter 3) by providing victims of discrimination, including those subjected to sexual harassment, access to trial by jury, compensatory damages for pain and suffering, and punitive damages if employers are proven to have acted with "malice or reckless indifference."

Small businesses are certainly not immune from sexual harassment. Unfortunately, such unwelcome behavior can occur in any company. Yet the penalties faced by small businesses are proportionately higher than those targeting large businesses. Limits vary from state to state, but consider the disparity in awards. A business with 15 employees could be assessed a maximum fine of $50,000 for a harassment conviction, or $3,333 per employee. A business with 500 employees could be fined $200,000, or $400 per employee. Which award do you think would have a greater effect on the business—$50,000 for a business of 15 or $200,000 for a business of 500?[7]

Because they can be held legally responsible not only for their own actions but also for the actions of their managers and employees, small businesses must prepare for potential problems by setting policies and procedures in advance of any complaint. Employees and managers need to be trained, as do subcontractors, because the business can be held liable for their actions as well. A business owner should be ready to investigate any complaint in a timely manner and poised to take appropriate action.

Workers' Compensation   Workers' compensation (also known by the shorthand term, *workers' comp*) is insurance that provides replacement income and medical expenses to employees who suffer work-related expenses or illnesses. This is a complex program that varies on a state-by-state basis. Any business with employees must purchase workers' comp either through a state fund or a private insurance company. Premiums are based on two major factors: industry classification and payroll. The number of claims that have been filed by your employees will affect your business's rates as well. Consequently, the financial ramifications of a claim being filed provide a powerful incentive for small businesses to create a safe workplace. Proper equipment, training in safe procedures, and instruction on how to act in emergencies are critical.

The costs of workers' compensation are now soaring to crisis levels. Nationwide, premiums increased by 50 percent in the first few years of the twenty-first century. Although relief is being sought, small businesses are especially hard hit by this trend because they cannot pass on these costs to their customers.[8] Factors such as increased health-care costs of treating claims and fear of terrorism also contribute to the rising premiums.[9]

Unemployment Compensation   All employers are required to contribute to an unemployment insurance fund. Employees who have been fired due to cutbacks in the workforce or because of a poor fit with the company are generally entitled to unemployment payments for a set period of time. Employees who are terminated for serious misconduct, such as theft or fraud, or who quit voluntarily are not entitled to benefits. Check with your state unemployment office for details on premiums and requirements in your area.

Occupational Safety and Health Administration (OSHA)   Congress passed the Occupational Safety and Health Act (OSHA) of 1970 to "assure, so far as possible, every working man and woman in the nation safe and healthful working conditions and to preserve our human resources."[10] OSHA has set workplace standards covering areas such as the following:

- Exposure to hazardous chemicals
- First aid and medical treatment
- Noise levels
- Protective gear—for example, goggles, respirators, gloves, work shoes, and ear protection
- Fire protection
- Worker training, and workplace temperatures and ventilation[11]

OSHA compliance inspections are conducted to investigate a reported accident, injury, or fatality at a worksite; when an employee complaint alleges a violation; or as part of a regular or programmed schedule of inspections. If you, as an employer, are cited for a violation, you may either correct the alleged violation, seek a variance, or appeal the penalty.

OSHA requires most employers with 11 or more employees to keep records of occupational injuries and illnesses. Employers must also post an approved state or federal OSHA poster and any citations, which must be displayed at or near the site of the alleged violation for three days or until corrected, whichever is later.

As a small business owner, you may request information from one of ten regional OSHA offices or ask for a free on-site OSHA-supported consultation through your state's labor or health department. No citations will be issued or penalties proposed during this visit, nor will the name of your firm or any information regarding your firm be given to OSHA. However, you will be expected to correct any serious job safety and health hazards identified as part of the consultation.

Licenses, Restrictions, and Permits

Because requirements for licenses and permits differ at the federal, state, regional, county, and city government levels, presenting a comprehensive list of all of them is not possible here. Nevertheless, we can offer some general guidelines for finding information on regulations at each level.

- Double-check license and permit rules. Check with the appropriate government agency directly—don't rely on real estate agents, sellers, or anyone else's opinion.

- At the federal level, get an employer identification number for federal tax and social security withholdings. File Form 2553 if you are forming a corporation. Check with the appropriate agency for your specific type of business. For example, if you are starting a common-carrier trucking company, you should contact the Interstate Commerce Commission.

- At the state level, professionals, such as lawyers, dentists, and architects, need professional licenses. You need to register for a state tax number with the Department of Revenue. You need an employer identification number for state tax withholding. Special licenses are usually needed for selling liquor, food, gasoline, or firearms.

- At the regional level, several counties may form regional agencies that oversee environmental regulations and water usage.

- At the local level, permits and licenses to comply with local and county requirements will vary from place to place. You need answers from the local level—the local chamber of commerce and lawyers are good sources of information. Offices to consult would include the following:

  - City or county clerk
  - City or county treasurer
  - Zoning department
  - Building department
  - Health department
  - Fire department
  - Police department
  - Public works department

- If your business involves the sale or preparation of food, you will need not only a permit from a local health department, but also regular inspections. Local health departments may also be involved with environmental concerns, such as asbestos inspections, radon testing, and water purity testing.

Zoning Laws   You need to be absolutely sure how a property is zoned before you sign a lease. If it is not zoned properly, you can sign the lease with a contingency clause that the property will be rezoned. You can also apply to the local zoning commission to obtain a *variance*, which allows you to operate without complying with the regulation or without having the regulation be changed.

> **zoning laws**
> Local laws that control where and how businesses may operate.

  Zoning laws control what a business can sell and where it can operate. They are typically used to control parking, waste disposal, and sign size and placement. You may not even be able to paint the building a certain color due to zoning restrictions. For example, a White Castle hamburger franchise in Overland Park,

Kansas, was not allowed to paint the building white because a zoning ordinance prohibited white buildings.

How do zoning laws affect home-based businesses, the fastest-growing segment in business (see Chapter 7)? Technology is making it possible for you to be productive at work from the comfort of your own living room. But are zoning boards comfortable with that idea? Yes, for the most part. Although some zoning ordinances prohibit home businesses, most don't. Restrictions on what you can and can't do on the property are more common. Most zoning laws seek primarily to maintain the residential nature of the surrounding neighborhood.

You should check zoning laws before you start your business, whether or not it is home based. At the zoning department at city hall, find out about not only the written laws but also the attitudes held by administrators, citizens, and the business community. Find out if other home-based businesses are allowed. If you disagree with a zoning ruling, you may be able to appeal to a variance board, the city council, or local commissioners.

Bankruptcy Laws

Bankruptcy is a remedy for becoming insolvent. When an individual or a business gets into a financial condition in which there's no other way out, the courts administer the estate for the benefit of the creditors. The Bankruptcy Reform Act of 1978 established eight chapters for businesspeople seeking the protection of bankruptcy. Three of these chapters—Chapters 7, 11, and 13—apply to most small business situations. Bankruptcy can accomplish two different objectives: *liquidation,* after which the business ceases to exist, and *reorganization,* which allows the business owner to file a plan with the court that offers protection from creditors until the debt is satisfied.

bankruptcy
A ruling granted by courts to release businesses or individuals from some or all of their debt.

Chapter 7 Bankruptcy

Chapter 7 bankruptcy means that the business is liquidated. All of the assets of the business are sold by a trustee appointed by the court. After the sale, the trustee distributes the proceeds to the creditors, who usually receive a percentage of the original debt. If any money is left over, it is divided among shareholders. About three of every four bankruptcy filings take place under Chapter 7.

Declaring bankruptcy does not necessarily leave you penniless and homeless. Most states have provisions that allow individuals to keep the equity in their homes, autos, and some personal property.

Other businesses that declare bankruptcy may provide an opportunity for you. For instance, imagine you are in business and one of your key suppliers goes bankrupt. What are your options? You could try to continue doing business with that firm for as long as possible. You could try to find a new supplier. Or you could use your knowledge of the bankrupt company and industry to your advantage, and buy the supplier at a bargain price, assuming you could operate the failed business more efficiently than the previous management.[12] Other strategic purchases could include buying a financially strapped competitor in an effort to increase your market share, or buying a business that is a customer in an effort to provide an outlet for your products.

The Bankruptcy Abuse Prevention and Consumer Protection Act of 2005 has caused some shifts in bankruptcy responsibilities. Individuals seeking Chapter 7 liquidation face increased responsibilities. While creditors have always had to show documentation of indebtedness—*proof of claim*—the burden is on the debtor to demonstrate that there is no reasonable alternative to the bankruptcy process. The debtor seeking liquidation must now prove an inability to pay his debts as they are due and demonstrate a good-faith attempt to resolve such a crisis without the court's help.

A controversial section in the Bankruptcy Code lies in the creation of a *means test* for eligibility to file under Chapter 7. The Bankruptcy Abuse Prevention and Consumer Protection Act requires a comparison of the debtor's income to the median income in the individual's home state. If the debtor's income is above the median and she is able to pay at least a minimal amount per month to creditors, she is now barred from Chapter 7 filing.[13]

Chapter 11 Bankruptcy

Chapter 11 provides a second chance for a business that is in financial trouble but still has potential for success. This type of bankruptcy can be either voluntary or involuntary. When you seek Chapter 11 protection, you must file a *reorganization plan* with the bankruptcy court. This plan includes a repayment schedule for current creditors (which may be less than 100 percent of the amounts owed) and indicates how the business will operate more profitably in the future. Only about 3 percent of bankruptcy filings take place under Chapter 11.

This reorganization protection keeps creditors from foreclosing on debts during the reorganization period. The business continues to operate under court direction. Both the court and the creditors must approve the plan, which also spells out a specific time period for the reorganization. If the business cannot turn operations (and profits) around, the likelihood of its switching to a Chapter 7 liquidation is great.

Chapter 13 Bankruptcy

Chapter 13 bankruptcy allows individuals, including small business owners, who owe less than $250,000 in unsecured debts and less than $750,000 in secured debts to pay back creditors over a three- to five-year period. As under Chapter 11, a repayment plan is submitted to a bankruptcy judge, who must approve the conditions of the plan. The plan must show how most types of debts will be repaid in full. Some types of debts can be reduced or even eliminated by the court. About one-fourth of bankruptcies are filed under the provisions of Chapter 13.

Although much of the negative stigma attached to declaring bankruptcy of any type has decreased, this course of action is still not an "easy way out." Bankruptcy stays on your credit report for at least seven years. It is expensive and time-consuming. Chapters 11 and 13 may be better than liquidation, but they are not a solution to all of your problems.

Contract Law for Small Businesses

contract
An agreement between two or more parties that is enforceable by law.

A **contract** is basically a promise that is enforceable by law. Contract law comprises the body of laws that are intended to make sure that the parties entering into a contract comply with the deal and provides remedies to those parties harmed if a contract is broken.

A contract does not have to be in writing to be enforceable. Although it is a good idea to get any important agreement down on paper to help settle future disputes, the only contracts that must be in writing are those that involve one of the following:

- Sale of real estate
- Paying someone else's debt
- More than one year to perform
- Sale of goods valued at $500 or more

Even written contracts do not have to be complicated, formal documents created by a lawyer. Although you may not want to rely on contracts that are too sketchy, a letter or memo that identifies the parties, the subject, and the terms and conditions of the sale can be recognized as a valid contract.

Elements of a Contract

The four basic conditions or elements that a contract must meet to be binding are legality, agreement, consideration, and capacity.

Legality   A contract must have a legal purpose. For instance, you can't make a contract that charges an interest rate higher than legal restrictions allow. At the same time, just because a deal is unfair, it is not necessarily illegal. You can't get out of a deal later if you offer to pay $1,500 for a used computer that is worth only $150.

Agreement   A valid contract has a legitimate offer and a legitimate acceptance—called a "meeting of the minds." If a customer tells you his traveling circus will pay your print shop $600 to print 200 circus posters and you say, "It's a deal," you have a legally binding contract. In this case, it is an oral contract, which is just as legally binding as a written one.

Consideration   Something of value must be exchanged between the parties involved in the contract. Without consideration, the agreement is about a gift, not a contract. In the preceding example, the $600 and the 200 posters are the consideration. If the circus owner picks up the posters, pays you the $600, and says, "Wow, for doing such a great job, come to the circus and I'll give you a free elephant ride," can you legally demand to ride the elephant later? No, you got what you agreed to—the $600—but there was no consideration for the bonus.

Capacity   Not everyone has the capacity to legally enter into a contract. Minors and persons who are intoxicated or who have diminished mental ability cannot be bound by contracts. This is an important point to remember when running a small business. For example, if you sell a used car to a person younger than the age of 18, you could end up with a problem. The minor could take the car, run it without oil, smash it into a tree, and then ask you for his money back. You would be legally obligated to return the money because a contract with a minor is not binding.

Contractual Obligations

What can you do if a party with whom you signed a contract doesn't hold up her end of the deal? This scenario is called **breach of contract,** and you have several

> *breach of contract*
> A violation of one or more terms of a contract by a party involved in the contract.

@ e-biz

Legal Answers Without a Retainer Fee

Looking for answers to legal questions? Although sometimes no substitute for a flesh-and-blood lawyer exists, they can be expensive, so check out these Internet sites first:

• The mother lode of business-law websites is 'Lectric Law Library (lectlaw.com). This site offers true one-stop shopping to answer your small business legal questions. Start with the library tour, where you will find information in thousands of stacks, including the Reference Room, Forms Room, Book Store, Laypeople's Law Lounge, Legal Professional's Lounge, and (most important to you) the Law for Business Lounge.

• Findlaw.com looks like a legal version of Yahoo! with more than 25,000 links. You will be most interested in the Small Business Toolbox (www.smallbiz.findlaw.com) with sample business plans, step-by-step checklists, downloadable legal forms, and documents.

• FreeAdvice.com uses the slogan, "The easy-to-use site for legal information." Not too catchy, but fairly accurate. Here you will find information on topics including bankruptcy, business law, employment, intellectual property, tax law, and small claims.

• At Lawoffice.com, West Group has compiled a site to help "businesses, professionals, and consumers navigate through legal issues that affect their professional and personal lives." The Law Pathfinders section includes a dictionary of more than 5,000 legal terms and links to print publications and other sites arranged by topic.

• Allaboutlaw.com offers more than 1,200 downloadable legal forms and documents.

• Nolo.com comes from the publisher of many great self-help guides and books on legal topics. The web site features downloadable forms and documents, legal software, a legal encyclopedia, a dictionary, and a Q & A section.

---

remedies available. Usually either money or some specific performance is used to compensate the damaged party. With either remedy, the intent of litigation is to try to put you back to where you were before the agreement was made.

Money awarded by a judge or arbitrator as a remedy for breach of contract is called **compensatory damages.** Go back to the circus poster example. If you were not able to complete the job as agreed and the circus owner had to pay someone else $800 to get the posters printed, you could be sued for $200 for breach of contract (probably in small claims court). Why $200? That amount represents the compensatory damages the circus owner suffered because you couldn't do the job for $600.

In some contract-dispute cases, money alone is insufficient to put a person back to his original state. In these cases, a judge may order a **specific performance** by the damaging party to make sure justice is done—in other words, requiring that party to do exactly what she agreed to do. Specific performance is awarded only if the item involved is unique and not substitutable. In this case, a judge will require the losing party to surrender the item in question.

Consider the case of buying an existing business for which the sales contract includes a *noncompete covenant*, which states that the previous business owner will not start or own a similar business within a specific geographic area for a certain amount of time. If the previous owner breaks the noncompete covenant and

> **compensatory damages**
> Money awarded by the courts to a party of the contract who has suffered a loss due to the actions of another party.

> **specific performance**
> A nonmonetary award granted by the courts to a party of the contract who has suffered a loss due to the actions of another party.

starts the same type of business, a single monetary award won't be enough. The judge can issue an **injunction,** which prohibits the previous owner from operating the new business for the duration of the agreement.

Watch the video clip that accompanies this chapter to see how a small business, Newbury Comics, used contract law to its advantage. Other legal and financial issues related to the subject are addressed in the video as well.

> *injunction*
> A court order that prohibits certain activities.

Laws to Protect Intellectual Property

Intellectual property is a broad term that refers to the product of some type of unique human thought. It begins as an idea that could be as simple as a new name or as complex as the invention of a new product. Intellectual property also includes symbols and slogans that describe your business or product and any original expression, whether it takes the form of a collection of words (like a published book), an artistic interpretation (like a videotape of a concert performance), or a computer program. These products of human thought have some value in the marketplace. A body of laws determines how, and for how long, a person can capitalize on his idea.

> *intellectual property*
> Property that is created through the mental skills of a person.

The forms of legal protection for intellectual property that will be discussed in this section are patents, copyrights, and trademarks. Although commonly used, the term *protection* may be misleading when we are discussing intellectual property, because it implies defense whereas patents, copyrights, and trademarks give the owner more offensive rights than defensive protection. They cannot prevent others from trying to infringe on your

"Safeguarded by the U.S. Constitution, intellectual-property protection encourages entrepreneurs to invent new ideas and products."

registered idea, but they can discourage such attempts by the threat of your taking them to court. Although these court challenges often do not prevail, the possibility that they might prevail reduces attempts to steal your intellectual property. In the United States, this right has been considered so essential a part of the country's economic functioning that it was written into the Constitution.[14]

Patents

A **patent** gives you the right to exclude someone else (or some other company) from making, using, or selling the property you have created and patented for a period of 17 years. To receive this protection, you have to file for a patent through the Patent Trademark Office (PTO). With a patent application, you must pay both filing fees and maintenance fees. Three maintenance fees must be paid 4, 8, and 12 years after the patent grant, or the patent will expire before 17 years.

> *patent*
> A form of protection for intellectual property provided to an inventor for a period of 17 years.

Although it is commonly believed that you have to hire a patent attorney to file a patent application, this is not the case. Actually, regulations require the PTO to help individuals who do not use an attorney. Hundreds of patents are granted each year to inventors who navigate the process solo. But just because you can complete the patent process without legal counsel, does that mean you should attempt it? It depends—on factors like your comfort level with processing "red tape." Patent attorneys charge $3,000 to $5,000 to prepare a patent application.

Reality Check

Protect Your IP or No?

There are some changing thought patterns for entrepreneurs regarding intellectual property (IP) as we enter the twenty-first century. In the past, companies have treated IP as a asset that must be kept out of the hands of others at all costs, but turning loose of that paranoia is becoming less the exception and more the rule.

This sounds counterintuitive given the amount of attention that is paid to the value of IP today, a value estimated at around $5.5 trillion—or about half of GDP—in the United States. The number of patent-related lawsuits filed in 2006 were just about twice the number filed in 1992, so companies are saying, "Keep your mitts off my good ideas."

But the bottom line (literally) is that that success of a business is rarely tied to success in protecting IP. Ninety-five percent of patents end up being of absolutely no commercial value. Even in the high-tech industry (where IP is everything), the rule of thumb in protecting patents is . . . don't bother. According to economics professor Glen Whitman,

"The faster the pace of innovation, the less important will be the patent." In other words, superb execution trumps IP protection every time.

Then why are companies so obsessed with patents? Because they don't really understand their own business. Danny Shader, CEO of Good Technology, maker of wireless communication software, says, "A lot of people think they're in the invention business, but they're really in the application business. Profitable innovation comes not from inventing a new product, but from having a team of smart employees who figure out how to do a better job every time they interact with customers."

The amount of information (movies, TV shows, books, music) available online is affecting attitudes toward IP. With downloads available on about every screen, business models are adapting to catch up. Do you think patent protection will become less important in the future? Why or why not?

SOURCE: From David H. Freedman, "Relax. Let Your Guard Down," *Inc.*, August 2006, 108–111. Copyright © 2006 Mansueto Ventures LLC, publisher of Inc. Magazine, New York, NY 10017. Reprinted with permission.

How many earth-changing widgets must you sell to cover that kind of overhead? If you are unsure of what the market for your widgets will be, books like *Patent It Yourself* by David Pressman contain all the instructions and forms you need to do it yourself.[15] Doing as much as you can yourself, while checking periodically with an attorney throughout the process, may be a reasonable compromise to offer you both expertise and cost savings.

Three types of patents exist. The most common type is the *utility patent,* which covers inventions that provide a unique or new use or function. If you could come up with a new way to keep shoes on people's feet without using laces, buckles, Velcro fasteners, zippers, or other ways currently used, you would need to file for a utility patent.

Whereas utility patents cover use, *design patents* protect unique or new forms or shapes. If the new shape also changes the function of the object, then you need to apply for a utility patent. If looks alone are different, you need a design patent. For example, if you were to design a ballpoint pen that looked like a fish, but which served no other function than that of a ballpoint pen, you would file for a design patent on your invention.

The third patent type is a *plant patent.* Such a patent covers living plants, such as flowers, trees, or vegetables that can be grown or otherwise reproduced.

What Can Be Patented?   The PTO reviews each application and decides whether to grant a patent on the basis of four tests, which come from the following questions:

- Does the invention fit a statutory class?
- Is the invention useful?
- Is it novel?
- Is it nonobvious?

The invention must fit into one of the five *statutory classes*—which means that you must be able to call it a machine, process, manufacture, chemical composition, or combination of those terms.

The invention must provide some *legal utility.* That is, it must be useful in some way. If the invention has some commercial value, this test shouldn't be difficult to pass. If it doesn't, you will have a hard time building your small business on it. The invention must be possible to build and be workable to be granted a patent. You have to be able to show the examiner that the invention will operate as you say it will.

The invention must be *novel.* It must be different from all other things that have previously been made or described anywhere else in the world (called *prior art*). Meeting this test can be difficult since the definition of *novelty* may be confusing to everyone involved. Three types of novelty that meet this requirement are those created by (1) physical difference, (2) a new combination of existing parts, or (3) the invention of a new use.

The invention must be *nonobvious.* Although this rule is also difficult to understand, it is an important one. It means that the difference between your invention and other developments (or prior art) must not be obvious to someone with common knowledge in that field. The novelty of your invention needs to produce new or unexpected results.

The flowchart in Figure 10.2 can help you visualize the tests your invention must pass to get a patent.

Patent Search   Before you file a patent application, you should conduct a *patent search* to save time and money later. You can conduct this search yourself, or you can hire a patent agent or patent attorney to do it for you. You are searching for existing patents for inventions that are or may be similar to yours.

Start by coming up with several keywords that could be used in describing your invention. These keywords will be run through the primary patent reference publication at the PTO in Arlington, Virginia, called *Index to the U.S. Patent Classification.* If you can't go to the PTO, you can search a Patent Depository Library. In these libraries, you can use the *Official Gazette of the U.S. Patent and Trademark Office.*

You can also conduct a patent search by subject or by specific patent via the Internet. Such a search is done through the Shadow Patent Office. For more information, visit the PTO's home page at www.uspto.gov through the Internet.

Patent Application   When submitting your patent application, you should include the following items:

1. Self-addressed postcard to show receipt of packet
2. Payment of the filing fee

3. Letter of transmittal

4. Drawings of your invention

5. Specifications, including

    a. Title or name of your invention

    b. Cross-reference of similar inventions

    c. Description of the field of your invention

    d. Prior art

    e. Features and advantages of your invention

    f. Drawing descriptions

    g. Description of how your invention works

    h. Conclusion

6. The claim, which specifies patent details that define the scope of your invention

7. An abstract, summarizing the whole project

8. A patent application declaration form that says that you are the true inventor

9. A statement that you have not transferred patent ownership to anyone else

10. An information disclosure statement and a list of prior art[16]

Your application will be reviewed by a PTO examiner in the order in which it is received, meaning that it could be months or years before the review begins. The examination process can take from one to three or more years with revisions and amendments. If your patent is approved, you will be notified, and a copy of the application will be sent to the U.S. Government Printing Office.

Copyrights

copyright
A form of protection for intellectual property provided to the creator of a literary, musical, or artistic work for a period of the creator's life plus 50 years.

A **copyright** is the protection of literary, musical, or artistic works. Copyright laws protect the expression of ideas, not the ideas themselves, because lawmakers want to encourage the dissemination of ideas while protecting the rights of the original owner.

The length of copyright protection is the life of the author plus 50 years. If your corporation is the owner of a book's copyright, it will continue as owner for 75 years after the first publication, or 100 years after creation.

You don't have to register your work to receive copyright protection, but it does strengthen your rights to do so. If registered, you don't have to prove actual damages to collect up to $500,000 if someone violates your copyright. The act of creating the work begins the copyright protection, whether or not it is ultimately published. If you do choose to register your work, all you need to do is complete the proper forms and send the fees to the Copyright Office along with a copy of your work.

Many small businesses create computer software. Should they seek a patent or a copyright for their creation? Actually, software could qualify for either or both forms of protection, so which would be better? A patented computer program is difficult for competitors to simulate or design around, and the protection lasts for 17 years, but consider the disadvantages: Patents can be expensive, require a lot of work to apply for and search, and take several years to obtain. Windows of opportunity open and shut quickly in the software market. Your software may be obsolete before a patent can even be granted.

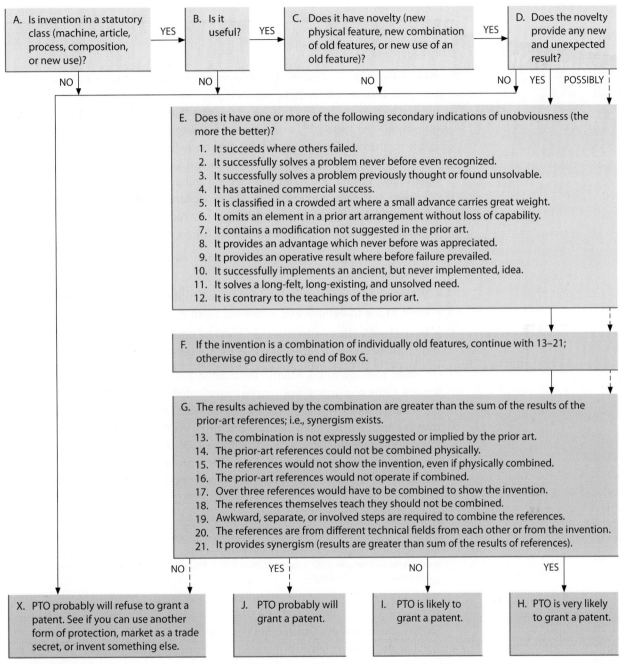

Figure 10.2

HOW DO YOU GET A PATENT?

Here Are the Steps Needed to Receive a Patent on Your Product.

SOURCE: From *Patent It Yourself*, Twelfth Edition, by David Pressman. 2006, p.111. Reprinted with permission from the publisher, Nolo. Copyright © 2006, http://www.nolo.com.

Copyrighting software is quick and inexpensive but doesn't provide the offensive punch of a patent. You can't copyright what a program does, only the specific way it is written. Thus competing small business programmers need merely to write the program for their software in a different manner to avoid copyright infringement.

Manager's Notebook

Exercise Your Trademark

When you've got a good thing, you want to keep it. That's why it's important for small business owners to register ideas and products as soon as possible and to monitor for any misuse of their trademarks. Designer Nancy Ganz introduced the Hipslip™, a product she created from nylon and DuPont's Lycra to provide extra support for the body-hugging garments that she designed. Ganz recognized that new ideas are quickly imitated, so she registered Hipslip with the PTO as soon as she coined the name.

Small business owners must be as vigilant as giants like Coca-Cola, Sony, or Adidas in monitoring for misuse of a registered trademark. But how do you achieve this ongoing awareness? Some suggestions follow:

- A press-clipping service can track references to products in articles and advertisements.
- When an infringement is found, send offending parties a letter notifying them of the trademark and informing them to cease and desist use of it.
- In extreme instances, legal action must be undertaken to recover proceeds that offenders have received using the trademarked name.

Since passage of the Madrid Protocol in 2003, the process of protecting a trade name has grown even more complicated. Now, in addition to checking a name with the PTO, state databases, and common-law uses, you can seek protection in up to 50 member countries via the international registry of the World Intellectual Property Organization. Of course, companies in member countries can do the same thing. Through one simple filing, a foreign company can acquire U.S. trademark protection for a trade name that you are using.

SOURCES: Jane Easter Bahls, "The Name Game," *Entrepreneur*, April 2004, 80; Nancy Ganz, "Protecting Your Good Name," *Nation's Business*, September 1995 6; Carl Geffken, "Protecting Your Intellectual Property," *GCI*, January 2004, 22–24; Eamonn Ryan, "Protecting Trademarks," *Finance Week*, 21 April 2004, 39.

---

brand
A name, term, symbol, design, or combination of these elements that clearly identifies and differentiates your products from those of your competitors.

trademark
A form of protection for intellectual property provided to the owner of a brand name or symbol.

What's the answer for "protecting" your software? Frankly, neither patents nor copyrights do a thorough job in this case. Protecting intellectual property for quickly changing industries and global markets is a serious problem that may become more so for small businesses and regulators in the near future.

Trademarks

A **brand** is a name, term, symbol, design, or combination of these elements that clearly identifies and differentiates your products from those of your competitors. A **trademark** is a registered and protected brand. Therefore, all trademarks are brands, but not all brands are trademarks. A trademark can include a graphic as well as a brand name. For example, not only is the Coke name protected, but the style of its script also makes it a trademark.

Your trademark rights remain in effect as long as you continue to use the trademark. This enduring nature offers an advantage over patents or copyrights. Trademarks are useful because they provide brand recognition for your product and are a good way to create an image in your customer's mind.

Because there are more than 1 million trademarks in use in the United States, how do you find one that isn't already taken? As with the patent search, you can either do the *trademark search* yourself or hire someone to do it for you. The problem gets more complicated with the trademark search, though, because a 1989 regulation change makes it possible to reserve a trademark before it is put into use.

Several businesses specialize in trademark searches of registered and unregistered marks, including the following: Trademark Service Corporation, 747 Third Avenue, New York, NY 10017, (212) 421-5730; Thompson & Thompson, 500 Victory Road, North Quincy, MA 02171-2126, (800) 692-8833; and Compu-Mark U.S., 1333 F Street NW, Washington, D.C. 20004, (800) 421-7881. You can conduct a search yourself with *The Trademark Register of the U.S.*, which is available in many libraries, or a similar directory. You can file for a trademark with the Patent and Trademark Office, Washington, D.C. 20231 (www.uspto.gov) with an application and a $325 fee. You can also register your trademark in your own state with the secretary of state at your state capitol.

Your trademark is worthless (and actually invalid) if you don't use it. Before your product is registered, use the symbol ™; after it is registered, use®.

Global Protection of Intellectual Property

Global protection of intellectual property has been a contentious issue for a couple of decades. Protection of trademarks, copyrights, and patents has had great difficulty crossing international borders. One of the driving forces in global protection has been the World Intellectual Property Organization (WIPO), which administers some 21 treaties covering intellectual-property protection, international filing systems, and trademark classification.[17] WIPO's roots actually stretch back to 1883 (yes, 1883) with the Paris Convention for Protection of Industrial Property and the 1886 Berne Convention for the Protection of Literary and Artistic Works.[18] WIPO is based in Geneva, Switzerland, and currently about 200 member nations depend on and defend its legal protections in the event of documented violations.

In 2004 WIPO launched downloadable software that allows patent applications to be filled out and submitted online. The software is called PCT-SAFE, where PCT stands for Patent Cooperation Treaty. This process could revolutionize patent filing—if applicants trust it. Advantages include faster filing (seconds compared with days), safety (encrypted so it cannot be stolen during delivery), and lower costs (no production of many copies, no mailing costs).[19]

Summary

- **Laws and regulations that affect small business**

Laws and regulations exist to protect competition, consumers, people in the workplace, and intellectual property; to allow bankruptcy; and to establish contracts. Specific laws that owners of small businesses should know include the Fair Labor Standards Act, the Civil Rights Acts of 1964 and 1991, the Immigration Reform and Control Act, the Americans with Disabilities Act, workers' and unemployment compensation, and the Occupational Safety and Health Act.

• Types of bankruptcy

The U.S. Bankruptcy Code is made up of nine chapters, only three of which apply to most small businesses (Chapters 7, 11, and 13). Chapter 7 uses liquidation, meaning that the business ceases to exist in an effort to provide the debtor with a fresh start. Liquidation involves selling all of the business assets and nonexempt personal assets and then distributing the proceeds among creditors. Chapters 11 and 13 allow the business owner to file a reorganization plan with the court that offers protection from creditors until the debt is satisfied.

• Elements of a contract

For a contract to be legally binding, it must have a legal purpose. Both parties must come to an agreement including a legitimate offer and a legitimate acceptance of that offer. Consideration, or something of value, must be exchanged. Finally, all parties must have the capacity to enter into a binding contract, meaning that they must not be underage, intoxicated, or of diminished mental ability.

• Ways to protect intellectual property

Patents, copyrights, and trademarks are legal ways to protect intellectual property. A patent grants an inventor the exclusive right to make, use, and sell an invention for a period of 17 years. A copyright provides legal protection against infringement of an author's literary, musical, or artistic works. Copyrights usually last for the author's life plus 50 years. A trademark is a legally protected name, term, symbol, design, or combination of these elements used to identify products or companies. Trademarks last for as long as they are in use.

Questions for Review and Discussion

1. Are the antitrust laws established in the late 1800s and early 1900s still pertinent in the twenty-first century? Why or why not?
2. How does the Federal Trade Commission protect consumers?
3. What rights does owning a patent protect? How do you get this protection?
4. What tests must an invention pass to receive a patent?
5. What is the difference between a copyright and a trademark? Between a trademark and a brand?
6. Name and explain the four elements that a contract must have to be valid.
7. List and briefly explain the laws that protect people in the workplace.
8. How are liquidation and reorganization used as different approaches to bankruptcy? What chapters of bankruptcy law accomplish these objectives?
9. What licenses are required by the owner of a small business?
10. What risk does an inventor assume when filing for a patent for an invention?

Questions for Critical Thinking

1. Compliance with government regulations is sometimes burdensome for small business owners; what can they (and you) do to change the laws and regulations that influence small business in order to lessen the burden?
2. Think of transactions you have entered into in the past: With whom were you agreeing, what was the agreement about, and what were the terms? When have you had a written contract with someone? When have you had an oral contract? Use several examples to analyze the process of buying a car, accepting a job, and ordering a pizza. What elements of contract law applied in each case?

Experience This . . .

Tired of boring, inside-the-box thinking? Do you think that the United States is becoming a nation more of Homer Simpsons than of Thomas Edisons? In fact, some people out there are solving problems that we didn't even know existed. Did you know that mechanical bat wings to provide aerodynamic lift for in-line skaters have been patented? How about the BinoCap, which builds binoculars onto the bill of a cap? Ted VanCleave has created a website called

Totally Absurd (www.totallyabsurd.com), complete with hilarious commentary on wacky inventions that have received U.S. patents. Of course, it can be easy to be funny when you're talking about toilet landing lights (they add "an almost mystical glow"), hair-braiding machines, hat tethers, and a diaper alarm. Visit this Totally Absurd website to lighten your day and stimulate your creativity.

What Would You Do?

The stories of companies like KFC, Coca-Cola, and McDonald's guarding their recipes for batter, syrup, and hamburger sauce are legendary. Triple-locked safes, binding contractual agreements, spies, and counterspies are all involved. A company's *trade secrets* are worth significant (sometimes staggering) amounts of money. Like any good secret, they are known to only a handful of people.

Many assets, such as chemical formulas, or specific designs are protected by patents. In exchange for the legal protection afforded by a patent, the patent holder must surrender the leverage of secrecy. That's because part of the patent-application process involves a full explanation of the process or product. The PTO publishes all patent applications within 18 months of their filing. Protecting a trade secret is complicated by the fact that, unlike patents, copyrights, and trademarks, trade secrets do not fall under federal jurisdiction. They are regulated by

individual state laws. Trade secrets must be *proved* to be secret to qualify for protection. At the very minimum, the owner must prove that procedures were in place to protect the information prior to any legal challenge.

SOURCE: Sabra Chartrand, "Patents," *The New York Times*, 5 February 2001, C-14.

Question

1. Imagine that you have developed a unique formula for a soft drink that, upon entering a person's mouth, analyzes the drinker's DNA to determine his favorite flavor, and then the drink instantly realigns its chemical composition to become that flavor. Write a two-page paper describing how you can best protect this trade secret. Will you patent it? Why or why not?

CHAPTER CLOSING CASE

INTELLECTUAL PROPERTY STOLEN—NOW WHAT?

Jonathan Hoffman rushed to the local Target store and stood dismayed before a shelf filled with books and flash cards. His employee, he quickly decided, had been right. The products looked uncomfortably similar to the ones made by his family's educational media company, School Zone Publishing. The composition, fonts, language, and concepts screamed copycat. Then he noticed the name of the competing publisher—Dogs in Hats—and it all made sense.

Dogs in Hats was a startup founded by Peter Alfini, School Zone's former vice president of national sales and marketing. Alfini had worked at School Zone for two years before resigning in February 2003, just a few months prior to Hoffman's trip to Target. The departure had stung, even more so when Alfini hired two former School Zone designers to join his new venture. Now Dogs in Hats' books and flash cards were sitting right next to

School Zone's in a chain that accounted for about 10 percent of School Zone's sales. Alfini says he started Dogs in Hats with his own ideas and resources, and that he had more than a decade of experience in educational publishing before joining School Zone. But it seemed clear to Hoffman that Alfini had used School Zone—its talent, marketing plans, equipment, and contacts—to get Dogs in Hats off the ground. Hoffman was furious.

He immediately called a meeting of his executive team—which includes his mother, Joan, the company's president and co-founder, and his sister, Jennifer Dexter, the vice president of design and development—and his attorney. They reviewed Alfini's products and came to the same conclusion: School Zone's intellectual property had been stolen and the company had little choice but to take Dogs in Hats to court.

Dexter and Barb Peacock, the company's director of design and development, began comparing School Zone's products with those of Dogs in Hats, looking for points of apparent trademark and copyright infringement. In one instance a School Zone alphabet flash card featured a drawing of a blond girl in pigtails with green bows and a yellow shirt collar and with a blue capital G on the card's flip side. A Dogs in Hats alphabet flash card was nearly identical, except for the girl's hair color, which was brown. "We were all very shocked," Peacock says. "Everything looked like ours."

When sales data from the summer season arrived, Hoffman's worst fears were confirmed. In one six-week period, when Dogs in Hats products were stocked at Target, sales of similar items made by School Zone dipped by 23 percent. Preparing the legal case became Hoffman's focus. When he suspected that a salesman was leaking information to Alfini, the case became his obsession. No longer sure of whom he could trust, he limited access to the copy room and closed the office on weekends and after hours. It was not the way he liked to manage. But he saw no other way.

In August 2003 School Zone filed a complaint in federal district court in western Michigan listing 84 allegations against Dogs in Hats, seeking payment for damages and attorneys' fees, and demanding that Alfini destroy materials using School Zone's copyrighted and trademarked material. In Dogs in Hats' October 2003 response to the complaint, Alfini denied most of the allegations, conceding only that he hired former employees of School Zone and was present at School Zone's offices after resigning.

Thus began an exhaustive discovery process that has lasted more than two years. By the beginning of 2005, School Zone had spent some $100,000 on legal filings and attorneys' fees. Joan Hoffman and Dexter were begging Hoffman to drop the case. But Jonathan kept thinking about what his father would have done. Jim Hoffman had founded School Zone in 1979 and died a few months before the Alfini affair began. "Jim Hoffman would have fire in his eyes," his son believed. The company's attorneys, meanwhile, warned that if School Zone did not defend its marks now, it would be more difficult to do so in the future. So Hoffman stuck with it.

In March 2005 a judge magistrate sent the parties into mediation. It shouldn't have surprised School Zone; western Michigan courts famously favor alternative means of resolving disputes. But Hoffman now faced a dilemma: whether to compromise and put the case behind him or to hold out for a shot at total victory in court.

What do you think? Hoffman's gut told him to litigate aggressively. But was that a smart move? Should he settle? Or should he press his case before a judge?

SOURCE: From Lora Kolodny, "Jonathan Hoffman Was Sure a Former Staffer Had Stolen His Company's Ideas," *Inc.*, September 2005, 55–56. Copyright © 2006 Mansueto Ventures LLC, publisher of Inc. Magazine, New York, NY 10017. Reprinted with permission.

Test Prepper

You've read the chapter, studied the key terms, and the exam is any day now. Think you're ready to ace it? Take this sample test to gauge your comprehension of chapter material. You can check your answers at the back of the book. Want more test questions? Visit the student website at college.hmco.com/pic/hatten4e and take the ACE and ACE+ quizzes for more practice.

Matching

_____ 1. legislation that prohibits company mergers or acquisitions that would stifle competition

_____ 2. government commission that regulates compliance of workplace laws

_____ 3. law that protects disabled Americans in the workplace

_____ 4. law that covers safety and health conditions in the workplace

_____ 5. insurance every business is required to purchase providing replacement income and medical expenses to employees who suffer work-related expenses or illnesses

_____ 6. benefit that employees who have been fired due to cutbacks or poor fit with the company can receive for a specific period of time

_____ 7. laws that control what a business can sell and where it can operate

_____ 8. bankruptcy option that allows the business to file a reorganization plan for a second chance

_____ 9. legal term for a contractual "meeting of the minds"

_____10. intellectual-property protection to the owner of a brand name or symbol

 ACE self-test   college.hmco.com/pic/hatten4e

a. OSHA

b. workers' compensation

c. unemployment compensation

d. Chapter 7

e. Chapter 11

f. Chapter 13

g. consideration

h. agreement

i. antitrust laws

j. EEOC

k. ADA

l. zoning

m. capacity

n. trademark

o. patent

p. copyright

Fill in the Blank

1. Laws to protect consumers have largely replaced the Latin term _____.

2. The law that sets a minimum wage for all covered employees, overtime pay for nonexempt workers, equal pay for men and women, and rules for child labor is the _____ _____ _____ Act.

3. Workers' compensation premiums are based on two factors: _____ and _____.

4. Bankruptcy stays on your credit report for at least _____ years.

5. A _____ judgment requires one party of a contract to do exactly what she has agreed to do.

## part 5

MARKETING THE PRODUCT OR SERVICE

Chapter 11   Small Business Marketing: Strategy and Research

Chapter 12   Small Business Marketing: Product

Chapter 13   Small Business Marketing: Place

Chapter 14   Small Business Marketing: Price and Promotion

Marketing your small business entails more than just personal selling or writing newspaper ads. Marketing involves every form of customer contact—plus much more. The theme of this book is creating a sustainable competitive advantage. The topics covered in Part 5 will form the basis for many of those advantages. All of them flow from one idea: You must understand how you serve your customers better than your competitors. **Chapter 11** explores small business marketing strategies and marketing research. **Chapter 12** highlights factors related to the products you sell. **Chapter 13** discusses location and layout. **Chapter 14** focuses on pricing and promotion strategies.

Small Business Marketing: Strategy and Research

After reading this chapter, you should be able to:

- Explain the importance of marketing to small businesses.

- Describe the process of developing a small business marketing strategy.

- Discuss the purpose of the market research process and the steps involved in putting it into practice.

"We are the market-share leader in turkey-flavored beverages." What??? Yep, that is what Peter van Stolk, CEO of Jones Soda, says about the success of the company's annual holiday novelty pack. During the holiday season, Jones makes soda flavors like Turkey and Gravy, Wild Herb Stuffing, Sweet Potato, and Green Pea. Mmmmmm.

Such flavors were enough to make Diane Sawyer and Joel Siegel gag on *Good Morning America.* Most companies don't go out of their way to make customers sick, but Jones Soda is not your normal company. Jones is known for offbeat marketing strategies. Including photos of customers on product labels.

Van Stolk got the idea for the unique flavors while on a road trip from Grand Rapids to Detroit, as he was trying to think of ways to boost cold-weather soda sales. It was October 2003, when the diet du jour was low-carbohydrate, so Peter dreamed up the idea of a soda that "tasted" like Thanksgiving dinner.

A marketing strategy that is offbeat can gain more attention than a traditional strategy—if done carefully, according to Rob Frankel, author of *The Revenge of Brand X: How to Build a Big Time Brand on the Web or Anywhere Else.* He goes

Peter van Stolk, CEO of Jones Soda, with Bottles of Jones Soda.

on to say that you need to know how tolerant your target market is, tolerance being measured in money. "`Crazy' becomes `too crazy' when the cash register stops ringing."

Not all of Jones Soda's marketing is outrageous—they also sell yummier flavors like Strawberry Lime, Crushed Melon, and Blue Bubblegum via traditional channels like Target, 7-11, and Kroger. But they do little traditional advertising because Van Stolk understands that his niche target market of teens and twenty-somethings responds better to offbeat tactics like music- and photo-sharing websites. This type of insight into one's target market is especially important for a small business with fewer marketing dollars to spread around. Jones Soda is a great example of consistency among all marketing variables: target market, product, place, price, and promotion.

For another example of understanding target markets, watch the video that accompanies this chapter about segmentation at Lake, Snell, Perry, and Mermin.

SOURCES: Ellen Neuborne, "Gag Marketing," *Inc.*, February 2006, 35–36; Jeff Cioletti, "An Impish 10-year-old," *Beverage World*, June 2006, 26–27; "Fight Attention Deficit," *Business Week*, 24 July 2006, 53; Heather Landi, "Beating the Odds," *Beverage World*, July 2006, 40.

Small Business Marketing

What do you think of when you hear the term *marketing*? Do you think of selling and advertising? Probably, but marketing is actually much more than just selling or advertising. Marketing involves all the activities needed to get a product from the producer to the ultimate consumer. Management guru Peter Drucker has stated that businesses have two—and only two—basic functions: marketing and innovation. These are the only things a business does that produce results; everything else is really a "cost."[1] This is just as true for the one-person kiosk as it is for the largest corporate giant.

Of course, some selling will always be necessary, but the goal of marketing is to come as close as possible to making selling superfluous.[2] A truly customer-driven company understands what consumers want in a product and provides it so that its products, to a great extent, sell themselves. Of course, this is not easy. To paraphrase President Lyndon Johnson, doing the right thing is easy; knowing the right thing to do is tough.

Marketing Concept

Many businesses operate today with a customer-driven philosophy. They want to find out what their customers want and then provide that good or service. This philosophy is called the **marketing concept.**

Businesses have not always concentrated their efforts on what the market wants. Before the Industrial Revolution and mass production, nearly all a business owner needed to be concerned about was making products. Demand exceeded supply for most goods, like boots, clothing, and saddles. People had to have these products, so about all a business had to do was to

marketing concept
The philosophy of a business in which the wants and needs of customers are determined before goods and services are produced.

"The essence of the marketing concept is to first find out what customers want and then supply it."

make them. This philosophy in which companies concentrate their efforts on the product being made is now called the **production concept** of business.

After the mid-1800s, when mass production and mass distribution became possible for manufactured products, supply began to exceed demand. Some selling was needed, but the emphasis remained on producing goods. World War II temporarily shifted resources from consumer markets to the military. After the war, when those resources were returned to the consumer market, businesses continued producing at capacity, and many new businesses were started. Managers found that they could no longer wait for consumers to seek them out to sell all they could make. Although these companies still emphasized making products, they now had to convince people to buy *their* products, as opposed to the competition's, which inaugurated the *selling concept* of business.

Early in the 1960s many businesses began to adopt the marketing concept, which, as just explained, emphasizes finding out what your customers want and need, and then offering products to satisfy those desires. PetMed Express showed that it understood the marketing concept on its way to grabbing the top spot on *Business Week*'s list of 100 Best Small Companies for 2004. PetMed created a whole new industry by selling pet medications via e-mail, phone, or fax, thereby allowing customers to bypass veterinarian practices.[3] Customers obviously appreciate the convenience of getting Fido's heartworm pills and the like online, because in just a few years PetMed has become the United States' largest pet pharmacy.

The business philosophy that broadens the view of the marketing concept is called **relationship marketing.** Here a business owner recognizes the value and profit potential of customer retention; therefore, the guiding emphasis is on developing long-term, mutually satisfying relationships with customers and suppliers.

Of Purple Cows

In your travels you have most likely passed by many cows: black ones, white ones, brown ones, or some combination thereof. Unless you have a specific reason for noticing them, such as being in the cattle business, very few cows probably stand out in your mind. In fact, most people would classify cows as boring. Author Seth Godin makes an analogy between most products that consumers see daily with cows: Consumers see so many products that seem to be alike that they are all boring. But a purple cow? Drive by one of those, even if it is in a field with a whole herd of black, white, or brown cows, and it would get your attention. What products stand out in your mind as different? Krispy Kreme doughnuts? Hard Candy cosmetics? Doing and creating things that are counterintuitive, phenomenal, and exciting are important ingredients to marketing small businesses.[4]

Small businesses can achieve the success that Godin discusses by avoiding the traps of convention and not being afraid to stand out from the crowd by offering unique products and marketing practices. "Purple cows" represent the creation of a competitive advantage or a *unique selling point (USP)*—topics that volumes have been written about. Take a look at Godin's *Purple Cow* for inspiration (you can read it in about an hour).[5]

Reality Check

And Now a Word from Our Sponsor . . .

Small business is about taking risks and breaking away from the pack. A marketing strategy that little 25-employee Rachel's Gourmet Snacks has used to enhance its company image is sports sponsorship—specifically, backing the Indy car team with driver Eddie Cheever, who won the 1999 Indianapolis 500. After beating 30-to-1 odds and outlasting 32 other drivers, Cheever pulled into the winner's circle with the "Rachel's" name across both his driving suit and his beautiful steel-blue car. Millions of fans saw that image.

The Olympic Games offer great exposure opportunities (the 2008 Beijing games are expected to draw 1 billion Chinese viewers, a half-million visitors, and 4 billion international viewers). It's pricey, though. To be an official sponsor in 2008 the bill can top $100 million, obviously out of reach for small businesses. But deals can be found at the national level. Jet Set Sports, a travel business from New Jersey is an "official sponsor" of the U.S. Olympic Committee for about $15 million for five years. Official Supplier is even cheaper. Remember Roots, the company that made those cool berets for the Winter Olympics in Turin? Imagine the exposure they got for only $5 million over four years.

Sponsorship at this level is not for the faint of heart among small business owners. It's a risky strategy for a financially struggling company to sign a three-year, multimillion-dollar sponsorship. But the image enhancement, visibility, and differentiation from competitors have proved awesome for Rachel's, the Bloomington, Minnesota, potato chip producer. Right after the race, the phone started ringing with new customers, new distribution outlets started contacting it, and employees had an extra bounce of pride in their steps.

Small businesses use marketing strategies and techniques to create and communicate their competitive advantage. Sponsorship is just one way (and it is most effective when used as part of a balanced marketing mix).

SOURCES: Max Chafkin, "Gold-Medal Marketing," *Inc.*, April 2007, 35–36; Harvey Meyer, "And Now, Some Words About Sponsors," *Nation's Business*, March 1999, 38–39; Andrew Rafalaf, "Leagues of Their Own," *Fortune Small Business*, March 2003, 76

Marketing Strategies for Small Businesses

Your **marketing strategy** should be decided in the early stages of operating your business. It should state *what* you intend to accomplish and *how* you intend to accomplish it. The marketing section of the business plan is a good place for the small business owner to identify marketing strategies. Any potential investor will carefully inspect how you have laid out the marketing action that will drive your business.

> **marketing strategy**
> What the marketing efforts of a business are intended to accomplish and how the business will achieve its goals.

A good marketing strategy will help you to be proactive, not reactive, in running your business. You can enhance your marketing plan by making sure that three bases are covered:

- Watching and understanding trends related to your customers, suppliers, demographics, and technology

- Having a vision that provides direction for your business

- Having an adaptable, flexible organization[6]

Small businesses in the service industries must pay special attention to marketing. When their service is one that customers could perform themselves, such as lawn mowing, a marketing strategy is critical. It is also often more difficult to differentiate or establish a brand image with services than with tangible products. Can the average car owner tell the difference between automatic transmissions that have been rebuilt by different shops? Probably not. A marketing strategy that communicates the benefits that consumers receive is crucial. However comprehensive or simple your marketing plan, it should include a description of your vision, marketing objectives, sales forecast, target markets, and marketing mix.[7]

Setting Marketing Objectives

Your marketing objectives define the goals of your plans. They can be broken into two groups: marketing-performance objectives and marketing-support objectives.[8] Objectives for *marketing performance* are specific, quantifiable outcomes, such as sales revenue, market share, and profit. For example, an objective of this type for a local insurance agency could be "to increase sales of homeowner's insurance by 10 percent for the next fiscal year." Objectives for *marketing support* are what you must accomplish before your performance objectives can be met, such as educating customers about your products, building awareness, and creating image.

Like any goal you want to accomplish in business, marketing objectives need to be (1) measurable, (2) action-oriented by identifying what needs to be done, and (3) time-specific by targeting a date or time for achievement.

Developing a Sales Forecast

sales forecast
The quantity of products a business plans to sell during a future time period.

Your marketing plan should include a **sales forecast,** in which you predict your future sales in dollars and in units—in other words, what your "top line" will be. If you are writing a business plan for a startup business, the sales forecast is one of the most important pieces of information you will gather. Why? Because that "top line" figure becomes the foundation for your pro forma income statements and cash-flow statement. From your projected revenues you will subtract your expenses and disbursements to see if and when you will make a profit.

Forecasting is difficult, but it will help you establish more accurate goals and objectives. Your sales forecast will affect all sections of your marketing plan, including the choice of appropriate channels of distribution, salesforce requirements, advertising and sales promotion budgets, and the effects of price changes.

A faulty sales forecast can do severe damage to a small business. Steve Waterhouse was an understandably excited sales manager when he reported in a budget meeting that one of his sales representatives had secured a $2 million order. Satisfying the order would require the company to invest $100,000 in new tools. The operations manager was not very excited, however, because the purchase order contained a clause allowing the customer to back out. The owner wisely decided to require a deposit for initial supplies before proceeding. After receiving $100,000 from the customer, the company purchased the required tooling. The customer then backed out of the deal. Crisis averted, but a close call nevertheless. What's the moral of the story? Be careful about projections based on "my sales rep says . . ."[9]

There are two basic ways to forecast sales: build-up methods and break-down methods. With a *build-up method,* you identify as many target markets as possible and predict the sales for each. Then you combine the predictions for the

Profile in Entrepreneurship

A Petunia by Any Other Name

Matt and Ronnie Horn, owners of Matterhorn Nursery in Spring Valley, New York, understand the challenges of marketing against some pretty tough competition. A Wal-Mart near Matterhorn sells a purple petunia for 26 cents; the Horns sell the same purple petunia for more than three times that price, 83 cents. Despite the price difference, on Mother's Day people form long lines at Matterhorn, while the Wal-Mart garden center is nearly empty.

To some people, a petunia is a petunia is a petunia. Matterhorn, however, has figured out how to create and merchandise plants and supplies in such a way that customers are happy to drive miles and pay premium prices. Everything is special at Matterhorn—right down to the dirt, which contains composted kelp and sea shells for $12.98 per bag compared with $4 at Wal-Mart.

Chain stores operate by moving huge volumes and offering few choices within product lines, including petunias. Matterhorn stocks miniature, giant, trailing, and spreading petunias—all in several colors. Also, nursery employees are generally better able to dispense expert advice. As Carol Miller, editor of a garden-center trade publication, says, "Most independent garden centers are run by plant people learning about retail; most mass merchants are businesspeople learning about plants."

Matt and Ronnie are battle-tested entrepreneurs who learned long ago that people will not go out of their way and pay premium prices for flats of conventional plants wedged into metal racks. On their 38 acres, which sit 25 miles north of New York City, they created ambiance. They use better soil, they give each plant more room to grow, and they nurture plants by hand rather than by machine. Matterhorn contains 18 wood-and-stone buildings to create a "village effect."

SOURCE: From "Marketing Panache by Cynthia Crossen, Plant Lore Invigorate Independent Garden Center's Sales," *Wall Street Journal*, May 25, 2004, p. B1. Copyright © 2004 by Dow Jones & Company, Inc. Reproduced by permission of Dow Jones & Co., Inc. via Copyright Clearance Center.

various segments to create a total sales forecast. For example, if you plan to open an ice cream shop, can you estimate how many ice cream cones you will sell in a year? Not very easily or accurately without some research. But you can estimate with some degree of accuracy how much you could sell in one day—especially if you spend several days outside an existing ice cream shop observing how many people go in and out, and roughly how much they are buying. From that daily sales figure, you can project sales for the week, month, and year. Would you expect to sell the same amount per day in April? July? October? January? Probably not, so you would come up with a daily sales projection at different times of the year to allow for seasonal fluctuations.

With some types of products, of course, it is difficult to estimate daily sales. Then what? You may be able to use a *break-down method*. For this approach, you begin with an estimate of the total market potential for a specific product or an entire industry. This figure is broken down into forecasts of smaller units until you reach an estimate of how large a market you will reach and how many sales you will make. For example, if industry information from a trade association for a product you consider selling shows that 4 percent of a population will be in the market for your product at any given time, how many units and

Creating Competitive Advantage

Sometimes the Best Marketing Strategy Is a Good Defense

We typically associate marketing with aggressive advertising campaigns designed to maximize growth, or open new markets, or gain market share from competitors. Marketing is a powerful offensive weapon—but it can be a valuable defensive tool also. And your business may need a defensive tool, because for every new business or product launched, there is an existing one (maybe yours) that must defend its position.

Greg Sutter, vice president of marketing for Datastream Systems, concentrates more attention on nurturing relationships with existing customers than attending trade shows or working up print advertising. He says, "To defend our position, we don't go wide; we go deep." In short, Datastream spends almost its entire marketing budget playing defense.

Not all customers are equal, though. They can be classified by their value (profitability) and their vulnerability (to competitors). Sutter will work most vigorously to retain customers who are both valuable and vulnerable. Customers who are valuable but not vulnerable are happy with the company, so they will maintain profit margins. Those who are neither valuable nor vulnerable are happy with the company but do not create profit. The business owner should try to make them valuable. An overlooked group are those customers who are vulnerable but not valuable, making them unprofitable and likely to leave. They should be encouraged out the door.

If you are smart in creating a defensive marketing strategy, you can keep competitors away from your turf, or even eliminate them. Some marketing tactics to consider:

- *Leverage your strengths.* If your small business has a hometown advantage over rivals, for example, capitalize on that.

- *Keep rivals guessing.* Moving targets are hard to hit, so innovate and put up barriers like patents and trademarks.

- *Know when to retreat.* Some markets and customers are not worth keeping, so move your resources elsewhere.

- *Make customer satisfaction a priority.* An old saying from ranching, "It doesn't take a good fence to keep in a happy horse," provides an analogy that can be applied to customers.

SOURCES: John Roberts, "Defensive Marketing," *Harvard Business Review,* November 2005, 150–157; Ellen Neuborne, "Playing Defense" *Inc.,* March 2006, 31–34. For more depth on this topic, read Al Ries and Jack Trout, *Marketing Warfare* (2005). This updated marketing classic focuses on how to beat the competition by out-thinking them, taking powerful examples from ancient military generals to modern guerrilla tactics.

---

dollars of sales could you realistically generate? Do enough people live in your area, or can you reach enough of the target market for your business to be profitable?

Marketers use many other models in sales forecasting; unfortunately, most don't apply well to small businesses because they depend on historical data. For example, **time series analysis** is a forecasting method that uses past sales data to discover whether product sales have increased, decreased, or stayed the same over periods of time. Cyclic, seasonal, and random factor analyses are variations on this model.

Like time series analysis, **regression analysis** uses extensive historical sales data to find a relationship between prior sales (the dependent variable) and one or more independent variables, such as income. With regression analysis, the intention is to develop a mathematical formula that describes a relationship between a product's sales and the chosen variable. The best we can hope for is to

time series analysis
A forecasting method that uses historical sales data to identify patterns over a period of time.

regression analysis
A forecasting method that predicts future sales by finding a relationship between sales and one or more variables.

identify an association, not to find proof or causation. Once a formula is established, you enter all necessary data into it to develop a sales forecast. Of course, because these models of time series and regression analysis depend so heavily on large amounts of historical data, they are useless in forecasting sales for new products.

Identifying Target Markets

Market segmentation is the process of dividing the total market for a product into identifiable groups, or **target markets,** with a common want or need that your business can satisfy. These target markets are important to your business because they consist of the people who are more likely to be your customers. They are the people toward whom you should direct your marketing efforts. Identifying and concentrating on target markets can help you avoid falling into the trap of trying to be everything to everyone—you can't do it.[10]

When asked about their target markets, many small business owners will respond, "We don't have specific target markets; we will sell to anyone who comes in the door." Of *course* you will sell to anyone who wants your product, but the point of segmenting target markets is to let the right people know about your product so that more people will want it. A market for your business must have three characteristics:

> **target markets**
> A group of people who have a common want or need that your business can satisfy, who are able to purchase your product, and who are more likely to buy from your business.

1. A need that your products can satisfy
2. Enough people to generate profit for your business
3. Possession of, and willingness to spend, enough money to generate profit for your business

To identify the most attractive target markets for your business, you should look for characteristics that affect the buying behavior of the people. Does where they live influence whether they buy your product? Does income, gender, age, or lifestyle matter? Do they seek a different benefit from the product than other groups do? These differences, called **segmentation variables,** can be based on geographic, demographic, or psychographic differences, or on differences in benefits received.

> **segmentation variables**
> Characteristics or ways to group people that make them more likely to purchase a product.

A small business owner should start (and occasionally revisit) the process of segmenting a market by committing to writing a description of "ideal" customers. For example, for a small accounting firm, that description could be "entrepreneurs in their early thirties to early fifties; owners of retail, service, or manufacturing firms with sales of $500,000 to $3 million." Ideal customer purchasing patterns could include this description: "When they are aware of a business need our accounting firm can solve, they want aggressive and innovative solutions. They don't have time to research solutions themselves." This preference pattern shows that our example accounting firm is segmenting on the basis of benefit received by customers. What makes such customers ideal ones for this firm? They actively want the skills of the professional services offered and are willing and able to pay for them.

Some methods of segmenting a market are more useful for certain businesses than others. For example, if males and females react to the marketing efforts of your business in the same way, then segmenting by gender is not the best way

"Big companies set their sights on mass markets, but entrepreneurial companies understand that the key to their success lies in satisfying niches."

mass marketing
Treating entire populations of people as potential customers for specific products.

market segmentation
Breaking down populations of people into groups, or target markets.

niche marketing
Segmenting populations of people into smaller target markets.

individualized marketing
Adjusting the marketing mix of a business to treat individual persons as separate target markets.

to identify a target market. When segmenting target markets, keep in mind that the reason for grouping people is to predict behavior—especially the behavior of buying from you.

A caveat for the future: Segmenting and targeting may not always be enough. The most common marketing strategy in the 1960s was **mass marketing,** or selling single products to large groups of people. Then, in the 1970s, **market segmentation** was used. Businesses took segmentation a step further in the 1980s with specialized **niche marketing,** which involves concentrating marketing efforts toward smaller target markets. The next step in the evolution of marketing came in the 1990s, with the emergence of **individualized marketing,** or customizing each product to suit the needs of individual customers. These trends in marketing techniques do not mean that businesses need to throw out every technique that has been used in the past. Rather, they indicate that businesses may need to add more tools to their marketing toolbox.

Two factors leading to more individualized marketing are clutter and technology. Clutter in traditional media channels (newspaper, direct mail, television, radio) has reached a point where "shotgun" approaches—the same message directed to no one in particular—do not stand out. Consider that the average American household has access to hundreds of television channels and spends more than 50 hours per week watching them. The American public also has more than 11,500 different magazines from which to choose. Add all the radio stations, catalogs, and direct mail that consumers absorb daily, and you begin to understand how incessantly consumers are bombarded with advertising. An individualized message to segments in need of your product has a better chance of being heard above the noise.

Technology is also allowing us to conduct more individualized marketing by allowing us to track our customers with more precision. Individualized marketing, if taken to an extreme, could mean treating each person as a separate market (offering different products, different advertising, and different channels to each). Although this tactic may not be practical, technology has certainly made it possible.

As "big box" stores get even bigger, the gap between mass markets and niches is actually growing larger as well. Big companies have to concentrate on mass markets to turn a profit. For this reason, large retailers—including supermarkets—are generally reducing the number of brands they stock. If a product is not a top-three brand, it is probably not SKU-worthy. Small businesses, in turn, must concentrate on niches to survive.[11]

A good place for you to start in obtaining specific information about your target market is at the Small Business Administration's home page (www.sba.gov). Here, under the category of Business Development/General Information and Publications, you'll find two files on marketing that are especially worth reading: "Knowing Your Market" and "Marketing Strategies for the Growing Business." Each provides basic background information on marketing topics for small business managers and owners.

When you're ready for more specific information on markets, check out the Census Bureau's website (www.census.gov). Here you'll find specific information by state and county regarding county business patterns and census information

@ e-biz
Get Found Online

What is truly essential in an Internet marketing strategy for your small business? Well, consider how *you* look for information. You search the Internet, right? Almost 134 million people in the United States regularly use search engines, and 63 percent look only at the first page of results. If you want your site to be on that first page, you need *search-marketing strategies,* including search-engine optimization (SEO) and pay-per-click (PPC) advertising. You need to give the search engines what they're looking for to be considered relevant. Then they'll place your site in the top results when people are searching for your product or service.

Here are some key *search-engine optimization (SEO)* strategies:

Find the hottest keywords for your market. Determining keywords is the starting point for any search-marketing campaign.

Plug keywords into the right locations in your copy and code. Your website is full of hot spots that search-engine spiders check regularly for keywords. Put your keywords in the headlines, subheads, and body copy of your Web pages. In your code, use them in anchor text, alt text, title tags, image tags, and meta tags. But use them sparingly: The old strategy of loading up your meta tags with keywords doesn't work anymore.

Use keywords that relate directly to your content. If you sprinkle keywords like "guaranteed weight loss" through your site that sells shoes, search engines will ignore you. Your keywords will work best if they reflect what your site is about.

Keep the spiders coming back by offering frequent new content. The more fresh, relevant content they find, the higher the search-engine spiders are likely to rank your site. Keep all the copy on your pages current, including any changes or updates to your business or products. And archive the newsletters or bulletins on your site. A blog or forum also keeps people heading back for daily updates and discussion.

Collect links from other sites that are considered reputable and relevant. Natural, relevant inbound links are search-engine gold. Put out "link bait"—quality content that contains a link back to your site. Distributing free articles and press releases is a great way to get quality inbound links. And don't forget the power of social networking. By using sites like Gather, MySpace, YouTube, and Second Life, you can drive new traffic to your website and get new sites linking to yours.

Use a site map to boost your ranking in Google, Yahoo!, and Windows Live Search. *Site maps* help spiders find their way through all your pages. And with the new site maps formatting protocol, the three search titans are giving site owners more clues than ever about how to help index their sites.

SEO should be at the core of your overall Internet marketing strategy. It's one of the most inexpensive (almost totally free) and effective approaches available. But SEO can be slow. If you don't want to wait for results in searches, another approach will get you targeted traffic faster: *pay-per-click (PPC)* advertising. Have you noticed sidebar listings when you do a search on Google or Yahoo!? These "sponsored results" are PPC ads that appear when people search using the keywords in the ads. PPC has some tremendous advantages for online businesses:

PPC ads show up immediately. You can drive traffic to your site right away, even if you haven't been indexed by search engines yet.

You pay only for results. No matter how many times your ad is displayed, you pay only when someone clicks on it. Watch your results carefully to determine how well each ad is converting and if it's worth continuing.

PPC is a great testing tool. You can run several ads simultaneously, allowing you to see very quickly which ones work best. Test your keywords this way, and use the best ones on your site to boost your organic search results.

With a combination of PPC and SEO you can make sure your target market will find you. No other set of strategies offers you so much scope as search marketing. You can dramatically improve your search engine rankings and direct quality, targeted traffic to your website—often without spending a single dime.

SOURCES: Derek Gehl, "Search Marketing 101," *Entrepreneur Magazine Online,* 29 March 2007, www.entrepreneur.com/ebusiness/ebusinesscolumnist/article176398.html; Lena L. West, "Becoming More Social," *Entrepreneur Magazine Online,* 9 April 2007, www.entrepreneur.com/marketing/onlinemarketing/article176798.html; Al Lautenslager, "Low-Cost Marketing Trends for 2007," *Entrepreneur Magazine Online,* 29 November 2006, www.entrepreneur.com/marketing/marketingideas/guerrillamarketingcolumnistallautenslager/article171214.html

for a specific county. As you're researching the viability of a target market, you can check for the number and types of businesses already operating and the demographic characteristics of that location's population. The Census Bureau is also fine-tuning its TIGER map service (http://tiger.census.gov), which provides census maps with street-level detail for the entire United States, all 50 states, and all counties in those states; cartographic design; and many other features. However, be aware that this site can be slow in creating the maps because of the large amount of data that must be transmitted.

Understanding Consumer Behavior

Whereas market segmentation and target marketing can tell you *who* might buy your products, it is also essential to your small business marketing efforts to understand consumer behavior—*why* those people buy. Information on consumer behavior comes from several fields, including psychology, sociology, biology, and other professions that try to explain why people do what they do. In determining why people purchase products, we will start with a stimulus-response model of consumer behavior called the *black box model* (see Figure 11.1). This model is based on the work of psychologist Kurt Lewin, who studied how a person's behavior is affected by the interactions of personal influences, such as inner needs, thoughts, and beliefs, and a variety of external environmental forces.

The *black box* is appropriate because it represents what goes on in the customer's mind that remains hidden from businesspeople. We can see the external factors that go in and the responses that come out, but we can't see the internal influences or the decision-making process.

As a small business owner, closeness to your customers is an advantage in understanding the internal influences in customers' minds. Their beliefs, attitudes, values, and motives, as well as their perceptions of your products, are critical to

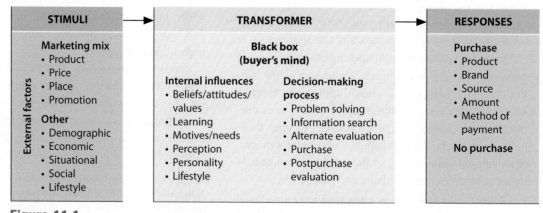

Figure 11.1

BLACK-BOX MODEL OF CONSUMER BEHAVIOR

Many Internal and External Factors Influence Consumer Behavior.

SOURCE: "The Black Box Model of Consumer Behavior," from Warren Keegan, et al., *Marketing* (Englewood Cliffs, NJ: Prentice Hall, 1992), 193. Reprinted by permission of Sandra Moriarty.

your success. A small business owner needs to be aware of the steps of the mental decision-making process that consumers use in satisfying their needs. We all use them, even if we are not conscious of every step. People usually buy products as a solution to some problem or need in their lives, not just for the sake of buying something.

Thus, the first step in the decision-making process that leads to a purchase is *problem recognition,* which occurs when we are motivated to reduce a difference between our current and desired states of affairs. For example, consider a young couple expecting their first child, who realize they do not have a way to record events for future memories. They have recognized a problem. Now they begin the second step in the decision-making process: an *information search.* What products exist that can solve the problem identified in the first step? This search will usually lead consumers to read advertising, magazine articles, and ratings like those found in *Consumer Reports.* They also talk with salespeople, friends, and family members to learn more about products that will satisfy their needs.

These information searches usually turn up several possible solutions, which lead the consumer to the third step: an *evaluation of alternatives.* The parents-to-be need a camera to capture little junior for posterity, but the choices of an analog 35 mm (SLR or point-and-shoot), a digital camera, or a camcorder (VHS, compact VHS, or 8 mm) leave them with six alternatives to evaluate. As a small business owner, you enter the customers' decision-making process by being in their **evoked set** of brands or businesses that come to mind when considering a purchase. For example, if you need a pair of shoes, how many businesses that sell shoes come to mind quickly? Those stores are your evoked set for shoes. If your business does not come into customers' minds as a possible solution to their problem, you probably can't sell them too much. The purpose of most advertising (including small business advertising) is to get products into a customer's evoked set.

> *evoked set*
> The group of brands or businesses that come to a customer's mind when she thinks of a type of product.

The most attractive alternative usually leads consumers to the fourth step, which is *purchase,* but many hidden factors can alter this decision. For example, the attitudes of other people can influence the purchase decision. If the prospective parents intended to buy a specific camera and learned that friends had trouble with that model, their decision to purchase would probably change.

Finally, the *postpurchase evaluation* occurs when the consumer uses the product and decides what his level of satisfaction is, which will affect your

Understanding Why Customers Behave the Way They Do Is Critical to Small Business Success.

cognitive dissonance
The conflict (i.e., remorse) that buyers feel after making a major purchase.

repeat sales. **Cognitive dissonance,** which, in this context, is the internal conflict we feel after making a decision, is a normal part of the process. If the parents in our example purchased a 35 mm SLR camera, you might expect them to later think about the motion and sound that they could have received from a camcorder. As a small business owner, you try to reduce cognitive dissonance with return policies, warranties, and assurance that the customer made the right choice.

Market Research

market research
The process of gathering information about consumers that will improve marketing efforts.

One of the major advantages that small businesses have over large businesses is close customer contact. Although this closeness can help you maintain your competitive advantage, you will also need a certain amount of ongoing **market research** to stay closely attuned to your market. If you are starting a new business, you will need market research even more.

The American Marketing Association (AMA) defines *market research* as the function that links the consumer, customer, and public to the marketer through information. That information can be used to identify and define marketing opportunities and problems; to generate, refine, and evaluate marketing actions; to monitor marketing performance; and to improve understanding of marketing as a process.

Not all market research conducted by small businesses is formal and intense. Most small business owners want to get information as quickly and as inexpensively as possible (see Figure 11.2). One survey showed that most spend between one and six months and less than $1,000 conducting market research on the last product or service they launched.

Market research can be as simple as trash and peanuts—literally. Owners of small restaurants often inspect outgoing waste to see what customers leave on their plates uneaten. Why? Because customers may order a dish like crayfish and

Figure 11.2
MARKET RESEARCH
EXPENDITURES

Small Businesses Often Spend Less Than $5,000 and Less Than Six Months Gathering Market Research for New Products.

SOURCE: Survey of 173 CEOs, 57 percent from companies with sales of $10 million or less, by *Inc.* and The Executive Committee, San Diego, 1992; Susan Greco, "Sales & Marketing," *Inc.,* July 1992, 118.

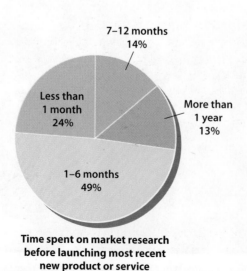

Time spent on market research before launching most recent new product or service

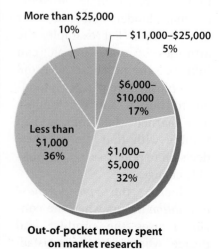

Out-of-pocket money spent on market research

pineapple pizza for the novelty, but if most don't actually eat it, it should be taken off the menu. One creative discount merchant conducted an in-store market research project using peanuts. During a three-day promotion, customers were given all the roasted peanuts in a shell they could eat while in the store. At the end of each day, the empty hulls on the floor provided information about traffic patterns of people moving through the store. Piles of shells in front of displays showed the merchandise that was attracting particular interest.[12]

> "One creative merchant conducted a secret marketing survey by giving his customers roasted peanuts. The piles of empty hulls on the floor showed him how people had moved through the store—and which displays had attracted the most attention."

There is one major factor signaling that small businesses should increase the amount of time and money they spend on market research: changing conditions. Because many markets and demographics change quickly, the businesses that emerge as winners are those that are *proactive* rather than *reactive*. Market research can give you information on what your customers are going to want as opposed to historical data that tell you what they used to want.

Some streetwise, down-and-dirty marketing research can be gathered from competitors. No, they will not voluntarily hand anything useful over to you, but you plant yourself in front of a competitor's store for a day or two, and notice how many people walk in. Now, how many walk out with a purchase? Can you get a feel for the average purchase size? This information could be very useful in making your sales projections if you have similar foot traffic.[13]

Small business owners who have been in business for longer than, say, two days have learned two things about market research: They need it, and it's expensive. An in-depth survey constructed, administered, and analyzed by a professional market research firm can easily cost $40,000 to $50,000. Denver-based Market Perceptions does those individualized surveys, but it has also created a less expensive alternative for its small business clients, a "shared survey" called the Colorado Opinion Tracker. It runs a monthly poll of 500 people and, for a fee, a small business owner can add her own questions. Two questions cost $1,250, with $500 being charged for each additional question. Small business owners get a 15 percent discount if questions need to run for more than one month. In addition to the small business owners' questions, Market Perceptions collects demographic information such as age, gender, and residence data to use as independent variables.

Fantastic Foods, of Petaluma, California, used ten questions in the Colorado Opinion Tracker to learn about Coloradoan eating habits and attitudes toward vegetarian meals. With this benchmark in hand, the company built a promotion encouraging people in the metropolitan Denver and Los Angeles areas to eat one vegetarian meal per week.

Now, at least in Colorado, small businesses can get the information they need at a price they can afford. Does a market research firm in your area conduct omnibus surveys?[14]

Market Research Process

The market research process follows five basic steps: identifying the problem, developing a plan, collecting the data, analyzing the data, and drawing conclusions (see Figure 11.3).

Figure 11.3
MARKET RESEARCH PROCESS

Conducting Research on Your Markets Involves a Logical Five-Step Process.

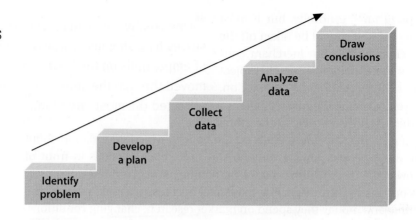

Identify the Problem The most difficult and important part of the market research process is the first step—identifying the problem. You must have a clearly stated, concisely worded problem to generate usable information. Many people (novice and experienced researchers alike) have trouble with this step because they confuse problems with symptoms. For example, if you go to a physician complaining of a fever, the physician could prescribe medication that would bring your fever down. That step would not cure you, however, because an infection or other problem is actually causing your fever. Your physician will search until the problem is found and then fix it—not just mask the symptom. Similarly, declining sales in your small business is not just a problem—it is a symptom of another, underlying problem that is its cause. That underlying problem is what you would want to try to uncover with your research. Has the competition increased? Do your salespeople need retraining? Have your customers' tastes changed?

Your marketing "problem" does not always have to be something that is wrong. It could be something that is lacking or something that could be improved. You can use market research not only to solve problems but also to identify opportunities. Whatever your goal, your ability to complete this first step of the research process is important in guiding the rest of your research efforts.

Planning Market Research Market research is often expensive, but a plan for how you will conduct your research project can help keep costs in check. Before you start, you must separate what is "critical to know" from what would be "nice to know." Your next step is to design a way to address the problem or answer the question that you have identified concerning your business. You can do it yourself, and you should keep it as simple as possible.

In planning your market research project, you need to do the following:

• Identify the types of information that you need.

• Identify primary and secondary sources of data.

• Select a sample that represents the population you are studying.

• Select a research method and measurement technique (phone survey, focus group, and so on) to answer your research question.

In conducting market research for your small business, you should choose a method that provides enough reliable data for you to make a decision with confidence. The method you choose must also use your limited time, money, and personnel efficiently.

Collecting Data   After you have identified the research problem and laid out a plan, you are ready to gather data. Although it sounds simple, don't get this order reversed. A common research error is to begin the process by gathering data and then trying to figure out what the information means and where to go with it—putting the cart before the horse. Determine what you need, and only then go get it. There are two basic types of data you may seek: secondary and primary.[15]

Secondary data are those that already exist, having been gathered for some other purpose. You should check secondary sources first, because they are less expensive than data gathered by conducting your own study. You may be able to solve your problem without an extended primary search.

> **secondary data**
> Marketing data that have been gathered, tabulated, and made available by an outside source.

The good news about secondary data is that the amount of available data is considerable. The bad news is that this mountain of information can prove overwhelming.

A good place to begin your search of secondary data is your local library. Online databases like Lexis-Nexis or ABI-INFORM allow you to enter key terms into the program and immediately receive titles, abstracts, and entire articles from journals and periodicals. The *Government Printing Office Monthly Catalog* contains report references from many government agencies, such as the Department of Commerce and the SBA, which may help you. The Department of Commerce also publishes *Selected Publications to Aid Business and Industry*. Check the *Encyclopedia of Associations* for the thousands of trade, professional, technical, and industrial associations that exist. These associations compile information that can be very relevant to your business.

You can get data on your personal computer from online computer services such as Dun & Bradstreet's home page, Yahoo!, or Dow Jones, publisher of *The Wall Street Journal,* which offers Dow Jones News/Retrieval. The latter service can help you scan the newspaper's daily Enterprise column, which is devoted to topics on small business. The SBA provides 24-hour access to information on services it provides, publications, training, trade fairs, and other programs through its electronic bulletin board, *SBA On-line* (www.sba.gov).

Among the best commercial sources of information are research and trade associations. Their information is industry specific and generally available only to association members, but it is thorough and accurate. If you are serious about getting into or being in business, the membership dues for these organizations are worthwhile investments. Check *Encyclopedia of Associations* (Gale Research) and *Business Information Sources* (University of California Press) at your local library to find relevant associations.[16]

Unfortunately, readily available secondary data are not always specific or detailed enough for your purpose, or they may be obsolete. In either case, you will need to gather your own primary data.

Primary data are qualitative or quantitative data that you collect yourself for your specific purpose. Both qualitative and quantitative data have their advocates and critics, but either can provide valuable information if collected and analyzed correctly.

> **primary data**
> Marketing data that a business collects for its own specific purposes.

Qualitative data refer to research findings that cannot be analyzed statistically. Such data are useful if you are looking for open-minded responses to probing questions, not yes-or-no answers.[17] They can be obtained through *personal interviews* or *focus groups* (groups of six to ten people), which provide considerable depth of information from each person. Qualitative data do not lend themselves to statistical analysis, however. Instead, they help you look for trends in answers or obtain specific or detailed responses to your questions.

Quantitative data are structured to analyze and report numbers, so as to help you see relationships between variables and frequency of occurrences. They are useful in providing information on large groups of people. Their less-probing questions yield results that can be analyzed statistically to show causation.

Small businesses that conduct business online (especially business-to-business operations) can obtain marketing research from the search engines that bring customers to their sites. Web reporting packages (such as WebTrends, Hitbox, and Core-Metrics) provide more data than most businesses can use. For example, you can track the exact phrases that are typed into the search bar that led to your site. What types of words are users entering to find your site? What words are misspelled repeatedly? (Hint: You should add the misspelled word to bring the people using it to your website.) What supplemental words are users adding into their search queries that you have not identified?[18]

Telephone interviews, personal interviews, and *mail surveys* are methods that small businesses commonly use to gather both types of primary data. Because the *questionnaire* is such a popular small business research tool, the following advice is offered to increase its usefulness and enhance response rates.

- Try to make the questionnaire visually attractive and fun to answer. This will help keep it from ending up in the recipient's wastebasket.

- Try to structure possible responses. Instead of asking open-ended questions such as, "What do you think of our product?" list answers that focus on specific issues such as reliability, quality, and price for respondents to check off.

- Don't ask for more than most people can remember. Annoying questions, like asking for the number of light bulbs a business uses in a year, can end the response.

- Don't have more than 20 words per question. People lose interest quickly if questions are too long.

- Be as specific and unambiguous as possible.

- Include a cover letter explaining the reason for the questionnaire. Say, "Thank you."

- Include a self-addressed, stamped return envelope to increase the response rate.

- Include a return date. A reasonable deadline will increase the number of responses and will let you know how long to wait before tallying the results.[19]

Other techniques of primary-data collection for small businesses are limited only by your imagination. The automobile license plates of many states show the county where the vehicle is registered. You can get an idea of where your customers live by taking note of the license plates in your parking lot. This information can help you determine where to aim your advertising. You can use the same technique by spending some time in your competitors' parking lots.

Telephone numbers can tell you where customers live, too. You can get them from sales slips, credit slips, or checks.

By running "lucky draw" contests, you can get a lot of information about your customers. Have them fill out cards with their names and addresses with the promise of a prize if their name is drawn from the box. You can plot these addresses on a local map to see your trade area for the price of a small giveaway prize.[20]

Small Business Decisions Based upon Data and Analysis are Almost Always Better Than Instinct Alone.

Advertisements that provide coded coupons or phrases in your broadcast advertising that customers can use to get a discount can help you determine the effectiveness and reach of your ads.

Data Analysis   Basically, *data analysis* is the process of determining what the responses to your research mean. Once data have been collected, they must be analyzed and translated into usable information. Your first step is to "clean" the data. This effort includes removing all questionnaires and other response forms that are unusable because they are incomplete or unreadable. Depending on the instrument or methodology used to gather data, you may need to code and examine the data to identify trends and develop insights. (An exhaustive description of data analysis is not appropriate for this text. For details of this process, refer to a source such as a market research text.)

For quantitative data, several software programs exist to aid in number crunching and transforming data into charts and graphs to make interpretation easier.

Presenting Data and Making Decisions   Market research that does not lead to some type of action is useless. Your research needs to aid you in making management decisions. Should you expand into a new geographic area? Should you change your product line? Should you change your business hours?

Conclusions based on your data analysis may be obvious. Data may fall out in such a way that you can see exactly what you need to do next to address the research problem identified in step 1.

Market research can provide you with information that will allow you to take proactive steps. This consideration is important because, as a small business owner, deciding what you need to do in the future is much more important than knowing what has happened in the past.

"In ten years of developing the minivan, we never once got a letter from a housewife asking us to invent one."

Limitations of Market Research

As important as market research can be for small businesses, it should be used with caution. Market research can provide you with a picture of what people currently know and expect from products or services, but it has limited ability to indicate what people will want in the future. Relying on market research exclusively for your marketing strategy and new product ideas is like driving a car while watching only the rearview mirror.

As noted in Chapter 1, small businesses provide many of the most innovative products that we use. Our economy and consumers depend on a stream of such innovations as fax machines, CD-ROMs, and minivans, but innovation does not come from market research. Peter Drucker notes that although the fax machine was designed and developed by U.S. companies, no U.S. companies began producing these devices for domestic consumption because market research indicated that there would be no demand for such a product.

When asking about a product that does not yet exist, Drucker says your question might go like this (in regard to the not-yet-produced fax machine): "Would you buy a telephone accessory that costs upwards of $1,500 and enables you to send, for one dollar a page, the same letter the post office delivers for 25 cents?" The average consumer would predictably say "no."[21] Hal Sperlich designed the concept of the minivan while he was working for Ford, but when Ford didn't believe a market existed for such a vehicle (based on its historical market research), he switched to Chrysler. Sperlich says, "In ten years of developing the minivan, we never once got a letter from a housewife asking us to invent one." To the skeptics, that proved a market didn't exist.[22]

Although market research works well for fine-tuning concepts for known products, customers don't have the foresight to ask for what they don't know about or don't know they need or want. As one axis of Figure 11.4 shows, there are two types of customer needs: those that customers can tell you about and those that customers have without realizing they have them. How many people were asking for DVD recorders, MP3 players, or GPS units ten years ago? The other axis of Figure 11.4 shows that there are two types of markets or customers for any given business: those served by the company's existing products and those not yet served—the company's potential customers. Market research can tell us the most about the

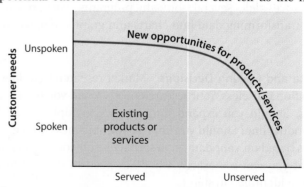

Figure 11.4

MATRIX OF CUSTOMER NEEDS AND TYPES

Market Research Is Most Effective When Used to Evaluate Existing Products That Satisfy Known Needs That Customers Can Talk About.

SOURCE: Adapted and reprinted by permission of Harvard Business School Press from "Seeing the Future First," by Gary Hamel and C. K. Prahalad. Competing for the Future. Boston, MA, 1994, p. 103. Copyright © 1994 by Harvard Business School Corporation. All rights reserved.

spoken needs of a served market, but much room for growth can be found by exploring the three other sectors. When you are driving a car, you need to check the rearview mirror occasionally, just as you should check your current and past markets with market research. But the ideal is to concentrate on defining markets rather than reacting to them. An entrepreneur must go beyond what market research can tell.

Summary

- **The importance of marketing to small businesses**

  Marketing involves all the points of contact between your small business and your customers. Marketing is how you find out what they want and need; it is how they are treated by you and everyone in your business; it is how you communicate with them through selling and advertising. What could be more important?

- **The process of developing a small business marketing strategy**

  Market segmentation is needed because no business can possibly be everything to everyone. Segmenting involves breaking down a population into target markets that have a common want or need that the business can satisfy. Target markets are the focus of a company's marketing efforts.

- **The purpose of the market research process and the steps involved in putting it into practice**

  Market research provides information about the people who are buying the products of a business. Conditions change, and the owner of a business must know about those changes to be proactive and maintain a competitive advantage. The steps of the market research process include problem identification, development of a plan, data collection, data analysis, and drawing conclusions. Market research can provide valuable information regarding people's current tastes, preferences, and expectations. It is useful in fine-tuning products that already exist for markets that are already known. Conversely, it is of limited use for markets that do not exist yet or for needs that customers do not realize they have.

Questions for Review and Discussion

1. Marketing plays a key role in a small business's success. Can a small business succeed without adopting the philosophy underlying the marketing concept? Why or why not?

2. What would happen to a business without a marketing strategy? Why?

3. What determines which type of sales forecast would be appropriate for a small business? Describe how a specific small business would implement the build-up approach.

4. Why is segmenting a niche market so crucial for a small business?

5. We all assume several different roles (parent, student, sibling, athlete, business owner, and so on) at any given time, and those roles affect our behavior as consumers. Describe how your various roles affect your purchases.

6. What is the significance of market research to the small business owner? How is market research defined, and what degree of complexity is necessary in the research plan for it to be valid?

7. Explain the market research process from a small business owner's perspective when he is trying to assess competitive advantage.

8. What types of data should be collected and analyzed to get a clear picture of the market for the good or service being produced?

9. Identify some valuable sources of information for the entrepreneur who is designing a market research plan to analyze competitive advantage.

10. What are some of the limitations of the process of market research? How can the entrepreneur offset these limitations?

Questions for Critical Thinking

1. Segmentation is the process of breaking a population down into smaller groups and marketing to them. Is it possible for a small business to oversegment its market? How would that be dangerous?

2. What do you think is the biggest limitation for small businesses conducting market research?

Experience This . . .

You decide that you need to create a survey to get customer feedback on a new product you have developed, but then you realize, "Oh, no! I've never created and administered a real survey before!" Go to your favorite search engine and conduct a search for "small business" and "market research." From your findings, create a bullet-point list of ten factors you should keep in mind when writing survey questions.

What Would You Do?

The bigger and stronger the competition is, the better a small business's marketing strategy needs to be. That being the case, Amilya Antonetti may need *your* help with a marketing strategy. Antonetti is starting a business to break into the $4.7 billion U.S. laundry detergent market, competing directly with the likes of Procter & Gamble. The niche of the detergent market that she is filling is hypoallergenic cleaning products, because her infant son had health problems aggravated by chemicals in the standard brands. She started her company, called SoapWorks, after conducting market research, primarily from other mothers of infants, and finding that many other families faced similar problems. Her annual advertising budget is limited to $60,000 (about what her huge competitors spend on one 30-second prime-time network TV ad), so she had to find different ways to let people know what SoapWorks would do for them.

Questions

1. If you were in Amilya Antonetti's place starting SoapWorks, what marketing strategy would you use to compete with Procter & Gamble and Clorox? How would you reach your target markets? How and where would you advertise? We talk about the power of word-of-mouth among our customers—how do you use it to your advantage as a small business marketer?

2. One of the biggest challenges SoapWorks faced was getting its products on the shelves of grocery stores. By 1999 they were in 2,500 stores from California to Florida, and the company had revenues of $5 million. How would you create such market penetration?

SOURCE: D. M. Osborne, "Taking on Procter & Gamble," *Inc.,* October 2000, 66–73.

CHAPTER CLOSING CASE

A FORK IN THE ROAD

Kevin Magenis hung up the phone, looked out his office window into his company's development lab, and thought about what he'd just heard. The callers were from Apple Computer, and they wanted to talk business. Magenis's startup, Cornice, had developed tiny hard drives with a one-inch platter for storing music or digital files. And it made them for a third of the price of rivals like IBM.

That's why the Apple execs called that afternoon in late 2002. Would Cornice be interested, they wanted to know, in supplying the drives for the iPod Mini, the new, smaller version of Apple's MP3 player? Digital music was still new, and no single player had emerged to dominate. But Apple was clearly the most innovative player on the scene, and hooking up with the company would definitely be a coup for Cornice.

Magenis was tempted. The problem was that Cornice was already working with two other makers of MP3 players, Thomson/RCA and Rio, and the Apple execs were insisting on an exclusive deal. Honoring that request would mean betraying two key clients.

Cornice, which is based in Longmont, Colorado, had been doing business with those two companies almost from the moment it was founded in 2000. At the time, Thomson and Rio were the leading manufacturers of MP3 players, both of them outselling Apple. Both companies had new products in the prototype stage designed around Cornice's hard drives, and Cornice expected the two clients to account for as much as 40 percent of its revenue. Cornice also was negotiating to supply drives, for non-music uses, to Dell, Hewlett-Packard, and Sony.

Indeed, digital music was just a tiny part of Cornice's business plan. The way Magenis and his team saw it, the real opportunity was in the much larger market for mobile phones—which they believed eventually would function as handheld computers, storing and sending all manner of data.

Still, Magenis knew he'd be a fool not to at least try to forge a relationship with Apple. He contacted some of his board members and told them about the offer. In addition to an exclusive arrangement, Apple also wanted Cornice to make some changes to its

technology; specifically, it wanted Cornice to design a new, double-sided drive capable of storing more information. That seemed reasonable. Nonetheless, the board members concluded it would be bad business to abandon Thomson and Rio. Instead, they decided to propose a compromise: Cornice would keep its two current customers, but the iPod would be the only other MP3-device manufacturer it would make drives for. (Apple declined to comment for this story.)

Over the next few months, Magenis made several trips to Apple's headquarters in Cupertino, California, and Apple's engineers came out to Cornice's Colorado offices. Magenis could sense how excited everyone at Apple seemed to be about the Mini; the iPod team was in constant contact with CEO Steve Jobs, and Magenis couldn't help but be thrilled when he got to meet the man in passing. In the back of his mind, Magenis fretted that Apple would fix the problems in the digital music business, and Cornice might miss out on being inside the market leader. "I could see it was going to be a hell of an effort on their part," he says.

But Magenis was also juggling nearly 40 other deals. Apple could consume only so much of his time. By the end of the year, Apple was getting impatient. The executives were friendly but insistent. Apple wanted to work with Cornice, but it absolutely refused to budge on the issue of exclusivity.

What do you think? Would it be completely nuts to say no? Should Cornice have chosen cell phones over the iPod?

SOURCE: From Michael Fitzgerald, "Why Cornice Said No, Thanks, to Apple," *Inc.*, October 2005, 59–60. Copyright © 2006 Mansueto Ventures LLC, publishers of Inc. Magazine, New York, NY 10017. Reprinted with permission.

Test Prepper

ACE self-test

college.hmco.com/pic/hatten4e

You've read the chapter, studied the key terms, and the exam is any day now. Think you're ready to ace it? Take this sample test to gauge your comprehension of chapter material. You can check your answers at the back of the book. Want more test questions? Visit the student website at college.hmco.com/pic/hatten4e and take the ACE and ACE+ quizzes for more practice.

Matching

_____ 1. the business philosophy driven by determining customer wants and needs before products are produced

_____ 2. the orchestrated efforts containing what you intend to accomplish and how you intend to achieve those goals

_____ 3. the top line of a business

_____ 4. estimating how many products you may sell by adding up the daily, weekly, and monthly projections

_____ 5. treating entire populations as potential customers for specific products

_____ 6. customizing a product or service to appeal to a specific person

_____ 7. the group of brands that come to mind when a customer thinks of a product type

_____ 8. data that have been collected, tabulated, and distributed by an outside source

_____ 9. the most important and difficult step in the marketing research process

_____10. the marketing function that links consumer, customer, and public with marketers

a. marketing concept

b. marketing strategy

c. time series analysis

d. secondary data

e. primary data

f. data analysis

g. decision making

h. marketing research

i. production concept

j. marketing objectives

k. mass marketing

l. individualized marketing

m. evoked set

n. sales forecast

o. build-up approach

p. niche marketing

q. problem identification

Fill in the Blank

1. Marketing objectives can be broken into two groups: marketing _____ and _____.

2. A type of marketing that is becoming more popular with small businesses, in which the business pays money to have its name associated with an event, is called _____ .

3. The remorse that some buyers feel after making a major purchase is called _____.

4. The faulty thinking of many small business owners regarding their target markets can be summarized as, "We don't have specific target markets; we will sell to _____ ."

5. Marketing research is valuable for fine-tuning products, but it is not so useful for _____ products.

Small Business Marketing: Product

Hattie Herzog was not a bride, but she felt like she had been left standing at the altar when she received a phone call saying that McDonald's was walking away from the partnership she thought they were heading toward. This budding entrepreneur had a new and exciting product with lots of potential, and McDonald's had the visibility and marketing savvy needed to make it become a huge success. Herzog's six-person company, ADT, had created the Shop 2000, an eye-popping 18- by 9-foot vending machine that dispenses 200 products, ranging from Diet Coke to disposable cameras to olive oil to computer disks.

Herzog had entered into a six-month test of the Shop 2000 with McDonald's with no money promised and no commitment extended. ADT provided a machine and technical support, and McDonald's chose the location—a busy site in the trendy Adams Morgan neighborhood of Washington, D.C. Herzog had worked for four years developing the innovative product without selling a single unit, so the pilot test represented a big chance for her. After the phone call that informed her of McDonald's decision to purchase the U.S. rights to a Belgian firm's similar product (oversized vending machines that offer the inventory of a mini-mart are more common in Europe and Japan), ADT was back to square one.

After reading this chapter, you should be able to:

- Define the term *marketing mix.*

- Discuss the different forms a product can take, and identify the five levels of product satisfaction.

- Explain the importance of purchasing and describe its procedures.

- Discuss the main concerns in selecting a supplier.

- Calculate how much inventory you need and when.

- Describe seven methods of inventory control.

Hattie Herzog.

The McDonald's test had provided Herzog with a wealth of valuable information about things like location, forms of payment, and product selection. Now she faced the lonely choice of what to do with that information—a common entrepreneurial dilemma.

Herzog made some product changes to the Shop 2000. In particular, she split the machine into modular units that would be easier to move and customize. The modular approach also allowed the machines to be placed in lobbies and covered areas that are protected from both the ravages of weather and vandalism. Herzog decided to approach colleges and hotels when seeking placements. Both venues offered large numbers of captive customers who needed a variety of items at all hours of the day. In 2005 testing began of the Shop 2000 on the factory floor of a potential partner in Greece. If successful, the machines will be placed on Greece military bases, especially on far-flung islands with no grocery stores. Herzog is still ADT's sole investor and remains optimistic about the future of her invention. Incidentally, McDonald's disbanded its innovative task force and dropped the vending experiment after a six-month test with the Belgian company in 2003.

Developing a new product is a long, difficult process for an entrepreneur and is filled with both ups and downs. Partnerships and collaborations with other companies are often necessary, but as Herzog says, "You don't necessarily marry everyone you date."

SOURCES: Patrick Cliff, "On the Rebound," *Inc.*, May 2006, 62; Michelle Leder, "Losing McDonald's," *Inc.*, March 2004, 44–46; Shelley Wolson, "Industry Looks Ahead: Automatic Innovation," *FoodService Director*, May 2003, 92; Matthew Swibel, "New from Mickey D's: Condoms," *Forbes*, December 2002, 60; Maryanne Murray Buechner, "Shop Around the Clock," *Time*, 18 November 2002, 96.

Using Your Marketing Mix

marketing mix
The factors that a business can change in selling products to customers—product, place, price, and promotion.

Marketing involves *all* the activities that occur from the time your product is made until it reaches the consumer. Your **marketing mix** consists of the variables that you can control in bringing your product or service to your target market. Think of them as the tools your small business has available for its use. The marketing mix is also referred to as the *Four Ps:* product, place, price, and promotion. You must offer the right *product* (including goods and services) that your target market wants or needs. *Place* refers to channels of distribution you choose to use, as well as the location and layout of your small business. Your *price* must make your product attractive and still allow you to make a profit. *Promotion* is the means you use to communicate with your target market. This chapter and the following two chapters will cover your use of the marketing mix to build and run your business.

Product: The Heart of the Marketing Mix

product
A tangible good, an intangible service, or a combination of these.

The product is at the heart of your marketing mix. Remember that **product** means tangible goods, intangible services, or a combination of these (see Figure 12.1).

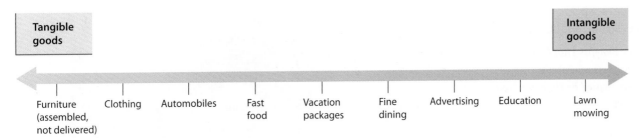

Figure 12.1

SPECTRUM OF GOODS AND SERVICES

Most Small Businesses Sell a Combination of Goods and Services.

Hiring someone to mow your lawn is an example of the service end of the goods-and-services spectrum. In this case, you don't receive a tangible good. An example of a tangible good would be the purchase of a chair that is finished and assembled, but not delivered. Thus, in this case, you don't receive any services. Many businesses offer a combination of goods and services. Restaurants, for instance, provide both goods (food and drink) and services (preparation and delivery).

When determining your product strategy, it is useful to think about different levels of product satisfaction. Products are the "bundle of satisfaction" that consumers receive in exchange for their money (see Figure 12.2). The most basic level of product satisfaction is its *core benefit,* or the fundamental reason why people buy products. For an automobile, the core benefit is transportation from point A to point B. With a hotel room, the core benefit is a night's sleep. To put this another way, people don't buy drills—they really buy holes.

The next level of product satisfaction is the *generic product.* For an automobile, the generic product is the steel, plastic, and glass. For the hotel, the building, the front desk, and the rooms represent the generic product.

The third level of product satisfaction is the *expected product,* which includes the set of attributes and conditions that consumers assume will be present. U.S. consumers expect comfortable seats, responsive handling, and easy starting from their cars. A hotel guest expects clean sheets, soap, towels, relative quiet, and indoor plumbing.

The *augmented product,* the fourth level of product satisfaction, is all the additional services and benefits that can distinguish your business. For example, night vision built into windshields, satellite-linked navigational systems in autos, and express checkout and health club facilities in hotels are product augmentations. Augmentations represent the sizzle that you sell along with the steak. The problem with product augmentations is that they soon become expected. When you have raised your costs and prices by adding augmentations, you open the door for competitors to come in and offer more of a generic product at a lower price. That's how the Motel 6 franchises became so successful—by offering a plain room for a low price when competitors were adding amenities that raised their cost structure and prices.

The fifth and final level is the *potential product.* It includes product evolutions to come. Not long ago, a DVD-R drive was a potential product for personal computers. It soon became a product augmentation and, very quickly, expected.

Figure 12.2

LEVELS OF PRODUCTS

The Benefits That Consumers Receive from Products Are Represented by Different Product Levels.

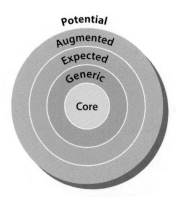

Thus the products that you develop and sell in your small business are more than just a combination of tangible features. Always keep in mind which core benefits customers receive from your product, how the actual product satisfies those core needs, and how you can augment your products to make them more appealing.

Developing New Products

Part of a marketer's job is managing products through the stages of their *life cycle* (see Figure 7.2, page 187). Trends like increased global competition and quickly changing customer needs have shortened product life cycles and increased the need for new products.[1] As a company's current products enter the stages of late maturity and decline, they need to be replaced with new ones in demand. What is new? Good question. Marketing consultants Booz, Allen & Hamilton group new products into six categories:

Jell-O Pudding Pops Are Line Extensions.

1. *New-to-the-world products.* These are products that have not been seen before, which result in entirely new markets. Ken Fischer developed and patented a marine paint that the U.S. Navy uses to keep its ships free of barnacles. The paint is made from a mixture of epoxy and cayenne pepper. Fischer came up with the idea for the paint after blistering his mouth on a Tabasco-covered deviled egg. He decided that animals would react the same way. He was right.[2]

2. *New product lines.* These are products that exist but are new to your type of business. For example, the addition of a coffee bar to your bookstore would be taking on a new product line.

3. *Additions to existing product lines.* These are products that are extensions of what you already sell. For example, creating Jell-O Gelatin Pops from existing Jell-O Pudding Pops would represent a product-line extension.

4. *Improvements in, revisions of, or new uses for existing products.* These are products that have had their value increased. Take the example of WD-40 spray lubricant. Although it was originally developed to prevent rust by displacing water, so many new uses have been found for it that the WD-40 Company holds an annual "Invent Your Own Use"

Profile in Entrepreneurship
The Customer Is King with "Shoppertainment"

The mantra for most re-tailers has been "the customer is king" for many years. Few small retail businesses ignore competitors who take a customer-centric approach to building a wide base of loyal customers. Of course, it sounds more simple than it is to satisfy customers on all the levels shown in Figure 12.2.

Jordan's Furniture, however, is a four-store chain in the Boston area that gets it. Their motto is "There's No Business That's Not Show Business." Brothers Barry and Eliot Tatelman share a magic touch combining shopping and entertainment into what they call "shoppertainment." Each store offers a unique array of interactive, sensory features that can do the impossible of turning furniture shopping into a family event.

At the Natick, MA, store, the Tatelmans have recreated a Mardi Gras celebration featuring kids' amusement rides, animatronic characters, and refreshment stands lining their version of Bourbon Street. From there, customers can journey through the couch section to take in a movie at the full-size IMAX movie theater located inside the store.

The highlight of the Reading store is the area titled Beantown covering 17,000 square feet and filled with a total of 280,000 pounds of Jelly Belly jellybeans. The 25 million jellybeans are used to construct Boston's Big Dig road construction project, the State House, and a full-size replica of Fenway Park's "Green Monster," with the Red Sox mascot clutching a New York Yankee. Obviously baseball fans, the brothers promise to give away furniture if the Sox win the World Series again. They have taken out a $20 million insurance policy in case the Sox do come through, and they are rooting for the home team so they can give away their wares.

Barry and Eliot are entrepreneurs who offer more than mattresses—they combine products, service, and fun. Watch the video clip that accompanies this chapter for more of their marketing antics.

SOURCES: Janet Groeber, "That's Entertainment," *Display & Design Ideas*, May 2005; "Jordan's to Give Away Furniture If Red Sox Win World Series," *Furniture Today*, 12 March 2007, 102; Robert Cashill, "That's Shoppertainment," *Lighting Dimensions*, March 2006, 32–36; Dan Berthiaume, "Connecting with the Customer," *Retail Technology Quarterly*, October 2005, 26a–29a.

---

contest. Besides quieting squeaky hinges and freeing zippers, the product also removes gum stuck in hair or carpet, and sticky labels from glass, plastic, and metal. The Denver Fire Department even used WD-40 to free a nude burglary suspect who got stuck while attempting to enter a restaurant through an exhaust vent.

5. *Repositioning of existing products.* These are products that have not changed except in customer perceptions. Many products are created with one purpose in mind but end up finding success in another arena—including Post-it Notes (originally created to mark pages in the inventor's church choir songbook) and Viagra (originally formulated to treat angina—chest pain associated with poor circulation to the heart). Developers at Gore-Tex (makers of waterproof outer clothing and Glide dental floss) tried to expand the use of the company's polytetrafluoroethylene (ePTFE) material to make cables for controlling puppets at Disney theme parks; it didn't work. It turns out, however, that ePTFE lasts five times longer than regular guitar strings. Now Elixir Strings are sold in more than half of all music stores in the United States.[3]

6. *Lower-cost versions of existing products.* These are products that provide value and performance similar to those of existing products but at a lower

*"I'm a pragmatist, Leon. Before I put a new
product on the market, I ask myself, 'Will it sell?'"*

cost. For example, food stands that sell hamburgers and hot dogs offer products similar to the big-name fast-food franchises but at a lower price, thereby enticing customers with their cost advantage.

Of course, increased risk is associated with the launch of new products. How many new products can you remember seeing on the shelves at the grocery store in the last year? Ten? Fifty? One hundred? Now think of how many of those you chose to adopt. However many you remember, it was surely far less than the 20,000 new food products and 5,000 nonfood items introduced each year.[4] Many of those new products did not survive. Nevertheless, despite the risk, innovation is the key to success. Innovation is part of being proactive in the marketplace.

Inventor's Paradox

At several points in this book you have been asked to project yourself into a scenario where you have come up with an idea for a new business and decide what you would do at that stage (maybe you are not projecting). Let's take up that discussion again with the following premise: You have developed a new product that fits into one of the six categories cited earlier. What are your options? The best alternative is to start and run your own business based on the new product—that option is the foundation of this whole book. But what other options exist?

Unfortunately, many product innovators believe that they simply need to generate an idea for a new product, service, or process, and Uber-Corporation X will pay them massive amounts of money for this idea. Sorry to disappoint you, but ideas are worth very little in the business world. In fact, most companies strongly discourage inventors from approaching them with ideas. Why? Because they have been approached by hundreds of people who want to cash in on undeveloped ideas. Of course, some people have convinced members of a large corporation that they are serious inventors who have marketable ideas, but lightning has struck in the same place twice, too. Just don't count on it happening.

Reality Check

Slotting Fees: Unfair for Small Businesses?

Did you pick up some of the great flavors of Lee's Ice Cream the last time you were in a grocery store? No? It's great stuff. It must be; the ice cream store in Baltimore has the highest gross sales per square foot of any ice cream stand in America. Sorry, but you couldn't buy it in any grocery store because of slotting fees.

What are slotting fees? They are fees paid by a manufacturer to ensure that a retailer places its products on store shelves. The practice of paying slotting fees has been around for about 20 years, mainly in the grocery business, but it has not been widely publicized. Manufacturers of all types have complained about slotting fees for years, but they keep their complaints to themselves for fear of retailer reprisals. Some companies, such as Pacific Valley Foods of Bellevue, Washington, are going public in saying that slotting destroyed 70 percent of its business.

Large grocery chains justify the practice by saying that the fees offset the expense and risk of putting new products on their shelves in place of proven products, and that they discourage random and poorly researched new products—in short, that they are a tool for improving distribution efficiency. Manufacturers say that slotting discourages product innovation, damages competition, destroys small food processors, and severely restricts product choices for consumers.

With the slim margins of the food industry, the payout period can be stretched up to five to seven years. Large food manufacturers can spread the fees [which can run as high as $50,000 per shop-keeping unit (SKU) per store in a chain] over many existing products, by charging slightly higher prices that go largely unnoticed. Because small producers must include slotting fees in the prices of their new products, they often can't afford to get their foot in the door (or products on the shelf).

One small company recently launched a new kind of meat product and *not counting slotting fees* had to pay a single grocery chain (1) $5,000 per item in warehouse costs, (2) $5,000 per item in quarterly newspaper ads, and (3) $86,000 in free samples. Thus a small manufacturer has put a $100,000 ante in before the product even reaches the store shelves. Even worse, if the product does not sell, the company has to buy it back!

A recent academic study found that slotting fees are used in both the consumer and the durable goods manufacturing industries, though different norms regarding slotting fees exist between product categories. This study evaluated several theoretical approaches regarding slotting fees including the efficiency school of thought, the market power school of thought, and even an approach that slotting fees are simply a new promotional tool from which manufacturers choose when allocating marketing resources.

Are slotting fees a way for grocery stores to shift the financial risk of new grocery products (80 percent of which fail) from the retailer to the manufacturer? Or are they a competition-stifling practice that unfairly punishes the smallest, most innovative companies?

SOURCES: P. F. Bone, K. R. France, and R. Russo, "A Multifirm Analysis of Slotting Fees," *Journal of Public Policy & Marketing*, Fall 2006, 224237; Barry Feig, "Too Clever by Half?" *Frozen Food Age*, January 2003, 20; Leonard Klie, "Slotting Fees Vary Among Products," *Food Logistics*, January/February 2004, 6; Richard Merli, "Slotting Just About Killed Us," *Frozen Food Age*, April 2000, 1, 12; Paul Bloom et al., "Slotting Allowances and Fees: Schools of Thought and the Views of Practicing Managers," *Journal of Marketing*, April 2000, 92–108; Chris White and Lisa Gerlich, "The Role of Slotting Fees and Introductory Allowances in Retail Buyers' New-Product Acceptance Decisions," *Academy of Marketing Science*, Spring 2000, 291–298.

If you do gain an audience with a corporate representative at which you can make a proposal and a presentation, you have a better chance of walking out with a **licensing agreement** than a check. Under a licensing agreement, the owner of intellectual property grants another person (or another company) permission to produce that product. In exchange, the inventor receives royalties, which constitute a percentage (generally 5 to 6 percent) of sales. The inventor relinquishes control over what the licensee does with the product. Your chances of getting a

> **licensing agreement**
> An agreement in which the owner of intellectual property grants another person (or another company) permission to produce that product.

licensing agreement are greatly improved if you are already producing the product and have established a track record of sales. Your chances of getting a licensing agreement dwindle if you are seeking a license because you don't have enough money to develop the product yourself.

Another alternative for an inventor may be **private-label manufacturing**. For example, Sears does not own a factory in which it builds its Craftsman tools. Instead, the company engages other companies to make the tools to its specifications and puts the Craftsman brand on them. This is where you, the tool inventor, could enter the picture. If you have designed a new tool that Sears does not currently have in its product line, you might be able to secure an agreement to produce that tool under the company's brand name. You will get only about one-half of the retail price, but at least you have a sales base from which to begin your operations. A serious downside to this strategy is that you have just one major customer, so your company's fortunes will hang on that firm's willingness to maintain the agreement.

Recall the Chapter 1 discussion of the symbiotic relationship between large and small businesses. Here is another possible connection where each party needs the other: Similar to private-label manufacturing, you could become an *OEM (original-equipment manufacturer),* a company that makes component parts or accessories for larger items.[5] For example, your firm might produce circuit boards for computer manufacturers or custom knobs for cabinet makers.

Importance of Product Competitive Advantage

Few would argue that the length of time many products have before they become obsolete has decreased rapidly over the past few years. Factors such as new technologies, increasing numbers of substitute products, quickly changing consumer tastes and preferences, and shifting consumption patterns all play large roles in this rapid phase-out of existing products. Small businesses are more vulnerable to product obsolescence because they typically depend on fewer key products and have fewer resources with which to develop new ones. In addition, the niche markets that small businesses serve can dry up or be lured away by a larger, low-cost competitor. The optimal scenario for these businesses features a steady stream of new products being developed to replace existing ones as they pass through the product life cycle.

Unfortunately, no one actually runs a business that operates within the optimal scenario. Instead, the best you can do is learn from other successful small businesses. A recent study illustrated some fundamental practices of small businesses that succeed in creating and retaining a competitive advantage. Notably, they maintain their focus on specialized products serving niche markets and rely on their existing core competitive advantage to enter new markets. A *sustainable competitive advantage* is based on something that firm does better than others—a *core competency.* To be classified as a core competency, a factor should satisfy three criteria:

1. Be applicable across a range of products
2. Be difficult for competitors to duplicate
3. Provide a fundamental and valuable benefit to customers

Assuming that their core competencies are intact, successful companies share some common characteristics that can be termed *best practices:* They

- *Leverage existing capabilities*—meaning they understand what they do well, and they use those skills to enter new markets.
- *Enter growth markets*—and thereby avoid cutthroat price competition and zero-sum games.
- *Target niche markets*—because, by definition, niche markets are less crowded with competitors than mass markets, and customers in niche markets are willing to pay premiums for specialized products.
- *Diversify*—so as to spread risk, or, as the cliché goes, they don't put all their eggs in one basket.
- *Add new capabilities*—by building a set of skills, such as technology, marketing, or distribution.
- *Establish strong top management leadership*—which will diversify and take other risks necessary to reposition their organizations when necessary.
- *Have a good workforce*—that is, employees who are skilled, flexible, and self-motivated.
- *Maintain high employee productivity*—and, thus, without adding employees, keep overhead costs low and product output high.
- *Have low overhead*—because they have a lean management structure, and they avoid major new investments in buildings and equipment by adding extra shifts and overtime.[6]

Packaging

If you are selling a packaged consumer product, think of packaging as your last chance to catch customers' attention—kind of like the last five seconds of marketing. Of course, packaging provides more than just a wrapper around your product; it can add value that benefits both you and your customers. Good packaging can make handling or storage more convenient. It can reduce spoilage or damage. Packaging can benefit your customers by making the product more identifiable and therefore easier to find on a crowded shelf.

POM Wonderful is a pricey pomegranate juice that is packaged in a fat, snowman-shaped bottle. Even though customers complain that it feels like it's about to fall out of their hand, they still shell out $4.39 per bottle.[7] Think the company could get that much if the juice was packaged in an aluminum can? Probably not.

Mitchells Luxury ice cream won the innovative packaging award at Grampian Food Forum Awards in England. Rather than using a standard ice cream tub, the firm created a rectangular tub with a perforated label that can be pulled back to access the fork built into the packaging. More important than the award, Mitchells has seen a 36 percent increase in its sales attributed directly to the packaging.[8]

Purchasing for Small Business

Your ability to offer quality goods at competitive prices depends on your purchasing skills. You need to seek the best value—the highest quality for the best price—for the goods, services, and equipment you purchase, because that is exactly what

"Your purchasing skills greatly affect your company's profitability, yet price is merely one of many factors you must consider."

your customers will be expecting when they purchase your products. Price is therefore merely one of many factors to consider. You should also consider the consistency of your suppliers' quality, their reliability in meeting delivery schedules, the payment terms available, product guarantees, merchandising assistance, emergency delivery and return policies, and other factors.

Purchasing Guidelines

The following questions provide guidelines for evaluating your small business purchasing and inventory control:

- Are you using the proper sources of supply?
- Are you taking advantage of all purchase discounts?
- How do you determine minimum inventories and reorder points?
- Have you run out of raw materials or finished goods?
- What is the record of your current suppliers for quality, service, and price?
- Are you using minimum quantities or economic ordering quantities?
- What are your inventory holding costs?
- Do you know your optimal average inventory? Does it guide your purchasing policy?
- Could you improve your purchasing to increase profits?
- What is your inventory turnover ratio? How does it compare with the industry average?[9]

To illustrate the importance of purchasing to the profit of your small business, suppose your business spends $500,000 annually, has yearly sales of $1 million, and enjoys a profit margin of 10 percent or $100,000. If you were able to decrease the costs of your purchases by 3 percent, you would save $15,000—increasing your profits by 15 percent. To see the same profit increase through sales revenue, you would have to generate $150,000 in additional sales, or a 15 percent increase. This means that a 3 percent savings on the cost of purchased items has the same impact on your bottom line as a 15 percent increase in sales.

Purchasing Basics

Whether you're purchasing inexpensive toilet paper for the employee bathroom or expensive components for your manufacturing process, you want to make good purchasing decisions—decisions that will get you the best possible product at the best possible price. To make your decisions wisely, it helps to know how the purchasing process *should* work. Let's look more closely at the steps in the purchasing process.

1. *Recognize, describe, and transmit the need.* If you're the only employee in your business, you'll have to rely on your own knowledge of your work processes to know *what* needs to be ordered and *when*. However, if your small business has other employees, you should train them to alert the person in charge of purchasing (yourself or another person whom you designate) of any needs. You'll probably

want to use a *purchase requisition* to standardize this process, a form that lists and describes the materials, supplies, and equipment that are needed. In addition, the purchase requisition should list the quantity needed, date required, estimated unit cost, budget account to be charged, and an authorized signature. This form should also have at least two copies: one for the person who does the purchasing and the other for the person requesting the items.

2. *Investigate and select suppliers and prepare a purchase order.* Once you know what's needed, you can begin to look for the best possible sources for obtaining the desired products. Because elsewhere this text describes the factors you need to examine in selecting a supplier, let's concentrate here on describing the *purchase order*, which is, in most instances, a legal contract document between you and the supplier—so you want to make sure you prepare it carefully.

Once you've selected a supplier, you should record on a serially numbered purchase order the quantity requirements, price, and delivery and shipping requirements accurately. If you have any quality specifications, they should also be described precisely. If you have any product drawings or other documents that relate to the order, these should be included as well. If you need to inspect sample products before an order is completed, be sure to specify what, when, and how much you want to sample. In other words, include all the data on your purchase order and word it so that it's clear to both you and the supplier what the specifications and expectations are.

You'll probably want to use a multipart purchase order form so that you and the supplier can keep track of the orders coming in and being fulfilled. In fact, purchasing experts say that *seven* is the minimum number of copies you'd want on a purchase order. Although you may consider this to be extreme, at least make sure that your purchase order form has enough copies so that both you and your supplier can keep track of the order in sufficient detail.

3. *Follow up on the order.* Although the purchase order represents a legal offer to buy, no purchase contract exists until the seller accepts the buyer's offer. The supplier accepts by either filling the order or at the very least notifying the purchaser that the order is being filled. By *following up* on the order by mail, e-mail, fax, or phone call, you can keep on top of its status. If the goods you ordered are critically needed, the follow-up can be doubly important. (For important orders, you'll want to get written verification that your order was accepted.) Besides being a good way to keep on top of your purchasing activities, the follow-up helps you maintain good relations with your suppliers.

4. *Receiving and inspecting the order.* Once the order is received, you should inspect it immediately to confirm that it is correct. The supplier should have enclosed a *packing slip* with the order that you can compare against your copy of the purchase order. You should check for quantity as well as quality of the goods. If someone other than yourself checks orders, you'll probably want to use a *receiving report form* that indicates what's included in the order—quantity and quality. In fact, even if you're the person who checks the order, it would be smart to have some way of noting the condition of the shipment, just in case you need this information in the future. If the order is correct, it's ready to go into inventory or into use. If there's a problem, you should contact the supplier immediately. Let the supplier know what the problem is and follow up with written *documentation* describing the problem. The supplier will let you know the procedure for handling the incorrect order.

5. *Completing the order.* The order isn't complete until you've paid the *invoice*—a bill that should be included with the order or might be sent later by the supplier—and prepared whatever accounting documents you need. Once you've completed this step, the purchasing process is complete.

Although the purchasing process as outlined here may seem burdensome and time-consuming, keep in mind that being an effective and efficient purchaser makes an important difference in your small business.[10]

Selecting Suppliers

Whom you buy from can be as important as *what* you buy. At the very least, supplier (or vendor) selection should be based on systematic analysis, not on guesswork or habit. Vendors are an important component of your operation.

Make-or-Buy Decision

A decision you must make in running your small manufacturing business is whether to produce your own parts and components or to buy them from an outside source. This choice is called the **make-or-buy decision**. Much of the decision rests on the availability and quality of suppliers.

The more specialized your needs or the more you need to hide design features, the more likely it is that you will have to make your own parts. But it is generally better to buy standardized parts (such as bolts) and standardized components (such as blower fans) rather than to make them.

The make-or-buy decision is not limited to manufacturing operations or functions. Service and retail businesses need to consider whether to outsource such functions as janitorial or payroll services. You could either use your own personnel for those services or hire another specialized business to produce them for you.

> *make-or-buy decision*
> The choice of whether to purchase parts and components or to produce them.

Investigating Potential Suppliers

Because the products you purchase become the products you sell, you want to be sure that you are dealing with the best suppliers available. But how do you do that? Tom Thornbury, CEO of Softub, a hot tub builder in California, asked that very question after his company had been burned by some bad vendors. His answer was to create a *vendor audit team* made up of ten employees from several areas of the business. The team spends from two hours to two days visiting and investigating the potential supplier.

Such thorough investigation is justified because companies like Softub are viewing their relationship with vendors as a long-term partnership. Since developing the audit team, product defects have dropped, and vendor turnover has been cut in half. To help the audit team remember everything it wants to look for, Softub developed a checklist (see Figure 12.3).[11] Factors you need to consider in developing your own checklist would include product quality, location, services provided, and credit terms.

A serious question that a small business owner must answer is whether to use one supplier or multiple suppliers. It takes time to investigate and analyze several potential suppliers, so many businesses are working toward building long-term relationships with fewer suppliers and vendors. An advantage for buyer and seller

Figure 12.3

VENDOR AUDIT CHECKLIST

The Checklist Softub Uses to Analyze Potential Suppliers Can Serve as an Example for Creating Your Own Checklist.

Source: From "The Smart Vendor-Audit Checklist," by Stephanie Gruner, *Inc.,* April 1995, pp. 93–95. Reprinted with permission of Gruner & Jahr USA.

SOFTUB'S MANAGERS POINT OUT THE VIRTUES OF THEIR VENDOR CHECKLIST

"We want to make sure a supplier's sales manager will work with its manufacturing people to meet our needs. When we hit a problem, the sales manager is our liaison. Does he have the influence to change schedules on the production line? Also, the vendor's ability to turn out a quality product is often reflected by the quality-control manager's experience. We want to know all about that."

"We check how busy vendors are in relation to their size. Say they're using only an eighth of a building's footage. Why is it empty? Did they lose business? The ones we'll end up doing business with can answer easily. And if you notice they don't have the proper space, you'll want to know where they keep their material. Will they have to leave it outside in the rain? They might show you a fancy brochure, and you find they're operating out of five garages."

"Once we went into a place where they said they made circuit boards, but they really specialized in making custom boards in very small volumes. We needed someone who could make thousands a month."

"When we get back to the office, we always check with other customers to ask if the supplier delivers on time or has quality problems."

"We don't have the expertise, the manpower, or the time to look into every procedure. If a large company (or the military) has done an audit on the supplier and given it a rating, it gives us a good idea if the supplier has sound systems and procedures in place. Why not let the big company do the work for us?"

Softub

VENDER SURVEY FORM

REPORTED BY: GARY ANDERSON

PROFILE

COMPANY NAME: ANY BOARD CO.   DATE: 12-14-93

ADDRESS
MAIN ST.
ANYTOWN, USA 12345

TELEPHONE: 800-555-5555
FAX #:
YEARS IN BUSINESS: 14
NUMBER OF EMPLOYEES: 170

SQUARE FOOTAGE OF BUILDING(S): 48,000 USA (60,000 IRELAND)
AGE OF BUILDING(S): 20 YRS
TYPE OF BUILDING(S): CONCRETE TILT-UP, OPEN BEAM CEILING AND IN GOOD CONDITION

PERSONNEL MET

CEO: JOHN G. DOE
PRESIDENT: AS ABOVE
SALES MANAGER: JACK B. DOE
SALES CONTACT: AS ABOVE
Q.C. MANAGER: JANE Q. PUBLIC
PRODUCTION MANAGER: JIM Z. SMITH
OTHERS: PRODUCT/ACCOUNT SPECIALIST

BUSINESS PROFILE

ANNUAL SALES IN DOLLARS: $10 MILLION
MAIN PRODUCT LINE: PRINTED CIRCUIT BOARDS
MINOR PRODUCT LINE: CABLE ASSEMBLIES
MAJOR CUSTOMERS: BENDEX, PACKARD BELL AND GEORGIA PACIFIC.

D & B REQUESTED:

Q.C. DEPARTMENT

EQUIPMENT CALIBRATED: ☑ YES ☐ NO
CALIBRATION TAGS IN PLACE: ☐ ATTACHED
TRAVELERS IN PLACE AT WORK STATIONS: ☑ YES ☐ NO
MILITARY OR ISO RATING: ISO 9000 U.L. F.C.C. C.S.A. F.D.A. T.U.V. (GERMANY) ☑ YES ☐ NO
TOTAL Q.C. EMPLOYEES: 8 + 1 MANAGER ☑ YES ☐ NO
GENERAL IMPRESSION: EXCELLENT, WELL LAID OUT, CALIBRATION EQUIPMENT IN GOOD SHAPE, INSPECTION LAB A-1 CONDITION AND STAFF IS VERY KNOWLEDGEABLE.

PRODUCTION

"Our impression of this supplier was really favorable, and we've learned from it, too. During our audit, we saw illustrated work instructions hanging in front of every station on the line. Each sheet had a checklist of things the operator was supposed to do. We started using similar instructions here. We asked the supplier to send one of its engineers to help us do it."

"We always request a Dun & Bradstreet report unless it's a mom-and-pop shop. Our chief financial officer also looks at the report. We want to know if the company owes more than it's worth. If it does, our finance department will call their finance people and ask more detailed questions."

"This company has the resources to make our product. But the 50% capacity would trigger us to check its financials and talk to its management, because it should be a little busier. We'd also ask how many shifts it's running, how many hours a day it's using certain machines, how many people it has now, and how many people it's had there before."

"If the place is messy and dirty, that's an indicator of the kind of service and product you're going to get. But if we see a board with tools hanging there so that when a tool is in use you see a black silhouette, that's a pretty good sign. It means people aren't wasting time looking for things, and they're probably not going to ship us a product with tie wraps in places where they don't belong."

"One big accident and a company can get sued and be out of business. Are first-aid charts posted on the walls? Are people wearing safety glasses? We want to know what a vendor is doing to prevent accidents. It's also a good indication of its management philosophy."

"International ratings are important because we sell our product overseas. If a vendor is already certified to sell in that country, we feel more confident that its product will pass inspection."

"If a vendor is doing preventive maintenance, there are records we can see. If machines are down, it could cost a company hundreds of thousands of dollars a day. Good companies will monitor their machines religiously."

___ION

CLEANLINESS:	EXCELLENT
ORGANIZED:	EXCELLENT
SQ. FOOTAGE:	43,000 APPROX.
CAPACITY PERCENTAGE OF TOTAL PRODUCTION:	50%

CAPACITY PERCENTAGE OF TOTAL PRODUCTION:

SAFETY DEVICES IN PLACE: ☑ GOOD

GENERAL SAFETY CONDITION: ☑ GOOD

GENERAL EMPLOYEE DEMEANOR: ☑ GOOD

EQUIPMENT CONDITION: ☑ YES

REGULAR MAINTENANCE SCHEDULES MAINTAINED: ☑ YES

DOES THE FACTORY APPEAR BUSY?: ☑ YES

IS THE EQUIPMENT RUNNING?: ☑ YES

ARE THERE STOCK PILES OF RAW MATERIAL?: ☑ YES

ARE THERE STOCK PILES OF FURNISHED GOODS?: ☑ YES

IS THE SHIPPING DOCK BUSY?:

☑ YES   ☐ NO
☐ AVERAGE   ☐ POOR
☐ AVERAGE   ☐ POOR
☐ AVERAGE   ☐ POOR
☐ NO
☑ YES   ☐ NO
☑ YES   ☐ NO
☑ YES   ☐ NO
☑ YES   ☐ NO
☑ YES

SUMMARY

HOW DOES VENDOR INTEND TO MEET OUR REQUIREMENTS?: THEY WILL RAMP UP TO MEET OUR REQUIREMENTS, 3 NEW EMPLOYEES AND 1 NEW FLOW SOLDER MACHINE.

OVERALL IMPRESSION: ☑ EXCELLENT   ☐ GOOD   ☐ AVERAGE   ☐ POOR

SHOULD SOFTUB DO BUSINESS WITH THIS COMPANY?: YES! NOTES: 1) REVIEW D & B WITH FINANCE 2) REVIEW WITH MANAGEMENT AND HAVE THEM VISIT ALSO 3) MAKE FINAL DECISIONS AFTER REFERENCE CHECKS.

VENDOR RATING
PLEASE CIRCLE ONE

1 – SHOULD NOT DO BUSINESS WITH
2 – CAUTION RATING
3 – AVERAGE

4 – GOOD RATING
(5) – WORLD CLASS RATING

WHITE – PURCHASING   CANARY – Q.C.   PINK – OPERATIONS

"The pink copy goes to operations. If the supplier is ISO 9000 certified or doing business with a *Fortune* 500 company, we'll request a copy of its quality manual."

when using a single source comes from a mutual dependence that benefits both companies. Another benefit of using a single source is the savings in paperwork from dealing with only one other business.[12]

An advantage of multiple-source purchasing is the competition between vendors to decrease prices and improve services offered. A lack of this competition can be a disadvantage of single-source purchasing if your one supplier becomes complacent or is unable to provide the goods you need when you need them.

Managing Inventory

Before considering how much inventory is needed, we should investigate the various meanings of the term **inventory**. Depending on the context, there are four common meanings of the term:

1. The monetary value of goods owned by a business at a given time. "We carry a $500,000 inventory."
2. The number of units on hand at a given time. "We have 1,000 yo-yos in inventory."
3. The process of measuring or counting goods. "We inventory the office supplies every month."
4. The detailed list of goods. "I need to look at the inventory on the computer."

> **inventory**
> Goods a business owns for the completion of future sales. Also, the act of counting the goods held in stock.

How Much Inventory Do You Need?

Managing inventory is like performing a balancing act. On one side of the scale, you have to keep an adequate supply of goods on hand. You don't want to shut down operations because you ran out of a needed part, and you don't want to lose a sale because customers find an empty shelf where they expected to find a product. On the other side of the scale, inventory represents money sitting idly on the shelf. And to complicate things further, the more you try to decrease the risk of running out of more obscure items, the more you increase the risk that some items will become obsolete.

Retail Business An important factor in considering the inventory needs of many small retail businesses is the time needed to get fresh inventory in and the cost of reordering. If you can replace inventory quickly at a reasonable price, you can hold down your inventory costs by keeping fewer items yourself.

Retailers should be aware of the *80-20 principle,* also called the *Pareto rule.* According to this rule, about 80 percent of the firm's revenue will come from about 20 percent of the inventory. This principle reminds the small retailer to concentrate on the "vital few" rather than on the "trivial many."

Service Industry Even service businesses that aren't retail based must consider their inventory needs. For instance, a restaurant needs appropriate food and beverages, cleaning fluids, table service equipment, and miscellaneous supplies, such as menus, toothpicks, cash register tape, and check slips. Financial services firms need adequate supplies of paper, pencils, accounting forms, and other types of office supplies. They might even need to have a supply of cash on hand to meet certain customer needs. Security firms need to keep items such as flashlights,

Reality Check

Money on the Shelf

Inventory represents money stacked on a shelf. Until it is sold, it does not generate cash—in fact, it ties up cash. Many small business owners fail to realize the direct impact that inventory has on cash flow. Lose track of your inventory, and your checkbook balance can hit zero in a hurry. Todd Heim, who owns Future Cure, Inc., of North Olmsted, Ohio, realizes how important inventory control is. Future Cure manufactures automotive paint spray booths. A typical booth contains more than 300 parts (some of which are big and expensive), so Heim has to manage inventory effectively.

Heim installed a state-of-the-art automated financial system that included a component to track inventory in detail. That feature allowed him to cut the inventory the company held in stock by 25 percent in a matter of months. That 25 percent decrease was almost exclusively dead stock, so employees spend less time scrambling and digging to find the parts they need. On top of decreasing inventory, better tracking has led to better stock selection, so parts are on hand when needed. Overnight shipping costs have dropped as well.

Before his automated inventory control, Heim would have a year's supply of some parts on hand and be completely out of others. As you see, inventory control means tracking individual items as well as the total.

If you run a retail business, rather than a manufacturing company like Future Cure, you have to be concerned about shrinkage. Alpha Bay, a Salt Lake City software company created a new Adaptive Integrated Retail System (AIRS) to help you prevent future losses. AIRS is an enterprise retail system that collects and allows users to manage inventory, streamline the supply chain, and analyze sales patterns from your desktop PC. A loss-prevention agent tool helps the user recognize, track, monitor, and report on employee theft, customer theft, administrative errors and vendor fraud.

SOURCES: J. Tol Broome, Jr., "The Benefits of Smart Inventory Management," *Nation's Business*, June 1999, 18–19; Leslie Taylor, "Manage Inventory and Prevent Theft—Right from Your Desktop," *Inc.*, 5 January 2007, www.inc.com.

mace or pepper spray, whistles or alarms, and, of course, office materials and supplies in their inventories. Auto repair shops must stock tires, batteries, wrenches, engine oil, grease, cleaning supplies, and other items. There are many other types of service businesses not mentioned here. The point is that small service-business managers should pay just as much attention to inventory control as their counterparts in manufacturing and retail.

Manufacturing Business   Inventory needs for a small manufacturer are different from those of retailers. Manufacturers' needs are based on production rate, lead time required to get in new stock, and the order amount that delivers the optimal economic quantity. Common techniques of manufacturers include just-in-time (JIT) inventory control and materials requirement planning (MRP), considered later in this chapter.

Costs of Carrying Inventory

There are several obvious and not-so-obvious costs of carrying inventory of any type. Financing is the most apparent cost of inventory. Because inventory is an asset, it must be offset by a liability—the cost of borrowing money or diverting your own cash from other uses. If you can sell merchandise and collect payment before you have to pay the supplier that provided you with the merchandise, you can avoid direct finance costs. Because that usually isn't the case, most inventory has a cash cost to the business.

Inventory **shrinkage** represents another cost to your business. Shrinkage can come from theft or spoilage. Employee theft and shoplifting by customers result in inventory that you had to pay for that is not available for sale. *Spoilage* is inventory you have purchased that is not fit for sale because of damage or deterioration.

Obsolescence, in which products become outdated or fall out of fashion, produces the same effect as spoilage: unrecoverable inventory costs caused by merchandise you can't sell. Such merchandise is known as *dead stock*. Obsolescence is a problem for a wide variety of businesses, but especially those in which styles, tastes, or technologies change quickly, such as clothing, automobile parts, and computer parts and accessories. You may be able to salvage some money from inventory that is obsolete (or on its way) through price reductions or recycling, but dead stock is still a major cost.

Holding costs are what you incur for keeping extra goods on hand—warehouse building expenses (either purchase and upkeep or rent), added utilities, insurance, and taxes on the building. In addition, there are expenses such as insurance on the value of the inventory and taxes on the inventory. Merchandise that spoils, becomes obsolete, depreciates, or is pilfered is considered part of the holding costs. Finally, you have interest expenses if you borrow money to pay for the goods.

Ordering costs are the expenses you incur in either ordering or producing inventory. Ordering costs tend to be fixed, meaning that they cost about the same no matter what quantity of goods you order. They include all the clerical expenses of preparing purchase orders, processing orders and invoices, analyzing vendors, and receiving and handling incoming products.

If holding costs were your only inventory expense, you would want to order as few items at a time as possible to minimize your cost of holding on to inventory. Ordering one part at a time would cut down on your storage expenses, but think of the cost in time, paper, and people needed to process that many order forms and receive goods one at a time; your total costs would go through the roof. Likewise, if ordering costs were your only inventory expense, you would want to send for as many goods as possible at one time to minimize your costs of ordering. Although your clerical needs would be cut by making out just one order, think of the size of the storage facility you would need and the cash-flow problems created by having all your money tied up in inventory.

In the real world, every business incurs both holding and ordering costs. Striving to maintain a balance between them is part of the difficult job of controlling inventory.

> " Inventory, like cash flow, can make or break your business. Because you may invest as much as 80 percent of your company's capital in inventory, you must manage it wisely. "

shrinkage	The loss of goods held in inventory due to theft or spoilage.
obsolescence	When products become outdated or fall out of fashion.
holding costs	Expenses related to keeping inventory on hand.
ordering costs	Expenses related to procuring inventory.

Controlling Inventory

Because inventory is such a significant expense, most businesses look carefully for ways to determine the appropriate levels of control for their inventory. *Inventory control* is the process of establishing and maintaining the supply of goods you

Figure 12.4

INVENTORY CYCLES

An Inventory Cycle Lasts from the Time the Goods Are Used or Sold Until They Are Replenished. The Reorder Point Indicates When You Need to Order Goods. The Reorder Quantity Is How Many Items You Wish to Put Back in Stock.

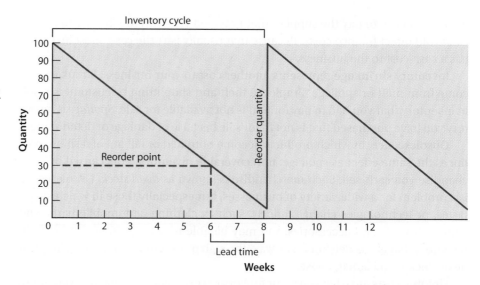

need to keep on hand. It is important because inventory represents about 25 percent of a manufacturing firm's capital and as much as 80 percent of a retailer's capital. Many techniques are used to control inventory, with the best choice depending on the type of business and the kind of inventory. Several techniques are described in this section.

Reorder Point and Quantity

Controlling your inventory begins with determining when you need to restock inventory and how much you need to reorder. These considerations are called the *reorder point* and the *reorder quantity,* respectively. The time period that begins when an item is at its highest desired stocking level, continues as the item is used or sold, and ends when it is replenished is called an **inventory cycle**.

Suppose you are a retailer who sells a certain product—Elvis Presley statuettes—with an average weekly demand of 10 units (see Figure 12.4). The **lead time** (time from order placement until delivery) is three weeks. You would need to reorder when inventory drops to 30 Elvises so that you don't completely run out before the ordered items arrive. The reorder quantity would be 100 statuettes, so you would have a 10-week supply of goods on hand at your highest desired stocking level.

Visual Control

Many small businesses operate without a formal or complex inventory control system. If you run a one- or two-person business that sells a relatively narrow selection of items, *visual control* may be the only inventory system you need. Visual inventory control means that you look at the goods you have on hand and reorder when you appear to be running low on items. It depends on your being in the business during most business hours and on your knowing the usage rate and reorder time needed.

Economic Order Quantity

Economic order quantity (EOQ) is a traditional method of controlling inventory that minimizes total inventory costs by balancing annual ordering costs with

inventory cycle
The period of time from the point when inventory is at its highest until it is replenished.

lead time
The period of time from order placement until the goods are received.

economic order quantity (EOQ)
A traditional method of controlling inventory that minimizes total inventory costs by balancing annual ordering costs with annual holding costs for an item.

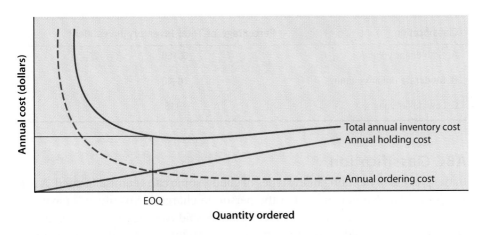

Figure 12.5
ECONOMIC ORDER QUANTITY

*Economic Order Quantity (EOQ)
Is a Way to Minimize Total
Inventory Expenses by Balancing
Holding Costs and Ordering
Costs.*

annual holding costs for an item. EOQ balances these two types of costs to minimize your total costs (see Figure 12.5).

Several models exist for the EOQ approach that go beyond the scope of this
book, so in practice you simply need to find a model that fits the cost structure of
your business and use it. The basic model of EOQ makes three assumptions:

1. You can't take advantage of volume discounts.

2. You can accurately predict annual demand.

3. Your average inventory level is equal to your maximum level minus your
   minimum level divided by 2.

If your business meets these assumptions, you can use the following formula:

$$EOQ = \sqrt{\frac{2DO}{C}}$$

where

   D = annual demand for the product (in units)

   O = average ordering cost for the product (in dollars per year)

   C = average holding cost for one of the products (in dollars per year)

To illustrate, imagine a sporting goods store that meets the three assumptions
stated previously. This store usually sells 12,000 pairs of hiking boots per year. Its
ordering costs are $10 per order. The holding costs run $0.96 per pair of boots per
year. The EOQ for hiking boots for this store would be 500.

$$EOQ = \sqrt{\frac{2 \times 12{,}000 \times 10}{0.96}}$$
$$= 500$$

This result tells us that to minimize total inventory costs and balance ordering
and holding costs, the sporting goods store would need to order 500 pairs of hiking boots at a time. In selling 12,000 pairs of boots and ordering 500 pairs each
time, the store would need to order hiking boots 24 times per year.

$$\text{Orders per year} = \frac{D}{EOQ}$$

$$24 = \frac{12{,}000}{500}$$

Table 12.1

ABC INVENTORY INVESTMENT CLASSIFICATION

Classification	Percentage of Total Inventory Investment
A. High dollar volume	60–80
B. Moderate dollar volume	10–40
C. Low dollar volume	5–15

ABC Classification

ABC classification
An inventory control system that classifies items based on the total dollar volume of sales each generates.

In the process of handling many types of goods, some can get misallocated. A reason for misallocation can be that the person in charge of inventory is paying as much attention to an item that costs $5 and is sold twice a year as to items that cost $500 and are sold many times per month. An inventory system that helps to allocate more appropriate time and attention to items is **ABC classification**. This system classifies items based on the total dollar volume of sales each generates. To calculate the total dollar volume, multiply the cost of an item by the number of units sold annually. The greater the weighted dollar volume generated by an item, the more attention you will want to give it in your inventory control.

Items that generate high dollar volume will be classified in the A category and will receive the highest priority. Proportionately less attention will be given to the moderate-dollar-volume goods in the B category, and low-dollar-volume items in the C category. A rule of thumb for percentage allocation for each group is shown in Table 12.1. The use of a computer database in your inventory control makes monitoring your ABC classification system relatively quick and easy to adjust if necessary.

Electronic Data Interchange

electronic data interchange (EDI)
The computerized application-to-application exchange to track items within a business in a standard data format.

perpetual inventory system
An inventory system that indicates how many units of an item are on hand at any given time.

Electronic data interchange (EDI) is an electronic means of inventory control. It is made possible through the use of UPC (Universal Product Code) *bar codes,* the black-and-white parallel bars on packaged goods. When goods are scanned into your inventory system by employees receiving them in a shipment or ringing them up as a sale at the cash register, the transactions are updated in the company's computer inventory program. By using this technology, you can track sales, determine what needs to be ordered, and transmit the inventory data to your suppliers through the same EDI system. EDI is one type of **perpetual inventory system**, which allows you to know how many items you have in stock at any given time.

There are a number of software programs you can use to help you better control your inventory. Peachtree Complete Accounting and Peachtree Accounting (Peachtree Software) are particularly good programs for tracking inventories and accounts receivable. You can also customize these packages to your unique inventory needs. Intuit's QuickBooks Pro is another popular software package that you can use to track inventory. These software packages are relatively inexpensive, ranging from $99 to $199. You might decide to invest a little more in a more extensive software/hardware package called SellWise from CAP Automation (www.capauto.com). This program (list price of about $1,500) handles sales, tracks customers, produces reports, orders, receives, controls inventory, and creates tags (bar codes). This package is particularly good for small retail businesses.

One of the latest software programs is called Big Business (www.bigsoftware.com); list price about $350 for a single user or $750 for multiple users on a network version). This program is ideal for many different small business applications because it integrates four critical business functions: sales, marketing, inventory, and finance. Its creators claim that it is perfect for individuals who have limited accounting knowledge. This program may be just the ticket for helping you control your inventory.

Regardless of the specific software that you choose to help you manage your inventory, be sure to select a package that you'll actually *use*. After all, this is one area of your business that you *can* control, so why not be effective and efficient at it?

Major retailers and packaged-goods companies such as Wal-Mart, Ace Hardware, Lowe's, and Target are pushing hard to clean up their product data and change their inventory processes to make *UCCnet* work. UCCnet is a nonprofit unit of the Uniform Code Council standards organization that seeks to establish a global online registry of product information. Manufacturers and retailers submit their product information and descriptions and share the data with their information technology departments. Then all UCCnet members (currently about 3,500 companies) can easily share consistent product data to drive down supply-chain costs, speed new product launches, maintain more accurate inventory data, and reduce inventory errors.[13]

For the UCCnet system to work, suppliers need to use *radio-frequency identification (RFID)* tags. These RFID tags could eventually make UPC bar codes obsolete. The integrated circuit in each tag sends information about an item via radio waves. Supermarket checkout could be eliminated completely, for example, as RFID scanners detect the items you have selected and deduct their costs from your credit card.[14]

How does RFID affect small business? First, two small companies, Matrics and Zebra Technologies, actually make the tags (remember that symbiotic relationship?). Second, Wal-Mart, the world's largest retailer, has demanded that its top 100 suppliers implement the technology with smaller suppliers to follow.[15] If your small business deals in consumer packaged goods, do you think it won't eventually have to comply with the new standard?

Just-in-Time

An inventory management system based upon the philosophy that well-run manufacturing plants do not require the stockpiling of parts and components is called **just-in-time (JIT)**. The basic idea underlying JIT is to reduce order sizes and to time orders so that goods arrive as close to when they are actually needed as possible. The intent is to minimize a business's dependence on inventory and cut the costs of moving and storing goods. JIT is used more frequently by producers than by retailers.

There are notable differences between a JIT approach and a more traditional approach (which you could think of as "just-in-case"). Table 12.2 highlights some of these differences.[16]

JIT works best in situations that allow accurate forecasting of both demand and production. Because JIT is based on actual rather than projected demand,

> *just-in-time (JIT)*
> A Japanese approach to inventory management that aims to reduce order sizes and to time orders so that goods arrive as close to when they are needed as possible.

Table 12.2

JIT AND TRADITIONAL
INVENTORY COMPARISON

JIT Inventory	Traditional Inventory
Small orders and frequent deliveries	Large orders and infrequent deliveries
Single-source supplier for a given part with a long-term contract	Multiple sources of suppliers for the same part with partial or short-term contracts
Suppliers expected to deliver product quality, delivery performance, and price; no rejects acceptable	Suppliers expected to deliver an acceptable level of product quality, delivery performance, and price
Objective of bidding is to secure the highest-quality product through a long-term contract	Objective of bidding is to find the lowest possible price
Less emphasis on paperwork	Requires more time and formal paperwork
Delivery time and quantity can be changed with direct communication	Changes in delivery time and quantity require new purchase orders

a small business may have to be in operation for a while before it can take advantage of this system, as a company called Lifeline Systems learned. When Lifeline first began making its voice-activated personal response devices, which allow people to call for help in an emergency, production lead time was 30 days from order to shipment. After the company adopted JIT, (total quality management (TQM), and manufacturing resource planning II (MRPII), which will be discussed shortly , that figure decreased to four days. As John Giannetto, corporate manager of materials and purchasing, stated, "What comes in the back door [in parts and materials] is gone four days after it gets here."[17] Keeping in line with JIT philosophies, Lifeline has cut the number of its suppliers from 300 to 75, 85 percent of which offer service and quality at a level that makes inspection unnecessary.

One caveat of JIT is that everyone involved *must* be able to do what they say they can, when they say they can do it. If you are operating with enough inventory to support one day's production, which is common with JIT, a single unexpected event—a trucking strike, a breakdown, or a shortage—can shut down your entire operation. Just-about-in-time or almost-in-time won't cut it.

Materials Requirements Planning

materials requirements planning (MRP)
Inventory control system that depends on computers to coordinate product orders, raw materials in stock, and the sequence of production.

Another new inventory control method for producers is **materials requirements planning (MRP),** which depends on computers to coordinate product orders, raw materials in stock, and the sequence of production. A master schedule ensures that goods are available at the time they are needed in the production cycle.

Whereas JIT is a *pull system,* based on the "pull" of actual customer demand, MRP is a *push system,* relying on the "push" of estimated demand. MRP is an inventory management technique that is appropriate when demand for some materials depends on the demand for others. For example, if your business makes customized mountain bikes, and you anticipate sales of 1,000 bikes next month, you know how many components you will need. You need 1,000 frames, 2,000 pedals, 4,000 wheel nuts, and so on. The demand for each of these items depends on the demand for bikes. Rather than keep all of those supplies in stock, as with EOQ, MRP allows you to determine the number of components and subassemblies needed and coordinate their ordering and delivery.

A more advanced control system that has evolved from MRP is *manufacturing resource planning II (MRPII),* which coordinates inventory management with all other functions of a business, such as marketing, accounting, financial planning, cash flow, and engineering. Because it is more complex and expensive, it is used mainly in large businesses. It is worth noting here, however, because techniques and processes used in big business often find their way into small businesses after a period of time.

Summary

• The marketing mix

The marketing mix consists of the variables that you can control in bringing your product or service to your target market. Also referred to as the *Four Ps,* it includes the *product* (including goods and services) that your target market wants or needs; the *place,* or the channels of distribution you choose to use, as well as the location and layout of your small business; the *price* that makes your product attractive and still allows you to make a profit; and the methods of *promotion* you use to communicate with your target market.

• The different forms a product can take and the five levels of product satisfaction

Products are tangible goods, intangible services, or a combination of these. The five levels of product satisfaction are the core benefit, the generic product, the expected product, the augmented product, and the potential product. The core benefit represents the value a customer gets from a product. The generic product is the simplest components from which a product is made. The expected product represents the characteristics that customers expect to find in a product. The augmented product contains the characteristics of a product that are over and above what customers expect to find. The potential product represents future product augmentations and developments.

• The importance of purchasing and its procedures

Purchasing is an important part of a small business because the goods or raw materials that you bring into your business become the products you will in turn have available to sell to your customers. A savings gained from the cost of purchased items has a larger effect on your profit level than an increase in sales revenue.

• Considerations for selecting suppliers

Small manufacturers must first decide whether to make the parts needed in their production or to purchase components from another business. Retailers must decide whether to hire personnel or to outsource needed services. Both of these are examples of the make-or-buy decision. Factors such as product quality, location of supplier, services that suppliers offer, and credit terms available need to be considered when selecting suppliers.

• How to determine inventory needs

If your small business requires inventory, you must maintain a balance between having enough goods on hand to prevent lost sales due to items being out of stock and having inventory dollars lying idle on a shelf. Retailers and manufacturers need to heed the

Pareto rule by paying attention to the "vital few" rather than the "trivial many" items in inventory. Shrinkage, obsolescence, holding costs, and ordering costs are factors to be considered in determining the inventory needs of your business.

- **Procedures for different types of inventory control**

To control your inventory, you must begin by determining your reorder point (when you need to reorder) and your reorder quantity (how much you need to reorder). Many small businesses depend on visual control to maintain inventory. Economic order quantity, ABC classification, electronic data interchange, just-in-time, and materials requirements planning are common tools for controlling inventory.

Questions for Review and Discussion

1. What factors should be considered when purchasing for a small business?

2. Explain how the Pareto rule is important to a small business owner.

3. How can shrinkage affect an inventory system?

4. Assume that you are the owner of the sporting goods store used in the example of EOQ inventory control on page 331. You typically sell 14,500 sweatshirts per year. Your ordering costs are $10 per order. Holding costs are $0.60 per sweatshirt per year. What is your EOQ for sweatshirts? How many sweatshirt orders would you place per year?

5. When would an ABC classification inventory system be appropriate?

6. Aside from reducing inventory levels, what does the JIT philosophy promote?

7. What is the difference between a pull system and a push system of inventory control?

8. Consider the make-or-buy decision. Give three examples of situations in which a business should make, rather than buy. Give three examples of situations in which a business should buy, rather than make.

Questions For Critical Thinking

1. Many small businesses are built around one product. What risks does this approach impose? How can small business owners minimize those risks? How can a small business develop new products?

2. Purchasing products or materials is obviously an important part of running a small business.

What are the pros and cons of developing a relationship with a single vendor from which to purchase most of your products versus using multiple vendors and not depending on just one other company?

Experience This . . .

Arrange with your instructor for your class to visit a local business (preferably a larger retail store, but still a small business or some type of manufacturing business that uses multiple materials or components). Check out its inventory system. How are items brought in (physically and paperworkwise)? How is inventory stored and tracked? How are vendors selected and evaluated? How are products chosen for the business to sell?

What Would You Do?

Costume Specialists, Inc.

Storybook characters like Madeline, Babar the Elephant, and even Stinky Cheese Man come alive under the watchful eye of Wendy Goldstein of Columbus, Ohio. Her company, Costume Specialists, fashions the complicated costumes for these characters from scratch and sells the creations to book publishers and bookstore chains. Each costume takes about 60 to 80 hours of artistic effort and costs up to $3,000 in materials and labor to produce. Goldstein's business brings in $600,000 annually.

Catch the Wave

Catch the Wave is a marketing information and graphics design firm located in Minneapolis. The company designs web pages for clients wanting to get on the Internet. Its 20 employees have varied experience in design, advertising, writing, photography, and computer graphics. Prices charged to clients depend on the sophistication and interactivity desired for their web sites. The popularity of the Internet and World Wide Web has sent the company's annual revenues soaring to $7 million. This figure is expected to continue to rise, as more and more clients want to "catch the wave."

Margaritaville Store

Of course, it has to be in Key West! Where else would you expect to find Jimmy Buffett's 400-square-foot shop, Margaritaville Store? And what would you expect to find there except T-shirts and other beach paraphernalia? The first store did so well that Buffett expanded the retail operation and even added a café in New Orleans. Total annual sales revenues for Jimmy Buffett's empire exceed $50 million. That's a lot of CDs, tapes, books, T-shirts, trinkets, and food—even in Margaritaville!

Questions

1. Select one of the companies described and write a short paper (no more than two pages) about the type of inventory control techniques that the business should use. Explain what would be an appropriate number of suppliers for this company and why you chose this number.

2. Effective inventory management also means being ready to cope with problems. Divide into groups based on the companies you selected in Question 1, and discuss how you could design an inventory system that would adapt to "shocks" like the ones described below.

Costume Specialists, Inc.

Your longtime supplier of flexible costume mouthpieces has just been purchased by a Japanese conglomerate that has strict purchasing guidelines and wants you to use EDI.

Catch the Wave

You were hoping it would never happen, but now it has. A computer virus has wiped out all but two of your firm's computers.

Margaritaville Store

Trouble in paradise comes in the form of hurricanes. Even though you've been lucky so far, the last hurricane season came a little too close for comfort.

CHAPTER CLOSING CASE

KEEPING THE BUSINESS SOCIAL

You couldn't blame Ben and Mena Trott for feeling satisfied, even a little smug. The couple's San Francisco software company, Six Apart, had helped fuel one of the Internet's hottest trends—blogging. And it had not one, but two hit products. Movable Type, designed for corporate users, boasted clients like Boeing (NYSE:BA) and General Motors (NYSE:GM). TypePad was a leading product for personal bloggers. By mid-2005, Six Apart had raised some $10 million in venture capital and had more than 100 employees.

But the Trotts were not satisfied. In fact, they were worried. Blogging was still big, but Six Apart was facing tough new rivals, most notably Wordpress, a popular new open-source product that could be downloaded free of charge. Meanwhile, the tech world seemed less interested in blogging than in social networking. Ventures like MySpace and Facebook were growing at astounding rates, and new sites were being showered with venture capital. The Trotts had a promising social networking idea of their own and were eager to diversify. But given the speed at which the market was moving, they didn't have much time.

The pair, high school sweethearts from Petaluma, California, scarcely could have imagined facing such issues when they launched Six Apart in October 2001. It was the early days of blogging, and Mena was enthralled. She wrote a blog called Dollarshort, in which she mused about her childhood and daily life, and started gaining new readers every day. Many of those readers were bloggers themselves, and both Mena and Ben, a programmer, could sense a trend emerging. They also were frustrated by the lack of good software for bloggers. So they built their own—naming it Movable Type, after Gutenberg's printing press. Working out of their apartment, they created a website and began selling the software as a download. "Almost 200 people downloaded it in the first hour," Ben says. "We were saying, 'This is real.'"

The trend indeed took off. By November 2005 some 41.5 million Americans were reading blogs every day, according to ComScore Media Metrix (the number has since swelled to 62.5 million), and Six Apart was a real company. Movable Type was sold as a basic software license; it's now priced at $150 for a five-seat annual license. TypePad, hosted over the Web and designed for less technically adept users, goes for $50 per user per year. The numbers added up fast. The company also acquired several small companies, including LiveJournal, a social networking site based in Portland, Oregon.

But the Trotts and their colleagues saw big changes happening. Wordpress was being downloaded at a rate of about 85,000 times a month, threatening Six Apart's market share, and other open-source rivals were emerging as well. In the age of free software, selling licenses and subscriptions seemed out of date. Meanwhile, everyone was buzzing about social networking—especially after News Corporation's $580 million purchase of MySpace.

Some executives at Six Apart wanted in on the action. The question was how to proceed. The company could put more money and manpower into LiveJournal. But though the site had nearly 12 million users, more than 75 percent of them were younger than 26—roughly the same demographic as Facebook, which has nearly 14 million users, and MySpace, which has more than 100 million. Did Six Apart, which had never built a community-oriented site of its own, really want to plunge scarce resources into competing against those two giants?

Executives at the company began analyzing the market. The point of networking sites, it seemed, was to amass as wide a network of "friends" as rapidly as possible. But aside from making users feel popular, what did those sites really offer, asked Brad Fitzpatrick, founder of LiveJournal and now Six Apart's chief architect. "It's like, 'Okay, I've declared my friends. What next?'" Why not enhance the experience by adding new functions, such as photo sharing, e-commerce, and, yes, blogging?

Just as important, the leading networking sites had proved profoundly alienating to adults. A huge audience of Web users was essentially excluded from the social networking craze, argued Barak Berkowitz, who had joined Six Apart as CEO in 2004. He suggested a social network for grownups, one that was geared toward helping users stay in touch with a smaller group of family, friends, and neighbors. It would capitalize on Six Apart's blogging expertise; indeed, it would be more like a blog network than a social network. That notion was especially appealing to Mena, who couldn't help but think about her own mother, Clare Grabowski, a 49-year-old administrative assistant in North Carolina. Why couldn't Clare have a social networking site of her own? And because it was aimed at a new, more mature market, the new site could comfortably coexist with LiveJournal.

Of course, launching the social networking site, dubbed Vox, would mean supporting four different products, each with its own revenue model. Some at the company wondered if Six Apart could handle it all. Nonetheless, the idea began to gain traction.

But Six Apart had to move fast. Scores of start-ups were jumping in with niche products of their own. What's more, Six Apart had just received an invitation to make a presentation at the upcoming Demo conference, to be held in Scottsdale, Arizona, in September 2005. For years the gathering had been the hottest place for a splashy new product launch; Ask Jeeves, TiVo, and PalmPilot all had made their debuts there. Six Apart already had been hard at work on a new version of TypePad. The developers would have to shift gears to work on the new product to get it ready for the conference—which was now less than a month away.

Was Six Apart ready to launch its own Social Networks?

SOURCE: From Patrick Cliff, "Six Apart Feared It Was Missing Out on the Next Big Thing—Social Networks," *Inc.*, March 2007, 61–64. Copyright © 2007 Mansueto Ventures LLC, publisher of Inc. Magazine, New York, NY 10017. Reprinted with permission.

Test Prepper

college.hmco.com/pic/hatten4e

You've read the chapter, studied the key terms, and the exam is any day now. Think you're ready to ace it? Take this sample test to gauge your comprehension of chapter material. You can check your answers at the back of the book. Want more test questions? Visit the student website at college.hmco.com/pic/hatten4e and take the ACE and AEE+ quizzes for more practice.

Matching

_____ 1. variables that a business owner can control in bringing goods to consumers

_____ 2. fees charged by grocery stores to put new products on their shelves

_____ 3. changing the perception that customers have of your product instead of changing the product

_____ 4. additions made to a product over and above the expected level

_____ 5. bundle of satisfaction that people receive in exchange for money

_____ 6. choice of whether to purchase parts or to produce them

_____ 7. the legal contract between buyer and seller

_____ 8. the loss of goods in inventory due to theft or spoilage

_____ 9. expenses related to procuring inventory

_____10. inventory system that shows the number of units on hand at any given time

a. marketing mix

b. repositioning

c. make-or-buy decision

d. obsolescence

e. augmented product

f. slotting fees

g. product

h. purchase order

i. holding costs

j. shrinkage

k. ordering costs

l. perpetual inventory system

m. ABC classification system

Multiple Choice

1. The last five seconds of marketing is
   a. advertising
   b. inventory control
   c. packaging
   d. closing

2. Fees charged by grocery retailers to ensure that products are placed on shelves are called
   a. slotting fees
   b. royalties
   c. ransom
   d. popping fees

3. Which of the following was *not* cited as a criterion defining a product's core competency?
   a. be applicable across a range of products
   b. be difficult for competitors to duplicate
   c. provide a fundamental benefit to customers
   d. produce huge cash flow to the business

4. Producing products under another company's name is called
   a. licensing
   b. private-label manufacturing
   c. franchising
   d. moonlighting

5. Jody runs a one-person business in which she hand-makes only three items. She keeps about two weeks' worth of items in inventory at any given time. Which type of inventory control should Jody use?
   a. EOQ
   b. visual control
   c. EDI
   d. MRP

Small Business Marketing: Place

Buck Knives is a three-generation family business started by a blacksmith apprentice named Hoyt Buck, who, in 1902, was tired of sharpening hoes and decided that making blades would be more interesting. He experimented for years until he developed a technique for tempering steel that made knife blades so sharp and hard that they would cut bolts. Hoyt and his oldest son, Al, formed H.H. Buck & Son Lifetime Knives in 1947, now Buck Knives. In 1964 Buck introduced the Folding Hunter model, which became the best-selling outdoor knife in America.

Buck grew into a $33 million business with 260 employees making more than a million knives a year under Hoyt's grandson, C.J. Buck Knives was an American legend, but in the late 1990s it was having some problems also: Profit margins had been gutted by Asian competitors, leaving the company short on cash; energy costs (key in tempering blades) were soaring; and labor costs in Southern California were through the roof. C.J. says, "We were losing money and there was no end in sight."

After reading this chapter, you should be able to:

- Describe small business distribution and explain how "efficiencies" affect channels of distribution.

- Explain how the location of your business can provide a competitive advantage.

- List factors in selecting a state in which to locate your business.

- List factors in selecting a city in which to locate your business.

- Discuss the central issues in choosing a particular site within a city.

- Compare the three basic types of locations.

- Explain the types of layout you can choose.

- Present the circumstances under which leasing, buying, or building is an appropriate choice.

At the Buck Knives Factory in Post Falls, Idaho, Just Outside Coeur d'Alene, Chairman Chuck Buck and CEO C.J. Buck Pose with a Display Case of Knives.

Energy deregulation in the spring of 2000 sent electricity prices bouncing from 12 cents per kilowatt-hour to 42 cents as speculators tried to manipulate the market. Workers' compensation, labor costs, and taxes were skyrocketing in California. C.J. explains, "Through no fault of what you've done or what you're doing, your workers'-comp premium is going to go from $250,000 a year to $400,000 to $650,000 over a three-year period. That's huge, and it's completely out of your control. You aren't guilty of bad practices, but the cost just goes up and up. Now, that's a scary thing." Something had to give. It occurred to C.J. that that "something" might be the unthinkable–move the company.

"It's a tough decision–especially for family-owned companies," he says. "Uprooting a company is a tough, tough thing to go through. You're uprooting families, uprooting kids." He struggled with the decision until September 11, 2001. Sales plunged to the point that 40 employees had to be laid off and C.J. took a 30 percent pay cut. He realized that moving a company is like having an operation to save your life–you have to move *before* it's too late.

Buck Knives started shopping for new locations, primarily in the Pacific Northwest, using a wish list of cheap electricity, good business climate, low taxes, plentiful labor supply, good transportation connections via highway, rail, and air–and high quality of life because he was moving people as well a business. In late 2001 Buck executives narrowed the search down to Post Falls, Idaho, population 21,400, and located just outside Coeur d'Alene.

Making the final decisions and preparations for the move was a long and grueling process. Selling the factory in El Cajon, California, finding just the right site in Post Falls, deciding how many employees to relocate (the final number was 75; 200 were given a year's notice and provided severance and retraining packages), and hundreds of other decisions took time. The groundbreaking ceremony for Buck's new factory happened in June 2004–over a year later than C.J. wanted. The first Buck knife produced in Idaho came off the line in February 2005. It was a Folding Hunter, the original source of Buck fame.

Despite all the hassle factors, the 1,500-mile move was worth it for Buck. C.J. is thrilled with the new surroundings. "It's delivered everything we hoped. Electric bills are roughly 30 percent what they would have been if Buck had stayed in California; workers' comp 10 percent; and labor costs 75 percent." The once struggling company is now thriving due to the transplant.

SOURCES: Chris Lydgate, "The Buck Stopped..." *Inc.*, May 2006, 86–95; Corinne Kator, "Thriving on Lean," *Modern Materials Handling*, February 2007, 33-34; "Idaho Beckons a Golden State Warrior," *Business Week Online*, November 24, 2003, www.businessweek.com.

Small Business Distribution

In this chapter, we will explore the role of product distribution, business location, and layout of your small business. In marketing terms, these functions are categorized as *place*. Of the *Four Ps* of the marketing mix, place, or *distribution*, is especially significant for your small business because an effective distribution system can make or save a small business as much money as a hot advertising campaign can generate. In fact, distribution is about the last real bastion for cost savings—as techniques for tracking and individualizing promotion improve, as manufacturing becomes more and more efficient, and as employee productivity rises. Your choice of **distribution channel** is especially important when entering international markets, where you are not likely to have as many options for distribution as in the U.S. market.

In marketing, *distribution* has two meanings: the physical transportation of products from one place to the next, and the relationships between intermediaries who move the products—otherwise called the *channels of distribution*. There are two types of distribution channels: direct and indirect (see Figure 13.1). With a **direct channel**, products and services go directly from the producer to the consumer. Buying sweet potatoes and corn at a farmer's market, or a pair of sandals directly from the artisan who made them, are examples of sales through a direct channel. Other examples are buying seconds and overruns from factory outlets or through catalog sales managed by the manufacturer.

Indirect channels are so called because the products pass through various intermediaries before reaching the consumer. Small businesses that use more

> *distribution channel*
> The series of intermediaries a product passes through when going from producer to consumer.

> *direct channel*
> A distribution channel in which products and services go directly from the producer to the consumer.

> *indirect channels*
> A distribution channel in which the products pass through various intermediaries before reaching the consumer.

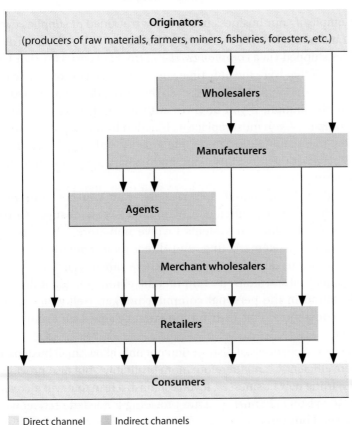

CONSUMER PRODUCTS

Figure 13.1
CHANNELS OF DISTRIBUTION

Channels of Distribution Are Systems Through Which Products Flow from Producers to Consumers.

dual distribution
The use of two or more channels to distribute the same product to the same target market.

agents
An intermediary who brings buyers and sellers together and facilitates the exchange.

brokers
An intermediary who represents clients who buy or sell specialized goods or seasonal products.

wholesalers
An intermediary who buys products in bulk from producers and resells them to other wholesalers or to retailers.

retailers
An intermediary who sells products to the ultimate consumer.

than one channel (such as a swimsuit producer selling to an intermediary like a retail chain and directly to consumers via catalog sales) are said to use **dual distribution.**

Intermediaries include agents, brokers, wholesalers, and retailers.

Agents bring buyers and sellers together and facilitate the exchange. They may be called *manufacturer's agents, selling agents,* or *sales representatives.*

Brokers represent clients who buy or sell specialized goods or seasonal products. Neither brokers nor agents take title to the goods sold.

Wholesalers buy products in bulk from producers and then resell them to other wholesalers or to retailers. Wholesalers take title to goods and usually take possession.

Retailers sell products to the ultimate consumer. Retailers take title and possession of the goods they distribute.

The key word for evaluating a channel of distribution is *efficiency*—getting products to target markets in the fastest, least expensive way possible. Did you realize that about three-fourths of the money spent on food goes to distribution?

Does adding intermediaries to the channel of distribution increase the cost of getting the product to the consumer? Or does "doing away with the middleman" always mean savings to consumers? Although the latter has become a marketing cliché, it is not always true. Adding intermediaries can *decrease* the price to the consumer if each intermediary increases the efficiency of the channel. You can do away with the middleman, but you can't replace his function. Someone still has to do the job.

For example, if your business needs half a truckload of supplies every month from your main supplier 400 miles away, should you buy your own truck or have the supplies shipped via a *common carrier* (a trucking company that hauls products for hire)? If that were the only time you needed a truck, of course it would be cheaper to have the supplies shipped, even though it adds an intermediary to your channel of distribution. If you do away with the middleman—in this case, the trucking company—you must replace its function by buying your own truck, paying a driver, maintaining the vehicle, filing paperwork, and so on. The question here is not *whether* the functions of an intermediary are performed; the question is *who* performs them.

You need to be prepared to revise the way you get your products to consumers because the efficiency of channels can change. Currently the fastest-growing distribution systems involve non-store marketing, including vending machines, telemarketing, and direct mail. Sometimes a break from the industry norm can create a competitive advantage for your business. When Michael Dell started Dell Computer, he eliminated all of the usual intermediaries found in the personal computer market. Dell advertised and sold directly to consumers. This distribution strategy shot Dell Computer into the *Fortune* 500.

Efficiencies in channels of distribution not only allow small businesses to offer goods more efficiently (and therefore more profitably), but also provide opportunities for starting new businesses. If you establish a firm that will increase the efficiency of an existing channel, you are providing a needed service, which is the basis for a good business.

Profile in Entrepreneurship
Advantage by Location

Pack St. Clair is the founder of Cobalt Boats, a maker of 20- to 36-foot runabouts that cost from $30,000 to $300,000. With their sleek lines and flowing power humps, Cobalts are widely admired as the Steinways of the runabout boat class.

If you want to see your boat as it is being made, what would you expect to drive by? Probably not miles of wheat fields. Cobalts are made as far from ocean tide as geographically possible—in Neodesha, Kansas, population 2,800. This is St. Clair's and Cobalt's home. It takes great confidence to build world-class boats so far from navigable water (the nearest decent-size lake is two hours away in Oklahoma). St. Clair built his competitive advantage based on the people wearing cowboy boots and big belt buckles who work in his company. At a recent company meeting, Pack's son and company president Paxson asked, "How many of you were raised on a farm, currently live on a farm, or still work some land or care for some animals?"

At least 60 percent of the men and women held up their hands.

Pack moved to Neodesha in 1970 due to economic incentives offered when Standard Oil vacated a large refinery. Cobalt moved into the buildings, but that wasn't the best part of the deal. It didn't take long for St. Clair to realize what he had tapped into: a group of self-reliant farmers with a powerful work ethic, can-do ingenuity, and—most importantly—an owner's mindset.

People who assert that high labor costs eliminate the possibility of attaining world-class manufacturing within the borders of the United States need to look toward the country's midsection. Rural living is different than city living. The younger St. Clair asks, "How often do company owners lament, 'If only I could get my people to think like me, think like an owner'? Farmers are owners of their own businesses; they understand that things have to get done and get done right or you'll pay for it later."

Surprising locations can yield surprising advantages.

SOURCE: John Grossmann, "Location, Location, Location," *Inc.,* August 2004, 82–86.

Location for the Long Run

Selecting a location for your business is one of the most important decisions you will make as a small business owner. Although not every business depends on foot traffic for its customers, just about any business can pick a poor location for one reason or another. For example, retail businesses need to be easily accessible to their consumers. A company that produces concrete blocks for construction must be located in an area that frequently uses that type of building material, if it is to keep down transportation costs. Manufacturing businesses need to consider locating near their workers, sources of raw materials, and transportation outlets.

People do not tend to go out of their way to find a business. Although Ralph Waldo Emerson had great literary success when he wrote, "If a man can make a better mousetrap than his neighbor, though he builds his house in the woods, the world will make a beaten path to his door," it's best not to take his advice literally when selecting a location for your business.

Figure 13.2

IDENTIFICATION OF REGIONAL
AND LOCAL MARKETS

*Choosing the Right Location for
Your Business May Be a Process
of Narrowing Down the Region,
State, City, and Neighborhood
That Are Right for You.*

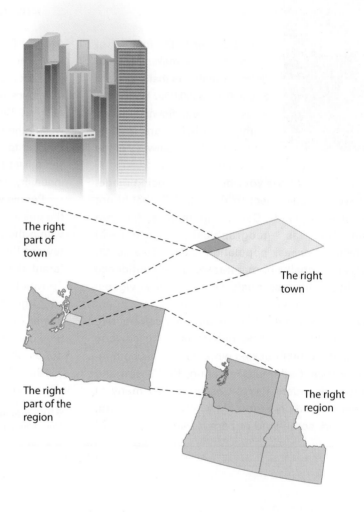

The right
part of
town

The right
town

The right
part of the
region

The right
region

This chapter will follow the building-location process from the broadest decisions (selecting a state or region) to the narrowest (designing a layout of your
facilities). There are four essential questions you need to ask:

1. What region of the country would be best for your business?
2. What state within that region satisfies your needs?
3. What city within that region will best suit you?
4. What specific site within that city will accommodate your business?

Don't automatically jump to the fourth question. By beginning the site-selection
process broadly and then narrowing your choices down, you can choose a location that meets the needs of your target market and is near other businesses that
are complementary to yours (see Figure 13.2).

To analyze a potential location for your business, you will want to consider the
specific needs of your business in conjunction with your personal preferences.
First establish the criteria that are essential to your success. Then list those that
are desirable but not mandatory. Examples of criteria include the following:

- Price and availability of land and water
- Quality and quantity of labor pool
- Access to your customers
- Proximity of suppliers
- Access to transportation (air, highway, rail)
- Location of competition
- Public attitudes toward new businesses
- Laws, regulations, and taxes
- Your personal preference regarding where to live
- Financial incentives provided (tax breaks, bond issues, guaranteed loans)
- Quality of schools
- Quality of life (crime rate, recreation opportunities, housing, cost of living, cultural activities)

State Selection

Most small business owners start and operate their businesses in the area where they currently live. Other people, however, are anxious to relocate to another part of the country (or world) to run their small businesses.

The United States is a collection of local and regional markets rather than one big market. Business conditions vary from place to place. Economic booms and recessions vary from region to region. Markets and people's tastes vary from region to region as well, and these regional differences may influence the decision about where you should locate your business. For example, your recipe for deep-pan pizza may not set your business apart from the competition in Chicago, where that style of pizza is already very popular. By contrast, it may make your business unique in Flagstaff, Arizona, or Biloxi, Mississippi.

Where do you find information to compare and contrast the economic performance of regions, states, and cities? Several sources are available. Every year *Inc.* magazine publishes its annual Metro Report, which ranks job growth, population growth, business starts, growth in personal earnings, and employment pool data. *Fortune* magazine regularly includes information on regional and state economies in its *Fortune* Forecast. *Business Week, Forbes, The Wall Street Journal, Entrepreneur,* and *USA Today* all regularly publish accounts of current regional and national information. The U.S. Census Bureau gathers data by geographic region every 10 years and maintains an extensive database. Census data are reported by several sources, including the *Survey of Buying Power,* which is published annually by *Sales and Marketing Management (SMM).*

The *SMM Survey of Buying Power* combines data on population, income, and retail sales for nine regions within the United States. The survey assigns a weight to each factor to calculate a *buying power index (BPI),* so that different markets can be compared. Table 13.1 illustrates an example of BPI by region, plus all the additional data available and further broken down to state, county, and city levels. The BPI allows you to compare any city, county, or state to the United States as a whole (U.S. = 100).[1]

Table 13.1

REGIONAL SUMMARIES OF POPULATION, EFFECTIVE BUYING INCOME, AND RETAIL SALES

| | 2005 Totals of U.S. Population by Age Group | | | | | | | | |
| | Population by Age Group (ooos) | | | | | | | | |
Region	Total Population (ooos)	% of U.S.	0–17 Years	18–24 Years	25–34 Years	35–49 Years	50 and Older	Total Households (ooos)	% of U.S.
New England	14,325.7	4.8538	3,278.7	1,345.7	1,773.6	3,043.9	4,523.8	5,596.9	5.0419
Middle Atlantic	40,436.3	13.7006	9,448.5	3,771.2	5,176.8	9,304.1	12,735.7	15,250.5	13.7383
East North Central	46,148.4	15.6306	11,473.8	4,596.4	6,033.7	10,322.3	13,722.2	17,773.3	16.0109
West North Central	19,725.4	6.6833	4,820.9	2,055.4	2,532.7	4,333.7	5,982.7	7,721.4	6.9559
South Atlantic	55,539.2	18.8180	13,381.7	5,312.9	7,406.3	12,446.5	16,991.8	21,538.5	19.4026
East South Central	17,501.8	5.9301	4,248.7	1,768.0	2,353.4	3,836.3	5,295.4	6,872.2	6.1908
West South Central	33,515.9	11.3560	9,095.7	3,533.5	4,734.4	7,241.8	8,910.5	12,204.1	10.9939
Mountain	19,930.7	6.7531	5,328.6	2,044.3	2,857.2	4,234.0	5,466.6	7,367.2	6.6364
Pacific	46,292.4	16.2691	12,391.3	4,773.0	6,872.2	10,901.8	13,078.4	16,683.6	15.0293
Total United States	295140.1	100.00	73,467.9	29,200.4	39,740.3	66,024.4	86,707.1	111,007.7	100.0000

| | 2005 U.S. Totals of Effective Buying Income | | | | | | | |
| | EDI by Income Group (ooos) | | | | | | | |
Region	2002 Total EBI ($ooo)	% of U.S.	Per Capita EBI ($)	Average Household EBI ($)	Median Household EBI ($)	$20,000–$34,999	$35,000–$49,999	$50,000 and Higher
New England	322,578,176	5.6664	22,517	57,635	43,810	1,083.3	1,046.9	2,396.4
Middle Atlantic	822,475,359	14.4473	20,340	53,931	39,798	3,170.9	2,854.1	5,846.1
East North Central	891,563,433	15.6609	19,319	50,163	39,700	4,033.3	3,553.1	6,547.5
West North Central	365,325,746	6.4157	18,516	47,302	37,882	1,882.4	1,592.5	2,607.0
South Atlantic	1,092,206,659	19.1854	19,666	50,710	38,842	4,972.5	4,187.5	7,731.6
East South Central	299,754,791	5.2655	17,127	43,618	33,551	1,700.3	1,279.0	1,993.9
West South Central	587,816,994	10.3254	17,538	48,166	36,422	2,885.2	2,308.6	4,027.0
Mountain	374,091,769	6.5712	18,770	50,778	39,825	1,744.8	1,471.2	2,712.4
Pacific	937,186,640	16.4622	19,518	56,174	43,043	3,475.5	3,175.8	6,896.8
Total United States	5,692,909,567	100.0000	19,289	51,284	39,324	24,984.2	21,468.7	40,758.7

| 2005 U.S. Totals of Retail Sales | | | | | | | |
| Retail Sales by Store Group | | | | | | | |
Region	2005 Total Retail Sales ($000)	% of U.S.	Per House hold Retail Sales	Food and Beverage Stores ($000)	Food Service and Drinking Establish- ments ($000)	General Merchandise ($000)	Furniture and Home Furnishings and Electronics and Appliances ($000)	Motor Vehicles and Parts Dealers ($000)
New England	234,225,395	5.5687	41,849	33,140,824	24,222,290	20,336,720	10,367,684	49,239,491
Middle Atlantic	550,824,774	13.0960	36,118	75,764,556	54,249,768	52,920,860	27,083,574	111,435,974
East North Central	645,469,156	15.3461	36,317	75,861,239	62,366,217	87,661,206	29,880,165	61,420,485
West North Central	301,403,465	7.1660	39,035	31,901,166	25,454,467	41,060,225	14,368,792	61,420,485
South Atlantic	776,963,666	18.4725	36,073	99,175,159	76,200,746	94,193,765	40,839,767	181,325,361
East South Central	226,952,515	5.3958	33,025	27,079,629	22,016,144	36,988,784	8,538,640	49,693,036
West South Central	486,476, 506	11.5661	39,862	49,554,070	45,215,853	74,899,677	23,045,275	117,303,381
Mountain	291,592,595	6.9327	39,580	35,274,732	27,876,517	39,447,796	15,653,517	63,002,741
Pacific	692,144,923	16.4561	41,487	92,167,642	75,758,998	91,765,990	41,970,578	147,205,305
Total United States	4,206,052,995	100.0000	37,890	519,919,017	413,361,000	539,275,023	211,747,992	919,862,988

SOURCE: From 2005 *Survey of Buying Power, Sales and Marketing Management,* September 2005, p. 62. Copyright © 2005 Nielsen Business Media Inc.

Another figure useful in helping you determine a location for your business is the **effective buying index (EBI)**. The EBI takes the census's figures for personal income and subtracts all personal taxes and deductions that are charged in each area. The result shows what is known as *disposable personal income,* or money that people have left over after taxes. This figure is especially useful if your business is based on a product or service that is more of a luxury than a necessity. You would want to locate a business that sells luxury goods in an area with a high EBI, because a higher average disposable income means that more people in the area are available to buy your goods.

> *effective buying index (EBI)*
> The amount of personal income after taxes and deductions made by people in a specific geographic area.

City Selection

To most business owners, what is going on in their own city or state is more important than what is going on in the $11 trillion U.S. economy.[2] The economic condition

	Sales/Advertising Indexes	
Sales Activity	Buying Power	Quality
115	5.4744	113
96	13.8925	101
98	15.5613	100
107	6.6934	100
98	18.8981	100
91	5.4369	92
102	10.9047	96
103	6.7166	99
101	16.4221	102
100	100.0000	100

SOURCE: From "2005 Survey of Buying Power," *Sales and Marketing Management*, September 2005, 62. Copyright © 2005 Nielsen Business Media, Inc.

of a particular city, state, or region is often much different than the national situation. Check out *Entrepreneur* magazine's annual rankings of top U.S. cities for small business. *Inc.* magazine ranks the best large, medium, and small metro areas for small business. Areas and cities seeing the strongest growth recently are those that are relatively affordable, in terms of housing, living expenses, and business costs.[3] Look at current issues of these magazines to catch up on the latest trends.

Let's look at the Fort Collins–Loveland metropolitan area of Colorado as an example of the specific demographic information available from the annual *SMM Survey of Buying Power* (see Table 13.2). You can compare population by age groups, retail sales by type of store, and percentages of effective buying income to those of other cities that you are also considering for your business location.

inshopping
The effect of more consumers coming into a town to purchase goods than leaving it to buy the same product.

If your business is involved in retail or service sales, a technique for comparing different locations based on residents' ability to convert personal income into retail purchases is the *sales conversion index (SCI)*.[4] This index allows small business managers to analyze a market area in relation to a benchmark area with similar income and non-retail spending characteristics. You can even examine specific categories of retail activity. The SCI measures the strength of the retail sector by calculating **inshopping**, which occurs when consumers come from outside the local market area to shop. A city with a weaker retail sector experiences **outshopping**, or consumers' tendency to go outside the community to shop.

outshopping
The effect of more consumers leaving a town to purchase goods than entering it to buy the same product.

Because it takes only a simple calculation of readily available secondary data, any business can use the SCI. The data can be found in *Sales and Marketing*

Retail Sales (in $ooo)	Fort Collins	Conversion Factor	SCI	Conversion Pueblo	Factor	SCI
Total retail sales	$2,049,038	1.12	83.58	$1,618,533	1.34	119.64
Food	297,362	.16	69.57	274,006	.23	143.75
Eating/drinking places	230,136	.13	86.67	177,150	.15	115.38
General merchandise	312,162	.17	73.91	272,906	.23	135.29
Furniture/ appliances	184,275	.10	166.67	71,467	.06	60.00
Automotive	412,627	.23	100.0	272,686	.23	100.00
Total EBI (in $000)	$1,831,934			$1,209,826		
Buying Power Index	.0508			.0349		

Table 13.2
RETAIL SALES BY STORE GROUP AND EBI TO CALCULATE SCI

Management's Survey of Buying Power (refer again to Table 13.2). To make the calculation, you need the following data:

- Total retail sales from the retail trade areas being examined (called the *subject area*).
- Retail sales for an appropriate *benchmark* unit.
- Retail sales for the subject and benchmark areas in each of the product categories.
- EBI for the subject and benchmark areas. (You will recall that EBI is equal to personal income minus personal tax and nontax payments).

Calculating the SCI takes five steps:

1. Determine the metropolitan area, the city in that metropolitan area, or the county to be examined (the subject area).
2. Establish the benchmark area to use for comparison.
3. Divide retail sales by the EBI for both the trade area and the benchmark area. This provides conversion factors.
4. Divide the subject area's conversion factor by the benchmark area's conversion factor after both are expressed as a percentage of EBI. The figure is the SCI.
5. Calculate the SCI for each of the retail categories from the *Survey of Buying Power:* food, eating and drinking places, general merchandise, automotive, drugs, and furniture, furnishings, and appliances.

An SCI greater than 100 indicates inshopping. The higher the SCI, the more desirable the location is. An SCI less than 100 suggests outshopping. The lower the number, the less desirable the location is. Using the data from Table 13.2, let's calculate the SCIs for Fort Collins, Colorado, and Pueblo, Colorado.

$$\text{Collins conversion factor} = \frac{2,049,038}{1,831,934} = 1.2$$

$$\text{Pueblo Conversion factor} = \frac{1,618,533}{1,209,826} = 1.34$$

$$\text{For Collins SCI} = \frac{1.12}{1.34} = .8358 \times 100 = 83.58$$

$$\text{Pueblo SCI} = \frac{1.34}{1.12} = 1,1964 \times 100 = 119.64$$

Because the SCI for Fort Collins is far less than 100, at 83.58, you can conclude that the city experiences substantial outshopping compared with Pueblo. Conversely, Pueblo, with its 119.64 SCI, enjoys considerable inshopping compared with Fort Collins. When Pueblo is used as the benchmark, the only Fort Collins store category that indicates inshopping is "Furniture/appliances," with an SCI of 166.67 (Table 13.2 again). This would be a very interesting piece of information for you to know if you were considering opening a furniture store and were trying to decide in which city to site your business. Calculation of SCI is worth the effort when you consider the importance and permanence of locating your business.

Site Selection

Whereas the total makeup of the U.S. marketplace is diverse and complex, neighborhoods tend to be just the opposite. People are generally more comfortable in areas where people like themselves live. Thus the cliché "opposites attract" doesn't usually hold true in neighborhoods. The reasons for this demographic fact can be a matter of practicality as much as of preference. People of similar income can afford similarly priced houses, which are generally built in the same area. Neighborhoods also tend to contain clusters of similar age groups, religious groups, families, and cultural groups. These factors distinguish one neighborhood from another. They are therefore important to consider in locating your business.

To distinguish different neighborhood types, Claritas Corporation has created a database program called PRIZM (Potential Rating Index for Zip Marketers).[5] For a neighborhood to be classified by the PRIZM program, it must be different enough from all others to be a separate segment, and it must contain enough people to be worthwhile to businesses. By using the ZIP + 4 codes combined with demographic data from the census, nationwide consumer surveys, and hundreds of interviews, PRIZM creates an accurate geodemographic segmentation system. In 2003 Claritas released a new version called PRIZM New Evolution (PRIZM NE) with designations such as "Young Digerati, Beltway Boomers, Multi-Culti Mosaic." By mining the 110 types of households in the United States, Claritas describes the increasingly diverse population. Want to see what PRIZM NE has to say about your ZIP code? Go to www.yawyl.claritas.com and click on "You Are Where You Live."[6]

Manager's Notebook

GIS: "Where" and "Who"

Businesses large and small are using geographic segmentation systems to analyze the demographics of target markets, choose new retail site locations, and optimize distribution routes. These systems start with millions of raw data points on individuals. Then, on the basis of these statistics, they divide the nation's households into groups based on similarities (the process is much like biologists' dividing plants and animals into orders, families, genera, and so on) and plot them on maps using *geographic information systems (GIS)* software.

The *Arizona Republic* newspaper takes the use of GIS to an art form for targeting advertising inserts to specific customers. They can include inserts into copies of the paper going to any single or combination of ZIP codes, streets, or circumference around an advertising company's store. For example, a store that sells swimming pool supplies can have inserts included only in newspaper subscribers who have pools within a specific distance from their store—or even more specifically, with an income of, say, $200,000.

The combination of business intelligence (BI) analytic software and GIS provide a level of information that has not been available to managers before. The *Republic* uses ArcGIS combined with an application named Market Focused II that contains subscriber information from circulation databases to pinpoint ads.

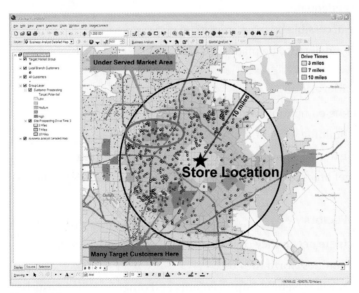

Arizona Republic

SOURCES: Gary H. Anthes, "Beyond ZIP Codes," *Computerworld*, 19 September 2005, 56–61; Sue Hildreth, "On the Corporate Radar," *Computerworld*, 2 April 2007, 25–26; Emma Rubach, "Where in the World?" *Precision Marketing*, 16 September 2005, 23–24.

Site Questions

Choosing the correct site involves answering many questions about each location being considered. You must find the right kind of site for your business. It must be accessible to your customers and vendors, and it must satisfy all legal requirements and economic needs of your business.

Type of Site

- Is the site located near target markets?
- Is the type of building appropriate for your business?
- What is the site's age and condition?
- How large is the trade area?
- Will adjacent businesses complement or compete with your firm?

Accessibility

- How are road patterns and conditions?
- Do any natural or artificial barriers obstruct access to the site?
- Does the site have good visibility?
- Is traffic flow too high or too low?
- Is the entrance or exit to parking convenient?
- Is parking adequate?
- Is the site accessible by mass transit?
- Can vendor deliveries be made easily?

Legal Considerations

- Is the zoning compatible with your firm?
- Does the building meet building codes?
- Will your external signs be compatible with zoning ordinances?
- Can you get any special licenses you will need (such as a liquor license)?

Economic Factors

- How much are occupancy costs?
- Are the amenities worth the cost?
- How much will leasehold improvements and other one-time costs be?

Traffic Flow

The number of cars and pedestrians passing a site strongly affects its potential for retail sales. If you are a retailer, you need to determine whether the type and amount of traffic are sufficient for your business. Fast-food franchises have precise specifications for number counts of vehicles traveling at specified speeds in each direction as part of their location analysis. State highway departments can usually provide statistics on traffic counts for most public roads.

Type of traffic is important, because you don't receive any particular benefit if the people passing your business are not likely to stop. For example, suppose you are comparing two locations for your upscale jewelry store—one in a central business district and the other in a small shopping center with other specialty stores in an exclusive neighborhood. Total volume of traffic by the central business district location will be higher, but you will enjoy more of the right type of traffic for your store at the small shopping center.

> "The volume of automobile and foot traffic, the speed of vehicles, and the presence of turn lanes and parking are factors to consider when choosing a location for a retail or service business."

Other businesses in the area will affect the type of traffic. This explains why you often see automobile dealerships clustered together. The synergy created from several similar businesses located together can be very beneficial, with customers coming to a specific area to "shop around" before buying. Your chances of attracting customers in the market for an auto will be much greater in a location with complementary competition than if your location is isolated.

Going Global

If you are considering expanding your operations into another country, you need information on the location of your foreign project. You can get background information and opinions on foreign locations from magazines and newspapers at your local library. Keep in mind that all local chambers of commerce and economic development groups exist to promote their area, not to criticize it, so view information received from them with a somewhat skeptical eye. The American Management Association and the American Marketing Association (and other organizations) sponsor seminars on opportunities and problems in foreign operations. The U.S. Department of State can be very helpful in telling you about political developments, local customs and differences, and economic issues in specific countries.

In addition to doing your research (and reviewing the information in Chapter 15), it is very important that you get to know the area personally before you establish operations abroad. Visit potential sites, meet with others in business there, and identify possible distribution sources before you consider setting up business in another country.

Finding information on the Internet to help you make intelligent location decisions about global markets is fairly easy. The U.S. government has created websites for various government agencies that can provide the small business owner with appropriate information. For instance, the Central Intelligence Agency server (www.odci.gov) provides access to the latest edition of the *CIA World Factbook,* which includes information about every country in the world, with details such as geography, climate, terrain, natural resources, religions, languages, and so forth.

In addition, you might want to access websites devoted to specific geographic locations once you've narrowed down your list of potential sites. For instance, you can access information about Vietnam, Latin America, China, the European Union, and Russia and Eastern Europe at the following addresses:

Vietnam: www.govietnam.com

Latin America: http://lanic.utexas.edu/

China: www.chinesebusinessworld.com

European Union: www.eubusiness.com

Russia: www.einnews.com/russia

Rostislav Ordovsky-Tanaevsky Blanco, a native of Venezuela, chose his father's homeland, the former Soviet Union, as the location for his chain of photo retail stores and restaurants. He's been called crazy by others, but Ordovsky-Tanaevsky has enjoyed the last laugh on those naysayers. His business, Rostik International, quickly garnered revenues in excess of $100 million and employed about 6,000 people. Ordovsky-Tanaevsky has become Moscow's leading restaurateur, operating a number of hamburger joints, pizzerias, New York–style delis, and theme restaurants. Achieving this level of success hasn't been easy. Site selection of any type is fraught with risks. But when you add in the uncertainties of a newly democratized society, you've increased the challenges. However, Ordovsky-Tanaevsky is a perfect example of how a global small business owner can bridge the uncertainties and develop successful businesses in locations where others fear to tread.[7]

Location Types

Service and retail businesses have three basic choices for types of locations: central business districts, shopping centers, and stand-alone locations.

Central Business Districts

The *central business district (CBD)* is usually the oldest section of a city. Although urban blight caused many businesses to desert CBDs in favor of the suburbs, many other CBDs have undergone a *gentrification* process, meaning that old buildings have been restored, or razed and replaced with new offices, retail shops, or housing. This planning and development, such as Denver's Larimer Square and Chicago's Water Tower Place, has created some of the best and most expensive locations for many types of retailers.

The advantages of locating in a CBD are that your customers generally will have access to public transportation; to a variety of images, prices, and services; and to many other businesses. The disadvantages can include parking availability, which is usually very tight and expensive; traffic congestion; possibly a high crime rate; older buildings; and sharp disparities between neighborhoods, in which one block can be upscale while the next is rundown.

Shopping Centers

Although concentrated shopping areas have existed for centuries, the last four decades have witnessed the "malling of America." Shopping centers and malls are centrally owned or managed, have balanced store offerings, and have their own parking facilities. **Anchor stores** are major department stores that draw people into the shopping center.

Over the last several decades, shoppers have come to demand the convenience of shopping centers. People living in the suburbs want to be able to drive to a location where they can park easily and find a wide variety of goods and services. Shopping centers have also gone through an evolutionary process, tending toward

anchor stores
A large retail store that attracts people to shop at malls.

Creating Competitive Advantage

Economic Action Downtown

When *Inc.* magazine and the Initiative for a Competitive Inner City (ICIC) compiled the Inner City 100 to open a window into the new U.S. economy, they were surprised at what they saw. Although many people assume that little economic activity occurs in inner-city neighborhoods well known for problems, the opposite is actually true. Inner cities are a hotbed of entrepreneurship. ICIC is founded on the premise that no matter what amount of social intervention—whether philanthropy, or charity, or government subsidization—is applied, communities cannot possibly be healthy unless the local economy works.

What competitive advantages could draw businesses to these areas? Harvard professor Michael Porter has studied inner-city businesses for a decade and has found that access to transportation and labor are their biggest advantages. The average labor turnover rate is less than 14 percent for inner-city businesses, compared with the national average of about 20 percent.

Darryl Hart created a supply-chain management company named Commodity Sourcing Group (CSG) in downtown Detroit, Michigan. CSG acts as intermediary between hospitals and vendors. In the process, it buys equipment, creates brochures, and trains employees for about 10 local businesses. In one case, CSG purchased over $50,000 worth of equipment for a small printing company so it could win a large contract. CSG then sold the equipment to the company with payment spread out over three years in addition to providing recruiting and training of employees to use it. CSG does well as a business—a business of doing good; it ranked number one on the *Inc.* Inner City 100 for 2006 with a revenue growth rate of 10,028 percent from 2000 to 2004 on revenue of $21.1 million in 2004 and 54 employees.

SOURCES: Leigh Buchanan, "The 2006 Inner City 100—Share the Wealth," *Inc.*, June 2006, 108–120; Mike Hofman, "Q&A with Michael Porter," *Inc.*, May 2004, 98–99.

larger centers offering more variety, wider selections, and more entertainment. Have megamalls like the West Edmonton Mall or the Mall of America gone too far in this evolutionary process? Have they reached the point of being "too big"? Ultimately, the consumer market will decide.

Advantages that shopping centers can offer to your business, compared with a CBD, include heavy traffic drawn by the wide variety of products available, closeness to population centers, cooperative planning and cost sharing, access to highways, ample parking, a lower crime rate, and a clean, neat environment.

A disadvantage of locating within a shopping center is the inflexibility of your store hours. If the center is open from 9 A.M. to 10 P.M., you can't open your store from noon until midnight. Your rent is often higher than in an outside location. The central management of the shopping center may restrict the merchandise you sell. Your operations are limited, membership is required in the center's merchant organization, and you face the possibility of having too much competition. Smaller stores may be dominated by anchor stores.

Shopping centers will continue to evolve rapidly. Aging centers are being renovated. As shoppers become more dependent on malls and shopping centers to supply their needs, more service-oriented businesses, such as banks, health clinics, day care centers, and insurance offices, will be located in malls.

Stand-Alone Locations

Drawing in and keeping customers are difficult tasks, especially if you choose a freestanding, or stand-alone, location. With a freestanding location, your business must be the customers' destination point. Therefore, your competitive advantage must be made very clear to them. You must have unique merchandise, large selections, low prices, exceptional service, or special promotions to get them in.

Advantages of stand-alone locations include the freedom to set your own hours and operate the way you choose. You may have no direct competition nearby. More parking may be available, and rent may be lower than what you would pay at a shopping center.

Disadvantages of having your business in a stand-alone location include the loss of synergy that can be created when the right combination of businesses is located together. You have to increase your advertising and promotional spending to get customers in your door. You can't share operating costs with other businesses. You may have to build rather than rent.

If the goods or services that you offer are destination-oriented products (like health clubs, convenience stores, or wholesale clubs), a freestanding location may be the right choice for your business.

Service Locations

With some exceptions, the location decision for service businesses is just as important as it is for businesses selling tangible products. Services tend to be hard to differentiate—that is, to show how one is different from another. People will not go out of their way to visit a specific service business if they think there is very little difference between services, so car washes, video rental stores, dry cleaners, and similar services must be *very* careful about the convenience of their locations. With service businesses that visit the customer (like plumbers, landscapers, and carpet cleaners), location is not critical.

Incubators

In the early 1980s government agencies, universities, and private business groups began creating business incubators to help new businesses get started in their area. Today, several hundred incubators operate in the United States, and their number is growing. Incubators offer entrepreneurs below-market rent prices, along with services and equipment that are difficult for start-up businesses to provide on their own. They encourage entrepreneurship, which contributes to economic development. Businesses are not allowed to take advantage of these benefits indefinitely, and they must "graduate" to outside locations as they grow.

"An incubator is an attractive place to start a new small business. It offers support services and such equipment as photocopiers, fax machines, and computers, which young businesses often cannot afford by themselves."

Choosing an incubator as your starting location can help you through the first months when your new business is at its most fragile. As noted earlier, a major advantage of incubators is that they charge lower than market rent. Other benefits follow.

Support Services Incubators typically make copy machines, computers, fax machines, and other equipment available for their tenants to share. These items

Reality Check

Incubation Variations

Business *incubators* come in two broad varieties: mixed-use and sector-focused. James Prinster and Steve Kramer needed the expertise of a mixed-use incubator when they set out to create a contract-electronics manufacturing company in Grand Junction, Colorado. They knew the manufacturing side of the business from being employees of such a firm, but they needed help in all other aspects. Starting in 2002 with revenues of $60,000, they quickly grew to $850,000 by 2004. Being located in an incubator was a huge advantage at this time because they could take over more space without moving the business. Finally, they did outgrow the incubator and moved into their own 6,000-square-foot building in Grand Junction.

An interesting variation on the traditional business incubator is emerging: creative incubators, such as the one offered by the Arts Council of New Orleans. This incubator's forte is helping creative startups find the right balance between pushing creative boundaries—by producing music, creating jewelry, or launching a theater company—and making smart business decisions with fiscal responsibility.

In addition to typical access to equipment, companies admitted to the Arts Council's Energy Program obtain access to a group health plan, workshops on business topics, fund-raising, and board development. Successful performance is expected, exemplified by 5 to 10 percent growth per year at a minimum. According to Chesley Adler, owner of a jewelry-design business located in the incubator, bouncing ideas off other businesspeople in the creative incubator has been invaluable.

For information on finding a creative incubator, try these websites:

- Arlington's Arts Incubator: www.arlingtonarts .org/incubator
- Chatham Creative Arts Incubator: http:// chathamarts.org/about.htm
- Cultural Development Corps Flashpoint: www.culturaldc.org/mather_arts.html
- Handmade in America: www.handmadeinamerica .org
- National Business Incubator Association: www.nbia.org

New ideas inevitably beget new ideas. As dot-com businesses grew in number and popularity, for example, new forms of "help" popped up to provide assistance to them and to cash in on this trend. Most notable were the Internet incubators, also known as *accelerators* or *startup rockets*. A common practice was for an incubator to take an equity position in the Internet business, but most have gone the way of the dot-com bust.

SOURCES: Michael Patterson, "Hatching for Success," *Business Week Online*, 8 December 2005; Nichole Torres, "Growing Up," *Entrepreneur*, December 2003, 120; Leonard Jacobs, "Deep Pockets Hatching New 'Arts Incubator,'" *Back Stage*, 27 February 2004, 2; Thea Singer, "Inside an Internet Incubator," *Inc.*, July 2000, 92–100.

can improve your productivity as a young business, but they would cost a lot of money if you had to buy them outright. In an incubator, you can have access to such equipment and pay only when and if you use it. Receptionists, secretarial support, and shipping and receiving services are also available on a shared basis, so you don't have to add to your payroll.

Professional Assistance   Incubators often negotiate reduced rates with needed professionals like accountants and lawyers. They also offer training in cash-flow management, marketing practices, obtaining financing, and other areas.

Networking   Incubators can put you in contact with other local businesses. A "family" atmosphere often develops between businesses located in incubators, because all are at roughly the same stage of development. This atmosphere usually leads to an esprit de corps among tenants.

Financing   Incubators often have financial assistance available or access to other funding sources such as revolving loan funds, which can provide loans at lower than market rates.

Layout and Design

After you have selected a site, you need to lay out the interior of your business. If yours is a type of business that customers visit, most of your management decisions will be directed toward getting customers into your business to spend money. No matter what type of business you run, this is where the activity happens. How your location is laid out and designed is important because it affects the image and productivity of your business.

Legal Requirements

The Americans with Disabilities Act (ADA) requires businesses to be accessible to disabled customers and employees, with businesses having more than 14 employees required to accommodate disabled job candidates in hiring. This law affects the way every business operates. Buildings constructed after January 26, 1993, must meet stricter requirements than those built earlier.

Some ADA requirements for customer accommodation include the following:

- Access ramps must be built where the floor level changes more than half an inch.
- Elevators are required in buildings of three stories or more and in buildings with more than 3,000 square feet of floor space per story.
- Checkout aisles must be at least 36 inches wide.
- Carpets of accessible routes must be less than one-half inch in pile.
- Toilet facilities, water fountains, and telephones must be accessible to people in wheelchairs.
- Self-service shelves, counters, and bars must be accessible to people in wheelchairs and to the visually impaired.[8]

Retail Layouts

The layout of your retail store helps create the image that people have of your business. It is important to display merchandise in an attractive, logical arrangement to maximize your sales and to make shopping as convenient as possible for your customers.

Three types of layouts are commonly used in retail stores in various combinations. The simplest type is the **free-flow layout**, which works well with smaller stores such as boutiques that sell only one type of merchandise (see Figure 13.3). As there is no established traffic pattern, customers are encouraged to browse.

free-flow layout
A type of layout used by small retail stores that encourages customers to wander and browse through the store.

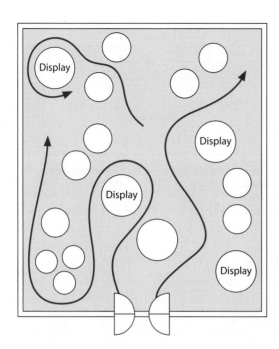

Figure 13.3
FREE-FLOW LAYOUT

The Free-Flow Layout Encourages Shoppers to Browse.

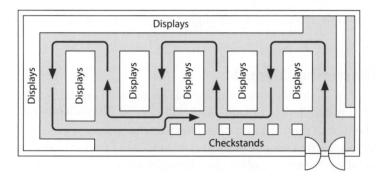

Figure 13.4
GRID LAYOUT

The Grid Layout Routes Customers up and down Aisles to Expose Them to a Large Quantity of Merchandise.

A **grid layout** establishes a geometric grid by placing counters and fixtures at right angles in long rows (see Figure 13.4). It effectively displays a large amount of merchandise with tall shelves and many shelf facings. Supermarkets and drugstores tend to be set up with this layout, because it suits customers who wish to shop the entire store by moving up and down alternate aisles. But if customers can't see over fixtures or if they want only one or two specific items, they may find this layout frustrating.

The **loop layout** has gained popularity since the early 1980s as a tool for increasing retail sales productivity (see Figure 13.5). The loop sets up a major aisle that leads customers from the entrance, through the store, and back to the checkout counter. Customers are led efficiently through the store so as to expose them to the greatest amount of merchandise. At the same time, they retain the freedom to browse or cross-shop. This layout is especially good for businesses that sell a wide variety of merchandise, because customers can be routed quickly from one department of merchandise to another.

grid layout
A type of layout used by retail stores to move customers past merchandise arranged on rows of shelves or fixtures.

loop layout
A type of retail layout with a predominant aisle running through the store that quickly leads customers to their desired department.

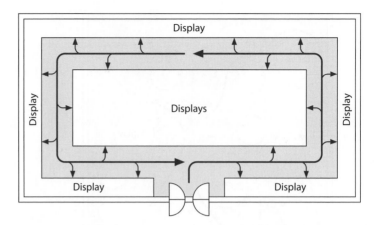

Figure 13.5
LOOP LAYOUT

*The Loop Layout Allows
Customers Quick Access to Any
Department in the Store.*

Service Layouts

Service businesses that customers visit, such as beauty shops and restaurants, need to be concerned about how their layout affects both their customers' convenience and the business's work flow. The image of these service businesses is just as strongly affected by layout as the image of retail stores is. Speed of service becomes more critical every year. Consider the decreasing amount of time needed for photo finishing—from one week, to two days, to one hour, to while you wait. Layout is critical to maintaining the speed and efficiency of service providers.

Manufacturing Layouts

The layout of a manufacturing business is arranged to ensure a smooth flow of work. The specific layout of your plant will depend on the type of product you make, the type of production process you use, the space you have available, and other factors, such as volume of goods and amount of worker interaction needed. There are three basic types of manufacturing layouts, which may be combined as needed.

process layout
A way to arrange a manufacturing business by placing all comparable equipment together in the same area.

Process Layout   With the **process layout**, all similar equipment and workers are grouped together so that the goods being produced move around the plant (see Figure 13.6). This layout is common with small manufacturers because of the flexibility it allows. The product being made can be changed quickly. An example of the process layout can be seen in a small machine shop, in which all the grinders would be in one area, all the drills would be in another area, and all the lathes would be in a third area. Restaurant kitchens commonly employ this type of layout as well, with the refrigerators in one place, the ovens in another, and a food preparation area elsewhere.

Another advantage of the process layout is that it minimizes the number of tools or equipment needed. For example, an assembly line (which uses a product layout) might require a company to purchase several grinding machines, one for each point where it is used on the assembly line. With a process layout, by contrast, only one or two grinders need be purchased, and all can be used in one area. Because the machines operate independently, a breakdown in one does not shut down operations.

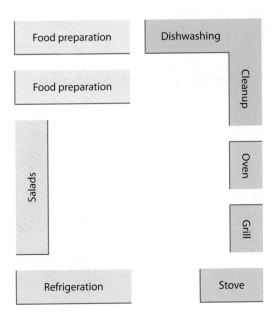

Figure 13.6

PROCESS LAYOUT IN A RESTAURANT KITCHEN

In a Process Layout, Similar Equipment Is Grouped Together in Areas to Complete Specified Tasks.

A disadvantage of the process layout is that when equipment is grouped together, increased handling is needed to move the product from one station to another when more than one task is performed. This effort can require additional employees. Because this layout is more general in nature, producing long runs of the same product would be less efficient than in the product layout.

Product Layout   With a **product layout**, you arrange workers, equipment, and activities needed to produce a single product in a particular sequence of steps (see Figure 13.7). A product layout is best when you are producing many standardized products or using specialized equipment. Auto assembly lines, textile mills, and other continuous-flow assembly lines in which raw material enters one end of the line and finished products exit the other end are examples of a product layout. Material handling costs can be decreased and tasks can often be mechanically simplified so that skilled labor is not needed.

> *product layout*
> A way to arrange a manufacturing business by placing equipment in an assembly line.

A restaurant that specializes in a product like bagels, pizzas, or cookies can make use of the product layout by moving through a sequence of steps to prepare the finished product. The kitchen can be arranged to store ingredients and mix the dough at one end of the counter before it is all moved to cold storage. Then batches can be removed and processed through a dough-rolling machine; prepared and mixed with other ingredients; and cooked, cut, and served in an assembly-line fashion. The layout works well for making that one product, but what if you want to diversify your menu to offer other food items like hamburgers, French fries, or tacos? You would have to set up separate product lines with new ovens, stoves, and counters for each new product—an expensive way to expand a menu.

A product layout is inflexible because it is costly and difficult to change the product that is being made. It is usually more expensive to set up than a process layout because more specialized machinery is needed. A breakdown anywhere

Figure 13.7

PRODUCT LAYOUT IN A PIZZA KITCHEN

In a Product Layout, Workers, Equipment, and Activities Are Laid out According to the Sequence of Steps Needed to Make the Product.

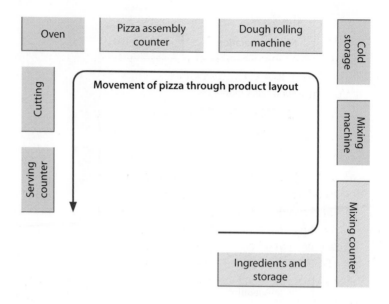

along the line can shut down the entire operation. The specialization needed for a product layout eliminates this option for most small businesses because of cost reasons.

Fixed Layout   In a **fixed layout**, the product stays in one spot, and equipment, material, and labor are brought to it as needed for assembly. Types of businesses using this layout include building construction, aircraft and shipbuilding, and other large, immovable product production.

> **fixed layout**
> A type of layout for a manufacturing business in which the product stays stationary while workers and equipment are brought to it.

Home Office

Is a home-based business right for you? It is becoming a popular option for business owners. Let's look at some advantages and disadvantages.

Advantages

- *Flexibility in scheduling personal, family, and business obligations.*
- *Low overhead expenses.* You are already paying for the space you live in and utilities.
- *No commute time.* Of course, that walk from the kitchen to the office can seem like a long one if you don't really feel like working.
- *Independence.* You can be your own boss and your own landlord. You have some degree of control over what work you accept and the schedule for doing it.
- *No office distractions.* A lot of time can be wasted in office settings chatting with people who "pop in."

Disadvantages

- *Interruptions.* It's hard for family and friends to understand that you really do have work to do.

- *Isolation.* Much of the social aspect of work can be lost without contact with others. A house can get very quiet and lonely.
- *Credibility.* Although home-based businesses are much more accepted now, being taken seriously as a business can be a challenge. This isn't a hobby, and you are not unemployed.
- *Work space.* Your working area may be cramped and not too private.
- *Zoning issues.* Be sure to check whether it is legal for you to operate a business out of your home.

Thirteen-year-old Zachary Durst and his ten-year-old sister Laura knew that a red scarf on their mother's home-office door meant "Mom is on the phone. Do not interrupt unless one of you needs a tourniquet." Christine Durst (Mom) runs Staffcentrix from her home. She organized an online network of "virtual assistants," who provide business support services. Durst loves the way she can manage both a family and a business from her home. As her children grew older, they became less resentful of the time she spent on her business. Being involved in the business helped, too. They did jobs like running the postage meter, which made them feel as if they were part of the action.

Durst is an example of a home-based business owner who takes a multitask-ing approach, rather than strictly separating her personal and professional roles. The approaches to running a home business are as varied as the millions of entre-preneurs who own them. Equipment needs vary almost as much.

You must make sure that it is legal to operate a home-based business where you live. Some communities have adopted tough restrictions, such as not allow-ing a home office even for work you bring home from your "real" office. More typical concerns involve complying with zoning regulations that govern parking, signage, and types of businesses allowed in residential areas. Check with your local zoning board.

Lease, Buy, or Build?

You have three choices of ownership for your location: leasing a facility, purchas-ing an existing building, or building your own. In this section, we will discuss the relative advantages of leasing or purchasing your building.

Leasing

A lease is basically a long-term agreement to rent a building, equipment, or other asset. The biggest advantage of leasing is the amount of cash you free up for other purposes. Not only do you avoid a large initial cash outlay through leasing, but you also reduce your risk during the startup period. Once your business is estab-lished, your needs may change. Leasing your business premises can give you the flexibility to move to a bigger, better, or more suitable location in the future.

A disadvantage of a lease is that it may prevent you from altering a building to fit your needs. You also do not have long-term assurance that you can stay in the same location. The owner may decide not to renew your lease at the end of the term or may increase your rent payments. Leased space in shopping centers commonly requires a monthly fee based on square feet of space, plus a percentage of gross sales.

Review any lease with your lawyer before signing it. This advice holds true for any legal document, but with a lease there is a tendency to think, "These forms are pretty much standard," and thus ignore the advice to review them first. Remember who drew up the document—the lessor. Whom do you think the conditions of the lease will favor? Not you, the lessee. You may need to negotiate the provisions of the lease, or *escape clauses*. These items can allow you to terminate the lease if your circumstances change drastically. You will also want to consider the lease's renewal options. Will the lease allow you to remain in the same location at the end of the lease period?

Leasehold improvements are important considerations to negotiate. They comprise the improvements you make to the property, such as upgrading lighting or plumbing, installing drop ceilings, building walls, and making other changes to the property. Of course, you cannot take these improvements with you when you leave, so try to negotiate rent payments in exchange for them. These are just a few factors you need to negotiate before signing a lease. Get all agreements in writing.

The best way to avoid disputes between landlords and tenants is for both parties to understand the lease agreement *before* it is signed. Because a lease will legally bind you for a long period of time, you should have the following questions answered to your satisfaction when you enter the deal:

1. *How long will the lease run?* The length of most leases is negotiable, with three to ten years being typical. In the past, landlords wanted the lease term to be as long as possible to hold down their vacancy rates. Now, in areas where vacant office space is at a premium, many businesses often want long leases as a hedge against rising prices. For example, in New York City an office tower may charge $60 per square foot for rent today, whereas the same offices rented for $16 per square foot only five years earlier.

2. *How much is the rent?* Be sure you know the dollar amount per square foot of space that the rent is based on for any location you consider. Find out how much you are paying for different kinds of space—you don't want to pay the same dollar amount for productive office space as you do for space like lobbies, hallways, mechanical areas, and bathrooms.

There are at least five types of leases, which calculate rent differently, though they are all based on square feet. In a **gross lease**, the tenant pays a flat monthly amount. The landlord pays all building operating expenses such as taxes, insurance, and repairs. Utility bills may or may not be included. In a **net lease**, the tenant pays some or all real estate taxes above the base rent. A **net-net lease** includes insurance on top of the base rent and taxes. A *net-net-net*, or **triple-net lease,** requires tenants to pay not only the base rent, taxes, and insurance, but also other operating expenses related to the building, such as repairs and maintenance. A **percentage lease**, which is common in shopping centers or other buildings that include many different businesses, requires tenants to pay a base rent plus a percentage of gross income.

3. *How much will the rent go up?* To protect against inflation, most landlords include an **escalation clause** in leases, which allows them to adjust rent according to the consumer price index (CPI) or some other scale. You should not agree to pay the full CPI increase, especially if you are already paying part of the building operating expenses.

4. *Can you sublease?* There are many reasons why you might not be able to stay in a location for the stated duration of the lease, including, at the extremes, a

leasehold improvements
Changes that make a property more valuable, such as painting, adding shelves, or installing new lighting.

gross lease
A lease in which the monthly payment made by the tenant remains the same and the landlord pays the operating expenses of the building.

net lease
A lease in which the tenant pays a base monthly rent plus some or all real estate taxes of the building.

net-net lease
A lease in which the tenant pays a base monthly rent plus real estate taxes and insurance on the building.

triple-net lease
A lease in which the tenant pays a base monthly rent plus real estate taxes, insurance, and any other operating expenses incurred for the building.

percentage lease
A lease in which the tenant pays a base monthly rent plus a percentage of their gross revenue.

escalation clause
A lease that varies according to the amount of inflation in the economy.

failure of your business or becoming so successful that you need to move to a larger space. If you must move, can you rent your space to another tenant who meets the same standards the landlord applies to all other tenants?

5. *Can you renew?* Unless a clause is written into your lease that guarantees you the first right to your space at the end of the lease term, the landlord has no legal obligation to continue it. A formula for determining the new rent payment might be included in the renewal clause, or you might pay current market rate.

6. *What happens if your landlord goes broke?* A *recognition,* or *nondisturbance, clause* can protect you from being forced out or into a new lease should the property change ownership.

7. *Who is responsible for insurance?* Landlords should be expected to carry a comprehensive policy on the building that includes casualty insurance on the structure and liability coverage for all public areas such as hallways and elevators. Building owners can require tenants to buy liability and content insurance.

8. *What building services do you get?* Your lease should state the specific services you can expect to receive, including any electricity use limits, cleaning schedules, and heating, ventilation, and air conditioning (HVAC). Note that, unlike residential rents, commercial space does not usually come with 24-hour HVAC service. (Monday through Friday from 8 A.M. to 5 P.M. and Saturday from 8 A.M. to 1 P.M. are normal.) This could produce some hot or cold working conditions if you work at other hours.

9. *Who else can move in?* Clauses can be written into leases that restrict direct competitors, or businesses that are exceptionally noisy or otherwise disruptive to others, from locating in adjoining spaces. Remember that such restrictions can become a problem to you if you need to sublease.

10. *Who pays for improvements?* Construction and remodeling become expensive quickly. Although you are usually allowed to make leasehold improvements, the building owner does not always have to pay for them. Improvements are an area wide open to negotiation in leases—make sure all agreements in this area are in writing.[9]

Before you make a commitment and sign a lease for your small business, you would be well advised to read *Leasing Space for Your Small Business* by Janet Portman and Fred Steingold (published by Nolo Press).

Purchasing

The decision to buy a building can be a difficult one. Ownership increases your upfront expenses and the amount of capital you need. The major expense of purchasing and remodeling can drain already stretched resources from other business needs.

With ownership, you gain the freedom of customizing the property any way you want. You know what your payments will be. At the same time, you are tied down to that location much more if you own rather than rent the property. Tax considerations enter the picture. Although lease payments are deductible business expenses, only depreciation on the building is deductible if you own it. Finally, the value of your investment is subject to the whims of the local real estate market. The value may appreciate or depreciate for reasons that have nothing to do with your own efforts. In the end, the choice comes down to economics and flexibility. Because most entrepreneurs are in business because of what they make or sell, and not in the "brick-and-mortar" business of real estate speculation, a majority will choose leasing.

Building

Building a new facility to meet your own specifications may be necessary if your business has unique needs or if existing facilities are not located where you need them, which may be the case in some high-growth areas.

As with buying an existing property, building a new facility greatly increases your fixed expenses. Will your revenues increase enough to cover these additional expenses? On the plus side, building a new facility may enable you to incorporate new technology or features that will lower your operating costs compared to using an older, existing building. Look at your *total* costs over the long term when making this decision.

Summary

- **Small business distribution and how "efficiencies" affect channels of distribution**

The purpose of a channel of distribution is to get a product from a producer to consumers as quickly and cheaply as possible. Because distribution represents such a large portion of the price of many products, selecting the most efficient channel will help keep costs down.

- **How the location of your business can be your competitive advantage**

Competitive advantages can be built on many factors. If the location choice of your business makes your product, good, or service more accessible to your customers, to the point where they buy from you rather than other sources, then location is your competitive advantage.

- **The crucial factors when selecting a state in which to locate your business**

In deciding where to locate your business, you should consider the price and availability of land and water, the labor pool from which you can hire employees, accessibility to customers and suppliers, closeness of competition, adequacy of transportation, public attitudes toward new businesses, taxes and regulations, your personal preference about where you want to live, financial incentives offered, and the quality of life available.

- **How to select a city in which to locate your business**

A city's sales conversion index (SCI) is calculated from *Survey of Buying Power* data to determine the amount of inshopping for a city compared to another benchmark location. Begin by determining a conversion factor for the considered city and the benchmark area by dividing total retail sales by the effective buying income for each place. Then divide the chosen city's conversion factor by the benchmark conversion factor. An SCI greater than 100 indicates inshopping—that is, more people come to that town to buy your type of product than go elsewhere.

- **The central issues in choosing a particular site within a city**

The most appropriate site for your business is determined by answering specific questions related to matching the needs of your business with the type of site, accessibility, legal considerations, and economic factors.

- **The three basic types of locations**

The three types of locations you may choose are central business districts (CBDs), shopping centers, and stand-alone locations. The CBD for most cities and towns includes the original "downtown" area, so it is usually the oldest urban section. Shopping centers can range from small strip malls that serve the local neighborhood to very large regional malls that draw customers from hundreds of miles. A stand-alone location places your business apart from other businesses.

• The types of layout you may choose

For retail businesses, a free-flow layout encourages customers to wander and browse through the store. A grid layout moves customers up and down rows of shelves and fixtures. A loop layout features a wide central aisle that leads customers quickly from one department to another. For manufacturing businesses, a process layout groups all similar equipment and jobs together and provides the flexibility needed by many small manufacturers. A product layout arranges equipment and workers in a specific sequence to produce products in a continuous flow. With a fixed layout, the product being made stays in one place, while equipment, materials, and labor are brought to it.

• Circumstances that make leasing, buying, or building appropriate choices

When deciding whether to lease, buy, or construct a building, you need to consider how long the building will be suitable for your business and whether you can afford to tie up your capital, which could be used for other purposes. Before leasing, you need to carefully examine the terms and conditions of the lease before signing it.

Questions for Review and Discussion

1. How can a small business owner create competitive advantage with a channel of distribution?

2. Why should the small business owner consider the demographics of an area when choosing a location for opening a new business? Name some sources of demographic information that are valuable tools to use in this evaluation.

3. When choosing a location for a new business, what are the most important criteria for the entrepreneur to consider? Explain the connection between type of business and location.

4. Why would a small business flourish in one area of the United States but fail in another region?

5. What is the SCI, and why should the small business owner become familiar with the way it is calculated and the information to be obtained from it?

6. Explain the importance of knowing the legal requirements of an area before attempting to open a small business.

7. What are some considerations that the entrepreneur should take into account if business is to be conducted in a foreign market?

8. What are the three location types and their subcategories? Give an example of a type of small business that would have the greatest chance of succeeding in each location type. State your reason for selecting that particular business type by giving specific advantages.

9. What is the ADA, and how does it affect the small business owner's site layout and design plan?

10. What are the main types of layout plans, and what should the entrepreneur focus on when designing the layout plan for a new business?

11. Compare and contrast the advantages and disadvantages of buying, building, or leasing space for a small business.

Questions for Critical Thinking

1. How can your business location affect customers' image and perception of your business?

2. The old adage "location, location, location" applies as well to cyberspace as it does to brick-and-mortar businesses. How does an Internet-based business influence its "location"? Which of the principles of location discussed in this chapter apply to e-businesses? What other factors do they have to deal with?

Experience This . . .

Choose a business you would like to start or own. If you are writing a business plan for this course, include this assignment in your business plan. Using graph paper (or simple architectural software if you have access to it), draw to scale the layout for your business. Include all office space, storage, restrooms, delivery, and so on, in addition to merchandise sell-ing and working areas. Also include the exterior elevation, showing parking and customer entrances. Review Figures 13.3 through 13.7; in your layout you need to label what merchandise or work will be done in each area. Include a written description of why you are using your chosen layout.

What Would You Do?

Jodi has a problem. She has decided to go into business for herself selling used books, videos, music CDs, and DVDs. She lives in a community of about 200,000 in the northeastern part of the United States. No other stores in the area specialize in the used products she will sell. Her community has a large regional shopping center with four anchor stores. Two sites the size she needs (approximately 2,000 square feet) are currently vacant in the mall.

The CBD is thriving, primarily with small, boutique-type stores. The atmosphere is pleasant, with many trees, flower beds, and artistic sculptures lining the streets. The Downtown Business Association does a good job of arranging events like parades and music festivals to draw people to the CBD. One site with 2,500 square feet is available in the CBD.

The community has two primary traffic arteries lined with stand-alone commercial businesses. One stand-alone site is available that has ample parking and a traffic count of approximately 80,000 cars per day passing at 35 mph. This site is the right size, but it is not available to lease; she would have to buy the building. Foot traffic in the mall is the highest, but restrictions and lease payments are by far higher than in the other locations. Not as many people pass by the downtown location, but rent is much cheaper as well.

Questions

1. From the information you have been provided, and considering the advantages and disadvantages of the different types of locations mentioned in this chapter, where would you recommend that Jodi locate? Provide justifications for your recommendation.

2. What additional information would you want to have to make this location decision?

CHAPTER CLOSING CASE

GOING BIG-BOX OR NOT?

The Problem: Lance Fried planned to sell his waterproof MP3 players in surf shops. But could he really say no to the big-box retailers?

At first, Lance Fried was elated. The CEO of Free style Audio had spent months slaving over his invention, a waterproof MP3 player designed specifically for athletes who want to rock out while surfing, swimming, water-skiing, or snowboarding. In classic bootstrap fashion, Fried had invested his personal savings and somehow convinced half a dozen friends to work for him for free. Now he heard some amazing news: Several major retailers—including Best Buy and Bass Sporting Goods—wanted to put his gadget on their shelves alongside popular players by giants like Apple and Sony. A deal with just a single big chain, Fried knew, could instantly push sales over $1 million.

But the more Fried thought about it, the more nervous he became. Pursuing mass retailers had never been part of the San Diego startup's plan. Instead, the idea always had been to start small, selling through specialty shops. Pursuing a big-box strategy meant crafting an entirely new business plan—one that would involve mass production and a potentially huge up-front investment. What's more, the retailers wanted the players in time for the holiday shopping season, which was just four months away.

Fried, an electrical engineer and product-design whiz who last served as CEO of an apparel company, got the idea for a submersible MP3 player while watching surfers near his home in Del Mar. Then, in late 2003, a friend dropped an iPod into a cooler full of water and ice, rendering the device useless. Fried got to work designing his waterproof player. By August 2004 a prototype was ready. It was lightweight (40 grams), with a 40-hour battery and 512MB of flash memory, capable of holding about 80 songs. The headphones wrap tightly around a swimmer's ears, and all of it is waterproofed using a proprietary technology. He planned to sell the units for $180 a pop.

Enter Greg Houlgate. A friend of Fried's who served on Freestyle's board and had worked as a sales strategist for a number of large sporting goods companies, including Callaway Golf, Houlgate showed the player to some of his contacts in the big-box retail world. "I've never had such a quick and positive response on any consumer electronics," he says.

The question was how—or for that matter, whether—to capitalize on that interest. Fried quickly convened a meeting of his three-man board at Jimmy O's, a local ocean-view hangout. Houlgate presented the good news to the third partner, Mike Brower. "Mass distribution gets your name out fast and gives you an instant hit," Houlgate said. "Your

vendors really start to take you seriously." That wasn't the only advantage. With mainstream retailers on board, it would be easier to attract investors. That appealed to Fried, who was growing tired of depleting his own bank account.

But Brower, CFO of the popular sunglasses company Spy Optic, was wary. He'd worked at plenty of sporting goods companies and had always succeeded by starting small, becoming a hit with an influential niche group, and going for bigger distribution deals only after that groundwork had been laid. How, he wondered, would Freestyle get its key customer groups—surfers and snowboarders, both of them notoriously anticorporate—into big, decidedly unhip retail outlets? And what would Freestyle have to give for the privilege of a good position on big-box shelves? "They'll make you a commodity if you don't know how to negotiate, asking for discounts that just kill your margins," Brower said.

Meanwhile, ramping up production would require a significant capital investment. How could Freestyle find that kind of money? Would the company's manufacturing partners be able to maintain quality if orders suddenly spiked? How would the company shout louder than competing MP3 player brands manufactured by corporate giants and backed by multimillion-dollar marketing campaigns?

Time was running out. The three-day action sports retail trade show—where independent retailers go to test and order new gear to sell at their surf, dive, skate, and snowboard shops—was just weeks away. Making a big splash at the show had always been part of Freestyle's plan. If Fried signed on for a big-box deal, that plan would have to change.

What do you think Lance should do?

SOURCE: From Lora Kolodny, "Case Study," *Inc.*, April 2005, 44–45. Copyright © 2006 Mansueto Ventures LLC, publishers of Inc. Magazine, New York, NY 10017. Reprinted with permission.

Test Prepper

You've read the chapter, studied the key terms, and the exam is any day now. Think you're ready to ace it? Take this sample test to gauge your comprehension of chapter material. You can check your answers at the back of the book. Want more test questions? Visit the student website at college.hmco.com/pic/hatten4e and take the ACE and ACE+ quizzes for more practice.

college.hmco.com/pic/hatten4e

Multiple Choice

1. Small business owners have access to a wealth of information about their local area in an annual issue of which business periodical?
   a. *Sales and Marketing Management*
   b. *Forbes*
   c. *Retailing Today*
   d. *Journal of Regional Economics*

2. When more people come to a community to shop for a type of item than leave it to buy the same product, the effect is called:
   a. outshopping
   b. inshopping
   c. conversion
   d. turnover

3. The government website for which of the following was recommended in this chapter as a detailed source of information on almost every country in the world that a company would want to enter?
   a. *Federal Reserve System Guide*
   c. *Department of Commerce Sourcebook*
   b. *CIA World Factbook*
   d. *Department of the Treasury Money Book*

4. Charlie wants to start a small machine shop. He plans to place all welding equipment in one area, all grinding and milling equipment in another area, and all drilling equipment in another area. What type of layout is Charlie using?
   a. fixed layout
   b. product layout
   c. process layout
   d. broken layout

5. Which of the following was *not* cited as an advantage of working in a home office?
   a. flexibility in scheduling
   b. low overhead expenses
   c. no commute time
   d. no interruptions

True/False

1. T F Neither agents nor brokers take title to goods.
2. T F The United States is more of a collection of local and regional markets than a single homogeneous market.
3. T F Almost all small businesses have the same needs when choosing a location.
4. T F Inner-city locations can have a competitive advantage because of transportation and labor sourcing issues.
5. T F A disadvantage of locating in a shopping mall is inflexibility in choosing your own hours.
6. T F Businesses that start their operations in incubators can stay there indefinitely.
7. T F Loop layouts are used for small boutiques.
8. T F A product layout provides greater flexibility for producing a wider variety of products.
9. T F A triple-net lease requires a tenant to pay a base monthly rent plus real estate taxes, insurance, and operating expenses.
10. T F Tenants must always pay for leasehold improvements.

## chapter 14

Small Business Marketing: Price and Promotion

Buzz. The type of marketing every business craves. Word-of-mouth. But how does a small business create it? First, people have to genuinely like your product: If it's bogus, it's not buzz. Not all products or businesses can generate buzz, of course. It's like catching lightning in a bottle.

Tia Wou did it. She worked in the fashion industry in the early 1990s and needed a bag like ones she had seen in her extensive travels in Asia, South America, and Europe. At the time designers were not interested in handbags, so Wou whipped out her sewing machine and combined a style from Japan with rich colors and textures from Bolivia into a bag that would sell in America. That effort spawned Tote Le Monde, as Wou teamed up with a friend from Bolivia, Aliaga, to market her bags.

Wou started with only two assets: a small, but energetic staff and an unwavering belief in her signature product—a chic but practical striped carryall bag made from recyclable plastic called Wootex. Knowing how the fashion world

After reading this chapter, you should be able to:

- Identify the three main considerations in setting a price for a product.

- Explain what breakeven analysis is and why it is important for pricing in a small business.

- Present examples of customer-oriented and internal-oriented pricing.

- Explain why and how small businesses extend credit.

- Describe the advertising, personal selling, public relations, and sales-promotion tools that a small business owner uses to compile a promotional mix.

Tia Wou.

works, Wou targeted the few retailers that set trends, not follow them. Armed with a few samples, she headed to New York to meet with buyers, landing deals with Barneys, Henri Bendel, and Saks Fifth Avenue. She also scored features in the celebrity bible *In Style* and the debut issue of *O, the Oprah Magazine*. Buzz built, and the sales of Tote Le Monde's products soared.

But Wou knew something else about buzz: It has a finite lifespan. When Monica Lewinsky (and just about everyone else) got into the handbag business in 2002, she knew the trend was over. Her company moved on to lifestyle products like bath products, luggage, and home decor, and phased out the fashion merchandise.

Wou is turning to a public relations firm to help spark new buzz about her products. Even a small firm like hers pays about $10,000 per year to get publicity and another $10,000 for samples to charity events or to celebrities and their stylists. Buzz can build quickly, so a business must be ready to ramp up production fast because "recognition without sales isn't a result."

To create buzz like Wou's on a regular basis, 26-year-old Tina Wells created and runs Buzz Marketing Group. The youth marketing agency generated revenue of $3.3 million in 2006 specializing in research, events, and promotions. Wells has been blazing a trail in youth marketing for a decade, founding her company, which was initially called The Buzz, in 1996. A little math tells you that she started the company at 16 years old. Buzz Marketing Group leverages its 10 employees. A BuzzSpotters network of more than 9,000 teens and tweens helps feed the company's research and keeps Wells in touch with what's happening.

SOURCES: Amanda C. Kooser, "Young Millionaires-Tina Wells" *Entrepreneur*, October 2006, 83–95; Linda Tischler, "Buzz Without Bucks," *Fast Company*, August 2003, 78–83; Nichole Torres, "Roamin' Holiday," *Entrepreneur*, September 2003, 102–105; Linda Tischler, "What's the Buzz?" *Fast Company*, May 2004, 76.

In the previous chapters, we discussed two of the Four Ps of marketing: product and place. In this chapter, we will investigate the third and fourth components of the marketing mix: price and promotion. We will consider why price is one of the most flexible components of a business's marketing mix, factors that must be considered in setting prices, strategies related to pricing, the use of credit in buying and selling, and ways to use the various media in communicating with your customers.

"Your total costs represent the minimum price you can charge for your goods or services. If you cannot cover your costs and make a profit, you will not stay in business."

We deal with prices every day. The coins you exchanged for a cup of coffee on the way to class, the tuition you paid for the semester, and the money you earn from a job all represent a form of price for goods and services.

The Economics of Pricing

Price is the amount of money charged for a product. It represents what the consumer considers the *value* of the product to be. The value of a product depends on the benefits received compared with the monetary cost. People actually buy benefits—they buy what a product will do for them. If consumers bought on price alone, then no Cadillac convertibles, Denon stereo receivers, or Godiva chocolates would ever be sold, because less expensive substitutes exist. People buy premium products like these because they perceive them to have higher benefits and increased quality that delivers value despite the higher cost. Typical consumers do not want the *cheapest* product available—they want the *best* product for the most reasonable price.

Price differs from the other three components of the marketing mix in that the product, place, and promotion factors all add value to the customer and costs to your business. Pricing lets you recover those costs. Although the "right" price is actually more of a range between what the market will bear and what the product costs, many elements enter into the pricing decision. For example, the image of your business or product influences the price you can charge.

Even though the pricing decision is critical to the success of a business, many small business owners make pricing decisions poorly. Total reliance on "gut feeling" is inappropriate, but so is complete reliance on accounting costs that ignore what is happening in the marketplace—what the competition is doing and what customers demand.

Three important economic factors are involved in how much you can charge for your products: competition, customer demand, and costs. Let's take a closer look at how each of these forces can affect your small business.

Competition

Your competitors will play a big part in determining the success of your pricing strategy. The number of competitors and their proximity to your business influence what you can charge for your products, because they represent substitute choices to your customers. The more direct competition your business faces, the less control you have over your prices. Direct competition makes product differentiation necessary, so that you compete on points other than price.

Proximity of competition can be a factor in pricing decisions for many small businesses. The closer the competition is geographically, the more influence it will have on your pricing. For example, if two service stations located across the street from each other had a price difference of 10 cents per gallon of gasoline, to which one would customers go? Conversely, the same price difference between stations located several miles apart may not have as dramatic an impact. Price competition presents a more difficult challenge for all businesses today, because customers have more access to information about you and your competitors than you had about your own business even five years ago.[1]

> "To survive in an industry dominated by giants, don't compete directly—differentiate. Offer your customers value—the best quality, service, and selection for their money."

The type of products sold will also have an impact on price competition. If you run a video rental business, then other video rental stores are not your only competition. In reality, your rivals include movie theaters, athletic events, and even the opera. Don't think of yourself as being in the video rental business—think of being in the entertainment business, because you are competing for entertainment dollars. Therefore, you should monitor not only what other video rental places are charging, but also what indirect, or alternative, entertainment services charge.

Today more small businesses are facing stiff competition from large chains like Wal-Mart and Kmart. Can small businesses compete with gigantic discount stores located in the same town? Of course they can. The key is to remain flexible. They probably can't compete on price for identical items—the discounters have economy-of-scale advantages from mass purchasing and distribution that can knock a small business out of a head-to-head price war. So competition must take place on other fronts. For example:

- Don't compete directly—differentiate.
- Specialize—carry harder-to-get and better-quality goods.
- Emphasize customer service.
- Extend your hours.
- Advertise more—not just products, but also your business.
- Work together with other small businesses.

Wal-Mart represents a formidable opponent for many small businesses. Its distribution system is the state-of-the-art in efficiency, linking manufacturers directly to individual stores. Its shrinkage (loss from theft and damaged goods) target is 1 percent,[2] whereas most retailers average 3 to 5 percent. Wal-Mart spends only about 0.5 percent of its sales revenues on advertising, relying mainly on word-of-mouth for publicity, compared with its major competitors, which spend about 2 percent on advertising. Wal-Mart's success is directly related to its efficiency, which goes straight to the bottom line. The company achieves a gross margin of 22 percent, compared with Sears's 30 percent. But Wal-Mart yields a 4 percent net profit margin—nearly double the rate for Sears. It's tough competition, but you can compete.

First of all, do not assume that "big box" stores such as Wal-Mart are winning the battle on price on every single item. If you do a price check, you will find that they are extremely price competitive on items that share the following traits: high household penetration (everyone buys them), large annual purchases (everyone buys a lot of them), and high purchase frequency (everyone buys a lot of them every week).[3] So, yes, you can forget about competing with discounters based on the prices of shampoo and laundry detergent. However, small businesses can be price competitive on certain other items, as well as offering superior product selection and variety.

Consider how Jayne Palmer took steps to ready her business, Gediman's Appliance, for the new competition when Wal-Mart moved to her area of Bath, Maine. She increased advertising by 30 percent. She added a computer to track her inventory and linked it into General Electric Credit so that she could order directly with better credit terms. She extended the store's hours. She offered more credit to her customers. She built a television viewing room with space for children to play on the floor. Finally, she cut the low-end appliances from her inventory to avoid competing directly with Wal-Mart on those items.

Demand

The second economic factor that affects the price you can charge for your products is *demand*—how many people want to buy how much of your product. Each

Reality Check

What Price Is Too Low . . . or Too High?

Damon Risucci is not a person who backs down from a challenge. When he started his first health club in 1990, he was only 24 and had more experience playing guitar than running a business. Synergy Fitness Clubs has since become a thriving operation, with three upscale New York City locations.

But when it came to raising prices, Risucci turned into the proverbial 97-pound weakling. For more than 10 years he kept his membership fees at $49.99 per month—about half of his competitors' rates—even though he had a rockin' Midtown Manhattan location and escalating rent and utilities. He says, "We thought our prices had to be low. It was almost a core belief."

Finally, after yet another month of reviewing financial statements and talking with staff and customers, Risucci gritted his teeth and did it: He raised monthly fees for new members to $57.99 and personal training sessions by 20 percent. The result? Not a single one of his 9,500 customers even threatened to leave. New customers have continued to join at the same, if not an increased, rate.

Risucci still offers great value, and his business represents another example of people being willing to pay for quality.

At some point, anyone selling anything will hear the objection, "We can't afford your price." How do you respond? Marketing entrepreneur Dann Ilicic, of Wow Branding, says, "We present three price options in our proposals. If they still say we're too expensive, that means we haven't demonstrated the value of what we're doing. Nothing's expensive if it provides you a return greater than the cost." Good observation—problems with price are not usually about price.

SOURCE: Stephanie Clifford, "Putting the Performance in Sales Performance," *Inc.*, February 2007, 87–95; Nadine Heintz, "Flexing Your Pricing Muscles," *Inc.*, February 2004, 25–26.

---

price you may choose for a product will be accompanied by a different level of demand. The number of units people will buy at different prices is called the **demand curve** (in economic terms a curve is often a straight line, as in Figure 14.1). The slope of that curve is called the *elasticity of demand*.

Price elasticity is the effect that price changes have on sales. The elasticity of demand for a product indicates how price sensitive the market is. **Price-elastic demand** means a *price-sensitive* market. **Price-inelastic demand** means that the market is *not price sensitive.*

If sales rise or fall more than prices rise or fall in percentage terms, demand for your product is price elastic. For example, assume that the demand for your computer software is elastic (see Figure 14.1 again). If you drop your price by 5 percent, you would expect sales to increase by more than 5 percent. Restaurant usage, personal computers, and airline travel all tend to have elastic demand. Price elasticity is far from absolute; products and segments vary in the degree of elasticity depending on how consumers perceive their need for the product.

If sales rise or fall less than prices rise or fall in percentage terms, demand for your product is price inelastic. You would expect the change in demand to be small after a change in your price (refer once more to Figure 14.1). A physician who increases the price of a medical procedure by 10 percent can expect the demand for that procedure to change by less than 10 percent. Health care is price inelastic (at least without government intervention). Both staple necessities and luxury

> **demand curve**
> The number of units of a product that people would be willing to purchase at different price levels.
>
> *price-elastic demand*
> Describes a market in which customers are price sensitive.
>
> *price-inelastic demand*
> Describes a market in which customers are not sensitive about the price.

Figure 14.1

DEMAND CURVES

When Demand for a Product Is Elastic, as with Computer Software, a Decrease in Price Will Cause an Increase in Demand.

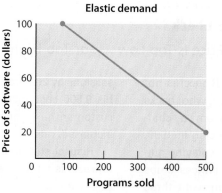

Elastic demand

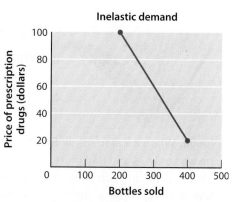

Inelastic demand

When demand for a product is elastic, as with computer software, a decrease in price will cause an increase in demand.

When demand for a product is inelastic, as with prescription drugs, a change in price will have little effect on the quantity demanded.

goods tend to have inelastic demand. If you absolutely have to have a product or service, you are less sensitive to price. If a product is truly a luxury, price becomes less of a concern. When demand for a product is inelastic, as with prescription drugs, a change in price will have little effect on the quantity demanded.

Three factors influence the price elasticity of demand for a product:

1. *Product substitutes.* The more alternatives that exist, the more price elastic a product tends to be.

2. *Necessity of the product.* Necessary and luxury goods tend to be price inelastic.

3. *The significance of the purchase to the consumer's total budget.* Cars and houses are elastic. Food and clothing are more inelastic.[4]

The theory of the elasticity of demand is important for small business owners to understand in setting prices. How easily your customers can do without your product or how readily they can use something else in its place will affect what you can charge. Market research can provide price-sensitivity information about your product.

Costs

Earlier we stated that the "right" price is actually a range of possible prices. What your competition charges and what consumers are willing to pay set the ceiling for your price range. Your costs establish the floor for your price range. If you cannot cover your costs and make a profit, you will not stay in business.

Your total costs fall into two general categories: fixed costs and variable costs.

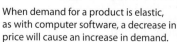

Total costs = Fixed costs + Variable costs

fixed costs
Costs that do not change with the number of sales made.

variable costs
Costs that change in direct proportion to sales.

Fixed costs remain constant no matter how many goods you sell. In the short run, your fixed costs are the same whether you sell a million units or none at all. Costs such as rent, property taxes, and utilities are fixed. **Variable costs**, in contrast, rise and fall in direct proportion to sales. Sales commissions, material, and labor tend to be variable costs.

Inc. magazine columnist Norm Brodsky (if you are not reading his monthly feature yet, start now) warns against falling into what he calls the *capacity trap*—that is, accepting a lower price than usual because you have unused capacity. Unused capacity can take the form of an empty warehouse, a truck that is sitting idle, or a machine that is used only occasionally. When the opportunity arises to sell that capacity at a reduced rate, few people would refuse. They think about the money to be made on something that would otherwise go to waste but ignore the problems they create by charging significantly less than the service is worth. Along the way, they ignore the *cost of capital;* we invest in items like trucks and warehouses to make more money from them than if we had bought something else. There are also *opportunity costs;* low-margin sales tend to crowd out high-margin sales. For example, if business is slow in your small job shop and you take on work at half your normal rate to avoid your machinery sitting idle, what happens when a full-pay job comes along? You don't have time to tackle it. Finally, do you think your existing customers won't find out that new customers are paying less than they are or have been for the same product or service? They will—and they will not be amused; they may feel betrayed. Certainly, they will demand the same discount. Bottom line: Don't erode your margins.[5]

Breakeven Analysis

By using the three cost figures discussed earlier in a breakeven analysis, you can try to find the volume of sales you will need to cover your total costs. Your **breakeven point (BEP)** in sales volume is the point at which your total revenue equals total costs. Calculating your breakeven point will allow you to set your prices above your total costs, creating profit.

> **breakeven point (BEP)**
> The point at which total costs equal total revenue and the business neither makes nor loses money.

Figure 14.2 is an example of a BEP graph. Notice that the fixed-costs line runs horizontally because fixed costs don't change with sales volume. The total-costs line begins where the fixed-costs line meets the *y*-axis of the graph, showing that your total costs are your fixed costs when you haven't sold anything. Total costs rise from that point at an angle, as variable costs and sales increase. The area between the total-costs line and the fixed-costs line represents your variable costs. The revenue line represents the number of units you will sell at any given price level—the demand curve for your product. The point at which the revenue line meets the total-costs line is your breakeven point. The area above the BEP between the revenue and total-costs lines shows profit. The area below the BEP between the revenue and total-costs lines represents loss.

The slope and shape of the revenue line for your business will vary depending on your customer demand. The information needed to draw this line can come either from sales history or, if hard data are not available, from your personal best "guesstimate" of how much people will buy. You can also plot other revenue lines based on different selling prices. The revenue line in Figure 14.2 is based on product sales. Let's use the example of compact disks (CDs) selling for $13 each. You can also find your BEP for units with the following formula:

$$\text{BEP (units)} = \frac{\text{Total fixed costs}}{\text{Unit price } - \text{ Average varible cost}}$$

where average variable cost equals total variable cost divided by quantity.

Using the data from Figure 14.2, we could calculate the BEP in units for a new CD of Christmas songs from Hatten and His Yodeling Goats. Total fixed costs to produce this musical masterpiece are $300. Variable costs run $7 per unit. Charging

Figure 14.2
BREAKEVEN ANALYSIS

When the Price of a Compact Disk is $13, the Breakeven Point (BEP) Would Be Reached When 50 CDs Are Sold and $650 of Revenue Are Generated.

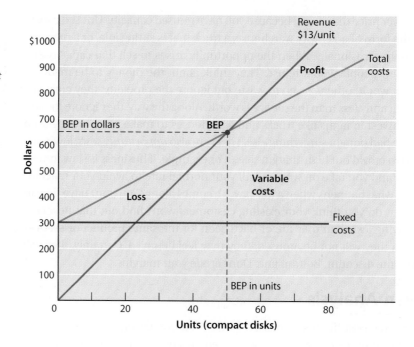

$13 per CD, we would have to sell 50 CDs to break even on the venture. (Would 50 people pay $13 to hear yodeling goats, or should Hatten keep his day job?)

$$\text{BEP (units)} = \frac{300}{13 - 7} = 50$$

To calculate the BEP point in dollars, we need to find the average variable cost of our product. This is done by taking the total variable costs ($350) and dividing by the quantity (50). The following formula is used to calculate the BEP in dollars:

$$\text{BEP (units)} = \frac{\text{Total fixed costs}}{1 - \dfrac{\text{Average variable costs}}{\text{Unit price}}}$$

For our struggling musician's CD, we would find that at $13 per CD, the BEP would be $650.

$$\text{BEP (dollars)} = \frac{300}{1 - \dfrac{7}{3}} = 650$$

What would happen to our BEP in dollars and our BEP in units if we changed the selling price to $20 each or $11 each? At $20 per CD, we would break even at only $400 in sales. At $11 per CD, we would break even at $880. Figure 14.3 illustrates what happens at different price levels.

Breakeven analysis is a useful tool in giving you a guideline for price setting. It can help you see how different volume levels will affect costs and profits. In reality, lines rarely run perfectly straight indefinitely. The usefulness of your analysis depends on the quality of your data. The most valuable information for figuring your BEP is the demand for your products at each price level, which is difficult to predict with precision.

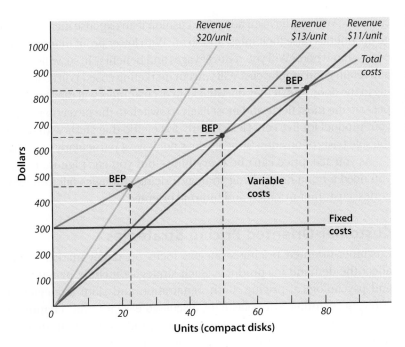

Figure 14.3
HOW PRICE CHANGES AFFECT THE BREAKEVEN POINT

When the Price of a Compact Disk Is Changed to $11 or $20, the Breakeven Point Also Changes.

Another use for breakeven analysis is to tell you how many units you need to sell to earn your desired return. If Hatten and His Yodeling Goats wanted a return of $1,000, how many units would need to be sold?

$$\text{Target return} = \frac{\text{Total fixed cost } + \text{ Desired profit}}{\text{Unit price } - \text{ Average variable cost}}$$

$$\$1,000 \text{ return} = \frac{300 + 1,000}{13 - 7} \, 217 \text{ units}$$

When the sales price is $13 per CD, 217 CDs would have to be sold to generate a return of $1,000.

Pricing-Setting Techniques

After taking competition, consumer demand, and your costs into consideration, you have made a start toward establishing your "right" price. You have a feel for what the price floor and price ceiling might be, but the price you finally choose will depend on the objectives and strategies you choose to pursue—what you are trying to accomplish in your business.

You have surely heard the old joke about the guy who buys 100 watermelons for $100 and sells them in bunches of 10 for $10. When asked how he expects to make money, he replies, "I'll make it up in volume." Okay, so it's not that funny, but you would be amazed how many people think they can grow their businesses merely by pricing their products cheaper than the competition. They assume that low prices will generate enough sales to make up for lower margins.

Setting your prices too low is a dangerous trap to fall into when starting a business. Take a hypothetical example: You think that some product is too expensive, so you decide to go into business selling that item for less than your competitors. If you sell for less, you have lower profit margins. Lower profit margins, in turn, mean less cash flow. Will you have an adequate cushion if an expense increases? After all, rents go up, utilities raise their rates, and so on. With lower profit margins, you need to cut costs—but where? Will you reduce wages and benefits? If, so, will you be able to hire and retain good employees? Will you cut marketing costs? Will customers keep coming in the door, and, if they do, what kind of customers will they be? Low-price shoppers are the most fickle and most likely to switch to the next company that can offer your product for five cents less. Clearly, a scenario that starts with using low price as the sole basis of business strategy does not have a particularly attractive outlook.[6]

As you see, price can't be everything—but you can't ignore it, either. Instead, you need a bona fide pricing strategy. Pricing strategies fall into two broad categories: customer oriented and internal oriented.

Customer-Oriented Pricing Strategies

Customer-oriented pricing strategies focus on target markets and factors that affect the demand for products. Such strategies include penetration, skimming, and psychological pricing. Both penetration and skim strategies are based on knowing customer price elasticity, discussed earlier in this chapter. If elasticity is low, it would make sense to price your new product high (within reason), because people will buy it regardless of the price level. If elasticity is high, a penetration strategy is more appropriate to drive greater sales volume.[7]

Suppose you have the following pricing objectives:

* Increase sales.
* Increase traffic in your store.
* Discourage competitors from entering your market.

penetration pricing
Setting the price of a new product lower than expected to gain fast market share.

To accomplish these objectives and gain rapid market share, **penetration pricing** is the most appropriate strategy. Penetration pricing entails setting prices below what you might expect to encourage customers to initially try your product. This strategy is designed to keep competition from entering the market for your product. Athough you make less profit on each unit, the tradeoff is to remove the incentive for competition to enter, thereby, it is hoped, helping you build a long-term position in the market.

Suppose that you have a different set of pricing objectives:

* Maximize short- or long-run profit.
* Recover product development costs quickly.

price skimming
Setting the price of a new product higher than expected to recover development costs.

If these are your objectives and you have a truly unique product, a strategy of **price skimming** may be appropriate. Price skimming involves setting your price high when you believe that customers are relatively price insensitive or when there is little competition for consumers to compare prices against. Skimming helps recover high development costs, so businesses with new-to-the-world inventions often use this strategy. Home electronics, for example, are often introduced using a skimming strategy. Think of the price declines in personal computers, cell phones, and DVDs. These products usually have high development costs, but their unit costs fall as production increases. Of course, consumers have to be willing to pay a premium to be one of the first to own these new products. Skimming is not a long-term strategy. Eventually competition forces prices down.

Finally, suppose you have these pricing objectives:

- Stabilize market prices.
- Establish your company's position in the market.
- Build an image for your business or product.
- Develop a reputation for being fair with suppliers and customers.

To accomplish these objectives, you may employ one of the **psychological pricing** strategies, which aim to influence the consumer's reaction toward prices of products. Such strategies include prestige pricing, odd pricing, and reference pricing.

psychological pricing
Setting the price of a product in a way that will alter its perception by customers.

People often equate quality with price, a belief that has led to a practice called **prestige pricing**. Prestige pricing is especially effective with goods whose quality is difficult to determine by inspection or for products that consumers have little solid information about. Products as diverse as jewelry, perfume, beer, and smoke detectors, or the services of law firms, can all be prestige priced.

prestige pricing
Psychological pricing strategy used with goods whose quality is difficult to determine by inspection or for products about which consumers have little solid information.

In an experiment at Stanford University, graduate students were given three unmarked bottles of beer. One bottle had a dime taped to it, one had nothing, and the third required payment of a dime. The students did not know that the beer in all three bottles was identical. The "premium" beer (the one that cost a dime) won the taste test. Some students even said the "discount" beer made them ill. Price does affect the image of a product.

We are more likely to see goods priced at $4.98, $17.89, or $49.95 than at $5.00, $18.00, or $50.00—this is **odd pricing**. Research has yet to prove a positive effect of odd pricing, but proponents believe that consumers see $99.99 as a better deal than $100.00. Sales of some products seem to benefit from *even pricing* if you are trying to convey the image of quality. For example, pricing a diamond ring at $18,000 gives the appearance of being above squabbling over loose change.

odd pricing
Psychological pricing strategy in which goods are priced at, say, $9.99 rather than $10.00 in the belief that the price will seem lower than it really is.

Reference pricing is common in retail goods for which consumers have an idea of what the price "should be" and have a "usual" price for that item in mind. As discussed already, a product's price is supported by the value it generates for the customer; with reference pricing, however, the price can be changed without affecting the value. For example, a 12-pack of Coca-Cola is a commodity well recognized by most shoppers, who have a good idea of what a package of 12 cans of Coke is worth. If the price is dropped, customers are attracted to the product; conversely, if it is raised above that reference point, they are repelled.

reference pricing
Psychological pricing strategy common in retailing goods for which consumers have an idea of what the price "should be."

If your customers are price sensitive to comparison prices of competing items, you may choose to use **price lining**. An example of price lining would be a men's clothing store that has ties at three different price points, such as $24.95, $33.95, and $44.95.

price lining
Grouping product prices into ranges, such as low-, medium-, and high-priced items.

Internal-Oriented Pricing Strategies

Pricing strategies that are internal oriented are based on your business's financial needs and costs rather than on the needs or wants of your target markets. If you use these strategies, make sure that you don't price your products out of the marketplace. Remember that consumers don't care what your costs are; they care only about the value they receive. Internal-oriented strategies include cost-plus pricing and target-return pricing.

markup
The amount added to the cost of a product in setting the final price. It can be based on selling price or on cost.

Cost-Plus Pricing   Probably the most common form of pricing is adding a specified percentage, a fixed fee, or **markup**, to the cost of the item. Although this type of pricing, called *cost-plus pricing*, has always been common in retailing and wholesaling, manufacturers also use this relatively simple approach. Markup can be based on either *selling price* or *cost*, and it is important to distinguish between the two.

For example, if an item costs $1.00 and the selling price is $1.50, the markup on selling price is 33.3 percent. Fifty cents is one-third of $1.50. However, using the same figures, the markup on cost is 50 percent. Fifty cents is one-half of $1.00. Markup based on cost makes your markup appear higher, even though the amounts are exactly the same. Most businesses base markup on selling price.

Effective use of markup depends on your ability to calculate the *profit margin* you need to cover costs. Formulas useful in calculating markup include the following:

$$\text{Selling price} = \text{Cost} + \text{Markup}$$
$$\text{Markup} = \text{Selling price} - \text{Cost}$$
$$\text{Cost} = \text{Selling price} - \text{Markup}$$

Target-Return Pricing   If you have accurate information on how many units you will sell and what your fixed and variable costs will be, *target-return pricing* will allow you to set your selling price to produce a given rate of return. To calculate a target-return price, add your fixed costs and the dollar amount you wish to make, divide by the number of units you intend to sell, and then add the variable cost of your product.

$$\text{Target return price} = [(\text{Fixed costs} + \text{Target return}) \div \text{Unit sales}] + \text{Variable cost}$$

As an example, suppose demand for your product is 5,000 units. To meet this demand, you need a target return of $100,000. Your fixed costs are $200,000 and your variable costs run $50 per unit. Using this strategy, your price would be

$$\frac{\$200,000 + \$100,000}{5,000} + 50 = \$6 + \$50$$
$$= \$110 = \text{Your selling price}$$

Creativity in Pricing

The importance of being proactive and creative in running your business is a theme that runs throughout this book. The need for creativity can apply to pricing as well. The key to creativity is breaking out of thought processes that keep you in ruts, such as the cliché, "That's not the way it's done in my type of business." To be creative in your pricing, look at techniques and practices of pricing used in different types of businesses and ask yourself, "How can that concept be applied to my business?" To begin this process, look at Table 14.1, the Creative Pricing Primer, compiled by Michael Mondello of Celestial Seasonings.[8] Take note of how each approach could apply to your business.

Credit Policies

After establishing your pricing practices comes an even more important task: deciding how you will get customers to pay for their purchases. Payment methods include cash, check, or credit.

Obviously, accepting only cash really cuts down on those bad debts. But the trend is toward consumers carrying *less* cash, not more, so a cash-only policy will probably turn off many customers who would like to purchase with another form of payment. Most small businesses accept checks with adequate identification, such as a phone number and driver's license number, in case the bank returns the check for insufficient funds. For bookkeeping purposes, checks are treated the same as cash and actually make bank deposits easier.

The main reasons for your small business to extend credit are to make sales to customers you would not have otherwise reached and to increase the volume and frequency of sales to existing customers.

Extending Credit to Your Customers

Should you extend credit to your customers? Good question. Do your competitors? Will your sales increase enough to pay the finance charges? Will sales increase enough to cover the bad debts you will incur? Can you extend credit and still maintain a positive cash flow? Will credit sales smooth out fluctuations in sales volume?

Credit is broken down into two basic categories: trade credit and consumer credit.

Trade Credit   **Trade credit** refers to sales terms that one business extends to another for purchasing goods. As a small business owner, consider trade credit from both directions—extended to you from vendors and that you may extend to your customers. If you can purchase goods/services and are allowed to take 30, 60, or 90 days to pay for them, you have essentially obtained a loan for those items for that time period. Many new businesses can take advantage of trade credit even when no other form of financing is available. Be warned, however, that habitual late payment or nonpayment may cause your suppliers to cut off your trade credit and place your business on a COD—cash on delivery—basis.

> *trade credit*
> Credit extended from one business to another.

If you extend credit to your business customers, you will need an accounts receivable system to keep cash flowing into your business. A very easy trap that growing new businesses fall into is the thought, "Get the sales now; work on improving profit margins later." This trap is especially serious for service businesses, whose largest expense is labor, which must be paid when the service is provided. Manufacturers also suffer from slow collection due to the long time lag between purchasing raw materials, labor, and inventory and the actual sale of the product. If you don't collect on sales, they aren't sales.

Trade credit can be offered in several forms: extended payment periods and terms, goods offered on consignment, payment not required until goods are sold. Credit lines are popular ways for one business to receive trade credit from another.

Consumer Credit   You have several choices regarding **consumer credit,** which is offered to your ultimate customers rather than to other businesses. You can carry the debt yourself, you can rely on a financial institution such as a bank to loan money to your customers, or you can accept credit cards.

> *consumer credit*
> Credit extended by retailers to the ultimate customers for the purchase of products or services.

If you wish to carry the debt yourself, you can set up an *open charge account* for customers. Customers take possession of the goods, and you bill them. Invoices are usually sent out monthly. You can encourage early payment by offering cash

Table 14.1   CREATIVE PRICING PRIMER

Pricing Approach	How It Works	Examples
1. Bundling or unbundling	Sell products or services together as packages or break them apart and price accordingly.	Season tickets; stereo equipment; car rentals charging for air conditioning
2. Time-period pricing	Adjust price up or down during specific times to spur or acknowledge changes in demand.	Off-season travel fares (to build demand); peak-period fees on bank ATMs (to shift demand)
3. Trial pricing	Make it easy and lower the risk for a customer to try out what you sell.	Three-month health club starter memberships; low, nonrefundable "pre-view fees" on training videos
4. Image pricing	Sometimes the customer wants to pay more, so you price accordingly.	Most expensive hotel room in a city; a private-label vitamin's raise in price to increase unit sales by signaling quality to shoppers
5. Accounting-system pricing	Structure price to make it more salable within a business's buying systems.	Bill in phases so no single invoice exceeds an authorization threshold; classify elements so pieces get charged to other line items.
6. Value-added price packages	Include free "value-added" services to appeal to bargain shoppers, without lowering price.	A magazine's offering advertisers free merchandising tie-ins when they buy ad space at rate-card prices
7. Pay-one-price	Unlimited use of a service or product, for one set fee.	Amusement parks; office-copier service contracts; salad bars
8. Constant promotional	Although a "regular" price exists, no one ever pays it.	Consumer electronics retailers' pricing always matching "lowest price" in town; always offering one pizza free when customer buys one at regular price
9. Price performance	Amount customers pay is determined by the performance or value they receive.	Money managers' being paid profits; offering a career-transition guide for $80 and allowing buyers to ask for any amount refunded after use
10. Change the standard	Rather than adjust price, adjust the standard to make your price seem different (and better).	A magazine clearinghouse's selling a $20 subscription for "four payments of only $4.99"
11. Shift costs to your customer	Pass on ancillary costs directly to your customer, and do not include those costs in your price.	A consulting firm's charging a fee and then rebilling all mail, phone, and travel costs directly to client
12. Variable pricing tied to a creative variable	Set up a "price per" pricing schedule tied to a related variable.	Children's haircuts at 10 cents per inch of the child's height; marina space billed at $25 per foot for a boat
13. Different names for different price segments	Sell essentially the same product, under different names, to appeal to different price segments.	Separate model numbers or variations of the same TV for discounters, department stores, and electronics stores
14. Captive pricing	Lock in your customer by selling the system cheap, and then profit by selling high-margin consumables.	The classic example: selling razors at cost, with all the margin made on razor blade sales
15. Product-line pricing	Establish a range of price points within your line. Structure the prices to encourage customers to buy your highest-profit product or service.	Luxury-car lines (high-end models enhance prestige of entire line but are priced to encourage sale of more profitable low end)
16. Differential pricing	Charge each customer or each customer segment what each will pay.	In new-car sales, a deal for every buyer; Colorado lift tickets sold locally at a discount, at full price for fly-ins
17. Quality discount	Set up a standard pricing practice, which can be done several ways.	Per-unit discount on all units, as with article reprints; discounts only on the units above a certain level, as with record clubs
18. Fixed, then variable	Institute a "just-to-get-started" charge, followed by a variable charge.	Taxi fares; phone services tied to usage
19. "Don't break that price point!"	Price just below important thresholds for the buyer, to give a perception of lower price.	Charging $499 for a suit; $195,000 instead of $200,000 for a design project

Note: Once you've been creative, make sure you're covered. The most important aspect of any pricing approach is that it be legal and ethical. Check with your legal counsel.

SOURCE: From "Naming Your Price," by Michael Mondello, *Inc.*, July 1992, p. 82. Reprinted with permission of Gruner & Jahr USA.

discounts or punishing late payment with finance charges. Open accounts must be managed carefully. As noted in Chapter 8, open accounts can absolutely kill cash flow and drain the life out of your business.

An *installment account* is frequently offered to customers who are purchasing big-ticket items (such as autos, boats, and appliances). Customers rarely have enough cash to pay up front for such items. With an installment account, they make a down payment and follow with monthly payments on the unpaid balance plus interest for an extended period of time. This type of financing is not quite as dangerous as the open account, because the product typically serves as collateral. Generally, small businesses exist to sell their products, whereas financial institutions are in business to sell money—so let them handle installment loans.

Alternatively, you may extend a *line of credit* to your customers. This system operates like a revolving credit account: You approve credit purchases for each customer up to a certain dollar limit. Lines of credit allow customers to buy goods without going through a new credit check for each purchase. Finance charges are paid on the unpaid balance monthly. Extending lines of credit can reduce the amount of paper in your credit application process, because a new application is not required for each purchase. This type of financing allows you to control the total amount of credit you extend.

To avoid the expense and inconvenience of maintaining your own accounts receivable, you can rely on *credit cards* as your source of consumer credit. Consumers' use of cash and checks is decreasing as a percentage of total consumer spending, whereas the use of credit and debit cards is skyrocketing. A survey by the American Bankers Association revealed that 52 percent of all in-store purchases today are made with debit or credit cards. Cash and checks account for 42 percent of such transactions. Debit cards alone account for 31 percent of all in-store transactions, exceeding the number handled with credit cards (21 percent) and checks (15 percent) and nearly equal to cash payments.[9]

A new player in consumer payment is *cell phones* used in place of cash. Customers buying a train ticket, picking up a newspaper, and grabbing a cup of coffee on their way to work just wave their handset and your business has their money. This practice offers a lot more convenience than the consumer fumbling for money and waiting for change, or using plastic and having to tap in numbers or sign a slip of paper.[10] If your target market is between the ages of 18 and 34 you may want to consider taking this type of payment, as younger people are four times more likely to carry a cell phone than cash.

Convenience for customers comes at a price for businesses, however. Businesses must pay a percentage of each sale to the credit card company handling the sale. Although card companies offer discount rates for small businesses, transaction and statement fees will increase the amount you pay. The percentage most small businesses pay to credit card companies varies according to the number of transactions made, but most small businesses are charged between 1.5 percent and 3 percent.[11] Total fees, including sales percentages and transaction and statement fees, can run as high as 6 percent.

Online Credit Checks   For business credit requests, the Yahoo! Web search site lists several merchant credit services that you can access through the Web links' capability. Just point your mouse to the one you want to investigate and click. In

Figure 14.4

SHOW ME THE MONEY

*The Longer Bills Go Unpaid, the
Less Your Chance of Collecting.*

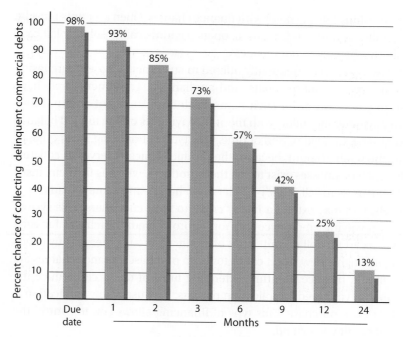

Figure 14.4

SHOW ME THE MONEY

*The Longer Bills Go Unpaid, the
Less Your Chance of Collecting.*

addition, Dun & Bradstreet provides a free search of millions of U.S. companies. Then, for a nominal fee, you can receive a Business Background Report that lists important credit information about the company you're investigating.

For about $300 per year, you can join the National Association of Credit Management, a membership organization that researches and reports on many small firms that are often overlooked by larger credit agencies. As a member, you can get a comprehensive report on a particular firm from the database, which includes about 6.5 million firms.

Collecting Overdue Accounts

Bill collecting is never fun, but it is critical for small businesses. Paul Mignini, Jr., president of the National Association of Credit Management, says that you will often hear customers' excuses like, "Times are tough; we're having a hard time making it." You should acknowledge their difficulty by saying, "I know times are tough. Let's get this settled before other bills get in the way." The longer bills go unpaid, the worse your chances of collecting on the debt (see Figure 14.4).

Begin your collection process by telephone if you don't receive a check after 30 days. Create a sense of urgency that the bill must be paid. Try to get a commitment for a certain amount by a specific day, like $100 by the 25th of the month. That puts the burden on the customer. If repeated calls lead you to believe that the customer is playing games, with little intention of paying what she owes, you have five choices: a letter service, an attorney, small claims court, a collection agency, or writing it off. Always remain professional and try to stay on friendly terms. You can say something like, "I really busted my tail to get the delivery to you on time. Will you please help us serve other customers by sending a check?"

To facilitate collections, pay attention to your invoices and credit applications. Always print your late-payment service charges on your invoices. Include a venue provision on your invoices if you are selling goods out of state so that any court case concerning the sale will be heard in a court of your choice. State the specific number of days a customer has to notify you of any problems with the shipment.

On your credit application form, ask customers to sign a release that authorizes creditors to disclose relevant information. This step will help you to spot credit problems in advance.

Promotion

The goal of a company's promotional efforts is to communicate with target markets. You have four major tools available when developing your *promotional mix:* advertising, personal selling, public relations, and sales promotions. The weight you choose to give to each of these tools will depend on your type of business.

Advertising

Advertising is a way to bring attention to your product or business by publishing or broadcasting a message to the public through various media. Your choices of media include the following:

Print media: newspapers, magazines, direct mail, Yellow Pages

Broadcast media: radio, television, or computer billboards

Outdoor media: billboards or posters placed on public and other transportation

The habits of your target market will affect your choice of advertising media. For example, if your target market is teenagers, radio and television would be the most appropriate choices. The nature of your product will also help to determine the media selected. Does advertising for your product need to include color, sound, or motion to make it more attractive? The cost of your advertising is another important factor in choosing media vehicles. You should look at the total dollar amount that an ad costs and the cost per thousand people exposed to the message.

Advertising is critical, but it has some real downsides, including slow feedback, expense, difficulty cutting through clutter, and difficulty creating a personalized message. Choosing the appropriate advertising medium for your message is important. Which one should you use? Let's take a look at your options (the percentage of total media dollars spent on each medium is shown in parentheses):

Newspaper (20.1 percent)

Advantages: Flexible; timely; covers local markets well; believable (because people read newspapers to get information); relatively inexpensive; can use color, coupons, or inserts.

Limitations: Short life of ad; number of ads per newspaper causes clutter; poor photo reproduction; low pass-along value (meaning that newspapers are rarely read by more than one person).

Profile in Entrepreneurship
Hitting the Streets

Shepard Fairey has something that many businesses want: the ability to get alternative-culture kids talking about mainstream brands. As a self-described "skatepunk" while a student at the Rhode Island School of Design, he began plastering the face of pro wrestler Andre the Giant on stickers and posters he created on local night spots. He aroused the curiosity of the community and created a following with his art. He didn't realize he was doing what marketers attempt to do.

In some circles Fairey is known as one of the most prolific and notorious street artists of his generation, creating memorable graphics that have spread through urban centers all over the world. He has gone on to form his own marketing design firm, Studio Number One. Fairey walks a fine line between art and commerce, between the underground world of graffiti art and the very mainstream world of selling products to consumers. He says, "Sometimes I feel like a double agent."

While in New York to address a conference called Creativity Now on the topic "The Commodification of Street Art," Fairey described himself as a capitalism-embracing entrepreneur. But later that same evening, he went out with some friends to do some "bombing," or putting up street images. While on a rooftop pasting up a six- by eight-foot poster, he got caught by police and was arrested for criminal mischief and trespassing—for the ninth time.

Shepard has a gallery exhibition titled "This Is Your God" that juxtaposes his signature graphics with dollar bills. Such works speak to a large group of people—people that Levis, Mountain Dew, Universal Pictures, Sunkist, Sony, Ford, and Pepsi (to list a few clients) have paid him to reach. *Supply & Demand: The Art of Shepard Fairey* is a hardcover book featuring more than 700 illustrations spanning the man's "Obey"-obsessive output from 1989 to 2006. Fairey is a maverick, a self-promoter, an artist, a skater, a risk-taker, a guerrilla marketer . . . an entrepreneur.

SOURCES: Rob Walker, "The Buzz Guru," *Inc.*, March 2004, 102–109; Sandra Dolbow, "Guerrilla Marketers of the Year—Landscape of the Giants," *Brandweek*, 12 November 2001, 25–32; "Blk/Mrkt Inc," *Creativity*, April 2003, 45; "Shepard Fairey's Giant Retrospective," *Creativity*, July 2006, 2.

Television (24.3 percent)

Advantages: Reaches large audience; combines sight, sound, and motion; perceived to be prestige medium.

Limitations: High absolute cost; several ads run together increases clutter and decreases impact; short exposure time.

Direct Mail (18.3 percent)

Advantages: Can be targeted very specifically; message can be personalized; less space limitations than other media.

Limitations: Perceived as "junk mail"; high relative cost; mailing lists are expensive and often inaccurate.

Radio (7.9 percent)

Advantages: Can be targeted to specific audience; low relative cost; short lead time so ads can be developed quickly.

Limitations: People are often involved with other activities and do not pay full attention to ad; people cannot refer back to ad; competition for best time slots.

Creating Competitive Advantage

Guppy in a Shark Tank: Small Business, Big Trade Shows

The 1.3 million-square-foot McCormick Place convention center in Chicago can seem like a very large place if you are a small business owner setting up for a trade show. Giant competitors set up booths that dwarf the displays of small businesses. Nevertheless, trade shows can generate big deals for small businesses.

Gregory Perkins uses bright lights, bold and colorful graphics, and ten-foot-tall displays to catch the attention of the 20,000 people attending Book Expo America. Perkins's business, Magic Image, sells African American greeting cards, calendars, and pocket planners. He does about a dozen shows a year, and they generate most of his $500,000 annual sales. At the 1998 Book Expo, Perkins caught a big fish of a deal when Target Stores placed a $30,000 order on the spot.

Research shows that trade shows can be more effective at generating sales than direct mail, telemarketing, or other sales strategies—but you have to develop some trade-show savvy. To improve your odds of success at trade shows, try the following:

- *Choose the right show.* Trade shows are specialized by industry, market, or product. Size, draw, and cost vary widely. Find shows that offer the right mix of audience, location, industry, and price.

- *Plan ahead.* E-mail, snail-mail a letter or postcard, fax, or phone the customers you want to pitch at the show. Let them know where your booth will be and how to reach you at the hotel. Don't just sit back and wait for people to approach you. Put forethought into your display. If you bought a ten-by ten-foot space, recreate that size before you go to the show to ensure that all the products you plan to take will fit and to decide how you want to display them.

- *Get a good spot.* You want a steady flow of foot traffic, so try to get an island location. Your chances of getting a good spot increase by registering early. You may have to pay a premium to be near the entrance or in a corner.

- *Pool resources with others.* Locating next to businesses with products that complement yours can build synergy. Perkins and five other business owners had their booths adjoin one another to strategically increase the presence of African American products. Each paid for his own space, but the combination made an impressive display for bookstores looking for their products.

- *Use the right stuff.* Your sales tactics at a show should be different than when you are on the floor or on the phone. You have only about 45 seconds to draw someone into your booth. You have to be quick and concise, and use the right buzzwords. Don't concentrate on talking to one customer at the expense of ignoring new people who wander in.

- *Follow up on leads.* Your intent is to turn contacts into sales contracts. Although you may close some deals in the booth, sealing even more will take persistence and patience. Stay in touch via your company newsletters to keep potential customers informed about your business.

Ready for a road trip? The three-day Small Business Expo in Auckland, New Zealand, is designed as a "business-to-business marketplace" for small and medium-sized businesses, providing all types of business solutions under one roof. Over 7,000 small business owners attend each year.

SOURCES: Michelle Wirth Fellman, "Small Booth, Big Show, Big ROI," *Marketing News*, 1 February 1999, 1; Karen Gutloff, "Show and Sell," *Black Enterprise*, July 1998, 105; Kate Meere, "Largest Event Ever Held for Small Business," *Chartered Accountants Journal*, November 2005, 16–17.

Magazine (5.1 percent)

Advantages: Target markets can be selected geographically and demographically; long life because magazines are often passed along; high-quality reproduction.

Limitations: Long lead time needed in purchasing ad; no guarantee of placement within magazine; higher relative cost than other print media.

Outdoor (0.7 percent)

Advantages: High, repeated exposure; low cost; little competition.

Limitations: Limited amount of message due to exposure time to ad; little selectivity of target market.

Yellow Pages (5.4 percent)

Advantages: People viewing ad are likely to be interested buyers; relatively inexpensive; effectiveness of ad easy to measure.

Limitations: All of your competitors are listed in the same place; easy to ignore small ads; may need to be listed in several sections.

Internet (1.8 percent)

Advantages: Good selectivity of target markets; inexpensive.

Limitations: Often negative reaction to advertising on computer networks; uncertainty of number of people reached.

Miscellaneous (14.4 percent)[12]

Known as *unmeasured media advertising,* miscellaneous advertising includes things like catalogs, ads on bus stop benches, and signage at sport fields. Many small businesses determine how much to spend on advertising by allocating a percentage of their total sales revenues. This percentage varies considerably by type of business (see Table 14.2).

Advertising Objectives   Different types of advertisements help to accomplish different objectives. You may be trying to do any of the following:

- *Inform* your audience of the existence of your business, your competitive advantage, or product features and benefits.

- *Persuade* people to take an immediate action—such as buying your product.

- *Remind* people that your business or product still exists. Get them to remember what they received from your business in the past so that it remains in their evoked set.

- *Change the perception* of your business rather than trying to sell specific products. Generally called *institutional advertising,* advertising with this objective aims to build goodwill rather than to make an immediate sale.

Table 14.2
ADVERTISING COSTS
BY BUSINESS TYPE

Industry	Ad Dollars as % of Operating Income
New and Used Car Dealers	1.1%
Furniture and Home Furnishing Stores	4.1%
Electronics and Appliance Stores	2.1%
Hardware Stores	1.6%
Food and Beverage Retail Stores	0.8%
Beer, Wine, and Liquor Stores	0.6%
Nonstore Retailers	3.4%
Software Publishers	6.1%
Commercial Banking	0.5%
Advertising and Related Services	5.1%
Food Services and Drinking Places	2.7%
Motor Vehicle Manufacturers	1.8%
Breweries	8.1%
Soft Drink Companies	3.1%

SOURCE: Leo Troy, *Almanac of Business and Industrial Financial Ratios, 2007* (Chicago: CCH Publishing, 2006).

It is a challenge to achieve these broad objectives with your advertising. Creating effective advertisements is both a science and an art. Originality, humor, and excitement can make your ad break through the clutter of other media, but, at the same time, these traits can obscure the real message of your ad. Communicating your message clearly while catching the viewer's attention is a tough balance to achieve. Consider these common strategies, all of which you might choose to achieve your advertising objectives:

- *Testimonials.* Use an authority or a personal testimony from a celebrity to present your message. Athletes and movie stars attract attention, but their public images can change rapidly and must remain consistent with that of your business.

- *Humor.* Humor can grab the viewer's attention, but be careful who bears the brunt of the joke or you could offend some group and generate negative publicity for your business. Advertising history is also full of some very funny ads that did not generate a single dollar of additional revenue.

- *Sensual or sexual messages.* According to the cliché, "Sex sells." Sex is certainly used in a lot of ads, but research shows that it is not an effective way to get a message across. As with humor, using sex to attract attention is worthless if it doesn't translate into sales.

- *Comparative messages.* Naming competitors in your advertising is legal and quite common. It can be a very powerful way to position your product in customers' minds against another known entity—although it also gives your competitor free exposure.

- *Slice-of-life messages.* These messages may use a popular song or a brief scene from life to position your product. Music is a great way to transport people mentally back to another time in their life. Nostalgia can help create a brand identity for your product.

- *Fantasy messages.* These messages present an idealistic self-image of the buyer. What you are trying to do is link a product with a desirable person or situation. Certainly, this is what almost every beer or soft-drink commercial attempts—the message is, "Drink this liquid and you will be beautiful, popular, and desirable." Right.

How do you tell if your advertising works? A common complaint among advertisers runs along this line: "I know that half of my advertising dollars are wasted, I just don't know which half." Measuring the effectiveness of your advertising is difficult. Is the cost of producing and running the ad justified by increased sales and profit? A few techniques might help you find out.

- *Response tracking.* Coded or dated coupons can let you compare different media, such as the redemption rate for coupons in newspapers compared with flyers handed out on the street.

- *Split ads.* Code two different ads, different media, or broadcast times to see which produces a greater response.

- *In-store opinions.* Ask in-store customers where they heard about your business, what they think, what you are doing right, and why they buy from you rather than from a competitor.

- *Telephone surveys.* Make random phone calls with numbers gleaned from customer files. Ask customers whether they have seen your advertising and what they think of it.

- *Statement questionnaires.* Drop a brief questionnaire in the monthly bills you send out to ask customers if they are satisfied with the product or service and how they found out about it.

Advertising Development   Most small business owners plan their own advertising programs, which is usually more appropriate for them than hiring a professional producer. Even if you choose to use an advertising agency, you should still take active control of your advertising campaign. Remember, you cannot afford to buy a solution to every problem you will face. This is true with your advertising. Spending money will not automatically get you better advertising. As Paul Hawkin has said, "The major problem affecting businesses, large or small, is a lack of *imagination,* not a lack of capital."[13] Don't let money replace creativity.

A common problem among self-produced advertisements is that business owners try to cram too much into them. Their reasoning is, "This space costs a lot of money, so I am going to use every minuscule part of it." The result is usually an ad that is busy, unattractive, and uninteresting. Simplicity should be the rule here. White space draws the reader's attention. The same principle applies to package design: It doesn't have to tell the consumer everything.

Even though self-produced ads are appropriate for many small businesses, owners should at least investigate the options and promotions that outside professional advertising services make available.

Advertising Agencies   To mount an effective campaign, you may want to consider consulting an advertising agency. These businesses can help you by conducting preliminary studies, developing an advertising plan, creating advertisements, selecting the appropriate media, evaluating the effectiveness of the advertising, and conducting ad follow-up.

A small agency that specializes in and understands your type of business may be a better choice for a small business than a large agency. Ask your friends and colleagues for recommendations, and get samples of the agency's work before signing a contract. Remember that fees are often negotiable, so the agency's fees may be flexible.

Media Agencies   You can create your own advertising and hire a media buyer to coordinate the purchase of print space or broadcast time for your ads. Why would you choose to use a media buyer? If you have identified your specific target market, a media buyer can help coordinate your media mix to reach that market. Suppose you have designed a new line of blue jeans targeted to urban females from 13 to 17 years old. A media buyer can tell you in which magazine, on which radio station, or on which television show to advertise.

Art and Graphic Design Services   If you design your own ads and write your own copy but lack the artistic skills needed to produce the final piece of art or film, an art service can handle this task for you. Like the art director in an advertising agency, this service needs to work closely with the person writing your copy to coordinate the message.

Other Sources   Radio and television studios, newspapers, and magazines with which you contract to run your advertising can also produce ads for you. Their services generally cost less than those of an advertising agency.

Personal Selling

Personal selling involves a personal presentation by a salesperson for the purpose of making sales and building relationships with customers. There are many products not large enough, complex enough, or differentiated enough to warrant personal selling, but for those products that do, this technique is the best way to close the deal.[14] Through personal selling, you are trying to accomplish three things: identify customer needs, match those needs with your products, and show the customers the match between their need and your product.

> "Personal selling, though costly, can be closely tailored to customer needs—making it an effective way to close a sale."

Cost is the biggest drawback to personal selling. When you calculate what it costs for a salesperson to contact each prospect, you see that this strategy is much more expensive than the cost per person for advertising. Another drawback is that salespeople have gained a poor reputation because of the high-pressure tactics and questionable ethics a few of them employ. The biggest advantage of using personal selling is the flexibility of the presentation that becomes possible. A trained salesperson can tailor a presentation to the prospect around three aspects of the product:

Features: What the product is.

Advantages: Why the product is better than alternatives.

Benefits: What the product will do for the customer.

Customer expectations are rising. A good product at a fair price, offered by a well-trained sales staff, backed by a responsive customer service department, is just the starting point in a competitive marketplace. For your business to stand out, its products need to be tailored to the particular needs of your customers. Fortunately, technology is helping to supercharge your sales performance. For example, many salespeople dread making cold calls, partly because they don't know much about the prospective customer they are about to call. You could Google the prospects, but that's not enough. Services such as Before the Call automatically scour Internet sites like Hoover's and Factiva as well as their own proprietary database for new articles. Before the Call can be incorporated with your sales systems like Salesforce.com and Oracle OnDemand to keep customer databases up-to-date and full of current information.[15] Such services could provide just the bit of information your salesperson needs to spark conversation.

The personal-selling process involves seven steps:

1. *Preapproach.* Before meeting with the prospective customer, a salesperson must acquire knowledge about the product and perhaps about the customer and his business.

2. *Approach.* Upon first meeting the customer, the salesperson tries to establish a rapport with her. People seldom buy from someone they don't trust, so a successful salesperson must first earn a customer's trust.

3. *Questioning.* To find out what is important to the customer, the salesperson will try to identify his needs as early in the process as possible.

4. *Demonstration.* The salesperson shows how the product will solve the customer's problem and meet her needs.

5. *Handling objections.* An effective salesperson will listen to what the customer is really saying. An objection shows that the customer is interested but needs more information. Would you raise objections to a salesperson if you were not really interested in a product? No, you would probably just walk away.

6. *Closing the deal.* When he senses that the customer is ready to buy, the salesperson should ask for the sale. Many sales are lost when a customer is ready to buy, but the salesperson continues to sell.

7. *Suggestion selling and follow-up.* An effective technique is *suggestion selling,* or recommending products that are complementary to those just sold. *Follow-up* with a phone call after the sale will build rapport and work toward creating a long-term relationship with the customer.

Public Relations

Public relations (PR) involves promotional activities designed to build and sustain goodwill between a business and its customers, employees, suppliers, investors, government agencies, and the general public.[16] **Publicity** is an aspect of PR consisting of any message about your company communicated through the mass media that you do not have to pay for. Generally, PR works by generating publicity.

PR involves a variety of communication formats, including company publications such as newsletters, annual reports, and bulletins; public speaking; lobbying; and the mass media. Each format can have an appropriate use and benefit for

publicity
An aspect of public relations consisting of any message about your company communicated through the mass media that you do not pay for.

"Here it is—the plain, unvarnished truth. Varnish it."
© *The New Yorker Collection 1999 Richard Cline*
from cartoonbank.com. All Rights Reserved.

your company's marketing effort. Table 14.3 shows some PR activities, their target audience, and their effects on your business.

A welcome change in the PR business has been firms that charge by pay-for-placement rather than retainer deals. PayPerClip is just such a firm based in Califon, New Jersey, that can help remove some of the mystery from PR bills. PayPerClip would receive $400 for a brief airing on a small market TV news show, $2,000 for a sizable story in a small trade magazine, and $8,900 for a full feature in *The Wall Street Journal.*[17]

Sales Promotions

Any activity that stimulates sales and is not strictly advertising or personal selling is called a *sales promotion*. Special in-store displays, free samples, contests, trade show booths, and the distribution of coupons, premiums, and rebates are examples of sales promotions. These activities enhance but do not replace your advertising or personal selling efforts.[18] They are most effective when used in intervals, because customer response decreases over time as customers become familiar with the promotions.

Ratchet Effect   Advertising and personal selling are used on a continuous basis, whereas sales promotions are intermittent. A strategy that combines all three can produce a *ratchet effect* on sales (see Figure 14.5). Advertising is used to increase customer interest, whereas personal selling is used to increase sales. Sales promotions at the point of purchase are usually employed to increase sales over a short period of time.

@ e-biz

Wadda Ya Lookin' At?

You put a lot of effort, time, and money into creating your business Web page. You try to make it an integral part of your promotional efforts. You have your dubya, dubya, dubya, dot all over the place for people to see. You know that if people don't find what they want on a Web page quickly, they move on. But what do people see when they come to your site? Try looking through their eyes—literally. A company called Eyetracking.com lets you do just that.

Eyetracking.com uses state-of-the-art technology to measure what Web page visitors see first, what they stop longest to look at, and how easily they find what they want.

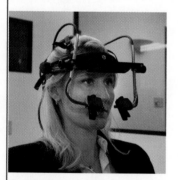

GazeStats Precisely Measures Eye Movement and Reactions.

Testers wear three head-mounted cameras, with a headset shaped like a bike helmet, which follow the eye at 250 observations per second. A technician tracks eye movements across a Web page and measures pupil dilation, which correlates with cognitive effort.

Analysis of these eye patterns and physical responses are used to create GazeStats, GazeTraces, and GazeTransitions to indicate site usability. GazeTransitions create a diagram that shows the order and progression with which the person being tested looks at Web page items. GazeStat shows the percentage of time testers' eyes spend looking at each location over a prescribed time. Go to www.eyetracking.com to see what draws, attracts, and keeps our eyes engaged on Web pages.

A recently patented process measures changes in the pupil diameter to determine the emotional state of a user as she engages with your product. Changes in the pupil indicate in real time and objectively whether he is reacting favorably to your product. Applications for this technology include measuring effectiveness of your TV commercials, online advertising, website design or branding, package design, and sponsorship and brand positioning.

SOURCES: www.eyetracking.com, May 19, 2007; Jason Toates, "What Makes Customers Click," *Ziff Davis Smart Business*, June 2000, 152; "Eyes Provide More Accurate MR with Improved, Proprietary Technology," *Research Department Report*, April 2000; Tessa Romita, "The Eyes Have It," *Business 2.0*, November 2000.

The Business Card An important image builder that is often overlooked and taken for granted is a 3½ -by 2-inch white rectangle—the business card. If done correctly and creatively, a business card not only provides information about your small business, but also becomes hand-to-hand advertising. When asked how small businesses can get noticed, David Avrin of Avrin Public Relations Group, recommends that they "shout a little bit louder, do a little better job and be a little more impressive than established companies who get by on reputation alone." Business cards are a good way for a small business to differentiate itself.[19]

Senior Moves, a Boulder, Colorado, company that specializes in moving services for senior citizens, sets its cards apart by using a different shape than normal. Rather than the standard rectangle, Senior Moves cards take the shape of Rolodex cards imprinted with the company's logo of a house on wheels. Co-owners Sarah

Table 14.3
RELATIONSHIP BETWEEN
MARKETING AND PUBLIC
RELATIONS

Target	PR Activities	Benefits to Marketing
Customers	Press releases	Increase name awareness
	Event sponsorship	Increase credibility
Employees	Newsletters	Improve communications
	Social activities	Decrease absenteeism and product defects
		Increase morale
Suppliers	Articles in trade publications	Improve image
	Promotional incentives	Improve delivery schedule
General public	News releases	Attract better employees
	Plant tours	Improve image to customers
	Support for community activities	Improve local relations
Government	Lobbying	Favorable legislation
	Direct mail	Less regulation
	Personal calls	

Dillon and Michael Lackey pass out about 200 cards per month. At $22 for 500 cards, that's cheap advertising.

Don't make the common mistake of trying to include everything there is to know about your business on the card. You don't have to include *every* phone, fax, and cell number the business owns. You do, however, need to include your website, because it provides a wealth of business information (doesn't it?), and, of course, your e-mail address.

Promotional Mix

In deciding how to combine each of your four tools into a promotional mix, you need to consider when each type of promotion may be appropriate. Advertising reaches so many people that it is good for creating awareness, but its power to stimulate action decreases quickly. Personal selling, by contrast, is the most effective tool for building customer desire for the product and prompting customers to take action. Because it requires one-on-one contact, however, it is less useful in creating awareness. Sales promotions are most effective with customers who are already interested in the product, but who may need prompting to make the purchase. Public relations builds awareness, but results in few immediate sales.

Figure 14.5

SHORT-TERM RATCHET EFFECT
OF SALES PROMOTION

*When Used with Advertising
and Personal Selling, Sales
Promotion Can Give a
Short-Term Boost to Sales.*

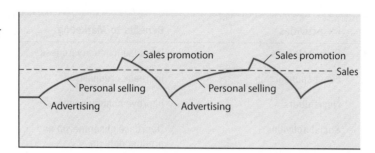

Summary

- **The three main considerations in setting a price for a product**

The economic factors that have the largest influence on pricing are the prices charged by competitors, the amount of customer demand for your product, and the costs incurred in producing, purchasing, and selling your products.

- **The importance of breakeven analysis**

Breakeven analysis ensures that your prices are set above total costs, allowing you to make a profit. It is also useful in estimating the likely demand for a product at different price levels. Finally, breakeven analysis shows how many units need to be sold to generate a target dollar return.

- **Examples of customer-oriented and internal-oriented pricing**

Customer-oriented price strategies, such as penetration pricing, skimming, and psychological pricing,

focus on the wants and needs of your target customers and the number of units of your product they will buy. Internal-oriented pricing involves setting your prices according to the financial needs of your business, with less regard for customer reaction.

- **Why and how small businesses extend credit**

Small businesses extend credit to their customers to realize sales that would not have been made without credit, and to increase the volume and frequency of sales to existing customers. Credit is extended through open charge accounts, installment accounts, lines of credit, and acceptance of credit cards.

- **Tools that a small business owner uses to compile a promotional mix**

A promotional mix is the combination of advertising, personal selling, sales promotions, and public relations that best communicate the message of a small business to its customers.

Questions for Review and Discussion

1. What strategies should be considered if a small business is setting prices for a product that is to be exported? How do these strategies differ from those used in a domestic market?

2. What advantages and disadvantages are involved for a small business offering sales on credit?

3. As the owner of a small, hometown drugstore, how would you prepare for a Wal-Mart being built in your area?

4. What can happen if the price of a product does not fit with the three other Ps of the marketing mix?

5. Should a small business owner's judgment be used to determine prices if so many mathematical techniques have been developed for that purpose?

6. Discuss the importance of remaining professional and friendly when trying to collect an unpaid bill.

7. What factors should be considered when a small business owner decides to advertise?

8. Discuss the personality traits that a good sales-person should have. What traits would detract from the personal-selling process?

9. Explain the ratchet effect on sales.

10. How would promotional mix decisions change for a small business that is expanding into a foreign market?

Questions for Critical Thinking

1. Much of the self-produced small business advertising is weak. Think of an example of a local small business that uses especially effective advertising. Why is it successful at communicating with its target market when so many are not?

2. Of the pricing techniques described in this chapter, which one do you think is most commonly used by small businesses? Why?

Experience this . . .

In this exercise we will walk through the steps of creating a print advertisement.

Step 1: Choose a concept. The following words commonly appear in advertising copy. Choose three or four words that will convey the message you want to send.

act	hurry	now	save
advantage	imagine	opportunity	thanks
benefit	invite	protect	today
convenient	know	proven	unique
discover	learn	results	valuable
exciting	limited time	reward	win
free	new	satisfaction	

Step 2: Work up the copy. Take the words you chose in step 1 and write several sentences to describe or promote your business, product, or idea. Your ad copy should answer five basic questions:

1. Who are you (and why should you be believed)?

2. What is your product?

3. How will it benefit the customer?

4. What do you want the customer to do?

5. Where can customers find or contact your business? Analyze your sentences. Is your tone conversational? (It should be.) Are you targeting a specific market? Do you communicate your features, advantages, and benefits? Is your copy specific or general? (Specific is better.) Do you address your business's competitive advantage? How can the copy be shortened?

Step 3: Sketch out the artwork. Not every print ad needs artwork, but based on the copy you have written in step 2, could a photo or drawing help customers visualize the point or the benefit you are providing? If so, sketch it out.

Step 4: Create a headline. Now you need to grab your potential customer's attention. A good headline can do the following:

• Ask a question. ("Are you tired of scrubbing tile and grout?")

• Offer a benefit. ("Cut your yard work in half.")

• Make a promise. ("No need to ever change filters again.")

• Identify a problem. ("Using harsh chemicals can be dangerous.")

• Set a scenario. ("They laughed when I sat down at the piano, until . . . .")

Write some headlines that attract attention and engage the reader to continue reading the copy. Make sure the headline meaning is clear.

Step 5: Pull it all together. Combine all the elements you created in the first four steps. Be sure you don't crowd too much in; white space draws attention. How does the finished product look?

What Would you Do?

Developing an effective marketing strategy can be tough. Without one, however, a small business will be fighting for survival. Read through the following two examples and answer the questions at the end.

DAPAT Pharmaceuticals

DAPAT is a small manufacturer of external analgesics (pain relievers) based in Nashville, Tennessee. Its main product, called Dr.'s Cream, faced this marketing challenge: In competition with much larger makers of over-the-counter remedies (such as Ben Gay), it had to find some ways to attract customers despite having only a small advertising budget.

Macromedia, Inc

Macromedia is also in a highly competitive field—software publishing. The company makes graphic arts software tools for graphic designers, CD-ROM developers, and people who need to make "flashy" presentations. Macromedia's products are full of technical "bells and whistles," but are they enough to compete effectively? Creating computerized dancing mice could be cool, but technology alone won't sell the product.

Questions

1. Working in teams of no more than three, choose one of the two examples to work on. Develop an outline for a comprehensive marketing strategy for the company and its product. Be specific in defining the product, place, price, and promotion aspects.

2. Once your team has developed its marketing strategy, find another team in the class that has worked on the same example. Take turns presenting your information to each other.

CHAPTER CLOSING CASE

GO BIG OR GO HOME

Chris Mendez's dry cleaning company was falling deeper into debt. Was new technology the answer?

By the end of 2004 Chris Mendez was tempted to give up. The owner of a chain of dry cleaning stores in central Florida, Mendez had grown up in the industry, learning his chops at his father's business in Apopka before striking out on his own in 1995. In just eight months he broke even; by the end of 2003, he had six storefronts and his own 1,400-square-foot dry cleaning plant. But in his eighth year, Mendez's business, Clothes Dr., was spinning out of control: He was losing $130,000 a year on revenue of $1.2 million; he had completely leveraged his house; and he was physically and emotionally exhausted. "I couldn't sleep at night," he says. "How many more things could go wrong? How many more people could quit? When would the boiler explode again?" Did the dry cleaning business really have to be so difficult? Mendez wondered.

Such thoughts couldn't have been farther from his mind when Mendez, at the age of 25, first set up shop in a newly developed area of Apopka, outside Orlando, just far enough from his father's store to avoid direct competition. He opened a second store in a nearby shopping center in 2001 and a third shortly thereafter. "I had a good credit history, so I was getting credit cards in the mail with zero-percent interest," Mendez recalls. "So over three years, I floated $100,000 to expand, and I paid it back as we grew."

But trouble was brewing at his original location. His landlord, uneasy about the potential environmental hazards of the widely used dry cleaning solvent perchloroethylene (or, as it's commonly known, perc), told Mendez he'd need to start using an alternative solvent or lose his lease. Mendez knew that no other solvent cleaned as well as perc, but he agreed nonetheless, and spent more than $63,000 on new equipment. He now thinks of it as "the Ford Pinto of dry cleaning machines. It took too long to clean the clothes, and they ended up smelling bad. That machine was killing me."

There were personnel problems as well. "I thought I could just train a person at one location, put him in one of my other stores, and have everything go smoothly," Mendez says. "But it didn't work out that way." Employees didn't show up, and Mendez found himself racing from store to store to put out fires. Nonetheless, Apopka's growing population continued to bring Mendez its dirty laundry and dry cleaning. "The new stores took off, but I just couldn't get the right crew to handle the volume of work," he says. "I started physically feeling it. I couldn't be in three places at once."

And then opportunity knocked. A dry cleaner in the nearby affluent suburb of Lake Mary called Mendez in mid-2002 and told him that she was retiring. Did Mendez want to buy her business, Dry Clean World? It included three storefronts and a dry cleaning plant that was permitted to use perc. To Mendez's wife, Merilyn, this was not an opportunity; it was a potential disaster. But Mendez was intrigued. If he bought it, he could move most of his cleaning equipment into his own building, begin cleaning with perc again, and never have to worry about fussy landlords. So Mendez took the plunge: he leveraged the house and convinced the owner of Dry Clean World to hold a note for $250,000 so that he could buy the business for $400,000.

It was a rocky transition. In 2003 plant improvements in Lake Mary and quality problems in Apopka put him $130,000 in the red; the following year wasn't much better. Plus, his rent went up, employees wanted raises, and utility rates increased. "I was getting pinched from every corner," he says. At one of his stores in Lake Mary, the rent rose so high that he closed the place and laid off two employees. His wife, a registered nurse whose salary was supporting the family, was losing patience.

Mendez's father commiserated with him, and in February 2005 the two decided to attend a trade show in Miami, where they planned to research point-of-sale systems for their businesses. Updated technology, they reasoned, might help them clamp down on expenses, manage their employees, and keep better track of customer data. Mendez arrived in Miami with just a flicker of optimism. By the time he left, it had been stoked into a bona fide flame. He had Jason Loeb to thank for that.

Loeb is the CEO of Sudsies.com, a Miami-based dry cleaner that had all but abandoned the traditional storefront dry cleaner's model. Loeb's business, with approximately $3 million in revenue, was almost entirely Web-based. He had one storefront and 10 trucks on the road, picking up and delivering dry cleaning and laundry to customers who scheduled and tracked their orders on his website. Loeb wasn't a typical dry cleaner, removing spots or hovering over the steam cleaner in the back of his plant. Instead, he had gone to great lengths to create brand recognition, to train and engage his employees, and to cultivate relationships with his customers.

After talking to Loeb, Mendez found that business as usual looked less and less attractive. He was intrigued by the prospect of closing additional stores and investing in delivery trucks and a Web-based customer tracking system modeled on Loeb's. There was risk involved, to be sure. Loeb had invested $250,000 to change his business model, and the venture was not instantly profitable. Mendez would need to build a website, master new technology, hire new staff, and retrain his existing employees. Trucks, however, would be far less expensive to run than storefronts, so he would vastly reduce his overhead while expanding his geographic reach. He also knew that door-to-door pickup and delivery was becoming increasingly popular among consumers; it could be just the way to differentiate his business from other dry cleaners.

What do you think Mendez should do? Invest in new technology or maintain status quo?

Test Prepper

college.hmco.com/pic/hatten4e

You've read the chapter, studied the key terms, and the exam is any day now. Think you're ready to ace it? Take this sample test to gauge your comprehension of chapter material. You can check your answers at the back of the book. Want more test questions? Visit the student website at college.hmco.com/pic/hatten4e and take the ACE and ACE+ quizzes for more practice.

Multiple Choice

1. When competing with a big-box retail store, a small business should do all but which of the following?
   a. differentiate products
   b. specialize with unique goods
   c. emphasize customer service
   d. try to undercut price on identical items

2. Customer-oriented pricing strategies include:
   a. breakeven analysis
   b. penetration pricing
   c. cost-plus pricing
   d. target-return pricing

3. Josh's business sells jewelry. He has installed granite counters and oak trim in his showroom. Josh charges more for his jewelry than other stores. What type of pricing strategy is Josh using?
   a. prestige pricing
   b. price lining
   c. odd pricing
   d. reference pricing

4. What do you have to give up if you choose to accept credit cards in your small business?
   a. nothing
   b. generally 5 to 6 percent
   c. 10 percent
   d. $5 per transaction

5. Julie is running a block of advertising for her small business. Her ads offer 50 percent off of everything in the store for the next two days only and free lunch between 11 A.M. and 1 P.M. What is Julie's advertising objective?
   a. inform
   b. persuade
   c. remind
   d. change perception

Fill in the Blank

1. Selling a group of products or options together as a package is called _____.

2. When launching her designer-bag company Tote Le Monde, Tia Wou created _____.

3. The elasticity of demand for a product indicates how _____ _____ the market is.

4. Entrepreneur and street artist Shepard Fairey said that sometimes he feels like _____ _____.

5. A good salesperson focuses on the fundamentals of _____, _____, and _____.

## part 6

Managing Small Business

Chapter 15   International Small Business

Chapter 16   Professional Small Business Management

Chapter 17   Human Resource Management

Chapter 18   Operations Management

In this section we will bring together all the phases of running your own business. Visualize yourself making the decisions needed to make it all happen as you read these chapters. Are there opportunities for your business in other countries? Many small businesses find that there are, especially via e-commerce. Foreign sales can be an excellent way to generate growth, and **Chapter 15** explores those possibilities. **Chapter 16** explains professionally managing your business through the various stages of growth it will experience. **Chapter 17** looks at managing your most valuable resource—people. **Chapter 18** covers the management of service and manufacturing operations.

## chapter 15

International Small Business

After reading this chapter, you should be able to:

- List factors to consider when preparing an international business plan.

- Name five ways for small businesses to conduct international trade.

- Analyze the advantages and disadvantages of exporting for small businesses.

- Discuss factors to consider when importing products and materials.

- Explain how small businesses can manage their finances in international trade.

- Articulate the cultural and economic challenges of international small business activity.

In 1973 Tony and Maureen Wheeler went on their honeymoon. And the trip wasn't simply a weekend at Niagara Falls. Tony had just received his master's degree from the London Business School, and Ford Motor Company had just offered him a job, but he deferred accepting for a year. The couple took a year-long trip to try to get the wanderlust out of their systems before "settling down." They bought a very used Austin minivan for $150 and still had $1,400 in savings. They drove across Europe and the Middle East to Afghanistan. There they sold the Austin and continued across Asia via train, bus, rickshaw, and boat, eventually ending up in Sydney, Australia, after spending a mere $6 per day. On this trip they kept a journal. Tony noted specific details. Maureen mused romantically. Their 96-page travel notebook became the foundation of a travel-guide empire called Lonely Planet.

When they returned to Australia flat broke, they were surprised to find people they knew asking them repeatedly, "How did you do that?" So they wrote a

Maureen and Tony Wheeler, Founders of Lonely Planet Travel Guides.

travel guide entitled *Asia on the Cheap* to tell adventurous, unconventional people just that—how they did it. They set up a tiny office in Melbourne, where they returned from far-flung expeditions to compile their notes in another book. Since the 1970s the Wheelers have compiled more than 400 guides touching every continent.

Like most small businesses starting out, Lonely Planet kept its overhead to a minimum. Maureen organized layouts and set the type herself. Tony packed shipping cartons and wrote. They both did it all. Their traveling and their business were done on a shoestring, which became the competitive advantage of their guides. People wanted to learn how to travel on the cheap and were willing to pay for it. The Wheelers loved to travel and write about their experiences. *South-East Asia on a Shoestring,* which sold 15,000 copies at $1.95 each, was followed by more shoestring guides for Hong Kong, Australia, Nepal, and Africa. The Wheelers thought they were over their heads with the India guide, because it was twice the length (700 pages) and twice the price ($10) of their other products, but it sold more than 100,000 copies in its first edition.

Tony recalls that in early days most of their books were about Asia, and a lot of their business was done in Asia. He remembers one Asian distributor who hated to pay for the books he imported via the more traditional methods. "'So much paperwork and bureaucracy, so many bribes to be paid,' he'd complain. 'It's much better I just pay you in cash anytime you're in the country.' So the invoices would mount up for a year or so, and then one day, in some back-street cafe, large rolls of greenbacks would be counted out across the table, and I'd stuff them into every available pocket."

In 1980 the Wheelers decided to get serious about their international business after the birth of their first child. They opened an office in Oakland, California, and one in London six years later. Lonely Planet was turning into a real business, gradually expanding its staff to 12 people.

Today Lonely Planet has gone high tech. Lonelyplanet.com supports the guidebooks with message boards, author blogs, Q&A columns, and medical advice. The website receives over 650,000 hits per day and has developed a reputation as one of the best travel sites around.

World events continue to conspire against the travel industry, but Lonely Planet forges ahead. Tony Wheeler says, "In the short term there's still the terrorist/SARS/Iraq madness impact to overcome, but in the longer term we're going to get back to the same old problems: not killing the golden goose by too much ill-planned tourism."

Although their company has certainly changed over their 30-plus years, the Wheelers' mission has not changed—getting unique information to travelers as

SOURCES: Tony Wheeler, "The Way We Were," *Publishers Weekly,* 12 March 2007, 66; Joanna Doonar, "It's Not Such a Lonely Planet," *Brand Strategy,* January 2004, 25–25; Maggie Overfelt, "Wanderpreneurs," *Fortune Small Business,* 21 April 2000, fsb.com; "Roughing It," *Fortune Technology Guide,* Summer 2000, 257; Michael Schuman, "The Not-So-Lonely Planet," *Forbes,* 22 May 1995, 104–108; Cade Metz, "How They Built It," *PC Magazine,* 8 February 2000, 147.

> quickly and accurately as possible. They love books as a way to carry around information but are receptive to the idea of changing formats. Maureen says that whatever way travelers learn about new places, the Wheelers hope it will be from Lonely Planet.

Preparing to Go International

When most people think of international business, they envision large, multinational corporations with operations all over the globe. A common conclusion is that small and medium-sized businesses are at a disadvantage in terms of their ability to compete internationally. Actually, research shows that the size of a business is not a barrier to entry into international markets; it merely limits the number of markets you can serve.[1] Having improper strategies, negative attitudes toward expansion abroad, or lack of experience may keep businesses out of the international game, but size does not have to be a factor. In fact, the same competitive advantages—your unique skills, talents, and products—that have made your business successful in local markets may create the same advantage in foreign markets.

> " The size of a business does not determine its ability to enter global markets, but it may influence the number and scale of markets a business can enter. "

Growth of Small Business

International trade is one of the hottest topics of the new millennium, but it is certainly not a new trend. Think of Marco Polo. Think of the great caravans of the biblical age carrying silks and spices.[2] Exporting is essential to the economic health of the United States, as international sales provide more than 30 percent of the country's domestic economic growth. Perhaps surprisingly, a full two-thirds of that boom comes from companies with fewer than 20 employees.

Not only can small businesses compete successfully in other countries, but they are also increasing their exports at a rate much faster than that of large businesses. A study by the U.S. Small Business Administration (SBA) showed that more than one-third of all U.S. small businesses were exporting, accounting for 96 percent of all U.S. exports. Clearly, small businesses are major players in international business (see Figure 15.1).

International Business Plan

To navigate these shifting international tides, you will, of course, need a business plan. As we discussed in Chapter 4, a solid business plan is behind most successful small businesses.

What do you need in an *international business plan?* Begin with everything that is included in a domestic plan. You have to have a unique product, a market (or preferably multiple markets) for your product, the managerial skills to take advantage of the opportunity you have identified, and the financial capability to do the deal. In addition to the business-plan content and analysis described in Chapter 4, the following information, at a minimum, is necessary to help you analyze your ability to go international and chart the best course to follow. Note that with any business plan, a balance between information and analysis are needed

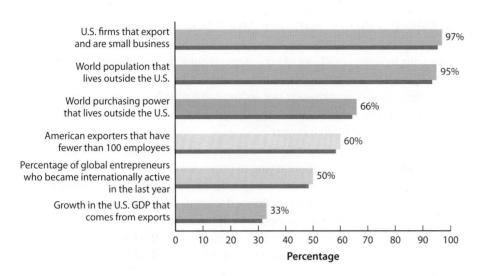

Figure 15.1

SMALL BUSINESS
GLOBALIZATION
BY THE NUMBERS

SOURCE: Allbusiness.com/FocusMagazine/Going
Global, U.S. Department of Commerce, and SBA
Office of Advocacy.

here. The first three items on the following list identify what you need to describe for a foundation exporting, while the rest discuss how you will become successful.

- A firm commitment to international trade
- An export pricing strategy
- A reason for exporting
- The most attractive potential export markets and customers
- Methods for entering foreign markets
- Exporting costs and projected revenues
- Financing alternatives to allow you to export
- Any legal requirements you need to meet
- The transportation method that would be most appropriate
- Any overseas partnership contacts and foreign investment capabilities[3]

One expert recommends that an international business plan should include both market entrance and exit approaches because markets that are difficult to leave can drain export sales profits.[4]

Take the Global Test

Taking your small business across national borders can be a good move. You've heard stories of others striking gold just over the horizon—but it's not easy. Your chances of building competitive advantage and therefore being successful in international business are good if you can pass this 10-part test.

1. *The "good reason" test.* If exporting is not part of your core business strategy, don't bother going international. A one-shot deal, even a big one, may not be worth the trouble. Software company Blue Pumpkin, which has operated internationally since its beginning in 1996, is an example of a company with a "good reason" for going global. Because Blue Pumpkin provides customer-service software to many *Fortune* 1000 firms that want to use it all over the world, it has to be global.

2. *Do you have the right stuff to pull this off?* To be taken seriously by foreign buyers, your business needs a certain degree of success at home. Depending on your industry, this level of achievement could be measured by market share, technical expertise, or brand awareness. In selling fishing lures, for example, brand awareness is key, so Kendall Banks makes sure that T-shirts for his Silver Buddy lures cover the BassMasters trade show in New Orleans for the benefit of foreign buyers.

3. *Can you identify a market?* Every country provides different sets of problems and customers. Forget about trying to enter more than one at a time. Randy Reichenbach has trouble competing in the Middle East against a competitor from Trieste, Italy, selling reconditioned surgery tables. Randy's U.S.–made tables are top-of-the-line, but the Italian models are great, too, and the strong euro makes their prices higher. Good news for Randy as the currency exchange rates tip the price advantage in his favor.

4. *Are you flexible?* With few exceptions, product modifications will need to be made. Carroll Mixon's Kelley Manufacturing makes digger shaker inverters for planting peanuts in Georgia (the U.S. state, not the Eastern European country). South Africa uses different row spacing that required product changes. Mixon had to determine whether the expense of modifying his product for export was worth it. Such modifications can be, if they are part of the overall strategy (see number 1 in this list).

5. *Can you find a good distributor?* Getting your products into the hands of end users in other countries is especially challenging for small businesses. Export managers and foreign distributors can prove very helpful in preparing you for the twists and turns in reaching markets, but they may also change the perception of your product.

6. *Can you cope with all the complexity?* Jim Hunt, president of Kabobs, makes frozen hors d'oeuvres for ritzy hotels. He says that "every shipment to Canada requires 40 pieces of paper, and you have to save all paperwork for at least three years." Another complexity is dealing with differing standards: If one of his appetizers is, say, 25 percent chicken, does it fall under Canada's chicken import quota? You get the idea.

7. *Can you brave the, shall we say, nonlegal barriers?* Roger Berkeley wanted his textiles from Weave Corporation to reach buyers in Italy. The problem is that Americans were banned from the annual trade show in Como, Italy. Berkeley fought through the problem by laying out his goods at a nearby villa and picking customers up directly at the trade show to drive them to his goods. Someone, he alleges, got his drivers arrested. That was enough, so he now focuses on a friendlier show in Belgium.

8. *Are you willing to extend credit or deal with currency turmoil?* Sure, you would prefer to be paid up front and in U.S. dollars, but that option is not always available. You are more likely to receive a bankable letter of credit, which slows your ever-critical cash flow. Then you face the volatility of currency exchange rates. Weave Corporation saw its sales plunge with the decline in value of the euro relative to the U.S. dollar because European rivals then had a price advantage.

9. *Are you ready to run a much different kind of company?* Exporting will inevitably change your company—and your life. Changes may be as simple as going in to the office at 4 A.M. for a foreign conference call because of time-zone differences.

10. *Do the rewards outweigh the costs?* This will be a personal decision that depends on what you want to get from the business, and your answer to this question may change from time to time. Many small business owners involved in international trade sometimes ask themselves, "What have I gotten myself into this time?" At other times, when sales are growing through the roof, you may feel like you're on top of the world.[5]

If you conclude from your planning and testing that you should proceed with your expansion into other countries, you have five basic choices: exporting, importing, licensing your product, establishing a joint venture, or setting up operations in the other country. Each of these options represents an increased level of commitment on your part, so let's look at your options in that order.

Establishing Business in Another Country

The vast majority of small business activity in the international market will be conducted via importing and exporting. Still, for the experienced, visionary, and adventurous businessperson, other options exist that represent an even greater commitment to global trade. Small businesses can license their products or services, form joint ventures or strategic alliances, or even set up their own operations to conduct business in other countries.

Exporting

The primary mechanism for small businesses to engage in international business is **exporting,** or sending the products they make to another country. Because of the importance of this option for establishing business in another country, we will cover direct and indirect exporting in more detail later in this chapter.

> *exporting*
> Selling goods or services in a foreign country.

Importing

Many small business owners recognize that not only do markets for their products exist in other countries, but their domestic markets can also be served by bringing in products from other countries via importing. Importing represents such a viable option for small business that we will discuss it in more detail later in this chapter.

International Licensing

As an exporter, you can stop exporting at anytime you wish. However, other forms of international business represent a larger commitment on your part. The next level of commitment above exporting in international business is **licensing** As a licenser you are contractually obligated to another business for a period of time.

Licensing offers a way to enter foreign markets by assigning the rights to your patents, trademarks, copyrights, processes, or products to another company in

> *licensing*
> The agreement that allows one business to sell the rights to use a business process or product to another business in a foreign country.

exchange for a fee or royalty. The two biggest advantages of licensing are speed of entry and cost. You can enter a foreign market quickly without investing virtually any capital. Licensing is similar to franchising domestically. Licensing agreements are generally written to endure for a specified period of time. A disadvantage of this approach is that your licensee may become your competitor after the agreement expires if it continues to use your licensed process without paying you for it.

International Joint Ventures and Strategic Alliances

joint venture
An agreement in which two businesses form a temporary partnership to produce a product or service in a market that neither could satisfy alone.

A foreign **joint venture** is a partnership between your business and a business in another country. As with any partnership, choosing the right partner is critical to the success of the venture. Each of you needs to bring something (products, knowledge, channel of distribution, access to a market, or other quality) to the venture that the other would not have alone.[6]

Partnerships of *any* type can be difficult (see Chapter 2). Joint ventures are often costly failures. A study by Columbia University shows a success rate of only 43 percent for such ventures, with an average life span of 3.5 years.[7] Despite the difficulties, joint ventures and strategic alliances are and will be needed to be competitive globally. Finding a local partner is the only way to enter some countries.

Seven advantages often work in combination to improve your chances of forming a successful joint venture:

1. Penetrating protected markets
2. Entering heavily concentrated industries
3. Lowering production costs
4. Sharing risks and high R&D costs
5. Preventing competitive alliances
6. Maximizing marketing and distribution channels
7. Gaining leverage over a supplier and strategic knowledge of a supplier's products

strategic alliances
A partnership between two businesses (often in different countries) that is more informal than a joint venture.

Strategic alliances are not exactly the same as joint ventures.[8] Lorraine Segil, of the Lared Group, specializes in establishing strategic alliances, helping to match small organizations with large ones through a chain of contacts in the United States, Europe, and Australia. The match is often made with a large, well-established company abroad that needs fresh ideas and products. Because many entrepreneurial firms have just such assets, but only limited capital, the result is often a profitable alliance for both.

Direct Investment

Once you have established your international operations, you may choose to set up a permanent location in another country. Opening an office, factory, or store in a foreign land is the highest level of international commitment you can make. Of course, you are making a significant financial investment that costs you money, but what other risk is involved with direct investment? Think about what might happen if you set up operations in a country experiencing political instability. What if a new political regime takes power? Will you be allowed to operate as you did before? Will you even be allowed to keep the assets you have invested in there? Perhaps not, on either count. Consequently, small businesses rarely start out their

Profile in Entrepreneurship
Hot Tchotchkes

Robert Kushner launched and now manages Pacific China Industries with different goals than many U.S.–based businesses entering China. He was not tempted by visions of 1 billion potential customers or a drive to take advantage of a low-wage, high-tech labor force. He did not enter with a splashy debut intended to impress officials in Beijing. He did not come with a bleeding-heart, "let's build a wonderful People's Republic" spirit. Kushner came to make money—and he has been successful at it, unlike most large corporations in China. Pepsi has been there for more than 20 years, for example, but has yet to turn a profit.

Kushner and his 15 employees develop and manufacture novelties. His tchotchkes (cheap, showy trinkets) include dancing rock stars that attach to dashboards, collapsible corkscrews, and sunglasses holders. They end up on the shelves of many U.S.

retailers. Kushner takes a very practical, fundamental approach to running his business. He expands only when it's financially possible to make a profit. He keeps overhead to a minimum by minimizing the number of expatriate staff, but he's careful about it.

One of the best-known competitive advantages is low labor rates, which is a major reason why major corporations relocate to China. Kushner warns that it's a major mistake to pay local managers too little. He says, "You have to pay managers top dollar, and you also should pay the inspectors at your plants well. Otherwise, you'll wind up with too much of your product going out the back door, and one day, you'll see your items for sale in the local market."

Even so, Kushner's products typically get knocked off by local competitors within three months. As a result, he must be constantly on the lookout for new markets for those products and be developing new products all the time.

SOURCE: Joshua Kurlantzick, "Promised Land," *Entrepreneur*, January 2004, 66–69.

global experience with direct investment. Exporting, licensing, or joint ventures are much more common vehicles.

Exporting

Exporting is defined as selling in another country the goods or services that you offer domestically. It is the most common way for small businesses to operate in other countries. Of all the ways to conduct business internationally that we are considering in this chapter, exporting provides the lowest levels of risk and investment, increasing your chances of being profitable. The SBA has identified both advantages and disadvantages of exporting. Advantages include the following:

- Increased total sales and profits
- Access to a share of the global market
- Reduced dependence on your existing markets
- Enhanced domestic competitiveness
- Opportunity to exploit your technology and know-how in places where they are needed
- Realization of the sales potential of existing products and extension of the product life cycle

Reality Check

Deepest Darkest Continent

So you think China is the only global growth market? It depends on your product and market. For PointCare Technologies, they need to be in Africa. Even though company founder Peter Hansen says that he sometimes needs State Department escorts for safety.

According to the World Bank's annual *Doing Business* report, nine of the world's worst places to do business are in Africa. This report looks at issues such as starting a business, dealing with licenses, employing workers, and registering property. The dubious honor of number 175 out of 175 countries went to the Democratic Republic of Congo, followed by the countries of Timor-Leste, Guinea-Bissau, Chad, and the Republic of Congo.

PointCare manufactures a device called the Aurica flow cytometer, which is used to measure CD4 levels (the blood cells most affected by HIV) in HIV patients. This is one of the few portable, simple-to-use, monitoring tools that can assist health agencies combat the AIDS epidemic. The device is about the size of a laser printer and requires no advanced medical degree to operate.

Hansen points out that although there are some very unstable sections of Africa, it is not a single place. Countries like South Africa, Namibia, Botswana, and Kenya have stable economies. PointCare needs to be there since 6 percent of the people in sub-Sahara Africa have HIV. Programs like President Bush's Emergency Plan for AIDS Relief assure that there is money available to purchase such products.

Even though his company has had problems getting established, Hansen says that the rewards for going to Africa are huge. He says, "We had an installation in a hospital in Kenya, and people cried. They were weeping. They told us, 'Finally we can do what we need to do!'" After a pause he adds, "Nobody's going to cry in Chicago."

SOURCE: Michael Fitzgerald, "Into Africa: Yes, You Can Do Business There," *Inc.*, February 2007, 46–47.

- Stabilization of seasonal market fluctuations
- Opportunity to sell excess production capacity
- Chance to gain information about foreign competition[9]

Disadvantages to exporting revolve around the additional responsibilities and obligations your business may incur. You may be required to do the following:

- Develop new promotional material suitable for foreign customers
- Forgo short-term profits in the interest of long-term gains
- Incur added administrative costs
- Allocate funds and personnel for travel
- Wait longer for payments than with your domestic accounts
- Modify your product or packaging
- Acquire additional financing
- Obtain special export licenses[10]

Only you can decide whether the disadvantages of global expansion outweigh the advantages. The timing of entering a foreign market may not be right, or you may be short on the cash needed to fund the expansion at this point. In any event, no hard-and-fast rules govern international expansion.

If you decide that exporting is right for your business, you have two methods that you can use: indirect exporting and direct exporting. Whether you choose to use intermediaries is the primary difference between the two.

Indirect Exporting

The simplest and perhaps most cost-effective way for a small business to export is to hire an export service company to market products abroad.[11] This method minimizes the financial and personnel resources needed to promote international sales. Using an intermediary reduces your risks and can help you learn the exporting process. Even if you start using indirect exporting, you may choose to set up an international sales staff once you develop the capital and expertise.

Of course, the fee charged by an export service company will reduce your profit margin, but the increased sales should offset this disadvantage. A more dangerous disadvantage is that you lose control by operating through an intermediary. Your company name and image are in the hands of this intermediary. Finally, the price the ultimate consumer pays may be increased by using intermediaries. You should negotiate what all costs, fees, and the final price will be up front in the contract.

There are several kinds of intermediaries for you to consider. Agents and brokers, export management companies (EMCs), export trade companies (ETCs), and piggyback exporting are all domestic-based intermediaries. Foreign-based intermediaries include foreign distributors and foreign agents.

Agents and Brokers   Both agents and brokers will put your company in touch with foreign buyers. They set up the deal, but they don't buy the products from you. They can also provide consultation on shipping, packaging, and documentation.

Export Management Companies   *Export management companies (EMCs)* provide a much broader range of services than agents or brokers, but they still do not take title to your goods. Instead, EMCs act as your own export department, conducting marketing research, arranging financing and distribution channels, attending trade shows, and handling logistics. These intermediaries will even use your company letterhead in all correspondence and provide customer support after a sale. EMCs are a good option for small businesses new to international trade.

Approximately 600 EMCs operate in the United States, each representing an average of 10 suppliers. For example, Transcon Trading Company, of Irmo, South Carolina, has made sales in more than 70 countries. Although it deals in animal health products most of the time, it also represents a company that makes go-carts and a firm that makes bug zappers. Transcon works comfortably in any region, thanks to the people on its staff, who speak 10 different languages.[12]

Export Trade Companies   *Export trade companies (ETCs)* perform many of the same functions as EMCs, and, in addition, generally take title to your goods and pay you directly. ETCs operate individually but may also join together to form cooperative groups of companies selling similar products.

Piggyback Exporting   If you can find another company that is already exporting, you may be able to make a *piggyback arrangement,* thereby taking advantage of

"I'M AT THE MERCY OF THE ORGANIZATION OF LEMON-EXPORTING COUNTRIES."

the international connections the other company has already established. If your products do not directly compete with the other company's products, it may simply add your product line to its own.

Foreign-Based Distributors and Agents   Using a distributor or an agent that is based in the foreign country rather than one that is based in the United States can provide the advantage of cultural and local knowledge that you may not be able to get elsewhere.

George Grumbles, president of Universal Data Systems, has been exporting electronic equipment for more than 25 years. He believes in building groups of local distributors in his foreign markets. Grumbles says, "You have to work through nationals [residents of the foreign country]. If you send U.S. folks into a foreign country, you have to expect it will take a couple of years for them to find their way around. Instead, you should find people who are embedded in the local economy."

Foreign agents do the same jobs overseas that manufacturer's representatives do in the United States. They work on commission within their sales region of specific countries. Local laws and customs vary greatly between countries, so you must be clear on what you can expect an agent to do legally. Some countries go to extremes in protecting their citizens from foreign companies.

Foreign distributors may sell on a commission basis or buy your goods directly. You and the distributor should work together to produce your marketing materials, because translating your packaging and promotional material into another language can be a problem.

Direct Exporting

With direct exporting, you do not use any intermediaries, unlike in indirect exporting. If you choose to use direct exporting as your method of selling your products in other lands, you have more control over the exporting process, greater potential profit, and direct contact with your customers. A point you must remember when considering any channel of distribution is that you can do away with the intermediary, but *someone* has to perform this function. If you choose not to use an intermediary for your exporting, then *you* have to perform those duties. You have to choose the target countries, arrange the most efficient channel of distribution, and market your product in the foreign country. Direct exporting is therefore riskier, more expensive, and more difficult than indirect exporting. Because you pay less in service fees or commissions, however, your potential profit could be greater.

In direct exporting, one approach could entail the use of sales representatives who sell your products and other (noncompeting) products on a commission basis. You may choose to use a distributor or to sell directly to the final consumer.

Selling your product in other countries can be a logical extension of your domestic business. Many business executives say that exporting is essentially no different from expanding into a new market in your own country. Of course, operating in other countries can create unique challenges, but taking care of "the basics" will help you meet those challenges. First you have to perform market research to determine who will buy your product and where those buyers are. Then you have to determine your channels of distribution and your prices.

Identifying Potential Export Markets

Successful marketing depends on your knowledge of the people and places with which you are dealing. In addition to the marketing research you would ordinarily conduct locally, marketing research in the international sector needs to include the following activities.

Find Countries with Attractive, Penetrable Markets Sometimes the largest trading partners of the United States may not be the best countries for you or your products. For example, Harden Wiedemann, of Assurance Medical, a provider of alcohol- and drug-testing services, was surfing around the Internet one day when he stumbled on information about growing alcohol-related problems in Argentina. A little more investigation revealed a sizable opportunity for his company.

Most small businesses begin their search for market information with U.S. government sources. Go to www.export.gov to find market research to learn your product's potential in a given market, the best prospects for success, and the market's business practices before you export. From the Market Research Library, you can check Market Research Reports, Country Commercial Guides, and Best Market Reports on any Industry, Region, or Country.

The SBA provides current market information to small businesses on foreign markets where their products are being bought and sold, and on which countries represent the largest markets. At www.sba.gov, you can find full-text versions of *SBA Exporting Guide* and *Primer on Exporting.*

Canada, China, and Mexico top the list of importers of products made in the United States (see Figure 15.2). More detailed information on foreign markets for small businesses is available through sources like the *CIA World Factbook* (see Figures 15.3, 15.4, and 15.5).

Figure 15.2

TOP 10 TRADE PARTNERS
OF THE UNITED STATES

*These 10 Countries Account for
63.5 Percent of Total U.S. Trade
for 2006.*

SOURCE: www.census.gov/foreign-trade/
statistics/country/top/index.html

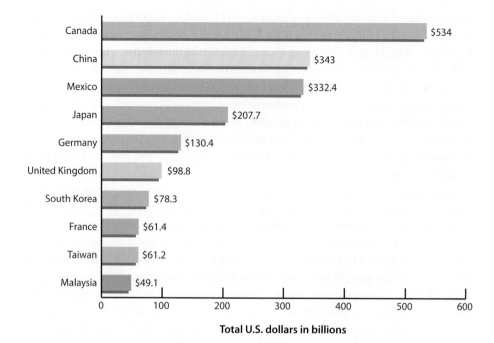

Total U.S. dollars in billions

Figure 15.3

CANADA AT A GLANCE

*For Information About the
United States' Largest Trading
Partner, Go to This Country's
Listing in The CIA World
Factbook (www.cia.gov/cia/
publications/factbook/
index.html).*

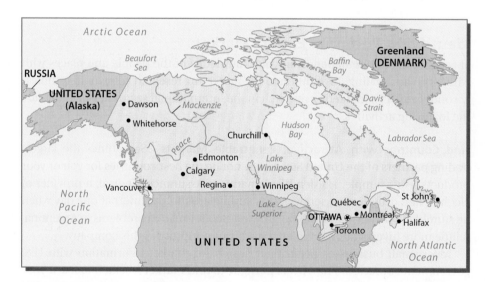

Economy—Overview: Canada
As an affluent, high-tech industrial society in the trillion-dollar class, Canada resembles the United States in its market-oriented economic system, pattern of production, and affluent living standards. Since World War II the impressive growth of the manufacturing, mining, and service sectors has transformed the nation from a largely rural economy into one that is primarily industrial and urban. The 1989 U.S.–Canada Free Trade Agreement (FTA) and the 1994 North American Free Trade Agreement (NAFTA) (which includes Mexico) touched off a dramatic increase in trade and economic integration with the United States. Given its great natural resources, skilled labor force, and modern capital plant, Canada enjoys solid economic prospects. Top-notch fiscal management has produced consecutive balanced budgets since 1997, although public debate continues over how to manage the rising cost of the publicly funded health care system. Exports account for roughly a third of GDP. Canada enjoys a substantial trade surplus with its principal trading partner, the United States, which absorbs about 85 percent of Canadian exports. Canada is the United States' largest foreign supplier of energy, including oil, gas, uranium, and electric power.

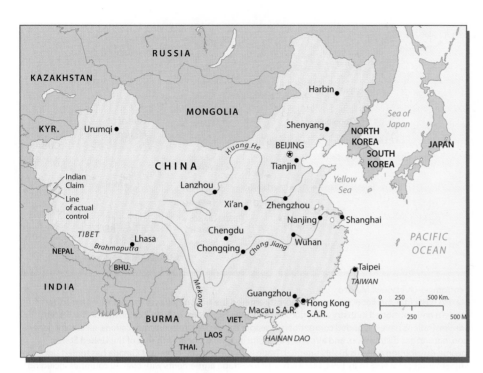

Figure 15.4
CHINA AT A GLANCE
For Information About the United States' Second-Largest Trading Partner, Go to This Country's Listing in The CIA World Factbook (www.cia.gov/cia/publications/factbook/index.html).

Economy—Overview: China

China's economy during the last quarter century has changed from a centrally planned system that was largely closed to international trade to a more market-oriented economy that has a rapidly growing private sector and is a major player in the global economy. Measured on a *purchasing power parity (PPP)* basis, China in 2006 stood as the second-largest economy in the world after the United States, although in per capita terms the country is still lower-middle-income, and 130 million Chinese fall below international poverty lines. Economic development has generally been more rapid in coastal provinces than in the interior, and there are large disparities in per capita income between regions. The government has struggled to (1) sustain adequate job growth for tens of millions of workers laid off from state-owned enterprises, migrants, and new entrants to the workforce; (2) reduce corruption and other economic crimes; and (3) contain environmental damage and social strife related to the economy's rapid transformation.

From 100 million to 150 million surplus rural workers are adrift between the villages and the cities, many subsisting through part-time, low-paying jobs. One demographic consequence of the "one child" policy is that China is now one of the most rapidly aging countries in the world. Another long-term threat to growth is the deterioration in the environment—notably air pollution, soil erosion, and the steady fall of the water table, especially in the north. China continues to lose arable land because of erosion and economic development. China has benefited, however, from a huge expansion in computer Internet use, boasting more than 100 million users at the end of 2005.

Foreign investment remains a strong element in China's remarkable expansion in world trade and has been an important factor in the growth of urban jobs. In July 2005 China revalued its currency by 2.1 percent against the U.S. dollar and moved to an exchange rate system that references a basket of currencies. In 2006 China had the largest current-account surplus in the world—nearly $180 billion. More power-generating capacity came about in 2006 as large-scale investments were completed. Thirteen years in construction, at a cost of $24 billion, the immense Three Gorges Dam across the Yangtze River was essentially completed in 2006 and will revolutionize electrification and flood control in the area. The 11th Five-Year Program (2006–10), approved by the National People's Congress in March 2006, calls for a 20 percent reduction in energy consumption per unit of GDP by 2010 and an estimated 45 percent increase in GDP by 2010. The plan states that conserving resources and protecting the environment are basic goals, but it lacks details on the policies and reforms necessary to achieve these goals.

Figure 15.5

MEXICO AT A GLANCE

For Information About the United States' Third-Largest Trading Partner, Go to This Country's Listing in The CIA World Factbook (www.cia.gov/cia/publications/factbook/index.html).

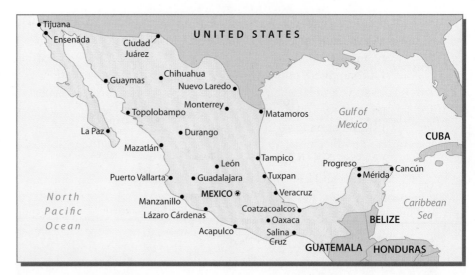

Economy—Overview: Mexico
Mexico has a free-market economy that recently entered the trillion-dollar class. It contains a mixture of modern and outmoded industry and agriculture, increasingly dominated by the private sector. Recent administrations have expanded competition in seaports, railroads, telecommunications, electricity generation, natural gas distribution, and airports. Per capita income is one-fourth that of the United States; income distribution remains highly unequal. Trade with the United States and Canada has tripled since the implementation of NAFTA in 1994. Mexico has 12 free-trade agreements with over 40 countries including Guatemala, Honduras, El Salvador, the European Free Trade Area, and Japan, putting more than 90 percent of trade under free-trade agreements. The new Felipe Calderon administration that took office in December 2006 faces many of the same challenges that former President Fox tried to tackle, including the need to upgrade the infrastructure, modernize the tax system and labor laws, and allow private investment in the energy sector. Calderon has stated that his top priorities include reducing poverty and creating jobs. The success of his economic agenda will depend on his ability to garner support from the opposition.

Define Export Markets That Match Your Product   After you have identified potential countries, you must find out if a need exists there that you can satisfy. Ask yourself these questions:

- How does the quality of products in the foreign country compare with that of your products?
- Will your prices be competitive?
- Can you segment customers?
- Are there political risks in the country you are considering?
- Will your products need any modifications?
- Will tariffs or nontariff barriers (restrictions or quotas) prevent your entry into the market?

The Department of Commerce and the SBA produce various publications and reports to help provide this information. The Department of State gathers information on foreign markets through consulates and embassies. Foreign affiliates of the U.S. Chamber of Commerce, called American Chambers of Commerce (AmChams), also collect and disseminate information.

Importing

When your small business is importing rather than exporting, the major focus of your activities shifts from supplying to sourcing. You need to identify markets making products for which you see a domestic demand.

Factors to consider when choosing a foreign supplier include its reliability in having products available for you, the consistency of product or service quality, and the delivery time needed to get products to you. A bank subsidiary office and the embassy of the supplier's home country are sources for this information.

As an importer, you must comply with the regulations and trade barriers of both the foreign country and the United States. You must make sure that your product can legally cross national borders. For example, cigars made in Cuba cannot be imported into the United States because of an embargo against that country. The United States also has established import quotas that limit the amount of products such as steel and beef that can be brought into this country. Such quotas are intended to protect domestic industries and jobs, although their results are not completely positive. Trade restrictions remain a topic of political discussion, and the debate will likely continue for years. You should try to stay as current as possible on trade and tariff regulations if you are involved in global trade.

Anthony Raissen knew from personal experience that he needed a product that could cleanse his breath, especially after eating the spicy foods that he loved. He found that gum, mints, candies, and other breath aids didn't do the job. These products tended to mask the bad breath as opposed to eliminating it. The same problem is faced by many people. During a trip to his native South Africa, Raissen was introduced to a group of chemists who had developed a formula of parsley-seed oil and sunflower oil that worked like magic on the bad-breath problem. Raissen bought the rights to the formula and returned to the United States to form BreathAsure, of Calabasas, California. Selling this product, Raissen's company has achieved annual sales revenues of nearly $18 million. In fact, responding to consumer demand, the company released Pure Breath, a version of the original BreathAsure product designed for dogs and cats—another obvious target market for this imported formula.[13]

Financial Mechanisms for Going International

Once you decide to enter the international trade game, you face challenges such as how to finance your expansion, how to pay your debts and get paid, and where to find information and assistance.

International Finance

Selling overseas is only half the challenge; the other half is finding the money to fill the order. Working capital may be needed for your new transaction level. Options for additional sources of capital include conventional financing, venture capital from investor groups, and prepayment or down payments from overseas buyers. To start looking for export financing, contact the Export-Import Bank (Eximbank) or the Small Business Administration (SBA).

The Eximbank is an independent federal agency that has been in existence for about 15 years and has developed eight programs designed to help small business engage in international trade.[14] One such program covers 100 percent of working capital for a commercial loan. It also offers export credit insurance to protect exporters, in case a foreign buyer defaults on payment. To get information on the Eximbank's lending and insurance programs, visit its website (www.exim.gov).

The SBA has several financial services for exporters, including an international trade loan program for short-term financing and the 7(a) business loan guarantee

Figure 15.6
INTERNATIONAL PAYMENT
TERMS, BY RISK TO SELLER

SOURCE: *IOMA'S Report on Managing Exports,*
December 2002, 1.

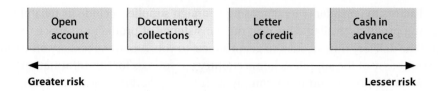

program for medium-term working capital and long-term fixed-asset financing. The SBA's free booklet on export finance is entitled *Bankable Deals.*

Managing International Accounts

A problem for most small businesses is getting paid. Small businesses rarely have the financial resources to carry excessive accounts receivable, which can be amplified by selling in other countries. In the United States the average number of days needed to collect accounts receivable is 42. That's quite a long time for a small business to have money outstanding, but the international branch of the National Association of Credit Management says that some countries average much longer waits. For example, you can expect to wait more than 120 days for payment from customers from Greece, Albania, and Lithuania. Companies from many less developed countries may take even longer to pay their bills.

Your primary financial concern as a global operator should be to ensure that you get paid in full and on time. Keep in mind that your foreign buyers will be concerned about receiving products that meet their specifications on time. Thus terms of payment must be agreed upon in advance in a way that satisfies both parties.

The primary methods of paying for international transactions are described next, presented in order from most secure for the exporter to least secure (see Figure 15.6).

Payment in Advance   Requiring clients to pay in advance provides the least risk to you, but unless you have an extremely specialized product, the buyer can probably get a better deal from someone else. Still, it is reasonable to negotiate partial payment or progress payments.

Letter of Credit   A letter of credit is an internationally recognized instrument issued by a bank on behalf of its client, the purchaser. It is a guarantee that the bank will pay the seller if the conditions specified are fulfilled.

Documentary Collection (Drafts)   Drafts are documents that require the buyer to pay the seller the face amount either when the product arrives (called a *sight draft*) or at a specified time in the future (called a *time draft*). Because title does not pass until the draft is paid, both parties are protected. Drafts involve a certain amount of risk but are cheaper for the purchaser than letters of credit.

Consignment   Selling on consignment means that you advance your product to an intermediary, who then tries to sell it to the final user. If you sell on consignment, you don't get paid until the intermediary sells the product. Consignment is risky because there is no way of knowing when, if ever, the goods will be sold.

@ e-biz

6.6 Billion Potential Customers

Do you think of your business as a local, mom-and-pop operation? It may not be for long. No matter how small you are, once you create a website, you may be attracting business from anywhere in the world. Did you know that

- Only one-third of Internet users live in the United States?

- One-third of Internet users prefer a language other than English?

- Customers are four times more likely to buy from a site that uses their own language?

- Most U.S. companies draw less than 10 percent of their e-commerce revenue from international users?

Many small businesses create a website by "concentrating on the English version first." This approach may be more expensive later, when you have to reengineer it for another language. Start by looking at major multilingual sites like those operated by Microsoft, MSNBC, ZDNET, and Symantec. See how they bring each language version into line with the base site. If you want to create a website that uses multiple languages, you need a company that translates languages on a Web page from a single database. To find one, go to InterPro (www.interproinc.com), RWS Group (www.translate.com), or TRADOS (www.trados.com).

Some other considerations:

- Keep the layout simple, and avoid cultural icons such as the American flag or the Russian hammer and sickle.

- Keep the page layouts and color choices similar throughout all the pages of your base site. This way you can use the base site as a template.

- Choose visual elements that can work across cultures.

- Do not lose sight of the purpose of your website. You want to communicate the benefits of your products or services to the customer, with the purpose of stimulating a response—like a purchase.

SOURCES: InterPro, RWS Group, and TRADOS websites; "Keys to Effective Translation and Localization," *World Trade*, May 2001; Laurel Delaney, "A Crash Course in Doing Business Abroad," *Fortune Small Business*, April 2001, fsb.com; Kenneth Klee, "Going Global?" *Fortune Small Business*, March 2001, 98–103;

Open Account Although commonly used in selling products in the United States, delivering goods before payment is required is very risky for international sales. If the creditworthiness of the buyers or the political and economic stability of their country is questionable, you stand to lose your entire investment, possibly without recourse.[15]

Countertrade and Barter

A problem encountered in trading with many economically emerging countries (such as many Eastern European and former Soviet countries) is that their currency is virtually worthless outside their borders. A solution to this problem may be **countertrade**. Although countertrade takes several forms, it is basically substituting a product for money as part of the transaction. Although countertrade is rarely a long-term solution, it may be a tool to make deals that could not be reached otherwise.[16]

The most common form of countertrade that small businesses can use is *barter*.[17] This type of trading has existed throughout history. Some creativity may

> **countertrade**
> The completion of a business deal without the use of money as a means of exchange. Barter is a common form of countertrade.

be needed to find a business that has complementary needs. Pepsico arranged creative trades within the former Soviet Union by trading soft drinks for vodka, which was worth much more on the open market than the ruble and was much easier to sell. You may make deals just as creatively.

The key to making money in countertrade is to have somewhere to sell the goods you receive in trade. Swapping your product for something you can't sell later is no bargain. The golden rule of countertrade is this: *Do not quote prices until the countertrade situation is clearly understood.*

Information Assistance

Where can you go on the Internet for help in going global?

- *U.S. Census Bureau (www.census.gov).* Great site for international trade statistics, export classification assistance, and profiles of exporting companies.
- *U.S. Department of Commerce (www.doc.gov).* One-stop shop for useful statistics on business, trade, and the world economic picture.
- *STAT-USA/Internet (www.stat-usa.gov).* This site is a single point of access to authoritative business, trade, and economic information from across the federal government.
- *U.S. Small Business Administration (www.sba.gov).* You've been sent here before, but this time you will find information on export assistance in the "Expanding" section.
- *International Logistics (www.export.gov/logistics/exp_internat_log_home.asp).* The U. S. government's international logistics homepage.
- *Currency Conversion Calculator (www.oanda.com).*
- *Foreign Incentives (www.export.gov).* One-stop site for info on trade leads, commercial serce specialist, marketing research, and advocacy.
- *Tradenet's Export Advisor (link through www.sba.gov).* Another one-stop shop for exporting. A joint venture with the SBA, Department of Commerce, and other agencies. Its credo is, "No business is too small to go global."

  Also see these sites:

- American Association of Exporters and Importers (www.aaei.org)
- Federation of International Trade Associations (www.fita.org)
- International Chamber of Commerce (www.iccwbo.org)
- International Federation of Customs Brokers Association (www.ifcba.org)
- International Organization for Standardization (www.iso.org)

The International Challenge

Success for many small businesses will depend increasingly on some degree of sales to markets in other countries. International business presents quite a few challenges, but, then, most entrepreneurs thrive on challenge. There are no hard-and-fast rules for going global, and space does not permit coverage of every situation you may face, but some issues you need to be aware of are cultural differences, global trading regions (especially NAFTA), the effect of the World Trading Organization (WTO), and ISO 9000 quality certification.

Understanding Other Cultures

The most important cultural factors you'll want to consider are language, religion, education, and social systems. Ask questions such as these:

- How do these factors differ from those in my home country?
- How does my business or product name translate into the language? (This issue could affect brand-name usage, advertising, and other promotions.)
- What are the recognized religious holidays and customs? (They could affect when, where, and how you conduct business.)
- What is the average educational level of your potential customers? (It could influence the type of employee training needed or packaging and advertising decisions.)
- What are the accepted and practiced social rituals, customs, and behaviors? (They could influence many different business decisions.)

And just where can you find this information? First, numerous books and other publications describe cultural customs and the differences among countries. A trip to your local library can uncover a wealth of sources. You could also contact international business professors or foreign-language professors at a local college. These individuals are typically highly knowledgeable about cultural factors or, at the very least, can point you toward other sources of such information. If you know someone who has visited or lived in the country you're investigating, most certainly talk to that person. Such firsthand knowledge is invaluable. Another source of information would be the U.S. Department of Commerce, which has a number of programs and services for companies interested in doing business in other countries.

When marketing your product globally, you must think and act globally. This means that you need to be sensitive to cultural beliefs that vary from country to country. Every culture has different accepted norms and ways of doing business. Not understanding and not following these norms can lead to embarrassment for you at best, and completely blowing your deal at worst. In the United States, for instance, a pat on the back says "attaboy," whereas in Japan it is a sign of disrespect. Nodding your head means "no" in Bulgaria, and shaking your head side to side means "yes," the opposite of American customs.[18]

Training the employees you send overseas can help them adjust to cultural differences so that they can perform their jobs better. Several types of programs are available that provide cross-cultural training beyond training in foreign language. These global training programs generally involve six overlapping categories: cultural awareness, multicultural communication, country-specific training, executive development, language courses, and host-country workforce training.[19]

Customs like gift giving are important to understand. Gifts from business partners are expected in some cultures, but they are considered offensive in others. Should you present the gift on the first meeting or afterward? In public or private? To whom? What kind of gift is appropriate? In Japan, gifts are exchanged to symbolize the depth and strength of a business relationship.[20] When dealing with a

A Diverse Group Engaging in Cultural Awareness/Multicultural Training

Japanese business, the first meeting is the appropriate time to exchange gifts; if you are presented with a gift, you are expected to respond with one in return. By contrast, gifts are rarely exchanged in Germany, Belgium, and the United Kingdom.

Exchanging business cards is no big deal, right? Wrong. Taking someone's card and immediately putting it in your pocket is considered very rude in Japan. You should carefully look at the card, observe the title and organization, acknowledge with a nod, and make a relevant comment or ask a question. In presenting the card, you should use both hands and hold it so the other person can read it. If English is not the primary language, you should have the information printed in the recipient's native language on the reverse side.

Language is another obvious problem. You are not expected to speak another language like a local, but making an attempt to learn some of the language can be a sign of good faith. Most trade specialists recommend that you employ a professional translator for written communication and always have one available when you travel for face-to-face meetings. It may cost a few hundred dollars per hour, but as Jeff Barger, president of CTS (Corporate Translation Services), says, "Look at the marketing dollars you spent to win a customer—are you going to skimp when you finally sit down with him?"[21] In addition to hiring an interpreter, don't rely on your memories of seventh-grade Spanish class—get documents professionally translated. Get free price quotes on translation services at www.buyerzone.com.[22]

Trade experts at Moran, Stahl & Boyer International, an international consulting firm, say that culture has two components: surface culture (fads, styles, food, and holidays) and deep culture (norms, attitudes, values, and beliefs). According to the tip-of-the-iceberg concept, only 10 to 15 percent of a region's culture is visible (see Figure 15.7).[23] This means you must look below the surface to identify forces that truly drive a culture.

As you can see, the cultural aspects of international business are very complicated and confusing, but their importance cannot be overstated. Doing your homework can prevent serious mistakes.[24]

"Since World War II, a major development in the world economy has been the creation of regional trade associations—the European Union, the Association of Southeast Asian Nations, and the alliance created by the North American Free Trade Agreement"

Pat McGovern states that when a small business ventures abroad, the CEO needs to be the point person, traveling frequently and acting boldly and enthusiastically. McGovern has the experience to back up what he says: In the forty years since the start of his business, IDG, he has averaged four months of

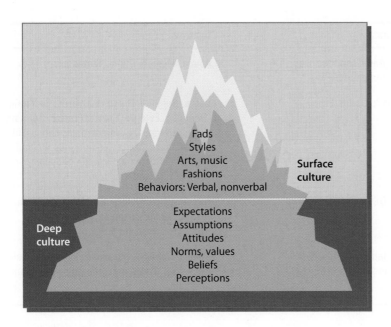

Figure 15.7
THE CULTURAL ICEBERG
Many Important Cultural Factors Are Not Easily Seen.

SOURCE: Kevin Walsh, "How to Negotiate European Style," *Journal of European Business*, July/August 1993, 45–47.

travel per year launching technology publications, events, and research from Antarctica to Zimbabwe.

Being the point person opening new territory is not an easy job. When McGovern first went to Changsha, capital of the Hunan province, business associates took him to a restaurant where the waiter decapitated a snake and poured its blood in everyone's glass. People in his party told him that toasting with the blood would make him a member of the "Hunan Mafia." McGovern says, "Fortunately, I have an iron stomach (I've also eaten monkey brains and scorpion), so I downed the stuff." It pays to be in the inner circle, as many of his Chinese business leaders today are from Hunan.[25]

International Trading Regions

Since World War II, a major development in the world economy has been the creation of regional trade groupings. That trend has accelerated in recent years. A trade region is established through agreements to create economic and political ties among nations usually located within a close geographic area. These agreements reduce trade barriers among countries within the region and standardize barriers with countries outside the region. They also are intended to increase competition within them, so that inefficient nationalized companies or monopolies will lose their protective walls and be forced to come up to speed. Table 15.1 identifies major trading regions and the member countries.

What effect do world regions have on you and your small business? The passage of the North American Free Trade Agreement (NAFTA) was intended to open markets and to reduce barriers for U.S. companies to send their products to Mexico and Canada. Regional agreements may also change your strategy for dealing with businesses in those countries. For example, because the European Union (EU) has higher tariffs and barriers for products coming from countries outside the region than for products that come from within, it might make sense to establish operations in

Table 15.1

MAJOR REGIONAL TRADE
ASSOCIATIONS

Association	Countries
North American Free Trade Agreement (NAFTA)	Canada, Mexico, United States
European Union (EU)	Austria, Belgium, Bulgaria, Cyprus, Czech Republic, Denmark, Estonia, Finland France, Germany, Greece, Hungary, Ireland, Italy, Latvia, Lithuania, Luxembourg, Malta, Netherlands, Poland Portugal, Romania, Slovakia, Slovenia, Spain, Sweden, United Kingdom
MERCOSUR	Argentina, Brazil, Paraguay, Uruguay, Venezuela; Bolivia, Chile, Columbia, Ecuador, and Peru are associate members
Association of Southeast Asian Nations (ASEAN)	Brunei, Combodia, Indonesia, Laos, Malaysia, Myanmar, Philippines, Singapore, Thailand, Vietnam

an EU country if you intend to do a lot of business there. Then you can sell in any of the 27 member nations under reduced barriers.

North American Free Trade Agreement   In 1993 Congress passed the North American Free Trade Agreement (NAFTA), which joined Canada, Mexico, and the United States into a free-trade area. One of the primary goals of NAFTA is to ultimately eliminate tariffs and nontariff barriers between the United States, Canada, and Mexico on nearly all qualifying goods.[26] Overall "Trade in Goods" among the United States, Canada and Mexico has grown from $297 billion in 1993 to $884.4 billion in 2006, an increase of 198%.[27]

A key word here is *qualifying.* Products will qualify for tariff elimination if they *originate,* as defined in Article 401 of NAFTA, in one of the three countries. For example, products that are made in Japan and are shipped through Mexico cannot enter the United States under preferential NAFTA duty rates. So you need to determine whether your products are originating goods. There are four primary ways for goods to qualify:

1. Goods wholly obtained or produced in a NAFTA country

2. Goods made up entirely of components and materials that qualify

3. Goods that are specifically cited in an article of the agreement (very few products are cited)

4. Goods that are covered under specific rules of origin for that product, as listed in NAFTA Annex 401 (the most common way to qualify)[28]

Your products need to be assigned a *harmonized system (HS)* number. The harmonized system classifies products so that their chapter, heading, and subheading numbers are identical for all three countries. See the example at the top of page 429.

Once you have determined the HS number for your products, you can find the specific NAFTA rule of origin that applies. Some specific rules of origin will call for

Chapter 95	Toys, games, and sports requisites
Heading 95.04	Table or parlor games
Subheading 9504.20	Articles for billiards and accessories
Tariff item 9504.20.21	Billiard tables

additional requirements. Usually such a requirement takes the form of a test of the product's *regional value content (RVC)*, which means that a certain percentage of the product's value has to originate in a NAFTA country. For example, if the rule specifies that a good must have at least 65 percent RVC, then you need to demonstrate that at least 65 percent of the good's value originated in either Canada, the United States, or Mexico.

If your products do qualify as originating goods, you need to complete a *certificate of origin* for each product. The importer of your products must have a valid certificate to claim preferential tariff treatment. The certificate of origin shows the names and addresses of the importer and the exporter, a description of the goods, the HS number, the preference criteria (how it qualified), the producer, the net cost, and the country of origin.

For help in determining a product's HS number, exporters can call the Census Bureau's Foreign Trade division (301-763-5210) or contact their Commerce Department district office. The Commerce Department's Industrial Trade Staff (202-482-5675) can determine the tariff rate and phase-out schedule for specific products. To learn about NAFTA rules of origin and other important provisions, exporters should obtain a copy of the NAFTA agreement online (www-tech.mit.edu/Bulletins/nafta.html) or from the U.S. Government Printing Office (202-783-3238). U.S. Customs has also set up a help desk offering assistance on how NAFTA affects a wide variety of issues (202-927-0097). The Trade Information Center (TIC) is a convenient first stop for new exporters, offering information on the export process (800-USA-TRADE).

World Trade Organization   The first global tariff agreement began in 1947 with the General Agreement on Tariffs and Trade (GATT). This agreement, which originally included the United States and 22 other countries, has grown to include 134 member countries that represent more than 90 percent of world trade. Since GATT's inception, it has gone through eight "rounds" of negotiations or meeting sites. The latest series of negotiations, called the Uruguay Round, lasted from 1986 until 1994. One of its provisions was to create a successor to GATT, called the World Trade Organization (WTO). Created in 1995, the WTO has broader authority over services and agricultural products than GATT. The WTO is seen as the arbiter of global trade with an agenda that focuses on nontariff barriers to trade.[29]

ISO 9000

Quality isn't a concern just among American managers within their own businesses; it is also an international issue. The International Standards Organization (ISO), based in Europe, has established 13,000 international quality standards for manufacturers' *methods* of product development.[30] These ISO standards are intended to minimize the need for on-site visits by vendors to verify that their suppliers are taking the proper step to ensure quality production. *ISO 9000 certification* relates to quality standards of production, not to the quality of the product itself. *ISO 14000 standards* relate to environmental issues.

The process of getting your business ISO certified is time-consuming, complex, and expensive. The procedure works like this: After you document all the steps of your operations that ensure the quality of goods and services, an auditing firm visits your company to conduct a process audit and a financial audit to determine whether you pass. Two follow-up audits per year are required to maintain certification.

Why would a small business bother? Lori Sweningson, owner of Job Boss Software, is taking her company through the ISO certification process because she wants to sell software in Europe. To get certified, Sweningson has budgeted $30,000 to $50,000 for consultant and auditor fees.[31] The payoff is expected to be the marketing tool of being ISO certified. She believes that ISO certification will soon be the minimum requirement for many international sales.

Currently large businesses and divisions of major corporations are the ones getting ISO certified, but small manufacturers are quickly following suit. Free information packets are available from the American Society of Quality Control (800-248-1946) or the American National Standards Institute (212-642-4900). Of course, you can also go right to the source (www.iso.ch) to find a wealth of information on ISO standards, principles, and forms—even business plans for public review. We will revisit the topic of ISO 9000 in more depth in Chapter 18.

Summary

- ### The components of an international business plan

In addition to everything included in your domestic business plan, your international business plan should specify your preferred method for entering foreign markets, markets that represent the best opportunities for your business, projected costs and revenues, any contacts you have in overseas partnerships or foreign investment, and any legal requirements or restrictions you must consider.

- ### Five ways for small businesses to conduct international trade

The five methods for small businesses to conduct international business are exporting, importing, licensing, joint ventures, and direct investment.

- ### The advantages and disadvantages of exporting for small businesses

The advantages of exporting are that it offers you a way to increase sales and profits, increase your market share, reduce your dependence on existing markets, increase your competitiveness in domestic markets, satisfy a demand for your products abroad, extend your product's life cycle, stabilize seasonal sales fluctuations, sell excess production capacity, and learn about foreign competition.

The disadvantages of exporting are the expense of changing your products and promotional material, the increased costs that cut into short-term profits, added administrative and travel costs, time needed to receive payment (which may be longer than for domestic accounts), the need for additional financing, and the increased paperwork involved.

Small business owners have a choice of two approaches to exporting: indirect and direct. Indirect exporting involves the use of intermediaries such as agents and brokers, export management companies, export trade companies, piggyback exporting, and foreign-based distributors and agents. With direct exporting, the small business owner makes all contacts and handles the logistics and paperwork of exporting alone.

• **Factors to consider when importing products and materials**

The focus of a small business in regard to importing is on finding international sources of products to satisfy its domestic customers. The small business owner must consider the reliability of the foreign supplier, the consistency of the product quality, and the additional time that will be needed to ship products from another country.

• **How small businesses can manage their finances in international trade**

In managing your finances for international trade, you must plan how to raise additional funds and how to get paid. Funding can come from your current commercial bank, from the Eximbank, or with assistance from the SBA. Methods for payment include payment in advance, by letters of credit, by draft, on consignment, and by open account.

• **The challenges of international small business activity**

Challenges you will face when going global include learning and adapting to cultural differences, dealing with provisions of trade regions and agreements like NAFTA and GATT, and ensuring the quality of your products to customers who are not familiar with you or your business, through compliance with international standards such as ISO 9000.

Questions for Review and Discussion

1. Discuss the difference between and the advantages and disadvantages of indirect and direct exporting.
2. What is the advantage of a strategic alliance over direct investment when entering a foreign market?
3. What information should a small business owner gather before deciding to export products?
4. Why is finding financial assistance for international expansion more difficult than finding such help for domestic expansion?
5. Why would a small business choose to license its products in other countries?
6. Choose three foreign markets and find out what the customs and courtesies for greetings are in those countries (possibly using the Internet as a source).
7. Imagine that you own a small manufacturing business. Identify the product that you produce and a foreign market that appears to represent an opportunity. What is one country that would pose a bigger risk?
8. Name a form of countertrade and indicate when it would be an appropriate strategy.
9. Discuss the differences and similarities between domestic-and foreign-based intermediaries.
10. What does the Eximbank do for potential exporters? For importers?

Questions for Critical Thinking

1. Now that the Internet has opened up international trade, especially for small businesses, what effect do you think it will have on trade standards for selling goods abroad? Do you expect an increase in nontariff barriers?
2. Which countries are riskier markets for small businesses to enter? Why? Where would you find information regarding political stability, financial risks, and cultural differences?

Experience This . . .

Locate a small business in your area that conducts business in another country (you may be surprised to find who your local global players are). Ask the owner what the greatest challenge has been in doing business across borders. Share your story with the class.

What Would You Do?

Refer to the chapter-opening vignette on Lonely Planet. The Wheelers built their business by describing travel in many countries around the globe. In the process, they created a website (www.lonelyplanet.com) that offers an incredible wealth of information for entrepreneurs. Choose a country that you believe has potential to be a market for the small business you wish to own. Working in teams of two, use Lonely Planet online to become "experts" on this country. Use all of the site's resources, such as Worldguide, Theme Guides, The Thorn Tree, and The Scoop. Once you have gathered this valuable information on Iceland, Singapore, or anywhere in between, prepare a two-page executive summary on the opportunities you find for your chosen country. Present your findings to your class.

CHAPTER CLOSING CASE

HYPERGROWTH NEEDED

With revenue flattening, David Galbenski needed a bold new plan.

By almost any measure, David Galbenski's company was a success. Contract Counsel, which Galbenski and a law school buddy, Mark Adams, started in 1993 from Galbenski's parents' basement in Royal Oak, Michigan, helps companies find lawyers on a temporary contract basis. The growth over the past five years had been furious. Revenue went from less than $200,000 to some $6.5 million at the end of 2003, and the company was placing thousands of lawyers a year.

And then the revenue growth began to flatten. The company grew just 8 percent in 2004 despite a robust market for legal services estimated at about $250 billion in the United States alone. Frustrated and concerned, Galbenski stepped back and began taking a hard look at his business. Could he get it back on the fast track? "Most business books say that the hardest threshold to cross is that $10 million sales mark," he says. "I knew we couldn't afford to grow only 10 percent a year. We needed to blow right through that number."

For that to happen, Galbenski knew he had to expand his customer base beyond the Midwest into large legal supermarkets such as Boston, New York, and Washington, D.C. He also knew that in doing so, he'd run into stiff competition from larger, publicly traded rivals. Contract Counsel's edge had always been its low price. Clients called when dealing with large-scale litigation or complicated merger-and-acquisition deals, either of which can require as many as 100 lawyers to manage the discovery process and the piles of documents associated with it. Contract Counsel's temps cost about $75 an hour, roughly half of what a law firm would charge, which allowed the company to be competitive despite its relatively small size. Galbenski was counting on using the same strategy as he expanded into new cities. But would that be enough to spur the hypergrowth that he craved?

At the time, Galbenski had been reading quite a bit about the growing use of offshore employees. He knew companies like General Electric, Microsoft, and Cisco were saving bundles by setting up call and data centers in India. But it was an article in the November 2004 *American Lawyer* titled "Briefed in Bangalore: Will India's Lawyers Help Re-shape the U.S. Legal Market?" that really opened his eyes. Law firms could offshore their work? Galbenski's mind raced with possibilities. He imagined tapping into an army of discount-priced legal minds that would mesh with his existing talent pool in the United States. The two workforces could collaborate over the Web and be productive on a 24/7 basis. And the cost savings could be massive.

Of course, there were big questions. Could he count on the quality of the work that came from overseas? Would language and cultural differences be a problem when it came to reviewing and coding documents for an upcoming trial? Would licensing be an issue? Using offshore workers was a risk—but the payoff was potentially huge.

Galbenski and his eight-person management team were preparing to meet for their semiannual strategic review meeting at the Thomas Edison Inn in Port Huron, about an hour from the company's office. The purpose of the two-day event was to decide the company's goals for the coming year. As he drove to the meeting, Galbenski struggled to figure out exactly what he was going to say. He was still undecided about whether to pursue an incremental and conservative national expansion or take a big gamble on overseas contractors. Could the company really afford to go global? Could it afford not to?

What do you think? Is outsourcing to India really the answer for Contract Counsel?

Test Prepper

You've read the chapter, studied the key terms, and the exam is any day now. Think you're ready to ace it? Take this sample test to gauge your comprehension of chapter material. You can check your answers at the back of the book. Want more test questions? Visit the student website at college.hmco.com/pic/hatten4e and take the ACE and ACE+ quizzes for more practice.

 college.hmco.com/pic/hatten4e

Matching

_____ 1. percentage of world population that lives outside the United States

_____ 2. product that Lonely Planet sells

_____ 3. the test you have passed if exporting is part of your core business strategy

_____ 4. an agreement in which two businesses form a temporary partnership

_____ 5. a company that will act as a small business's export department

_____ 6. the top trading partner of the United States

_____ 7. a viable component of international trade in which products are brought into a country

_____ 8. the completion of a business deal without the use of money

_____ 9. accepted norms and ways of doing business

_____10. certification of a manufacturer's methods of product development

    a. dating service

    b. 80 percent

    c. travel guides

    d. just because

    e. China

    f. joint venture

    g. 95 percent

    h. good reason

    i. licensing

    j. ISO 9000

    k. EMC

    l. broker

    m. Mexico

    n. importing

    o. theft

    p. WTO

    q. Canada

    r. indirect exporting

    s. countertrade

    t. culture

True/False

1. T F Lonely Planet is a successful international small business started with a multimillion-dollar IPO.

2. T F Small businesses are major players in international business.

3. T F Before achieving success in another country, almost every small business is successful locally first.

4. T F International licensing is very similar to domestic franchising.

5. T F The vast majority of small business activity in the international market is conducted via importing and exporting.

6. T F The primary difference between direct and indirect exporting is the use of intermediaries.

7. T F *The CIA World Factbook* shows that Mexico has a huge middle class.

8. T F The United States has established import quotas for items such as steel and beef to protect its domestic producers.

9. T F An internationally recognized instrument issued by a bank on behalf of its client is called a letter of credit.

10. T F The existence of international trade regions really has no effect on the way small businesses conduct international trade.

Professional Small Business Management

When Hillary Johnson took over as editor of a small newspaper, she knew she was entering a whole new world. She had never been in charge of an organization before. In fact, the term "in charge" seemed foreign to her. She had run her household on a model based more on negotiation, persuasion, consensus building, and reward than on intimidation, orders, or forcefulness. Johnson found the office environment to be as welcoming and friendly as a pirate ship. For many years, the management style there had been based on aggressive, militaristic, alpha-male behavior. Staffers told her that they had rarely been praised (because, it was believed, compliments foster weakness) and were often pitted against one another (divide and conquer). In addition, displaying a lack of courtesy toward one's subordinates was considered a privilege of rank. A young writer complained that she had to fetch coffee for her female boss every day.

A veteran manager friend gave Johnson a copy of the management best-seller, Sun Tzu's *The Art of War,* to help her whip her staff into shape and hit

After reading this chapter, you should be able to:

- Describe the functions and activities involved in managing a small business.

- Explain the stages of small business growth and their consequences for managing your business.

- Discuss the significance of leadership and motivation in regard to employees of small business.

- Discuss time and stress management as they relate to small business.

Hillary Johnson.

those production deadlines. Reading the book, she found missives like, "All warfare is based on deception," "Speed is the essence of war," "Take advantage of the enemy's unpreparedness," and—the one that really got her attention—"Throw your soldiers into a position from whence there is no escape, and they will choose death over desertion." Now, how was she supposed to use that idea in managing her six-person staff?

The only way to run a business is like the military is run, right? Johnson had seen workplace behavior that was almost gladiatorial while watching Donald Trump's *The Apprentice,* whose participants acted as if life and death depended on the emperor's thumb being up or down. Still, such an approach didn't fit *her.*

Then one day Johnson accidentally stumbled upon the management tome that would be her guiding beam—all because she spilled mango juice on her favorite blouse. She picked up a copy of a book called *Home Comforts: The Art and Science of Keeping House* by Cheryl Mendelson (who cleans for recreation when not practicing law or teaching philosophy at Columbia University). Although written as a serious guide to cleaning, cooking, and organizing, not business management, *Home* Comforts provided Johnson with many helpful management metaphors.

For example, Johnson found directives such as, "If you don't know anything about food, or fabric, you are putting a great deal of control over your life into the hands of strangers whose interest in you is entirely commercial"—the point being that ignorance is crippling. She read, "Where shining, sweet-smelling kitchens are equipped with the latest labor-saving devices, cooking has been transformed into an art that everyone can be proud to master." Johnson realized that her newspaper office bore much greater similarities to a busy household than to an armed encampment. She said to herself, "Wouldn't my goals as a manager be far better served by treating the office more like a kitchen and less like a war room and fostering a sense of egalitarianism and pleasure in the *process* as well as the *outcome*?"

What Johnson learned had nothing to do with gender, or hormones, or right ways of thinking or wrong ways of thinking. What she discovered, from a very unexpected source, was the crucial small business manager's lesson: Find out which management approach fits your own personal style, and apply it to the situation.

You would do well to look up the lead source article for this chapter-opening vignette to discover what other jewels Johnson gleaned from the household analogy. Then look for your own management guide (*besides* this book). It may be in the bicycle-repair section, the astrophysics section, the zoology section—almost any section—of the bookstore.

SOURCES: Hillary Johnson, "The Next Management Revolution," *Inc.,* July 2004, 78–83; Sarah Vowell, "I Won't Launder My Dish Towels," *Time,* 13 March 2000, 78; Laura Shapiro, "All in a Day's Housework," *Newsweek,* 11 November 1999, 96.

Managing Small Business

Businesses of every size must be managed or they will cease to exist. Although there are many similarities between managing a large business and managing a small one, significant differences also exist. Managing a small business is a complex job. You have to perform many activities well without the resources available to your large competitors. The expectations of customers, associates, and employees are increasing to the point where small businesses can rarely survive without understanding the tools and practices of professional management. In this chapter, we will investigate the processes of managing a growing business, of leading people, and of facing the concerns of a small business owner.

Four Functions of Management

The major functions of **management** are generally accepted to be *planning, organizing, leading,* and *controlling*. To some extent, a manager performs these functions whether he is in charge of a large or a small operation, a for-profit or a nonprofit organization, or a retail, service, or manufacturing business.

> **management**
> The process of planning, organizing, leading, and controlling resources in order to achieve the goals of an organization.

These four functions are *continuous* and *interrelated* (see Figure 16.1). In other words, managers do each of them all the time. You don't have the luxury of getting out of bed in the morning and saying, "I think I am going to just organize today." Rather, you will have to do some planning, some organizing, a lot of leading, and some controlling every day.

These four functions are interrelated in that their achievement occurs as part of a progressive cycle. Planning begins the process, as the manager determines what to do. Organizing involves assembling the resources (financial, human, and material) needed to accomplish the plan. Leading is the process of getting the most output possible from those resources. Controlling is comparing what was initially planned with what was actually accomplished. If a deviation exists between what was planned and what was done (which is almost always the case), a new plan is needed, and the cycle begins again.

What Managers Do

Management is getting things done through people. When running a small business, you will have to spend a certain amount of time performing the actual duties and daily tasks of the business—probably more during the early stages in the life of the business and less later. You must decide where to strike a balance between doing and managing. This doesn't mean that managers don't "do" anything.

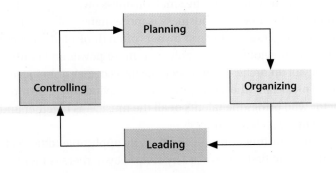

Figure 16.1
FOUR FUNCTIONS
OF MANAGEMENT
The Functions of Managing a Business Are Continuous and Interrelated.

@ e-biz

Help Me, Help Me, Help Me

Managing a small business can be tough and lonely. Where can a small business owner go on the Internet to get help? Is there anywhere an entrepreneur can gain insight into the daily nitty-gritty of running a business? A place to chat with others about difficult situations?

Several small business portals have sprung up to go past advice and offer real online service. Portals are gateways to a wealth of resources.

- allbusiness.com. At this self-described one-stop resource for growing businesses, you will find the following topics: Business Advice, Professional Journals, Business Bloggers, Forms & Agreements, Tools & Services, and Industry Centers.

- bizjournals.com. Bizjournals is the online media division of American City Business Journals, the nation's largest publisher of metropolitan business newspapers. Characterized among the "Best of the Web" by *Forbes* magazine, bizjournals' archives contain 1.25 million business news articles published since 1996. Bizjournals' sites have more than 4 million unique monthly visitors.

- startupjournal.com. From the publishers of *The Wall Street Journal,* it's not just for big businesses anymore. Good small business portal.

- www.toolkit.cch.com. CCH Business Owner's Toolkit. Good portal for startups, less so for existing businesses. Good information on marketing, taxes, incorporation, financing, employees—all the stuff you need for starting a business.

- Workz.com. Good, comprehensive site for running an online business—from accepting credit cards to creating banner ads. Over 1000 articles, templates, and tools targeted specifically for small businesses are available.

- inc.com. *Inc.* magazine is one of the best small business magazines going—and their website is packed with useful info and full-text article archives.

- money.cnn.com/magazines/fsb/. *Fortune Small Business* magazine combines the credibility that *Fortune* has created over decades of business journalism and focuses on practical application for running your own business.

- fastcompany.com. *Fast Company* magazine combines two things in each issue: cutting-edge cool and depth of coverage. Good combo.

- money.cnn.com/magazines/business2. *Business 2.0* magazine provides lots on leveraging technology for your small business. Good e-commerce, Web design, and tech strategy.

- businessweek.com/smallbiz. We normally associate *Business Week* magazine with big business and the economy, but their online section has great small business tactics.

Rather, it means that the time that you spend on the daily tasks like selling or writing new software or cleaning machinery is time when you are not managing. Those tasks have to be done, and the small business owner is usually the one who has to do them, but managing a business is more than a collection of tasks.

First-time managers and business owners often think of management as doing the job they have previously done, only with more power and control. Rather, to use the analogy of an orchestra, a novice business owner or manager must move from being a musician who concentrates on playing one instrument to being the conductor who brings the talents of all the musicians together and knows the capabilities of every instrument.[1]

Although the four functions are as generally applicable today as they were in 1916 when they were first articulated by Henri Fayol, there is more to describing what managers *do*. Henry Mintzberg has gone into considerable depth searching for descriptions of how managers spend their time.[2]

First, rather than being reflective, systematic planners, managers tend to work at an unrelenting pace on a wide variety of activities that are brief and have little continuity. The front-line managers in Mintzberg's study averaged 583 activities per eight-hour day—one activity every 48 seconds. Half of CEOs' activities lasted less than nine minutes, and only 10 percent took longer than an hour.

Second, rather than managers having no regular duties to perform, Mintzberg found that managers spend a lot of time on regular duties, such as performing rituals and ceremonies, negotiating, and dealing with the external environment. They receive visitors, take care of customers, and preside at holiday parties and other rituals and ceremonies that are part of their job, whether the business is large or small.

Third, even though management is often viewed as a technological science, information processing and decision making remain locked in the manager's brain. Managers are people who depend on judgment and intuition more than on technology. Computers are important for the business's specialized work, but managers still greatly depend on word-of-mouth information to support almost all of their decisions. A manager's job is complex, difficult, and as much an art as a science.

Mintzberg suggests several important skills that a manager needs to master so as to plan, organize, lead, and control successfully:

- Develop relationships with peers
- Carry out negotiations
- Motivate subordinates
- Resolve conflicts
- Establish information networks and then disseminate information
- Make decisions in allocating resources under conditions of extreme uncertainty
- Most important, be willing to learn continually on the job[3]

As a manager, you must use your resources *efficiently* and *effectively*. The difference is more than an exercise in semantics. *Effectiveness* means achieving your stated goals. Having a helicopter fly you everywhere you go (across town to meetings, to the grocery store, to a ball game) is an effective way to travel. You get where you intend to go. But, of course, with the reality of limited resources, effectiveness cannot be your only goal. You need *efficiency*, too—making the best use of your resources to accomplish your goals. In running a small business, you have to get the job done, but you have to contain costs as well. Wasting your limited resources—for instance, on helicopter rides—even though you achieve your goals, will lead to bankruptcy just as fast as if you were not making sales. A small business manager must balance effectiveness and efficiency to be competitive.

Katherine Allen of Springfield, Missouri, runs a company that specializes in oil-cleanup products and services. She estimates that half of her company's nearly $4 million in annual sales comes from exports to locations ranging from Singapore to São Paulo. Because her business is in a field traditionally dominated by men, she's had to expend significant time and energy in building this global business. Allen says, however, that her company's success in global markets is due to her efforts to understand her markets and her customers. This type of knowledge is invaluable for any small business owner seeking to expand into global markets.[4]

Small Business Growth

Growth is a natural, and usually desirable, consequence of being in business. Growth of your business can take several forms, albeit not necessarily all at once. You may see evidence of it in revenues, total sales, number of customers, number of employees, products offered, and facilities needed. It is something to be expected and planned for as your business evolves, but it should not be an end in itself. Bigger is not necessarily better. A sunflower is not better than a violet. And growth brings changes that may not always be positive ones.

As your business makes upward progress, you will experience "growing pains" just as people do as they move through childhood, adolescence, and adulthood. Signals of growing pains can be jobs that are not delivered on time, costs that rise out of control, or feelings that chaos is reigning. Such signals can indicate that your business has grown to a point where your staff or operating structure cannot satisfy the rising demands. Breakdowns in customer service and product quality soon follow.[5] Managing growth is a difficult part of managing a small business because of the transitions needed as your business passes from one stage to another.

Your Growing Firm

When a business grows in size by increasing its number of employees and its volume of sales, the way it is managed must also change. As it evolves from a bare-bones startup to an expanded, mature firm, it may pass through roughly five stages.[6] Naturally, not all small businesses are the same size at startup, nor do they all seek to achieve the same level of growth in maturity. Even so, these five stages provide a way to understand the changing needs of your business.

In the first, or *existence* stage, the owner runs the business alone (see Figure 16.2). Although not every business begins with one individual running (and being) the entire business, it is not uncommon. In fact, technology is making the solo type of business much more common than ever before. Online networks have allowed the creation of electronic cottage industries out of people's homes. Thus, although some people intentionally keep their businesses at the solo size, it also represents the first stage of growth.

A business reaching the second stage, *survival,* has demonstrated that it has a viable idea; at this point, the key problem shifts from mere existence to generation of cash flow. Now the entrepreneur is no longer responsible for just her own efforts. Carrie Wong labored through this stage as founder and sole employee of the Practical Gourmet, an upscale bakery in Aurora, Oregon. She made all the goodies, delivered them in her Subaru wagon, and pitched creations to restaurants. When local newspapers ran features on her business, sales really took off to the point that she was working 90-hour weeks. Says Wong, "This was insane. I had to stop taking on more clients or just go for it." That meant hiring her first employee—a scary move. An entrepreneur is plagued with questions: Who do I hire? How do I

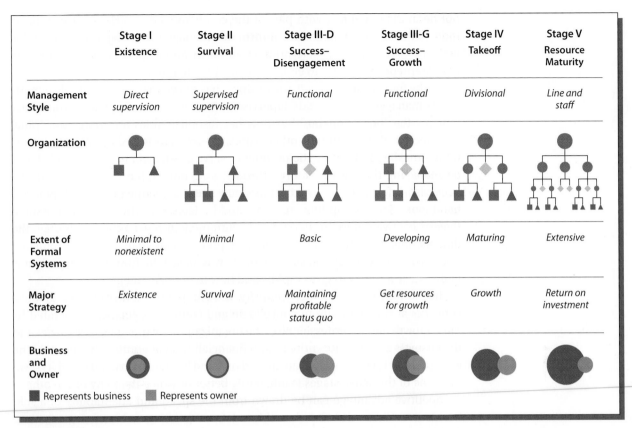

Figure 16.2
STAGES OF BUSINESS GROWTH

Businesses Tend to Evolve Through Five Stages as They Grow from Single-Person Firms to Full-Fledged Businesses.

SOURCE: Reprinted by permission of *Harvard Business Review*. Exhibit. From "Five Stages of Small Business Growth," by Neil C. Churchhill and Virginia L. Lewis, May–June 1983. Copyright © 1983 by the Harvard Business School Publishing Corporation; all rights reserved.

find someone who will care as much about the business as I do? What if the business goes in the tank?

Fortunately for Wong, she met Todd Wieweck, a pastry chef in Scottsdale, Arizona, who worked out well. Today she concentrates on sales while he runs the kitchen. If all goes as planned, Wong will offer profit sharing to Wieweck soon. She understands the importance of rewarding employees beyond a standard paycheck. However, she also required Wieweck to sign nondisclosure and noncompete agreements to protect her recipes. She plans to hire more people soon. "I don't have to be the smartest person in the world to expand this business," she says. "I just need to be smart enough to hire the right people to help me do it."[7]

When the business grows to the point where employees operate within several departments, the entrepreneur must either become a professional manager or hire managerial expertise. In this third stage, *success,* the owner accepts a degree of disengagement as a level of supervision is added—employees to lead departments or divisions. Care must be taken that these supervisors understand the culture of the business they are joining and will work toward building it. At this point, the entrepreneur is performing less of the daily production personally and may not be in direct contact with part of the company's efforts. He must turn loose more of the "doing" and assume more of the "managing." Giving up control in this way can be difficult, but delegation of authority and responsibility is something an entrepreneur must do to enable the business to grow.

In the fourth stage, *takeoff,* the business has grown to include multiple departments managed by numerous supervisors. As in the preceding stages, the owner remains the "head honcho," but now her responsibilities are more conceptual than technical in nature. In other words, rather than focusing on daily operations—making and selling the product or service—she will more intensely focus on managing the bigger picture—through long-range planning and overseeing supervisors, for instance. The business now needs someone to establish policies, handbooks, job descriptions, training, and budgets, and the owner will assume those executive duties. In this stage the entrepreneur must either go through the difficult metamorphosis of becoming a professional manager, hire someone else to run the business and step out of the way, or sell the firm. The key problems in this stage are how to grow rapidly and how to finance that growth.

In the fifth stage, *resource maturity,* the company has arrived. The greatest concerns at this point are to consolidate and control the finances generated by rapid growth and to professionalize the organization. By this stage, the owner and the business are separate entities, both financially and operationally. The child the entrepreneur bore has grown up, moved out, and has taken on a full life of its own.

None of these five stages is inherently better or worse than any of the others. Competitive advantage can be drawn from the speed and adaptability of a solo business or from the muscle achieved from growing a larger organization. Problems can also occur at every stage, although their magnitude is intensified when growth occurs too rapidly. Cash flow can turn negative, quality can suffer, and employees can lose sight of the vision of the business in cases of too rapid growth. Growth has to be managed, and it is not a heresy to try to limit the size of your business.

Transition to Professional Management

The transition from entrepreneur to professional manager is difficult, because the skills or characteristics that were needed to establish and run the business in the startup phase are not always the same skills needed to manage a larger business.[8] The transition from an entrepreneurial style of running a business to a managerial approach can be complicated by a variety of factors:

- A highly centralized decision-making system in which few or none of the business decisions are made by employees
- An overdependence on one or two key individuals, with little delegation
- An entrepreneur's inadequate repertoire of managerial skills and training in all areas of the business
- A paternalistic atmosphere within the company that leads to employees' reluctance to act without clearance from the entrepreneur[9]

In a recent study conducted by the National Federation of Independent Business (NFIB), 4,603 small business owners shared their insights about their most significant problem during the previous year of operation (see Table 16.1).

Table 16.1
WHAT'S BUGGING YOU? PROBLEMS FACING SMALL BUSINESS OWNERS BY ORDER OF IMPORTANCE

Measures of Small Business Problem Importance						
Problem	Rank	Mean Rating	Standard Deviation	Percent "Critical"	Percent "Not a Problem"	2000 Rank
Cost of Health Insurance	1	1.75	1.42	65.6	3.4	1
Cost and Availability of Liability Insurance	2	2.86	1.82	30.1	6.4	13
Workers' Compensation Costs	3	3.03	2.06	32.8	11.8	7
Cost of Natural Gas, Propane, Gasoline, Diesel, Fuel Oil	4	3.03	1.88	26.1	8.3	10
Federal Taxes on Business Income	5	3.05	1.79	23.2	6.8	2
Property Taxes (Real, Personal or Inventory)	6	3.18	1.85	22.7	7.7	new
Cash Flow	7	3.25	1.84	21.6	7.1	9
State Taxes on Business Income	8	3.35	1.93	20.2	10.5	6
Unreasonable Government Regulations	9	3.35	1.87	19.5	8.7	4
Electricity Costs (Rates)	10	3.42	1.75	15.1	7.5	19
Locating Qualified Employees	11	3.55	2.02	18.8	14.0	3
Poor Earnings	12	3.56	1.94	18.6	9.2	20
FICA (Social Security Taxes)	13	3.59	1.85	14.3	10.5	5
Cost of Supplies/Inventories	14	3.59	1.73	11.7	8.2	17
Frequent Changes in Federal Tax Laws and Rules	15	3.72	1.80	12.7	9.1	11
Telephone Costs and Service	16	3.72	1.70	9.7	7.7	15
State/Local Paperwork	17	3.73	1.80	11.6	9.3	12
Federal Paperwork	18	3.74	1.85	12.2	10.6	8
Unemployment Compensation (UC)	19	3.80	2.00	14.4	15.3	28
Fixed Costs Too High	20	3.80	1.81	11.4	10.5	22
Cost of Outside Business Services; e.g., Accountants, Lawyers, Consultants	21	3.89	1.75	8.5	9.9	21
Competition from Large Businesses	22	3.90	2.03	15.3	15.8	24
Highly Variable Earnings (Profits)	23	3.93	1.84	10.6	11.5	27
Ability to Cost-Effectively Advertise	24	3.95	1.93	11.0	15.4	34
Projecting Future Sales Changes	25	3.95	1.72	7.4	10.9	26

SOURCE: From Bruce D. Phillips, "Small Business Problems and Priorities," NFIB Research Foundation/Wells Fargo, 15 June 2004, www.nfib.com/page/researchFoundation. Reprinted with permission of the author.

These owners evaluated 75 potential business problems and assessed their severity on a scale of 1 for a "Critical Problem" to 7 for "Not a Problem." A mean (average) was calculated from the responses for each problem.

A recent *Inc.* article identified attributes that distinguish professionally managed small businesses. To achieve professional standards, you should do the following:

- *Be automated.* Computers can efficiently track items like inventory, expenses, and customers; use technology wisely.

- *Be competitive.* Being small no longer means you will have less competition—you have to produce quality.

- *Be resourceful.* There is no shortage of services available to tap for assistance and for tools you may lack.

- *Be planned.* Sophisticated marketing information such as demographic mapping is no longer affordable by only the largest businesses.

- *Be experienced.* More "corporate refugees" are starting small businesses with incredible connections, talent, and management experience every year.

Small businesses can no longer operate unmolested in anonymity. Competition raises standards. As one small business owner put it, "Running a business is like playing a video game. You work and scramble to reach the next level, only to find out that the game speeds up and everything gets even harder."

The Next Step: An Exit Strategy

To every thing there is a season. There comes a time that every business must end. Unfortunately for many entrepreneurs, the arrival of this time means that the business could not sustain itself or them any longer and must cease to exist for that unhappy reason. But for many others, the business appears capable on continuing indefinitely. Then the question becomes, how long will *you* last? How will you and the business part ways?

Just as you needed a plan to start this deal, so you need a plan to finish it. An exit strategy must be well-planned, because it could take years to execute to completion. You have three broad choices, with many themes and variations upon each: You can sell, merge, or close. None of the three is especially easy, but whether or not you have a strategy, you will exit sooner or later.

Consider these exit options:

- *Sell to a financial buyer*—someone like you who wants to buy and run a business.

- *Sell to a strategic buyer*—a company that wants to expand into your industry or market. Perhaps a competitor wants to buy more market share. Such a buyer is more likely to pay market value than an individual financial buyer and may want you to stay on and run the daily operations.[10]

- *Sell to a key employee or group of key employees.* This kind of deal is similar to selling to an individual buyer, but employee-buyers tend to be more intimately familiar with what they are purchasing. They will drive the price down, how ever, because they feel they deserve a lower price due to their years of service.

- *Sell to all employees via an employee stock ownership plan (ESOP).* This strategy is a great option for the seller if the business has a key group of motivated employees. You are much more likely to receive market price or even a premium because the ESOP will be based on a formal business valuation by a professional.

- *Take the company public.* This step takes a tremendous commitment, both physically and financially, to comply with all elements of the Securities Exchange Commission (SEC) requirements.

- *Create a family succession.* This tactic is a popular, highly desired option. But the question must always be asked, "Are my family members up to it?" A better transition may be to hire an outside CEO to mentor the kids.[11]

- *Undertake a planned liquidation.* This approach would involve running the business until the day you're done; then you sell the assets. It takes a lot of planning and patience and can be an emotional roller coaster.

Next comes *valuation,* in which the company's worth is in the eye of the beholder. There are as many ways to value a business as there are businesses, but the three most common are the *market approach* (what others have paid for comparable businesses), the *asset-based approach* (essentially the cost to recreate the operating assets of the business), and the *income approach* (how much a buyer could make from the business) (see Chapter 6).

Business valuation is a complex topic. A good article on this subject was written by Larry Kanter: "The Definitive Valuation Guide—What's Your Company Worth Now?" *Inc.,* January 2007, 98–105. In addition, the following websites offer useful information:[12]

- *www.conference-board.org.* The Conference Board collects and publishes information on the U.S. economy.

- *www.bizcomps.com.* This fee-based site offers small business transaction sales data contained in databases organized by state. The databases are updated annually with each region's sales data over the past ten years.

- *www.dnb.com.* The Dun & Bradstreet Business Information Report (fee-based) provides detailed company data.

- *www.corporateinformation.com.* This site will search company names to bring up links to related web sites for those businesses.

- *www.nacva.com.* This site is operated by the National Association of Certified Valuation Analysts.

> " Leadership abilities are crucial for small business owners because they work so closely with people—employees, vendors, and customers. "

Leadership in Action

Small businesses need managers who are also leaders, because building an organization requires every employee to contribute to productivity and efficiently use every resource. Owners of small businesses must be very visible leaders because they work closely with their people. Jim Schindler, CEO of ESKCO, Inc., says that leaders of small businesses are building a different foundation than their counterparts in large organizations. The small business owner's "character, his vision, what he brings to the equation has a lot more direct impact."[13]

Jim Kouzes, president of Tom Peters Group/Learning Systems, says that the foundation of small business leadership is *credibility.* He sums up his concept with one sentence: "If people don't believe in the messenger, they won't believe in the message."[14] How do you build credibility? Kouzes prescribes an acronym—DWWSWWD (Do What We Say We Will Do).

A lot of literature on management is devoted to an ongoing debate over management versus leadership. The debate began with a now famous statement from Warren Bennis: "American businesses are overmanaged and underled."[15] Management has been depicted as unimaginative, controlling, rigid, analytical, orderly, and focused on problem solving, whereas leadership is seen as visionary, passionate, creative, flexible, and charismatic.[16] Are these labels useful? Not really, because running a small business takes a combination of *both* qualities. Vision without analysis produces chaos, and orderliness without passion produces rigid complacency. **Leadership** is the inspirational part of the many things a manager must do through directing and influencing team members—along with an amount of planning, directing, and controlling.

Where do small businesses find the next generation of leaders? Andy Medley and Scott Hill, owners of Indianapolis-based holding company CIK Enterprises, with 80 employees, grow their own. They run a manager's book group that meets weekly to discuss the theories of Jim Collins, Jack Stack, and other business thinkers. They call the program The Incubator. Managers nominate candidates based on enthusiasm, drive, and smarts. Only 10 percent of employees can participate at any given time. Those that come through to be future leaders will thrive, having been endued with an understanding of the company culture. Hill states that "even if they don't want to do management, they'll come through saying, 'Hey, I learned a lot,' and they'll be better able to help in any way they can."[17]

leadership
The process of directing and influencing the actions of members within a group.

Andy Medley and Scott Hill Stay Current in Small Business Practices via Their Management Book Group.

Leadership Attributes

The magazine *Management Review* conducted a study to determine the attributes that business leaders need. Its findings are summarized here.

Vision   Having a mental picture of where the company is going, a vision, will always be an important part of leadership. Moreover, a good leader is able to describe that vision to others so that everyone is headed in the same direction. A person with a vision that can't be put into action is a dreamer, not a leader.

Communication   Constant communication is needed for a leader, not only to find out what is going on but also to let others know about it. The ability to communicate clearly ranks as one of the most important attributes a leader must possess.

Integrity   Leaders must have inner strength and demonstrate honest behavior in all situations. People will not follow a leader who lacks integrity unless they are moved by fear. Leaders need to be dedicated to doing what they know is right.

Trust   The bond of trust between leaders and followers must run in both directions. Leaders need to be able to trust their people, and at the same time they themselves must be trustworthy.

Commitment   Loyalty to one's company is more precarious in today's climate of economic uncertainty. With this being the case, it is more important than ever that leaders be seen as caring about the business and the employees. Passion for what is good for both the business and the workers can't be faked.

Entrepreneurial Evolution

Contrary to much of what management literature and many consultants say, there is more than one right way to run a new entrepreneurial business. The key is to recognize your style and match your strategy to your business goals.

You can be a successful business owner as a *Classic* manager—involved in every aspect and every decision of the business. You may be reluctant to admit you are a Classic for fear of receiving criticism for not delegating (not seen as politically correct). Actually, this is a very legitimate way to run your business. The biggest problem with this style is not the lack of delegation, but acting like a Classic while deluding yourself into thinking you are using a team approach. Delegating is fine, not delegating is fine—but don't *pretend* to delegate, because then no one will be happy.

You can run your business as a *Coordinator*—operating without a single employee and farming out everything from accounting, to sales, to manufacturing. Do what you enjoy or what you do well, and subcontract out the rest.

Your style may be that of an *Entrepreneur + Employee Team*—you, plus a team of employees. This style gives you both control and the ability to grow. Authority can be delegated to key employees, but you retain final control is retained yourself.

What we as a society define as a business leader changes over time. In the 1950s the so-called corporate man ruled, thinking "inside the box" was rewarded, and mavericks were disdained. Business leaders in the 1990s swung toward entrepreneurs, people who stood apart from the crowd because of their creativity. In the twenty-first century, a diversity of people, backgrounds, and styles epitomize leadership. Management in this century poses challenges that have not been seen in the past. To deal with them, a blend of male and female traits are needed—both intuition and focus on bottom line, both people skills and analytical strength.

Still, some things don't change. Some leadership traits apply no matter what decade you live in: You have to set standards and live up to them, you need to innovate, and you need to execute. What is your leadership style? Take a quiz at www.entrepreneur.com/quiz/leaderstyle to find out.

SOURCES: Carol Tice, "Building the 21st Century Leader," *Entrepreneur,* February 2007, 64–69; Rieva Lesonsky, "Entrepreneur Evolution," *Entrepreneur,* February 2007, 10; Ronald E. Merrill and Henry D. Sedgwick, *The New Venture Handbook,* 2nd ed. (New York: AMACOM, 1993).

Creative Ability   Good leadership involves creating something that didn't exist before. A person must have a positive mind-set in order to see creative opportunities and different ways to do things.

Toughness   Often a manager is aware of the difficult choices or changes that must be made for the health of the business but is unable to make them. Such indecisiveness translates into a lack of leadership. A leader needs a certain amount of toughness to make unpopular decisions or to stand against the majority when necessary. A successful leader is able to set high standards and refuse to compromise them.

Ability to Take Action   Small business leaders must realize that without action, all of the foregoing attributes are mere academic rhetoric. Leadership attributes need to be practiced consistently to be effective. The subject of leadership is easy to talk about, but a challenge to demonstrate.[18]

Negotiation

The art of negotiation is what you do while running your small business, from the time the idea pops into your head until the day you harvest it. *Negotiation* can be defined as the communication process in which two or more people come together to seek mutual agreement about an issue. When you are raising money, hiring employees, shopping for computer systems, or signing contracts, you are negotiating. You are communicating with other people to get the job done. Whenever two or more people get together to exchange information for the purpose of changing their relationship in some way, they are negotiating. From merging onto the freeway in rush-hour traffic, to scheduling an appointment with a client, to deciding which television program to watch with your family, negotiation is involved.[19]

Every negotiation ends with one of four possible outcomes:

- *Lose-lose.* Neither party achieves his needs or wants.
- *Win-lose.* One counterpart loses and the other wins.
- *Win-win.* The needs and goals of both parties are met, so they both walk away with a positive feeling and a willingness to negotiate with each other again.
- *No outcome.* Neither party wins or loses, which most likely leaves both parties willing to return to the negotiating table at a later date.[20]

Negotiation is so important to businesses of all sizes that we can see the free enterprise system at work by considering the sheer number of books written on the subject. *Getting to Yes* has sold 3.5 million copies in the 22 years since it was first published. *The Power of Nice* , *The Negotiation Tool Kit, The Art and Science of Negotiation, You Can Negotiate Anything,* and *Negotiating Rationally* are other popular examples. Virtually every one of these books includes some simplistic examples, such as the Parable of the Orange, which goes like this: Two people each want an orange and agree finally to split the fruit in half. But it turns out that one side simply wanted the juice, and the other side wanted the rind. If only they had worked together to solve the problem, each side could have gotten what it wanted. Okay, so such simplistic solutions don't often turn up in the world of business. Nevertheless, there are some great pieces of advice in these tomes. Here's a sampling of some of the best:

- Stay rationally focused on the issue being negotiated.
- Exhaustive preparation is more important than aggressive argument.
- Think through your alternatives. The more options you believe you have, the better your negotiating position.
- Spend less time talking and more time listening and asking good questions. Sometimes silence is your best response.

- Let the other side make the first offer. If you're underestimating yourself, you might make a needlessly weak opening move.

- Some gurus advocate a bit of play-acting. Always seem put off at your rival's offer. Play up the importance of factors you don't really care about so that it will seem like a bigger deal when you concede on them. Seem more befuddled than you are so that your opponent will underestimate you.[21]

Delegation

By **delegation** of authority and responsibility, a manager gives employees the power to make many decisions that she would otherwise have to make, thereby giving her time to concentrate on more important matters. Delegation *empowers* employees, meaning that it increases their involvement in their work. Also, by holding employees more accountable for their actions, delegation allows managers to maximize the efforts and talents of everyone in the company.

> *delegation*
> Granting authority and responsibility for a specific task to another member of an organization; empowerment to accomplish a task effectively.

Many small business owners are either unwilling or unable to delegate for several reasons. For entrepreneurs who have started a business, giving up control is difficult. Owners often know the business more thoroughly than anyone else and feel as if they *have* to make all the decisions so as to protect the business. They may feel that subordinates are unwilling or unable to accept responsibility. In reality, this attitude may become a self-fulfilling prophecy. If employees' attempts to take responsibility or to show initiative are squelched too often, they will either stop trying to show initiative or will leave the business.

Some small business owners simply misunderstand the meaning of management. They believe the only way to get the job done right is to do it themselves. That is a commendable attitude, but it can be counterproductive to being an effective manager, which, by definition, is someone who needs to get things done through other people.

Delegation is not the same as abdication. Nor is empowering people the same as instituting a pure democracy, where you simply count votes and the majority rules. In using delegation and empowerment, an effective leader is trying to encourage participation and take advantage of shared knowledge so that everyone can contribute. Of course, consensus can't always be reached, so sometimes the leader has to make a decision and go with it.

When you assign tasks, make sure you clarify exactly what is expected: when the job should be done, what performance level is expected, and how much discretion is allowed. Your employees need feedback control for their own sake and for yours. Controls help monitor employees' progress by letting them know how they are doing and preventing mistakes before they happen.

Motivating Employees

The word *motivation* comes from the Latin *movere,* which means "to move." For our purposes, **motivation** is the reason an individual takes an action in satisfying some need. It answers the question of why people behave the way they do.

> *motivation*
> The forces that act on or within a person that cause the person to behave in a specific manner.

Motivation Theories   Some people say that one person cannot motivate another, that one can merely create an environment for self-motivation. Whether this is the case or not, as a small business manager, you will be interested in encouraging

Creating Competitive Advantage
Motivating Without Breaking the Bank

Many small businesses, from specialty coffee shops to CPA firms, are dependent on hourly employees for the operation of the business and contact with customers. Think about what is expected of these employees, who are making only $7 to $8 per hour. They are expected to spend eight hours per day providing quick, friendly, and superior service to every customer. They are expected to be diligent, honest, and sacrifice their personal time (often with little or no notice) to cover a shift they were not scheduled for. The bottom line is that business owners expect their hourly employees to be as motivated about their businesses as they are. It is no surprise that a survey of 500 small and midsize business owners by Arthur Anderson's Enterprise Group showed that retaining and motivating workers is their biggest challenge. More than 48 percent of respondents placed this concern at the top of their problem list.

In response, many small business owners are creating "work/life" policies to sustain a competitive advantage in hiring employees. Work/life issues can include on-site child care, time-off policies, flextime, job sharing, and personal days. The problem is this: How do you afford to offer such perks on limited revenues and razor-thin margins? The answer comes from the same source as many other solutions—creativity. For example:

- Graham Weston, 42, co-founder and CEO of Rackspace Managed Hosting, which hosts Web applications for other firms from San Antonio, hands top performers the keys to one of his cars, a BMW M3 convertible, for a week. Weston says, "If you gave somebody a $200 bonus, it wouldn't mean very much. When someone gets to drive my car for a week, they never forget it."

- David Williams, CEO of Merkle, a database-marketing agency in Lanham, Maryland., with $114 million in annual sales, pays for his 851 employees to take classes during *business* hours on subjects ranging from computer programming to public speaking.

- Richard Caturano, president of Boston accounting firm Vitale Caturano, offers workers free gourmet dinners and Saturday lunches during the busy season, and a concierge service for errands such as picking up dry cleaning.

SOURCES: Pofeldt, Elaine, "Better Bosses," *Fortune Small Business* October 2006, 90–93; Tom Macon, "Motivating the Troops," *Specialty Coffee Retailer*, March 1999, 10–11.

motivation for your employees. Many theories on motivation exist, and a thorough examination of each is not appropriate for this text, but you can obtain more information on the subject from texts on principles of management or organizational behavior. Here we will summarize two of the most well-known and accepted theories.

One of the best known is *Maslow's hierarchy of needs.* Psychologist Abraham Maslow stated that people have in common a set of universal needs occurring in order of importance. The lowest-level needs are *physiological* (food, water, air, sleep, sex, and so on). *Safety and security* needs are the next level, followed by *social* needs, *esteem* needs, and the highest-level needs for *self-actualization.*

As a small business owner, you should be aware of the fact that your employees will not always manifest these needs in the same order. People will be at different levels of needs at different times—sometimes simultaneously—so a variety of ways to motivate their behavior is needed. For example, the use of money to motivate is often misunderstood, especially in terms of Maslow's hierarchy.

Money is generally seen as providing for basic physiological needs and not being important to the higher-level needs. In fact, money is actually a motivator because it buys the time and resources needed for self-actualization.[22]

The biggest contribution of Maslow's theory to motivating employees is its recognition that people have needs that "pop up" and continue to require attention until they are satisfied. If a lower-level need pops up for an employee, he will not be able to concentrate on a higher-level need until the lower-level need is fulfilled. For example, if an employee receives a phone call from a school nurse informing him that his second-grade child had an accident and broke her arm on the playground, a safety need has popped up. This employee will probably not be very productive on the job until he can be sure the situation is under control, either by going to the school in person or by making other arrangements. Any effort to interfere with his handling of this need will create frustration and antagonism, which will undermine your employee's motivation and damage his attitude toward work.[23]

Another important motivational theory is *Herzberg's motivation-hygiene theory.* This theory is important to the small business owner because it recognizes that the factors producing job *satisfaction* are not the same as the factors producing job *dissatisfaction.* Herzberg called things that cause people to feel good about their job *motivators* and things that cause people to feel bad about their job *hygiene factors.* By eliminating hygiene factors on the job (such as unfair or inadequate company policies), you may create contentment among employees but not necessarily motivate them to excel (see Figure 16.3). To truly motivate your people, you need to create an opportunity for them to achieve.[24]

Look at the factors listed in Figure 16.3 that cause satisfaction on the job: achievement, recognition, the work itself, and responsibility. These provide intrinsic rewards to people. The practical application of Herzberg's theory gives a small business manager some direction in keeping employees satisfied on the job. Satisfaction may not translate directly into motivation, but it is a significant component in keeping employees on the job.

Motivation Techniques   A key to motivating the employees of your small business is to know what is important to them. For instance, if you provide a motivational reward that they do not want, it is a kind of inadvertent punishment. Say you promise a "sweet year-end bonus" for the top performer for the month of December. You will probably set up healthy competition that increases morale and achievement. But if your sweet bonus turns out to be a fruitcake—and your employees don't care for fruitcake—don't expect your next incentive to be motivational.

Bill Mork is the owner of Modern of Marshfield, a furniture maker located in Marshfield, Wisconsin. Mork followed the popular advice of using recognition instead of cash to reward participants in his new employee-suggestion program. From the suggestions received, Mork and other managers picked a "colleague of the month," who was awarded with a special parking space and a big handshake in front of all the gathered employees.

The number of suggestions that came in as a result of the new program was underwhelming. One winner pleaded not to be chosen again, to avoid embarrassment and being called a "brown nose" by coworkers. As a result, Mork changed the

Figure 16.3

JOB SATISFIERS
AND DISSATISFIERS

The Factors or Experiences That Cause People to Feel Satisfied with Their Jobs (Motivators) Are Distinctly Different from Those That Create Job Dissatisfaction (Hygiene Factors). This Chart Records Factors Affecting Job Attitudes as Reported in 12 Investigations.

SOURCE: Reprinted by permission of Harvard Business Review. From "One More Time: How Do You Motivate Employees?" by Frederick Herzberg, January 2003. Copyright © 2003 by the Harvard Business School Publishing Corporation; all rights reserved.

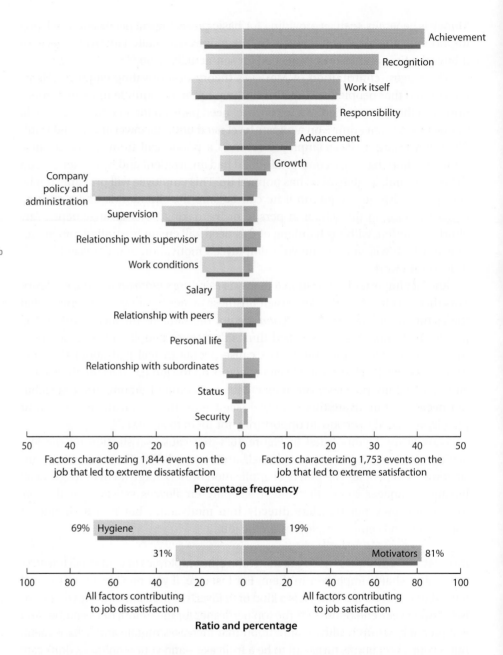

whole program and added cash bonuses at each step. For any cost-saving suggestion made by an employee that was implemented by the company, the employee was given a bonus worth 10 percent of the estimated savings. An additional 10 percent of the savings was added to a fund to be split among all suggestion makers at the end of the year. Anyone who had contributed a suggestion was eligible for prize drawings, whether or not the suggestion was implemented. The "colleague of the month" is now chosen by previous winners rather than by managers.

Employees have taken a very different attitude toward the program since bonus checks were added.[25] Modern's sales have almost doubled. Each year Mork pays out $10,000 in rewards for about 1,200 suggestions submitted by 100 employees. Although that may sound like a lot of money, Mork estimates the savings generated by the suggestions to be five times that amount. This example suggests an answer to that long-asked management question, does money motivate? Apparently, at a very visceral level, *yes!*

Motivation Myths   So many motivation theories have been put forth that some misconceptions have resulted:

- *All employees need external motivation.* Some employees have such a strong internal drive that external techniques will not increase their motivation—though they still need your support, backing, and guidance.

- *Some employees don't need any motivation.* Motivation is the force that prompts every action—we all have to have motivation; it just comes from different sources.

- *Attempts to motivate always increase performance and productivity.* If our attempts to motivate involve incentives that employees do not desire, they can decrease performance. And some incentives can increase happiness and morale without producing an increase in productivity.

- *Money always motivates people.* Base salary is generally not a long-term motivator. A person who receives a raise may temporarily work harder but will soon rationalize, "I'm *still* getting paid less than I'm worth," and return to her previous level of productivity.

- *Intrinsic rewards provide more motivation than money.* As seen in the Bill Mork example, money—as a one-time bonus—*does* motivate at a visceral level.

- *Fear is the best motivator.* Workers who are afraid of a boss will work hard in the boss's presence, but may not have the business's best interests in mind. The best workers will also be looking for another job—so fear may drive out the very people the business needs the most.

- *Satisfied workers are always productive.* Happy people do not necessarily produce more. The goal of employee motivation is not to create a country-club or amusement park-atmosphere. Rather, the goal is to get everyone in the company to maximize his efforts so as to increase contributions (and earnings).

- *This generation of workers is less motivated than the last.* Most generations hold this attitude toward the following generation. While members of the so-called X generation have been mislabeled as "slackers," they have already produced notable entrepreneurs, including many who have been used as examples throughout this book.

Can You Motivate?

To determine how effective you are at motivating, ask yourself the following questions (project yourself being in charge of others, if necessary):

- Do you know what motivates each of the people who report to you?

- To what extent are they motivated by money?

- To what extent are they motivated by recognition?

Profile in Entrepreneurship
Smooth Operator

While enjoying an Earth, Wind, and Fire concert when he was only nine years old, Marcus Johnson discovered his life's passion: to make quality music like that of his favorite band. "My number one objective is to create classic sounds," says the now 32-year-old entrepreneur, whose office and fully equipped recording studio are stationed in Silver Spring, Maryland.

Specializing in contemporary jazz, Johnson's 12-employee independent label is leaving its imprint on the music industry with its blend of smooth grooves and soul-stirring beats. Since the label's founding two years ago, several of the artists on its eight-person roster have secured Top 20 spots on contemporary jazz charts. In the last year, Marcus took a leap into the R&B realm with female vocalist YahZarah, whose debut album, *Blackstar*, quickly hurdled its way up the *Billboard* charts, peaking at number 44. The company, which garners most of its revenues from record sales, touring, and renting out its studio rooms for $80 to $500 per hour, generated $400,000 in revenues in 2002 and projected revenues between $650,000 and $700,000 for 2003.

Johnson's venture into the music business began while he was a Georgetown University student simultaneously pursuing a law degree and a master's degree in business administration. During a summer internship with MCA Records, the accomplished pianist, who had studied music since the age of six, learned the ins and outs of the recording industry firsthand. Johnson borrowed $1,000 from his sister plus $2,000 from friends and family to release his debut album, *Lessons in Love.*

He was searching for investors when he met Three Keys co-owner Robert L. Johnson at a jazz festival in Rehoboth Beach, Delaware. The BET founder invested $3 million to finance the Three Keys Music recording label and build a state-of-the-art studio. "Bob Johnson plays an integral role in the success of our company," says Marcus of his partner. "But not just because of his investment. There are times I don't know what to do, and I know that I can always ask him for guidance."

Although business is currently booming, Johnson isn't ready to rest on his laurels, even with success on the horizon. He distinctly recalls the hardships he faced and the revenues he lost when he stopped touring so that he could focus on building the business side of his company. "That year, there was no product released until the third quarter," he says. "Without [that] or the performance revenues, it made for a very lean time. I don't want to go through that again."

"I like to follow the Japanese model of business," he adds. "Whatever is not good, let's make it better, and whatever is good, let's make it great."

SOURCE: From *Black Enterprise*, "Hitting the High Note," by Demetria Lucas and Alan Hughes. Copyright © 2004 by Graves Ventures LLC. Reproduced with permission of Graves Ventures LLC via Copyright Clearance Center.

- To what extent are they motivated by opportunity for growth?
- Have you done anything in the last week that was intended to motivate someone else?
- Have you done anything lately that would undermine an employee's motivation—such as embarrassing or criticizing an employee in front of others?
- Have you praised anyone today?

Employee Theft

Can you spot a thief in your business as easily as you can in the cartoons (you know, the guy with beady eyes, slick black hair, and droopy mustache)? Of course you can't. But employee theft accounts for greater financial losses than fire each year. And small businesses are especially vulnerable because they have fewer defenses.

Fraud and other employee crime costs employers more than $400 million per year. Men commit three-fourths of the offenses, even though they represent only 54 percent of all employees. In 90 percent of the cases in which people steal from their company, the employer would probably have described the person as a trusted employee.[26] So what is a small business owner to do?

- Get a good small business insurance policy covering outside theft, employee theft, and/or computer fraud.

- Screen out potential problem employees at the hiring stage by administering a standardized test that indicates level of integrity (available from career counseling centers).

- Create a culture of honesty with a written code of ethics and conduct. Instruct employees in how to spot problems and what to do about them (tell you). A culture of integrity is best created by your and other managers' demonstrating it.

- Minimize the amount of cash on hand, and put excess cash in a safe.

- Change the times and routes you take to the bank for making deposits.

- Never schedule an employee to work alone.

- Let everyone know that you look at every deposit and every check. Make sure that you get monthly bank statements delivered to your desk unopened.

- The most important point for small business: Divide up financial tasks. The person who keeps the books should not be the same person who keeps the money.

Special Management Concerns: Time and Stress Management

Beyond the standard functions of management lie many other duties and responsibilities. Besides running your business, you also have personal, family, and social activities to tend to. You must be a good manager of time and be able to keep stress at acceptable levels.

"You can't store, hoard, or buy time—so you had better use it wisely!"

Time Management

As noted earlier, management is the *effective* and *efficient* use of resources. Most of us in business focus on our money: How much do I need? Where can I get it? We take the risking of our money seriously. But lost money can be made back.[27] What is a small business owner's most precious and most limited resource that can't be replaced? Time. No one seems to have enough of it, yet everyone has the same amount—24 hours per day, 168 hours per week, 8,760 hours per year. You can't store it, rent it, hoard it, sell it, or buy any more of it. So you had better use it wisely.

Few of us use time as effectively or as efficiently as possible. The key to effective time management for a small business owner is establishing priorities, investing time in what is important in life—and in the business. Thus time management is a goal-oriented activity. It requires that you prioritize what needs to be accomplished in any given day. Following are some indications that you are having problems with time management:

- You are frequently late for or forget meetings and appointments.
- You are consistently behind in responsibilities.
- You don't have enough time for basics—eating, sleeping, family.
- You are constantly working and still miss deadlines.
- You are often fatigued, both mentally and physically.

How can you improve your effectiveness in using your time? A good starting point is to conduct a *time audit*. A time audit makes as much sense as conducting a financial audit, yet few small business managers can account for their minutes as precisely as they can their dollars. Why? They don't have time to conduct a time audit!

Begin your time audit by keeping a log to record your activities. Break days down into 15-minute intervals and keep track of what you do for about two weeks. When the log is complete, you can analyze how you have spent your time. Did you accomplish your most urgent needs? Which activities were a waste of time and could be eliminated? In the end, the time audit should help you prioritize activities and set daily goals.

After you conduct your time audit, use these tips to your advantage:

- *Make a to-do list.* Write down and rank by importance what you want to accomplish each day. The return you receive will be many times greater than the small amount of time you invest in this exercise.
- *Eliminate time wasters.* Combine similar tasks and eliminate unnecessary ones.
- *Remember Parkinson's law.* "Work expands to fill the time available." If you schedule too much time to accomplish something, you'll probably set a pace to take that amount of time.
- *Know when you are most productive.* We all have a daily cycle. Some of us are "morning people." Some are "night owls." Schedule your work so that you handle your most demanding problems when you are at your best.

How late is late? Every culture has its own concept of time. In an experiment at California State University–Fresno, 200 students were surveyed in California and Brazil about their definition of "early" and "late." American students believed they were "late" for a lunch date when they made a friend wait for 19 minutes, compared with 34 minutes for the Brazilians. Does this finding mean anything to your small business? Yes, groups form "temporary cultures" that can be used to influence their attitude toward time.[28] Since perceptions of lateness vary, you need to clarify exactly what time employees are expected to be at work, to be back from lunch, and to show up for meetings.

Stress Management

One of the most ambiguous words in the English language is **stress.** There are almost as many interpretations of this term as there are people who use it, but technically the stress response is actually the unconscious preparation to fight or flee that a person experiences when faced with a demand. Common usage leads us to think of stress as a negative thing, as if it were something to be avoided, yet there is a positive side to stress. Positive stress (called eustress) stimulates us to face challenges, motivates us to achieve, and adds excitement to life, as when you are anticipating a wedding or vacation. It produces favorable chemicals in our body—endorphins, serotonin, and dopamine—and is necessary for life and health. But the negative side of stress, called **distress** entails unfavorable psychological, physical, or behavioral consequences, and this is the stress that we must learn to manage.

For a situation to create distress for a person, two conditions are necessary: Its outcome must be uncertain, and it must be a matter of importance to the person. Very few (if any) small businesses are "sure things" guaranteed to produce the outcome that the owner desires. Because small businesses are almost always the sole means of support for their owners, saying that they are extremely important to the owners is not an understatement. Therefore, both conditions causing distress exist in running a small business.

Other sources of stress that small business owners encounter include role conflict, task overload, and role ambiguity. *Role conflict* exists when we are faced with a situation that presents divergent role expectations. For example, a two-day business trip to meet with a potential client could help you land a large new account and prove very profitable for your business. But suppose taking the trip would cause you to miss your second grader's school play. The result is role conflict. The desire to attend both the meeting and the play—to be both a focused entrepreneur and a loving parent—creates a stressful internal conflict.

Task overload is another source of stress for a small business owner. More is expected of you than time permits—a common scenario in a small business. Unfinished work can be a sign of overload. In a business climate that calls for leaner organizations, work can pile up and more work be taken on before existing jobs are finished. Unfinished work creates tension and uneasiness. If the pattern of taking on more and more continues, eventually an accumulation of unfinished work produces stress and decreases performance.

Role ambiguity occurs when you are not entirely sure what you should do in a situation. Owning a small business generally means that you don't have anyone to consult when problems arise and that you will have to make decisions on a wide variety of topics. Some people have a higher tolerance or preference for ambiguity than others, but it still produces stress.

Stress is cumulative—it builds up. Sales declining at the business, a key employee being unhappy, a child having discipline problems, and the transmission going kaput in the family car all can combine to form a lot of stress. Individual stressors that could be handled by themselves may combine and become overwhelming.

> **stress**
> Emotional states that occur in response to demands, which may come from internal or external sources.
>
> **distress**
> The negative consequences and components of stress.

Practicing Relaxation Techniques Can Help You Be a More Productive Manager.

Stress cannot, and should not, be eliminated from everyday life, but it must be managed. General recommendations for controlling your stress level include the following.

Preventive Stress Management Attempt to modify, reduce, or eliminate the source of distress. Any changes you can make in your schedule or role as business owner can help prevent distress from building to a dangerous level.

Relaxation Techniques A few minutes of concentrated relaxation will prevent a build-up of distress. Practice a five-step relaxation exercise. First, sit in a comfortable position in a quiet location. Loosen any tight clothing. Second, close your eyes and assume a passive, peaceful attitude. Third, relax your muscles as much as possible—beginning with your feet and continuing to your head—and keep them relaxed. Fourth, slowly breathe through your nose and develop a quiet rhythm of breathing. After each exhale, quietly say "one" to yourself. Fifth, continue relaxing muscles and concentrate on breathing for 10 to 20 minutes. Open your eyes occasionally to check the time. It will take practice for you to learn to ignore distracting thoughts during relaxation, but soon this exercise can help you reduce stress.[29]

Social Support Systems Working in an environment that provides social and emotional support can help us deal with distress. Relationships within the workplace, family, church, and clubs provide emotional backing, information, modeling, and feedback.

Physical Exercise A person's physical condition affects his response in stressful situations. Aerobically fit people have more efficient cardiovascular systems and better nervous system interaction, which allows them to deal with and recover from stressful events more quickly.[30]

If (once you own your own business) you find yourself struggling with any of the varied topics in this chapter from motivating employees to battling stress and cannot win the struggle alone, you may want to consider a fast growing trend in small business—hiring a business coach.[31] The practice is not unusual; managers have sought outside counsel ever since Machiavelli first advised a young prince. The number of business coaches has grown from 2,000 in 1996 to over 10,000 in 2007.[32]

Summary

- **The functions and activities of managing a small business**

Managers plan, organize, lead, and control. To accomplish these functions, they perform many activities, such as developing relationships, negotiating, motivating, resolving conflicts, establishing information networks, making decisions, and continually learning.

- **The stages of growth and their consequences for your business**

In the earliest stage of many businesses' life, the entrepreneur acts alone. Many entrepreneurs even prefer to keep their businesses as one-person organizations. In the second growth stage, employees are added, so the entrepreneur often acts as a coach in getting work accomplished through other people. In stage three, a new layer of supervision is added, so the entrepreneur does not directly control all the people or activities of the business. In the fourth stage, takeoff, the business has grown to include multiple departments managed by numerous supervisors. By the fifth stage, the owner and

the business are separate entities, both financially and operationally.

- **The significance of employee leadership and motivation to small business**

Leadership means inspiring other people to accomplish what needs to be done. Leadership is part of a manager's job of providing the vision, passion, and creativity needed for the business to succeed.

Because management is getting things done through people, a small business manager must be able to motivate employees. The manager must therefore understand employees' behavior and recognize what is important to them. Maslow's and Herzberg's theories provide small business managers with frameworks for understanding motivation.

- **Time and stress management as they relate to small business**

Besides running your business, you must be a good manager of time and be able to keep stress at acceptable levels.

Questions for Review and Discussion

1. Give examples of efficiency and effectiveness in managing your everyday life.

2. Discuss some of the skills or characteristics that are needed by a manager in the startup phase of a business and explain how they differ from the skills or characteristics needed later to manage a larger, established firm.

3. Study the management styles mentioned in Manager's Notebook, "Entrepreneurial Evolution." Which one best describes you? Explain. Do you recognize a different style in managers you have worked for in the past?

4. What is motivation? Can managers really motivate employees?

5. Which exit strategy discussed in the chapter would you consider ideal? What would a downside of that strategy be?

6. Are you a good manager of time in your personal life? How will this affect your ability to manage your time as a business owner?

7. Give examples of stress, eustress, and distress

8. How can the owner of a small business apply Maslow's hierarchy of needs to working with employees?

9. What are positive and negative aspects of delegation?

10. As a business owner, in which of the leadership attributes discussed in the text are you the weakest? How could you help yourself improve in this area? How could others help you? What is your strongest leadership skill?

Questions for Critical Thinking

1. Review the five stages of business growth. Which of these five would you aspire to for your own business? Be prepared to justify your answer.

2. Refer to the chapter opening story about Hillary Johnson. She found managerial wisdom in a seemingly unrelated book on housecleaning.

The highest level of learning anything is the ability to connect divergent topics. Describe at least two areas you are knowledgeable about (from a hobby, personal interest, or previous job) and explain how you will relate them to your management style.

Experience This . . .

Experience can be the best teacher. See what you can learn from others' experience. Contact five small business owners in your community for a one-question mini-interview. Ask them what they would do differently if they could build their business all over again. You—and they—may be surprised at the responses.

What Would You Do?

Ten years ago, Linda Turner was in an exercise class and saw a pregnant woman struggling through her routine. After class, Turner asked the woman if she knew of any products that would help her be more comfortable. Because none existed, she began developing a prototype of the Bellybra—a support device designed for women in their third trimester. The Bellybra has tank-top shoulder straps and fits snugly all the way down below the wearer's enlarged stomach area. Turner experimented with different fabrics, including white lace and CoolMax fabric that pulls heat away from the body.

The Bellybra prototypes tested well with consumers, but because Turner was a stay-at-home mom, she was not able to build a company at that time. She licensed the product to a company called Basic Comfort and became the firm's first employee. As the success of the Bellybra increased, Turner eventually left on friendly terms to go out on her own. She sold 1,000 units in her first year and 10,000 units in her second year. Some growth rate! She has now expanded her focus from obstetricians and gynecologists to selling on her Internet site (www.bellybra.com).

Questions

1. Linda Turner will face different challenges as her company progresses through the five stages of growth described in this chapter. Describe how you believe her business would change in each stage.

2. Business growth that occurs too quickly can present some significant problems and challenges compared with a business that grows at a slow, steady pace (of course, zero growth or decline makes for a whole new set of problems). Describe the challenges of hypergrowth that Turner could face and explain how she should respond as a small business owner.

CHAPTER CLOSING CASE

FAMILY MATTERS

When the bank called in a loan, Larry Cohen had to act fast to save the family business. Was replacing his nephew with a more seasoned executive the answer?

Larry Cohen had an unsettling meeting with his bankers at the Chicago headquarters of Cole Taylor Bank in December 2003. Accurate Perforating, the Chicago-based metal company owned by Cohen's family, had run out of operating capital. The bank, which had loaned Accurate $1.5 million two years earlier, gave Cohen, the company's president, two choices: liquidate the business or find a new lender. Cohen was shocked by the ultimatum. "They were basically going to put us out of business," he says.

For decades, Cohen and his father, Ralph, who founded Accurate in 1940, had focused on one thing: putting as many holes in as many sheets of metal as possible. They bought the metal from steel mills in the Chicago region, perforated it, and sold it in bulk to distributors, which then sold it to metal workshops. There the metal was fabricated and finished—that is, cut, folded to specification, and painted—and sold to manufacturers of products like speaker grilles and ceiling tiles. "We were really just selling tonnage," Cohen says. "We stayed away from sophisticated products, and as a result we wound up in a very competitive situation where the only thing we were selling was price."

When a global steel surplus held down prices in the 1980s and 1990s, Accurate's business model became increasingly unsustainable. The company's manufacturing costs climbed while its prices stayed flat, squeezing its once healthy margins. Rather than switch to the more profitable niche of fabricating, finishing, and selling metal directly to manufacturers, as had many of Accurate's rivals, the company survived through militant budgeting. "If we couldn't pay cash, we didn't do it," recalls Cohen, who was unwilling to invest in the equipment required to become a fabricator. During those lean years, Accurate's employees built perforating machines from scratch—repairing them only when absolutely necessary—and used outmoded manufacturing processes developed by Ralph Cohen in the 1940s.

Sales hovered between $10 million and $15 million for more than 20 years.

Accurate was decades behind the competition in terms of both technology and business strategy by the time Cohen's 36-year-old nephew, Aaron Kamins, the only member of the family's younger generation working at the company, took over day-to-day operations as general manager in 2001. "There was a culture here that resisted change," Kamins says. "Everyone was comfortable with what they were doing. We were making a living and that was that." Kamins, who had worked on Accurate's factory floor since graduating from college, hoped to steer the company in a new direction. In 2002, with Cohen's approval, he borrowed $1.5 million from Cole Taylor Bank to purchase Semrow Perforated & Expanded Metals, a business in Des Plaines, Illinois, that produced and sold fabricated products. He hired two of the company's top executives, Mike Beck and Mike Zarnott, to oversee the division, along with 10 of Semrow's 40 factory workers.

In 2002 the small division sold $1.5 million worth of fabricated metal directly to manufacturers. But Beck, Accurate's director of new product development and engineering, and Zarnott, the company's director of sales and marketing, had bigger aspirations. They begged Kamins to revamp Accurate's website and invest in e-mail marketing to promote sales of finished metal. Kamins, though, was worried about diverting too much time and money away from the core commodity business, and Cohen agreed. "Everything I said about marketing Aaron thought was rubbish," says Zarnott, who struggled with a marketing budget of $15,000 a year. "The people running this company didn't have enough skills or education to run a modern manufacturing outfit."

The situation became dire after the invasion of Iraq in March 2003. That spring, Accurate's customers became skittish, and orders fell by 50 percent. The bank "strongly recommended" that the company hire a consultant, recalls Kamins, who retained the Stonegate Group, a turnaround firm in Deerfield, Illinois, that the bank recommended. Stonegate advised him to renegotiate payment schedules with vendors. Meanwhile, Cohen liquidated half a million dollars in personal real estate to pay overdue bills. To cut costs, the company laid off 13 of its 85 employees.

Despite the turnaround efforts, Accurate lost more than $500,000 in 2003. During the fateful meeting with Cole Taylor that December, the bank agreed to give Cohen a few weeks to devise a plan, and he immediately began looking for a new lender. He bought some more time by rounding up an additional $400,000 in loans from friends—just enough to purchase three months' worth of steel. He had 90 days to make some serious decisions about Accurate's future.

Cohen was convinced that Accurate could thrive with the right business model, so liquidation seemed too dramatic. Another alternative was to continue cutting costs and hope for a rebound in steel prices, which was a strong possibility due to growing demand from China. Beck and Zarnott's idea of scaling back the commodity business to focus on selling finished metal seemed like the smartest long-term strategy. But it would take huge amounts of time and money to perfect the new manufacturing process, retrain factory workers, cultivate new clients, and revamp Accurate's nuts-and-bolts image.

The most difficult question Cohen faced was whether to replace his nephew with a more seasoned executive. He wondered if Kamins, whom he had groomed but who had little formal business training, could lead a turnaround. "I worried that we would just continue repeating all the mistakes that we had made," Cohen says. An outsider would offer a fresh perspective, but hiring a CEO would be expensive and time-consuming. Cohen felt like the owner of a baseball team with a losing manager. "I didn't know if a new guy would do a better job," he says. "I just knew the old guy wasn't doing a good job."

What do you think? Does Aaron Kamins deserve one last chance to save the company?

SOURCE: From Max Chafkin, "Case Study," *Inc.*, June 2006, 58–60. Copyright © 2006 Mansueto Ventures LLC, publisher of Inc. Magazine, New York, NY 10017. Reprinted with permission.

Test Prepper

You've read the chapter, studied the key terms, and the exam is any day now. Think you're ready to ace it? Take this sample test to gauge your comprehension of chapter material. You can check your answers at the back of the book. Want more test questions? Visit the student website at college.hmco.com/pic/hatten4e and take the ACE and ACE+ quizzes for more practice.

college.hmco.com/pic/hatten4e

Matching

_____ 1. getting things done through other people

_____ 2. a website that provides a "one-stop shop" on a specific topic

_____ 3. how well a person achieves stated goals

_____ 4. the achievement of goals while making the best use of resources required

_____ 5. the stage of business growth at which the business has grown to include multiple departments managed by numerous supervisors

_____ 6. the stage of business growth at which a business may add its first employees

_____ 7. the process of directing and influencing the action of members within a group

_____ 8. the entrepreneurial management style in which the entrepreneur operates without employees and outsources many functions of the business.

_____ 9. the reason an individual takes an action

_____ 10. the communication process whereby two or more people come together to seek mutual agreement about an issue

a. portal

b. efficiency

c. takeoff stage

d. delegation

e. effectiveness

f. management

g. leadership

h. motivation

i. survival stage

j. classic

k. coordinator

l. negotiation

Fill in the Blank

1. Small business owners have to do each of the four functions of management all the time; therefore, to them, these functions are _____ and _____.

2. Stages of business growth range from _____ to _____ _____.

3. Entrepreneur Marcus Johnson likes to take whatever is average and make it _____, and take whatever is good and make it _____.

4. The exit strategy of selling to all employees is a(n) _____.

5. Granting authority and responsibility for a specific task to another member of an organization is called _____.

## chapter 17

Human Resource Management

After reading this chapter, you should be able to:

- Discuss the importance of hiring the right employees.

- Describe the job-analysis process and the function of job descriptions and job specifications.

- Evaluate the advantages and disadvantages of the six major sources of employee recruitment.

- Describe the four tools commonly used in employee selection.

- Discuss the need for employee training and name the seven methods of providing this training.

- Explain the two components of a compensation plan and the variable elements of a benefits system.

- Profile an effective sequence for disciplining and terminating employees.

Elizabeth Brandt knows a lot about being a veterinarian but is a lousy HR manager. Within a year of opening All Creatures Veterinary Hospital in Salem, Massachusetts, she saw half of her initial employees quit. Brandt blamed herself. She was not sure of the right interview questions to ask, so she ended up hiring technicians who didn't fit the jobs. Even though she offered health insurance, Brandt couldn't lure top talent with the kinds of benefits larger employers could provide: 401(k)s, dental insurance, health spending accounts. But then Brandt found a solution to her HR woes: Take the entire staff off the payroll.

No, she didn't fire them. Instead, All Creatures (creaturehealth.com) enlisted the help of a professional employer organization (PEO), Integrated Staffing (integratedstaffing.com). PEOs are essentially *employee-leasing* firms in that they

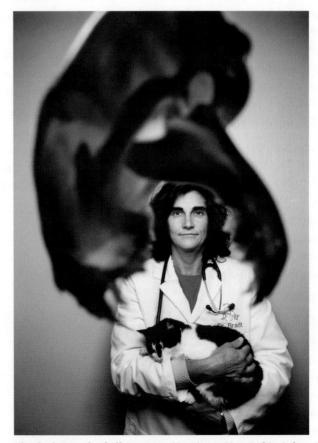

Elizabeth Brandt of All Creatures Veterinary Hospital in Salem, Mass.

function as the legal employer (or co-employer) of your staff for purposes of payroll, benefits, and HR. By combining the employees of many businesses, a PEO can often offer better rates on health and workers' compensation insurance, while giving employees big-business-style benefits. For the business owner, PEOs take on the headache of payroll taxes, regulatory compliance, and a gamut of HR issues, from hiring, to drafting an employee handbook, to mediating conflicts.

Although PEOs have been around since the early 1980s, the industry has been growing at 15 to 20 percent annually over the past several years, according to the National Association of Professional Employer Organizations (napeo.org), an industry trade group. Originally, PEOs administered only basic payroll services and benefits programs. But over the past few years, after some very visible bankruptcies, many have undergone makeovers to improve their credibility. Now PEOs are becoming one-stop shops for small businesses to outsource their whole HR function so as to concentrate on core competencies.

PEO services typically require a one-time startup fee and then an ongoing percentage of payroll, which can fluctuate from less than 5 percent to more than 15 percent, depending on the services and the average worker salary. About 40 percent of all businesses that go the PEO route are able to upgrade their total benefit packages to their employees.

SOURCES: Julie Sloane, "Cure Your HR Ills," *Fortune Small Business,* March 2007, 64–65; David Drucker, "Outsourcing HR," *Financial Planning,* February 2006, 61–62; Fiona Haley, "PEOs to the Rescue," *Black Enterprise,* July 2006, 62; Max Chafkin, "Fed Up With HR?" *Inc.,* May 2006, 50–52.

Hiring the Right Employees

Are *human resource management (HRM)* issues important to small businesses? Can small business owners afford the time and cost of developing formal recruitment, selection, training, and benefits programs? Perhaps the more appropriate question is whether small business owners can afford *not* to spend the time and money on such programs? In today's marketplace, some of the most valuable resources and competitive advantages a small business has are its employees.

In a recent Roper Organization study, small business owners reported that their biggest problems were finding competent workers and motivating them to perform.[1] Part of the problem in finding employees is the cost involved. According to the Families and Work Institute, a nonprofit research group based in New York, hiring and training costs to replace a nonmanagerial employee typically average 75 percent of a year's pay.[2] To make matters worse, 50 percent of all new hires last an average of only six months in their new positions.[3] As alarming as these figures are, they do not include other potential costs, such as defending against charges of discrimination, the loss of customer satisfaction, low employee morale, and wrongful-discharge suits. Once you find people to hire, you must find ways to retain and motivate them, which costs money. These costs may also increase as you implement more employee incentive and benefit plans.

All told, the costs and risks associated with HRM issues are too great for any company to ignore. Small business owners need to realize that their most valuable assets walk out the door at closing time.

Job Analysis

The recruitment process involves attracting talented individuals to your company. To achieve this goal, you must be able to (1) define the positions to be filled and (2) state the qualifications needed to perform them successfully. This endeavor requires that you conduct a job analysis, prepare a job description, identify a list of job specifications, and identify alternative sources of employees.

The **job analysis** indicates what is done on the job, how it is done, who does it, and to what degree. It is the foundation on which all other HR activities are based and, if necessary, defended in court. Although no single job-analysis technique has been endorsed by the courts or the Equal Employment Opportunity Commission (EEOC), both entities urge—and in some cases require—that the information from a job analysis be used to ensure equal employment opportunity.

The first step in completing the job analysis is to gain the support and cooperation of employees, because they often know best what the job involves. The next step is to choose the jobs that should be analyzed. Generally, the amount of time and money you have available, and the importance of the particular job to the company's overall success, will determine the order and the number of jobs you will analyze.

Step 3 involves identifying the job-analysis technique or techniques you will use to obtain information about each job. Although numerous techniques exist, for reasons of cost, ease of use, and time savings, the most commonly used technique is the questionnaire. Questionnaires typically seek to gather the following information: identification facts about the job, skill requirements, job responsibilities, effort demanded, and working conditions. Once you have analyzed your jobs, you are ready to prepare the job description and job specifications.

Job Description

A **job description** identifies the duties, tasks, and responsibilities of the position. Although a standard format for the job description (often termed the *position description*) does not exist, it is generally agreed that each job description should include the following elements:

- *Job identification.* The job title, location or department within the company, and date of origin should be included in this introductory section. This section might also include the job code, salary range, pay classification, and analyst's name.
- *Job summary.* This summary should outline the jobholder's responsibilities, the scope of her authority, and superiors to whom she is to report.
- *List of essential duties.* Although this list may contain both essential and nonessential duties, the Americans with Disabilities Act (ADA) requires that each be clearly identified, because employment decisions may be based only on the essential components of the job (see Chapter 10).

> *job analysis*
> The process of gathering all the information about a particular job, including a job description and the job specifications.

> *job description*
> A written description of a non-management position that covers the title, duties, and responsibilities involved for the job.

- *Task statement.* Task statements detail the logical steps or activities needed to complete the overall duties. These statements should focus on the outcomes or results rather than on the manner in which they are performed. For example, a loading-dock worker might "*move* 50-pound boxes from the unloading dock to the warehouse" rather than "*lift* and *carry* 50-pound boxes from the unloading dock to the warehouse." Task statements help to identify the knowledge, skills, abilities, and educational levels needed to perform the job and help to establish performance standards for the position. In addition, these statements are valuable in complying with various federal and state employment provisions.

General working conditions, travel requirements, equipment and tools used, and other job-related data may also be included in the job description. To preserve your status as an *at-will employer,* which gives you the right to discharge an employee for any reason (discussed further later on in this chapter), you may add a *general-duty clause,* such as "and other duties as assigned," or "representative tasks and duties" to indicate that your list is not comprehensive. Figure 17.1 shows an example of a typical job (position) description.

Job Specifications

The **job specifications** indicate the skills, abilities, knowledge, and other personal requirements a worker needs to successfully perform the job. In writing the specifications, take care to ensure that the stated requirements are truly necessary for successful performance of the job. For example, in some cases, stating that a college degree is a requirement for a given job may be difficult, if not impossible, to prove if questioned by an EEOC representative. For this reason, you may wish to add a qualifier, such as "or equivalent," and limit the specifications to those that are truly job related and necessary. Job specifications are often integrated into the job description, as shown in Figure 17.1.

> **job specifications**
> The identification of the knowledge, skills, abilities, and other characteristics an employee would need to perform the job.

Under Title VII and other anti-discrimination laws, you have a very limited right to hire on the basis of gender, religion, or national origin. If a job has special requirements that make such discrimination necessary, those requirements are called *bona fide occupational qualifications (BFOQs).* Race can never be a BFOQ.[4]

> " Small business owners must realize that the most valuable assets of a company are its employees. "

Employee Recruitment

You may recruit employees from a variety of sources, each of which has advantages and disadvantages. The six major sources are help-wanted ads, employment agencies, Internet job sites, executive recruiters (headhunters), employee referrals, and relatives or friends.

Advertising for Employees

Help-wanted ads in newspapers, trade publications, or storefronts generate a large number of responses, but generally the quality of applicants is not equal to that generated by other sources. Nevertheless, ads reach a wider, more diverse audience than other techniques, which may be needed to ensure equal opportunity representation or an adequate supply of employees with unique or specialized skills.

Figure 17.1

SAMPLE JOB DESCRIPTION

SOURCE: Material adapted from "Sample Job Description: Marketing Manager," www.job description.com. Reprinted by permission of KnowledgePoint.

Job Title: Marketing Manager

Department: Marketing

Reports to: President

Status: Nonexempt

Summary: Plans, directs, and coordinates the marketing of the company's products and/or services by performing the following duties personally or through subordinate supervisors.

Essential Duties and Responsibilities: Include the following. Other duties may be assigned.

- Establish marketing goals to ensure market share and profitability.
- Develop and execute short- and long-range marketing plans.
- Research, analyze, and monitor internal and external factors in order to capitalize on market opportunities and ensure positive competitive position.
- Plan and oversee execution of advertising and promotion internally and through advertising agencies.
- Develop and monitor pricing strategies.
- Accountable for profit/loss ratio and market share in relation to preset standards.
- Establish controls and corrective actions needed to achieve marketing objectives within prescribed budget.
- Recommend changes of organization in marketing team as needed to respond to threats and opportunities.
- Conduct market research relative to target markets and product development.
- Prepare monthly marketing activity reports.

Supervisory Responsibilities: Manage three subordinate supervisors who supervise a total of five employees. Supervise two nonsupervisory employees. Carry out supervisory responsibilities in accordance with the company's policies and applicable laws. Responsibilities include interviewing, hiring, and training employees; planning, assigning, and directing work; appraising performance, rewarding, and disciplining employees; and addressing complaints and resolving problems.

Qualifications: The employee must be able to perform each essential duty satisfactorily. The requirements listed below are representative of the knowledge, skill and/or ability required. Reasonable accommodations may be made to enable individuals with disabilities to perform the essential functions.

- *Education and experience:* Master's degree or equivalent, or a minimum of four years' related experience and/or training, or combination of education and experience.
- *Language skills.* Ability to read, analyze, and interpret common technical and industry literature, financial statements, and legal documents. Ability to respond to common inquiries and complaints from customers, regulatory agencies, or members of the business community. Ability to present information to company or public groups.
- *Mathematical skills.* Ability to apply advanced mathematical concepts, such as exponents, logarithms, quadratic equations, and permutations. Ability to apply statistical operations, such as frequency distributions, determination of test reliability and validity, analysis of variance, correlation techniques, sampling theory, and factor analysis.
- *Reasoning ability.* Ability to define problems, collect data, establish facts, and draw valid conclusions using abstract and concrete variables.
- *Physical demands.* While performing the duties of this job, the employee is regularly required to sit and talk or listen. The employee is frequently required to use hands to finger, handle, or feel. The employee is occasionally required to stand, walk, and reach with hands and arms. Reasonable accommodations may be made to enable individuals with disabilities to perform the essential functions.

Employment Agencies

Located in all states and most large cities, *government-funded employment agencies* focus primarily on assisting blue- or pink-collar employees, so they may not always offer the candidates you want. On the positive side, they allow you to obtain screened applicants at no cost. On the negative side, the quality of applicants may not be equal to that generated by some other sources. *Private employment agencies* can be useful in helping you find more skilled employees. Fees for professional and management jobs are usually paid by you, the employer.

Internet Job Sites

Online job-posting sites like Monster.com, Yahoo!'s HotJobs.com, and Careerbuilder.com provide access to millions of potential employees. Prices to list jobs vary by geographic location, industry, and the package you select.

Executive Recruiters (Headhunters)

Executive recruiting, or so-called headhunting, firms can be useful for small businesses looking for a key person or two rather than candidates for the manual-labor or other lower-level positions that government agencies concentrate on. These firms search confidentially for people who are currently employed and usually not actively seeking another job. Their services can be expensive.

Employee Referrals

Because your employees know the skills and talents needed to work in your company, they can be a good source for finding people to fill slots. This inside-track approach to recruiting is not very costly and can generate qualified, highly motivated employees as long as your current employee morale is high and your workforce is somewhat large and diversified. On the downside, exclusive use of this source may perpetuate minority underrepresentation or create employee cliques. Moreover, in cases where the referral is not hired or does not work out, the referring employee may become resentful.

Scott Glatstein relies on the referral approach almost exclusively in his $2.5 million consulting firm, Imperatives. Glatstein says that the number one benefit of this approach is hiring a better quality employee who becomes productive quicker and has superior skills. He says, "People aren't going to recommend people who [will] make them look bad in the eyes of their employers."[5]

Relatives and Friends

The advantage of hiring relatives or friends is that you generally know beforehand of their abilities, expertise, and personalities. At the same time, no approach is more laden with long-term repercussions. The effects of a poor decision may be felt long after the desk has been cleared and the nameplate changed. According to Peter Drucker,

- Family members working in the business must be at least as able and hardworking as any unrelated employee.
- Family-managed businesses, except perhaps for the very smallest ones, increasingly need to staff key positions with nonfamily professionals.

- No matter how many family members are in a company's management, no matter how effective they are, one top job must be filled by a nonrelative.

- Before the situation becomes acute, the issue of management succession should be entrusted to someone who is neither part of the family nor part of the business.[6]

Other Sources

Job fairs, trade association meetings, and specialized Internet sites run by professional organizations (accountants, environmental specialists, and so on) can be good sources of potential employees. Finally, don't forget the simple things, such as putting a "help wanted" sign in the window or a notice on the employee bulletin board.

Obviously, hiring employees in a foreign location presents special challenges. Unless you have a lot of firsthand knowledge about or experience in the country where you'll be hiring employees, you'd be wise to get assistance and advice from local experts. That's what Eli E. Hertz, founder of Hertz Computer Corporation in New York, did. When Hertz wanted to expand into Israel, he purchased a small distributor there to handle his computer equipment. Because of the nature of the business, potential employees needed technological as well as cultural understanding. Hertz felt that this approach was the best option for him in expanding into this market.[7]

Joel Spolsky, of Fog Creek Software, wants to hire the best of the best software developers. He knows that the top 1 percent can easily be 10 times more productive than the average developer in inventing new products, save months of work by creating shortcuts, and when there are no shortcuts, plow through coding problems "like a monster truck at a tea party." He has had success recruiting talent while still in college by hiring interns (*paid* interns, at $750/week, plus free housing, free lunch, free subway passes, relocation expenses, and various other benefits). More than half of Fog Creek's developers started as interns, then were recruited for full-time work.[8]

Hiring decisions should not be made in haste. An incorrect decision can be costly to you and your business. Almost without exception, you are better off holding out for the *best* employee, rather than filling a position quickly. Keep the following factors in mind when trying to hire the best.

- Keep your focus on hiring the best.
- Have a written job description.
- Use a written rating system so that you don't forget about attributes of early candidates.
- "Overqualified" is better than "underqualified."
- A person with a long history of self-employment will, in all probability, return to self-employment as soon as possible. Hire this person as a consultant if you need her skills.
- Test specific skills and industry knowledge. You want to observe the candidate performing the work to be done (as closely as it can be duplicated) during testing.
- Check the candidate's background and all references thoroughly.
- Keep a written record of all terms of employment.

Selecting Employees

Once you have a pool of applicants from which to choose, you should match the applicants with the job requirements outlined in your job description and specifications. Four commonly used tools for selecting employees are the application form and résumé, the selection interview, and testing.

Application Forms and Résumés

Application forms and résumés contain essentially the same information. Both contain the candidate's name, address, telephone number, education, work experience, and activities. The difference between them is that applications are forms prepared by your company, whereas résumés are personal profiles prepared by job candidates, but they both have the following four purposes:

1. To provide a record of the applicant's desire to obtain the position
2. To provide a profile of the applicant to be used during the interview
3. To provide a basic personnel record for the applicant who becomes an employee
4. To serve as a means of measuring the effectiveness of the selection process

The application form need not be complex or long to achieve these objectives. It must, however, ask enough of the right questions to enable you to differentiate applicants on the basis of their knowledge, skills, and ability to perform the job. In addition, the application form should provide the names of potential references and obtain the applicant's permission for you to contact each reference to discuss qualifications and prior job performance. Finally, it should include a notice that you are an *at-will employer* (discussed further later on in this chapter) and may therefore discharge an employee for cause or no cause and that any misinformation provided on the application form is grounds for immediate dismissal.

A caveat on résumés: They are sometimes the best fiction written, so view them with some degree of skepticism. You want to believe what people tell you, but check out all the facts, and contact previous employers.

Time and money constraints will prevent you from interviewing every candidate. Applications and résumés give you a screening tool to decide who to bring in for the next stage of the selection process—the interview.

Interviewing

Considered by many employers to be the most critical step in the selection process, the personal interview gives you a chance to learn more about the applicants; to resolve any conflicts or fill in any gaps in the information they provided; and to confirm or reject your initial impressions of them, drawn from the application or résumé. The interview also gives you a chance to explain the job and company to the applicant. Always remember that you are selling your company to the potential employee as well as determining his suitability to join your company. If the applicant is a good fit, you want her to join your firm. But even if you don't hire this applicant, the image you create may well lead to another suitable person through a word-of-mouth referral.

Don't Even Ask!

EEOC and other government guidelines set parameters for what you can and can't ask in an interview. You are limited basically to information concerning how the person would handle the job and provide value to the company—no "small talk" for the sake of conversation. Unless clearly related to the job, avoid questions like these:

- "When did you graduate from high school?"
- "How many kids do you have?"
- "Where were you born?"
- "Do you own or rent your home?"
- "How long have you lived there?"
- "Have you ever been arrested?" (You can ask whether the applicant has ever been convicted of a felony.)
- Questions regarding current or past assets, liabilities, credit rating, or bankruptcy.
- Questions regarding the applicant's state of health or medical conditions.
- "Have you ever filed a workers' compensation claim?"
- "Can you leave a photo of yourself with us?"
- "Would any religious obligations prevent you from working any day of the week or holidays?"
- "Would your family object to your working at night?"
- "You think you can keep up with these kids around here?"
- "Do you have any kind of disability that would require reasonable accommodation?"
- "How did you learn to speak that foreign language?"
- "Do you own a car?"
- "How did you lose that leg?"

SOURCE: Material adapted from Donald A. Phin, "Questions to Avoid During an Interview," www.lawthatworks.com. Reprinted by permission of the author.

To conduct an effective interview, you should do the following:

Be Prepared Start by thoroughly reviewing the job description and job specifications. You must know what your needs are before you can find a person to fulfill them. Next, review the candidate's application form. Look for strengths and weaknesses, areas of conflict, and questions left unanswered or vaguely worded.

Set the Stage for the Interview Arrange to hold the interview at a time and location demonstrating its importance. The location should provide privacy and comfort, and present the right image of your company. It should allow you to talk without interruptions. Taking telephone calls, answering employee questions, or

Business Interviews Provide Information to Both Employer and Employee.

working on another task while conducting the interview does little to ease the fears of the applicant and simply does not facilitate good communication or present a good image.

Use a Structured Interview Format   Develop a set of questions to ask each candidate so that you can compare their responses. The job description and specifications should be the source of the majority of your questions. Such a format will allow you to collect a great deal of information quickly, systematically cover all areas of concern, and more easily compare candidates on the basis of similar information.

Use a Variety of Questioning Techniques   Although closed-ended questions are appropriate when looking for a commitment or for verifying information, they are very limiting. Consequently, you should use open-ended or probing questions that are related to the job. For example, rather than asking, "Do you like working with figures?" you may wish to probe with the question, "What is it that you like about working with figures?" Open-ended, probing questions encourage the applicant to talk, providing you with a wealth of information and insight into the applicant's ability to communicate effectively.

No Matter the Type of Question, Make Sure That It Is Job Related   The EEOC requires that all job-interview questions be nondiscriminatory in nature. In other words, they must be devoid of references to race, color, religion, sex, national origin, or disability, and they must be job related. You should be able to relate each interview question to one or more of the items in your job description or job specifications and to show how the information obtained from the questions will be used to differentiate candidates.

Keep Good Records, Including Notes from the Interview   The EEOC construes any selection device as a test, and if a test results in underrepresentation of a protected group, it must be validated. Therefore, if the interview results in underrepresentation, the interview process must be validated. In the case of most small business owners, the problem is not one of questionable behavior or wrongdoing within this area, but rather one of inadequate documentation. You must be able to show that your decision to hire or not to hire was based on a sound business reason or practice as proven by your interview notes.

Testing

Employee testing has long been used by U.S. businesspeople to screen applicants. For the most part, prior to the 1971 Supreme Court decision in *Griggs* v. *Duke Power Co.,* employers were fairly free to do as they pleased in this matter.[9] Today, however, employers must be able to prove that their tests and other selection criteria are valid predictors of job performance. This can be done, according to the Supreme Court and the EEOC, through statistical or job-content analyses.

For small business owners, the process of statistically validating a test is generally far too time-consuming and expensive. Therefore, short of eliminating all tests, two options remain: purchasing preprinted tests from commercial vendors that have conducted the necessary standardization studies to ensure test reliability (although ultimate liability still rests with the employer) or using content-based tests. Although it is not an absolute defense, you are more likely to be able to prove a test's validity if the test is a sample or measure of the actual work to be performed on the job. For example, if a clerk's job involves counting back change to customers, then asking an applicant to count back change as a test is probably content-valid and its use is therefore permitted.

Regardless of the type of test used, rarely should you use the results of a single test or indicator as the sole reason for hiring or not hiring an applicant. In addition, all test results should be kept strictly confidential and in a file other than the employee's personnel file. Commonly used tests include the following:

Achievement Tests   Achievement tests are given to measure the specific skills a person has attained as a result of his experiences or education. These tests are easy and inexpensive to administer and score. Proving validity and job-relatedness, however, is another matter. Therefore, you should have a very compelling, business-related reason to justify their use during the selection process.

Performance (Ability) Tests   Performance tests are administered to assess the applicant's ability to perform the job. The tests provide direct, observable evidence of performance. They are also easily administered, relate directly to the job, and are relatively inexpensive to conduct. Validity is generally not an overriding issue with performance testing.

Physical Examinations   Often considered the last step in the screening process, physical examinations are given to discover any physical or medical limitations that might prevent the applicant from performing the duties of the job.

The ADA states that physical examinations can be given only after a conditional offer of employment and only if they are administered to all applicants in the particular job category.[10] In addition, you cannot disqualify individuals as a result of such examinations unless the findings show that the person would pose a "direct threat" to the health and safety of others.[11] All medical findings must be kept separately from general personnel files and be made available only to selected company personnel on a need-to-know basis.

Drug Tests   Organizations are increasingly using drug tests to screen applicants. According to a recent survey, 64 percent of reporting firms administered drug tests as part of their health and safety programs.[12] Although tests for illegal use of drugs are not considered tests under the ADA and are therefore not subject to its regulations, many state legislatures have imposed conditions under which drug tests may be administered, samples tested, and results used. Generally, to justify the cost and privacy concerns caused by these tests, you must be able to demonstrate a strong need for safety within your workplace or services.

Honesty Tests   The 1988 Employee Polygraph Protection Act essentially outlawed the use of voice stress analyzers and other devices in most business situations. As a result, employers have increasingly relied on paper-and-pencil honesty tests. So far, these tests remain suspect in terms of their validity, and the courts have yet to rule decisively on their use. Several congressional committees are also looking into restricting or outlawing their use as a preemployment tool. Unless you have an overriding reason for employing this kind of test—for example, unless the employee will have ready access to merchandise or money—the use of an honesty test is not recommended without proper legal advice. Court rulings on honesty testing do vary from state to state.

Which Tests to Use?   There are thousands of employee evaluations for you to choose from, but which one(s) should you use? Following are some of the most extensively validated, most respected instruments for cognitive ability and personality:

1. *Watson-Glaser Critical Thinking Appraisal.* This widely used cognitive test measures problem-solving skills, creativity, and other factors with 40 difficult questions ($10 to $20 per test).

2. *Wesman Personnel Classification.* This cognitive exam uses a combination of verbal and numerical questions to evaluate employees for decision-making roles ($7 to $15 per test).

3. *Multidimensional Aptitude Battery II.* This 303-question test of general mental ability, developed in 1998, is administered in 100 minutes. It measures ability to reason, plan, and solve problems ($190 for 25 tests).

4. *Wonderlic Personnel Test.* This classic test, developed in 1937, is probably most familiar to those who follow the NFL draft, as the football league administers it to college recruits. It takes only 12 minutes and is most appropriate for entry-level to mid-level jobs ($10 per test).

5. *NEO Personality Inventory-Revised.* This personality test measures respondents on five scales: neuroticism, extroversion, openness to experience, agreeableness, and conscientiousness ($245 for 25 tests).

6. *16PF.* This personality test targeted for leadership positions includes 185 items measuring 16 personality factors ($8 to $30 per test).

7. *Hogan Personality Inventory.* This personality test consists of true-false questions that measure seven personality scales, such as ambition and prudence. This test has been around for about three decades, so responses can be compared to those of people actually doing most jobs in the United States ($25 to $175 depending on the amount of detail in report).[13]

Temporary Employees and Professional Employer Organization (PEO)

Today many small business owners are recognizing the benefits of hiring temporary employees. In the past, agencies such as Kelly Services and Manpower, Inc., were generally called upon only when someone in the company went on vacation or demand suddenly exceeded capacity. Although these are still the most popular reasons for using temporary services, other motivations include the need to fill new or highly specialized positions, to ensure a full workforce during periods of labor shortages, and to take advantage of the growing pool of workers who like the flexibility and challenge of working for multiple employers.

The employment costs of temporary employees are often lower than those associated with permanent or full-time employees. The employment agency generally takes care of all federal and state reporting and record-keeping requirements, thereby lowering the company's overhead costs. In addition, training and other costs, such as workers' compensation, unemployment insurance, and fringe benefits, are paid by the agency rather than by the company. Finally, once the job has been completed in the case of seasonal demands, temporary workers can be laid off quickly and with fewer concerns for wrongful-discharge claims.

A relatively recent trend in HRM are *employee-leasing* firms called *professional employer organizations (PEOs),* as seen in the chapter opener. The PEO becomes the legal employer, handling employee-related duties, including recruiting, hiring, payroll tax paperwork, and provision of benefits. The handling of benefit packages, especially health insurance, is usually what makes outsourcing the HR function attractive to small businesses. Because employees are part of a larger group with an employee leasing company than they would be with a small business, they can obtain insurance coverage that is otherwise unavailable or prohibitively expensive. For the small business owner, the cost savings associated with not providing benefits and other HRM functions may outweigh the associated fees.

Despite the cost savings, many business owners are understandably reluctant to turn over responsibility of their most important assets—employees—to an outside company, so cost is seldom the only factor in this decision. PEOs may be a viable alternative for your small business if you can pick the right company, and you can get assistance in choosing a PEO company from the National Association of Professional Employer Organizations (napeo.org).

Placing and Training Employees

Every employee, no matter how experienced, will need to be introduced to the methods and procedures of the job and the rules of your company. This process of introduction is called **employee orientation.** Many organizations mistakenly leave the orientation of new hires to coworkers on an informal, as-time-permits basis. This casual approach often results in an incomplete orientation, and it cannot be formally documented in the event of a wrongful-discharge claim. A formal orientation will, by contrast, ensure that the new hire is welcomed to the company in a positive, complete, and cost-effective manner.

> *employee orientation*
> The process of helping new employees become familiar with an organization, their job, and the people they will work with.

The orientation should be comprehensive and spread over several days. *Hard issues,* which are relatively easy to cover, include specifics such as the way in which the job is to be performed, the company's policies and procedures, and a discussion of pay and fringe benefits. *Soft issues* might include the organization's interest in making a profit, producing a quality product, being socially responsible, and providing a safe, efficient, team-oriented work environment. These soft issues establish the tenor of the employment relationship and generally make the difference between an "acceptable" and a "good" employee. The sessions at which soft issues are discussed should be kept short, generally not exceeding two hours, and should be spread over several days if the employee is to truly learn and grow from the orientation experience.

When an employee reports to work for the first time, she has many needs, some of which are more immediately pressing than others. For example, the fear of not being at the right place at the right time or of saying the wrong thing to the wrong person generally far outweighs concerns over fringe benefits or the company's plan for future growth. Consequently, the order of the orientation presentation should be directed toward fulfilling the most pressing needs first.

William Brodbeck, president and CEO of Brodbeck Enterprises of Platteville, Wisconsin, preaches the importance of employee training and orientation for reducing employee turnover and thus being able to keep service levels high. His company owns and operates eight supermarkets, for which a highly systematic training program is in effect for new hires. The company's basic training and orientation session is 6.5 hours long. Cashiers receive another 38.5 to 40 hours of training on top of the basic training, deli employees get another 33 hours, and seafood workers receive an additional 47.5 hours of training. Brodbeck feels strongly that his company's commitment to training and orientation makes a difference in the customer service his supermarkets provide.[14]

Employee Training and Development

Often overlooked by managers is the use of **employee training** and **development** as a motivating tool. Training involves increasing the employee's knowledge and skills to meet a specific job or company objectives. It is usually task and short-term oriented. Development, by comparison, is more forward looking, providing the employee with the knowledge, skills, and abilities needed to accept a new and more challenging job assignment within the company.

> *employee training*
> A planned effort to teach employees more about their job so as to improve their performance and motivation.
>
> *employee development*
> A planned effort to provide employees with the knowledge, skills, and abilities needed to accept new and more challenging job assignments within the company.

A trained workforce can give your business a competitive advantage that, once gained, is not easily duplicated by competitors. That advantage can be maintained and enhanced through an ongoing training and development program.

Manager's Notebook

Sixty-Second Guide to Training Your First (or Fiftieth) Employee

Good help may be hard to find, but your work as a small business owner is not finished after they accept your job offer. Every employee, regardless of experience, must make the transition from new hire to fully integrated staff member. A well-designed orientation and training program can help expedite this process, and reduce the likelihood of turnover.

In just 60 seconds, we'll show you how to lay the foundation for an orientation and training program tailored to your business.

0:60   Define the Job

Training and orientation actually begin with the hiring process. Each position should have a written job description detailing specific responsibilities, performance and evaluation criteria, relationships with other functions within the business, etc.

0:51   Then Define the Training Needs

While a job's title and basic functions may be the same from one business to another, your business may have specific processes, equipment, policies, and production standards. Determine which elements require hands-on training, classroom formats, manuals, or a combination of approaches. Depending on your time commitments and communications skills, it may be worthwhile to hire an experienced HR trainer and/or writer to prepare these materials.

0:42   Assign a Mentor

If you already have an employee on staff performing similar tasks, ask him to help guide the new hire through training and orientation. Beyond simply helping with "learning the ropes," the mentor can answer questions and monitor the new employee's progress. Even if you also delegate evaluation responsibility to this person, stay involved with the process as much as possible. There's nothing like encouragement from "the boss" to help motivate a new employee.

0:34   Be Patient

Even veteran workers may need time adjusting to new work environments, processes, and expectations. Allow sufficient time to get up to speed, but also be alert to problems such as repeated mistakes or inconsistent performance. The solution may be as simple as some follow-up guidance, additional practice, and closer oversight. The small business experts at SCORE can help you gauge the effectiveness of your training and orientation program, and offer valuable suggestions for improvement.

0:21   Make Training a Two-way Street

Encouraging questions and feedback during orientation and training may sound like a no-brainer. But what you may not be aware of is that you should be prepared to learn something yourself. New employees can provide a fresh perspective on the way your business operates. Along with gaining additional help, you may have also hired someone who can take the lead in implementing changes that will benefit your company and your customers.

0:09   Keep it Coming

The training process should continue throughout the employee's career with your company. A comprehensive professional development program will help your entire staff acquire skills and knowledge that will keep your business competitive.

SOURCE: Reprinted with permission of SCORE Association, www.score.org.

Such a program helps prevent boredom and, consequently, increases retention rates for qualified personnel. Not only are turnover costs reduced but, over a period of time, the overall level of employee morale is raised. Finally, training and development assure your firm a place in tomorrow's competitive environment. New employee skills and abilities will inevitably be required as the business expands into new product lines, acquires new technologies, and strives to maintain or reach a higher level of customer service.

Ways to Train

Depending on the objectives of your training program, several techniques are available. The seven most common methods are on-the-job training (OJT), lecture, conferences, programmed learning, role-playing, job rotation, and correspondence courses.

On-the-Job Training   Everyone from the mail clerk to the company president experiences *on-the-job training (OJT)* from the time he joins a company. This type of training entails learning the job while you are doing it. OJT is effective, but the small business owner should try to ensure that it is not the *only* type of training provided. The most familiar types of OJT are coaching and mentoring, in which a new employee works with an experienced employee or supervisor. This practice not only instructs new employees on how to operate equipment, but also ideally builds a bond between that employee, her mentor, and the business.

Lecture   *Lecturing* involves one or more individuals communicating instructions or ideas to others. The technique is often used because of its low cost, the speed with which information can be covered, and the large number of individuals who can be accommodated in each session. Employee participation is limited, however, and no allowance is made for individual employee differences.

Conferences   Also termed *group discussions*, the *conference* technique is similar to the lecture method, except that employees are actively involved in the learning. Although this technique produces more ideas than lecturing does, it takes more time, and only a limited number of participants can participate.

Programmed Learning   *Programmed learning* or instruction is achieved through use of a computer or printed text. The employee receives immediate feedback and learns at her own speed. This method works well for almost any type of training. However, outside materials must generally be purchased, and the learner must be self-directed and motivated for this technique to be effective.

Role-Playing   In the *role-playing* method, employees take on new roles within the company, acting out the situation as realistically as possible. If the sessions are videotaped, playing back the tapes allows for employee feedback and group discussions. Some employees find the technique threatening, and not all business situations lend themselves to this type of training.

Job Rotation   *Job rotation* allows employees to move from one job to another within the company. In addition to ensuring that employees have a variety of job skills and knowledge, the technique provides management with trained replacements in the event that one employee becomes ill or leaves the company. On the downside, job rotation does not generally provide in-depth, specialized training.

Correspondence Courses   This technique is especially useful for updating current knowledge and acquiring new information. Generally sponsored by a professional association or university, the employee receives prepackaged study materials to complete at his own pace. In addition to providing individualized learning, this training technique is applicable to a variety of business topics. However, the employee must be motivated to learn, and course costs may be high.

Compensating Employees

Employees expect to be paid a fair and equitable wage. Determining what is fair and equitable is a challenging and ongoing task that involves primarily two components: wages and benefits.

> "Wages and incentives—including health care and other benefits—are necessary to keep employees alive, healthy, and motivated."

Determining Wage Rates

Based on the Fair Labor Standards Act (FLSA), employees are classified as either exempt or nonexempt. *Exempt employees* are not covered by the major provisions of the FLSA, which specifies minimum wage, overtime pay, child labor laws, and equal-pay-for-equal-work regulations. Most exempt employees are paid on a straight salary basis. *Nonexempt employees,* however, must be paid a minimum wage set by Congress (or your state government, if higher). These payments may take the form of hourly wages, salary, piecework rates, or commissions.

Hourly Wages   Most organizations pay their nonexempt employees an hourly wage (a set rate of pay for each hour worked). Exempt employees are not paid on an hourly basis but rather a straight salary.

All-Salaried Employees   Some organizations are moving to an *all-salaried workforce.* These companies pay both exempt and nonexempt employees a salary (a fixed sum of money). Although still subject to FLSA provisions, this type of compensation plan removes the perceived inequity between the two "classes" of employees and fosters a greater esprit de corps.

Piecework Rates   Unlike salaried or hourly wage rates, the piecework rate is a *pay-for-performance* plan. Under a piecework rate, the employer pays an employee a set amount for each unit he produces. Some employers pay, as an incentive, a *premium* for units produced above a predetermined level of production. For example, an employee might receive $2 per unit for the first 40 units produced and $2.25 for any units above 40. Other plans might pay a straight rate for all units— say, $2.15—once the standard output quota of 40 units has been surpassed.

Commissions   Commissions represent another type of pay-for-performance scheme. Some jobs, especially those in sales, are not easily measured in terms of units produced. Under a straight commission plan, the employee's wages can be based solely on her sales volume. Because employees often cannot control all of the external variables that affect sales, employers are increasingly paying these workers on a base-salary-plus-commission basis. Employees tend to favor this combination approach in which they are provided with a degree of income security during slow sales periods.

Still other employers are allowing their employees to "draw" against future commissions. This means that an employee may receive an advance from the employer during a slow sales period and repay the advance (draw) out of commissions earned during the remainder of the pay period or, in some cases, future pay periods. Such draws are particularly effective if sales fluctuate from month to month or from quarter to quarter.

Jim Lippie, CEO of consulting firm Thrive Networks of Concord, Massachusetts, paid salespeople via commission, but wanted to foster more teamwork. He considered switching them to salaries, but was concerned about decreasing motivation. Lippie then created a quarterly commissions pool shared equally by the six salespeople. Approximately one-third of their total compensation is tied to the performance of the whole sales team, and the rest is salary. Lippie says, "We've become much better at sharing information while spreading around both incentives and the risks."[15]

Incentive-Pay Programs

An *incentive-pay program* is a reward system that ties performance to compensation. Two common types of incentive-pay programs involve the awarding of bonuses and profit-sharing programs. **Bonuses** are generally doled out on a one-time basis to reward employees for their high performance. They may be given to either an individual employee or a group of employees. Bonuses are frequently awarded when an employee meets objectives set for attendance, production, cost savings, quality, or performance.

To be an effective motivator, a bonus must be tied to a specific measure of performance. The reason for which the bonus is being awarded must be communicated to employees at the time they are informed that they will receive it. The bonus should be paid separately from the employee's regular paycheck to reinforce its specialness. In this way, the bonus is less likely to be viewed by employees as an extension of their regular salary and something to which they are automatically entitled.

Under most **profit-sharing plans** employers make the same percentage of salary contributions to each worker's account on a semiannual or annual basis. The percentage of contributions varies according to the amount of profits earned, making the system highly flexible. Most employers believe these plans serve to motivate workers by giving them a sense of partnership with the employer. Profit-sharing

bonuses
A one-time reward provided to an employee for exceeding a performance standard.

profit-sharing plans
A plan in which employees receive additional compensation based on the profitability of the entire business.

Profile in Entrepreneurship
Cooking up a Cause

One of Miami's hottest chefs, Lorena Garcia was born, raised, and graduated from law school in Venezuela. She credits family gatherings spent entertaining family and friends as her career inspiration. "Bringing loved ones together to enjoy wonderful food—it's natural—it is something that has always fulfilled me."

In 2005 Lorena started an ambitious venture named Elements. Tierra [Earth] featured an eclectic blend of Latin and Asian-inspired dishes in the heart of Miami's design district. In addition to Tierra, Garcia opened Agua [Water], a convenience store, Fuego [Fire], a catering business and Aire, [Air] an office headquarters of sorts for Garcia's marketing.

Lately Lorena has also lent her talent to a bigger cause—the health and social problems caused by childhood obesity. Since 2004, Garcia, 37, has conducted free cooking workshops for children in southern Florida. "I love kids and I love cooking, so I put these passions together." Garcia created "Big Chef, Little Chef," a non-profit organization that teaches children 8 to 12 year olds how to give their favorite treats a nutritious twist. She was inspired to start Big

Chef Little Chef by her nephews and nieces, who, like many kids, were eating fattening prepackaged meals. "I want kids to know about nutrition and make food they can be proud of and will love to eat. Getting them involved in preparing their own meals and having a great time doing it is the first step in getting them to make dietary changes."

Lorena's charismatic personality and contagious enthusiasm for great food has caught the attention of many and landed her in front of the camera. She hosted several nationally syndicated shows on the Gems and Mun2 television networks. Lorena is currently the host of "El Arte del Buen Gusto," one of the highest rated shows on MGM's 'Casa Club TV' airing both in the U.S. and Latin America. She also appears weekly on Telemundo's nationally syndicated morning show "Cada Dia con Maria Antonieta." Lorena has also caught the eye of companies like Nestle and Splenda. Nestle tapped the chef to host the nationally syndicated segment, "Cocinando con Nestle," and she is the spokeswoman for SPLENDA® No Calorie Sweetener.

SOURCES: Andrea C. Poe, "Nutritious Meals Cook Up an Idea," *Entrepreneur Magazine*, August 2007, p. 91; Idy Fernandez, "Earthly Delights," Hispanic Magazine Online, February 2006, http://www.hispaniconline.com/magazine/2006/february/la_buena_vida/spice.html; "Big Chef, Little Chef," http://cheflorenagarcia.com/bclc.html

plans are a mainstay of many small business owners' compensation plans. According to Mac McConnell, owner and president of Artful Framer Gallery, a $600,000 business with a staff of eight, "A company can never be too small to benefit from a well-designed profit-sharing plan."[16]

Benefits

benefit
Part of an employee's compensation in addition to wages and salaries.

An employee **benefit** consists of any supplement to wages and salaries. Health and life insurance, paid vacation time, pension and education plans, and discounts on company products are examples. The cost of offering and administering benefits has increased greatly in recent decades—up from 25.5 percent of total payroll in 1961 to about 38 percent today. Often employees do not realize the market value and high cost of the benefits they receive.

According to a survey by the Employee Benefit Research Institute, Americans' satisfaction with their benefit packages is declining.[17] Fewer than 50 percent of survey respondents said that they were completely satisfied with their package, down from a high of 70 percent who reported being satisfied in 1991. At the same time, the number of respondents who were satisfied with the level of benefits but wanted a different mix of benefits increased to 27 percent, up from 15 percent in 1991. Health care coverage, vacation or other time off, and life insurance were the three areas in which most respondents desired to see changes made.

As an employer, you are required by law to

- Give employees time off to vote, serve on a jury, and perform military service.
- Comply with all workers' compensation requirements.
- Withhold FICA taxes from employees' paychecks and pay your own portion of FICA taxes, providing employees with retirement and disability benefits.
- Pay state and federal unemployment taxes, thus providing benefits for unemployed workers.
- Contribute to state short-term disability programs in states where such programs exist.
- Comply with the Federal Family and Medical Leave Act (FMLA) if your business has 50 or more employees.

While you may need to in a competitive job market, you are not required to provide

- Retirement plans
- Health plans (except in Hawaii)
- Dental or vision plans
- Life insurance plans
- Paid vacations, holidays, or sick leave[18]

With this increasing discontent and call for a new mix of benefits, the challenge for small business owners is to provide a mix of benefits that is both affordable for the employer and motivational for employees.

Flexible Benefit Packages   Because all employees do not have the same needs, a *flexible-benefit package,* or *cafeteria plan,* allows each employee to select the benefits that best suit his financial and lifestyle needs. Employees generally favor such plans due to their flexibility and pretax benefits.

Increasingly, flexible-benefit packages not only provide employees with a menu of benefits from which to choose, but also include choices between taxable and nontaxable benefits. Under the latter, IRS-approved plans, employees are allowed to purchase benefits with pretax dollars. In this way, they can reduce their taxable income while at the same time increasing their benefit options.

The advantages of flexible plans are not realized without additional costs. As the number and mix of benefits increase, so do administrative costs associated with activities such as record keeping, communications with employees, and compliance with government regulations. A second, but no less important, concern is that employees may select the wrong mix or types of benefits. Often employees do not worry about their benefits until they are actually needed, generally in response to a major illness or accident. Yet the law does not allow benefit choices to be changed during the plan year, so employees often find that their benefit options do not match their immediate needs.

Health Insurance   One of the most common and most highly valued employee benefits is health insurance. According to Dallas Salisbury, president of the Employee Benefit Research Institute, "There's no question that workers value health insurance benefits above all others."[19] In response, employers are increasingly providing employee health care coverage, although many are also opting for a copayment plan of some type. Sixty-seven percent of all small private employers provide some form of medical care coverage.[20]

In an attempt to hold down the growing costs of health insurance, many small business owners are joining cooperative *health maintenance organizations (HMOs)* or *preferred provider organizations (PPOs)*. Under an HMO system, a firm signs a contract with an approved HMO that agrees to provide health and medical services to its employees. In return for the exclusive right to care for the firm's employees, the HMO offers its services at an adjusted rate. Unfortunately, employees often object to these plans because they are restricted to using the health care specialists employed or approved by the HMO.

To overcome this objection, some companies are switching to PPOs. With a PPO, a firm or group of firms negotiates with doctors and hospitals to provide certain health care services for a favorable price. In turn, member firms encourage their employees, through higher reimbursement payments, to use these "preferred" providers. Employees tend to favor PPOs because they can use the doctor of their choice.

Retirement Plans   To assist employees in saving for their retirement needs, employers provide them with retirement, or pension, plans. Such plans present employees with an accumulated amount of money when they reach a set retirement age or when they are unable to continue working due to a disability. Four common options are individual retirement accounts, simplified employee pension plans, 401(k) plans, and Keogh plans. Another, less common option is the *412(i) plan*.

- *Individual Retirement Accounts.* Individual retirement accounts (IRAs) allow employees under age 50 to make tax-exempt contributions up to a maximum of $3,000 per year into their own accounts.

- *Simplified Employee Pension Plans.* A simplified employee pension (SEP) plan is similar to an IRA but is available only to people who are self-employed or who work for small businesses that do not have a retirement plan.

- *401(k) Plans.* Named after Section 401(k) of the 1978 Revenue Act, 401(k) plans allow small businesses to establish payroll reduction plans that are more flexible and have greater tax advantages than IRAs. As was true of the foregoing plans, the amount deferred and any accumulated investment earnings are excluded from current income and are taxed only when finally distributed (usually when the worker retires).

- *Keogh Plans.* A Keogh plan is a special type of retirement account for self-employed individuals and their employees.

- The relatively unknown *412(i) plan* (named for section of IRS code) is designed for small business owners with 20 or fewer employees planning to retire within 10 years. It is a defined-benefit plan that allows you to accumulate significant retirement assets in a short period of time.

A 412(i) is ideal for small business owners in their peak earning years who have saved less for retirement than they would like. Contributions are based on age and income and can be as high as $350,000 per year. In general, the older you are, the more you can contribute. The plan is fully insured, which means it is funded with a combination of life insurance and annuities, or annuities alone.[21]

For a review of retirement plans, see Table 17.1.

Child Care and Elder Care   As the number of dual-income families continues to increase and the concern over family values grows, more and more employees are looking to their employers for help in managing what is often called the *work–family balance*. For example, in a recent survey of employees, 68 percent of respondents said they would be willing to contribute to a benefit program that allowed them to set aside money before taxes to pay for health care or child care

Table 17.1
RETIREMENT PLAN PREVIEW

	Eligibility	Funding Responsibility	Annual Contributions per Participant	Vesting of Contributions	Administrative Responsibilities
Simple IRA	Businesses with 100 or fewer employees that do not currently maintain any other retirement plan	Funded by employee salary-reduction contributions and employer contributions	3% employer match; employee contributions to maximum of $10,000	Immediate	No employer tax filings
SEP-IRA	Any self-employed individual, business owner, or individual who earns any self-employed income	Employer contributions only	Up to 25% of compensation, to maximum of $42,000	Immediate	Form 5498 and IRS testing
401(k)	Any business; employees who have worked at least 1,000 hours in the past year	Primarily employee salary-reduction contributions and optional employer contributions	Combined employer and employee contributions to maximum of $42,000	Determined by employer	Form 5500 and special IRS testing to ensure plan does not discriminate in favor of highly compensated employees
Defined-Benefit Plan—Keogh	Any self-employed individual, business owner, or individual who earns any self-employed income	Generally employer contributions only	Maximum annual retirement benefit of $170,000 or 100% of 3-year average compensation	May offer vesting schedules	Form 5500

SOURCE: "Small Business Retirement Plans," *Entrepreneur Magazine Online*, www.entrepreneur.com/humanresources/compensationandbenefits/article79282.html, 2007.

expenses.[22] Apparently employers are listening, as nearly eight out of ten major U.S. employers now offer some form of child care assistance.[23]

This aid takes many forms, of which the most common types are flexible work schedules, flexible spending accounts that allow workers to set aside a portion of their pretax earnings to pay for child care costs, resource and referral services, and, to a much lesser extent, company-sponsored day-care centers. Employers that offer child care assistance generally do so for one or more of the following reasons: to accommodate employee requests, thereby increasing employee morale; to retain high-performing employees; to improve recruiting efforts; to reduce employee absenteeism and tardiness; and to increase employee productivity.

Another big issue is *elder care*. As the life expectancy rates rise, a "sandwich" generation finds itself caring for both children and parents simultaneously. Benefits for elder care are becoming more and more needed.

Miscellaneous Benefits   The number and variety of employee benefits are determined by the employer's generosity and ability to pay. Benefits provided by firms with fewer than 49 workers represented 25.6 percent of total compensation, whereas those provided by firms with 500 or more workers amounted to 32.9 percent.[24] Figure 17.2 summarizes the types of benefits that employees of small private establishments have access to and the percentages that participate.

Note that under the Uniformed Services Employment and Reemployment Rights Act, an employer is required to take back Reservists, Guard members, and other employees who have been away on active military service for periods of five years or less.[25] Employers are not required to pay employees for their service while on military leave, but they are required to provide health care benefits to the employee and dependents that they would otherwise lose due to military leave.

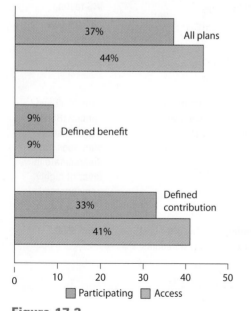

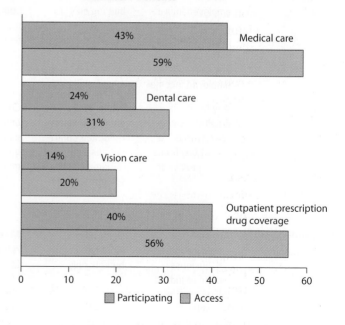

Figure 17.2

ACCESS AND PARTICIPATION RATES OF WORKERS

NOTE: The access rate represents the percent of employees offered the benefit, and the participation rate represents the percent of employees that receive the benefit.
SOURCE: U.S. Department of Labor, U.S. Bureau of Labor Statistics, *National Compensation Survey: Employee Benefits in Private Industry in the United States*, Tables 1 & 2, March 2006; www.bls.gov/ncs/ebs/sp/ebsm0004.pdf

When Problems Arise: Employee Discipline and Termination

Despite your best efforts at maintaining harmony in the workplace, sometimes problems may arise. When they do, you need policies established for discipline or dismissal of employees.

Disciplinary Measures

Discipline involves taking timely and appropriate action to change the performance of an employee or group of employees. The purpose of discipline is to ensure that company rules and regulations are consistently followed for the well-being of both the company and its employees. A fair and just disciplinary procedure should be based on four components: the employee handbook, performance appraisal, progressive approach, and appeal process.

Employee Handbook   The **employee handbook,** or *policy manual,* provides a comprehensive set of rules and regulations to inform employees of their rights and responsibilities in the employment relationship. To be effective, the rules and regulations must be up-to-date, easily understood, and, most importantly, communicated to employees. An effective way to achieve this latter goal is to go over the employee handbook during employee orientation and have employees sign a statement acknowledging its receipt.

> *employee handbook*
> Written rules and regulations informing employees of their rights and responsibilities in the employment relationship.

Following are suggestions for what to include in your employee handbook:

- *The disclaimer.* Every employee handbook should have a disclaimer (it's a good idea to include it at the beginning and the end) specifying that the handbook is not a contract of employment. Without such a notice, a fired employee might attempt to sue you for breach of contract. Lawyer Robert Nobile recommends including a disclaimer such as the following: "This handbook is not a contract, express or implied, guaranteeing employment for any specific duration. Although we hope that your employment relationship with us will be long term, either you or the company may terminate this relationship at any time, for any reason, with or without cause or notice."[26]

- *Employment policies.* Describe work hours, regular and overtime pay, performance reviews, vacations and holidays, equal employment opportunities, and other items that affect employment.

- *Benefits.* Relate insurance plans, disability plans, workers' compensation, retirement programs, and tuition reimbursement.

- *Employee conduct.* Explain your expectations on everything you classify as important, from personal hygiene to dress codes to employee development.

- *Glossary.* Every company has its own terms and jargon. Explain terminology important to your business. For example, Ashton Photo distinguishes between late ("not completed on time in a given department"), delayed ("production of a job has been suspended, awaiting information from the customer"), and on hold ("production of a job has been suspended for accounting reasons").

- *Organization chart.* Include charts and job descriptions to give employees a sense of their place in the organization and how all the parts of the business fit together.

In your employee handbook, don't try to include specifics on what people should do in every possible situation. You just want to communicate the broader principles of what the company believes in and how it expects people to perform.

Performance Appraisal   A well-designed **performance appraisal** system is the second essential component of a fair and just disciplinary policy. Not only does a sound performance-appraisal process document the need for possible discipline, but it also affords management the opportunity to address problem areas before they become disciplinary concerns. In addition, a well-defined performance-appraisal process will help to fulfill the third tenet of a good disciplinary procedure: a system of progressive penalties, discussed next.

Progressive Approach   Increasingly, managers are moving away from the "hot-stove" principle of discipline, in which discipline is immediate and of consistent intensity, to the **progressive approach** in which discipline is incremental and increasingly forceful. Under most progressive systems, managers first issue an oral (informal) reprimand, then a written warning (formal notice), followed by suspension, and finally discharge. Arbitrators and the courts generally favor progressive discipline over that of the hot-stove approach, except in cases of gross misconduct, such as theft or assault, when immediate discharge is warranted. Note that a record of any disciplinary action should be placed in the employee's file even if the reprimand is verbal. A written record is essential if termination occurs and to ensure that the discipline is in accordance with a union contract, if one exists. Write out what happened, what was said by both parties, and when it happened as soon as practical—after all, memories fade. Steps for a progressive disciplinary approach include the following:

- *Determine whether discipline is needed.* Is the problem an isolated incident or part of an ongoing pattern?

- *Have clear goals to discuss with the employee.* You should discuss the problem in specific terms. Indirect comments will not make your point clear. You must also state what you expect the employee to do. If the employee has no idea about your expectations after discussing a performance problem with you, she is likely to repeat past performance.

- *Talk about the problem in private.* Public reprimand is embarrassing both for the employee and for everyone who witnesses it. If you chastise an employee in public, you will lose trust and respect not only from that individual but also from those who observe the act.

- *Keep your cool.* A calm approach will keep a performance discussion more objective and prevent distraction by irrelevant problems.

- *Watch the timing of the meeting.* If the problem is not obvious and you schedule the meeting far in advance, the employee will spend time worrying about what is wrong. Conversely, if the problem is obvious, the meeting should be scheduled to give the employee plenty of time to prepare.

- *Prepare opening remarks.* Performance meetings will be more effective if you are confident in your opening remarks. Think them out in advance and rehearse them.

- *Get to the point.* Beating around the bush with small talk does more to increase the employee's anxiety level than to reduce it.

---

performance appraisal
A process of evaluating an employee's job-related achievements.

progressive approach
Discipline that is applied to employees in appropriately incremental and increasingly forceful measures.

Firing an Employee

Firing employees is never a pleasant duty, and few managers handle the process well. That's because, whatever the facts of the dismissal, most managers feel bad about letting someone go. Ironically, expressing feelings of remorse can be cruel, because it gives the employee false hope. Instead, the best way to deal with the termination is to make it a quick, unambiguous act. Spell out exactly why you are letting the employee go, state clearly that the decision is final, and explain the details of the company's notice policy or severance. Then ask the employee to leave by the end of the week if possible (so that his presence won't demoralize the rest of the staff) and to sign a letter of acknowledgment, which will make it more difficult for him to reopen the discussion—or to sue. Above all, resist any attempts to turn the discussion into an argument.

Icebreaker. I'm sorry to have to give you some bad news: Your job here is being terminated. *If for economic reasons:* I think you'll find the terms of the severance quite generous. I have also prepared a letter of reference, which I'll give you at the end of this meeting.

Fired for Poor Performance. Please understand that this decision is final. You haven't made any real progress with the problems we discussed at your last two performance reviews. I'm sure you'll be able to put your skills to better use in a different position. If you'll sign this letter that says you understand our discussion, we can put this matter behind us.

Laid off for Economic Reasons. Unfortunately, this decision is final. Please understand that it's purely an economic move and no reflection on your performance. I'll be happy to make that clear to any new employers you interview with. If you'll just sign this letter outlining what I've just said, we can get this unhappy business over with.

Gets Angry. You've got some nerve getting rid of me this way. This company might not be in such a mess if it didn't treat its employees so shabbily.

Gets Defensive. You're singling me out. I've performed as well as anyone else—better, in fact, considering the new accounts I just landed.

Gets Personal. How could do this to me? We're friends. You've come over to my house for dinner. Isn't there something you can do?

Absorb Anger. I'm sorry to hear that you feel that way. Everyone here, including me, wanted to see your position work out. Unfortunately, it hasn't. Why don't you take a few minutes to look over this letter and then sign it.

Deflect Defense. As I've said, this is purely an economic decision. You were simply the last one hired. *Or:* Your skill in lining up new clients doesn't make up for your consistent problems with our existing accounts.

Deflect Guilt. I feel bad about this, but it is strictly a business decision. My personal feelings don't count. As your friend, I'll do everything I can to help you land another job. For now, though, I need you to take a look at this letter and then sign it.

Demands More Severance. I'm not going to sign anything until we talk about this severance package. It isn't nearly enough, considering how long I've worked here.

Threatens Legal Action. I'm not going to sign anything until I speak to my lawyer. I think there are some issues that I need to get some legal advice on.

Asks for Another Chance. Isn't there something I can do to reverse this decision? I need this job. I promise my work will improve. Please give me another chance.

End Discussion. You're welcome to discuss the severance offer with someone higher up, although I have to warn you that they're the ones who set the terms. *Or:* Of course. You have every right to speak with your attorney first. I'll hold on to the check and the paperwork until I hear from you. *Or:* I'm terribly sorry, but the decision really is final. [*Stand up.*] Good luck in the future.

SOURCE: Stephen M. Pollan and Mark Levine, "Firing an Employee," *Working Woman,* August 1994, p. 55. Reprinted with permission of Stephen M. Pollan.

- *Allow two-way communication.* Make sure the disciplinary meeting is a discussion, not a lecture. You can get to the heart of the problem only if the employee is allowed to speak. Your intent is to arrive at a solution to a problem, not to scold the employee.

- *Establish a follow-up plan.* You and your employee need to agree to a follow-up plan to establish a time frame within which the employee's performance is to improve.

- *End on a positive note.* Highlight the employee's positive points so that he will leave the meeting with a belief that you want him to succeed in the future.[27]

Appeal Process   The final component of an effective disciplinary program is an **appeal process.** The most common appeal process in nonunion companies relies on an *open-door policy,* a procedure whereby employees seek a review of the disciplinary decision at the next level of management. For such a process to be effective, it must involve a thorough and truly objective review of the facts of the case by an executive of higher rank than the supervisor who applied the discipline. Open-door policies are appropriate for companies with many employees and levels of management. In the majority of small businesses, however, the only level of management is you—the owner. In that case, if an employee feels unjustly treated and is not satisfied with your decision, her only recourse is through the courts.

Dismissing Employees

Because dismissing an employee is the most extreme step of discipline you can exercise, it must be taken with care. Your legitimate reasons for dismissing an employee may include unsatisfactory performance of the job or changing requirements of the job that make the employee unqualified.

When it comes to discharging an employee, what you can and cannot do will be influenced to a large degree by two considerations. First, the decision to discharge an employee must be based on a job-related reason or reasons, not on race, color, religion, sex, age, national origin, or disability. Second, your ability to legally discharge an employee and the manner in which you may do so will be highly dependent on your *at-will* status Under the **at-will doctrine** unless an employment contract is signed, an employer has great leeway in discharging an employee, in that she has the right to discharge the employee for a good reason, a bad reason, or no reason at all. Within the past decade, however, the courts and some state legislatures have imposed one or more of the following restrictions on at-will employers. Check the laws of your state to find which apply to your business. And remember that an employee cannot be fired for union-related activities, even if a union does not exist in the company.

Implied Contract   An employer may be restricted in discharging an employee if an *implied contract* exists as a result of written statements in the company's employment application, employment ads, employee handbook, or other company documents. Verbal statements by company representatives to employees may also erode an employer's at-will status, as may an employee's record of long-term employment with the firm.

appeal process
A formal procedure allowing employees to seek review of a disciplinary measure at a higher level of management.

at-will doctrine
essentially means an employee hired for an indefinite period may be discharged for any or no reason, cause or no cause, unless specifically prohibited by law.

Good Faith and Fair Dealing   The *good faith and fair dealing* exception holds that the employer must have acted fairly and in good faith in discharging the employee. For example, an employee cannot be fired simply because he is about to become vested in the company's pension plan.

Public Policy Exception   Under the *public policy* exception, employers cannot discharge workers for exercising a statutory right, such as filing a workers' compensation claim, or performing public service, such as serving on a jury. Nor can an employee be fired for refusing to break the law or engaging in conduct that is against or her beliefs— for example, refusing to falsify an employer's records to cover up possible misconduct on the part of the company.

Proving Just Cause   In the event that a terminated employee seeks legal redress by filing a lawsuit against your business, whether or not you have acted in a manner consistent with the at-will principle will be decided by a judge. In all cases, you should be able to provide evidence of *just cause* for the dismissal, which generally implies *due process* and *reasonability* on your part. You are likely to have just cause if you can do the following:

- Cite the specific work-rule violation and show that the employee had prior knowledge of the rule and the consequences of violating it.
- Show that the work rule was necessary for the efficient and safe operation of the company and was therefore a *business necessity.*
- Prove that you conducted a thorough and objective investigation of the violation and, in the process, afforded the employee the opportunity to present his side of the story.
- Document that the employee was given the opportunity to improve or modify her performance (except in cases of gross misconduct or insubordination, when it is unnecessary).
- Show that there was sufficient evidence or proof of guilt to justify the actions taken.
- Show that you treated the employee in a manner consistent with *past practices.*
- Demonstrate that the disciplinary actions taken were fair and reasonable in view of the employee's work history.
- Document that the disciplinary action was reviewed by an independent party either within or outside the company prior to being implemented.

Summary

- **The importance of hiring the right employees**

Some of the most valuable resources and competitive advantages a small business has are its employees. There are too many costs and risks involved in HR issues not to pay attention to them.

- **The job-analysis process and the function of job descriptions and job specifications**

Job analysis is the process of determining the duties and skills involved in a job and the kind of person who should be hired to do it. A job description is part of the job analysis; it lists the duties, responsibilities, and reporting relationships of a job. Job specifications are another part of the job analysis; they identify the education, skills, and personality that a person needs to have to be right for a job.

• The advantages and disadvantages of the six major sources of employee recruitment

Help-wanted advertising reaches numerous potential applicants, but many of them will not be right for the job you are trying to fill. Employment agencies prescreen applicants so that you do not have to deal with as many people. The agencies run by the government are usually appropriate only for positions requiring lower-level skills. Private employment agencies and executive recruiters (headhunters) offer more expensive services but can help you find people with higher-level skills. Internet job sites offer limited resources, for a fee. Employee referrals are effective because your current employees know the skills and talents needed, but hiring in this manner can create cliques and build resentment if the new hire does not work out. Moreover, it can lead to underrepresentation of protected groups. Hiring friends and relatives gives you the advantage of knowing their abilities and expertise, but personal relationships can become strained on the job.

• The four tools commonly used in employee selection

In the selection process, you narrow the applicant pool generated by recruitment by trying to match the needs of your business with the skills of each person. Application forms and résumés, interviews, and testing are the most common tools of selection.

• The need for employee orientation and training and the seven methods of satisfying that need

To become a better, more productive worker, every employee needs to have his knowledge and skills enhanced through orientation and training. On-the-job training, lecture, conferences, programmed learning, role-playing, job rotation, and correspondence courses are seven common techniques.

• The two components of a compensation plan and the variable elements of a benefits system

Employees can be compensated for their efforts with hourly wages, straight salary, or on the basis of piecework or commission plans. Incentive-pay programs offer a way to motivate and reward employees above their base pay by paying bonuses or profit-sharing amounts. Common benefits included as part of a compensation package are flexible-benefit plans, health insurance, pension plans, and child care accounts. The most common pension plans adopted by small businesses are individual retirement accounts (IRAs), simplified employee pension (SEP) plans, 401(k) plans, and Keogh plans.

• An effective sequence for disciplining and terminating employees

The progressive disciplinary system, favored by many managers today, begins with an oral reprimand, followed by a written warning, then suspension without pay, and, finally, termination from the company.

Questions for Review and Discussion

1. What is the difference between a job analysis and a job description?

2. When would you, as a small business owner, prefer to receive a résumé than an application form?

3. How is the use of temporary employees different from employee leasing? What are the advantages and disadvantages of each?

4. What are the differences between hard and soft issues during a job orientation? Is one more important than the other?

5. List the advantages of a flexible-benefit package to employees and to the employer.

6. Explain the four components of an effective disciplinary system.

7. Define "at-will" employment status.

8. Discuss three key pieces of legislation that are used to prevent job discrimination.

9. What factors influence the type and amount of employee benefits that a small business can offer?

10. Review the section on training new employees. Give examples of types of jobs that would best lend themselves to each training method.

Questions for Critical Thinking

1. As a young entrepreneur, you may soon be in the position of hiring one or more of your college friends in your own business. What are the advantages of hiring your friends? What are the potential pitfalls?

2. Hiring an employee is a big step for a small business. How can you make a wise hiring decision if so many limitations are put on the interview questions you can legally ask?

Experience This . . .

Find a copy of a small business's employee handbook, either from your current job or from a local small business owner (it may be interesting just to find out how many don't even have one). Compare the sections in this handbook with the "Employee Handbook" section in this chapter. Is everything that an employee would need to know included in this handbook? What is missing? Does everything included in this handbook appear to comply with employment law?

What Would You Do?

Todd owns and manages a T-shirt shop in a small resort town. He has two full-time employees who have been with the business for more than three years. He also employs as many as five part-time employees, depending on the tourist season. They help him keep the shop open from 10 A.M. to 9 P.M. seven days a week. Todd opens the shop every day but typically has his employees close. Whoever closes the store follows a checklist of closing procedures, including ringing out the cash register, filling out the bank deposit, and putting the daily receipts in the safe, with $300 kept in a separate cash bag for the next day's opening cash on hand. As with many businesses, the cash drawer is often off by a small amount, but usually no more than a couple of dollars.

One day Todd opened the store and found that the cash drawer was short $35 for the previous day. Todd called a meeting that afternoon and told all seven employees that they would each have to chip in $5 to cover the shortage and that any time there was a shortage, they would have to split the reimbursement. Todd walked out of the room. The seven employees sat in disbelief.

Questions

1. Is Todd within his legal rights to take this action? If his actions are legal, what are some possible consequences?

2. How would you have handled the situation if you were Todd?

CHAPTER CLOSING CASE

SWITCH TO AN HSA OR NOT?

White Stone's health care costs were out of control. Then the quintuplets arrived.

In January 2004, in a Knoxville hospital, Shannon van Tol gave birth to Tennessee's first quintuplets: Meghan, Willem, Isabella, Ashley, and Sean. Amid the cigars, balloons, and donated diapers, Guille Cruze, CEO of the White Stone Group—the software company where the quints' father, Willem, worked—was both elated and worried.

Willem van Tol had worked as a programmer at White Stone for more than three years and, like many of the firm's 70 full-timers, had enrolled his family in the company's health care plan. The year leading up to the quintuplets' arrival had included a great deal of medical care, including fertility treatments, three ultrasounds a week, eight weeks of bed rest in the hospital, and extended stays for the newborn babies.

All told, the medical bills added up to more than $2 million. Cruze knew that his insurer, Blue Cross Blue Shield, would pass some of the costs back to him. But when he received his renewal notice a few months later, he was stunned. His annual premium had shot up more than 30 percent, from $290,000 to $380,000. For a company with $8 million in revenue, that extra $90,000 was going to hurt. "Willem said he was sorry," says Cruze, who tried to reassure his employee. "I told him that it was okay, that we would live and die as a team."

Privately, Cruze wondered what to do. When he hired his first few employees in 1997, he covered 100 percent of their health care expenses. Every year since, insurance premiums had gone up, forcing him to scale back. By 2004, he was covering 95 percent of expenses for single employees and 55 percent for families. With this latest increase looming, Cruze was fed up. What if premiums jumped another 30 percent next year? In a moment of frustration, he considered doing away with health benefits altogether, but he soon realized that such a drastic step would destroy the close-knit culture he had spent years cultivating.

Cruze called dozens of insurance carriers for quotes, and they all told him that a $400,000 annual health insurance bill was the norm for a company White Stone's size. The situation seemed hopeless. Then he read about an interesting alternative: health savings accounts. HSAs let individuals save money for health care expenses using pretax dollars. The accounts seemed like a good deal for employees. They could roll over any money remaining at the end of the year and take the accounts with them if they should leave White Stone. They could also withdraw funds for nonmedical expenses, though they'd have to pay income tax and a 10 percent penalty. After age 65, they could withdraw anything remaining, paying only income tax.

There was one big drawback: HSAs are used in conjunction with qualified health plans with low premiums and high deductibles—between $1,000 and $5,100 for individuals and between $2,000 and $10,200 for families. (Unlike flexible spending accounts, HSAs limit employees to one health plan.) Cruze could save a bundle by taking advantage of the low premiums, but he worried that his employees might resent the high deductibles, or forgo necessary medical treatments to avoid paying them. The only way to get around that problem, he figured, would be to cover the deductible himself. After doing some calculations, he figured out he'd still wind up paying about $400,000 a year.

Cruze was torn. On the one hand, he liked the idea of HSAs. He'd much rather deposit money into his employees' accounts than continue filling an insurance company's coffers. But HSAs were a new concept, and he worried that his employees would be confused and even intimidated by the complex model. In many ways, it would be easier to stick with a traditional plan and either absorb the entire increase or ask employees to pony up a bigger percentage of the premium payments. By November 2004, as the renewal date for the company's insurance policy loomed large, employees began speculating about the fate of their health benefits. Cruze had to make a decision fast.

What do you think? Are HSAs a good idea for White Stone?

SOURCE: From Darren Dahl, "A Health Insurance Dilemma," *Inc.,* November 2005, 53–54. Copyright © 2006 Mansueto Ventures LLC, publisher of Inc. Magazine, New York, NY 10017. Reprinted with permission.

Test Prepper

college.hmco.com/pic/hatten4e

You've read the chapter, studied the key terms, and the exam is any day now. Think you're ready to ace it? Take this sample test to gauge your comprehension of chapter material. You can check your answers at the back of the book. Want more test questions? Visit the student website at college.hmco.com/pic/hatten4e and take the ACE and ACE+ quizzes for more practice.

True/False

1. T F Professional employer organizations (PEOs) offer a way for small businesses to outsource HR functions.

2. T F A job description should include a list of tasks associated with each duty required.

3. T F The purpose of employee recruitment is to build a large enough pool of applicants to hire a qualified employee.

4. T F Résumés are a source of highly accurate and reliable information about an applicant.

5. T F During an interview you should make the candidate feel comfortable by asking questions about his family and hobbies.

6. T F Honesty tests have not been proven statistically valid or reliable enough to depend on for hiring decisions.

7. T F Employee training and development can be thought of as enhancing an existing competitive advantage.

8. T F Based on the Fair Labor Standards Act, employees are classified as either exempt or nonexempt.

9. T F The most highly valued employee benefit is a pension plan.

10. T F With a progressive approach, discipline is incremental and increasingly forceful.

Fill in the Blank

1. Having current employees recommend new potential employees is called _____ _____.

2. The government agency that sets most employment guidelines is the _____ _____ _____ _____.

3. A job's special requirements based on gender, religion, or national origin that legally allows an employer to hire on those bases constitute a _____.

4. The training that an employee receives in the course of completing her job and receiving coaching/mentoring is called _____ _____ _____.

5. A one-time reward an employee receives for exceeding a performance standard is a _____.

## chapter 18

Operations Management

After reading this chapter, you should be able to:

- List the elements of an operating system.

- Describe how manufacturers and service providers use operations management.

- Explain how to measure productivity.

- Recount the methods of scheduling operations.

- Discuss the role of quality in operations management.

- Identify the three ways to control operations.

Now, these are not your ordinary doughnuts. Although the minifactory bakeries are now covering North America like a glaze, they started in North Carolina, and when people who grew up in the South talk about them, they get a far-off look in their eyes. Comfort food remembered from their childhood.

Krispy Kreme doughnuts have a glaze so delicate that it melts under your fingers. They are so airy that you can't lift one without denting it. You can't enter their store without smiling.

Krispy Kreme combines the science of operations management with the passion of art. Customers stand in line to watch the production process through multiple viewing windows. A parade of doughnuts floats through the fryer, flipping over automatically halfway through the cooking process. Once they are cooked, a conveyor whisks the doughnuts out of the hot shortening and into a waterfall of glaze.

Whether the doughnuts are kneaded, cooked, and filled in Toronto, Ontario, Las Vegas, Nevada, or New York City, every container of doughnut mix, icing, and filling comes by truck from the headquarters on Ivy Avenue in Winston-Salem, North Carolina. The fryers, conveyors, and proofing boxes are all made by hand in the company's equipment department. The Krispy Kreme goal comes down to one word—*consistency*—the hallmark of operations management.

A Krispy Kreme Production Line.

Customers want a doughnut purchased anywhere to taste exactly the same. They also want a doughnut purchased on July 13, 2008, to taste just like one purchased on July 13, 1937. That level of consistency is not as easy to achieve as you might think—it takes superb operations management.

Krispy Kreme is so obsessed with consistency that before a batch of wheat flour is allowed into the building, a core sample is taken to a second-floor lab to analyze moisture content, protein, and ash. If a 25-ton truckload of flour falls outside the parameters of set tolerance ranges, the whole delivery is rejected. And it happens a couple of times each month.

Consistency is not achieved via the lab alone. Adjacent to the lab is a baking lab where Ben Parker and Andrew Henry make doughnuts from every single 2,500-pound batch of mix that comes through each day. Batches that are rejected (which happens about once per month) become food for a lucky bunch of pigs. Patience is needed as much as diligence to achieve consistency. A warehouse the size of a Home Depot holds the mix to season for approximately one week.

Mike Cecil, Krispy Kreme minister of culture (yes, his real job title), has some great stories of doughnut obsession. He tells of a man traveling from Florida back out West with a car full of camera gear, equipment, and luggage. He also had a bunch of Krispy Kreme boxes. Someone broke into his car and stole all the doughnuts—but left all the expensive equipment. Three hundred and fifty cases of Krispy Kremes are loaded on a U.S. Army C-130 Hercules every Wednesday and flown to a NATO base in Keflavik, Iceland. They go into the commissary on Friday morning and are gone by noon.

Some fun facts about Krispy Kremes:

- Vernon Rudolph sold the first one on July 13, 1937, from a rack in the back seat of his 1936 Pontiac.
- In less than two minutes, enough doughnuts are made to stack as high as the Empire State Building.
- In one year, Krispy Kreme bakes enough doughnuts to circle the earth twice.

How about a Krispy Kreme sandwich? So far, such creations—usually a burger patty or a fried chicken breast between a sliced Krispy Kreme glazed doughnut "bun"—have been limited to minor-league baseball games and state fairs. But two years of declining sales and sliding market share make new products critical to long-term company success. The chain's newest product offering, a whole-wheat glazed doughnut was "well received." Krispy Kreme soon will introduce a zero-transfat doughnut as well. In addition to new food offerings, Krispy Kreme is introducing a new beverage program featuring its Chillers frozen drinks, which boast a Kremey line and a Fruity line.

SOURCES: Sarah E. Lockyer, "Krispy Kreme Plans Foreign Expansion, New Beverage Line," *Nation's Restaurant News*, 23 April 2007, 9; Sarah E. Lockyer, "Krispy Kreme Looks to Climb Out of the Hole With New Strategy" *Nation's Restaurant News*, 16 November 2006, 4; Sarah Lockyer, "Krispy Kreme Sweetens Pot with New Offerings," *Nations' Restaurant,* 21 June 2004, 1; Charles Fishman, "The King of Kreme," *Fast Company,* October 1999, 262–278; Kevin Libin, "Holey War," *Canadian Business,* 21 August 2000, 34–41; Jacque White Kochak, "Another Go Around," *Restaurant Business,* 15 August 2000, 81–90; Scott McCormack, "Sweet Success," *Forbes,* 7 September 1998, 90–91; Nancy Brumback, "The Hole Story," *Restaurant Business,* February 2004, 32–33.

This chapter focuses on *operations management,* sometimes referred to as *OM* and the processes associated with it. The function of operations management has evolved over the last few decades from a narrow view of production, inventory, and industrial management into a broader concept that includes services. Indeed, the management of production and operations is critical to all small businesses; not just those involved in manufacturing. Every business performs an operations function—the processes and procedures of converting labor, materials, money, and other resources into finished products or services.

Elements of an Operating System

Operations management systems contain five basic elements: inputs, transformation processes, outputs, control systems, and feedback. These elements must be brought together and coordinated into a system to produce the product or service—the reason for the business to exist.

Inputs

inputs
All the resources that go into a business.

The **inputs** in an operations management system include all physical and intangible resources that come into a business. Raw materials are necessary as the things that will become transformed in a business. A company that makes in-line skates, for instance, must have polymers, plastics, and metal. Skills and knowledge of the people within the organization are other inputs. A management consulting firm, for example, needs people with special expertise. The in-line skate manufacturer needs trained workers to fabricate the product. Likewise, money, information, and energy are all needed in varying degrees. Inputs are important to the quality of the finished product of the business. Remember the computer cliché, "Garbage in—garbage out." The idea holds true for operations management, too: You can't produce high-quality outputs from inferior inputs.

Transformation Processes

transformation processes
What a business does to add value to inputs in converting them to outputs.

Once we have identified the inputs of a business, we can look at the processes that are used to transform them into finished products. **Transformation processes** are the active practices—including concepts, procedures, and technologies—that are implemented to produce outputs. Dry cleaners, for instance, take soiled clothing (inputs) and use chemicals, equipment, and know-how to transform them into clean clothing (the outputs of the business).

Outputs

outputs
The tangible or intangible products that a business produces.

Outputs, the result of the transformation processes, are what your business produces. Outputs can be tangible, such as a CD, or intangible, such as a doctor's diagnosis.

Since a business's *social responsibility,* or obligations to the community, has become as serious a matter as product-liability and other lawsuits, we need to

Reality Check
Stretching the Supply Chain

Shelving Concepts is a privately held company in business since 1987. Founded by Tom Amoruso, the company has grown into one of the top 100 small businesses in Houston, Texas. Tom's background in installation and sales of office filing systems, mobile storage systems, and industrial metal shelving has helped the company increase sales every year. Tom still personally oversees each sale!

Amoruso is used to working with suppliers, but he is learning that buying one of your suppliers is another matter altogether. Amoruso acquired the assets of manufacturer Dixie Shelving along with another former supplier, Dura Rack, at auction for $100,000. He bought the company names, phone and fax numbers, website addresses, and Dixie Shelving's equipment. He purchased Dura Rack's name for potential future use, but not its equipment. "I would always tease [Dixie Shelving's owners] and say, 'If you're ever interested in selling, I'd be the guy to buy,'" says Amoruso, who's delving into manufacturing for the first time because he sees wide growth opportunities.

For Shelving Concepts, lower production costs are one big advantage of buying a former supplier. They used to pay 22 cents to make a certain type of shelving clip; now they can manufacture it for 4 cents under their own roof. Buying the assets of a former supplier, however, requires new skill sets. "All of your accumulated experience may not only be worth little here, it may actually mislead you."

Amoruso has invested $270,000 into upgrades on Dixie Shelving's manufacturing equipment since July and says he could spend as much as $300,000 before everything's up and running. He's learning about manufacturing, and his workload is now double because he's effectively running two businesses. Manufacturing "is a whole new game," he says. The Dixie Shelving purchase has also put Amoruso in the interesting position of supplying his main competitors, some of whom remain apprehensive about sharing their price lists. "There are two dealers struggling with it," he says.

What Tom Amoruso is adjusting is his company's value chain (or supply chain), which are based on the assumption that everyone who touches a product or service adds some value to it. So farmers add value by growing and harvesting grain; truckers or railroads add value by hauling the grain to grain elevators, which add value by storing the grain and distributing it to the manufacturers, who add value by turning it into finished products. Along the way, a lot of other people join the value chain, from ad agencies to supermarkets.

The question that entrepreneurs must ask when they consider buying a supplier or a customer is "are we *really* adding value or just passing things down the line?"

SOURCES: Chris Penttila, "Buying a Suppliers's Company," *Entrepreneur*, April 2006; www.shelvingconcepts.com/aboutus; Watts Wacker, "A Valuable Proposition," *Entrepreneur*, June 2001; "People to know,"*Modern Materials Handling*, October 2005, 18.

consider *all* the outputs a business produces—not just the beneficial or intended ones. When we look at the big picture of the transformation process, we see that employee accidents, consumer injuries, pollution, and waste are also outputs.

control systems
The means to monitor input, transformation, and output so as to identify problems.

Control Systems

Control systems provide the means to monitor and correct problems or deviations when they occur in the operating system. Controls are integrated into all three stages of production—input, transformation, and output (see Figure 18.1).

Figure 18.1
CONTROL SYSTEMS

Every Type of Business Takes Inputs and Transforms Them into Outputs.

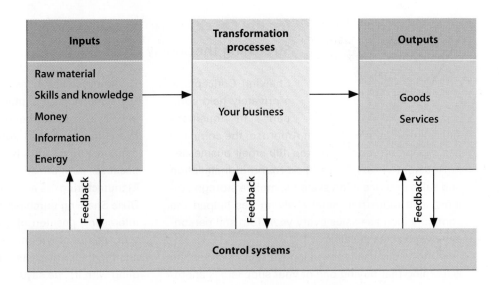

An example of a control system would be the use of electronic monitors in a manufacturing process to tell a machine operator that the product is not being made within the allowed size tolerance. In service companies, employee behavior is part of the transformation process to be controlled. A bank manager, for instance, might hire people to pose as new bank customers and then report back to the manager on the quality of service they received from tellers or loan officers.

Feedback

feedback
Communication tools to connect control systems to the processes of a business.

Feedback is the information that a manager receives in monitoring the operation system. It can be verbal, written, electronic, or observational. Feedback is the necessary communication that links a control system to the inputs, transformation, and outputs.

Types of Operations Management

Production broadly describes what businesses of all types do in creating goods and services. Computer hardware and software companies, health care providers, and farmers are all involved in production. Manufacturing is just one type of production, making goods as opposed to providing services or extracting natural resources. One of your highest priorities as a manager is to ensure that **productivity**—which is the measure of production, or output per worker— remains high. It is important to measure productivity so as to control the amount of resources used to produce outputs.

productivity
The measure of outputs according to the inputs needed to produce them; a way to determine the efficiency of a business.

Operations Management for Manufacturing Businesses

Manufacturing businesses can be classified by the way they make goods and by the time spent on making them. Goods can be made from analytic or synthetic systems, using either continuous or intermittent processes.

Analytic systems reduce inputs into component parts so as to extract products. For example, automobile-salvage businesses buy vehicles from insurance companies or individuals to dismantle them for parts or scrap iron to sell. **Synthetic systems**, by contrast, combine inputs to create a finished product or change it into a different product. Thus, restaurants take vegetables, fruits, grains, meats, seafood, music, lighting, furniture, paintings, and a variety of human talents to create and serve meals.

Production by a **continuous process** is accomplished over long periods of time. Production of the same or very similar products goes on uninterrupted for days, months, or years. Microbreweries and wine makers are examples of small businesses that produce goods via a continuous process.

Production runs that use an **intermittent process** involve short cycles and frequent stops to change products. Small businesses using intermittent processes are also called *job shops.* Custom printing shops and custom jewelry makers are examples.

Can small businesses compete in a manufacturing sector long associated with gigantic factories? Yes, primarily because automation makes flexible production possible. Computers assist small manufacturers in determining raw material needs, scheduling production runs, and designing new products. Automation allows the retooling of production machines in seconds, rather than hours or days, so that shorter batches can be produced profitably. Machines can be programmed to perform many combinations of individual jobs and functions, rather than just one. With the help of computers, products and processes can be designed at the same time, rather than designing a product and then figuring out a way to make it.

Many small businesses are benefiting from the number of large businesses that are examining what they do best, determining that manufacturing is not their strongest suit, and farming out production to smaller specialty firms. For example, your new Dell computer did not come from a Dell computer factory—none exists. Dell concentrates on marketing, buying computer components from different companies, and assembling them in a warehouse.[1] This type of flexible contract production opens up many opportunities for entrepreneurs.

Manufacturing is already evolving past flexible production, however, to **mass customization**, which means tailoring products to meet the needs of individual customers. As an example of mass customization, suppose a customer in need of a new business suit steps into a kiosk-like device where an optical scanner measures his body. As soon as he chooses a fabric and style, the order is beamed to the plant, where lasers cut the material and machines sew it together. The suit could be ready and shipped directly to the customer in a matter of days.[2]

Operations Management for Service Businesses

As pointed out earlier, service providers need and use operations management just as much as product manufacturers do. Both types of businesses take inputs and produce outputs through some type of transformation process. However, operations processes differ from one product and service to another, and some overlap. For example, manufacturers often offer repair services. Restaurants offer food products as well as services.

analytic systems
Manufacturing system that reduces inputs into component parts so as to extract products.

synthetic systems
Manufacturing system that combines inputs to create a finished product or change it into a different product.

continuous process
A production process that operates for long periods of time without interruption.

intermittent process
A production process that operates in short cycles so that it can change products.

mass customization
A production process that allows products to be produced specifically for individual customers.

Table 18.1
PRODUCT AND SERVICE
OPERATIONS SYSTEMS

Inputs	Transformation	Outputs	Feedback
Restaurant			
Food	Cooking	Meals	Leftovers
Hungry people	Serving	Satisfied people	Complaints
Equipment			
Labor			
Factory			
Machinery	Welding	Finished products	Defects
Skilled labor	Painting	Services	Returns
Raw material	Forming	Waste products	Market share
Engineering	Transporting		Complaints
Management			
Buildings			

Traditionally, all service businesses were seen as intermittent-process businesses, because standardization didn't seem possible for businesses such as hair salons, accounting firms, and auto service centers. Today, in an effort to increase productivity, some service businesses are adopting continuous processes. For example, Merry Maids house cleaners, Jiffy Lube auto service, Fantastic Sam's family hair-cutting salons, and even chains of dentists located in malls are all using manufacturing techniques of continuous production. A notable difference between service and manufacturing operations is the amount of customer contact involved. Many services, such as hair salons, require the customer to be present for the operation to be performed. Consider the examples of product and service operations systems in Table 18.1.

What Is Productivity?

According to Chapter 16, as a manager, you are involved in planning, organizing, leading, and controlling. But how do you tell if and when you are reaching the goals that you have set? You can measure your success by assessing your *productivity,* which is an expression of efficiency. Productivity, or efficiency, can be described numerically as the ratio of inputs used to outputs produced, such as output per labor-hour. The higher the ratio, the more efficient is your operating system. You should constantly look for ways to increase outputs while keeping inputs constant or to keep outputs constant while decreasing inputs.

Ways to Measure Manufacturing Productivity

Productivity can be measured for your entire business or for a specific portion of it. Because many inputs go into your business, the input you choose determines the specific measure of productivity. Total productivity can be determined by dividing total outputs by total inputs:

$$\text{Total productivity} = \text{Outputs/Labor} + \text{Capital} + \text{Raw materials} + \text{All other inputs}$$

If your software company sold $500,000 worth of software and used $100,000 in resources, your total productivity ratio would be 5. But you may not always want to consider all of your inputs every time. For example, because materials may account for as much as 90 percent of operating costs in businesses that use little labor, materials productivity would be an important ratio to track.

$$\text{Materials productivity} = \text{Outputs/Materials}$$

If 4,000 pounds of sugar are used to produce 1,000 pounds of candy, the materials productivity is 1,000 divided by 4,000, or 0.25, which becomes a base figure for comparing increases or decreases in productivity. Stated simply, you can increase the productivity of your business by increasing outputs, decreasing inputs, or a combination of both. Most productivity improvements come from changing processes used by your business, from your employees accomplishing more, or from technology that speeds production.

Productivity ratios can be used to measure the efficiency of a new process. Suppose that you run a furniture shop with a productivity ratio of 1:

$$\text{Output/Input} = \text{Number of tables/Hours} = 100/100 = 1$$

You have invented a new process that will save 20 percent on your labor costs. Now you can still produce the same number of tables (100) but take only 80 hours to produce them. Your new productivity ratio is 1.25:

$$\text{New productivity ratio} = 100/80 = 1.25$$

Unfortunately, your new process ends up increasing defects in the tables. To correct these defects, you have to increase labor-hours to 120. Your productivity ratio is now 0.833:

$$\text{Corrected productivity ratio} = 100/120 = 0.833$$

Your corrected productivity ratio shows that it is back to the drawing board for your new process.

Ways to Measure Service Productivity

"Ergonomics is the key to worker productivity. Make sure that there is a healthy fit between people and equipment."

Productivity in the U.S. service sector has been flat over the last decade, with a growth rate averaging only 0.2 percent.[3] This statistic is even more significant when you remember that almost 80 percent of the U.S. workforce is employed in the service sector.

Productivity in service-related businesses has not grown as rapidly as productivity in manufacturing businesses because service businesses are more labor intensive. Factories can substitute machines for people and increase output. Can service businesses do the same?

Actually, to some degree they can. Rick Smolan, president of Wildfire Communications, has developed an electronic device that can totally automate

Profile in Entrepreneurship

It's Not Easy

The story of Victor and Janie Tsao has all the makings of a classic entrepreneurship tale. The pair, who emigrated from Taiwan, started the company that would become Linksys in their garage in 1988 (entrepreneurs love working in garages—just ask Hewlett and Packard). Their story concludes with a $500 million buyout by Cisco Systems. In between were 20 years of hard work, calculated risks, and 70-hour workweeks.

The Tsaos are very goal oriented. Janie worked in information technology at Carter Hawley Hale, and Victor was MIS director of Taco Bell. Both were determined to be independent by the time they reached age 40. Searching for a product on which to build their own business, they settled on an unsolved problem: Printer cables could extend only about 15 feet before the data started to degrade. Working with a Taiwanese manufacturer, the Tsaos developed a system using telephone wire to extend that range to 100 feet. They also made a product that would allow multiple PCs to connect with multiple printers.

Victor quit his job with Taco Bell two years later after investing $7,000, the only startup capital Linksys needed. The company's product lines expanded to include printer-to-PC connectors, PC-to-PC Ethernet hubs, cards, and cords that allowed individuals and small businesses to connect their computers together. Victor often worked 100-hour weeks, taking intermittent naps on the office floor, managing operations and finances. Janie handled sales. Victor took no salary until the mid-1990s, while the family got by (raising two boys) on Janie's salary of $2,000 per month. The company grew steadily without taking on any debt or outside investors.

Linksys's break came in 1995, when Microsoft built networking functions into its new release of Windows 95. With that move, it suddenly became simple to network, and Linksys's market potential exploded. What the company desperately needed was national distribution—a difficult nut for a small business to crack. But Janie succeeded at RetailVision, an electronics trade show. Unable to meet with Best Buy's buyer in regularly scheduled sessions, she tracked him down in the hotel hallway. He loved the presentation and made a $2 million order on the spot. Janie stayed calm and cool until she reached her rental car, where she let out an uncharacteristic scream of joy.

That's the experience of entrepreneurship—everything from the discomfort of sleeping on the floor to moments of pure exhilaration. The Tsaos were *Inc.* magazine's Entrepreneurs of the Year.

SOURCES: Ian Mount, "Be Fast, Be Frugal, Be Right," *Inc.*, January 2004, 64–70; "CRN Interview—Victor Tsao, Linksys," *CRN*, 24 March 2003, 20.

telephone communications. By blending computer, telephone, and voice-recognition technology, Wildfire receives and directs calls wherever you are, takes messages, and maintains your calendar and Rolodex—and does it all by responding to your voice. Smolan and others who are always on the phone but rarely in an office use Wildfire instead of a personal secretary. "Secretarial work is just not good use of a human being," according to Smolan.[4]

Besides technological innovation, another key to enhancing productivity in a service business is making sure your employees are comfortable. **Ergonomics** studies the fit between people and machines. "The human body is simply not designed to sit. Yet between 70 percent to 75 percent of today's workforce is sitting and working on computers," says corporate ergonomist Rajendra Paul.[5] Lighting levels, furniture size and height, and the location of computers and telephones are important factors to consider when designing your workstations. Given the myriad physical differences and varying employee needs, you may need to consider

> *ergonomics*
> The study of the interaction between people and machinery.

chairs with adjustable armrests and footrests, keyboards and mouse pads that adjust to the correct height and angle, and nonglare monitor screens.

Management style is another key factor in improving the quality and quantity of service workers' output. At Mountain Shadows, Inc., in Escondido, California, owner H. Douglas Cook knew that keeping his employees' productivity high meant that he had to stay out of the way and let his employees do their jobs. Cook has a special interest in Mountain Shadows, a residential facility for the developmentally disabled, because not only is he its owner, but his son Brian is also a resident there. The facility's 105 residents range in age from 7 to 63, and almost all of them use wheelchairs. Mountain Shadows is, by necessity, a highly labor-intensive operation. Yet Cook doesn't interfere with the 170 employees. Instead, he has introduced an open management style that recognizes the importance of the employees. By doing so, he has dramatically reduced employee turnover, which in turn has increased his workers' efficiency.[6]

What About Scheduling Operations?

Scheduling is a basic operations management activity for both manufacturing and service businesses that involves the timing of production. The purpose of scheduling is to put your plans into motion by describing what each worker has to do.

Scheduling is necessary to maximize levels of efficiency and customer service. For example, if a beauty shop schedules one haircut every 30 minutes, although each could actually be done in 20 minutes with no decrease in quality, the operator could be working one-third more efficiently. Three haircuts could be produced per hour rather than two. In contrast, a shop that schedules too much work cannot complete jobs on time, resulting in poor customer service

" SINCE THE SCHEDULE REORGANIZING, WE HAVEN'T YET FIGURED OUT
WHAT TO DO WITH HARRIS. "

www.CartoonStock.com

and probably losing future business from customers who become aggravated by having to wait for their appointments. If you can schedule the exact amount of work to meet your customer demand at a given time, you will optimize your resources.

Scheduling Methods

Most business operations use forward scheduling, backward scheduling, or a combination of the two methods. With **forward scheduling**, materials and resources are allocated for production when a job order comes in. Any type of custom production in which the product changes or in which demand is unknown in advance needs forward scheduling. **Backward scheduling** involves arranging production activities around the due date for the product. You take the date on which the finished product must be delivered, then schedule in reverse order all material procurement and work to be done.

Henry L. Gantt devised a simple bar graph for scheduling work in any kind of operation. Developed in 1913, it still bears his name: the *Gantt chart*. This chart can be used to track the progress of work as a product makes its way through various departments (see Figure 18.2). It allows you to see the time required for each step and the current status of a job.

forward scheduling
Scheduling in which materials and resources are allocated for production when a job order comes in.

backward scheduling
Scheduling that involves arranging production activities around the due date for the product.

Figure 18.2
GANTT CHART

Stages of Work in Building a House Can Be Scheduled in a Gantt Chart.

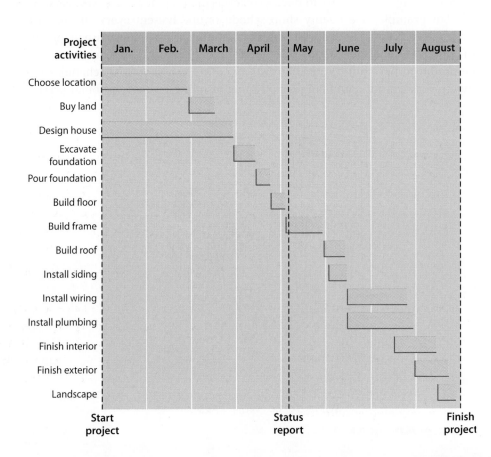

Reality Check
How Good Is Good Enough?

If 99.9 percent accuracy were good enough. . .

- The Internal Revenue Service would lose 2 million documents per year.

- *Webster's Third International Dictionary of the English Language* would have 315 misspelled words.

- 12 newborn babies would go home with the wrong parents daily.

- 107 medical procedures would be performed incorrectly every day.

- 114,500 pairs of new shoes would be mismatched each year.

- 2,488,200 books would be printed each year with no words.

- Telephone companies would send 1,314 calls to the wrong number each minute.

- 5,517,200 cases of soft drinks would be made every year with no fizz.

- Two airplanes would crash at Chicago's O'Hare International Airport every day.

Routing

Scheduling involves routing, sequencing, and dispatching the product through successive stages of production. **Routing** shows the detailed breakdown of information explaining how your product or service will be produced. *Routing sheets* are the paper copies, and *routing files* are the electronic versions of this information. Needed information could include tooling specifications and setups, number of workers or operators needed, the sequence in which steps are to be taken, and control tests to be performed.

> *routing*
> Information showing the steps required to produce a product.

Sequencing

Sequencing is the critical step of determining the order in which a job will go through your production system. Sequencing is most important when the job involves more than one department of your business, because a holdup in one department could cause idle time for another. Drafting a Gantt chart is a good way to track the flow of jobs between departments.

> *sequencing*
> The order in which the steps need to occur to produce a product.

Dispatching

Dispatching is the act of releasing work to employees according to priorities you determined in planning the work sequence. Taxi companies often use *first-come, first-served* priority dispatching rules. A tailor may use an *earliest due date* rule, in which the order due first is dispatched first. A company that assumes that orders that will take the longest will be the largest (and most profitable) will use a *longest processing time* priority dispatching rule. Companies that make significant profit from handling charges and that reduce costs by completing more orders will use a *shortest processing time* priority dispatching rule.

> *dispatching*
> Allocating resources and beginning the steps to produce a product.

Quality-Centered Management

There is no quality more important to businesses today than just that—quality. In the recent past, many U.S. businesses lost tremendous market share to foreign companies for one reason: They had not paid enough attention to quality. Now, few industries and businesses, large or small, can afford *not* to pay attention to quality.

To manage a small business focused on quality, you must keep two things in mind about what the word **quality** means. First, from your customers' perspective, *quality* is how well your product or service satisfies their needs. Second, from your business's standpoint, *quality* means how closely your product conforms to the standards you have set.

> **quality**
> How well a good or service meets or exceeds customers' expectations, or the degree to which a product conforms to established tolerance standards.

Six Sigma in Small Business

A common way that companies measure the quality of a product is to keep close track of the **defect rate**. A defect rate is the number of goods produced that were out of the company's accepted **tolerance range**—the boundaries of acceptable quality. But how good is good enough? Is 99 out of 100 good enough? With a 1 percent defect rate, consider this: The U.S. Postal Service would lose more than 18,000 pieces of mail per hour!

Perfection is not possible, but companies need to strive for it—that is, for zero defects. **Six sigma** is the term that has come to signify the quality movement, not just in manufacturing, but throughout entire organizations. In statistical terminology, *sigma* denotes the *standard deviation* of a set of data. It indicates how all data points in a distribution vary from the mean (average) value. Table 18.2 shows different sigma levels and their corresponding defects per million.[7]

With a normal distribution, 99.73 percent of all the data points fall within three standard deviations (three sigma) of the mean. Pretty good, but that is just for one stage of the production process. Products that have to go through hundreds or thousands of stages could still come out with defects.

If you choose six-sigma defects as your production goal, you will have 99.99966 percent of your products within your specification limits—only 3.4 defects per million! Even if your product has to go through 100 different stages, the defect rate will still be only 3,390 defects per million.

> **defect rate**
> The number of goods produced that are outside the company's boundaries of acceptable quality.
>
> **tolerance range**
> The boundaries a manager sets in determining the acceptable quality of a product.

> **six sigma**
> The tolerance range in which only 3.4 defects per million are allowed.

Table 18.2
SIGMA LEVELS AND DEFECT RATES

Sigma Level	Defects per Million
3.0	66,810.0
3.5	22,750.0
4.0	6,750.0
4.5	1,350.0
5.0	233.0
5.5	32.0
6.0	3.4

The concept of six sigma is not limited to producing goods in your small business. You can also apply it to customer satisfaction in your service business. Consider a company with 1,000 customers and 10 employees (or stages) that can affect customer satisfaction. The difference between three sigma (499 dissatisfied) and four sigma (60 dissatisfied) is 439 dissatisfied customers. That represents 44 percent of your entire customer base![8]

Let's take a closer look at the basic components of a six-sigma quality program and the activities and tools needed to practice them.

Basic Components   The basic components of a six-sigma program include the actual improvement process and quality measurement. The actual improvement process involves the following steps:

1. Define products and services by describing the actual products or services that are provided to customers.

2. Identify customer requirements for products or services by stating them in measurable terms.

3. Compare products with requirements by identifying gaps between what the customer expects and what she is actually receiving.

4. Describe the process by providing explicit details.

5. Improve the process by simplification and mistake-proofing.

6. Measure quality and productivity by establishing baseline values and then tracking improvement.

Those quality measurements should include process mean and standard deviation, capability index, and defects per unit. Variance analysis is an important part of getting the most out of six sigma. *Multivariate analysis (MANOVA)* is used to identify how variation affects the process and product performance. *Analysis of variance (ANOVA)* is used to identify where in the process this variation occurs (by location, person, or process step). *Regression analysis* is used to determine the magnitude of the effect these factors have on the process and to identify potential root causes of variation.[9]

Quality Activities and Tools   The quality activities encompass ongoing management processes that businesses need to practice in a six-sigma program. They include participative management, short-cycle manufacturing, designing for manufacturing benchmarking, statistical process control (SPC), and supplier qualification. The improvement tools and analytical techniques include flow-charts (schematic representations of an algorithm or a process), Pareto charts (charts used to graphically summarize and display the relative importance of the differences between groups of data), histograms (the graphical versions of tables that show what proportion of cases fall into each of several or many specified categories), cause-and-effect diagrams (diagrams, also known as fishbone diagrams because of their shape, that show causes of certain events), and experimental designs (the designs of all information-gathering exercises where variation is present, whether under the full control of the experimenter or not).

The speed at which e-business is conducted fits like a glove with six-sigma principles, because these principles are aimed at enabling businesses to deliver just what customers need when they want it.

@ e-biz
Six-Sigma Online

www.6-sigma.com This site created by the Six Sigma Academy offers a good look within the academy and training provided. Start with a click on "What is Six Sigma?" A wealth of information on training and the six-sigma philosophy is provided. "News and Reviews" reveals which companies have implemented the process and describes how it has affected their operations.

www.isixsigma.com This site provides information on how to implement quality strategies into your business. Clicking on "Methodologies" will take you to a variety of papers describing differing quality methodologies.

www.sixsigma.de Start with the site-map link at the top of the page, where you will find an outline of site topics. It is easy to navigate from there. You may be interested in the detailed boundary conditions with graphics of six sigma.

www.thequalityportal.com Here you will find a wide range of quality-related items, including plenty of information on six sigma. Click on "Six Sigma" for a description of what this concept is, why it is important, when to use it, how to use it, and what a six-sigma black belt is.

www.sixsigmaonline.org Looking for six-sigma cerification? This site offers online certifications—with Yellow, Green, and Black Belts to boot. Six-sigma training encourages individuals to stop what they are doing, examine how well they have done it, and then implement improvements to iron out defects.

Small businesses that would like to achieve six-sigma status must work diligently to reduce the incidence of defects. Those that do will find six sigma to be not just a strange phrase, but the means toward achieving the ultimate goals of improved manufacturing and increased customer satisfaction.[10]

Quality Circles

quality circles
The use of small groups of employees to analyze products and processes in an effort to improve quality.

A popular technique for improving quality relies on **quality circles**, which seek to involve everyone within the organization in decisions that affect the business. Small groups of employees meet regularly to discuss, analyze, and recommend solutions to problems in their area, after they receive training in problem solving, statistical techniques, and organizational behavior.

How Do You Control Operations?

The issue of quality affects the entire production process, so controls need to be built in at every stage. *Feedforward quality control* applies to your company's inputs. *Concurrent quality control* involves monitoring your transformation processes. *Feedback quality control* means inspecting your outputs. Each will be discussed here.

"Small businesses must monitor their productivity closely to stay competitive and to remain profitable."

feedforward quality control
Quality control applied to a company's inputs.

Feedforward Quality Control

Control of quality begins by screening out inputs that are not good enough. **Feedforward quality control** depends strongly on the *total quality management*

(TQM) principles stating that every employee is a quality inspector and is responsible for building better, long-term relationships with suppliers. When you have a long-term relationship with suppliers, they can help you achieve higher quality standards by continuously improving their products. Teamwork with your employees and cooperation with suppliers are keys to feedforward control.

Concurrent Quality Control

Concurrent quality control involves monitoring the quality of your work in progress. To facilitate this type of monitoring, many small businesses are realizing the value of the international quality standards known as **ISO 9000** (pronounced ICE-oh 9000), discussed also in Chapter 15. The purpose of the ISO 9000 standards is to document, implement, and demonstrate the quality assurance systems used by companies that supply goods and services internationally.[11]

ISO standards do not address the quality of your specific products. Rather, compliance with them shows your customers (whether consumers or other businesses) how you test your products, how your employees are trained, how you keep records, and how you fix defects. ISO standards are more like generally accepted accounting principles (GAAP) than they are a spinoff of TQM.[12] Certification in the United States comes from the American National Standards Institute, 11 West 42nd Street, New York, New York 10035 (212-642-4900).

American Saw, of East Longmeadow, Massachusetts, an 800-employee, family-owned business, was the first in its industry to receive ISO certification. Tim Berry, quality control manager, believes that because the company took the steps necessary to become certified, its product defects have decreased, communication has improved, and workplace accidents have been reduced.[13] What's more, meeting the standards will ease entry into foreign markets and cut costs. Unfortunately, the up-front costs of certification can be high for small businesses. American Saw, for example, laid out $60,000 for outside consultants and registrars.

Richard Thompson, of Caterpillar, states, "Today, having ISO 9000 is a competitive advantage. Tomorrow, it will be the ante to the global poker game."[14] Small businesses may find themselves between the proverbial rock and a hard place relating to certification and costs if the larger companies that buy their products require certification before they will purchase from the small business. Some suggestions for dealing with costs follow:

- *Negotiate consultation prices.* Different consultants and registrars charge different amounts. Consultation prices are on the way down, so shop around. Always make sure that the consultant you select is familiar with your particular industry, however.

- *Request customer subsidies.* If the company you are selling to is pushing its suppliers for certification, it may help you become certified. A primary customer of Griffith Rubber Mills, of Portland, Oregon, paid the entire certification bill because it needed the technology.

> *concurrent quality control*
> Quality control applied to work in progress.
>
> *ISO 9000*
> The set of standards that certifies that a business is using processes and principles to ensure the production of quality products.

- *Look for consultant alternatives.* A local college may be able to help set up an ISO networking group.
- *Consider your need for full certification.* You may be able to save money if it is more important to your suppliers for your business to meet ISO standards than to have full certification.[15]

An important tool for monitoring the quality of a product while it is being produced (concurrent control) is **statistical process control (SPC),** the process of gathering, plotting, and analyzing data to isolate problems in a specified sample of products. Using SPC, you can determine the probability of a deviation being a simple, random, unimportant variation or a sign of a problem in your production process that must be corrected.

For example, if you are producing titanium bars that need to be 1 inch in diameter, not every single bar will measure *exactly* 1 inch. You need to calculate the probability that various deviations will occur by chance alone or because of some problem. If a sample bar measures 1.01 inches, you wouldn't be too concerned, because that amount of variation occurs by chance once in every 100 products. But if a sample bar measures 1.05 inches, a variation that occurs by chance only once in 10,000 products, you know a problem needs correction in your production process. See the *control chart* in Figure 18.3 for this example. A control chart consists of the following:

- Points representing averages of measurements of a quality characteristic in samples taken from the process and shown over a period of time
- A center line, drawn at the process mean
- Upper and lower control limits (called *natural process limits*) that indicate the threshold at which the process output is considered statistically unlikely

Another powerful tool for concurrent control is **benchmarking,** which allows the comparisons necessary for measurement. To identify or measure a competitive advantage for your small business, you must have a comparison base. Your products, services, practices—almost anything related to your business that can be measured—can be benchmarked. Where can you find benchmark information? First, visit your local library reference section to

---

statistical process control (SPC)
The use of statistical analysis to determine the probability of a variation in product being random or a problem.

benchmarking
the process of comparing key points within your business with comparable points in another external entity

---

Figure 18.3
CONTROL CHART

Control Charts Are Used to Distinguish Random from Nonrandom Variations in the Production of Goods.

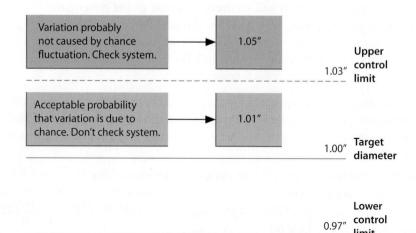

find *RMA Annual Statement Studies*. RMA is second to none for providing small business industry averages. In addition, industry groups and trade associations often publish industry averages in journals, magazines, and newsletters.

Benchmarking can be used to improve every facet of your business. Some examples follow:

Production Process

- Methodology
- Equipment needs
- Assembly time
- Inspection
- Parts availability
- Facility needs
- Personnel needs
- Quality control
- Cost considerations
- Returns and repairs

Customer Service

- Goods and services availability
- Warranties and guarantees
- Cost considerations
- Returns, repair, and replacement
- Feedback mechanisms (surveys, toll-free free numbers, etc.)

Feedback Quality Control

Inspecting and testing products after they are produced is called **feedback quality control**. Quality control inspectors may be used to check products. Rejected products will be either discarded, reworked, or recycled.

A problem with many types of product inspection is that the product can no longer be used because it has to be cut up, taken apart, or disassembled to test and measure it. However, nondestructive testing of several metal and plastic parts is being perfected by using laser ultrasound and other electromagnetic and acoustic-based methods.[16]

> *feedback quality control*
> Inspecting and testing products after they are produced.

Summary

- ### Elements of an operating system

In developing a system for producing your product or service, your business takes inputs such as raw materials, skills, money, information, and energy, and transforms them in some way to add value to product outputs. You need to receive feedback at every stage to control the process.

- ### How manufacturers and service providers use operations management

Operating systems used by manufacturers are either analytic (systems that take inputs and reduce them into component parts to produce outputs) or synthetic (systems that combine inputs in producing outputs). The processes that manufacturers use are either continuous or intermittent. A continuous process produces the same good without interruption for a long period of time. An intermittent process is stopped with some frequency to change the products being made. Service businesses also take inputs and produce outputs through some transformation process. Most have used intermittent processes, but some have adopted continuous processes in an effort to increase productivity.

• How to measure productivity

The ratio of inputs used to produce outputs is called *productivity*. Productivity measures the efficiency of your entire business or any part of it. It can be improved by changing processes used by your business, by getting your employees to accomplish more, or by using some type of technology that speeds production. To calculate productivity, simply divide outputs by inputs.

• How to schedule operations

Scheduling involves planning what work will need to be done and determining what resources you will need to produce your product or service. Forward scheduling is accomplished by having resources available and ready as customer orders come in. Backward scheduling is used when you plan a job around the date when the project must be done. Gantt charts are a useful backward-scheduling tool.

• Building quality into operations

A company's tolerance range denotes the boundaries of acceptable quality. The defect rate indicates the number of products made that fall outside the tolerance range. Six sigma establishes a tolerance range of only 3.4 defects per million products produced. Statistical process control (SPC) is a procedure used to determine the probability of a deviation being a simple, random, unimportant variation or a sign of a problem in your production process that must be corrected.

• How to control operations

Controlling operations enables you to measure what is being accomplished in your business. Feedforward quality control applies to your company's inputs. Concurrent quality control involves monitoring your transformation processes. Feedback quality control relies on inspecting your outputs.

Questions for Review and Discussion

1. Discuss the elements of an operations management system. What would happen if the control system were not included? The feedback?

2. What is the difference between flexible production and mass customization?

3. Define *productivity*.

4. How can ergonomics be tied to productivity?

5. Explain the difference between forward and backward scheduling.

6. Define *six sigma* both technically and as used as a business standard.

7. What types of small businesses would benefit from having ISO 9000 certification?

8. Give examples of products that would be suited to each of the dispatching rules.

Questions for Critical Thinking

1. This chapter concentrated on both productivity and quality. In running your small manufacturing business, can you increase both, or aren't they mutually exclusive?

2. You have read about ISO 9000 certification in both Chapter 15 and this chapter. Bearing in mind that such certification is both time-consuming and expensive, describe what type of small business should pursue it.

Experience This . . .

Some things are just better understood by seeing them, rather than by reading about them or visiting them online. For this exercise, lobby your instructor for a class plant tour of a local manufacturing business. Write a two- to three-page paper describing its feedforward, concurrent, and feedback control systems.

What Would You Do?

Reread the chapter-opening vignette about Krispy Kreme. This vignette provides a lot of information about the company's products and processes. Find related articles about the company and visit its website (www.krispykreme.com).

Questions

1. Using Figure 18.1 and Table 18.1 as models, describe Krispy Kreme's inputs, transformation process, outputs, feedback, and control systems.

2. How would you apply six-sigma principles to making doughnuts?

CHAPTER CLOSING CASE

MADE IN THE U. S. OF A.

The problem: Magnetech wants to triple its workforce. But with manufacturing waning, skilled workers are very hard to find.

Don't tell John Martell that manufacturing is dying in the United States. His company, Magnetech Industrial Services, is thriving, with eight locations and revenue of $25 million. Founded in 2000, the company, based in South Bend, Indiana, specializes in making, servicing, and repairing industrial magnets and electric motors of all sizes. It's precisely the sort of old-school industrial production that has been headed overseas for years, and Martell is proud that he's been able to keep 170 skilled laborers gainfully employed and his company on the upswing in the face of tough economic conditions.

Martell, 49, frequently walks the 25,000-square-foot factory floor of his South Bend headquarters, where 22 of his workers, all of them members of the International Brotherhood of Electrical Workers, strip, test, and remanufacture engines for clients ranging from steel producers to city governments. But Martell began to recognize something worrisome—Magnetech, it was increasingly clear, had a labor problem. No, the workers were not restive, nor were pickets lining up outside. Instead, too many of his employees were gray-haired veterans of the industry. Eventually they'd be retiring. And it was less than

clear where he'd find the next generation of industrial workers to replace them.

Martell's fears were confirmed last spring when he and his management team did a quick, informal study of the workers at all eight locations—four in Indiana and others in West Virginia, Ohio, Wisconsin, and Alabama. The result: At least 80 percent of the employees were well into their forties. "We have an issue," Martell observed.

And it was a big one. Martell had major plans for Magnetech. While other U.S. manufacturers have been downsizing and moving operations offshore, Martell saw revenue hitting $100 million by 2007—a feat that would require tripling the company's workforce. The question was where he would find the next generation of workers. Back when American manufacturing was robust, most new workers came through union apprenticeship programs. After graduating from high school, mechanically inclined kids who weren't college bound were brought on by the industrial locals to learn alongside journeymen.

To say that things have changed since then would be a major understatement. Manufacturing job losses totaled 257,000 in 2003 and more than 3 million since 1998. A scant 13.5 percent of U.S. workers belong to a union, and many of the apprenticeship programs

---

have faded away. At the same time, technological innovations require more training than in the past. All of this put Magnetech in a Catch-22 that it didn't create and couldn't solve. "There is a Rust Belt mentality that says, 'It'll die,'" says Martell. "We want to show that there is a future in industrial manufacturing."

With no union apprentices to hire, Martell has found most of his new workers through word-of-mouth or newspaper ads. He also woos skilled laborers from competing firms. But those tactics are short-term fixes at best. Too often Magnetech has been relying on workers who may be skilled in one part of the job but do not understand the entire process—precisely what a strong apprenticeship program teaches.

All of which led Martell to ask himself, if Magnetech was going to sink resources into recruiting workers, wouldn't it make at least as much sense to invest in an in-house education program of its own? If the unions were no longer training apprentices, perhaps Magnetech would have to do it itself. What should he do?

SOURCE: From Patrick J. Sauer, "Case Study," *Inc.*, January 2005. Copyright © 2006 Mansueto Ventures LLC, publisher of Inc. Magazine, New York, NY 10017. Reprinted with permission.

Test Prepper

ACE self-test

college.hmco.com/pic/hatten4e

You've read the chapter, studied the key terms, and the exam is any day now. Think you're ready to ace it? Take this sample test to gauge your comprehension of chapter material. You can check your answers at the back of the book. Want more test questions? Visit the student website at college.hmco.com/pic/hatten4e and take the ACE and ACE+ quizzes for more practice.

Multiple Choice

1. Raw materials, employee skills, money, information, and energy are all that businesses use in production.
   a. inputs
   b. outputs
   c. outputs
   d. transformation process

2. Kerri is opening a microbrewery in which she will be making 20 barrels of low-carb, nonalcoholic brew at any given time. What type of process is Kerri using?
   a. analytic system
   b. synthetic system
   c. continuous process
   d. intermittent process

3. Jerry wants to keep productivity high in his job shop. He should look for ways to increase outputs while:
   a. keeping inputs constant
   b. decreasing inputs
   c. increasing costs
   d. decreasing revenue

4. Bruno's Bongo Shoppe sold $500,000 worth of bongos and used $150,000 of resources. What was Bruno's productivity ratio?
   a. 1.5
   b. 33.3
   c. 2.67
   d. 3.33

5. The use of statistical analysis to determine the probability of a variation in a product being a random occurrence or a continuous problem is known as:
   a. ISO 1400
   b. statistical process control
   c. ISO 9000
   d. benchmarked process control

True/False

1. T F The key word describing Krispy Kreme's success is "consistency"—the hallmark of operations management.

2. T F High-quality outputs can be produced from inferior inputs.

3. T F Only manufacturing businesses use the transformation process—not service businesses.

4. T F In the Reality Check titled "Stretching the Supply Chain," Shelving Concepts improved its business profitability by buying the manufacturer that it used to purchase shelving from.

5. T F A business monitors and corrects problems and deviations through control systems.

6. T F Small businesses operating printing shops and custom jewelry shops use an intermittent process.

7. T F Productivity can be measured only in terms of total outputs and total inputs.

8. T F A tolerance range consists of the boundaries that a manager sets for acceptable quality for a product.

9. T F Feedforward quality control involves the inspection of finished products.

10. T F Benchmarking involves comparison of anything that can be measured.

Complete Sample Business Plan

Cameo's Fine Jewelry & Timepieces
Business Plan

Table of Contents

Executive Summary 520
Concept History and Background 521
   The Product 521
   The Idea 522
   Experience 522
Goals and Objectives 522
Marketing Plan 523
   Consumers and Demand—Market Identification 523
   Total Number of Jewelry Customers 524
   Total Number of Cameo's Customers 524
   Competition 524
   Strengths and Weaknesses 525
   Geographic Market 526
   Pricing Policy 527
Legal Requirements 527
Form of Ownership 528
Organization, Management, and Staffing Plan 529
   Organization Chart 529
   Employee Requirements 529
Special Considerations 530
   Facility Needs 530
   Education and Training Needs 530
   Grand Opening Event 531
Appendix A: Industry Analysis 531
   Market Size 531
   Competitive Analysis 533
   Demographic Issues. 534
   Industry Trends 536
   Laws or Legal Issues 537
   Barriers to Entry 538
   Factors That Make the Industry Attractive 539
Works Cited 539

Executive Summary

Cameo's Fine Jewelry & Timepieces is designed to be the Western Slope of Colorado's finest, most exquisite jewelry store available. Located in the heart of Grand Junction, Cameo's will offer jewelry and watches from world-renowned artists and designers from countries known for their quality jewelry, such as Switzerland, Germany, Italy, and the United States.

Galleries will feature the work of Cartier, Rolex, Pippo Italia, Hearts on Fire, Paul Klecka, and many more. Many of the pieces found in these galleries are exquisite enough to number fewer than 100 in the world.

The experience our customers receive through our atmosphere and customer service will be as fine as the jewelry itself. Our retail format will take on the elements of both a gallery and a lounge. Saltwater fish tanks will enhance the environment, and a wine and cocktail bar will be available to our customers. The sales staff and on-duty gemologist will be able to assist in finding that perfect piece of jewelry, and if it's not available, they will be able to order it or create a custom piece. Socials will invite the community to come enjoy the galleries and become more educated about the different qualities of jewelry.

Our first social event will be held to celebrate our grand opening. This event will encourage community members to come see the jewelry, store, and meet the staff. Two Rivers Winery will also take part by offering wine and hors d'oeuvres. Our grand opening will immediately define Cameo's as Grand Junction's finest jewelry store.

Grand Junction serves as an ideal location. As the largest city on the Western Slope of Colorado, it acts as a retail hub for the surrounding communities. Since Cameo's will be the only jewelry store in this area that offers this level of quality, it will draw customers from a four-county region including Mesa, Garfield, Delta, and Montrose counties.

These four counties, grown to 2006 figures, have a total population of 254,666. After taking into account age, percent of population who purchase jewelry, yearly weddings, and salary, there are 101,096 jewelry consumers within this geographic market. My goal is to obtain a 1 percent market share during the first year of business, which would provide 1,011 customers.

With this market penetration, and an average jewelry purchase of $2,000, Cameo's would sell $2,022,000 worth of products in the first fiscal year. The cash position at the end of the first fiscal year will equal $460,052, making this a very attractive and profitable venture to pursue.

Cameo's defining strengths will be that of location and facility as well as inventory. Besides being located in Grand Junction, Cameo's will be housed in a 6,850-square-foot renovated building on 4th and Main. Being downtown means that Cameo's will fall under the guidance of the Downtown Partnership. The purpose of the Downtown Partnership is to oversee the promotion of the downtown area and provide community-benefiting events. Some events held downtown include an October fest, a farmer's market, parade of lights, and an art hop.

Cameo's exclusive inventory will also set it apart from other jewelry stores. Many pieces in inventory will be rare or hard to find and certainly the only ones available within this geographic market. I will also carry brands such as Cartier, which will make me the only retailer of this product in western Colorado.

There are several things that make the jewelry industry as a whole very attractive, including strong growth, a stable position, and new product creation, innovation, and trends. Currently the jewelry industry is growing annually at a rate of 9 percent, allowing for more retail outlets in one geographic region.

Jewelry is very stable because it is never going away nor is it a fad item. Jewelry is often considered a necessity in times of marriage and anniversary, and is often used as a gift. There are many new jewelry products entering the market all the time that are technologically, fashion, and trend driven, which creates an increase in demand.

My passion for watches, and the jewelry industry, combined with previous work experience will enable me to make this business a success. Previous employment has provided me with experience in the necessary functions of this business including management, marketing, event planning, and financials.

My skills in marketing and event planning will prove most beneficial to the startup of this business. The product costs in this industry are very high, and general knowledge is low; therefore, providing information and educating the consumer is crucial. Special events will draw consumers into the store in order to show them what it has to offer.

As I had previously mentioned, I have a love for watches and have made collecting them a hobby of mine. Since I am already interested in watches, I have developed a strong knowledge of the products, brands, and industry.

Due to my experiences and interests, I will be able to satisfy this niche market by offering a fine product at a quality location. With this plan, financial outlook, and market growth, I know I will be able to maximize profits and turn this venture into a success.

Concept History and Background

The Product

Cameo's Fine Jewelry & Timepieces is going to sell very fine jewelry and watches crafted by world-renowned artists and designers from Switzerland, Germany, Italy, and the United States. This product line will include Swiss and Italian-made watches from Cartier, Breitling, Rolex, Tag Heuer, Patek Phillipe, Pippo Italia, Montblanc, and Movado. Jewelry collections, which will also include wedding sets, will feature Aaron Basha, Hearts on Fire, Paul Klecka, Steven Kretchmer, and Yvel.

The three-diamond ring and tension-set diamonds will focus on modern style, while the Santos De Cartier will represent the first wristwatch created in 1904. Hearts on Fire diamonds are the world's most perfectly cut diamonds, which allows them to reflect and retract light like no other. Galleries will feature rare and exotic pieces, many of them numbering fewer than 100 in the world.

The service customers receive will be as extraordinary as the jewelry itself. Our sales staff will meet customer's needs through customization, special orders, and education. Our on-duty gemologist will be available to service, repair, educate, and clean customer's jewelry and watches. The atmosphere in the store will be that of a fine gallery mixing the elements of a lounge. A wine and cocktail bar will be available to serious and returning customers. Organized socials will invite the community to come and see the galleries as well as provide education about the different qualities of jewelry.

Currently there is no comparable product on the Western Slope of Colorado, and the service provided will far outdo any other jewelry store. The knowledge base of the staff will also far exceed what is currently available.

The Idea

The idea to start a fine jewelry store in Grand Junction, Colorado, came after I had to go elsewhere to find the engagement ring I wanted. When I finally found the ring, it came from a very fine jewelry store that is like nothing the Grand Valley has to offer. The environment, sales staff, and product in this store were all very exquisite, offering only the finest jewelry and watches.

When I returned to Grand Junction, I realized the closest place to find jewelry like this is either in Aspen or Vail, about a two-hour drive away. Grand Junction is already a shopping destination for the Western Slope, and I saw a need for a finer jewelry store. The Grand Valley is a fast-growing community and also has a high percentage of retired couples. Because of this, I believe the market is strong enough to support such a store.

I also have a passion for fine timepieces and how they work, which is why I have a desire to start a jewelry store. Part of this venture would fulfill a hobby of mine in watch collecting.

Experience

As I mentioned previously, watch collecting is a hobby of mine; therefore, I already have a knowledge base regarding the products and brands.

Experience I have gathered through previous employment includes management, marketing, event planning, and financials.

My experience in marketing will be especially crucial in this new business because of the high product cost and general lack of knowledge for this industry. Education about diamonds and watches will prove critical in the early stages of customer development. Special events will also need to be organized in order to draw customers into the store and discover what it has to offer.

Management is another key factor in this new business, since I will be overseeing the day-to-day operations as well as human resources.

Goals and Objectives

Short-Term (First Year)

- To establish a customer base of 1,100
- To have three in-store promotional events to create excitement, educate the consumer, and increase customer base
- To establish a qualified team of employees
- To develop strong relationships with suppliers, my banker, accountant, and lawyer

- To establish a reputation of being Grand Junction's finest, most exclusive jewelry store

Long-Term

- To increase my customer base by 10 percent annually
- To raise additional capital to increase the product line
- To pay off small business loans
- To increase marketing to attract new customers
- To become the number one jewelry store in Grand Junction by sales

Marketing Plan

Consumers and Demand—Market Identification

The main market that is available to support Cameo's Fine Jewelry & Timepieces encompasses a four-county region that surrounds the business itself. The business is located in Grand Junction, Colorado, which resides within Mesa County. Grand Junction is the largest city on the Western Slope of Colorado, which makes it a retail hub for the surrounding communities. Being the finest jewelry store on the Western Slope, Cameo's will mainly draw from the following communities: Mesa County, Garfield County, Delta County, and Montrose County. The total population of these four counties is 221,312, with an average growth rate of 9.1 percent.

The market for a jewelry store is broken into several segments that include gender and age with a focus on income and marital status. In the four-county region men make up 49.9 percent of the population and women 51 percent. The age category of 25–44 includes 27.3 percent, and the age category of 45+ includes 39 percent. The average age is 38. Among the men, 58.3 percent are married; among the women, 54.3 percent are married. The median household income is $37,725, with a per capita income of $18,592.

Cameo's male customers are likely to purchase watches and gifts of anniversary, and wedding sets. Watches are one of the few items at Cameo's that will be intended for the man himself. The men that purchase these high-end watches will include collectors/enthusiasts and those with an annual salary of $75,000 or more. Men are likely to purchase jewelry as a gift for a woman, especially a wife, which includes jewelry for the anniversary or another holiday/birthday. The last type of purchase consists of wedding sets or engagement rings, and will be made by the man making a proposal.

Female customers are more likely to make jewelry purchases for themselves, or for a wedding. Women will buy any range of jewelry for themselves, and will purchase men's wedding bands for their fiancés. The majority of women buying jewelry for themselves will also have an annual salary of $75,000 or more.

People in the age group of 25–44 are most likely to make a purchase for a wedding that would include an engagement ring, wedding band, or set. The median age of marriage in the United States is 27, and the average engagement ring sells for $2,000. Gifts in this age category would be intended primarily for an anniversary. People in the 45+ age category would make more purchases for themselves and for gifts.

This market has been chosen based on the reasons for jewelry purchases as well as income levels. Being an exclusive jewelry store, offering a premium product, it will attract customers who are among the wealthiest in the community. I have chosen Grand Junction, and the four-county region, to locate my business because there is no other jewelry store in the area that offers this level of quality, therefore allowing me to capture this niche market.

Total Number of Jewelry Customers

The total population in Cameo's geographic market when grown to 2006 numbers is 254,666. The total population 25 years of age and older is 168,844. Of this, 84,253 are males and 86,110 are females. In 2004, 58 percent of the American population had made a jewelry purchase within the previous six months. By this standard, the four-county region has 97,929 jewelry consumers.

There are 18,788 single men and 14,294 single women. On average, 1 percent of a city's total population will wed each year, equating to 2,547 weddings per year in this market. In Grand Junction, there are 620 individuals with a mean annual salary that exceeds $75,000.

Using these figures, there are 101,096 jewelry consumers within Cameo's geographic market.

Total Number of Cameo's Customers

For the first year of business, as Cameo's establishes a reputation and gains market share, I believe it can sustain a 1 percent share. A 1 percent share of the market would provide 1,011 customers for the first year of business.

Competition

Analysis of the Competition				
Competitors	Price	Location	Facility	Direct (D) or Indirect (I)
Page-Parsons Jewelers	High	Same	Worse	D
Brink's Fine Jewelry	High	Same	Worse	D
Zales Jewelers	Middle	Better	Worse	D
Kay Jewelers	Middle	Better	Worse	D
Sam's Club	Middle/High	Better	Worse	I
Mesa Jewelers	Middle	Better	Worse	D
House of Diamonds	Middle	Worse	Worse	D
Gordon's Jewelry	Middle	Better	Worse	D
Samuels Jewelers	Middle	Better	Worse	D
Big J Jewelry & Loan	Low	Same	Worse	I

Failed Jewelry Stores			
Name	**Location**	**Reason for Failure**	**Comments**
Anker Scott Jewelry Fine Jewelry Liquidators	Mesa Mall moved to 729 North Ave		Owner: Scott Anker 1970–2004
Bush Jewelry	2441 Belford Ave		
Cook L Jewelry Inc.	418 Main Street		
A Touch of Gold	435 Main Street		
Randall's Custom Jewelry	158 N Mesa Ave		
Park Lane Fashion Jewelry			
Anderson Jewelry	1127 North Ave		
Schubach Jewelers	Mesa Mall		
Otero Jewelers	Mesa Mall		
Dale Smith Jewelry	1150 N. 25th suite B		
Golden Era Jewelry	635 Main Street		
Peyton Jewelers	440 Main Street		

Trends: Most failed jewelry stores are located in one of three areas: North Avenue, Mesa Mall, or Main Street.

Strengths and Weaknesses

Strengths

1. Location—Cameo's Fine Jewelry & Timepieces will be located in the heart of downtown Grand Junction on Main Street. Downtown Grand Junction offers shopping, restaurants, art and sculptures on the boardwalk, a beautiful tree-lined street, fairs, and events. Some events offered downtown include an October fest, a farmer's market, parade of lights, and an art hop.

   The downtown area is overseen by the Downtown Partnership, which consists of a partnership between the Downtown Association, the Downtown Development Authority, and the City of Grand Junction. The purpose of the Downtown Partnership is to oversee the promotion of the downtown area and provide community-benefiting events. The Downtown Partnership also offers gift cards that are accepted at all the downtown retail outlets.

   The downtown area is a place that appeals to both locals and tourists. The large amount of walking traffic will make my business visible and easily accessible. This location will cater to many "walk-ins."

2. Facility—My chosen facility is a newly renovated building on 4th and Main. The building has been beautifully renovated and offers wonderful street appeal. The space I will be purchasing sits on the corner of the street,

making it visible on two sides. There is the main-street level as well as a basement. At 6,850 square feet, this facility will allow me to have an extensive inventory.

I also have the benefit of managing the interior design. Since it is a new building, I can incorporate a modern theme into the interior, which will make it the finest jewelry store in Grand Junction by appearance.

3. Price—Offering only high-quality jewelry will mean that my store fits into a high-price category. There are fewer high-priced jewelry stores in Grand Junction than there are middle- to low-priced. This means that consumers looking for an exclusive piece are very limited as to where they can go.

4. Inventory—My inventory will consist of very fine jewelry and timepieces, many of which are very hard to find. One product I will offer is the Cartier Timepiece, which will make my store the only one in Mesa County offering this brand. This will hold true for the majority of my brands.

My collection will truly set my store apart from any other jewelry store in the Grand Valley and will certainly differentiate my store from those found in the mall.

Weaknesses

1. Competitors—There are already several jewelry stores located in Grand Junction that have established rapport with the community and have a loyal customer base. These stores include other jewelry stores, discount stores, mass merchandisers, and club stores. My business will be "the new guy in town" and will certainly face pressure from the competition.

I will overcome this weakness through promotion, publicity, and exclusivity. I will promote my business as being the finest jewelry store in Grand Junction as well as having products that aren't offered at any other local jewelry store. I will also become involved in community events in order to build relationships and gain trust among the community members.

2. Lack of reputation—Since I will be starting a new business with no affiliation to a large chain, I will lack a reputation at the start of the business. Consumers like going to a store they know and trust, especially when it comes to big-ticket items. Other jewelry stores might be known for their product line, knowledge base, or guarantees.

In order to overcome this weakness, I will need to be very particular about forming the reputation that I desire and can uphold throughout the life of the business. I need to prove to customers that I can be trusted, and if they have any problems with a product, I will take care of them. In order to build a reputation, I will need to hire employees that can adopt the guiding principles of the business, and I need to train them on those principles.

Geographic Market

Cameo's Fine Jewelry & Timepieces will be the exclusive jewelry store for the Western Slope of Colorado; therefore, it will draw from a large geographic area.

The majority of the consumers will come from a four-county region including Mesa County (the county of the business location), Garfield County, Delta County, and Montrose County. These four counties have a total combined population of 221,312, and an annual growth rate averaging 9.1 percent.

Pricing Policy

My pricing policy will implement several different pricing strategies in order to maximize profits and the consumer's perception of value. At the opening and continuing for the first two weeks of business, I will use a form of market-penetration pricing. Instead of discounting all items in the store; however, I will have a "name your price" event in conjunction with my grand opening. During this event, all items will be priced at their normal retail value, but consumers will be given the power to name their price. The sales staff will have authority to bargain with customers in order to give them a desired price, while still making a profit. This technique will create excitement and customer interaction far better than just simply discounting the items from the start.

After two weeks of business, the products' normal retail prices will be implemented based on status quo pricing of local competitors. Negotiating prices will still be allowed but on a very limited basis. In order to be eligible to talk down a price, the customer must be buying multiple items, or be a frequent shopper who makes big-ticket purchases. The sales staff will be trained to be very conservative in discounting prices.

Discounted items will be available only once a year at an annual sales event. This most likely will take form as an Anniversary Sale. This yearly sale will be designed to renew excitement about the store as well as clean out old inventory. Not all items will be discounted; rather, only the items that aren't selling and a few loss leaders. An annual sales promotion will give consumers something to look forward to, as well as generate hype.

The most influential price leaders in my geographic region would be Page-Parsons Jewelers and Sam's Club. Page-Parsons offers a similar product as my store and has been in business for many years. Consumers will certainly compare my product and prices to those of Page-Parsons. Sam's Club is a member-only warehouse that offers fine jewelry at competitive prices. Sam's Club lacks customer support, but offers a good price.

The information in this marketing plan was derived from Appendix A: Industry Analysis.

Legal Requirements

Employer/Employee Regulations
1. Fair Labor Standards Act (FLSA)
2. Equal Pay Act (EPA)
3. Immigration Reform and Control Act (IRCA)
4. Federal Unemployment Tax Act (FUTA)
5. Occupational Safety & Health Administration Act (OSHA)
6. Title VII Civil Rights Act

7. Americans with Disabilities Act (ADA)

8. Pregnancy Discrimination Act

9. Age Discrimination in Employment Act (ADEA)

10. Older Worker Benefit Protection Act (OWBPA)

11. Regulatory Flexibility Act (RFA)

12. Small Business Regulatory Enforcement Fairness Act of 1996 (SBREFA)

13. Paperwork Reduction Act of 1980

14. Small Business Paperwork Relief Act of 2002

15. Consumer Protection Laws

16. Social Security

17. Federal Insurance Contributions Act (FICA)

18. Consolidated Omnibus Budget Reconciliation Act of 1985 (COBRA)

19. Employee Retirement Income Security Act (ERISA)

Insurance
Unemployment Insurance

1. Worker's Compensation

2. Commercial Automobile Insurance

3. General Business Liability

4. Property Insurance

5. Errors and Omission/Professional Liability Insurance

Legal Forms

1. SS-4 Federal employer identification number (FEIN)

2. CR100 The Colorado Business Registration Form

3. CR0100 Retail Sales Tax License

4. Immigration and Naturalization Services I-9

5. W-4 Employee's Withholding Allowance Certificate

6. W-2 Wage and Tax Statement

7. Form 8109 Wage Withholding and Social Security/Medicare Taxes

8. Form 941 Total wages paid, taxes withheld and due, and taxes deposited

9. DRP 1098 Colorado Income Tax Withholding Tables

10. Form 940 Total Unemployment Tax Liability

11. Form UITR-1 Unemployment Insurance Tax Report

12. UITR-1(a) Unemployment Insurance Report of Workers Wages

Form of Ownership

The form of ownership I am going to use for this business is a limited liability company (LLC). The reason I am choosing this form of ownership is because it limits owner liability, and it avoids double taxation.

If, after establishing a successful track record, I want to expand in the future, I could incorporate my business in order to raise additional capital.

Organization, Management, and Staffing Plan

Organization Chart

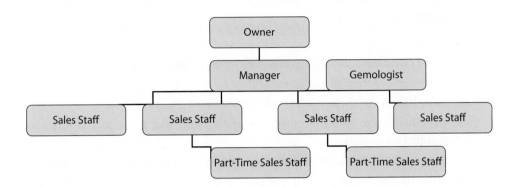

Employee Requirements

There are three types of employees at Cameo's, which include a manager, a gemologist, and a sales staff. Each job will have its own set of expectations, responsibilities, and duties. Following is a job description for each type of employee.

Manager

1. Act as a vital link between owner and sales staff
2. Assist the owner in duties such as inventory, promotions, and community relations
3. Solve problems as they arise in a professional and efficient manner
4. Relay important product information/news to the sales staff
5. Create and maintain the sales staff schedule
6. Assist the sales staff as needed
7. Must be able to use a point of sale system and take payments in order to complete a transaction
8. Responsible for data input and management of a customer database system
9. Update the sales staff on new policies, procedures, and events
10. Must follow all policies and procedures as outlined in the employee handbook

Gemologist

1. Work with the sales staff and/or customer to clean and repair jewelry
2. Responsible for creating accurate estimates on jewelry repair
3. Work with the sales staff and/or customer to create custom jewelry
4. Must be a certified jeweler, and be able to create accurate appraisals

5. Must be able to use a point-of-sale system and take payments in order to complete a transaction
6. Responsible for data input and management of a customer database system
7. Must have a strong knowledge of jewelry and the industry
8. Must follow all policies and procedures as outlined in the employee handbook

Sales Staff

1. Assist customers in finding the jewelry that is right for them
2. Must demonstrate strong sales skills
3. Must have a strong knowledge of jewelry and the industry
4. Must be able to use a point-of-sale system and take payments in order to complete a transaction
5. Responsible for data input and management of a customer database system
6. Must be able to work with the gemologist in placing custom orders and repairs
7. Must have exceptional customer service skills in the sense of creating and maintaining relationships
8. Must follow up on every sale with a letter or phone call
9. Must be able to negotiate with customers
10. Must follow all policies and procedures as outlined in the employee handbook

Special Considerations

Facility Needs

The facility I have chosen to locate Cameo's is in downtown Grand Junction on the northwest corner of 4th and Main. This space is part of a multi-unit building that has both office/retail space as well as residential units. I will be leasing suite number 104 from Reed Building Development, LLC, for $11.00 per square foot annually with triple net. Suite 104 is a corner unit, making it visible from both 4th and Main. This lease will include the main-level floor plus a basement. The main level has 4,550 square feet, and the basement has 2,300 square feet, for a total of 6,850 square feet.

In order to make this facility suitable for the needs of a jewelry store, there will have to be significant remodeling. Plans for the remodel include paint, lighting, flooring, a security system, offices, bathroom, and fish tanks. I will also need to purchase and install display cases, furniture, a complimentary bar, and artwork.

For signage, I will need two exterior signs (one on each side of the building), window decals, and interior signage. The window decals and interior signs will mainly promote the brands of jewelry that are in inventory.

Education and Training Needs

All staff members will be required to attend training, which will be held the week prior to opening. I will work closely with the manager prior to sales staff training, so that he or she will be able to assist in the training process as well. Training will consist of the fundamental job duties as well as the vision for the company and its atmosphere.

Each staff member will receive a copy of the policies and procedures handbook, which will have all the expectations of employment as well as procedures for fulfilling the job duties. Throughout training, I will use role playing between team members in order for the staff to practice each step of their required duties.

A focus on the vision of the company, and the desired reputation, will be stressed to the employees during training. In order to establish and maintain a specific reputation, all team members must work together towards that goal.

Grand Opening Event

Cameo's grand opening event will take place on Saturday, August 5, 2006 from 3–9 pm. The purpose of the event will be to create a social atmosphere in which community members can come see the store, its inventory, and meet our staff.

At the event, we will implement a "name your own price" sales strategy. Customers will have the opportunity to negotiate prices with our sales staff, in order to obtain a reasonable discount. We won't use pressure to make sales at this event; rather, our real intention is to create awareness within the community. The "name your own price event" will continue for two weeks following our grand opening event.

Two Rivers Winery will also be at the event, offering wine and hors d'oeuvres. Once again, this event will be designed to meet the community and let them know that we want to be part of the community; not just another business.

Advertising for this event will include sending postcards (see promotional piece) to homes with a value of $250,000 or greater, a banner that spans across Main Street in front of the store, as well as window displays. On the day of the event we will use balloons and streamers inside and outside the store to gain attention.

Appendix A: Industry Analysis

The NAICS definition for the "specialty retail" category of jewelry stores (NAICS 44831) is as follows: "This industry comprises establishments primarily engaged in retailing one or more of the following items: (1) new jewelry (except costume jewelry); (2) new sterling and plated silverware; and (3) new watches and clocks. Also included are establishments retailing these new products in combination with lapidary work and/or repair services."

Market Size

The U.S. retail jewelry industry is a rapidly growing one and has recently proven resilience during economic downturns. In 2003–2004 this industry had revenues of $27,310 million with 16,750 enterprises, and an average annual revenue increase of 9 percent.

The Jewelry Consumer Opinion Council (JCOC) conducted a survey in May of 2004. The council polled Americans, asking them about their custom jewelry purchases and interests. The survey found that 58 percent of Americans have purchased jewelry in the last six months, and 37.6 percent plan on making a jewelry purchase in the next six months. Of these consumers, 43.4 percent own at least one piece of one-of-a-kind jewelry.

Gold jewelry sales hit $16.3 billion in 2003, which is an increase of 2.5 percent from 2002. The year of 2003 also marked the thirteenth consecutive year of gold sales increases. Gold bracelets contributed an increase in dollar sales volume of 8.2 percent and 6.8 percent in unit volume. Gold earrings jumped 2.6 percent in sales volume and 6.6 percent in unit sales.

During the economic downturn in 2001, diamond jewelry retail sales showed incredible resilience, declining only 1 percent from 2000 (the year of 2000 had a market increase of 12 percent). This was the first time in over a decade that the overall diamond jewelry market experienced a drop in sales on an annual basis. In the past decade, the diamond jewelry market doubled, reaching $26.1 billion in 2001 retail sales.

The decline in 2001 was not due to consumers refraining from purchasing a diamond, but rather was influenced by consumers watching their spending. This is proved by a volume increase of 2 percent in 2001 while the average ticket price declined 3 percent. This goes to show that although the United States was in a time of economic downturn, consumers still were willing to pay for the heartfelt gift of a diamond. In fact, during 2000–2001, 43 percent of the adult population, 85 million in all, bought jewelry.

Diamond engagement rings play a huge role in the market size for diamonds. In 1999, 1.66 million pieces were sold, equating to revenues of $3.318 billion. While the number of pieces sold remained about the same, there was an 11 percent increase in value from 1997. The average diamond engagement ring sold for about $2,000 compared with $1,804 in 1997. In 2001, 84 percent of all U.S. brides acquired a diamond engagement ring, which drove retail sales 5 percent higher than in 2000. Each year an average of 2.3 million couples are married in the United States.

The table below represents the average value of diamond engagement rings for first-time marriages by age, and the increase from 1997 to 1999.

Age Group	1999	1997	Percentage Increase
18–24	NA	NA	0%
25–34	$2,983	$2,774	7%
35+	$3,312	$2,291	36%

For second marriages the bride received a ring with an average value substantially less than that received by first-time brides. Brides of 18 to 24 years old received a ring averaging $1,953. For those in the 25–34 age category, ring value averaged $2,128, and for those in the 35+ category, it averaged $2,028. The average age of a U.S. bride is 25.3 and 26.9 for the groom.

The table below represents the diamond cut and percentage sold for engagement rings.

Diamond Cut	Percentage Sold
Round Brilliants	57%
Marquises	26%
Emeralds/Squares	8%
Pear Shapes	4%
Heart Shapes	3%
Ovals	2%

Swiss watch exports fell by 4.4 percent globally in 2003; however, Swiss watch exports to the United States gained 1.1 percent. Total watch exports dropped 8.4 percent or by 2.2 million pieces globally in 2003. The total number of exported watches in 2003 was 24.6 million.

The jewelry industry has a huge market, as shown by eBay, which considers its jewelry and watch category to be a top-2 category within its online auction house, having transactions totaling $1.6 billion in the third quarter of 2005.

Competitive Analysis

A competitive analysis based on the Five Forces Model of Competition follows:

Intensity of Rivalry Among Existing Competitors—Moderate

1. *Buyer costs to switch brands is low (increases rivalry).* Switching from one brand to another has little cost to the consumer, and is greatly affected by personal preference.

2. *Competitors implement strong buyer incentives (increase rivalry).* Many competitors use discounts, gifts, and attractive financing options to lure in buyers. This greatly increases rivalry as it reduces profit margins.

3. *Advertisement is strong (increases rivalry).* Advertising campaigns are strong among the large players, which creates the perception that the smaller jewelers don't exist.

4. *Buyer demand is growing rapidly (reduces rivalry).* The jewelry industry is growing rapidly at an annual revenue growth rate of 9 percent (2003–2004). This allows a greater number of competitors to survive in the same market.

5. *High product differentiation and customer loyalty (reduces rivalry).* The jewelry industry has a very wide range of products. Each competitor carries slightly different pieces at different price levels. Customization is also very common in the jewelry industry. Customers are generally loyal to the jewelry store that offers pieces to match their style and price range, as well as exceptional customer service.

Threat of Entry by New Competitors—Strong

1. *Existing industry members are increasing their market size (increases threat).* The large industry members are expanding rapidly and looking for ways to enter new geographic markets.

2. *Newcomers can expect to earn attractive profits (increases threat).* The jewelry industry has high profit margins, as well as a proven track record of remaining financially stable. Mass merchandisers have also found jewelry to be very profitable, therefore increasing their supply.

3. *Buyer demand is growing rapidly (increases threat).* Demand for jewelry continues to increase every year.

4. *Entry barriers are high (reduces threat).* Inventory and location can be very costly for a new jewelry store, which may reduce entrants into the industry.

Pressure from Substitute Products—Fierce

1. *Good substitutes are readily available and emerging (increases pressure).* Synthetic diamonds are gaining in popularity with technological advances that improve clarity. There are many metal-type options available, including yellow gold, white gold, titanium, steel, and platinum.

2. *Substitutes are attractively priced (increases pressure).* Costume jewelry, or "fakes," are becoming more attractive and of a higher quality. These pieces are considerably less expensive than fine jewelry. Many watchmakers are imitating Swiss design while offering their timepieces for a fraction of the cost.

Bargaining Power of Suppliers—Strong

1. *Small number of suppliers (increases power).* The diamond market is controlled by an overseas supplier that limits the quantity supplied.

2. *Brand names are very valuable (increases power).* For example, there is only one producer of official Rolex Watches.

3. *Industry members account for a big fraction of suppliers' total sales (reduces power).* The suppliers rarely sell directly to the end consumer; therefore, they depend on retail outlets to purchase and sell their product.

4. *Seller/supplier relationships are advantageous (reduces power).* The act of working together between the supplier and seller provides for an improved market on both ends.

Bargaining Power of Buyers—Weak

1. *Brand reputation is very important (reduces power).* Buyers are willing to pay for a particular brand like Rolex or Cartier.

2. *Particular suppliers offer a product that has exceptional quality (reduces power).* Swiss watches or Italian jewelry offer unmatched quality and excellence that can solicit premium prices.

Demographic Issues

These demographics will focus on the geographic market in which the majority of my target population resides. The geographic market includes four counties in Western Colorado: Mesa County (where the business is physically located), Garfield County, Delta County, and Montrose County.

Demographics 2000 Census	Mesa	Garfield	Delta	Montrose	Totals/ Averages
Total Population	116,255	43,791	27,834	33,432	221,312
Population growth to 2004	8.9%	10.8%	7%	9.7%	9.1%
Percentage of Males	49%	51.4%	50.2%	49.2%	49.9%
Percentage of Females	51%	48.6%	49.8%	50.8%	51%
Percent of ages 16–24	14%	13.7%	10.8%	12.2%	12.7%
Percent of ages 25–44	26.7%	33%	23.6%	25.8%	27.3%
Percent of ages 45–64	23.7%	22.1%	26.5%	25%	24.3%
Percent of ages 65+	15.2%	8.8%	19.7%	15.2%	14.7%
Average age (years)	38.05	34.34	41.32	38.31	38
Percent high school grads	30.3%	26.9%	34%	33.4%	31.2%
Percent some college/AA	32.7%	34.6%	28.5%	28.6%	31.1%
Percent bachelor's degree	14.6%	17.6%	12.5%	13.3%	14.5%
Percent graduate degree	7.3%	6.2%	5.1%	5.4%	6%
Median household income	$35,864	$47,016	$32,785	$35,234	$37,725
Per Capita Income	$18,715	$21,341	$17,152	$17,158	$18,592
Male, never married	24.8%	25.1%	17.5%	21.9%	22.3%
Male, married	58.3%	55.4%	60.9%	60.2%	58.7%
Male, divorced	10%	11.7%	10.6%	10.6%	10.7%
Female, never married	19%	19.6%	12.7%	15.1%	16.6%
Female, married	54.3%	56.8%	60%	57.6%	57.2%
Female, divorced	12.8%	14.1%	12.3%	13%	13.1%
Unemployment rate, 2004	5.1%	4.4%	5.2%	5.1%	5%

*2000 Census, U.S. Census Bureau

Below is a table of occupations in Grand Junction, Colo. that have a mean annual salary of $75,000 or greater.

Mean Annual Salary; Grand Junction, CO		
Occupation Title	Number Employed	Mean Annual Salary
Computer Software Engineers	60	$80,990
Chief Executives	180	$90,900
Lawyers	240	$86,630

Occupation Title	Number Employed	Mean Annual Salary
Dentists	40	$123,370
Family and General Practitioners	60	$100,750
Surgeons	40	$144,510
Total/Average	620	$104,525

2001, U.S. Bureau of Labor Statistics

Industry Trends

Contributing to the growth in the jewelry industry is the increased availability of jewelry at the retail level. Jewelry has become an affordable luxury for men and women and a wonderful gift available at all price ranges. Pam Danziger, president of Unity Marketing, says, "The jewelry market is becoming more democratic in the past decade as good-quality and high-design jewelry is now available at a much wider range of retailers. After all, Wal-Mart Stores, with over $2 billion in jewelry sales in 2000, is now the nation's largest jewelry retailer."

Women have a significantly higher purchase incidence of jewelry than men: 48 percent compared to 36 percent. Men do, however, spend significantly more than women on their jewelry purchases, and most purchases by men are for gifts. Purchase incidence is also highest among young adults (18–24) and declines with age.

Jewelry stores are still the preferred choice for fine jewelry, but costume-jewelry buyers are more likely to go to discount stores or mass merchandisers. Also, the age group of 18–34 is more likely to make a jewelry purchase through a mass merchandiser than the older age groups.

A marketing trend developed by the World Gold Council (WGC) and Jewelry.com is intended to drive more sales by coining "May Is Gold Month." This promotion will use sales, events, advertisements, and sweepstakes to increase sales. These events will take place at jewelry retailers across the country during May.

Diamond jewelry continues to be a very popular item during the Christmas holiday, resulting in increases of 4 percent in value and 7 percent in volume. The Christmas season accounts for 28 percent of all women's diamond jewelry sold in 2001 and 22 percent of sales.

In 2001 a demand for jewelry showcasing larger stones was increasing rapidly. The Three-Stone Diamond Anniversary Ring, introduced in early 2000, was designed to signify a couple's past, present, and future. The Three-Stone Ring quickly established itself as a classic "must have" piece, and it experienced a growth rate in pieces sold of 28 percent. Three-Stone Rings now account for one out of every ten diamond-only ring purchases in the United States.

In response to this demand, other, similar jewelry styles became available, including the Three-Stone Diamond Necklace and the Three-Stone Diamond Earrings. This diamond-jewelry category sustained growth rates of 34 percent in volume.

Listed below are the top picks of the nation's top fashion editors at the Couture Jewellery Collection and Conference. These choices reflect the latest trends and styles in the jewelry industry.

- Dramatic yet tailored designs, not daring, but definitely eye-catching;
- Yellow gold returns with a rush: glamorous designs with warm-colored gems;
- Estate jewelry influences, such as lavalieres, filigree, woven chain;
- Bold rings with hefty colored gemstones;
- Textures, satin finishes, meshy flexible constructions;
- Diamond-intensive brooches, hearts, stars, butterflies, lots of diamond pave;
- The white heat of platinum, sometimes with diamonds, sometimes alone;
- Resurgence of coral and turquoise, sometimes with pearls;
- New necklace shapes: lariats, longer lengths and dramatic bibs;
- Color in all forms: colored gemstones, colored gold, pastel-toned pearls;
- Fancy-cut gemstones and briolettes;
- Wrist-wrapping bracelets such as bangles, cuffs, and coils;
- Longer and more dramatic earrings, less demure, more drama;
- Versatility: stackable, reversible and convertible designs.

Laws or Legal Issues

In the jewelry industry, as in any nonhazardous retail industry, there are several legal regulations that must be followed in order to run a lawful entity. Below is an extensive list of employer/employee regulations, insurance requirements, and legal forms that must be filed by the employer.

Employer/Employee Regulations

1. Fair Labor Standards Act (FLSA)
2. Equal Pay Act (EPA)
3. Immigration Reform and Control Act (IRCA)
4. Federal Unemployment Tax Act (FUTA)
5. Occupational Safety & Health Administration Act (OSHA)
6. Title VII Civil Rights Act
7. Americans with Disabilities Act (ADA)
8. Pregnancy Discrimination Act
9. Age Discrimination in Employment Act (ADEA)
10. Older Worker Benefit Protection Act (OWBPA)
11. Regulatory Flexibility Act (RFA)
12. Small Business Regulatory Enforcement Fairness Act of 1996 (SBREFA)
13. Paperwork Reduction Act of 1980
14. Small Business Paperwork Relief Act of 2002
15. Consumer Protection Laws
16. Social Security
17. Federal Insurance Contributions Act (FICA)
18. Consolidated Omnibus Budget Reconciliation Act of 1985 (COBRA)
19. Employee Retirement Income Security Act (ERISA)

Insurance

1. Unemployment Insurance
2. Worker's Compensation
3. Commercial Automobile Insurance
4. General Business Liability
5. Property Insurance
6. Errors and Omission/Professional Liability Insurance

Legal Forms

1. SS-4 Federal employer identification number (FEIN)
2. CR100 The Colorado Business Registration Form
3. CR0100 Retail Sales Tax License
4. Immigration and Naturalization Services I-9
5. W-4 Employee's Withholding Allowance Certificate
6. W-2 Wage and Tax Statement
7. Form 8109 Wage Withholding and Social Security/Medicare Taxes
8. Form 941 Total wages paid, taxes withheld and due, and taxes deposited
9. DRP 1098 Colorado Income Tax Withholding Tables
10. Form 940 Total Unemployment Tax Liability
11. Form UITR-1 Unemployment Insurance Tax Report
12. UITR-1(a) Unemployment Insurance Report of Workers Wages

Barriers to Entry

There are three main barriers to entry in the jewelry industry: strong competition, high startup costs, and finding knowledgeable/qualified employees.

There is already an abundance of jewelry stores, consisting of retail jewelry, mass merchandisers, discount stores, and club stores. With all of these outlets to purchase jewelry from, the market is very close to saturation. These competitors have also already established a clientele base.

The high startup costs in the jewelry industry include inventory, location of the business, and the interior design/display. Inventory for a fine jewelry store is very expensive and may also sit, unsold, for an extended period of time.

The physical location of the business is also expensive, especially for the retail industry. A jewelry store needs to have ample floor space with an attractive interior and exterior, and needs to be located in a retail district with street appeal that will be visible to the consumer.

The interior displays are very costly as well. Jewelry stores need attractive showcases with special lighting to accentuate the diamonds. The store should be comfortable, clean, and well organized.

Lastly, finding qualified employees in this industry can be very difficult. Employees need to be knowledgeable, friendly, helpful, and have the ability to sell. They also need a sense of fashion to help create settings and custom designs. A jewelry store with an on-duty gemologist needs to make sure that that person is certified and extremely knowledgeable of all the products and custom design.

Factors That Make the Industry Attractive

The entrance into the jewelry industry is attractive due to its strong growth, stable position, and opportunity for new product creation, innovation, and trends. As noted in the *Market Size* section of this industry analysis, the jewelry industry is growing rapidly every year in both volume and sales. This growth will allow for an increased number of retail outlets in a given geographic market.

This industry is also very stable, because jewelry is never going away, nor is it a fad item. Jewelry is considered a necessity for most people in times of marriage and anniversaries. Jewelry is also commonly used as gifts, which oftentimes means that people are willing to spend a high-dollar amount for the item. For these reasons, the jewelry industry was even able to remain stable during the economic fall of 2001.

There are also new jewelry products entering the marketplace all the time, which creates demand. These new products are technologically, fashion, and trend driven. The fashion trends for jewelry change virtually every year, which again spurs an increase in demand.

Works Cited

Business Wire. (2002). U.S. Diamond Jewelry Market Remains Strong Despite Economic Downturn in 2001, According to the Diamond Information Center. Retrieved November 3, 2005, from http://www.findarticles.com/p/articles/mi_m0EIN/is_2002_April_2/ai_84331472

Colored Stone. (2004). One-of-a-Kind Jewelry Study. Retrieved on November 3, 2005, from http://www.tucsonshowguide.com/stories/jul04/selling2.cfm#1

Couture Jeweler. (2005). Your Couture Jewellry Trend Report. Retrieved on November 3, 2005, from http://www.couturejeweler.com/couturejeweler/trend_reports/index.jsp

Diamond Registry. (1999). Latest Statistics on the U.S. Diamond Jewelry Market–Focus on the Diamond Engagement Ring. Retrieved November 3, 2005, from http://www.diamondregistry.com/News/stats.htm ePodunk Inc. (2005). Retrieved November 2, 2005, from www.epodunk.com

IBISWorld. (2004). Industry Snapshot. Retrieved November 3, 2005, from http://www.ibisworld.com/snapshot/industry/default.asp?page=industry&industry_id=1075

JCK-Jewelers Circular Keystone. (2005). Jewelry and Watches Accounted for $1.6 Billion in Quarterly Business for eBay. Retrieved on November 3, 2005, from http://www.jckgroup.com/article/CA6276690/jck?section=Internet+Update

Mar-Nel Productions. (2005). Statistics for the Wedding Industry. Retrieved on November 3, 2005, from http://www.afwpi.com/wedstats.html

Professional Jeweler. (2004). Swiss Exports Drop in 2003. Retrieved November 2, 2005, from http://www.professionaljeweler.com/archives/articles/2004/may04/0504ts.html

Professional Jeweler. (2004). U.S. Gold Jewelry Sales up 2.5%; Gold Month set to Launch in May. Retrieved November 3, 2005, from http://www.professionaljeweler.com/archives/news/2004/042104story.html

Sound Vision. (2005). Statistics on Weddings in the United States. Retrieved on November 3, 2005, from http://www.soundvision.com/info/weddings/statistics.asp

Unity Marketing. (2001). Jewelry Sales Reach $39.8 Billion. Retrieved on November 3, 2005, from http://retailindustry.about.com/library/bl/q2/bl_um041701.htm

U.S. Bureau of Labor Statistics. (2005). Retrieved on November 3, 2005, from http://www.bls.gov/lau/home.htm

Notes

CHAPTER 1

1. Small Business Administration, Office of Advocacy, "Frequently Asked Questions," June 2006, www.sba.gov/advo

2. Ibid.

3. Small Business Administration, Office of Advocacy, "Small Business Economic Indicators," June 2006, www.sba.gov/advo

4. Small Business Administration, Office of Advocacy, "Frequently Asked Questions," June 2006, www.sba.gov/advo

5. Small Business Administration, "Guide to SBA's Definition of Small Business," 28 September 2006, www.sba.gov/size/indexguide.html

6. Small Business Administration, Office of Advocacy, "Small Business Economic Indicators for 2002," June 2003, 21.

7. www.hoover.com, 28 September 2006.

8. John A. Byrne, "How Entrepreneurs Are Reshaping the Economy and What Big Companies Can Learn," *Business Week,* Enterprise Edition, October 1993, 12–18.

9. Anonymous, "The Great Hollowing-out Myth," *Economist,* 21 February 2004, 27.

10. Laura D'Andrea Tyson, "Outsourcing: Who's Safe Anymore?" *Business Week,* 23 February 2004, 26.

11. Byrne, 14.

12. Small Business Administration, Office of Advocacy, "Frequently Asked Questions,," 3 November 2006, www.sba.gov/advo

13. *Statistical Abstract of the United States* (Washington, DC: U.S. Government Printing Office, 1997), 560–561.

14. Small Business Administration, Office of Advocacy, "Frequently Asked Questions,," 3 November 2006, www.sba.gov/advo

15. Ibid.

16. Small Business Administration, Office of Advocacy, *The Small Business Economy: A Report to the President* (Washington, DC: U.S. Government Printing Office, 2006).

17. Ibid. 121.

18. Nichole L. Torres, "Leader of the Pack," *Entrepreneur,* March 2006.

19. Small Business Profile: United States, December 2006, www.sba.gov/advo

20. Ying Lowery, "Dynamics of Minority-Owned Employer Establishments, 1997–2001," *Small Business Research Summary No. 251,* February 2005.

21. Ying Lowery, "Women in Business: A Demographic Review of Women's Business Ownership," *Small Business Research Summary No. 280,* August 2006.

22. Faye Rice, "How to Make Diversity Pay," *Fortune,* 8 August 1994, 79–86.

23. J. A. Schumpeter, *Capitalism, Socialism, and Democracy* (New York: Harper & Row, 1943).

24. Joshua S. Gans, David H. Hsu, and Scott Stern, "When Does Start-up Innovation Spur the Gale of Creative Destruction?" *RAND Journal of Economics,* Winter 2002, 571–586.

25. "Report Examines Small Business Innovative Activity," *The Small Business Advocate,* December 1993, 10.

26. "Small Serial Innovators: The Small Firm Contribution to Technical Change," 27 February 2003, www.sba.gov/advo

27. Dun & Bradstreet Corporation, Business Failure Record, as reported in "Business Failures by Industry: 1990 to 1998," *Statistical Abstract of the United States* (Washington, DC: U.S. Government Printing Office, 2001), 561.

28. Andrew L. Zacharakis, G. Dale Meyer, and Julio DeCastro, "Differing Perceptions of New Venture Failure: A Matched Exploratory Study of Venture Capitalists and Entrepreneurs," *Journal of Small Business Management,* July 1999, 1–14.

29. "Avoiding the Pitfalls," *Wall Street Journal Report on Small Business,* 22 May 1995, R1.

30. Richard Monk, "Why Small Businesses Fail," *CMA Management,* July/August 2000, 12–13; Udayan Gupta, "How Much?" *The Wall Street Journal,* 22 May 1995, R7; Stephanie N. Mehta, "Small Talk: An Interview with Wendell E. Dunn," *The Wall Street Journal,* 22 May 1995.

31. Jack Welch & Suzy Welch, "The Danger of Doing Nothing.," *Business Week,* 10 July, 2006

32. John Case, "The Wonderland Economy," *The State of Small Business,* 16 March 1995, 29.

33. James Aley, "Debunking the Failure Fallacy," *Fortune,* 6 September 1993, 21.

34. Brian Headd, "Redefining Business Success: Distinguishing Between Closure and Failure," *Small Business Economics,* vol. 21, 2003, 51.

35. "Marriages and Divorces 1900–2001," InfoPlease.com, U.S. Department of Health and Human Services, National Center for Health Statistics. Web: www.cdc.gov/nchs/

36. Steven Burd, "Graduation Rates and Student Mobility," *Chronicle of Higher Education,* 2 April 2004, A22.

CHAPTER 2

1. Robert Hisrich, "Entrepreneurship/Intrapreneurship," *American Psychologist,* February 1990, 209.

2. P. VanderWerf and C. Brush, "Toward Agreement on the Focus of Entrepreneurship Research: Progress Without Definition," *Proceedings of the National Academy of Management Conference,* Washington, DC, 1989.

3. Denis Gregoire, Martin Noel, Richard Dery, and Jean-Pierre Bechard, "Is There Conceptual Convergence in Entrepreneurship Research? A Co-Citation Analysis of Frontiers of Entrepreneurship Research, 1981–2004," *Entrepreneurship Theory and Practice,* May 2006, 333–372.

4. Carol Moore, "Understanding Entrepreneurial Behavior: A Definition and Model," in *Academy of Management Best Paper Proceedings,* edited by J. A. Pearce II and

R. B. Robinson, Jr., 46th Annual Meeting of the Academy of Management, Chicago, 1989, 66–70. See also William Bygrave, "The Entrepreneurial Paradigm (I): A Philosophical Look at Its Research Methodologies," *Entrepreneurship: Theory and Practice,* Fall 1989, 7–25, and William Bygrave and Charles Hofer, "Theorizing About Entrepreneurship," *Entrepreneurship: Theory and Practice,* Winter 1991, 13–22.

5. A. Shapiro and L. Sokol, "The Social Dimensions of Entrepreneurship," in *Encyclopedia of Entrepreneurship,* edited by. J. A. Kent, D. L. Sexton, and K. H. Vesper (Englewood Cliffs, NJ: Prentice-Hall, 1992).

6. J. A. Schumpeter, *History of Economic Analysis* (New York: Oxford University Press, 1934).

7. William Gartner, "'Who Is an Entrepreneur?' Is the Wrong Question," *Entrepreneurship: Theory and Practice,* Summer 1989, 47. See also J. W. Carland, F. Hoy, W. R. Boulton, and J. A. C. Carland, "Differentiating Entrepreneurs from Small Business Owners: A Conceptualization," *Academy of Management Review,* 1984, 354–359; William Gartner, "What Are We Talking About When We Talk About Entrepreneurship?" *Journal of Business Venturing,* 1990, 15–28.

8. Steven Covey, *The Seven Habits of Highly Effective People* (New York: Simon & Schuster, 1989), 95.

9. Peter Drucker, *Innovation and Entrepreneurship: Practice and Principles* (New York: Harper & Row, 1985).

10. Jess McCuan, "It's Good to Be King," *Inc.,* December 2003, 32.

11. Sanjay Goel and Ranjan Karri, "Entrepreneurs, Effectual Logic, and Over-Trust," *Entrepreneurship Theory and Practice,* July 2006, 480.

12. Jon Goodman, "What Makes an Entrepreneur?" *Inc.,* October 1994, 29.

13. David C. McClelland, *The Achieving Society* (New York: Van Nostrand Reinhold, 1961). See also David C. McClelland, "Achievement Motivation Can Be Developed," *Harvard Business Review,* November/December 1965; David Miron and David McClelland, "The Impact of Achievement Motivation Training on Small Business," *California Management Review,* Summer 1979, 13–28.

14. Robert Brochhaus and Pamela S. Horwitz, "The Psychology of the Entrepreneur," in *The Art and Science of Entrepreneurship,* edited by Donald Sexton and Raymond W. Smilor (Cambridge, MA: Ballinger, 1986), 25–48.

15. T. S. Hatten, "Student Entrepreneurial Characteristics and Attitude Change Toward Entrepreneurship as Affected by Participation in an SBI Program," *Journal of Education for Business,* March/April 1995, 224–228.

16. Michael O'Neal, "Just What Is an Entrepreneur?" *Business Week* (Enterprise Edition), 1993, 104–112.

17. NFIB Foundation/American Express Travel, *A Small Business Primer.*

18. Jerome Katz, "The Institution and Infrastructure of Entrepreneurship," *Entrepreneurship: Theory and Practice,* Spring 1991, 85–102.

19. Mark Weaver, Pat Dickson, George Solomon "Entrepreneurship and Education: What Is Known and Not Known About the Links Between Education and Entrepreneurial Activity," *The Small Business Economy—A Report to the President,* December 2006, 119.

20. "Best Schools for Entrepreneurs—Top 25 Undergrad Programs" *Entrepreneur,* October 2006, 102–103.

21. Fred Steingold, *Legal Guide for Starting and Running a Small Business,* 7th ed. (Berkeley, CA: Nolo Press, 2003).

22. James W. Reynolds and Steven Frost, "Uniform LLP Amendments Make Welcome Changes to Revised Uniform Partnership Act," *Journal of Limited Liability Companies,* Spring 1997, 189; James Hopson and Patricia Hopson, "Helping Clients Choose the Legal Form for a Small Business," *The Practical Accountant,* October 1990, 67–84.

23. Steingold.

24. "Legal Structure and Registration," *The Colorado Business Resource Guide* (Denver, CO: SBA and Colorado Office of Economic Development and International Trade, 2004), 4.4.

25. William Copperthwaite, Jr., "Limited Liability Companies: The Choice of the Future," *Commercial Law Journal,* Summer 1998, 222–239.

26. James Hamill and Jennifer Olson, "Much Ado About 'Nothings,'" *Tax Advisor,* July 1999, 506–514.

CHAPTER 3

1. For a more complete discussion of corporate social responsibility, see R. Griffin, *Management,* 8th ed. (Boston, MA: Houghton Mifflin, 2005). See also Archer Carroll, "The Pyramid of Corporate Social Responsibility: Toward the Moral Management of Organizational Stakeholders," *Business Horizons,* July/August 1991, 39–48; and Richard Rodewald, "The Corporate Social Responsibility Debate: Unanswered Questions About the Consequences of Moral Reform," *American Business Law Journal,* Fall 1987, 443–466.

2. O. C. Ferrell and John Fraedrich, *Business Ethics: Ethical Decision Making and Cases,* 2nd ed. (Boston, MA: Houghton Mifflin, 1994), 67.

3. Milton Friedman and Rose Friedman, *Free to Choose* (New York: Harcourt Brace Jovanovich, 1980); Milton Friedman, *Capitalism and Freedom* (Chicago: University of Chicago Press, 1963), 133.

4. "Social Responsibility: 'Fundamentally Subversive'?" interview with Milton Friedman, 15 August 1006, www.businessweek.com. Online Extra.

5. Milton Zall, "Small Business and the EEOC: An Overview," *Fleet Equipment,* March 2000, BIZM4.

6. Jack Gordon, "Rethinking Diversity," *Training,* January 1992, 23.

7. Cait Murphy, "Keeping Small Business Off the Street," *Fortune Small Business,* November 2003, 18.

8. Ken Rankin, "SEC Seeks to Ease Section 404 Burden," *Accounting Today,* 27 November 2006, 1, 33.

9. Mary-Kathryn Zachary, "Another Blonde, Another Situation, Another Outcome," *Supervision,* November 2003, 21.

10. 29 CFR 1604.11(a).

11. Jan Bohren, "Six Myths of Sexual Harassment," *Management Review,* May 1993, 61–63.

12. Ellyn Spragins, Maggie Overfelt, and Julie Sloane, "Dangerous Liaisons," *Fortune Small Business,* February 2004, 62.

13. Ibid.

14. Stuart Dawson, John Breen, and Lata Satyen, "The Ethical Outlook of Micro Business Operators," *Journal of Small Business Management,* October 2002, 302–313.

15. Jeannine Reilly, "Charitable Works Sells at a Number of Firms," *Arizona Daily Star,* 11 September 2000, 16.

16. Cheryl Dahle and Alison Overholt, "Social Capitalists," *Fast Company,* January 2004, 45–57.

17. Anne Murphy, "The Seven (Almost) Deadly Sins of High-Minded Entrepreneurs," *Inc.,* July 1994, 47–51.

18. Lisa Miller, "Ethics: It Isn"t Just the Big Guys," *Business Week Online,* 28 July 2003.

19. Ferrell and Fraedrich, 10.

20. George Manning and Kent Curtis, *Ethics at Work: Fire in a Dark World* (Cincinnati: South-Western Publishing, 1988), 74.

21. Miller, "Ethics: It Isn"t Just the Big Guys."

22. "Should You Put It in Writing?" *Nations Business,* March 1998, 37.

23. Manning and Curtis, 77.

24. David H. Freeman "The Technoethics Trap," *Inc.,* March 2006, 69–70.

25. Scott Baca and Erin Nickerson, "Ethical Problems, Conflicts, and Beliefs of Small Business Professionals," *Journal of Business Ethics,* November 2000, 15–24.

26. Richard Kaleba "Strategic Planning: Getting from Here to There," *Healthcare Financial Management,* November 2006, 74–78.

27. Charles Toftoy and Joydeep Chatterjee "Mission Statements and Small Business" *Business Strategy Review,* November 2004, 41–44.

28. Tom Peters, *Thriving on Chaos* (New York: Knopf, 1988).

29. Robert Linnman and John Stanton, "Mining for Niches," *Business Horizons,* May/June 1992, 43–51.

30. Fran Tarkenton and Joseph Boyett, "Taking Care of Business," *Entrepreneur,* February 1990, 18–23.

31. Anil Gupta, "Business-Unit Strategy: Managing the Single Business," in *The Portable MBA in Strategy,* edited by Liam Fahey and Robert Randall (New York: Wiley, 1994), 84–107.

32. Michael Porter, "Know Your Place," *Inc.,* September 1991, 90–95.

33. David Cravens and Shannon Shipp, "Market-driven Strategies for Competitive Advantage," *Business Horizons,* January/ February 1991, 90–95.

34. Porter.

35. Robert Hartley, *Marketing Mistakes,* 9th ed. (New York: Wiley, 2004), 2.

36. Leslie Cauley, "Perils of Progress," *Wall Street Journal Report—Technology,* 27 June 1994, R12.

37. David Menzies, "The Museum of Mortal Marketing Mistakes," *Marketing,* 23 April 2001, 9.

38. John Czepiel, *Competitive Marketing Strategy* (Englewood Cliffs, NJ: Prentice-Hall, 1992), 41.

39. Fred Amofa Yamoah, "Sources of Competitive Advantage: Differential and Catalytic Dimensions," *Journal of American Academy of Business,* March 2004, 223–227.

40. Michael Porter, *Competitive Advantage: Creating and Sustaining Superior Performance* (New York: Free Press, 1985).

41. Jenny McCune, "In the Shadow of Wal-Mart," *Management Review,* December 1994, 10–16.

42. Stephanie Clifford, "It's 2006! Whatchagonna Do About It?—You Can't Our Wal-Mart Wal-Mart," *Inc.,* January 2006, 84.

43. Aodheen O'Donnell, Audrey Gilmore, David Carson, and Darryl Cummins, "Competitive Advantage in Small to Medium-Sized Enterprises," *Journal of Strategic Marketing,* October 2002, 205–223.

44. Oren Harari, "The Secret Competitive Advantage," *Management Review,* January 1994, 45–47.

45. M. A. Lyles, J. S. Baird, J. B. Orris, and D. E. Kuratko, "Formalized Planning in Small Business Increasing Strategic Choices," *Journal of Small Business Management,* April 1993, 38–50.

46. Kenneth Hatten and Mary Louise Hatten, *Strategic Management: Analysis and Action* (Englewood Cliffs, NJ: Prentice-Hall, 1987), 13.

CHAPTER 4

1. David Gumpert, *How to Really Start Your Own Business* (Needham, MA: Lauson Publishing, 2003).

2. Bo Burlingham, "How to Succeed in Business in 4 Easy Steps," Inc., July 1995, 30–45.

3. Emily Barker, "The Bullet-Proof Business Plan," *Inc.,* October 2001, 102–104.

4. Nicole Gull, "Plan B (and C and D and . . .)," Inc., March 2004, 40.

5. William A. Sahlman, "How to Write a Great Business Plan," *Harvard Business Review,* July/August 1997, 98.

6. "Did Somebody Say 'Small?'" *Fortune Special Issue,* Summer 1999, 142.

7. *Guidelines for Entrepreneurs,* pamphlet, Colorado Small Business Development Center.

8. Copeland, Michael V. "How to Make Your Business Plan the Perfect Pitch," *Business 2.0,* September 2005, 88.

9. Kayte Vanscoy, "Unconventional Wisdom," *Smart Business for the New Economy,* October 2000, 78–88.

10. William Sahlman, "How to Write a Great Business Plan," *Harvard Business Review,* July/August 1997, 101.

11. Nicole Gull, "Plan B (and C and D . . .)," *Inc.,* March 2004, 40.

12. Ralph Alterowitz and Jon Zonderman, Financing Your New or Growing Business, *Entrepreneur Mentor Series* (Irvine, CA: Entrepreneur Press, 2002), 113.

13. Guy Kawasaki, "Needbucks.com," *Forbes*, 10 January 2000, 188; Scott Clark, "Great Business Plan Is Key to Raising Venture Capital," *Portland Business Journal*, 31 March 2000, 36; and Dee Power and Brian Hill, "Six Critical Business Plan Mistakes," *Business Horizons*, July/August 2003, 83.

CHAPTER 5

1. Thomas Dicke, *Franchising in America: The Development of a Business Method, 1840–1990* (Chapel Hill, NC: University of North Carolina Press, 1992), 13.

2. PricewaterhouseCoopers, "Economic Impact of Franchised Businesses," study for the International Franchise Association Educational Foundation, 2004, www.franchise.org/edufound/researchef.asp

3. Robert Justis and Richard Judd, Franchising (Cincinnati: South-Western, 1989).

4. www.franchisehandbook.com

5. U.S. Department of Commerce.

6. Andrew Caffey, "Hey, Get a Clue!" *Entrepreneur*, January 2004, 112–118.

7. Andrew Sherman and Karen Dewis, "Guidelines for Investing in, or Acquiring, an Established Franchising System," *Buyouts*, 1 December 2003, 34.

8. Ibid., 300.

9. David Kaufmann, "The Big Bang," Entrepreneur, January 2004, 86.

10. Ibid.

11. Kevin Butler, "Franchise Reform on Horizon?" *Investor's Business Daily*, 29 July 1999, A1.

12. Sam Dhir and Dawn Bruno, "Global Franchising: Making Good Business Sense," Franchising World, April 2004, 20.

13. Thomas Dambrine, "Less Is More," *Franchising World*, April 2004, 14.

14. Charles Weeks, "Searching for New Markets? Look South," *Franchising World*, March 2004, 61.

15. Pei Liang and Sun Zhixian, "What Entry Vehicle Will You Select in China?" *Franchising World*, March 2004, 65.

CHAPTER 6

1. David Gumpert, *How to Really Start Your Own Business*, 4th ed. (Needham, MA: Larson Publishing, 2003), 4.

2. Bill Broocke, "Buy—Don't Start—Your Own Business," *Entrepreneur Magazine Online*, 22 March 2004, www. entrepreneur.com/your_business

3. Glen Cooper, "Six Places to Search," May 2004, www.bizbuysell.com/guide

4. David Wold, *NxLevel Guide for Entrepreneurs* (Denver: US West Foundation, 2000), 76.

5. Richard Parker, "Due Diligence—Investigating a Business," 27 May 2004, www.bizquest.com/articles

6. Peter McFarlane and Deborah Gold, "Do the Due," *CA Magazine*, August 2003, 37–42.

7. Andrew Dolbeck, "Diligence Where It's Due," *Weekly Corporate Growth Report*, 28 July 2003, 1.

8. Dalia Fahmy "Deal Jitters?" *Inc.*, October 2005, 48.

9. Bill Broocke, "Buy—Don't Start—Your Own Business," *Entrepreneur.com*, 22 March 2004.

10. RMA Annual Statement Studies (Philadelphia: Robert Morris Associates).

11. Larry Kanter, "What's Your Company Worth Now?" *Inc.*, January 2007, 98–105.

12. Fred Steingold, *Legal Guide for Starting and Running a Small Business*, 7th ed. (Berkeley, CA: Nolo Press, 2003), 10/17.

13. John Johansen, "How to Buy or Sell a Business," *Small Business Administration Management Aid, No. 2.029* (Washington, DC: U.S. Small Business Administration, Office of Business Development).

14. Richard Parker, "Valuing a Business," May 2004, www.bizquest.com/articles

15. "Valuation Methodologies," May 2004, www.bizquest.com/articles

16. Bart Basi and Roman Basi, "Placing a Value on Business," *Industrial Distribution*, March 2004, 55–57.

17. William Bygrave, *The Portable MBA in Entrepreneurship*, 2nd ed. (New York: Wiley, 1997), 63–66.

18. Family Firm Institute, "Family Business in the U.S.," www.ffi.org

19. John Ward and Craig Aronoff, "Two 'Laws' for Family Businesses," *Nation's Business*, February 1993, 52–53.

20. David Wold, ed., *Nxlevel Guide for Entrepreneurs*, 3rd ed. (Denver, CO: U.S. West Foundation, 2000), 108.

21. George Rimler, "How to Professionalize the Family Business," *Air Conditioning, Heating & Refrigeration News*, 19 June 2000, 28.

22. Matthew Fogel, "A More Perfect Business," *Inc.*, August 2003, 44.

23. Jeffrey Barsch, Joseph Gantisky, James Carson, and Benjamin Doochin, "Entry of the Next Generation: Strategic Challenges for Family Members in Family Firms," *Journal of Small Business Management*, April 1988, 49–56.

24. Ernesto Poza, "Heirs and Graces in a Family Business," *Business Week Online*, 12 September 2003.

25. David Bork, "If Family Members Ask for a Job," *Nation's Business*, April 1992, 50–52.

CHAPTER 7

1. Andrew Rohm and Fareena Sultan, "The Evolution of E-Business," *Marketing Management*, January 2004, 32.

2. Amy Wilson Sheldon, "Strategy Rules," *Fast Company*, January 2001, 165–166.

3. Robert McGarvey, "Reality Check," *Entrepreneur's Start-Ups*, September 2000, 53.

4. Peter Labrow, "Back to Business Basics," *IT Training*, May 2004, 38.

5. Michael Perkowski, "Is E-Business Finally Living Up to Its Hype?" *CIO Insight,* September 2003, 73–81.

6. American Association of Home-Based Businesses, www.aahbb.com

7. David Bangs and Linda Pinson, *The Real World Entrepreneur Field Guide* (Chicago: Upstart Publishing, 1999), 474.

8. Nichole L. Torres, "No Place Like Home," *Entrepreneur's Start-Ups,* September 2000, 38–45; Heather Lloyd-Martin, "Oh, Give Me a Home," *Entrepreneur's Start-Ups,* October 2000, 42–45; Susan Gosselin, "Feeling Right at Home," *Business First of Louisville,* 14 May 2004; Kimberly McCall, "Home-Based Business: Is It for You?" *Inc.* online, www.inc.com/articles

9. Bureau of Labor Statistics, "Work at Home in 1997," www.bls.gov/newsrelease

10. All data on *Inc.* 500 companies come from *Inc. Special Issue,* Fall 2003.

11. Diane Goldner, "Ahead of the Curve," *The Wall Street Journal Small Business Edition,* 22 May 1995, R16.

12. John Case, "Why 20 Million of You Can't Be Wrong," *Inc.,* April 2004, 102.

13. David Kopcso, Robert Ronstady, and William Rybolt, "The Corridor Principle: Independent Entrepreneurs Versus Corporate Entrepreneurs," in *Frontiers of Entrepreneurship Research,* 1987 (Wellesley, MA: Babson College, 1987), 259–271.

14. Tim Blumerntritt, "Does Small and Mature Have to Mean Dull? Defying the Ho-Hum at SMEs," *Journal of Business Strategy,* vol. 25 (1), 2004, 27–33.

15. Phaedra Hise, "Where Great Business Ideas Come From," *Inc.,* September 1993, 59–60.

16. Neil A. Martin, "Invincible Spirit," *Success,* October 1994, 24.

17. Michael Treacy and Fred Wiesema, "How Market Leaders Keep Their Edge," *Fortune,* 6 February 1995, 88–98.

18. Colin Barrow, "People Count," *Director,* March 2004, 25.

CHAPTER 8

1. David Wallace, "Sarbanes-Oxley Sets Standard for Small Companies," *Rural Telecommunications,* March/April 2004, 68–73.

2. Karen Klein, "Where Accounting Isn't a Dirty Word," *Business Week Online,* 30 July 2002, www.businessweek.com

3. "Making Sense of Your Dollars," *Home Office Computing,* November 1993, 79–88.

4. Allen Beck, "The Cash Method for Small Business," *Tax Advisor,* October 2002, 623.

5. For an overview of FASB, see Craig Schneider, "Who Rules Accounting?" CFO, August 2003, 34–40.

6. Rick Telberg, "Mom and Pop Shops," *Journal of Accountancy,* July 2003, 49.

7. Kathryn Stewart, "On the Fast Track to Profits," *Management Accounting,* February 1995, 44–50.

8. Jay Finegan, "Corporate Cost Cutters," *Inc.,* August 1995, 28.

9. C. J. Prince, "Catch Your Cash," *Entrepreneur,* June 2004, 57.

10. New York Society of CPAs, "10 Ways to Improve Small Business Cash Flow," *Journal of Accountancy,* March 2000, 14.

11. Daniel Akst, "The Survival of the Fittest," *Fortune Small Business,* February 2002, 77.

CHAPTER 9

1. Dale D. Buss, "Growing More by Doing Less," *Nation's Business,* December 1995, 18–24.

2. Art Beroff and Dwayne Moyers, "On Their Terms," *Entrepreneur's Be Your Own Boss,* February 2004.

3. Crystal Detamore-Rodman, "Truth and Consequences," *Entrepreneur's Be Your Own Boss,* October 2003.

4. Crystal Detamore-Rodman, "The Burden of Borrowing," *Entrepreneur,* April 2003.

5. U.S. Small Business Administration, Office of Business Development, "The ABCs of Borrowing," *Management Aids Number 1.001* (Washington, DC: U.S. Government Printing Office).

6. Andrew Sherman, "Understanding the Different Sources of Capital," National Federation of Independent Business, 13 December 2001, www.nfib.com
   Catherine Curan, "Factoring Gets a Face-lift," *Inc.,* February 2006, 38–40.

7. www.sba.gov/financing

8. www.sba.gov

9. Jeffrey Moses, "Five Steps to Take When a Lender Says No," National Federation of Independent Business, 27 May 2003, www.nfib.com

10. David Newton, "Raising Money from Family and Friends," *Entrepreneur,* 26 January 2004, www.entrepreneur.com/articles

11. "Angels: A Funding Source for Firms with Limited Revenue," National Federation of Independent Business, 22 April 2003, www.nfib.com

12. Andrew Sherman, "Understanding the Different Sources of Capital, Part II," National Federation of Independent Business, 20 December 2001, www.nfib.com
    Dalia Fahmy, "Want Power and Money?" *Inc.,* April 2006, 44–46.

13. G. Baty, *Entrepreneurship*: Playing to Win (Reston, VA: Reston Publishing, 1990), 157–159.

14. Jeffry A. Timmons, *New Venture Creation,* 6th ed. (Homewood, IL: Irwin, 2003).

CHAPTER 10

1. 8 USC 1324 (a).

2. 8 USC 1324 (B) (g) (2) (B) (iv) (I)–(III).

3. "Does Small Biz Want Immigration Reform?" *Business Week Online,* May 10 2006, 4.

4. Ibid., C4.

5. Ibid., 19–20.

6. Justin Martin and Matthew Phan "Why the Disabilities Act Exasperates Entrepreneurs," *Fortune Small Business,* May 2005, 52–54.

7. William Jackson, Geralyn McClure-Franklin, and Diana Hensley, "Sexual Harassment: No Immunity for Small Business," Proceedings of 1995 Small Business Consulting Conference, Nashville, TN, 161–165.

8. Barry Shanoff, "Feeling the Burn," *Waste Age,* April 2004, 38.

9. Roberto Ceniceros, "Workers Comp Surcharge for Terrorism Risks Sparks Debate," *Business Insurance,* 12 April 2004, 1.

10. 29 USC 651 (b).

11. Fred Steingold, *Legal Guide for Starting and Running a Small Business,* 7th ed. (Berkeley, CA: Nolo, 2003), 15/30.

12. Alan Zeiger, "Bankruptcy Can Also Mean Smart Investment," *Management Review,* May 1992, 36–39.

13 Rozane DeLaurell and Robert Rouse, "The Bankruptcy Reform Act of 2005: A New Landscape," *The CPA Journal,* November 2006, 36–39.

14. "Constitution of the United States of America," Article I, Section 8, in Daniel J. Boorstin, *An American Primer* (Chicago: University of Chicago Press, 1966), 94.

15. David Pressman, *Patent It Yourself,* 12th ed. (Berkeley, CA: Nolo Press, 2006).

16. Ibid.

17. Carl Geffken, "Protecting Your Intellectual Property," *GCI,* January 2004, 24.

18. Tim Studt, "Protecting Your Intellectual Property," *R&D Magazine,* April 2004, 22.

19. James Nurton, "WIPO Launches Online Filing Option for PCT," *Managing Intellectual Property,* March 2004, 59.

CHAPTER 11

1. Peter Drucker, *People and Performance: The Best of Peter Drucker on Management* (New York: Harper's College Press, 1977), 90.

2. Ibid., 91.

3. Amy Barrett, "Hot Growth Companies," *Business Week,* 7 June 2004, 86–90.

4. Sean Moffitt, "In Pursuit of Purple Cows," *Marketing,* 17 May 2004, 25.

5. Seth Godin, *Purple Cow: Transform Your Business by Being Remarkable* (New York: Portfolio, 2002).

6. David Cravens and Shannon Shipp, "Market-Driven Strategies for Competitive Advantage," *Business Horizons,* January/February 1991, 53–61.

7. Holly O'Neill, "Back-to-Basics Best for Small Companies," *Marketing News,* 27 March 2000, 12.

8. Ronald Nykiel, *Marketing Your Business: A Guide to Developing a Strategic Marketing Plan* (New York: Hayworth Press, 2003).

9. Michele Marchetti, "Advanced Planning," *Sales and Marketing Management,* May 2004, 16.

10. Ken Wong, "Do We Really Get It?" *Marketing,* 26 April 2004, 7.

11. Adam Hanft, "In Praise of Niche Marketing," www.inc.com, May 2004.

12. J. Ford Laumer, Jr., James Harris, and Hugh Guffey, Jr., "Learning About Your Market," *Management Aid No. 4.019,* Small Business Administration Management Assistance Office.

13. Stever Robbins, "Down and Dirty Market Research," 12 August 2002, www.entrepreneur.com

14. Dina Bann, "Companies Use Shared Approach to Collect Low-Cost Marketing Data," *Denver Rocky Mountain News,* 21 February 1999, 46.

15. Sunny Crouch and Matthew Housden, *Marketing Research for Managers,* 3rd ed. (Burlington, MA: Butterworth-Heinemann, 2003).

16. Laura Tiffany, "Researching Your Market," 7 August 2001, www.entrepreneur.com

17. Ibid.

18. Ron Belanger, "Using Search Engine Marketing as Market Research Tool," *B to B,* 8 March 2004, 20.

19. U.S. Small Business Administration, www.sba.gov/starting_business/marketing/research.html

20. Allan Magrath, *The Six Imperatives of Marketing: Lessons from the World's Best Companies* (New York: AMACOM, 1992), 40–41.

21. Oren Harrari, "The Tarpit of Marketing Research," *Management Review,* March 1994, 42–44.

22. Gary Hamel and C. K. Prahalad, "Seeing the Future First," *Fortune,* 5 September 1994, 70.

CHAPTER 12

1. Teresa Costa Campi, Agusti Segarra Biasco, and Elisabet Marsal, "The Location of New Firms and Life Cycle of Industries," *Small Business Economics,* April/May 2004, 265.

2. William Barbach, "Developments to Watch," *Business Week,* 28 June 1993, 85.

3. Danielle Sacks, "The Gore-Tex of Guitar Strings," *Fast Company,* December 2003, 46.

4. Frozen Food Digest, July 1997, 20. also Stephanie Thompson, "No News Is Bad News for Food Biz." *Advertising Age,* 8 August 2005, 1–21.

5. Don Debelak, *Bringing Your Product to Market* (Irvine, CA: Entrepreneur Media, 2001), 100.

6. Christopher J. Sandvig and Lori Coakley, "Best Practices in Small Firm Diversification," *Business Horizons,* May/June 1998, 33–40.

7. Kenneth Hein and Michael Applebaum, "Get a Grip . . . Packaging Dept.," *Brandweek,* 17 May 2004, 50.

8. "Ice Cream Collaboration Comes Up Trumps," *Printing World,* 29 April 2004, 24–25.

9. Verona Beguin, ed., Small Business Institute Student Consultant's Manual (Washington, DC: Small Business Administration, 1992), Appendix F7.

10. Donald W. Dobler, David N. Burt, and Lamar Lee, Jr., *Purchasing and Materials Management,* 5th ed.

(New York: McGraw-Hill, 1990), 50–64; Barry Render and Jay Heizer, *Principles of Operations Management* (Upper Saddle River, NJ: Prentice-Hall, 1995), 406–415.

11. Stephanie Gruner, "The Smart Vendor-Audit Checklist," *Inc.*, April 1995, 93–95.
12. Leslie Marell, "Key Clauses to Reduce Risks with Sole/Single-Source Suppliers," *Supplier Selection & Management Report*, April 2002, 5–11.
13. Laurie Sullivan, "Slow to Sync," Informationweek.com, 7 June 2004, 57–59.
14. Nicholas Varchaver, "Scanning the Globe," *Fortune*, 31 May 2004, 114–119.
15. Marc L. Songini, "Wal-Mart Shifts RFID Plans," *Computerworld*, February 26, 2007, 14.
16. Sang Lee and Marc Schniederjans, *Operations Management* (Boston: Houghton Mifflin, 1994), 256.
17. Julie Candler, "Just-in-Time Deliveries," *Nation's Business*, April 1993, 64–65.

CHAPTER 13

1. "The Power of Buying Survey," *Sales and Marketing Management*, September 2002, A1.
2. *CIA World Factbook*, 2004, www.cia.gov
3. Joel Kotkin, "Top 25 Cities for Doing Business in America," Inc., March 2004, 93–99.
4. Gary Brockway and W. Blynn Mangold, "The Sales Conversion Index: A Method for Analyzing Small Business Market Opportunities," *Journal of Small Business Management*, April 1988, 38–48.
5. Michael Weiss, *The Clustering of America* (New York: Harper & Row, 1988).
6. "Claritas Introduces PRIZM Segmentation System," *Retail Merchandiser*, November 2003, 7.
7. Niklas von Dachne, "Ears to the Ground," *Success*, December 1995, 14.
8. Bradford McKee, "Achieving Access for the Disabled," *Nation's Business*, June 1991, 31–34.
9. Robert Cunningham, "Ten Questions to Ask Before You Sign a Lease," *Inc. Guide to Small Business Success*, 1993 supplement issue.

CHAPTER 14

1. Geoffrey Colvin, "Pricing Power Ain't What It Used to Be," *Fortune*, 15 September 2003, 52.
2. Edward Welles, "When Wal-Mart Comes to Town," *Inc.*, July 1993, 76–88.
3. David Wellman, "Wal-Mart Is Not About Price," *Frozen Food Age*, January 2002, 8.
4. Paul Argenti, *The Portable MBA Desk Reference* (New York: Wiley, 1994), 313.
5. Norm Brodsky, "The Capacity Trap II," *Inc.*, December 2003, 55–57.
6. Rhonda Abrams, "Competing on Price Alone," *Inc.com*, August 2002.
7. George Cressman, "Reaping What You Sow," *Marketing Management*, March/April 2004, 34–40.

8. Michael Mondello, "Naming Your Price," *Inc.*, July 1992, 80–83.
9. Steven Marlin, "Who Needs Cash?" *Information Week*, 22 December 2003, 20–23.
10. "A Cash Call," *The Economist*, February 17, 2007, 71–73.
11. Michael Jalili, "Merchant Fees Catching State Legislators' Eye," *American Banker*, April 30, 2007.
12. Robert Coen, "U.S. Advertising Volume," *Advertising Age*, 20 May 1996, 24.
13. Paul Hawkin, *Growing a Business* (New York: Simon & Schuster, 1987), 33.
14. John Anderson, "The Ultimate Sales Force," *Inc.*, June 2004, 75–80.
15. Alex Salkever, "We're Now in the Era of Sales 2.0," *Inc.*, December 2006, 110–115.
16. Jane Applegate, "Building Your Business with PR," *Working Woman*, December 1993, 69.
17. Stephanie Clifford, "Goodbye Retainers," *Inc.*, October 2006, 35–38.
18. Larry Light, "Promotion Has Bigger Role Than Ads, But 'Short-Term Bribes' Are Suicide," *Advertising Age*, 29 March 1993.
19. Rachel Miscall, "Pick a Card," *Denver Business Journal*, 23 October 1998.

CHAPTER 15

1. Johnathan Calof, "The Impact of Size on Internationalization," *Journal of Small Business Management*, October 1993, 60–69.
2. Laura Tiffany, "Import/Export," *Entrepreneur*, 28 June 2001.
3. Small Business Administration, *Breaking Into the Trade Game: A Small Business Guide to Exporting*, 3rd ed., (2006), www.sba.gov/international
4. "How to Take Your Company Global," 11 December 2003, www.entrepreneur.com
5. Kenneth Kale, "Going Global?" *Fortune Small Business*, March 2001, 98–103.
6. Anil K. Gupta and Vijay Govindarajan, "Managing Global Expansion: A Conceptual Framework," Business Horizons, March/April 2000, 45–54.
7. Ibid.
8. Ted Rakstis, "Going Global," *Kiwanis*, October 1991, 39–43.
9. "How to Take Your Company Global," 11 December 2003, www.entrepreneur.com
10. Courtney Fingar, "The ABCs of EMCs," *Export Today's Global Business*, May 2001.
11. Tom Stein, "The Sweet Smell of Success," *Success*, December 1995, 23.
12. Gene Goudy "Ex-Im Bank," Business Credit, November//December 2003, 48–50.
13. Breaking into the Trade Game, 86.
14. Dan West, "Countertrade," *Business Credit*, April 2002, 48–51.
15. Matt Schaffer, "Countertrade as an Export Strategy," *Journal of Business Strategy*, May/June 1990, 33–39.

16. "Understand and Heed Cultural Differences," *Business America*, September 1992, 30–31.

17. Julie Demers, "Crossing the Cultural Divides," *CMA Management*, September 2002, 28–30.

18. Ibid.

19. Moira Allen, "Talking Heads," *Entrepreneur*, January 2001.

20. Mie-Yun Lee, "Decipher Tricky Documents with a Translation Service," *Entrepreneur*, 28 January 2002.

21. Kevin Walsh, "How to Negotiate European-Style," *Journal of European Business*, July/August 1993, 45–47.

22. Ellen Neuborne, "Bridging the Cultural Gap," *Sales and Marketing Management*, July 2003, 22.

23. Pat McGovern, "How to be a Local, Anywhere," *Inc.*, April 2007, 113–114.

24. Trilateral Customs Guide to NAFTA (Ottawa, Ontario, Canada: Department of Customs, Excise, and Taxation, 1994), 1.

25. http://www.export.gov/fta/NAFTA/fact_sheet.asp, 30 May 2007.

26. NAFTA Rules of Origin (Ottawa, Ontario, Canada: Department of Customs, Excise, and Taxation, 1994), 1.

27. Robert Zoellick, "Customs and the WTO: Moving Closer," *Journal of Commerce*, 31 May 2004, 28.

28. Leslie Brokaw, "ISO 9000: Making the Grade," *Inc.*, June 1993, 98–99.

29. Ibid., 99.

CHAPTER 16

1. Linda Hill, "Hardest Lessons for First–Time Manager," *Working Woman*, February 1994, 18–21.

2. Henry Mintzberg, "The Manager's Job: Folklore and Fact," *Harvard Business Review*, March/April 1990, 163–176.

3. Amy Barrett, "It's a Small (Business) World," *Business Week*, 17 April 1995, 96–101.

4. Jacquelyn Denalli, "Keeping Growth Under Control," *Nation's Business*, July 1993, 31–32.

5. Neil C. Churchill and Virginia Lewis, "The Five Stages of Small Business Growth," *Harvard Business Review*, May/June 1983, 30–50.

6. Eric Wahlgren, "The First Employee," *Inc.*, February 2004, 30–31.

7. Donna Fenn, "When to Go Pro," *Inc.*, 500, 1995, 72.

8. Gerald Brown, "Strategy or Not, You'll Exit Sooner or Later," *Air Conditioning, Heating, and Refrigeration News*, 23 January 2003, 75–79.

9. Glen Baker, "Getting Out," *New Zealand Business*, June 2004, 12–15.

10. Rod Burkert, "A Good Deal Depends on Preparation," *Journal of Accountancy*, November 2003, 47.

11. Theodore Kinni, "Leadership Up Close," *Industry Week*, 20 June 1994, 21–25.

12. Theodore Kinni, "The Credible Leader," *Industry Week*, 20 June 1994, 25–26.

13. Warren Bennis, "Why Leaders Can't Lead," *Training and Development Journal*, April 1989, 35–39.

14. Genevieve Capowski, "Anatomy of a Leader: Where Are the Leaders of Tomorrow?" *Management Review*, March 1994, 10–17.

15. Leigh Buchanan, "Grow Your Own," *Inc.*, March 2007, 42–44.

16. Ibid.

17. Peter Barron Stark and Jane Flaherty, "How to Negotiate," *Training and Development*, June 2004, 52–55.

18. Ibid.

19. Rob Walker, "Take It or Leave It: The Only Guide to Negotiating You Will Ever Need," *Inc.*, August 2003, 81.

20. Patricia Buhler, "Managing in the New Millennium," *Supervision*, December 2003, 20.

21. For examples of applying Maslow's hierarchy of needs in small businesses, see Mark Hendrichs, "Motivating Force," *Entrepreneur*, December 1995, 68–72.

22. Frederick Herzberg, "One More Time: How Do You Motivate Employees?" Harvard Business Review, January 2003, 87–97.

23. Michael Cronin, "Motivation the Old Fashioned Way," *Inc.*, November 1994, 134.

24. Steven H. Appelbaum, Jennifer Cottin, Remy Paré, Barbara T. Shapiro, "Employee Theft: From Behavioural Causation and Prevention to Managerial Detection and Remedies," *Journal of American Academy of Business, Cambridge*, Sepember 2006, 175–182.

25. Norm Brodsky, "The Most Important Resource," *Inc.*, February 2006, 61–62.

26. Alison Stein Wellner, "The Time Trap," *Inc.*, June 2004, 42.

27. Martha Davis, Matthew McKay, and Elizabeth Robbins Eshelman, *The Relaxation and Stress Reduction Workbook*, 2nd ed. (Oakland, CA: New Harbinger Publications, 1982).

28. Kenneth Hart, "Introducing Stress and Stress Management in Managers," *Journal of Managerial Psychology*, vol. 5 (2), 1990, 9–16.

29. Mark Henricks, "Put Me In!" *Entrepreneur*, June 2007, 85–86.

30. Alison Stein Wellner, "Do You Need a Coach?" *Inc.*, April 2006, 86–93.

CHAPTER 17

1. *The Wall Street Journal*, 20 March 1990, A1.

2. Aaron Bernstein and Paul Magnusson, "How Much Good Will Training Do?" *Business Week*, 22 February 1993, 77.

3. Martin John Yate, *Hiring the Best: A Manager's Guide to Effective Interviewing* (Holbrook, MA: Bob Adams, 1998), 18.

4. Fred Steingold, *The Employer's Legal Handbook*, 5th ed. (Berkeley, CA: Nolo Press, 2002), 1/13–1/14.

5. Mark Hendricks "You Know Who?" *Entrepreneur*, May 2007, 89–90.

6. Peter F. Drucker, "How to Save the Family Business," *The Wall Street Journal*, 19 August 1994, A10.

7. Amy Barrett, "It's a Small (Business) World," *Business Week*, 17 April 1995, 96–101.

8. Joel Spolsky, "There's a Better Way to Find and Hire the Very Best Employees," *Inc.*, May 2007, 81–82.

9. *Griggs v. Duke Power Company*, 401 U.S. 424 (1971).

10. John S. O'Connor and Carlene Warner, "How to Develop Physical Capacity Standards," *Personnel Journal New Product News Supplement*, May 1996, 8, 10.

11. Ibid.

12. "SHRM–BNA Survey No. 59: Human Resource Activities, Budgets, and Staffs: 1993–94," *HR Bulletin to Management*, 30 June 1994, 31.

13. Jess Blumberg and Stephanie Clifford, "The Science of Hiring–Choose Your Weapon," *Inc.*, August 2006, 90–98.

14. Frank Hammel, "Tackling Turnover," *Supermarket Business*, October 1995, 103–108.

15. "Ask Inc.," *Inc.*, June 2006, 61.

16. Jill Andresky Fraser, "Financial Strategies," *Inc.*, November 1993, 137.

17. Stephen Huth, "The Perfect Storm?" *Employee Benefit Plan Review*, January 2001, 14–15; www.ebri.org

18. "The Basics of Employee Benefits," *Entrepreneur Magazine Online*, www.entrepreneur.com/humanresources/compensationandbenefits/article80158. html, 2007.

19. *Public Attitudes on Flexible Benefits* (Washington, DC: Employee Benefit Research Institute, 1994), 10.

20. Lynn Miller, "Small Companies Pushed to Offer Health Benefits," *HR Magazine*, June 2001, 18.

21. Peter D'Arruda, "A 412(i) May Be The Answer," *CPA Wealth Provider*, January 2007, 22–23.

22. *Public Attitudes on Flexible Benefits*, 20.

23. "Employees Pitch in for Working Parents," *Parents*, July 1994, 132.

24. United States Department of Labor, Bureau of Labor Statistics, Employer Costs for Employee Compensation-March 2007, Table 8. Employer costs as a percent of total compensation: Private industry workers, by establishment employment size, http://www.bls.gov/ncs/ect/home.htm

25. Allison Bell, "Uncle Sam Asks Bosses For Help," *National Underwriter*, April 19, 2004, 4.

26. "Essentials of an Employee Handbook," How-To section, www.allbusiness.com

27. Material adapted from D. Day, "Training 101: Help for Discipline Dodgers," *Training and Development*, May 1993, 19–22.

CHAPTER 18

1. Shawn Tully, "You'll Never Guess Who Really Makes . . . ," *Fortune*, 3 October 1994, 124–128.

2. Otis Port, "Custom-made, Direct from the Planet," *Business Week, 21st-Century Capitalism Edition*, 18 November 1994, 158–159.

3. Ronald Henkoff, "Make Your Office More Productive," *Fortune*, 25 February 1991, 72–84.

4. Dan Gutman, "Always in Touch," *Success*, March 1995, 54.

5. "Office Ergonomics: Not the Same as in a Plant," *Industry Week*, 5 December 1994, 37.

6. Michael Barrier, "You Have a Purpose in Life," *Nation's Business*, September 1995, 13–14.

7. Gwen Fontenot, Alicia Gresham, and Ravi Behara, "Using Six Sigma to Measure and Improve Customer Service," Proceedings of 1994 National Small Business Consulting Conference, Small Business Institute Director's Association, San Antonio, 1994, 298–304.

8. Ibid., 303.

9. Gregory Watson, "Six Sigma: Analyze Sources of Variation," *Manufacturers' Monthly*, May 2004, 20–21.

10. John Welch, "Timeless Principles," *Executive Excellence*, February 2001, 3–4; Fred R. McFadden, "Six-Sigma Quality Programs," *Quality Progress*, June 1993, 37–42; Gwen Fontenot, Ravi Behara, and Alicia Gresham, "Six Sigma in Customer Satisfaction," *Quality Progress*, December 1994, 73–76; Jim Carbone and Thomas Pearson, "Measure for Six Sigma Success," February 2001, 36–40.

11. *Breaking into the Trade Game: A Small Business Guide to Exporting* (Washington, DC: U.S. Small Business Administration, 1994), 94.

12. Ronald Henkoff, "The Hot New Seal of Quality," *Fortune*, 28 June 1993, 116–117.

13. Michael Barrier and Amy Zuckerman, "Quality Standards the World Agrees On," *Nation's Business*, May 1994, 71–72.

14. Henkoff, "The Hot New Seal," 116.

15. Barrier and Zuckerman, 72.

16. Steven Ashley, "Nondestructive Evaluation with Laser Ultrasound," *Mechanical Engineering*, October 1994, 63–66.

Answers to Test Preps

CHAPTER 1

Multiple Choice

1. a   **2.** b   **3.** d   **4.** a   **5.** c

Fill in the Blank

1. 50   **2.** $6 million   **3.** more than doubled
4. diversity   **5.** business failure

CHAPTER 2

Matching

1. p   **2.** l   **3.** d   **4.** a   **5.** k   **6.** b   **7.** m   **8.** q
9. e   **10.** g

True/False

1. F   **2.** T   **3.** F   **4.** F   **5.** F   **6.** T   **7.** F   **8.** F
9. T   **10.** T

CHAPTER 3

True/False

1. T   **2.** F   **3.** F   **4.** T   **5.** T   **6.** F   **7.** T   **8.** T
9. F   **10.** T

Fill in the Blank

1. strategic thinking   **2.** strengths/opportunities
3. don't do anything!   **4.** mission statement
5. competition

CHAPTER 4

Multiple Choice

1. d   **2.** b   **3.** a   **4.** c   **5.** c

Fill in the Blank

1. interrelated   **2.** meteorite   **3.** business plan
4. assumptions   **5.** investment

CHAPTER 5

Matching

1. c   **2.** h   **3.** b   **4.** e   **5.** f   **6.** i

True/False

1. F   **2.** T   **3.** T   **4.** T   **5.** T   **6.** F   **7.** F   **8.** T
9. F   **10.** F

CHAPTER 6

Multiple Choice

1. b   **2.** a   **3.** c   **4.** d   **5.** c

Fill in the Blank

1. holdback   **2.** skeptical   **3.** goodwill
4. negotiation   **5.** succession

CHAPTER 7

Matching

1. a   **2.** m   **3.** d   **4.** e   **5.** c   **6.** g   **7.** i   **8.** k
9. b   **10.** l

Multiple Choice

1. b   **2.** c   **3.** a   **4.** b   **5.** d

CHAPTER 8

Matching

1. a   **2.** q   **3.** d   **4.** d   **5.** t   **6.** m   **7.** l   **8.** p
9. e   **10.** f

True/False

1. F   **2.** F   **3.** T   **4.** T   **5.** T   **6.** F   **7.** T   **8.** T
9. F   **10.** F

CHAPTER 9

Multiple Choice

1. d   **2.** b   **3.** a   **4.** c   **5.** b

Fill in the Blank

1. higher   **2.** capacity   **3.** LowDoc   **4.** service
5. initial public offering

CHAPTER 10

Matching

1. i   **2.** j   **3.** k   **4.** a   **5.** b   **6.** c   **7.** l   **8.** e
9. h   **10.** n

Fill in the Blank

1. caveat emptor   **2.** Fair Labor Standards
3. industry classification and payroll   **4.** seven
5. specific performance

CHAPTER 11

Matching

1. a **2.** b **3.** n **4.** o **5.** k **6.** l **7.** m **8.** d
9. q **10.** h

Fill in the Blank

1. performance, support **2.** sponsorship
3. cognitive dissonance **4.** anyone
5. existing, new

CHAPTER 12

Matching

1. a **2.** f **3.** b **4.** e **5.** g **6.** c **7.** h **8.** h
9. k **10.** l

Multiple Choice

1. c **2.** a **3.** c **4.** b **5.** b

CHAPTER 13

True/False

1. T **2.** T **3.** F **4.** T **5.** T **6.** F **7.** F **8.** F
9. T **10.** T

Multiple Choice

1. a **2.** b **3.** b **4.** c **5.** d

CHAPTER 14

Multiple Choice

1. d **2.** b **3.** a **4.** b **5.** b

Fill in the Blank

1. bundling **2.** buzz **3.** price sensitive **4.** double
agent **5.** features, advantages, benefits

CHAPTER 15

Matching

1. g **2.** c **3.** h **4.** f **5.** k **6.** q **7.** n **8.** s
9. t **10.** j

True/False

1. F **2.** T **3.** T **4.** T **5.** T **6.** T **7.** F **8.** T
9. T **10.** F

CHAPTER 16

Matching

1. f **2.** a **3.** e **4.** b **5.** c **6.** i **7.** g **8.** j
9. h **10.** l

Fill in the Blank

1. continuous; interrelated **2.** existence; resource
maturity **3.** better; great **4.** ESOP (employee stock
ownership plan) **5.** delegation

CHAPTER 17

True/False

1. T **2.** T **3.** T **4.** F **5.** F **6.** T **7.** T **8.** T
9. F **10.** T

Fill in the Blank

1. employee referral **2.** EEOC (Equal Employment
Opportunity Commission) **3.** BFOQ (bona fide
occupational qualification) **4.** OJT (on-the-job
training) **5.** bonus

CHAPTER 18

True/False

1 T **2.** F **3.** F **4.** T **5.** T **6.** T **7.** F **8.** T
9. F **10.** T

Multiple Choice

1. a **2.** c **3.** a **4.** d **5.** b

Photo Credits

Index

AAFD. *See* American Association of Franchisees and Dealers (AAFD)

AAHBB. *See* American Association of Home-Based Businesses (AAHBB)

AAMCO Transmissions, 125

ABC classification, defined, 332

ABI-INFORM, 135, 305

Accelerators, 359

Account analysis, 229

Accounting
  basics of, 207–215
  defined, 203–204
  double-entry, 207
  methods of, 209
  small business, 203–205

Accounting equations, 209

Accounting records, 210–214

Accounting software, 208

Accounting systems, 203–204, 207

Accounts payable, defined, 250

Accounts receivable, 162, 163, 227–229

Accounts receivable factoring, 248

Accrual-basis method, defined, 209

Accurate, 461–462

Ace Hardware, 333

Achievement tests, 474

Action
  affirmative, 64
  as leadership attribute, 448

Action plan, strategic planning and, 73

Activity ratios, 217–218, 221

ADA. *See* Americans with Disabilities Act (ADA)

Adams, Mark, 432

Adams, Scott, 14

Adaptability, successful entrepreneurs and, 39

Adaptive Integrated Retail System (AIRS), 328

ADEA. *See* Age Discrimination in Employment Act (ADEA)

Adidas, 282

Adler, Chesley, 359

Adobe, 233

ADT, 313–314

Advancement, small business success and, 15

Advertising
  business plan and, 105
  competitive analysis and, 78, 79
  at Jones Soda, 291
  for market research, 307
  marketing strategies and, 296, 301
  PPC, 299
  as promotion, 389–395
  recruitment and, 467

Advertising agencies, for promotion, 395

Advertising development, for promotion, 394

Advertising fees, 142–145

Advertising funds, 143

Advertising objectives, for promotion, 392–394

AFA. *See* American Franchisee Association (AFA)

Affirmative action, 64

Africa, international small business in, 414

African Americans
  firms owned by, 11, 12
  small business finance and, 253

Age, legal environment and, 266

Age Discrimination in Employment Act (ADEA), 64

Agencies, recruitment and, 469

Agents, 344, 415, 416

Aging accounts receivable, 162, 163

Aging schedules, defined, 227

AgraQuest, Inc., 258

Agreement, contract and, 275

Agriculture
  business failure and, 18
  small business size and, 6

AIRS. *See* Adaptive Integrated Retail System (AIRS)

Alaska Natives
  firms owned by, 11, 12
  small business finance and, 253

Alfini, Peter, 285–286

Alipour, Eshan, 114

All Creatures Veterinary Hospital, 464–465

Allen, Katherine, 439–440

Allison, Eric, 114

All-salaried employees, 480

Alpha Bay, 328

AMA. *See* American Marketing Association (AMA)

Ambiguity, successful entrepreneurs and, 39

AmChams. *See* American Chambers of Commerce (AmChams)

American Apparel, 179

American Association of Exporters and Importers, 424

American Association of Franchisees and Dealers (AAFD), 134

American Association of Home-Based Businesses (AAHBB), 182

American Bankers Association, 387

American Chambers of Commerce (AmChams), 420

American Flatbread Company, 38

American Franchisee Association (AFA), 134, 143

American Indians, firms owned by, 11, 12

American Lawyer, 432

American Management Association, 65, 355

American Marketing Association (AMA), 302, 355

American National Standards Institute, 430, 511

American Saw, 511

American Society of Quality Control, 430

Americans with Disabilities Act (ADA), 64, 268–269, 269, 360, 466, 474–475
Amoruso, Tom, 499
Analysis
  account, 229
  breakeven, 110, 112–114, 379–381
  competitive, 73, 76–84, 191–192
  cross-sectional, 220–221
  data, 307
  environmental, 73, 74–76, 102–103
  external, 73, 75–76
  industry, 102–103
  internal, 73, 76
  job, 466–467
  market, 181, 191
  multivariate, 509
  ratio, 216, 221
  regression, 296–297, 509
  SWOT, 74, 84, 104 (*See also* Environmental analysis)
  time series, 220, 221–222, 296
  variance, 509
Analysis of variance (ANOVA), 509
"Analysis paralysis," 188
Analytic systems, defined, 501
Anchor stores, defined, 356
Andretti, Mario, 14
Angels, small business finance and, 253–254
Anheuser-Busch, 2, 7, 151
ANOVA. *See* Analysis of variance (ANOVA)
Antitrust laws, defined, 264
Antonelli, Heather, 259–260
Antonetti, Amilya, 310
Apollo 13, 25
Appeal process, defined, 490
Appendix, in business plan, 114
Apple Computer, 9, 82, 310–311, 370
Application forms, selecting employees through, 471
Approach, personal selling and, 396
Arbitration, partnerships and, 49
Arizona Republic newspaper, 353
Arlington's Arts Incubator, 359
Armstrong, Lance, 16
Art and Science of Negotiation, The, 448
Art of War, The (Tzu), 435
Art services, for promotion, 395
Artful Framer Gallery, 482
Arthur Anderson's Enterprise Group, 450
Articles of incorporation, 50, 51
Articles of partnership, 46, 47, 48–49
Arts Council, 359
ARTS PDF, 233
Ashton Photo, 487
Asia on the Cheap, 407
Asian Americans, firms owned by, 11, 12
Ask Jeeves, 339

Aspiration, social responsibility and, 67
Asset Growth Partners, Inc., 229
Asset-based approach, exit strategy and, 445
Assets
  defined, 207
  long-term, 237
  return on, 219, 221
  short-term, 237
  tangible, 162, 165, 166–167, 168
  thinning the, 169
Associated Business Systems, 96–97
Assumptions, in business plan, 108
Assurance Medical, 417
Atmosphere, competitive analysis and, 78, 79
AT&T, 14, 185
At-will doctrine, defined, 490
At-will employer, 467, 471
Audience, in business plan, 97
Audit checklist, 325–326
Audit notice, 206
Audit team, 324
Augmented product, of product satisfaction, 315
Australia, franchising in, 146
Automation, operations management and, 501
Autonomy, small business finance and, 256
Availability schedule, 229
Average collection period, 217, 221
Avocations, starting new business and, 189
Avrin, David, 398
Avrin Public Relations Group, 398

Baby Boom, 25
Backward scheduling, defined, 505
Bad Ass Coffee, 131
Badu, Erykah, 236
Baechler, Mary, 37
Baechler, Phil, 37
Bailey, George, 24
Balance sheet
  accounting equations and, 209
  defined, 110, 111, 112, 211–212
  OnGoal, 232
  pro forma, 241
  small business finance and, 237
  Stereo City, 212
Balance-sheet methods of valuation, defined, 166
Balloon notes, defined, 246
Bank loans, 245
Bank of America, 91, 259
Bankable Deals, 422
Banking, financial records and, 206–207
Bankruptcy
  Chapter 7, 273–274
  Chapter 11, 274
  Chapter 13, 274

defined, 273
    at Eminence Style, 259–260
    franchising and, 140
    at Morrow Snowboards, 120
    at Westbeach, 119, 121
Bankruptcy Abuse Prevention and Consumer Protection
    Act of 2005, 274
Bankruptcy Code, 274
Bankruptcy laws, 273–274
Bankruptcy Reform Act of 1978, 273
Banks
    cash flow and, 229
    commercial, 245–246
Bar codes, 332, 333
"Bargaining power of buyers," 80, 103
"Bargaining power of suppliers," 80, 103
Barger, Jeff, 426
Barneys, 374
Barnum. P. T., 156
Barter, 423–424
Basic Comfort, 460
Baskin-Robbins, 144
Bass Sporting Goods, 370
BassMasters trade show, 410
Baty, G. B., 256
Bayley, Julian, 189
Beck, Jason, 10
Beck, Mike, 461, 462
Before the Call, 396
Belgium, international small business and, 426
Benchmarking, 78, 509, 512–513
Benefits, 482–486, 487
Benefits to community, in business plan, 108–109
Bennis, Warren, 446
BEP. See Breakeven point
Berkeley, Roger, 410
Berkowitz, Barak, 338
Berman, Lyle, 90
Berne Convention for the Protection of Literary and
    Artistic Works, 283
Berra, Yogi, 73
Berry, Tim, 511
Best Buy, 370, 504
Best practices, 321
Better Business Bureau, 135, 157
Beyer, Jon, 60
BFOQs. See Bona fide occupational qualifications
    (BFOQs)
Big Apple Bagels, 131
Big Business, 333
Big Chef Little Chef, 482
Big-box deal, 370, 371
Big/large businesses, small businesses vs., 13, 302
Billabong, 120
BinoCap, 285

Birch, David, 21
BizPlanit.com, 96
Black, Bruce, 114
Black-box model, 300
Blacks. See African Americans
Blogging, 337–338
Blue Cross Blue Shield, 494
Blue Pumpkin, 409
Boeing, 337
Boelts Bros. Associates, 66
Bona fide occupational qualifications (BFOQs), 467
Bonuses, defined, 481
Book Expo America, 391
Book value, 162, 166
Bootstrapping, 94, 255
Booz, Allen & Hamilton, 316
Boris, Jon, 175
Borrowing, cash flow and, 230
Boston Beer Company, 2, 3, 7
Bottom Line Consultants, 259
BPI. See Buying power index (BPI)
Bradley, Bryan, 248
Brainstorming, 198
Brand, defined, 282
Brandt, Elizabeth, 464–465
Brazil, franchising in, 146
Breach of contract, defined, 275–276
Break-down methods, 294–296
Breakeven analysis, 110, 112–114, 379–381
Breakeven point (BEP), 113, 379, 381
BreathAsure, 421
Bridge on the River Kwai, The, 25
British Columbia Business Service Centre, 96
Brochures, business plan and, 105
Brodbeck, William, 477
Brodbeck Enterprises, 477
Brodsky, Norm, 95, 378
Brokaw, Tom, 198
Brokers, 344, 415
Brooks, Mel, 44
Brower, Mike, 371
Buchanan, Leigh, 16
Buck, Al, 341
Buck, Hoyt, 341
Buck, Pete, 135
Budgets, cash, 224–227
Buffett, Jimmy, 337
Building, for small business location, 368
Build-up methods, 294–295
Bulk purchasing, franchising and, 133
Bulk-sales provisions, 158
Bureau of Labor Statistics, 10, 183
Burke, Richard, 16
Burton, 120
Bush, George, 255

Bush, Herbert Walker, 255
Business Background Report, 388
Business brokers, defined, 155
Business card, promotion and, 398–399
Business density, defined, 11–12
Business ethics, defined, 67
Business failure, 17–20
Business Information Sources (University of
    California Press), 305
Business management, defined, 19
"Business opportunity" scams, 155
Business organization, 42–53
    corporation as (*See* Corporation)
    partnership as, 45–49
    sole proprietorship as, 43–45
Business ownership. *See* Small business ownership
Business plan, 93–122
    contents of, 101–114
    defined, 95
    examples of, 99–100, 115
    guidelines for writing a, 97–101, 115
    purpose of, 95–97
    review process for, 114–118
    sample of, 519–540
    starting new business and, 191
    strategic planning *vs.,* 87–88
Business Plan Center, 96
Business skills, management team and, 107
Business Source Premier, 135
Business strategy, 67–72, 181
Business termination, defined, 19–20
Business Valuation Resources, 161
Business Week, 28, 292, 347
Business-buyout alternative, 152–155
Business-format franchising, defined, 128
Business-level goal, 86
BusinessWeek magazine, 68
Buying, an existing business. *See* Existing business
Buying power index (BPI), 347
Buy-sell agreement, 47
Buzz, 373–374
Buzz Marketing Group, 374
Bylaws, of corporations, 51–52

C corporation, 49, 51, 52, 53
Cable Internet connections, 182
Cafeteria plan, 483
Calderon, Felipe, 420
Callaway Golf, 371
Canada
    franchising in, 146
    international small business and, 417, 418, 427,
        428, 429
Canada Free Trade Agreement, 418

CAP Automation, 332
Capacity
    contract and, 275
    earning, 142
    price and, 378–379
    small business finance and, 238
Capacity trap, defined, 378–379
Capital. *See also* Money
    business failure and, 18, 19
    for business plan, 95–96, 110, 111
    corporations and, 50, 51
    defined, 207
    forms of, 240–243
    franchising and, 130, 132
    intellectual, 17
    partnerships and, 46, 47
    small business finance and, 237–240, 244–257
    small business success and, 16
    sole proprietorships and, 45
    startup, 16–17, 238
    working, 237
Capital intensive, defined, 180
Capitalist system, small business success and, 15
Capitalization rate, 167
Carnegie, Andrew, 8
Carrot Capital Business Plan Challenge, 61
Carrot Capital VentureBowl, 114
Carter Hawley Hale, 504
Cartridge World, 131
Cash, 384–385, 387
Cash budgets, defined, 224–227
Cash flow
    defined, 111, 222–223
    discounted, 166
    franchising and, 133
    managing, 222–2230
    statement of, 212–214
Cash flow fundamentals, 223–224
Cash flow management tools, 224–227
Cash flow statement, Stereo City, 213
Cash forecasts, 224. *See also* Cash budgets
Cash on delivery (COD), 227, 385
Cash-basis method, defined, 209
Cash-flow statement
    accounting equations and, 209
    defined, 110–111
    sales forecast and, 294
Cash-to-cash cycle, 223, 224
Catch the Wave, 337
Caterpillar, 511
Caturano, Richard, 450
Cause-and-effect diagrams, defined, 509
Caveat emptor, 165, 264
CBD. *See* Central business districts (CBD)

CBIs. *See* Certified business intermediaries (CBIs)

CBO. *See* Characteristics of Business Owners (CBO)

CCH Business Owner's Toolkit, 96

Cease-and-desist orders, defined, 264

Cecil, Mike, 497

Cellular phones, 182, 387

Census Bureau, 10, 21, 298, 300, 347, 424, 429

Central business districts (CBD), 356, 357

Central Intelligence Agency, 355

Century 21 Real Estate, 131

CEOs, starting new business and, 184, 185

Certificate of origin, 429

Certified business intermediaries (CBIs), 156

Certified development company, defined, 249–250

Certified public accountant (CPA), 145, 206

Chamber of Commerce, 101, 420

Chandler, Sam, 233

Change
    business failure and, 20
    competitive analysis and, 79
    ethical responsibility and, 66
    small business success and, 15

Channels of distribution, 343–344

Chapter 7 bankruptcy, 273–274

Chapter 11 bankruptcy, 274

Chapter 13 bankruptcy, 274

Character, small business finance and, 239

Characteristics, of successful entrepreneurs, 39

Characteristics of Business Owners (CBO), 21

Charterlink, 120

Chase Manhattan Bank, 182

Chase Manhattan Mortgages, 91

Chatham Creative Arts Incubator, 359

Check, 384–385, 387–388

Cheever, Eddie, 293

Cher, 189

Chevrolet, 127

Child care, 485–486

Childbirth, legal environment and, 267

China. *See* Republic of China

Chizen, Bruce, 233

Christiansen, Clayton M., 187

Chrysler, 308

CIA World Factbook, 355, 417, 418, 419, 420

CIK Enterprises, 446

Cisco, 432, 504

Citizen Kane, 24, 25

City selection, for small business, 349–352

Civil Code of Russia, 146

Civil Rights Act (CRA) of 1964, 64, 267, 268

Civil Rights Act (CRA) of 1991, 270

Civil rights laws, 10

Claritas Corporation, 352

Clayton Act of 1914, 264

Clean Air Foundation, 61

Clemens, John K., 24, 25

Clinton, Bill, 255

Clorox, 310

Closed-ended questions, 473

Closely held corporation, defined, 49

Closing the deal, 169, 396

Clothes Dr., 402

Cloudveil, 175–176

Clutter, marketing strategies and, 298

Coaching, 479

Cobalt Boats, 345

Coca-Cola, 282, 285, 383

COD. *See* Cash on delivery (COD)

Code of ethics, defined, 68–69

Cognitive dissonance, defined, 302

Cohen, Larry, 461–462

Cohen, Ralph, 461

Cold Stone Creamery, 124–125, 131

Cole Taylor Bank, 461, 462

Coleman, Bessie, 235–236

Collateral, small business finance and, 239

Colleges/universities
    business plan and, 101
    U.S. economy and, 10

Collegiate Poker Tour Events Inc., 10

Collusion, defined, 264

Color, legal environment and, 266, 267

Colorado Opinion Tracker, 303

Colt, Samuel, 7

Comakers, defined, 244

Combined Resource Technology (CRT), 222

Comerica, 125

Commerce Department, 429

Commercial banks, small business finance and, 245–246

Commercial finance companies, small business finance and, 246–248

Commissions, 481

Commitment
    business failure and, 20
    as leadership attribute, 446
    self-employment and, 36, 37
    social responsibility and, 62
    successful entrepreneurs and, 39

Commodity Sourcing Group (CSG), 70, 357

Common carrier, defined, 344

Common-size financial statement, defined, 211

Communications
    franchising and, 133
    as leadership attribute, 446
    small business size and, 6

Community
    business plan and, 108–109
    strategic planning and, 74
Community development, business plan and, 109
Company information, in business plan, 102
Comparative messages, as advertising objective, 393
CompareInterestRates.com, 91
Compensating balance, 242
Compensation
    cash flow and, 230
    self-employment and, 36
    unemployment, 271
    workers', 270–271, 483
Compensatory damages, defined, 276
Competition
    in business plan, 104
    competitive analysis of, 73, 76–84
    five basic forces of, 79–81
    laws for, 264
    price and, 375–376
    small business finance and, 254
    social responsibility and, 64
    U.S. economy and, 9
    between vendors, 327
Competitive advantage
    benefits of, 82–83
    business plans and, 114
    creating, 83–84
    creativity and, 190
    defense as, 296
    defined, 13, 76–77, 79
    due diligence and, 153
    green marketing as, 72
    human resource management and, 477
    of inner cities, 70, 357
    marketing mix and, 320–321
    motivation as, 450
    product, 81–82, 320–321
    small business success and, 13–15
    starting new business and, 182
    strategic planning and, 73
    sustainable, 320
    trade shows as, 391
Competitive advantage cycle, 83
Competitive analysis, 73, 76–84, 191–192
Competitive environment, environmental
    analysis and, 75
Competitive weaknesses, 77
Compounding, 242
Compu-Mark U.S., 283
Computers
    notebook, 182
    operations management and, 501
ComScore Media Metrix, 338

Concurrent quality control, defined, 511–513
Conduct, employee, 487
Conferences, human resource management and, 479
Confidence, successful entrepreneurs and, 39
Consensual-relationship agreement, 65
Consequences, social responsibility and, 64–65
Consideration, contract and, 275
Consignment, international small business and, 422
Construction
    business failure and, 18
    small business size and, 5, 6, 7
Consumer behavior, marketing strategies and,
    300–302
Consumer credit, defined, 385, 387
Consumer Product Safety Act, 265
Consumer Product Safety Commission, 64
Consumer protection, social responsibility and, 64
Consumer protection movement, 64
Consumer Reports, 301
Consumers
    laws for, 264–265
    social responsibility and, 64
Contents, of business plan, 101–114
Continuity, partnerships and, 47
Continuous process, defined, 501
Contract
    agreement and, 275
    breach of, 274–277, 275–276
    capacity and, 275
    consideration and, 275
    defined, 274
    implied, 490
    legality in, 275
    love, 65
Contract Counsel, 432–433
Contract laws, 274–276
Contractual obligations, 275–277
Control
    concurrent quality, 511–513
    feedforward quality, 510–511
    franchising and, 133
    locus of, 39
    loss of, 133
Control chart, 512
Control systems
    in business plan, 106
    business-buyout alternative and, 154
    defined, 499–500
    strategic planning and, 73, 87
Controlling, in professional small business
    management, 437, 439, 502
Convenience, credit cards and, 387
Cook, Brian, 505
Cook, H. Douglas, 505

Coopers & Lybrand, 236
Copyright Office, 280
Copyrights, 164, 280–282, 285, 286, 411
Corbin, Stampp, 267
Core benefit, of product satisfaction, 315
Core competency, 320–321
Core-Metrics, 306
Cornice, 310–311
Corporate angels, defined, 253
Corporate outsourcing, 182
Corporate Translation Services (CTS), 426
Corporation, 42, 43, 45, 49–53
  C, 49, 51, 52, 53
  closely held, 49
  forming a, 51–52
  forms of, 52–53
  LLC as, 53
  non-profit, 53
  partnerships and, 47
  public, 49
  S, 49, 51, 52, 53
Correspondence courses, human resource
  management and, 480
Corridor principle, defined, 188
Cosmi Corporation, 52
Cost-control systems, 203
Cost-plus pricing, defined, 384
Cost(s)
  fixed, 378
  of franchise, 130, 141
  holding, 329
  of inventory, 328–329
  opportunity, 257, 379
  ordering, 329
  price and, 378–379
  of startups, 141, 192
  variable, 378
Costume Specialists, Inc., 337
Counterfeiting, 262–263
Countertrade, 423–424
Coupons4Everything.com, 24
Cousins, Brian, 175–176
Covenants, 244
Cover page, in business plan, 101
Covey, Steven, 32
CPA. See Certified public accountant (CPA)
Creation, entrepreneur and, 29
Creative ability, as leadership attribute, 446
Creative destruction, defined, 15
Creative Pricing Primer (Mondello), 384, 386
Creativity
  franchising and, 130
  in pricing, 384
  starting new business and, 190

Credibility, professional small business
  management and, 446
Credit, 245, 384–389
Credit cards, 251, 388, 402–403
Credit policies, 384–389
Credit scoring, 244
Credits, 207
Critical risks, in business plan, 108
Crosby, Vern, 153
Cross-sectional analysis, 220–221
CRT. See Combined Resource Technology (CRT)
Cruze, Guille, 494
CSG. See Commodity Sourcing Group (CSG)
CTS. See Corporate Translation Services (CTS)
Cultural Development Corps Flashpoint, 359
Culture
  defined, 62
  international small business and, 425–427
Currency, in China, 419
Currency Conversion Calculator, 424
Current ratio, 160, 161, 216, 221
Customer base, business-buyout alternative and, 154
Customer intimacy, defined, 193, 194
Customer service, 194–195, 513
Customer-oriented pricing strategies, 382–383
Customers
  competitive analysis and, 79
  credit policies and, 385–388
  environmental analysis and, 76
  as king, 317
  market research and, 308–309
  service for, 194–195
  small business success and, 15

Dairy Queen, 125, 146
DAPAT Pharmaceuticals, 402
Data
  accounting systems and, 203–204
  financial, 102
  for market research, 304, 305–307
  primary, 305–307
  qualitative, 306
  quantitative, 306, 307
  secondary, 305
Data analysis, 307
Datastream Systems, 296
De Abrew, Karl, 233
Dead Poets Society, 25
Dead stock, 162, 329
Debit cards, 387
Debits, 207
Debt
  business failure and, 18
  consumer credit and, 385–386

credit cards and, 251, 388
   legal environment and, 274
   small business finance and, 240–243
   sole proprietorships and, 45
Debt financing
   defined, 241–243
   lenders/investors and, 256
   sources of, 244–250
Debt funds, 240
Debt ratio, 218, 221
Decision making
   business ethics and, 67
   business plan and, 106
   managers and, 439
   marketing strategies and, 300
   partnerships and, 48
Decision-making process, 301
Decisions
   for franchising (*See* Franchising)
   for starting new businesses (*See* New business)
   for taking over existing businesses (*See* Existing business)
Defect rate, defined, 508
Defensive marketing strategy, 296
Delegation, professional small business management and, 449
Deliveries, cash flow and, 230
Dell, 85, 193, 311, 344, 501
Dell, Michael, 344
DeLuca, Fred, 135
Demand
   elasticity of, 377
   marketing concept and, 291–292
   price and, 376–378
Demand curve, defined, 377
Demand note, defined, 246
Democracy in America (Tocqueville), 4
Demonstration, personal selling and, 396
Denver Fire Department, 317
Deontology, defined, 66
Department of Commerce, 145, 252, 253, 262, 305, 420, 424, 425
Department of Justice, 268
Department of Revenue, 272
Department of State, 355, 420
Depot, 56
Design, of small business, 360–364
Design patents, defined, 278
Desire, small business finance and, 256
Determination, successful entrepreneurs and, 38
Development, human resource management and, 477, 479
Dexter, Jennifer, 286
Differentiation, 83

Dillon, Sarah, 398–399
Direct channel, defined, 343
Direct exporting, 416–417
Direct investment, international small business and, 412–413
Direct mail, as promotion, 390
Direction, of business plan, 96–97
Directory of Operating Small Business Investment Companies, 253
Disability
   legal environment and, 266, 268
   partnerships and, 49
Disabled Access Credit, 269
Disabled person, defined, 268
Discipline, employee, 487–491
Disclosure statement, 136, 139–142
Discount rate, defined, 166
Discounted cash flow, defined, 166
Discrimination
   civil rights laws and, 10
   legal environment and, 267, 268, 270
   social responsibility and, 64
Dismissing employees, 490–491. *See also* Employee termination; Firing employees
Disparate impact cases, defined, 270
Dispatching, defined, 507
Dispatching rule, 507
Disposable personal income, defined, 349
Dispute settlement, partnerships and, 49
Disputes, franchising and, 133
Dissatisfaction, job, 451–452
Distress, defined, 457
Distribution. *See* Small business distribution
Distribution channel, defined, 343
Distributors, international small business and, 416
Diversity
   social responsibility and, 64
   workforce, 10–13
Dividends, defined, 243
Dixie Shelving, 499
Documentary collection (drafts), international small business and, 422
Documentation, 323
Dogs in Hats, 285–286
Doing Business report, 414
Double taxation, corporations and, 50–51, 52
Double-entry accounting, defined, 207
Dow Jones, 305
Downsizing, defined, 9
Drafts, international small business and, 422
Draw, partnerships and, 49
Drew, Ernest, 12–13
Drucker, Peter, 20, 33, 291, 308, 469–470
Drug tests, 475

Dry Clean World, 403
DSL, 182
Dual distribution, defined, 344
Ducey, Doug, 125
Due diligence, 145, 153, 157
Due process, 491
Duke Power Co., Griggs v., 474
Dun & Bradstreet, 17, 18, 160, 220, 231, 305, 388, 445
Dunkin' Donuts, 138
DuPont, 282
Dura Rack, 499
Duration, of partnership, 49
Durst, Christine, 365
Durst, Laura, 365
Durst, Zachary, 365
"Dynamics of Minority-Owned Employer Establishments, 1997-2001," 11

Earliest due date rule, 507
Earning capacity, franchising and, 142
Ebert, Roger, 24
EBI. *See* Effective buying index (EBI)
E-business
   business plans and, 96
   customers through, 423
   defined, 180
   environmental analysis and, 75
   Eyetracking.com and, 398
   legal answers and, 276
   marketing strategies and, 299
   online financing and, 245
   portals and, 438
   SEO/PPC advertising and, 299
   six sigma and, 509
   starting new business and, 180–182
Economic development, business plan and, 109
Economic environment, environmental analysis and, 75
Economic order quantity (EOQ), 330–331
Economic responsibility, as social responsibility, 63
Economics of pricing, 374–379
Economy, small businesses in, 7–10
Economy of scale, defined, 8
EDI. *See* Electronic data interchange (EDI)
Edison, Thomas, 194, 285
Education
   business ownership and, 40, 41, 42
   international small business and, 425
   U.S. economy and, 10
Educational services, small business size and, 7
EEO. *See* Equal employment opportunity (EEO)
EEOC. *See* Equal Employment Opportunity Commission (EEOC)
Effective buying index (EBI), 349, 351
Effective rate of interest, 242

Effectiveness, defined, 439
Efficiency. *See also* Productivity
   defined, 439
   distribution and, 344
   franchising and, 130
80-20 principle, 327
Elasticity of demand, defined, 377
Elder care, 485–486
Electric services, small business size and, 6
Electronic data interchange (EDI), of inventory, 332–333
Elements, 482
Elevator pitch, 235
Elizabeth, 25
EMCs. *See* Export management companies (EMCs)
Emerson, Ralph Waldo, 345
Eminence Style, 259–260
Employee Benefit Research Institute, 482, 484
Employee conduct, 487
Employee development, defined, 477
Employee discipline, 487–491
Employee handbook, defined, 487–488
Employee orientation, defined, 477
Employee Polygraph Protection Act, 476
Employee protection, social responsibility and, 64
Employee recruitment, 467–470
Employee referrals, recruitment and, 469
Employee stock ownership plan (ESOP), 32, 444–445
Employee termination, 487–491
Employee testing, 474–476
Employee theft, 455
Employee training, defined, 477
Employee-leasing firms, 464–465, 476
Employees. *See also* Personnel
   all-salaried, 480
   business failure and, 20
   business-buyout alternative and, 154
   buying existing business and, 164
   code of ethics for, 68
   compensating, 480–486
   dismissing, 490–491 (*See also* Employee termination; Firing employees)
   environmental analysis and, 76
   exempt, 480
   exit strategy and, 444
   firing, 489 (*See also* Employee discipline; Employee termination)
   hiring, 465–466
   international small business and, 425
   nonexempt, 480
   OBM and, 225
   placing/training, 477–480
   selecting, 471–476
   small business success and, 17

social responsibility and, 64
temporary, 476
Employers
at-will, 467, 471
commissions and, 481
employee testing and, 474
incentive-pay programs and, 481
Employment agencies, recruitment and, 469
Employment policies, 487
Encyclopedia of Associations (Gale Research), 305
Endorsers, defined, 243–244
Energy, successful entrepreneurs and, 39
Enthusiast angels, defined, 254
Entrepreneur magazine, 14, 41, 134, 135, 148, 347, 350
Entrepreneurial angels, defined, 253–254
Entrepreneurial event, 31
Entrepreneur-manager relationship, 28–31
Entrepreneurs
assessment for, 30–31
college students as, 40
defined, 29
ethics/business strategy and, 68, 69
professional manager *vs.,* 442
social, 66
traits of successful, 38–39
Entrepreneur's Start-Ups magazine, 183
Entrepreneurship, 27–60
American Flatbread Company and, 38
bootstrapping and, 255
business organization and (*See* Business organization)
business planning and, 109
China and, 413
customers and, 317
defined, 28, 66
Edison and, 194
entrepreneur-manager relationship and, 28–31
Fairey and, 390
Garcia and, 482
Goya Foods and, 170
Johnson and, 454
Linksys and, 504
location and, 345
Matterhorn Nursery and, 295
self-employment and, 35–42
small business manager and, 29
startup process and, 31–34
Stonyfield Farms and, 67
Subway and, 135
Trek bikes and, 16
Entrepreneurship process, 31–34
Environment
competitive, 75
economic, 75

legal (*See* Laws)
legal/regulatory, 75 (*See also* Laws)
social responsibility and, 64
sociocultural, 75
technological, 75
Environmental analysis, 73, 74–76, 102–103
Environmental factors, defined, 33
Environmental protection, social responsibility and, 64
Environmental Protection Agency (EPA), 64
Environmentalism, 72
EOQ. *See* Economic order quantity (EOQ)
EPA. *See* Environmental Protection Agency (EPA); Equal Pay Act (EPA)
Equal Employment Opportunity Commission (EEOC), 64, 65, 267, 270, 466, 467, 472, 473, 474
Equal employment opportunity (EEO), 64, 265–266
Equal Pay Act (EPA), 64
Equipment
business-buyout alternative and, 154
for existing business, 162
starting new business and, 192
Equity
owner's, 207, 238, 241
return on, 220
small business finance and, 240–243
Equity financing
defined, 243
lenders/investors and, 256
sources of, 251–255
Equity funds, 240
ERC. *See* Ethics Resource Center (ERC)
Ergonomics, defined, 504
Escalation clause, defined, 366
Escape clauses, defined, 366
Escrow settlement, 169
ESKCO, Inc., 445
ESOP. *See* Employee stock ownership plan (ESOP)
ESPN: The Magazine, 28
ETCs. *See* Export trade companies (ETCs)
"Ethical edge," 70
Ethical responsibility, 63, 65–66
Ethics, 60–74
business, 67
business strategy and, 67–72
code of, 68–69
defined, 62, 65
under pressure, 69–72
social responsibility/strategic planning and, 61–62
TerraCycle and, 61
virtue, 66
Ethics Resource Center (ERC), 67
European Union (EU), 356, 427
Evaluation, in business plan, 104–106

Evaluation of alternatives, in decision-making process, 301
Even pricing, defined, 383
Evoked set, defined, 301
Excel, 208
Exclusive territory, 138, 141, 142, 144–145
Executive recruiters (headhunters), recruitment and, 469
Executive summary, in business plan, 102
Exempt employees, defined, 480
Exercise, as stress management, 458
Eximbank. *See* Export-Import Bank (Eximbank)
Existence stage, of growing firm, 440
Existing business, 151–177
  advantages of buying, 152–154
  business-buyout alternative and, 152–155
  closing deal on, 169
  disadvantages of buying, 154–155
  family business as, 169–172
  finding, 155–156
  intangible assets and, 163–164
  paying for, 165–168
  personnel for, 164
  seller of, 165
  tangible assets and, 162
  terms of sale and, 168–169
  what to look for in, 156–161
Existing products, 316–318
Exit strategy, 109, 444–445
Expansion, franchising and, 133
Expectations, franchising and, 130–131
Expected product, of product satisfaction, 315
Expense ratios, 160
Experience
  franchising and, 140
  management team and, 107
  starting new business and, 188
Experimental designs, defined, 509
Export management companies (EMCs), international small business and, 415
Export markets, 417–420
Export trade companies (ETCs), 415
Export-Import Bank (Eximbank), 421
Exporting, 413–420
  advantages of, 413–414
  defined, 411, 413
  direct, 416–417
  disadvantages of, 414
  indirect, 415–416, 417
  markets for, 417–420
  piggyback, 415–416
External analysis, 73, 75–76
"Extreme skiing," 39
Eyetracking.com, 398

Facebook, 338
Facilities, in business plan, 106
Facsimile machines, 182
Factiva, 396
Factoring, defined, 248
Failure, business, 17–20, 151
Fair Debt Collection Practices Act, 265
Fair Labor Standards Act (FLSA), 266–267, 480
Fairey, Shepard, 390
Families and Work Institute, 36–37, 465
Family
  business and, 37
  exit strategy and, 445
  incubators and, 359–360
  recruitment and, 469–470
  small business finance and, 252
Family business, 169–172
Family Business magazine, 172
Fantastic Foods, 303
Fantastic Sam's, 502
Fantasy messages, as advertising objective, 394
FAQs. *See* Frequently asked questions (FAQs)
Farkas, Alex, 40
FASB. *See* Financial Accounting Standards Board (FASB)
Fast Company, 15, 66
Fast-growth startups, 183, 185
Fayol, Henri, 438
FBI, 189
FDA. *See* Food and Drug Administration (FDA)
Feasibility, of business plan, 95, 114
Federal Family and Medical Leave Act (FMLA), 483
Federal loan programs, small business finance and, 248–250
Federal Trade Commission Act of 1914, 264
Federal Trade Commission (FTC), 64, 139, 142, 143, 264, 265
Federation of International Trade Associations, 424
Feedback
  defined, 500
  successful entrepreneurs and, 39
Feedback quality control, defined, 513
Feedforward quality control, defined, 510–511
Ferguson, Gil, 231
Ferris, Matt, 114
FICA, 206, 483
Finance/financing. *See also* Small business finance
  business failure and, 18, 19, 20
  business-buyout alternative and, 154
  credit cards for, 251
  debt (*See* Debt financing)
  equity (*See* Equity financing)
  incubators and, 360
  international, 421–422
  online, 245

small business (*See* Small business finance)

small business size and, 6, 7

Financial Accounting Standards Board (FASB), 210

Financial assistance, franchising and, 128, 141

Financial buyer, exit strategy and, 444

Financial condition, of existing business, 158–159

Financial data, in business plan, 102

Financial health, of existing business, 161

Financial plan, in business plan, 109–114

Financial ratios, 216, 220–222

Financial records, importance of, 205–207

Financial Research Associates, 212, 220

Financial statements

accounting systems and, 204

analyzing, 215–222

common-size, 211

franchising and, 142

OBM and, 225

pro forma, 214

to run business, 214–215

small business finance and, 240

Financial Status Checklist, 214–215

Financial Studies of the Small Business, 220

Financial vocabulary, 240–244

Financial/legal management, 201–287

accounting records and (*See* Accounting records)

financial statements and (*See* Financial statements)

legal environment for (*See* Laws)

small business finance and (*See* Small business finance)

Fingerhut, Allan, 56–57

Fingerhut, Ron, 56

Fingerhut, Rose, 56

Firing employees, 489. *See also* Employee discipline; Employee termination

First Avenue, 56–57

First-come, first-served priority dispatching rules, 507

Fischer, Ken, 316

Fishing, business failure and, 18

Fitzpatrick, Brad, 338

Five Cs of credit, 238–239

504 loan program, 249

Fixed asset turnover, defined, 217–218

Fixed costs, defined, 378

Fixed layout, defined, 364

Fixed-rate loan, 242

Flexibility

corporations and, 53

home-based businesses and, 182

loans and, 243

small business success and, 13–14

successful entrepreneurs and, 39

Flexible benefit packages, 483

Floor planning, defined, 246–247

Flowcharts, defined, 509

FLSA. *See* Fair Labor Standards Act (FLSA)

FMLA. *See* Federal Family and Medical Leave Act (FMLA)

Focus groups, for market research, 306

Focus strategies, 83

Fog Creek Software, 470

Follow-up, personal selling and, 396

Food and Drug Administration (FDA), 64

Forbes, 347

Ford, 82, 308, 390, 406

Ford, Henry, 8

Foreclosing, legal environment and, 274

Foreign Incentives, 424

Forestry, business failure and, 18

Fortune 500 companies, 1, 4, 32, 344

Fortune 1000 companies/firms, 253, 409

Fortune magazine, 347

Fortune Small Business, 15, 134

Forward scheduling, defined, 505

Founder's Syndrome, 38

Four Ps, 314, 342–343, 374

412(i) plan, 484, 485

401(k) plans, 484, 485

France

franchising in, 146

international small business and, 418

Franchise. *See also* Franchising

cost of, 130

defined, 125

opening a, 128–133

selecting a, 134–145

Franchise agreement, defined, 142–145

Franchise fee, 142–145

Franchise Handbook, The, 134

Franchise trade journal, 134

Franchisee

bulk purchasing and, 133

capital and, 132

control and, 133

defined, 125, 127

disputes and, 133

learning and, 129

opening franchise and, 128–132

overdependence and, 131

poor performance of, 132

profit sharing and, 133

revenue and, 132

standards and, 129

termination and, 132

Franchising, 124–150, 152

advantages of, 128–130, 132–133

business-format, 128

disadvantages of, 130–132, 133

facts about, 126
information about, 125–127
international, 145–146
product-distribution, 127
Franchising Code of Conduct, 146
Franchising Opportunities World, 134
Franchising systems, 127–128
Franchisor
  bulk purchasing and, 133
  capital and, 132
  control and, 133
  defined, 125, 127
  disputes and, 133
  efficiency and, 130
  growth and, 130
  learning and, 129
  marketing expertise and, 128
  opening franchise and, 129, 132–133
  overdependence on, 130–131
  poor performance and, 132
  profit sharing and, 133
  revenue and, 132
  standards and, 129
Franchisor venue provisions, 143
Frank, Byron, 56, 57
Frankel, Rob, 290
FranNet, 135
Fraud
  franchising and, 131
  professional small business management and, 455
Freedom, franchising and, 130
Free-flow layout, defined, 360, 361
Freestyle Audio, 370–371
Frequently asked questions (FAQs), 68–69
Frerick, Diana, 251
Fried, Lance, 370–371
Friedman, Milton, 63
Friends
  recruitment of, 469–470
  small business finance and, 252
FTC. *See* Federal Trade Commission (FTC)
Function-level goal, 86
Future Cure, Inc., 328

GAAP. *See* Generally accepted accounting
  principles (GAAP)
Gag rules, 143
Galbenski, David, 432–433
Gantt, Henry L., 505
Gantt chart, 505, 506, 507
Gantz, Nancy, 282
Garage.com, 235
GarageTek, 148–149
Garcia, Lorena, 482

Gas services, small business size and, 6
Gates, Bill, 9
GATT. *See* General Agreement on Tariffs and
  Trade (GATT)
Gay, Martha, 182
GazeStats, 398
GazeTraces, 398
GazeTransitions, 398
GDP. *See* Gross domestic product (GDP)
Gediman's Appliance, 376
General Agreement on Tariffs and Trade (GATT), 429
General Electric, 194, 432
General Electric Credit, 376
General ledger, defined, 210
General management, entrepreneur and, 29
General Motors, 1, 8, 337
General Nutrition Centers (GNC), 125, 137
General partnership, defined, 46
General-duty clause, 467
Generally accepted accounting principles (GAAP),
  210, 511
Generic product, of product satisfaction, 315
Geographic information systems (GIS) software, 353
Geographic location, in business plan, 106
George, Robert, 69, 70
Germany, international small business and, 418, 426
Getting to Yes, 448
Giannetto, John, 334
GIS software. *See* Geographic information systems
  (GIS) software
Glaser, Rob, 179
Glatstein, Scott, 469
Glengarry Glen Ross, 25
Global protection, for intellectual property, 283
Global test, for international small business, 409–411
Glossary, in employee handbook, 487
GNC. *See* General Nutrition Centers (GNC)
Go Computers, 185, 186
Goal setting, strategic planning and, 73, 84–87
Goals
  business plan and, 112
  business-level, 86
  code of ethics and, 68
  at Cold Stone Creamery, 125
  function-level, 86
  marketing strategies and, 294
  strategic planning and, 84–87
Godin, Seth, 292
Goldstein, Wendy, 337
Good faith and fair dealing, 491
Good Morning America, 290
Good Technology, 278
Goods, tangible *vs.* intangible, 315
Goodwill, 164, 165, 167, 168

Google, 91
Gottemoller, Meg, 182
Government lenders, small business finance and, 250
Government Printing Office Monthly Catalog, 305
Government Regulation on Franchising, 146
Government-funded employment agencies, 469
Goya Foods, 170
Grabowski, Clare, 338
Grand Casinos, 90
Graphic design services, for promotion, 395
Great Game of Business, The (Stack), 225
Great Harvest Bakery, 74
Great Plains, 207
Green marketing, 72
Grid layout, defined, 361
Griggs v. Duke Power Co., 474
Grittith Rubber Mills, 511
Gross domestic product (GDP), 170, 278, 418, 419
Gross lease, defined, 366
Group discussions, human resource management
   and, 479
Groupe Danone, 67
Growth
   corporations and, 51
   defined, 32
   entrepreneurship process and, 32, 33, 34
   franchising and, 125, 130, 133
   small business, 408, 440–445
   in U.S. economy, 9–10
Grumbles, George, 416
Guaranteed loans, 249
Guarantors, defined, 244
Guerrero, Bill, 40
Guides, for business plans, 101

Habitat for Humanity, 66
Hammacher Schlemmer, 114
Handmade in America, 359
Hanks, Tom, 189
Hansen, Peter, 414
Harassment, sexual, 65, 270
Hard Candy, 292
Hard issues, human resource management and, 477
Hardball Manifesto, 85
Harmonized system (HS), 428, 429
Hart, Darryl, 357
Hartley, Robert, 81
Harvard Business Review article, 85
Harvest
   defined, 32
   entrepreneurship process and, 33, 34
Hawaiians. *See* Native Hawaiians
Hawkin, Paul, 394
Headhunters. *See* Executive recruiters (headhunters)

Health insurance, human resource management
   and, 484
Health maintenance organizations (HMOs), 484
Health savings accounts (HSAs), 494
Health services, small business size and, 7
Healthcare benefits, 486
Heim, Todd, 328
Henri Bendel, 374
Henry, Andrew, 497
Hernandez, Leo, 231
Hertz, Eli E., 470
Hertz Computer Corporation, 470
Herzberg's motivation-hygiene theory, 451
Herzog, Hattie, 313–314
Hewlett-Packard, 311
H.H. Buck & Son Lifetime Knives, 341
Hill, Scott, 446
Hilldun, 248
Hilton Hotels and Resorts, 131
Hilton Inn, 130
Hipslip™, 282
Hiring, 465–466, 470
Hirshberg, Gary, 67
Hirshberg, Meg, 67
Hi-Shear Technology, 202–203
Hispanics
   firms owned by, 11, 12
   small business finance and, 253
Histograms, defined, 509
History of the World, Part I (Brooks), 44
Hitbox, 306
HMOs. *See* Health maintenance organizations
   (HMOs)
Hobbies, 189, 215
Hoechst Celanese, 13
Hoffman, Jim, 286
Hoffman, Joan, 286
Hoffman, Jonathan, 285–286
Hogan Personality Inventory, 476
Holdback money, 169
Holding costs, defined, 329
*Home Comforts: The Art and Science of Keeping
   House* (Mendelson), 436
Home Depot, 61
Home office, 364–365
Home-based businesses, 182–183, 273
Hon, Frankie, 120, 121
Honesty tests, 475
Hoosiers, 24
Hoover, 396
Horn, Matt, 295
Horn, Ronnie, 295
Houlgate, Greg, 371
Hourly wages, 480

Houston, Whitney, 251
Howard, James, 229
Howell, Bill, 240
H&R Block, 125
HS. *See* Harmonized system (HS)
HSAs. *See* Health savings accounts (HSAs)
Human development, business plan and, 109
Human resource management, 464–495
   compensating employees and, 480–486
   employee recruitment and, 467–470
   hiring and, 465–466
   job analysis and, 466–467
   selecting employees and, 471–476
Humor, as advertising objective, 393
Hunsan Company, 189
Hunt, Jim, 410

IBM, 1, 8, 185, 310
Ice Culture, 189
ICIC. *See* Initiative for a Competitive Inner City (ICIC)
Idealism, defined, 66
IFA. *See* International Franchise Association (IFA)
iFranchise Group, 149
Illicic, Dann, 377
Image
   in business plan, 98
   business-buyout alternative and, 154
   competitive analysis and, 78
Immigration and Naturalization Service
   regulations, 267
Immigration Reform and Control Act (IRCA),
   167–168
Imperatives, 469
Implementation, 31, 32, 33, 34
Implied contract, 490
Importing, 411, 420–421
In Style, 374
Inc., 15, 24, 25, 28, 40, 70, 91, 95
   existing business and, 161
   franchising and, 134
   operations management and, 504
   place and, 347, 350, 357
   price/promotion and, 378
   professional small business management and, 444, 445
   small business finance and, 238, 258
   starting new business and, 183, 184, 185
Incentive-pay programs, 481–482
Income
   disposable personal, 349
   partnerships and, 46
   self-employment and, 36
   taxes for, 195–196
   U.S. economy and, 8
Income approach, exit strategy and, 445

Income statement
   accounting equations and, 209
   defined, 210–211
   OnGoal, 232
   sales forecast and, 294
   Stereo City, 211
Income-statement methods of valuation, 166, 167
Inconsistency, franchising and, 133
Incorporator Pro, 52
Incubators, as small business location, 358–360
Independence
   partnerships and, 47
   self-employment and, 35, 36
Independent audit, 160
Independent contractor, defined, 196
Index to the U.S. Patent Classification, 279
Indirect channels, defined, 343–344
Indirect exporting, 415–416, 417
Individual retirement accounts, 484
Individualized marketing, defined, 298
Indonesia, franchising in, 146
Industrial Property Law, 146
Industry analysis, in business plan, 102–103
Industry experience, small business finance and, 256
Industry Norms and Key Business Ratios, 220, 231
Industry weakness, business failure and, 18, 19
Inexperience, business failure and, 18
Information
   about franchising, 134–135, 141
   accounting systems and, 203–204
   for financial records, 206
   small business success and, 17
Information processing, managers and, 439
Information search, in decision-making process, 301
Information technology (IT), 181
Initial capital requirements, 237
Initial public offering (IPO), 32, 255
Initiative for a Competitive Inner City (ICIC), 70, 357
Injunction, defined, 277
Innovation
   defined, 66
   entrepreneurs and, 29, 39
   entrepreneurship process and, 31, 32, 33, 34
   management, 15
   of new products, 318
   process, 15
   product, 15
   service, 15
   small business marketing and, 291
   small business success and, 14–15
Innovator's Dilemma: When New Technologies Cause Great Firms to Fail, The (Christiansen), 187
Inputs, defined, 498
Inshopping, defined, 350

Installment account, defined, 387
Installment loans, defined, 246
Installments, buying existing business through, 169
Institute of Management and Administration, 135
In-store opinions, for advertising, 394
Insurance
    business failure and, 18
    in buying businesses, 157
    cash flow and, 230
    health, 484
    leasing and, 367
    small business size and, 6, 7
Insurance companies, small business finance
    and, 248
Intacct Small Business, 208
Intangible assets, 162, 163–164, 165, 167–168
Intangible goods, 315
Integrated Staffing, 464
Integrity, as leadership attribute, 446
Intellectual capital, defined, 17
Intellectual property, 142, 164, 277–283
    copyrights and, 280–282
    defined, 277
    global protection of, 283
    patents and, 277–280
    trademarks and, 282–283
Interest rate
    defined, 241
    maturity and, 242
    small business finance and, 249
Intermediaries
    distribution and, 344
    international small business and, 415, 416
Intermediate-term loan, 242, 246
Intermittent process, defined, 501
Internal analysis, strategic planning and, 73, 76
Internal Revenue Service (IRS), 4, 44, 50, 52, 53,
    179, 195, 196, 206, 215, 269, 483, 507
Internal-oriented pricing strategies, defined, 383–384
International Brotherhood of Electrical Workers, 515
International Business Brokers Association, 156
International business plan, 408–409
International Chamber of Commerce, 262, 424
International Federation of Customs Brokers
    Association, 424
International finance, 421–422
International Franchise Association Educational
    Foundation, 126
International Franchise Association (IFA), 127, 134
International franchising, 145–146
International licensing, defined, 411–412
International logistics, 424
International Organization for Standardization, 424
International small business, 406–434

    challenges for, 424–430
    establishing, 411–413
    exporting for (See Exporting)
    financial mechanisms for, 421–424
    importing for, 411, 420–421
    preparing for, 408–411
International Standards Organization (ISO),
    429–430, 512
International trade, 408
International trading regions, 427–429
Internet
    Catch the Wave and, 337
    e-business on, 180–182
    environmental analysis and, 75
    goals and, 86
    going global and, 355
    incubators and, 359
    international small business and, 423, 424
    languages on, 423
    marketing strategies and, 299
    professional small business management and, 438
    as promotion, 392
    recruitment and, 470
    Second Life and, 179
Internet job sites, 469
Interstate Commerce Commission, 272
Interstate stock sale, defined, 254
Interviewing, human resource management and,
    471–474
Interviews, for market research, 306
Intrastate stock sale, defined, 254
Intuit Professional Accounting Solutions, 205, 332
Inventors, 318–320
Inventory
    business-buyout alternative and, 154
    cash flow and, 229
    costs of, 328–329
    defined, 327
    of existing business, 162
    managing, 327–329
    for manufacturing business, 328
    for retail business, 327
    for service industry, 327–328
Inventory control, 329–335
    ABC classification and, 332
    defined, 329
    EDI and, 332–333
    EOQ and, 330–331
    JIT and, 333–334
    MRP and, 334–335
    reoder point/quantity and, 330
    visual control and, 330
Inventory cycle, defined, 330
Inventory turnover, defined, 217

Investment
  franchising and, 141
  international small business and, 412–413
  return on, 219
Investors
  choosing, 256–257
  small business finance and, 240
IPO. *See* Initial public offering (IPO)
IRA, 484, 485
IRCA. *See* Immigration Reform and Control Act (IRCA)
Ireland, international small business and, 418
IRS. *See* Internal Revenue Service (IRS)
ISO. *See* International Standards Organization (ISO)
ISO 9000 standards, 430, 511
ISO 14000 standards, 430
IT. *See* Information technology (IT)
It's a Wonderful Life, 24, 25
It's Just Lunch Dating Service, 131

Jacobs, Bert, 191
Jacobs, John, 191
Jacobs & Prosek, 198–199
Japan, international small business and, 418, 425–426, 428
Jazzercise, 131
Jerry Maguire, 24
Jet Set Sports, 293
Jian's BizPlanBuilder Interactive, 101
Jiffy Lube, 502
JIT. *See* Just-in-time (JIT)
Job analysis, defined, 466–467
Job Boss Software, 430
Job description, 466–467, 468
Job fairs, recruitment and, 470
Job rotation, human resource management and, 480
Job shops, defined, 501
Job specifications, defined, 467
Jobs, Steve, 9, 311
John, Elton, 189
John Deere Company, 13
Johnson, Hillary, 435–436
Johnson, Lyndon, 291
Johnson, Marcus, 454
Johnson, Robert L., 454
Joint venture, 49, 412, 413
Jones Soda, 290–291
Joos, Bill, 235
Jordan's Furniture, 317
Journals
  accounting records and, 210
  accounting systems and, 204
Jungle, The (Sinclair), 64
Junk bonds, defined, 9
Just cause, 132, 491
Just-in-time (JIT), 328, 333–334

Kabobs, 410
Kamins, Aaron, 461, 462
Kanter, Larry, 445
Kaplan, Jerry, 185
Karaoke Star Store & Stage, 251
Keaton, Diane, 25
Kelley Manufacturing, 410
Kelly Services, 476
Kendall Banks, 410
Kennedy, Robert, 14
Kentucky Fried Chicken (KFC), 146, 285
Keogh plans, 484, 485
Kerry, John, 255
KFC. *See* Kentucky Fried Chicken (KFC)
KidSmart Vocal Smoke Detector, 114
Kmart, 376
Knives, Buck, 341–342
Knouf, Craig, 96–97
Knowledge
  small business success and, 15
  successful entrepreneurs and, 38
Koch, Jim, 2–3
Kongo Gumi, 152
Koreans, business density and, 11
Kouzes, Jim, 445
KPMG, 262
Kramer, Steve, 359
Krispy Kreme, 292, 497–498
Kroc, Ray, 145
Kroger, 291
Kumon Math & Reading Centers, 131
Kushner, Robert, 413

Labor force, in business plan, 106
Labor intensive, defined, 180
Lachenauer, Rob, 85
Lackey, Michael, 399
Lands' End, 194
Languages
  international small business and, 423, 425, 426
  website for, 423
Lared Group, 412
Large businesses. *See* Big/large businesses
Laser printers, 182
Latin America, website for, 355
Laws
  antitrust, 264
  bankruptcy, 273–274
  licenses/restrictions/permits and, 272–273
  to promote fair business competition, 264
  to protect consumers, 264–265
  to protect intellectual property (*See* Intellectual property)
  to protect workplace (*See* Workplace)

for small business, 263–364
social responsibility and, 63–65
zoning, 272–273
Layout(s)
competitive analysis and, 78, 79
fixed, 364
loop, 361
manufacturing, 362–364
process, 362
retail, 360–361
service, 362
of small business, 360–364
Lead time, defined, 330
Leadership
defined, 446
management *vs.*, 446
product, 193, 194
professional small business management and, 445–454
Leadership attributes, 446–448
Leading, in professional small business management, 437, 439, 502
Leasehold improvements, defined, 366
Leases/leasing, 164, 247, 365–367
Leasing Space for Your Small Business (Portman and Steingold), 367
Lecturing, human resource management and, 479
Ledbetter, Pierce, 55
Leddy, Patrick, Jr., 144
Ledgers
accounting records and, 210
accounting systems and, 204
Lee's Ice Cream, 319
Legal circumference, small business finance and, 257
Legal environment. *See* Laws
Legal form of business, 192
Legal management. *See* Financial/legal management
Legal obligations, social responsibility and, 63–65
Legal requirements, for small business location, 360
Legal utility, patents and, 279
Legality, in contract, 275
Legal/regulatory environment, environmental analysis and, 75
Lenders
choosing, 256–257
loan rejection by, 250–251
Lesonsky, Rieva, 14
Letter of confidentiality, 159, 160
Letter of credit, international small business and, 422
Leverage, defined, 240
Leverage ratios, 218–219, 221
Levi Strauss, 151, 390
Lewin, Kurt, 300
Lewinsky, Monica, 374
Lexis-Nexis, 135, 305

Liability/liabilities
business-buyout alternative and, 154
buying existing business and, 169
defined, 207
limited, 51
personal, 36
small business finance and, 240
unlimited, 45, 46
Licenses
legal environment and, 272–273
starting new business and, 195
Licensing, 411–412, 413
Licensing agreement, 319, 412
Life cycle, of product, 316
Life is Good, 191
Lifeline Systems, 334
Lifestyle, self-employment and, 35
Limited, The, 9
Limited liability, 51
Limited partnership, 46, 47–48
Limited partnership agreement, 47
Limited-liability company (LLC), 43, 48, 49, 51
Limited-liability partnership (LLP), 48
Limited-liability protection, 50, 52
Lincoln, David, 71
Lincoln Laser Company, 71
Linden Lab, 178–179
Line of credit, defined, 245, 387
Linksys, 504
Lippie, Jim, 481
Liquidation
defined, 273
exit strategy and, 445
legal environment and, 274
Liquidation value, 166, 167
Liquidity ratios, 216–217, 221
Litigation, franchising and, 140
Little & Co., 183
Little League, 66
LiveJournal, 338
LLC. *See* Limited-liability company (LLC)
LLP. *See* Limited-liability partnership (LLP)
Loan application process, 244
Loan Bright, 90–91
Loan officers, business plans and, 98
Loan restrictions, 244
Loan security, defined, 243–244
Loans
bank, 245
debt financing and, 241–243
fixed-rate, 242
guaranteed, 249
installment, 246
intermediate-term, 242, 246

long-term, 242, 245

policy, 248

rejection of, 250–251

SBA, 249, 250

secured, 247

self-liquidating, 245

short-term, 242, 245, 246, 247

terminology for, 243–244

unsecured, 245

unsecured term, 246

variable-rate, 242

Location types, 356–360

Location(s). *See also* Place

business plan and, 106

business-buyout alternative and, 154

competitive analysis and, 78, 79

geographic, 106

human resource management and, 472–473

service, 358

of small business, 193, 345–347

stand-alone, 358

Locus of control, defined, 39

Lodging Hospitality, 77

Loeb, Jason, 403

Logistics, for starting new business, 181

Logos, franchising and, 142

Lonely Planet, 406–407, 432

Longest processing time priority dispatching rule, 507

Longevity, business, 17

Long-term assets, defined, 237

Long-term loan, 242, 245

Loop layout, defined, 361

Loss of control, franchising and, 133

Losses, partnerships and, 48

Lotus Development, 185

"Love contract," 65

Lowe's, 333

"Lucky draw" contests, 307

Lump-sum payment, 168–169

M&A. *See* Mergers and acquisitions (M&A)

Maaco Auto Painting & Bodyworks, 131

Macro-aging schedule, defined, 227

Macromedia, Inc., 402

Madrid Protocol, 282

Magadan, businesses in, 93–94

Magazine, as promotion, 392

Magenis, Kevin, 310–311

Magic Image, 391

Magnetech, 515–516

Mail surveys, for market research, 306

Major League Baseball, 28

Make-or-buy decision, defined, 324

Make-or-buy policy, in business plan, 106

Management

business failure and, 19, 72

defined, 437

financial/legal (*See* Financial/legal management)

four functions of, 437

general, 29

human resource (*See* Human resource management)

leadership *vs.,* 446

operations (*See* Operations management (OM))

participative, 509

professional small business (*See* Professional small business management)

quality-centered, 508–510

small business (*See* Small business management)

stress, 457–458

time, 455–456

total quality, 334, 510–511

Management innovation, 15

Management style, 505

Management team, in business plan, 107

Managers, explained, 437–440

Managing international accounts, 422–423

Managing small business, 405–516, 437–440

human resource management (*See* Human resource management)

international small business (*See* International small business)

operations management (*See* Operations management (OM))

professional small business management (*See* Professional small business management)

MANOVA. *See* Multivariate analysis (MANOVA)

Manpower, Inc., 476

Manufacturer's agents, 344

Manufacturing

business failure and, 18

inventory for, 328

operations management for, 500–501

private-label, 320

production *vs.,* 500

short-cycle, 509

small business size and, 5, 6, 7

Manufacturing and operations plan, 106

Manufacturing layouts, for small business location, 362–364

Manufacturing resource planning II (MRPII), 334, 335

Marble Slab Creamery, 137

Margalith, Abby, 189

Margalith, Ethan, 189

Margaritaville Store, 337

Market analysis, starting new business and, 181, 191

Market approach, exit strategy and, 445

Market opportunity, in business plan, 102

Market Perceptions, 303

Market research, 302–309
Market Research Library, 417
Market research process, 303–307
Market segmentation
   in business plan, 104
   defined, 298
Market share, in business plan, 105
Market trends, in business plan, 104
Marketing, 289–404
   green, 72
   individualized, 298
   mass, 298
   niche, 298
   place and (*See* Place)
   price and (*See* Price)
   products and (*See* Product(s))
   promotion as (*See* Promotion)
   public relations and, 399
   relationship, 292
   research for, 302–309
   strategy for (*See* Marketing strategies)
   youth, 374
Marketing concept, defined, 8, 291–292
Marketing expertise, franchising and, 128
Marketing Mistakes (Hartley), 81
Marketing mix
   competitive advantage and, 320–321
   defined, 314
   inventor's paradox and, 318–320
   marketing strategies and, 300
   packaging and, 321
   place and, 342
   product and, 314–321
Marketing objectives
   in business plan, 105
   marketing strategies and, 294
Marketing plan
   in business plan, 105–106
   marketing strategies and, 293, 294
   starting new business and, 193
Marketing strategies, 293–302. *See also* Strategy/
   strategies
   consumer behavior and, 300–302
   defensive, 296
   defined, 86, 293
   Internet, 299
   marketing objectives and, 294
   sales forecast and, 294–297
   sponsorship as, 293
   target markets and, 297–298, 300
Marketing-performance objectives, 294
Marketing-support objectives, 294
Market/marketing research, 84, 104–106, 302–309
Markup, defined, 384

Marrone, Pam, 258
Marshall, Carmia, 235–236
Martell, John, 515–516
Maslow, Abraham, 450
Maslow's hierarchy of needs, 450–451
Mass customization, defined, 501
Mass marketing, defined, 298
Materials requirements planning (MRP), 328, 334–335
Mathy, Jon, 114
Matrics, 333
Matterhorn Nursery, 295
Maturity
   defined, 32, 242
   entrepreneurship process and, 33, 34
   loans and, 246
MCA Records, 454
McClellan, Steve, 56, 57
McClelland, David, 39
McConnell, Mac, 482
McCormick, Cyrus, 126
McDonald, Micky, 119–121
McDonald's, 125, 129, 131, 141, 145, 146, 164, 285,
   313–314
McGovern, Pat, 426–427
McGregor, Michael, 175
Medallion Construction Company, 69
Media, promotion through, 389
Media agencies, for promotion, 395
Medical conditions, legal environment and, 267
Medley, Andy, 446
Meineke Car Care Centers, 131
Members, corporations and, 53
Men
   business ideas from, 188
   employee theft by, 455
   self-employment of, 10
Mendelson, Cheryl, 436
Mendez, Chris, 402–403
Mendez, Merilyn, 403
Mentoring, 479
Mercedes-Benz, 164
"Merger mania," 9
Mergers and acquisitions (M&A), 254
Merkle, 450
Merry Maids, 131, 138, 502
MESBICs. *See* Minority enterprise small business
   investment companies (MESBICs)
Mexico
   franchising in, 146
   international small business and, 417, 418, 420, 427,
      428, 429
Meyers, Jack, 56–57
Micro-aging schedule, 227, 228
Microloan program, 250

Micromanagement angels, defined, 254
Microsoft, 9, 423, 432, 504
Mignini, Paul, Jr., 388
Miller, Carol, 295
Minimum wage, 267
Mining, small business size and, 5, 6, 7
Minority enterprise small business investment
    companies (MESBICs), 253
Minority-owned firms, 11, 12
Mintzberg, Henry, 439
Miscellaneous promotion, 392
Misrepresentation, business-buyout alternative
    and, 154
Mission statement, 73–74, 84, 86
Misunderstanding, franchising and, 131
Mitchells Luxury ice cream, 321
Mixed-use incubators, 359
Mixon, Carroll, 410
Modern of Marshfield, 451
Mondello, Michael, 384, 386
Money. *See also* Capital
    contracts and, 276
    franchising and, 134
    holdback, 169
    human resource management and, 471
    inventory as, 328
    as motivation, 453
    small business finance and, 240, 258
    starting new business and, 181
Moonlighting policy, 183
Moot Corporation, 96, 114
Morality, business ethics and, 67
Moran, Chris, 222
Mork, Bill, 451–453
Morrow Snowboards, 120
Motivation, professional small business management
    and, 449–454
Mountain Dew, 390
Mountain Shadows, Inc., 505
Movable Type, 337–338
Movies, small business lessons from, 24–25
*Movies to Manage by: Lessons in Leadership from Great
    Films* (Clemens), 24
MRP. *See* Materials requirements planning (MRP)
MRPII. *See* Manufacturing resource planning II (MRPII)
MSNBC, 423
Multidimensional Aptitude Battery II, 475
Multiple method, for buying existing business, 165–166
Multivariate analysis (MANOVA), 509
Murray, Bill, 25
Murray, Ian, 255
Murray, Shep, 255
MYOB Plus, 208
MySpace, 338

Nader, Ralph, 64
NAFTA. *See* North American Free Trade Agreement
    (NAFTA)
NAICS. *See* North American Industrial Classification
    System (NAICS)
NASA, 95
National Association of Certified Valuation Analysts, 445
National Association of Credit Managment, 388, 422
National Association of Professional Employer
    Organizations, 465, 476
National Business Ethics Survey, 67
National Business Incubator Association, 359
National Federation of Independent Business (NFIB), 17,
    188, 252, 264, 268, 442
National Football League, 28
National Hockey League, 28
National origin, legal environment and, 266, 267
National Venture Capital Association (NVCA), 245
Native Americans, small business finance and, 253
Native Hawaiians, firms owned by, 11
Natural process limits, 512
NCAA football teams, 28
Need to achieve, defined, 39
Negative cash flow, 212, 214
Negative covenants, 244
Neglect, business failure and, 18
Negotiating Rationally, 448
Negotiation, professional small business
    management and, 448–449
Negotiation Tool Kit, The, 448
Neighborhoods, for small business, 352
Neiman Marcus, 248
NEO Personality Inventory-Revised, 475
Nespole, Linda, 202–203
Nestle, 482
Net lease, defined, 366
Net profit margin, defined, 219
Net worth, defined, 207
Net-net lease, defined, 366
Net-net-net lease, defined, 366
Networking, incubators and, 359–360
New Balance, 194
New business, 178–200
    getting started with, 190–196
    startups for, 179–180, 185–190
    types of, 180–185
Newbury Comics, 277
News Corporation, 338
Newspaper, as promotion, 389
New-to-the-world products, 316
"Next Stop..." Businesstown, 96
NFIB. *See* National Federation of Independent
    Business (NFIB)
Niche marketing, defined, 298

Nike, 28

Nobile, Robert, 487

Noble, John, 181

Nolo Press, 52

Noncompete clause, defined, 165

Noncompete covenant, defined, 276–277

Nondisturbance clause, defined, 367

Nonexempt employees, defined, 480

Non-minority-owned businesses, 12

Nonobvious invention, defined, 279

Non-profit corporation, defined, 53

Nonwhite businesses, 11, 12

Nordstrom, 40

Norma Rae, 25

North American Free Trade Agreement (NAFTA), 75, 145, 418, 425, 427, 428–429

North American Industrial Classification System (NAICS), 5, 7

North of the Border Business Plan, 96

Notebook computers, 182

Novelty, patents and, 279

Nutrition Labeling and Education Act, 265

NVCA. *See* National Venture Capital Association (NVCA)

Nylon magazine, 236

O magazine, 374

Objections, personal selling and, 396

OBM. *See* Open-book management (OBM)

Obsolescence, defined, 329

Occupational Safety and Health Act (OSHA), 271

Odd pricing, defined, 383

OEM. *See* Original-equipment manufacturer (OEM)

Offbeat marketing strategies, at Jones Soda, 290

Office of Advocacy, 11, 12, 15, 241

Office of Economic Research, 11

Official Gazette of the U.S. Patent and Trademark Office, 279

Official Supplier, 293

O'Hare International Airport, 507

OJT. *See* On-the-job training (OJT)

Olympic Games, marketing strategies and, 293

OM. *See* Operations management (OM)

"One child" policy, 419

One Flew over the Cuckoo's Nest, 25

OnGoal, 231, 232

Online credit checks, defined, 387–388

Open charge account, 385

Open account, international small business and, 423

Open-book management (OBM), 225

Open-door policy, defined, 490

Open-ended questions, 473

Operating cycle, 223

Operating expenses, business failure and, 18, 19

Operating ratio, 161

Operating system, elements of, 498–500

Operational excellence, defined, 193

Operations management (OM), 496–516

    controlling, 510–513

    for manufacturing businesses, 500–501

    operating system elements and, 498–500

    productivity and, 502–505

    quality-centered management and, 508–510

    scheduling and, 505–507

    for services businesses, 501–502

    types of, 500–502

Operations plan. *See* Manufacturing and operations plan

Opportunity cost

    price and, 379

    small business finance and, 257

Opportunity/opportunities

    environmental analysis and, 75

    market, 102

    starting new business and, 185

Optimism, successful entrepreneurs and, 39

Oracle OnDemand, 396

Ordering costs, defined, 329

Orders, purchasing and, 323–324

Ordovsky-Tanaevsky Blanco, Rostislav, 356

Organization

    business (*See* Business organization)

    home-based businesses and, 182

Organization chart

    in employee handbook, 487–488

    management team and, 107

Organizing, in professional small business management, 437, 439, 502

Orientation toward the future, successful entrepreneurs and, 39

Original-equipment manufacturer (OEM), 320

OSHA. *See* Occupational Safety and Health Act (OSHA)

Outdoor, as promotion, 392

Outdoor media, promotion through, 389

Outputs, defined, 498–499

Outshopping, defined, 350

Outsourcing, 9, 182

Overdependence, franchising and, 130–131

Overdue accounts, 388–389

Overhead, home-based businesses and, 182

Owner's equity, 207, 238, 241

Ownership. *See* Small business ownership

Pacific China Industries, 413

Pacific Islanders, firms owned by, 11, 12

Pacific Valley Foods, 319

Packaging, marketing mix and, 321

Packing slip, 323

Palm Pilot, 182

Palmer, Jayne, 376
PalmPilot, 339
Palo Alto Software's Business Plan Pro, 101
Pareto charts, defined, 509
Pareto rule, 327
Paris Convention for Protection of Industrial
    Property, 283
Parker, Ben, 497
Participation, franchising and, 142
Participative management, 509
Partners, small business finance and, 252
Partnership Maker, 52
Partnership(s), 42, 43, 45–49, 50, 52, 53
    articles of, 46, 47, 48–49
    at First Avenue, 56
    general, 46
    international small business and, 412
    limited, 46, 47–48
    limited-liability, 48
    small business finance and, 252
    taxes for, 196
Passion, successful entrepreneurs and, 38
Patent and Trademark Office, 283
Patent application, 279–280
Patent Cooperation Treaty (PCT), 283
Patent Depository Library, 279
Patent It Yourself (Pressman), 278
Patent search, 279
Patent Trademark Office (PTO), 277, 279, 280,
    281, 282, 285
Patent(s)
    defined, 277
    design, 278
    for existing business, 164
    international small business and, 411
    legal environment and, 277–280
    plant, 278
    small business success and, 15
    steps to receive, 281
    trade secrets and, 285
    utility, 278
Paul, Rajendra, 504
Pay-for-performance plan, 480, 481
Payment in advance, international small business
    and, 422
Pay-per-click (PPC) advertising, 299
PayPerClip, 397
PC Law Library, 52
PCT. *See* Patent Cooperation Treaty (PCT)
PCT-SAFE, 283
PDAs. *See* Personal digital assistants (PDAs)
Peachtree, 207, 208, 332
Peacock, Barb, 286
Peacock, Dexter, 286

Pearl, David S. II, 262–263
Penetration pricing, defined, 382
PEO. *See* Professional employer organization (PEO)
Pepsi, 390
Percentage lease, defined, 366
Performance, franchising and, 132
Performance (ability) tests, 474
Performance appraisal, defined, 488
Performance intention, 29
Perkins, Gregory, 391
Permits
    legal environment and, 272–273
    starting new business and, 195
Perpetual inventory system, defined, 332
Personal digital assistants (PDAs), 182
Personal funds, small business finance and, 252
Personal liability, self-employment and, 36
Personal selling, 395–396
Personnel, for existing business, 164. *See also*
    Employees
Peters, Tom, 24, 74
PetMed Express, 292
Philanthropic goodwill, 63, 66–67
Philanthropy, 66, 74
Phillips, Bruce, 264
Physical examinations, 474–475
Physical exercise, as stress management, 458
Piecework rates, 480–481
"Piercing the corporate veil," 50
Piggyback exporting, international small business
    and, 415–416
P&L statement. *See* Profit-and-loss (P&L) statement
Place. *See also* Location
    as business location, 345–347
    in business plan, 105
    city selection and, 349–352
    distribution and, 342–345
    home office as, 364–365
    layout/design and, 360–364
    lease/buy/build and, 365–368
    location types and, 356–360
    as marketing mix, 314
    site selection and, 352–356
    state selection and, 347–349
Plank, Kevin, 27–28
Planning, 59–126
    business failure and, 20
    for business plan (*See* Business plan)
    business-buyout alternative and, 154
    ethics in (*See* Ethics)
    floor, 246–247
    in professional small business management, 437,
        439, 502
    social responsibility and (*See* Social responsibility)

starting new business and, 190, 191–193

strategic (*See* Strategic planning/plan)

Plan(s)

action, 73

business (*See* Business plan)

cafeteria, 483

employee stock ownership, 32, 444–445

financial, 109–114

412(i), 484, 485

401(k), 484, 485

international business, 408–409

keogh, 484, 485

manufacturing and operations, 106

marketing (*See* Marketing plan)

pay-for-performance, 480, 481

profit-sharing, 481–482

reorganization, 274

retirement, 484–485

simplified employee pension, 484, 485

Plant patent, defined, 278

Play It Again Sports, 131, 137

Pledging, 248

Plug-in business, 233

Point of view, in business plan, 98

PointCare Technologies, 414

Policy loans, defined, 248

Policy manual, 487. *See also* Employee handbook

POM Wonderful, 321

Porter, Michael, 70, 79–80, 103, 357

Portman, Janet, 367

Positioning: The Battle for Your Mind (Ries), 199

Positive covenants, 244

Postpurchase evaluation, in decision-making process, 301–302

Potential product, of product satisfaction, 315

Potential startups, 185–190

Power of Nice, The, 448

Poza, Carlos, 145

PPC advertising. *See* Pay-per-click (PPC) advertising

PPOs. *See* Preferred provider organizations (PPOs)

PPP. *See* Purchasing power parity (PPP)

PR. *See* Public relations (PR)

Practical Gourmet, 440

Pratt's Guide to Venture Capital Success, 253

Preapproach, personal selling and, 396

Preferred provider organizations (PPOs), 484

Pregnancy, legal environment and, 267

Premium, 481

Prepaid expenses, 237

Presidents Chain Store Corporation, 125

Presley, Elvis, 330

Pressman, David, 278

Prestige pricing, defined, 383

Price, 374–389. *See also* Pricing

breakeven analysis and, 379–381

competition and, 375–376

costs and, 378–379

credit policies for, 384–389

defined, 374

demand and, 376–378

economics of, 374–379

as marketing mix, 314

pricing-setting techniques for, 381–384

purchasing and, 322

selling, 384

Price lining, defined, 383

Price skimming, defined, 382

Price-elastic demand, defined, 377

Price-inelastic demand, defined, 377

PriceWaterhouseCooper, 236

Pricing. *See also* Price

in business plan, 105

competitive analysis and, 78, 79

cost-plus, 384

creativity in, 384

economics of, 374–379

even, 383

odd, 383

penetration, 382

prestige, 383

psychological, 383

reference, 383

target-return, 384

Pricing-setting techniques, 381–384

Primary data, 305–307

Prime rate, 241

Primer on Exporting, 417

Prince, 56

Principal, defined, 241

Prinster, James, 359

Print media, promotion through, 389

Prior art, defined, 279

Private employment agencies, 469

Private placements, small business finance and, 254

Private-label manufacturing, defined, 320

PRIZM, 352

Pro forma balance sheet, 241

Pro forma financial statements, defined, 214

Problem recognition, in decision-making process, 301

Problem solving, diversity and, 12–13

Problems, small business finance and, 256

Process innovation, 15

Process layout, defined, 362

Processes, international small business and, 411

Procter & Gamble, 310

Product competitive advantage, 81–82, 320–321

Product innovation, 15

Product layout, defined, 362–364

Product leadership, defined, 193, 194
Product life cycle, defined, 187
Product lines, 316
Product operations systems, 502
Product-distribution franchising, defined, 127
Production, defined, 500
Production concept, defined, 292
Production process, 513
Productivity, defined, 500, 502–505. *See also* Efficiency
Productivity ratios, 503
Product(s)
    augmented, 315
    in business plan, 103–104
    competitive analysis and, 78, 79
    defined, 314
    developing new, 316–318
    existing, 316–318
    expected, 315
    export markets for, 420
    generic, 315
    international small business and, 411
    inventory and (*See* Inventory)
    marketing mix and, 314–321
    new-to-the-world, 316
    potential, 315
    purchasing and, 321–324
    selecting suppliers for, 324–327
Professional advice, franchising and, 145
Professional angels, defined, 254
Professional assistance, incubators and, 359
Professional employer organization (PEO), 464–465, 476
Professional guidance, franchising and, 128–129
Professional manager, entrepreneur *vs.*, 442
Professional small business management, 435–463
    employee theft and, 455
    four functions of, 437
    growth and, 440–445
    leadership in, 445–454
    managing small business and, 437–440
    time/stress and, 455–458
Profit ratios, 161
Profit sharing, franchising and, 133
Profit trend, 160
Profitability ratios, 219–220, 221
Profit-and-loss (P&L) statement, 110, 111–112, 113, 210
Profits
    business failure and, 18, 19
    corporations and, 50–51
    for existing business, 158–159
    partnerships and, 48
    self-employment and, 35
Profit-sharing plans, defined, 481–482
Programmed learning, human resource management
    and, 479

Progressive approach, defined, 488, 490
Progressive Grocer, 77
Promotion, 389–400
    advertising as, 389–395
    in business plan, 105
    as marketing mix, 314
    personal selling as, 395–396
    PR as, 396–397
    promotional mix and, 399
    sales, 397–400
Promotional mix, 389, 399
Proprietorship, 42, 43–46, 50
Prosek, James, 198–199
Prosek, Jennifer, 198–199
Protection
    consumer, 64
    employee, 64
    environmental, 64
    global, 283
    limited-liability, 50, 52
    trade, 64
Proven product, franchising and, 128
Psychological pricing, defined, 383
PTO. *See* Patent Trademark Office (PTO)
Public corporations, defined, 49
Public figure arrangements, franchising and, 141
Public offerings, small business finance and, 254–255
Public policy, 491
Public relations (PR), 396–397, 399
Publicity, defined, 396
Puerto Ricans, business density and, 12
Pull system, 334
Purchase, in decision-making process, 301
Purchase obligations, franchising and, 141
Purchase order, defined, 323
Purchase requisition, defined, 323
Purchasing
    bulk, 133
    of small business location, 367–368
Purchasing power parity (PPP), 419
Pure Food and Drug Act, 64
Purple Cow (Godin), 292
Purple Rain, 56
Purpose, of corporations, 51
Push system, 334
Putnam Investments, 181

Qualified applicant, defined, 268
Qualitative data, defined, 306
Quality, defined, 508
Quality circles, defined, 510
Quality control, franchising and, 129–130
Quality-centered management, 508–510
Quantitative data, 306, 307

Quantity, reorder, 330
Quarterly Franchising World, 134
Queen Mother of Business Plan Sites, The, 96
Questioning
   human resource management and, 473
   personal selling and, 396
Questionnaire
   for advertising, 394
   for job analysis, 466
   for market research, 306
Questions
   about franchising, 136, 138–139
   open-ended, 473
Quick ratio (acid-test) ratio, 216–217, 221
QuickBooks, 206, 208, 332
Quicken, 207
Quicksilver, 120

Rabin, Craig, 10
Race, legal environment and, 266, 267
Race norming, defined, 270
Rachel's Gourmet Snacks, 293
Racing Strollers, 37
Rackspace Managed Hosting, 450
Radio, as promotion, 389, 390
Radio frequency identification (RFID), 262, 333
Raissen, Anthony, 421
Ramada Inn, 128
Ratchet effect, 397, 400
Ratio analysis, 216, 221
Ratio(s)
   accounting systems and, 204
   activity, 217–218, 221
   in balance sheet, 111
   current, 160, 161, 216, 221
   debt, 218, 221
   expense, 160
   financial, 216, 220–222
   leverage, 218–219, 221
   liquidity, 216–217, 221
   operating, 161
   productivity, 503
   profit, 161
   profitability, 219–220, 221
   quick (acid-test), 216–217, 221
   times interest earned, 218–219
Readiness Assessment Guide, for entrepreneurs, 30–31
Real estate
   business failure and, 18
   small business size and, 6, 7
RealNetworks, 179
Reasonability, 491
Reasonable accomodation, defined, 268
Recapitalization, defined, 254

Recognition clause, defined, 367
Reconciliation component, 225
Recruitment, employee, 467–470
Reebok, 28
Reference pricing, defined, 383
Regional value content (RVC), 429
Regression analysis, 296–297, 509
Regulations, starting new business and, 195
Reichenbach, Randy, 410
Reilly, Jim, 175–176
Relationship marketing, defined, 292
Relationships
   entrepreneur-manager, 28–31
   small business success and, 15
supplier, 154
Relatives, recruitment of, 469–470
Relaxation techniques, as stress management, 458
Religion
   international small business and, 425
   legal environment and, 266, 267
Renewal of agreement, 143, 144
Reorder point, of inventory, 330
Reorder quantity, of inventory, 330
Reorganization, defined, 273
Reorganization plan, 274
Replacement value, 166
Replacements, 56
Representations and warranties policies, 157
Republic of China
   franchising in, 146
international small business and, 413, 414, 417, 418, 419
   website for, 356
Research
   franchising and, 134–136, 138–139
   market/marketing, 84, 104–106, 302–309
Resource maturity stage, of growing firm, 442
Response tracking, for advertising, 394
Responsibility/responsibilities
   business ethics and, 67
   corporations and, 53
   economic, 63
   ethical, 63, 65–66
   partnerships and, 48
   social (*See* Social responsibility)
Restrictions
   for franchising, 130, 141
   in legal environment, 272–273
Résumés, selecting employees through, 471
Retail business, inventory for, 327
Retail layouts, for small business location, 360–361
Retail trade
   business failure and, 18
   small business size and, 5, 6, 7
Retail Trade Act, 146

Retailers, defined, 344
RetailVision, 504
Retirement benefits, 486
Retirement plans, 484–485
Return on assets, 219, 221
Return on equity, defined, 220
Return on investment, 219
Revenge of Brand X: How to Build a Big Time Brand on the Web or Anywhere Else, The (Frankel), 290
Revenue, franchising and, 132
Reverse engineering, 78
Review process, in business plan, 114–118
RFID. *See* Radio frequency identification (RFID)
Richmond, Mike, 269
Ries, Al, 199
Right of first refusal, 47, 132
Rio, 311
RISE business, 68
Risk assumption, entrepreneur and, 29
Risk taking, successful entrepreneurs and, 39
Risks
    in business ownership, 17–22
    in business plan, 108
    in buying businesses, 157, 165, 167, 168
    of developing new products, 218
    in entrepreneurship process, 31
    in international small business, 422
    marketing strategies and, 293
    of self-employment, 36–37
    of small business finance, 252
Risucci, Damon, 377
"Rivalry among existing competitors," 80, 103
RMA Annual Statement Studies, 113, 160, 214, 220, 231, 513
Robert Morris Associates (RMA), 160, 212, 214, 220, 231
Rocky Mountain Chocolate Factory, 131
Rogers, Will, 14
Role ambiguity, 457
Role conflict, 457
Role-playing, human resource management and, 480
Rolling Stone magazine, 198
Roots, 293
Roper Organization, 465
Rosborough, Greg, 40
Rosedale, Philip, 178–179
Rostik International, 356
Roth Distributing, 16
Routing, defined, 507
Royalty fees, 142–145
Rudolph, Vernon, 497
Runner's World magazine, 37
Russakoff, Richard, 259
Russell, 28
Russia, 146, 356

Russian-American Business Training Centers, 93
RVC. *See* Regional value content (RVC)
RWS Group, 423

S corporation, 49, 51, 52, 53
Sabian, 152
SABMiller, 7
Safe Handling, 240
Sageworks' ProfitCents, 208
Sahlman, William, 107
Saks Fifth Avenue, 374
Salaries, of partnership, 49
Sales and Marketing Management (SMM), 347
Sales conversion index (SCI), 350, 351, 352
Sales forecast, defined, 294–297
Sales methods, competitive analysis and, 78, 79
Sales promotions, 397–400
Sales representatives, 344
Salesforce.com, 390
Salisbury, Dallas, 484
Sanitary services, small business size and, 6
Sarbanes-Oxley Act, 64, 157, 205
Satisfaction
    job, 451–452
    product, 315
Sawyer, Diane, 290
SBA. *See* Small Business Administration (SBA)
SBA Exporting Guide, 417
SBA Express program, defined, 250
SBA loan, 249, 250
SBI. *See* Sports Brand International (SBI)
SBO. *See* Survey of Business Owners (SBO)
Scams, in buying existing businesses, 155
Schedule flexibility, home-based businesses and, 182
Schedule(s)
    aging, 227
    availability, 229
    macro-aging, 229
    micro-aging, 227, 228
Scheduling, 505–507
Schenk, George, 38
Schindler, Jim, 445
Schmidt, Scott, 39
School Zone Publishing, 285–286
Schreter, Susan, 24
Schumpeter, Joseph, 15
SCI. *See* Sales conversion index (SCI)
SCORE. *See* Service Corp of Retired Executives (SCORE)
Search-engine optimization (SEO), 299
Search-marketing strategies, 299
Sears, 8, 9, 259, 320, 376
SEC. *See* Securities and Exchange Commission (SEC)
Second Life, 178–179
Secondary data, defined, 305

Sector-focused incubators, 359

Secured loan, defined, 247

Securities and Exchange Commission (SEC), 49, 254, 445

Segil, Lorraine, 412

Segmentation variables, defined, 297

Seinfeld, Jerry, 86, 189

Selected Publications to Aid Business and Industry, 305

Self-discipline, home-based businesses and, 182

Self-employment, 10, 12, 14, 35–42
　　pros/cons of, 35–36
　　risks of, 36–37
　　successful entrepreneurs in, 38–39
　　taxes for, 195

Self-incorporation kits, 50

Self-liquidating loans, 245

Selling agents, 344

Selling concept, 292

Selling price, 384

SellWise, 332

Semrow Perforated & Expanded Metals, 461

Senior Moves, 398

Sensual/sexual messages, as advertising objective, 393

SEO. *See* Search-engine optimization (SEO)

SEP plans. *See* Simplified employee pension (SEP) plans

Sequencing, defined, 507

Serendipity, starting new business and, 189–190

Service businesses, operations management for, 501–502

Service Corp of Retired Executives (SCORE), 101, 251, 478

Service industry, inventory for, 327–328

Service innovation, 15

Service layouts, for small business location, 362

Service locations, as small business location, 358

Service operations systems, 502

Service policies, in business plan, 106

Service productivity, measuring, 503–505

Service sector, defined, 8

Services
　　business failure and, 18
　　in business plan, 103–104, 106
　　competitive analysis and, 78, 79
　　marketing mix and, 315
　　small business size and, 5, 6, 7

Settlement attorney, 169

7-11, 291

Seven Habits of Highly Effective People, The (Covey), 32

7(a) program, 249

Sex, legal environment and, 266, 267

Sexual harassment, 65, 270

Shader, Danny, 278

Shadow Patent Office, 279

Shakespeare, 24

Shareholders, corporations and, 52

Sharper Image, 114

Shaw, George Bernard, 14, 33

Shelving Concepts, 499

Sherman Antitrust Act of 1890, 64, 264

Shop 2000, 313–314

"Shoppertainment," 317

Shopping centers, as small business location, 356–357

Short-cycle manufacturing, 509

Shortest process time priority dispatching rule, 507

Short-term assets, defined, 237

Short-term loan, 242, 245, 246, 247

Shrinkage, 328, 329

Shukla, Amita, 114

Shuman, Marc, 148–149

SIC. *See* Standardized Industrial Code (SIC)

Siegel, Joel, 290

Sight draft, international small business and, 422

Sign-A-Rama, 131

Simple IRA, 485

Simplified employee pension (SEP) plans, 484, 485

Simply Accounting, 208

Sinclair, Upton, 64

Singer, Isaac, 126

Single-entry accounting, defined, 207

Sistahs of Harlem, 235–236

Site selection
　　franchising and, 141
　　for small business, 352–356

Six Apart, 337–339

Six sigma, defined, 508–510

16PF, 476

Size
　　of small business, 5–6
　　small business finance and, 256, 257
　　small business success and, 16

Skills, of management team, 107

SkyMall, 114

Slater, Samuel, 7

Slice-of-life messages, as advertising objective, 394

Slotting fees, 319

Small business
　　big/large businesses *vs.,* 13, 302
　　contract law for, 274–276
　　defined, 4–7
　　diversity in, 10–13
　　facts about, 4, 5
　　ownership of, 10–13
　　planning in (*See* Planning)
　　risks in, 17–22
　　size definitions of, 5–6
　　social responsibilities of, 62–67
　　success in, 13–17
　　types of industries as, 6–7
　　in U.S. economy, 7–10

Small Business Administration (SBA), 4, 5, 7, 11, 12, 15, 41
  business plan and, 96, 101
  existing business and, 155
  international small business and, 408, 413, 417, 420–422, 424
  small business finance and, 241, 249–250, 253, 259
  small business marketing and, 298, 305
Small Business Development Center, 17, 31, 101
Small business distribution, 342–345
Small Business Expo, 391
Small business finance, 235–261. *See also* Finance/financing
  capital requirements for, 237–240
  financial vocabulary for, 240–244
  finding capital for, 244–257
Small business growth, 440–445
Small business investment companies (SBICs), 253
Small business management, 27–60
  business organization and (*See* Business organization)
  defined, 28–29
  entrepreneur-manager relationship in, 28–31
  self-employment and, 35–42
  startup process for, 31–34
Small business managemetn process, defined, 32
Small business manager, entrepreneurship and, 29
Small business marketing. *See* Marketing
Small business ownership
  preparing for, 40–42
  small business, 10–13
  of small business location, 367–368
  workforce diversity and, 10–13
Smith, Adam, 63
SMM. *See* Sales and Marketing Management (SMM)
SMM Survey of Buying Power, 350, 351
Smolan, Rick, 503–504
Smoothie King, 148
Snip 'N Clip, 148
SoapWorks, 310
Social Capitalist Awards, 66
Social entrepreneur, 66
Social networking, 338
Social responsibility, 60–67, 73, 74
  defined, 62
  ethics/strategic planning and, 61–62
  of small business, 62–67
  of Stonyfield Farms, 67
  of TerraCycle, 61
Social Security taxes, 206
Social services, small business size and, 7
Social support systems, as stress management, 458
Social systems, international small business and, 425
Society of Human Resource Management, 65

Sociocultural environment, environmental analysis and, 75
Soft issues, human resource management and, 477
Softub, 324, 325–326
Software
  accounting, 208
  for business plans, 101
  for corporations, 52
  patents for, 280–281
Sole proprietorship, 42, 43–46, 195, 207
Sony, 282, 311, 370, 390
Sources and uses of funds, defined, 110
South Korea, international small business and, 418
South-East Asia on a Shoestring, 407
Spain, franchising in, 146
Spaniards, business density and, 12
SPC. *See* Statistical process control (SPC)
Special Olympics, 66
Specific performance, defined, 276
Sperlich, Hal, 308
Splenda, 482
Split ads, for advertising, 394
Spoilage, defined, 329
Spolsky, Joel, 470
Sponsorship, marketing strategies and, 293
Sports Brand International (SBI), 175–176
Sports sponsorship, marketing strategies and, 293
Springfield Remanufacturing Company, 225
Spy Optic, 371
St. Clair, Pack, 345
St. Clair, Paxson, 345
Stack, Jack, 225
Staffcentrix, 365
Stalk, George, Jr., 85
Stand-alone locations, as small business location, 358
Standardized Industrial Code (SIC), 5
Startup capital, 16–17, 238
Startup costs, 141, 192
Startup process, model of, 31–34
Startup rockets, 359
Startups
  about, 179–180
  business failure and, 21
  business-buyout alternative and, 152–153
  fast-growth, 183, 185
  increased, 9–10
  myths/realities of, 186
  planning and, 191–193
  potential, 185–190
  small business management and, 31–34
Starving Student Moving Company, 189
State lenders, small business finance and, 250
State selection, for small business, 347–349
Statement of cash flow, 212–214

Statement questionnaires, for advertising, 394
Statistical process control (SPC), 509, 512
Status, small business finance and, 257
STAT-USA/Internet, 424
Statutory classes, for patents, 279
Steingold, Fred, 367
Stereo City, 211, 212, 213, 216, 217, 218, 219, 220, 221
Stewart, Martha, 199
Stock, corporations and, 49, 50, 51
Stock offerings, small business finance and, 254
Stolberg, Ted, 9
Stonegate Group, 461–462
Stonyfield Europe, 67
Stonyfield Farms, 67
Strategic alliances, defined, 185, 412
Strategic alternatives, strategic planning and, 73, 84
Strategic buyer, exit strategy and, 444
Strategic circumference, small business finance and, 256
Strategic planning/plan, 72–88
    in action, 87–88
    business plans *vs.,* 87–88
    competitive analysis and, 76–84
    control systems and, 87
    defined, 62, 72
    environmental analysis and, 74–76
    goal setting/strategies and, 84–87
    mission statement for, 73–74
    social responsibility/ethics and, 61–62
    strategic alternatives and, 84
    TerraCycle and, 61
Strategy/strategies
    for cash-flow management, 227–230
    customer-oriented, 382–383
    exit, 109, 444–445
    internal-oriented pricing, 383–384
    marketing (*See* Marketing strategies)
    search-marketing, 299
    for strategic planning, 73, 84–87
Stratford, Kerry, 66
Straub, Russell, 90–91
"Street Smarts," 95
Stress, defined, 457
Stress management, 457–458
Studio Number One, 390
Style Channel, 236
Subway, 131, 135, 137, 141
Success, in small business, 13–17, 151
Success stage, of growing firm, 441–442
Sudsies.com, 403
Suggestion selling, personal selling and, 396
Sullivan, Stephen, 175–176
Sunkist, 390
Supplier qualification, 509

Supplier relationships, business-buyout alternative and, 154
Suppliers, for products, 324–327
Supplies, cash flow and, 230
Supply, marketing concept and, 291–292
Supply & Demand: The Art of Shepard Fairey, 390
Support services, incubators and, 358–359
Survey of Business Owners (SBO), 10
Survey of Buying Power, 347
Survival stage, of growing firm, 440–441
Sustainability, social responsibility and, 67
Sustainable competitive advantage, 320
Sutter, Greg, 296
Sweningson, Lori, 430
SWOT analysis, 74, 84, 104. *See also* Environmental analysis
Symantec, 423
Symbols, franchising and, 142
Synergy Fitness Clubs, 377
Synthetic systems, defined, 501
Szaky, Tom, 60

Table of contents
    in business plan, 102
    for disclosure statement, 140
Taco Bell, 504
Taco Time, 131
Taiwan, international small business and, 418
Takeoff stage, of growing firm, 442
Talents, of management team, 107
Tanenbaum, Stephen, 40
Tangible assets, 162, 165, 166–167, 168
Tangible goods, 315
Target, 83, 236, 285, 291, 333, 391
Target markets
    in business plan, 104
    defined, 297
    marketing strategies and, 297–298, 300
Target-return pricing, defined, 384
Task overload, 457
Tatelman, Barry, 317
Tatelman, Eliot, 317
Tax advantage
    for corporations, 52, 53
    for partnerships, 46
    for sole proprietorships, 44
Tax requirements, financial records and, 206–207
Tax returns, for existing business, 159
Tax/taxes
    accounting systems and, 205, 206
    ADA and, 269
    human resource management and, 483
    for income, 195–196
    for partnership, 195

Social Security, 206
  starting new business and, 195–196
  unemployment, 196
TCBY Enterprises, 145
Team
  audit, 324
  management, 107
Technical skills, management team and, 107
Technological environment, environmental analysis
  and, 75
Technology
  home-based businesses and, 182, 273
  marketing strategies and, 298
  small business growth and, 440
  U.S. economy and, 8, 9
Telecommunications, U.S. economy and, 8
Telephone surveys, for advertising, 394
Television, as promotion, 389, 390
Temporary employees, 476
Tenacity, successful entrepreneurs and, 39
Terminal value, defined, 166
Termination
  business, 19–20
  employee, 487–491
  franchising and, 131–132, 144
Terms of sale, for existing business, 168–169
TerraCycle, 60–61
Testimonials, as advertising objective, 393
Testing, employee, 474–476
Thai, Hung Van, 189–190
Theft, employee, 455
Thinning the assets, 169
Thompson, Richard, 511
Thompson & Thompson, 283
Thomson/RCA, 311
Thornbury, Tom, 324
"Threat of new entrants," 80, 103
"Threat of substitute products or services," 80, 81, 103
Threats, environmental analysis and, 75
Three Keys Music, 454
Thrive Networks, 481
TIC. *See* Trade Information Center (TIC)
TIGER map service, 300
Time
  accounting systems and, 206
  corporations and, 52
  franchising and, 134
  human resource management and, 471, 472
  lead, 330
  starting new business and, 180
Time audit, 456
Time draft, international small business and, 422
Time management, 455–456
Time series analysis, 220, 221–222, 296

Timeline, in business plan, 108
Times interest earned, 218–219, 221
Times interest earned ratio, 218–219
Timing, of cash flows, 223–224
Timmons, Jeffry A., 256
TiVo, 339
Tocqueville, Alexis de, 4
Tolerance range, defined, 508
Tom Peters Group/Learning Systems, 445
Total asset turnover, 221
Total quality management (TQM), 334, 510–511
Totally Absurd, 285
Tote Le Monde, 373–374
Toughness, as leadership attribute, 446–447
Toyota, 85, 179
TQM. *See* Total quality management (TQM)
Trade associations, 134, 212, 305, 470
Trade credit, defined, 250, 385
Trade Information Center (TIC), 429
Trade protection, social responsibility and, 64
Trade secrets, 285
Trade shows, 391, 403, 504
Trademark Register of the U.S., The, 283
Trademark Service Corporation, 283
Trademarks
  counterfeiting and, 262–263
  defined, 282
  for existing business, 164
  franchising and, 142
  international small business and, 411
  legal environment and, 282–283, 286
  trade secrets and, 285
Tradenet's Export Advisor, 424
TRADOS, 423
Traffic coverage, starting new business and, 181
Traffic flow, around small business, 354–355
Training
  employee, 477
  franchising and, 141
  for GarageTek, 149
  human resource management and, 477–480
  international small business and, 425
  on-the-job, 479
  opening franchise and, 129
Transcon Trading Company, 415
Transfer, franchising and, 131–132
Transformation processes, defined, 498
Translation services, international small business
  and, 426
Transportation
  business failure and, 18
  small business size and, 6
Triggering event, 31, 32, 33, 34
Triple-net lease, defined, 366

Trott, Ben, 337–338
Trott, Mena, 337–338
Trout: an Illustrated History (Prosek), 198
Trump, Donald, 436
Trust, as leadership attribute, 446
Trusts, legal environment and, 264
Trustworthiness, successful entrepreneurs and, 38
Truth-in-Lending Act, 265
Tsao, Janie, 504
Tsao, Victor, 504
T-Shirt Makeovers, 236
Tuleh's, 248
Turner, Linda, 460
Twain, Mark, 75, 266
Twelve Angry Men, 25
Twelve O'Clock High, 25
TypePad, 337–339
Tzu, Sun, 435

UCCnet, 333
UFOC. *See* Uniform Franchise Offering Circular (UFOC)
Unanue, Andy, 170
Under Armour, 27–28
Undercapitalization, 236
Undercapitalized, 214
Undue hardship, defined, 268
Unemployment compensation, 271
Unemployment tax, 196
Uniform Code Council, 333
Uniform Commercial Code, 158
Uniform Franchise Offering Circular (UFOC), 142
Uniform Partnership Act (UPA), 45, 48
Uniformed Services Employment and Reemployment Rights Act, 486
Unique selling point (USP), 292
United Kingdom, international small business and, 418, 426
United Way, 66
Universal Data Systems, 416
Universal Pictures, 390
Universal Product Code (UPC), 332, 333
Universities. *See* Colleges/universities
Uniweld, 262–263
Unlimited liability, 45, 46
Unsecured loans, defined, 245
Unsecured term loans, defined, 246
UPA. *See* Uniform Partnership Act (UPA)
UPC. *See* Universal Product Code (UPC)
UPS Capital, 125
Uruguay Round, 429
U.S. Commercial Service, 145
U.S. Constitution, 266
U.S. Customs, 429
U.S. Department of Justice, 269

U.S. Government Printing Office, 280, 429
U.S. Secret Service, 189
U.S. Ski Team, 28
U.S. Steel, 8
USA Today, 347
USP. *See* Unique selling point (USP)
Utilitarianism, defined, 66
Utility patent, defined, 278

Valuation
   exit strategy and, 445
   income-statement methods of, 166, 167
Value/values
   defined, 374
   of mission statements, 74
   social responsibility and, 62
   terminal, 166
van Stolk, Peter, 290–291
van Tol, Shannon, 494
van Tol, Willem, 494
VanCleave, Ted, 285
Vanderbilt, Cornelius, 8
Variable costs, defined, 378
Variable-rate loan, 242
Variance, defined, 272
Variance analysis, 509
Vasquez, Albert, 66
Vendors, 324. *See also* Suppliers
Venture capital firms, small business finance and, 252–253
Venture Connect, 258
Vermicomposting, 60
Vesper, Karl, 40
Vibe magazine, 236
Vietnam, website for, 355
Vineyard Vines, 255
Virtue ethics, defined, 66
Vision, as leadership attribute, 446
VisiVas, 114
Visual control, of inventory, 330
Vitale Caturano, 450
Vocabulary, financial, 240–244

Wage rates, 480–481
Wall, Jonathan, 181
Wall Street Journal, The, 134, 149, 305, 347, 397
Wal-Mart, 1, 9, 61, 83, 85, 295, 333, 376
Warnock, John, 233
Waterhouse, Steve, 294
Watson-Glaser Critical Thinking Appraisal, 475
WD-40 Company, 316–317
Weave Corporation, 410
Webber, Carmen, 235–236
Websites, for multiple languages, 423

Webster's Third International Dictionary of the English Language, 507
WebTrends, 306
Wells, Tina, 374
Wells Fargo, 91
Wenner, Jann, 198
Wesman Personnel Classification, 475
Westbeach Sports, 119–121
Weston, Graham, 450
Wettach, Megan, 40
What About Bob?, 25
Wheeler, Maureen, 406–407
Wheeler, Tony, 406–407
White Castle, 272–273
White Stone Group, 494
Whitman, Glen, 278
Whitney, Eli, 7
Wholesale trade
    business failure and, 18
    small business size and, 5, 6, 7
Wholesalers, defined, 344
Wiedemann, Harden, 417
Wieweck, Todd, 441
Wildfire Communications, 503–504
Williams, Darwyn, 222
Williams, David, 450
Window of opportunity, defined, 187
WIPO. *See* World Intellectual Property Organization (WIPO)
Wireless modems, 182
Women
    business ideas from, 188
    businesses owned by, 12
    self-employment of, 10, 12
Women-owned firms, 11
Wonderlic Personnel Test, 475
Wong, Carrie, 440–441
Work, business failure and, 20
Workers' compensation, 270–271, 483
Work-family balance, 485

Workforce diversity, 10–13
Working capital, 237
Working hours, self-employment and, 36
"Work/life" policies, 450
Workplace, 265–271
    ADA and, 268–269
    CRA and, 267, 270
    FLSA and, 266–267
    IRCA and, 267–268
    laws protecting, 265–271
    OSHA and, 271
    unemployment compensation and, 271
    workers' compensation and, 270–271
World Bank, 414
World Intellectual Property Organization (WIPO), 282, 283
World Trade Organization (WTO), 425, 429
World Wide Web, Catch the Wave and, 337
Wou, Tia, 373–374
Wow Branding, 377
WTO. *See* World Trade Organization (WTO)

Yahoo!, 134, 305, 387
Yale Alumni Magazine, 199
Yellow pages, as promotion, 392
You Can Negotiate Anything, 448
Youth marketing, 374

Zarnott, Mike, 461, 462
ZDNET, 423
Zebra Technologies, 333
Zerofootprint, 61
Zildjian, Armand, 152
Zildjian, Avedis III, 152
Zildjian, Craigie, 151, 152
Zildjian, Debbie, 151, 152
Zildjian, Robert, 152
Zildjian Cymbal Company, 151
Zoning laws, defined, 272–273
Zoo Doo, 55